REPORTING AND WRITING:
BASICS FOR THE 21ST CENTURY

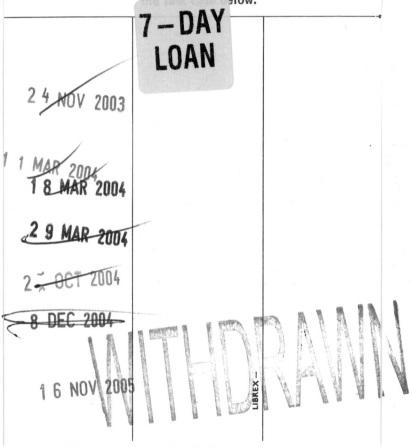

REPORTING AND WRITING:
BASICS FOR THE 21ST CENTURY

CHRISTOPHER SCANLAN
THE POYNTER INSTITUTE

Harcourt College Publishers

Fort Worth Philadelphia San Diego New York Orlando Austin San Antonio
Toronto Montreal London Sydney Tokyo

Publisher	Earl McPeek
Acquisitions Editor	Stephen Dalphin
Project Editor	Laurie Bondaz
Art Director	Garry Harman
Production Manager	Cindy Young

Cover credit: Brian Salibury

ISBN: 0-15-505378-7
Library of Congress Catalog Card Number: 99-61041

Address for Domestic Orders
Harcourt College Publishers, 6277 Sea Harbor Drive, Orlando, FL 32887-6777
800-782-4479

Address for International Orders
International Customer Service
Harcourt, Inc., 6277 Sea Harbor Drive, Orlando, FL 32887-6777
407-345-3800
(fax) 407-345-4060
(e-mail) hbintl@harcourtbrace.com

Address for Editorial Correspondence
Harcourt College Publishers, 301 Commerce Street, Suite 3700, Fort Worth, TX 76102

Web Site Address
http://www.hbcollege.com

Harcourt College Publishers will provide complimentary supplements or supplement packages to those adopters qualified under our adoption policy. Please contact your sales representative to learn how you qualify. If as an adopter or potential user you receive supplements you do not need, please return them to your sales representative or send them to: Attn: Returns Department, Troy Warehouse, 465 South Lincoln Drive, Troy, MO 63379.

Printed in the United States of America
0 1 2 3 4 5 6 7 8 032 9 8 7 6 5 4 3 2

Harcourt College Publishers

Dedicated to journalists of the 20th and 21st centuries, and their teachers.

About the Author

An award-winning reporter for two decades, Christopher Scanlan is director of writing programs at The Poynter Institute in St. Petersburg, Fla. where he teaches professional and student journalists. He is the editor of *Best Newspaper Writing* and *How I Wrote the Story*. Scanlan began his career reporting for small daily newspapers in his native Connecticut and earned a master's degree from Columbia University Graduate School of Journalism in 1974. He was a staff writer for *The Providence Journal*, where he helped launch the paper's writing improvement program, feature writer for the *St. Petersburg Times* and national correspondent for Knight Ridder Newspapers in Washington, D.C. Winner of 16 awards for reporting and writing, including a Robert F. Kennedy award for international journalism, Scanlan publishes articles, essays and short fiction in numerous magazines, textbooks and online sites. He is a frequent writing coach in newsrooms around the country.

PREFACE

Starting as a reporter 25 years ago, without experience or the benefit of a single journalism class, I was forced to begin a search for ways to get better at my craft. Since then, I've learned from hundreds of reporters, editors, writers, coaches and teachers, yet I continue to seek ways to hone this craft every day. *Reporting and Writing: Basics for the 21st Century* is your guide to the knowledge, skills and attitude of the professional journalist. Whether this is the start or the continuation of your education as a journalist, my hope is you'll find this a useful and inspiring companion on the lifelong journey of learning and discovery that every good journalist takes.

Foremost in your mind at this point may be this question: How do reporters get information and then manage to shape that information into stories that are clear and, at their best, approach the power of literature? Unfortunately, journalism, like most writing, is shrouded in myth. This book's goal is to demystify the process of reporting and writing. You'll find out how reporters do their job—how they think, act and produce newsworthy stories. You'll learn how to report, interview, write and revise your stories—not just for a grade—but to prepare you to succeed as a journalist in the 21st century.

Not long ago, reporters known as "legmen" collected information and funneled it to "rewritemen" who fashioned it into stories. Today, reporters of *both* sexes must be able to perform *both* jobs with equal skill. But it's not enough to know how to write an engaging story or conduct an effective interview. Reporters must now be as familiar with computer databases and electronic mailing lists as they are with telephone books. Once clear lines are blurred. Newspaper reporters find themselves delivering their stories in front of television cameras in their newsrooms. Broadcast and print journalists are reporting online as their news organizations reach out to their audiences on the Internet. Whatever the medium or tools, journalists in the 21st century will need the same basic skills as those needed in the 20th century and even earlier: reporting, critical analysis and writing. The lessons of this book are necessary for anyone interested in being a journalist, no matter whether the news is conveyed by a computer, a newspaper, or a radio or television broadcast. Delivery and distribution may change, but at the heart of journalism are the people for whom it is a calling. The people you will meet in these pages work for newspapers, radio and television stations, and online news sites. Like every good journalist I know, they share a common ground: They are driven to learn about life, to ask hard questions, to listen to the answers, to report the news and tell the stories of our times. In a free society, they play a challenging but important role. And, as many are quick to tell you, they have a lot of fun doing it.

Whether flashing a bulletin over a laptop computer equipped with a wireless modem or doing a live stand-up, reporters must still demonstrate the ability to collect information with speed and accuracy, analyze its significance, and then communicate the news with clarity, vigor and grace. That is this book's essential message. To bring it home, we'll explore the following three things in great detail: process, coaching and storytelling.

PROCESS.   News writing may seem magical, especially to a beginner, but it's not magic. It's a *process*—a series of rational steps, actions and decisions that can be described, learned and repeated to produce consistently excellent work. By making the processes of reporting and writing for print, broadcast and online news transparent, you'll learn not only how to cover a meeting or write a feature story, but also what it's like to do these things to make a living, what's challenging and rewarding about such work, what feelings it evokes and how you can be successful at your job.

COACHING.   Pioneered by Donald M. Murray, a Pulitzer Prize–winning journalist and teacher, and spread worldwide by my colleagues at The Poynter Institute, the *coaching* movement is based on another simple premise: The power to recognize a story's problems and the means to fix them lie inside you as the writer. By asking good questions a coach, whether yourself, a teacher, editor, or fellow writer, can help you uncover what you already know instinctively. Just as process reveals how reporters work, coaching gives you the help and guidance needed to produce your best work. Each chapter includes "The Coaching Way," that features coaching techniques and tips to guide the student and teacher.

STORYTELLING.   At a time when consumers of news are bombarded with information, *Reporting and Writing: Basics for the 21st Century* emphasizes the importance of *storytelling* as an effective means to connect with readers and as a way for students to realize their own creative potential. Success in journalism requires more than a mastery of basics. Most successful reporters are able not only to obtain the facts of a story, but also to present those facts in prose that is clear, vivid and, occasionally, unforgettable. Lessons are illustrated with examples written by student and professional print, broadcast and online reporters.

How This Book Is Organized

Reporting and Writing: Basics for the 21st Century is aimed at the beginning journalism student. Recognizing, however, that instructors have unique preferences about how they teach their course, the book is structured so chapters can be used in whatever manner proves most feasible. I welcome comments, suggestions, corrections and all feedback. Please send e-mail to **cscanlan@poynter.org**. Basic skills, theories and approaches to news covered in newswriting and reporting courses are explored in detail in the following 15 chapters:

1. *News Thinking in a Changing World*
2. *The Reporter's Toolbox*
3. *A Process Approach to Reporting and Writing*
4. *Finding and Writing a Lead*
5. *Story Forms: Shaping the News*
6. *Learning to Listen: Building Interviewing Skills*
7. *Making Connections: Diversity and the News*
8. *Reporting and Writing Broadcast News*
9. *Writing Online News*
10. *First Assignments*
11. *Doing the Right Thing: Libel, Privacy and Ethics*
12. *Storytelling On Deadline*
13. *On the Beat*
14. *Numbers and the Beginning Journalist*
15. *Getting—And Keeping—A Job*

OTHER FEATURES

These pedagogical features are designed to bring real-world journalism into the classroom:

A LIFE IN JOURNALISM.   Brief sections, contributed by working and student journalists, engage students by placing subject material in a true-to-life context.

CONVERSATIONS.   These are tightly focused interviews with veteran and beginning reporters and editors who share techniques and strategies for success as well as showing students how working journalists apply the book's lessons in real-life situations. Professionals aren't the only voices in this book. Drawing on the experiences of my own students, the book also includes the voices of beginners who share many of your concerns and aspirations.

READINGS.   A list of relevant books and articles follows each chapter, pointing students to further resources.

STORY EXAMPLES.   The text includes scores of examples from print, broadcast and online news, ranging from student work to award-winning journalism. These demonstrate current examples of story types and forms journalists must master. Many are accompanied by annotations, comments by the reporter, or "How I Wrote the Story" accounts that reveal to students the process students and professionals employ to report and write.

GLOSSARY OF ESSENTIAL TERMS. Each chapter includes a list of definitions for terms, concepts and newsroom jargon.

HOTLIST. More than 200 references for the student and teacher of up-to-date resources on the World Wide Web and elsewhere on the Internet are included. Sites relevant to particular teaching material are referenced in the margins. A complete hotlist follows each chapter. Each hotlist item has been reviewed and annotated. Reflecting the fluid nature of the Web, a regularly updated hotlist will be available on a Web site devoted to this book at **www.hbcollege.com**. I would greatly appreciate notification about outdated links by e-mail at **cscanlan@poynter.org**.

Reporting and Writing: Basics for the 21st Century is written with one eye on the future—where the news business is heading—and one eye on the past—where the hard-won and valuable lessons have already been learned by generations of journalists. Thus, ethical decision-making skills, cultural competence and a recognition of the vital role that diversity awareness plays in reporting and writing, and math skills are all emphasized in separate chapters. Written on the edge of a new century, this book is designed to be a timely and relevant manual for a changing world which draws on the important lessons of yesterday and the promise of tomorrow. Chapters focusing on broadcast and online news, and many examples from those platforms, reflect the reality that tomorrow's journalists must adapt to the new technology. Many are already meeting that challenge, as the rising number of online campus newspapers attests. A world of opportunities will be available for professionals who are open-minded and can bring to the newsroom a combination of traditional and new media skills. Advice and resources to guide your job search in traditional and new media—including the best way to prepare a job portfolio, conduct yourself in job interviews and locate job openings—are included in the book's final chapter.

Journalism is an important, exciting profession. Even, perhaps especially, in a new age, there still will be a need for someone to provide understanding as well as information, to make sense out of the stream of knowledge cascading through whatever distribution channels emerge in the coming decades. *Reporting and Writing: Basics for the 21st Century* provides the skills you'll need to succeed as the news industry enters its most challenging era. Together we'll teach and learn from each other. Let's start.

ACKNOWLEDGMENTS

As every reporter knows, behind every byline stands a long list of people whose contributions and assistance were instrumental and often unacknowledged. I am grateful and proud to belong to a community of journalists, teachers and learners whose support, guidance and extraordinary care have enriched my professional and personal life. It is my privilege to acknowledge their contributions to this book and no exaggeration to say it would not exist without their help. Of course, I bear responsibility for any errors. My thanks to you all and apologies to anyone I inadvertently fail to include in the following list.

Journalism teachers helped launch and sustain my career. At Columbia University Graduate School of Journalism, Melvin Mencher taught me the role of a journalist in a democracy and wrote the textbooks that guided my reporting and teaching, as they have for untold numbers of journalists and educators.

I have learned my most important lessons about writing and life from Donald M. Murray, professor emeritus at the University of New Hampshire, and former writing coach at *The Providence Journal,* where I soaked up everything he offered as his liaison to the newsroom staff. His teachings on writing process, coaching and storytelling fill a shelf of books and, as anyone who knows his work and ideas will see, are at the core of this book.

Christine Martin, as director of writing at the Perley Isaac Reed School of Journalism at West Virginia University, and co-director of The Poynter Institute's summer fellowship program in reporting and writing, has shared her passion for teaching and writing and taught me how to learn from our students. The approach to beat reporting in this book owes a direct debt to Martin and to Barbara Zang of The University of Missouri.

Jane Harrigan of the University of New Hampshire shared her passion for language and teaching. Her colleague, Lisa Miller, shared her knowledge of computer-assisted reporting. I relied heavily on the work of Mitchell Stephens, of New York University, for historical material. With Philip Meyer, of the University of North Carolina, I share the hope that tomorrow's journalists will value numeracy as much as literacy. Fortunately for this math-challenged writer, Meyer also shared his patient instruction and a review of the chapter on numbers and the beginning journalist.

Trevor Brown, dean of the Indiana University School of Journalism, offered valuable insights into the role of audiences. James Carey, of Columbia University, shared his research on the relationship of the telegraph and news writing.

John Sawatsky of Carleton University in Ottawa, Canada, opened my eyes and ears to a new way of looking at interviewing.

Sreenath Sreenivasan of Columbia University has been a generous and helpful guide to the emerging world of online news.

Rick Wilber, of the University of South Florida, has been a generous guide to the worlds of publishing and teaching while also providing inspiration through his own writing.

For two decades, newspaper and magazine editors gave me the assignments, editing, tough talk and gentle encouragement that every reporter craves. I have been especially fortunate to have worked with editors who were also some of my best teachers. Joel Rawson of *The Providence Journal* taught me how to tell stories and why a good editor edits people, not words. At the Knight Ridder Washington Bureau, Doug Clifton, Clark Hoyt and Rich Oppel gave me the opportunity to reach a national audience while Bob Shaw, Vicki Sue Gowler and Charles Green helped make my stories worthy of one. I am grateful to Evelynne Kramer of *The Boston Globe Magazine* and Sylvia K. Burack of *The Writer* for their support.

Newsroom training editors provide daily inspiration and education for time-pressed journalists and, in several cases, the opportunity for a former journalist to teach and learn in their newsrooms. My thanks to Gail Bulfin of the Fort Lauderdale *Sun-Sentinel*, Michael Schwartz of the *Atlanta Journal-Constitution,* Jack Hart of *The Oregonian,* Joe Grimm of the *Detroit Free Press,* Jean Patman of Gannet Suburban Newspapers, Adell Crowe of *USA Today* and their counterparts at newspapers around the country.

Several papers allowed me to reprint materials from their in-house publications, including *The Oregonian*'s "Second Takes" edited by Jack Hart, the Freep Academy on the *Detroit Free Press* Web site maintained by Joe Grimm, and *The Providence Journal*'s "Power of Words" Web site established by Bob Wyss.

My thanks also to the editors and newsrooms staffs who have helped me develop many of the lessons in this book during workshops and coaching sessions, including Sandra Mims Rowe and Peter K. Bhatia of *The Oregonian,* Jim Willse of the Newark *Star-Ledger,* Andrew Alexander of Cox Newspapers Washington Bureau, Deborah Howell of Newhouse Newspapers Washington Bureau, and the Singapore *Straits Times.*

A longtime print journalist would have no hope of including essential material on broadcast journalism without the aid of outstanding practitioners and teachers. Deborah Potter, formerly of CBS News and CNN, now an outstanding teacher, played a pivotal role by framing the chapter with her ideas and giving it shape with sections on reporting and writing that demonstrate her special qualities as a journalist, teacher and colleague. John Larson, West Coast correspondent for NBC's *Dateline,* teaches new lessons about storytelling every time he's on air and graciously shared his insights about enterprise reporting that can help any journalist regardless of medium. Donna Rowlinson of the Fort Lauderdale *Sun-Sentinel* shared that newspaper's program for helping print reporters make the shift to television. Tiffany Murri, a Poynter reporting fellow who now reports for KIVI-TV in Boise, Idaho, was especially generous with her scripts and experiences as a broadcast journalist.

I also needed help to understand the emerging world of online news and received it from Michael Rogers, editor of newsweek.com, Glenn McClaren, assistant editor of the Fort Lauderdale *Sun-Sentinel* online edition, former Poynter fellow David Ho of the Wall Street Journal Interactive Edition, Mary Beth Regan of Cox Newspapers Washington Bureau, Jonathan Dube of *The Charlotte Observer,* and Bill Mitchell founding editor of the *San Jose Mercury News* Merc Center who now directs The Poynter Institute's online site.

Jane Kirtley of The Reporters Committee for Freedom of the Press generously reviewed the chapter on libel and privacy and made excellent suggestions and revisions. Judy Gerber of the News Watch Project of the Center for the Integration and Improvement of Journalism reviewed the diversity chapter and also secured permission for me to reprint the project's diversity glossary in the appendix.

Each summer, Chief Goliath Davis and William Doniel, chief of public information, of the St. Petersburg Police Department, and their officers, help my students understand the world of law enforcement.

This book would not be possible without the unstinting support of my colleagues on the faculty and staff at The Poynter Institute. Jim Naughton, our president, not only supported this enterprise but edited the first draft with the same care he brought during his 19 years as an editor of *The Philadelphia Inquirer.* His Poynter predecessor, president emeritus Robert Haiman, generously shared his history of newsroom ethics. Roy Peter Clark and Karen Brown Dunlap, my colleagues in the writing and editing department, have been a steady source of ideas, collaboration, laughter and support. Bob Steele, Keith Woods and Aly Colón have been my teachers in the areas of ethics and diversity and shared their excellent lessons. Kenny Irby provided his photography tips and photographic skills. Nora Paul's writings and research on computer-assisted journalism have been a strong influence. I appreciate Paul Pohlman's and Bill Boyd's and Billie Keirstead's steady encouragement.

The Poynter Institute library staff, Kathy Holmes, David Shedden, Sandra Allen, and Sandra Johnakin, aided my research efforts countless times with their usual skill, patience and good cheer. Special thanks to Tom Lowe, Leslie Pelley, Tommy Carden, Monique Saunders and Latisha Williams.

Nancy Stewart, the Writing Program Assistant, kept me connected to my work and the Institute. Marty Gregor kept me connected to the outside world. Priscilla Ely, Larry Larsen and Anne Conneen helped with digitizing the book's photos. Joyce Barrett copyedited the manuscript. Lanette Miller and Rick Nesman kept me online.

Dr. Rod Jones, my chiropractor, kept my back adjusted.

Student journalists and their professors at several colleges helped me test teaching materials, including Rick Wilber's journalism class at the University of South Florida, Maria Vesperi's class at New College and an Adelphi University class taught by Doreen Carvahal of *The New York Times.*

I owe a great debt to the hundreds of writers, editors, producers, photographers, visual journalists and educators who have taught and learned with me at The Poynter Institute, including Stephen Buckley, Kevin McGeever, Tom French, Jeff Klinkenberg, Anne Hull, Nelle Nix, Michael Clapp and Kelly Ryan. Matt Schudel of the Fort Lauderdale *Sun-Sentinel Magazine* took time from his own writing to copyedit the book.

Perhaps my best teachers were the editors, reporters, photographers and artists at the papers and magazines I have worked or freelanced for, especially *The Providence Journal,* the *St. Petersburg Times* and Knight Ridder Newspapers Washington Bureau. In St. Petersburg, Andrew Barnes has supported me in my roles as a reporter and teacher. Two photographers, Andrew Dickerman in Providence and Ricardo Ferro in St. Pete, taught me unforgettable lessons about courage and how to better see a story. Berkley Hudson has encouraged me since we were journalism students together. A special thanks to Peter Perl of *The Washington Post,* my first bureau chief, who has remained a constant friend and journalistic role model.

My thanks to the newspapers, television station and online sites who let me reprint their stories, photos and other materials.

Thanks also to the American Society of Newspaper Editors and the scores of writers who have been my teachers in the pages of the *Best Newspaper Writing* that I have had the fortune to edit since 1994. Their work and practices enrich this book, especially those of Donna Britt, David Zucchino, Rick Bragg, Susan Trausch, Tom Hallman, David Waters, Eileen McNamara, Martin Merzer, Ken Wells, Mitch Albom, Terry Jackson and David Maraniss.

A very special thanks to the nearly 80 Poynter reporting and writing fellows who, since 1994, helped me develop and refine the lessons of this book and shared with me their work, insights and friendship as they launched their careers.

This book would not have been possible without the community of scholars, writers and passionate amateurs who have made the Internet a university, coffeehouse, library, art museum and community of global proportions.

Finally, a group of academic reviewers carefully read and reacted to a draft of this book: Sandra Combs Birdiett, Wayne State University; Glen L. Bleske, California State University at Chico; Barbara Hipsman, Kent State University; Christine Martin, Western Virginia University, Rick Wilber, University of South Florida; and Wendy Williams, The American University. Their devotion to teaching a new generation and their useful and inspiring suggestions for how to make this book help accomplish that goal deeply influenced the shape and content of the final product.

Among the many people who assisted me, a smaller group deserves special recognition. Don Murray, my mentor, teacher and friend, has for nearly two decades given me the ultimate compliment of treating me as an equal.

At Harcourt College Publishers, Carol Wada and her successor, Stephen Dalphin, shared my vision for this book and more important, their belief in me when my own wavered. Cathlynn Richard, my development editor, gave me steady encouragement, deadlines, feedback, ideas, and the attention to prose that made me the envy of other authors. I'm grateful to Laurie Bondaz, my project editor, for her attentiveness, care and support.

The faith, love and support of my mother, Alice S. Harreys, and my five brothers and sisters and their families have sustained me.

My wife, Kathy Fair, and our daughters, Caitlin, Lianna and Michaela, bring joy and meaning to my life. It is the lucky writer who has a spouse who writes and edits as well as mine. I am a writer today because she has believed in me.

CONTRIBUTORS

The following journalists and journalism educators contributed material to this book. The author bears ultimate responsibility for its contents. (Contributors' affiliations are current as of January, 1999.)

Jacqui Banaszynski
The Seattle Times

Deborah Barfield
Newsday

Rhea Borja
Richmond Times-Dispatch

Mitch Broder
Gannett Suburban Newspapers

Stephen Buckley
The Washington Post

Richard Erin Caddell
Institutional Investor

Gerald Carbone
The Providence Journal

Rebecca Catalanello
Charlestown Daily Mail

Bill Coats
St. Petersburg Times

Rhonda Cook
Atlanta Journal-Constitution

Lisa Demer
Anchorage Daily News

Jonathan Dube
The Charlotte Observer

Lillian Dunlap
University of Missouri

Karin Fischer
Charlestown Daily Mail

Thomas French
St. Petersburg Times

Mark Fritz
Los Angeles Times

Judy Gerber
News Watch Project

Gerry Goldstein
The Providence Journal

Frank Greve
Knight Ridder Newspapers

Jack Hart
The Oregonian

Dave Herzog
The Providence Journal

David Ho
Wall Street Journal Interactive Edition

Erin Hoover
The Oregonian

Holly Kurtz
The Orlando Sentinel

John Larson
NBC *Dateline*

Scott Libin
KTSP-TV

Christine Martin
West Virginia University

Linah Mathabane

Glenn McLaren
Fort Lauderdale *Sun-Sentinel*

Michelle McClellan
The Oregonian

Bill Mitchell
Universal New Media

Tiffany Murri
KIVI-TV

Elizabeth Osder
iXL

Richard Peacock
Charlestown Daily Mail

Deborah Potter
NewsLab

Michael Rogers
Newsweek.com

Donna Rowlinson
Fort Lauderdale *Sun-Sentinel*

Kelly Ryan
St. Petersburg Times

Matt Schudel
Fort Lauderdale *Sun-Sentinel*

Jeremy Schwartz
Imperial Valley Press

John Silcox

Thomas Stinson
Atlanta Journal-Constitution

Heather Svokos
Lexington Herald-Leader

Greg Toppo
The Associated Press

David Von Drehle
The Washington Post

Dan Wiederer
The Naperville Sun

FOREWORD
BY
DONALD M. MURRAY

In 1981 I was appointed Writing Coach to *The Providence Journal*. At the first meeting I was aware of a reporter who didn't know what a writing coach was, but seemed certain he didn't need any professor type to help with his writing. His face was quizzical, his body language skeptical, his questions critical but betraying an obsession with the "writing process"—a term he did not then know.

I feared he would expose my ignorance and asked who he was. "Chip Scanlan, one of our top reporters." My fears increased. I was not only a former journalist turned teacher, I was a writer who was—and is—still an apprentice to the writer's craft. I wasn't sure I had anything to teach an experienced reporter.

Eighteen years earlier I had been hired to establish a journalism program at the University of New Hampshire, but was also assigned to teach teachers of writing. Since junior high school, I had read books about writing and when I was hired I knew how to write, but didn't really know how I wrote, how others wrote or even how to teach writing.

Searching for a way to structure my classes, I turned to stories I had written for magazines on systems engineering in the early days of what was known as The Missile Crisis. I remembered how intercontinental missile designers saw missile guidance systems as a series of black boxes. To my astonishment, I found the engineers might not know what happened in the box, but they knew if they connected them, they could produce a result and eventually study how the electronic devices worked within each black box.

I could write publishable copy but to *understand* writing, I needed to look inside my own three black boxes that included: what prepared me to write, the writing itself and the inevitable revision. So, I began to study the *process* of writing. In those days, I did thirty—yes, 30—revisions of each magazine article I wrote. I had those precomputer drafts on hand, and I was able to examine them until I understood the black box of revision. Then I moved to prewriting, the more public process of reporting and preparing to write, and finally, to the most mysterious black box of all—when idea becomes draft.

In addition to my own drafts, I studied the writing process of published writers and of my best students. I began to write articles and books for teachers, then later for students, on the writing process. As a professor, I was invited to profess at conferences and workshops and soon found myself part of what began to be known as the "writing process" movement. I was invited to work with writers at *The Boston Herald* and called myself a "writing coach," a term that stuck as I moved on to *The Boston Globe, The Providence Journal* and other newspapers, where I worked with publishing writers and editors to study the reporting, writing and editing process of the various departments of the newspaper.

I discovered the obvious—that students had very different writing strengths and problems, and very little awareness of their particular strengths and weaknesses. Teaching them en masse proved a difficult task but individually, in conference, they could be given the kind of attention—coaching—given professionals such as opera singers.

Of course I was instructed as much as—often more—than those I coached. I was particularly instructed by the tough questions from that reporter in Providence, Rhode Island, Christopher Scanlan. I would make a glib generalization and he would nail me: What did I mean? Why? How did I know that? Give an example? What about writing on deadline? What about writing a long takeout? I tried to answer and counter attacked, asking him questions about his writing process and inviting him to coach me on my own writing. Our questions developed into conversations and he soon became a colleague and a friend. I was the consultant who blew in, blew off and blew out. He became the in-house authority who ran the program to improve writing day to day, studying the writing process at work, demonstrating how coaching could take place on deadline—all while he continued to be one of the paper's top reporters.

He became my personal writing coach as we shared drafts, writing questions and answers, tricks of our shared trade. In the years since 1981, he has become my closest colleague in the study of the writing process and in developing the techniques of coaching writers. He has an instinct for scholarship, an enormous appetite for information about writing, and the detachment of a true craftsperson who can stand back from his own drafts, articulating what works and what needs work.

We taught each other to lower our standards at the beginning of the process, to write early, to respect the instructive failure, to tell each other exactly what kind of reading—line-by-line or overall, for order or voice—that we needed at that stage of our writing process.

Then, when he was at the peak of his game as a reporter in Washington, The Poynter Institute for Media Studies made an inspired selection and appointed Christopher Scanlan Director of Writing. Suddenly he had an opportunity to continue his career as a publishing writer, to follow his instincts as a scholar of the writing process, and to develop his skill as a writing coach by teaching others to coach.

I have followed his development as a teacher—we talk almost every day—and have observed it firsthand both at Poynter and at professional meetings. He has become a master instructor of the writing process and the coaching method of teaching writing. He is also a master learner who has continued to follow his extraordinary curiosity about the writing process. He has been the colleague who has most instructed and inspired me.

Now I have had the delight of reading this cumulative work in which Christopher Scanlan demonstrates his ability to write with energy, clarity and grace; documents his profound understanding of how effective reporting becomes effective writing; and shows teachers how to coach students so they can coach each other.

I have learned from every chapter—the more a writer knows, the more he can learn—but I have especially learned from his seminal chapter on storytelling, his chapter on math that I need so much, and from the way he connects the old lessons of journalism with the new demands of the 21st Century. He has been my personal guide into the rapidly developing world of electronic reporting and writing.

This is the best journalism textbook I have read and the one I would use if I returned to the classroom. I recommend it to working journalists and to the teachers of those who will become working journalists. Christopher Scanlan's book is built on his personal experience as both writer and writing coach—and he writes so well that he inspires as well as instructs.

****

Donald M. Murray, who won a Pulitzer Prize for editorial writing, established the journalism program at the University of New Hampshire. He has published more than ten books on the writing process and its teaching as well as poetry and fiction. His column, Over 60, appears each week in *The Boston Globe*.

The Coaching Way: How to Get the Most Out of This Book

As a reporter, you'll confront daily challenges that will test your intelligence, energy, courage and sense of what is right and wrong. Although this may sound like it's a pretty tough territory to enter, fortunately, I have news for you.

You understand all your problems.

You have all the solutions to all those problems.

These are startling statements coming at the beginning of a textbook designed to help teach the craft of news reporting and writing. But such philosophy is the heart of this book. "The Coaching Way," as I refer to it, is based on the coaching approach pioneered by professor and journalist Donald M. Murray and further developed and spread worldwide by me and my colleagues at The Poynter Institute, a school for professional and student journalists in St. Petersburg, Fla.

Coaching is based on the idea that the power to recognize a story's problems as well as the means to fix them lie within the person reporting and writing the piece. This doesn't mean you won't need teachers, editors, classmates or colleagues to help you master the range of skills needed to report and write the news with power, clarity and grace. These relationships form the heart of the one-on-one coaching that will help you produce your best work. The best writers often say that the more they write, the more they realize how little they know about writing.

What "The Coaching Way" does is place the ultimate responsibility for learning on you. It also recognizes that the person who cares most about your success must be you. Coaching requires active participation rather than sitting back and waiting for others to tell you what to do. The search for answers must begin with you. Fortunately, coaching can help you achieve success by drawing on two basic skills you already possess: the ability to ask questions and the ability to listen to the answers.

What's the news? What's the story? What works in this story? What needs work? Where can you go to find that information? Who can you talk to about this story? Those are the kinds of open-ended questions that good editors and teachers have always used to get the best from their reporters and students. "The Coaching Way" asks you to help yourself and others do the same.

Effective listening requires empathy, the ability to identify with another person's point of view and to communicate that understanding. It requires a range of other skills and qualities, too, such as flexibility, confidence, a willingness to experiment, a keen awareness of another's situation and a genuine desire to help someone else achieve his or her goals.

For me, the qualities of a good coach are best described in the obituary of a *New Yorker* magazine editor named Robert Gerdy:

"He was generous, he was sensitive, he was tactful, he was modest, he was patient, he was imaginative, he was unfailingly tuned in. ... He found his own joy in helping other people bring their writings to a state of something like perfection."

In every chapter of this book, you'll find sections labeled "The Coaching Way," which contain lists of questions, along with tips and techniques designed to help you discover what you may already know about your story, what you may still need to find out, and where or who to go to for information and guidance. These questions can also be used to help other classmates or colleagues diagnose problems in their stories and devise solutions.

One of the best ways to learn your craft is to share the lessons learned when the reporting and writing go well. "The Coaching Way" uses three questions to guide your explorations of successes that can be described, shared and, best of all, repeated. They are:

1. What surprised you?

2. What did you learn?

3. What do you need to learn next?

These three questions are the diagnostic tools that I ask students and professional journalists to use to write accounts of successful reporting and writing experiences. Throughout the book you will find examples of these accounts entitled "How I Wrote the Story," written by students like yourself and by other professional journalists and myself as I continue to learn my craft. By focusing on what works and what may need work in our stories, we can repeat our successes rather than merely trying to avoid another failure. You will be encouraged to write your own stories, to become what my colleague, Roy Peter Clark, calls "a reflective practitioner," someone who doesn't just do the job of reporting and writing but also thinks about it in ways that regularly lead to the next level of competence. By practicing "The Coaching Way," you'll discover within yourself everything you need to produce your best work—and to help others do the same.

For more information about coaching, see:

Murray, Donald M. *A Writer in the Newsroom*. St. Petersburg, Fla.: The Poynter Institute, 1996.

Clark, Roy Peter and Don Fry. *Coaching Writers: Editors and Reporters Working Together*. New York: St. Martin's Press, 1992.

Geisler, Jill. *The Writing Coach in the Broadcast Newsroom*. St. Petersburg, Fla.: The Poynter Institute. Available online at MACROBUTTON HtmlRes Anchor **http://www.poynter.org/research/lm/lm_writecoach.h**.

Pohlman, Paul. *Coaching Skills: A Media Leadership Handout*. St. Petersburg, Fla.: The Poynter Institute. Available online at **http://www.poynter.org/research/lm/lm_coach.htm**.

CONTENTS

CHAPTER 3: A PROCESS APPROACH TO REPORTING AND WRITING   58

CHAPTER 4: FINDING AND WRITING A LEAD   115

CHAPTER 5: STORY FORMS: SHAPING THE NEWS   152

CHAPTER 8: REPORTING AND WRITING BROADCAST NEWS 262

CHAPTER 9: WRITING ONLINE NEWS 291

CHAPTER 10: FIRST ASSIGNMENTS   328

CHAPTER 11: DOING THE RIGHT THING: LIBEL, PRIVACY AND ETHICS   372

CHAPTER 14: NUMBERS AND THE BEGINNING JOURNALIST   513

CHAPTER 15: GETTING—AND KEEPING—A JOB   543

REPORTING AND WRITING: BASICS FOR THE 21ST CENTURY

News Thinking in a Changing World

Chapter Focus

News judgment—the ability to recognize and report news of interest and importance to an audience—is the foundation of good journalism and a skill that can be mastered.

Chapter Lessons

- What is news?
- What is news judgment?
- How do you decide whether something is newsworthy?
- What are the elements of news?
- Why is so much news bad?
- Where and how do you find news?
- Developing your news senses
- Knowing your audience
- Seeing news as culture
- How technology changes the definition of news
- News thinking: The Coaching Way

What's the News?

What's the news? It's the very first question the journalist must ask. It's the hardest one for beginners to answer.

What shall I write about? What do people in my community—the readers of my newspaper, the audience for my news broadcast, the browsers of my news Web site—need to know? From the flood of information that modern society generates, what do I report on? What's the most important aspect of the story I'm covering? When there seem to be 15 different ways to write a story, how do I choose the right one?

For beginning reporters, the mystery of what is a news story is often the first—and highest—hurdle to be cleared. It requires **news judgment,** one of many journalistic terms presented in this book. (You'll find these terms defined in the glossary at the end of each chapter.) News judgment is the ability to recognize and communicate news of interest and importance to an **audience.** It requires **critical thinking** and creativity. Learning the skill of news judgment takes time, experience, patience, lots of practice and some mistakes, but it can be learned. As with most things in life, the more you do it, the better you get at it. So let's get to it:

In the town of Pleasantville yesterday, police reported two motor vehicle accidents. Your job is to decide which one is more newsworthy.

1. A motorist pulling out of a parking space at the local mall backed into a parked car, denting the rear fender and breaking a taillight. No one was hurt, and the drivers exchanged information about their insurance companies.

2. A drunk driver ran a stop sign at a busy intersection and collided with a school bus carrying the high school band to a concert. Three students were taken to the hospital, one with serious injuries. The driver was arrested.

I know what you're thinking: Give me a break, a 5-year-old could answer that one. (For any 5-year-olds reading this, the answer is number 2.) It's a no-brainer, I agree. But that's the point. Once you become practiced at deciding what makes something news, or more importantly, *why* something is news, it will become a reflex action. (Later in the chapter, we'll return to the Pleasantville example to learn why the school bus accident is more newsworthy than the fender bender at the mall.)

"In most newsrooms, the nature of news, like language itself, is taken for granted," says Max Frankel, a retired executive editor of *The New York Times.* When journalists report and write a story, when their editors choose the stories for the front page, when a television news director decides the order for a news broadcast or when a content developer selects the headline links for a news site on the Internet, they all work, as Frankel puts it, "like chefs preparing a sauce—no recipes needed."

How to get to that point—no recipes needed—is the subject of this chapter. By the time you finish it, you will have a better sense of what the new reporter needs to know to make effective news judgments: the unspoken, common knowledge that people have in the newsroom.

What editors and news directors, as well as readers and viewers, want from reporters is the ability to think critically, to be able to size up a situation and report with authority, knowledge and accuracy about an event, a development or an issue in a way that helps people understand. Think of it as News Thinking, the foundation of all that follows in reporting and writing the news. For anyone interested in working in the communications field, whether in news, public relations or advertising, knowing how news professionals decide what to report is an essential skill. As news consumers, all of us can benefit by understanding why one story is considered newsworthy, even if we don't agree with the decision.

WHAT IS NEWS?

Another multiple choice question:
    News is:

1. Verified information that is relevant to public life.—Ellen Hume

2. What protrudes from the ordinary.—Walter Lippman

3. The departure from normal.—Leo Rosten

4. What I say it is.—David Brinkley

5. all of the above

When it comes to the definition of news, everybody has an opinion. An online news site called the Morrock News Service features a long list of definitions. That's why the correct answer is number 5, "all of the above," although that doesn't cover it, either. News is "probably as old as mankind, perhaps older," argues sociologist Robert E. Park in the essay *News as a Form of Knowledge.* "The lower animals were not without a kind of communication which was not unlike news. The 'cluck' of the mother hen is understood by the chicks as signifying either danger or food, and the chicks respond accordingly." In that way, we are all reporters of one kind or another, like children communicating the news of family matters to our parents and siblings. Until the 1830s, news consisted largely of information of interest to the wealthy and powerful. "Most newspapers were little more than excuses for espousing a political position, for listing the arrival and departure of ships, for familiar essays and useful advice, or for commercial or legal announcements," says historian Daniel Boorstin.

FIND MORE QUOTES ABOUT THE DEFINITION OF NEWS ONLINE AT http://morrock. com/newsdef. htm

The definition of news changed with the 1833 appearance of the *New York Sun.* It cost a penny, was aimed at the working class filling the cities and looked beyond political and shipping news, as journalism scholar Leon Sigal says, "to sample the rich variety of everyday social life in the city—crimes, accidents, the occasions of high and low society." News became a commercial product, and story forms, such as the human-interest story, developed as a kind of marketing tool written to sell papers.

News is also a business, a multibillion-dollar industry that employs tens of thousands. News is the backbone of America's 1,500 daily newspapers, 1,550 television stations and a growing number of electronic outlets from America Online to Webcasting products such as PointCast, an electronic delivery service that, unlike newspapers, which appear on doorsteps once a day, comes in a steady electronic push. This new technology is transforming the way news is gathered, organized, presented and distributed. As a reporter in the 21st century, you will use the skills of news thinking and news judgment you develop to play a major role in the ongoing evolution of news.

Spend some time studying the history of news. Not enough reporters do that. One of the most comprehensive survey texts, and good

VISIT THE NEWSEUM ONLINE AT http://www. newseum.org

"The news media are clearly now covering more of the society, moving away from institutional coverage of buildings and trying to make the news more relevant to audiences. With the end of the Cold War and other social and economic changes, the relevance of many traditional stories change, naturally moving the press in other directions."
—"CHANGING DIRECTIONS OF NEWS," THE COMMITTEE OF CONCERNED JOURNALISTS

READ MORE ONLINE AT http://www. journalism.org/ lastudy.htm

reading, too, is Mitchell Stephens' *A History of News.* You can also visit, in person or via cyberspace, the Newseum, an Arlington, Va., museum created by the Freedom Forum and devoted to journalism. It's a must-see stop for gatherers and consumers of news.

Even a brief acquaintance with the history of news will demonstrate that you are part of a long tradition. As a professional class, reporters didn't appear until the early 19th century. Before that, journalists were also publishers of their own publications. The development of the penny press created a demand for a journalist who visited government offices and police stations, crime scenes and legislatures and chronicled the doings of government and society, high and low.

Today the journalist is a knowledge worker who gathers information from databases as well as interviews and whose role is to gather, select, analyze and present that information in a coherent, accessible way to make sense of the ever-expanding information glut.

As a rookie reporter, I flipped through dozens of police and fire reports every day. Most were written in confusing legalese or jargon favored by cops and firefighters. (Why, for example, were burning buildings said to be "fully involved"?) I had to decide which incident to write about, to pick one burglary over another, to focus on one car accident out of 10 that happened the previous day. I didn't have much time, either. I had to identify the news, quickly and correctly, and then race back to the paper to write the story. It was hard, often frustrating, work. When I made the wrong choice I was called to task by my editors, fellow reporters and, most painfully, by my sources, the public officials, police officers and ordinary citizens I was writing about. I know now that what I experienced as a newcomer to journalism was not at all unusual.

Journalists must look at the world differently from most people. That takes getting used to. We are trained observers who play an important role in society: We inform the public about the events, developments and issues that affect daily life. We are constantly making assessments about what's going on around us, trying to understand the meaning that lies beneath the surface. Journalists can't sit back and watch the world go by. We are on duty all the time. For the newcomer to journalism, that can be an immense responsibility and a daunting challenge. It requires quick intelligence, a wide range of knowledge, incessant curiosity and persistence in the face of difficulty. We reporters don't just observe, however. We must assess, analyze what we observe and learn, and then we have to communicate our observations in stories that faithfully, accurately and thoroughly tell the news of the day. We reporters aren't stenographers, simply recording what people are saying and doing. We are reviewers of public life. We are constantly listening and assessing, probing, seeking to understand, going beneath the surface.

DEVELOPING CRITICAL THINKING SKILLS

The *San Jose Mercury News,* located in California's Silicon Valley, is one of the news industry's new media pioneers. Yet when the paper's editor was asked what training he believes reporters and journalism students need, he didn't mention computers. He talked about critical thinking. "I do not think we have to train people in the fine points of online journalism," Jerry Ceppos said. "If we teach kids how to think critically, organize their thoughts and put them down on paper or whatever material, that is far more important."

Critical thinking is the act of drawing inferences or conclusions from a body of information. It's the "art of taking charge of your own mind," as some teachers put it. It's using your analytical reasoning power in the pursuit of facts and the quest for truth and being open-minded enough to change your mind in the face of conflicting evidence. As a reporter, you will be bombarded with messages and points of view by politicians, advertisers, activists and many others—this candidate is the best for the job, my plan for school reform is the smartest, our widget is the most state-of-the-art on the market, abortion is murder/a woman's choice. The list goes on and on. As a writer, you will need to be willing to revise a story, no matter how much work you've already done on it, if the facts change the focus. Your job is to help your readers and viewers sort out the conflicting claims and gain a better understanding.

Critical thinking as a field of knowledge traces back some 2,500 years to Socrates, the Greek philosopher. Socrates showed how empty meaning often lies behind the persuasive arguments of those in authority. He accomplished this by using tools and techniques that belong in every journalist's toolbox: probing questions, search for evidence, willingness to question assumptions and focus on what people do as well as what they say. Critical thinking skills are essential at a time of accelerating change. When every day brings a new development in technology, health, education and other areas, journalists especially must equip themselves with the ability to examine and analyze so they can help their audiences make sense of those changes.

If you've taken a philosophy course, you're already familiar with critical thinking as a concept and some of its terms, such as fallacious appeals, sweeping generalizations and *ad hominem* attacks. If you've ever used a computer search engine, such as Infoseek or Excite, you've used critical thinking. When you typed "Clinton and Lewinsky" to research a paper, you've used a term of Boolean logic—*and*—that relies on the same basic terms and concepts of critical thinking. What you may not have realized is how important those lessons could be to your future as a journalist. Now is the time to get acquainted—or reacquainted—with this vital topic. Read one of the books or articles cited in the "Readings" section of this chapter or browse Internet links on critical thinking in this chapter's "Hotlist." A good beginning is Mission: Critical, a Web site maintained by David Mesher, a teacher

"Critical thinking is thinking about your thinking while you're thinking in order to make your thinking better."
—RICHARD PAUL, CENTER FOR CRITICAL THINKING AND MORAL CRITIQUE, SONOMA STATE UNIVERSITY

FOR FURTHER INFORMATION ABOUT CRITICAL THINKING ONLINE, VISIT http://www.criticalthinking.org

LEARN MORE ABOUT CRITICAL THINKING ONLINE FROM "MISSION CRITICAL," AN INTERACTIVE TUTORIAL, AT http://www.sjsu.edu/depts/itl AND THE REYNOLDS SCHOOL OF JOURNALISM AT THE UNIVERSITY OF NEVADA AT RENO AT http://www.unr.edu/unr/journalism/pro.home.html

"Although we
can't predict
how this new
media
landscape will
look in the
future, we can
be sure of the
skills the
journalists of
the new world
will need. First
and foremost,
they'll need to
be able to
think. They will
need to be able
to write, to
collect and
analyze
information,
and to present it
in a creative
fashion."
—FACULTY
STATEMENT,
REYNOLDS
SCHOOL OF
JOURNALISM,
UNIVERSITY OF
NEVADA AT RENO

at San Jose State University at **http://www.sjsu.edu/depts/itl/**. It offers readings, exercises and links to other useful sites, including the Reynolds School of Journalism at the University of Nevada at Reno, which has made critical thinking a foundation of its program.

Knowledge and critical thinking skills will produce the final element, the confidence that will enable you to identify the news quickly and fashion a report that answers the five W's—"who, what, where, when and why?"—as well as "how?" and the most important, "so what?"

Defining what news is has never been more important than it is today.

News is not fiction or poetry or a term paper, although, at its best, it displays the power, beauty and discipline of all three. News is everything from a high school volleyball score to Dennis Rodman's latest outburst on the basketball court, from a vote tally to the foreign policy debates within the State Department, from the stock market tables to the opening of a new megastore in town.

News is a commodity that is likely to increase in value because, as Michael Gartner, one of America's most thoughtful editors, says, people "want to know what is going on in the world, in their world, in their neighborhood."

News is what happened yesterday. It's what's happening today and what will happen tomorrow. News is what somebody wants everybody to know. News is what someone else wants to hide. News is information about the way we live and the way we ought to live. News is what important people say and do. News is what ordinary folks say and do. News is what people care about and what people should care about. News is information. News is knowledge. News is history. News is negative. News is positive. News is what people chat about at lunch counters and online.

News helps people make the choices that citizens face in a democracy—to vote, to petition the government, to exercise constitutional rights. News protects the public from abuses by governments and private institutions. News helps parents, children, students, investors, homeowners, renters.

In the exercises at the end of this chapter, you will be asked to come up with your own personal definition of news. Here is mine: **News** is an ongoing, constantly updatable record of change.

A LIFE IN JOURNALISM

As a journalist, you must find news that people want—and need—to know. It may be helpful for you to think of how you first experienced news as a child, as Rhea R. Borja, a beginning journalist, recalls in the essay on p. 7.

THREE BASIC ELEMENTS OF NEWS

So what makes something news? Journalists look for three basic elements. News is:

1. Timely

BEGINNINGS

Rhea R. Borja

RHEA R. BORJA IS A REPORTER FOR THE *RICHMOND TIMES-DISPATCH*.

The news was a mystery to me; I wondered how reporters got to each event in such a short time, whether it was a train wreck in India, a monetary crisis in France, or a fire down the street. It seemed that reporters were omnipresent, like Big Brother in Orwell's novel *1984*. They also seemed glamorous in a world-weary, caustic way. Their faces and their tones said, *We are very important. Pay attention.*

I don't remember reading newspapers or newsmagazines in grade school very much. I did produce a "newspaper" when I was 9. I handwrote it on thick white drawing paper. I wrote about the arguments I had with my brother, the very public divorce of our next-door neighbors, and some of the closed-door conversations of my parents. My readers were the other kids in the neighborhood. It had a very brief life; my parents found out after the first few issues, much to my chagrin and their horror.

I wanted to be either a concert pianist or a writer when I grew up. The former I knew was a fantasy, but the latter seemed reachable. Plus, one had a much, much larger audience. But back then I wanted to write fiction, mistakenly thinking that people like Hemingway and Chekhov were real writers and that reporters were not. But as I got older and started reading writers like Calvin Trillin and Maureen Dowd, I knew I was wrong.

My personal definition of news: current information about a community that not only informs, but also educates and inspires people.

2. Important

3. Interesting

NEWS IS TIMELY

Just as the word implies, news is "new." It's the vote that just occurred, the game that just ended, the war that just broke out, the verdict just in, the election just decided, the fact, event or development that provides what journalists call the **peg,** or reason to publish or broadcast news. It's what you didn't know when you went to bed or when you last turned on the television or went online. It's the fresh angle, the latest word, the most recent development.

Mark Fritz
(AP/Wide
World Photos)

More than two centuries ago, the first American newspapers "defined news as letters from travelers who had witnessed important events in Philadelphia or London or Paris and sent back a report by horse or clipper ship," says political columnist Richard Reeves. But after the first telegraph linked newspapers in Washington, D.C. and Baltimore in 1844, timeliness became an essential ingredient of news. The scoop soon followed. Newsboys screaming, "Extra, read all about it!" on city street corners have been replaced by live coverage of the Gulf War, the nearly instantaneous transmission of the Starr report on President Clinton's sex life and headlines streaming across personal computers connected to the Internet. Television stations still claim bragging rights about who was first to broadcast a breaking story. And the desire to beat the competition, like some primal urge, still beats in the hearts of newspaper journalists even though they long ago surrendered the chance to be first to the telegraph, radio and television. Long before CNN broadcast the opening explosions of the Gulf War live from Baghdad in January 1991, newspapers had "ceased to be the way people actually *discovered* something," says Geneva Overholser, a veteran newspaper editor who served as newsroom critic, known as an **ombudsman,** for *The Washington Post.* Think about the way you learned of the major news of the last five years: the O. J. Simpson verdict, the Oklahoma City bombing, the presidential election results, the Monica Lewinsky scandal, your favorite team's victory.

The dictionary defines news as "a report of a recent event." Even so, something that occurred long ago may become timely. Archaeological finds routinely make the headlines: At the turn of the last century, an influenza virus killed at least 20 million people worldwide. The long-forgotten 1918 epidemic became front page news in March 1997 after scientists reported that they had found fragments from the Spanish flu virus in the formaldehyde-soaked lung tissue of a man who died 79 years earlier. But whatever the time frame, news stories need to feel as fresh as bread straight from the oven, not the day-old loaf marked down to half price.

NEWS IS IMPORTANT

News matters. Reporters, news directors and editors know that readers and viewers will be asking: "So what? Why should I care?" As the world becomes more complex, the job of the journalist broadens to include explaining news. It's not enough to simply report events; the reporter has a responsibility to also help the reader understand why this information matters—or should. When *The New York Times* reported the discovery of genetic material from the 1918 flu, it was quick to discuss the relevance. The story's fourth paragraph points out that researchers "hope that understanding the genetic code of the Spanish flu virus might help scientists prepare for the next influenza virus, which many scientists think is coming soon." The story provides context. With it, readers can understand why they should care about a pandemic that occurred decades before they were born.

As a reporter, you will have to anticipate readers' demand for relevance, whether it's a story about a burglary on their street or a scientific discovery on another continent. The ability to analyze events, developments and trends, to make connections that help people gain a better understanding of what it means to be alive today, is one of the aspects about journalism that makes it so challenging and rewarding. "Many readers say they look to the paper not for notification that something happened, but for context, meaning, perspective," Overholser says. "They want to know what difference it will make to them: Who played, what comes next, what the various views are about, what took place."

Names, the saying goes, make news. People are killed in automobile crashes every day; only Princess Diana's death consumed the news columns and broadcasts for days. People are familiar with celebrities and so will be interested in news about them. Studies have shown that journalists focus principally on well-known personalities. But I believe the lifeblood of news is the ordinary people whose actions influence the news and whose lives are affected by it. Joel Rawson, executive editor of *The Providence Journal*, says journalists need to write the story that reveals a trend through the people who are living it. He calls it making "a new stencil" for the news. News isn't just what officials say and do. It's what regular folks say and do as well.

NEWS IS INTERESTING

"News," an editor once declared, "is anything that makes a reader say, 'Gee Whiz.'" In many newsrooms, it's the "Hey, listen to this!" rule at work, the story that makes a reader, listener or viewer take notice and want to spread the word to a friend. At the heart of the news-gathering process is discovery. Reporters are the explorers of the 21st century, on the hunt for information that will interest people. The reporter has to have a sense of what people find interesting. That means talking to people about what they care about. Use yourself, your friends and colleagues as a barometer of interest.

Remember the two vehicle accidents in the town of Pleasantville at the start of this chapter? In one, a motorist pulling out of a parking space at the local mall backed into a parked car, denting the rear fender and breaking a taillight. No injuries reported. In the other, a drunk driver ran a stop sign at a busy intersection and collided with a school bus carrying the high school band to a concert. The accident left three students hurt, including one with serious injuries. Police arrested the driver. I asked you to decide which one was more newsworthy and apologized for the no-brainer quality of the question. I also promised to return to the example to explore the reasons why the second accident is more newsworthy. The short answer is that it includes the three essential elements of news. Let's take a closer look at the kind of thinking that a journalist does when considering whether something is news:

1. It's timely. The news happened yesterday, so chances are good that readers don't know about it unless they witnessed the incident or they had friends or family involved in the accident.
2. It's important. An accident at a busy intersection that injured children riding in a school bus is a serious incident that a community needs to

know about, not merely those who have a personal connection. Drunk driving is recognized as a serious social problem. It's a significant event that raises issues of important public interest.

3. It's interesting. There's nothing out of the ordinary about a fender bender in a mall parking lot. On the other hand, school buses are not normally involved in serious accidents, fortunately. The fact that the students were band members on their way to a concert—an exciting occasion—lends the story an added poignancy.

With any story, you should be able to articulate the thought process behind your news judgment. Being able to do so will help you make the kind of quick decisions that responsible journalism requires. It will also help you produce the kind of stories that provide meaning in a complex world. Remember the three basic elements of news: timeliness, importance and interest. Frame them as questions:

Is it new?

Is it important?

Is it interesting?

FIRST, THE BAD NEWS

"Why is news always about the bad stuff?" "Why can't you report anything positive?" As a reporter, you will be confronted by such questions from sources, and also from friends, family and neighbors. Criticism of negative reporting is a major reason why journalists are held in low regard. "News is never good; it's always bad things," a young North Carolina woman told the Raleigh *News & Observer* when it surveyed community attitudes toward the news media. I know what she means. There are times when reading my local paper or watching the 11 o'clock news leaves me feeling hopeless. The steady diet of crime, tragedy, greed and depravity sickens me.

But consider this analogy suggested by writer and journalism teacher Rick Wilber. What if, on the front page of the paper today, the lead headline reports that 15 flights took off safely from the airport in your community? The anchor on the six o'clock news reports that every school bus driver in town picked up and dropped off young passengers without incident. Tomorrow the stories are repeated: Fifteen flights took off safely; 25,000 workers showed up on time at the local factory. And so on. After a while, you'd probably stop reading the paper or turning to the TV news. One of the essential characteristics of news is that it focuses on the exceptional, the out-of-the-ordinary. That is the idea behind the cliché that "Dog Bites Man" isn't news, but "Man Bites Dog" is. In a way, the newspaper is the ironic reflection of something very positive: Most things go right, and when they go wrong—one plane out of a thousand winging its way to Paris explodes over the Atlantic Ocean, one argument out of hundreds turns murderous, one teen-ager out of an entire high school opens fire in a crowded cafeteria—the news sits up and takes notice.

William Raspberry, the syndicated columnist, regularly takes his colleagues in the news business to task for the steady and unrelenting diet of bad news. Whenever he visits a town he asks for examples of programs that are working, young people who are succeeding, neighborhoods that are fighting back against crime. Usually, he says, journalists are hard-pressed to come up with any. No wonder that even the most sympathetic critics of the news media, such as Overholser, say it's almost impossible to come away from the newspaper without feeling that everything is in disarray, "that nothing works—not politics, not government, not the economy. Certainly not schools or cities. And television news, with its 'if it bleeds, it leads' philosophy is even worse." News is not just a record of society's failures. It must be a record of its achievements.

But everything is relative. When Liggett and Meyers, maker of Chesterfield, L&M and Lark cigarettes, acknowledged in March 1997 that smoking does cause cancer, it was bad news for the tobacco industry and good news for antismoking activists. In the same way, the same day's report that the House of Representatives voted again to ban partial-birth abortions was good news for opponents of abortion, bad news for proponents of abortion rights. News, like beauty, is in the eyes of the beholder.

Delivering bad news will always be part of your job as a journalist. But it can't be the only thing on the menu.

DEVELOPING YOUR NEWS SENSES

Good reporters are often said to have a "nose for news." Thinking effectively and imaginatively about news requires using your senses, although they're not limited to the sense of smell. Developing your news senses will help you better understand the basic elements of news. They heighten your awareness.

- News has a sense of AUDIENCE. The reporter knows for whom the story is written and what the reader cares about, whether it's an increase in property taxes or the score of the championship game.

- News has a sense of RELEVANCE. News matters to people because it is information they need or believe is important, if not vital, to their daily lives. In November 1998, the *St. Petersburg Times* reported that fewer Canadian tourists, so-called "snowbirds" who flee frigid weather for Florida's sunny warmth, were expected during the coming winter. Why is this relevant to the newspaper's readers? Because Canadian tourists supply millions of dollars to the local economy. Fewer tourists mean fewer jobs, lower profits, less traffic—all of interest to that paper's audience.

- News has a sense of TIME. One of the reporter's jobs is to orient people. News always includes a time element. When did an event happen?

When will it happen? The news storyteller uses chronology as a tool to organize information. Stories may focus on a day in the life, the final minutes before an airplane crash or the behind-the-scenes battle to win support for controversial legislation.

■ News has a sense of DRAMA. News is action. What people do. At the heart of all drama is conflict, the struggle that humans engage in from their first breath. News is a chronicle of conflicts from the battlefield to the floor of Congress. Journalists cover wars, skirmishes, infighting, battles for supremacy and legislation, struggles for civil rights and protection from pollution.

The news media are criticized for focusing too much on violent conflicts—crime, war, political intrigues and social unrest. While they can't turn a blind eye to the struggles that pit individuals and groups against each other, the media must also focus attention on lesser-noticed but equally dramatic struggles that go on every day. There's powerful drama in the struggle of a blind child to attend school with sighted classmates, as I learned when I wrote about Jed Barton, who was blinded at birth but attended regular school, rode a bicycle and attended summer camp with kids who could see. Mitch Albom of the *Detroit Free Press* wrote about Kevin Jones, a high school senior in Detroit whose mother supports the family by working as a janitor. You develop a sense of drama by asking what's at stake.

■ News has a sense of PEOPLE. News is the daily chronicle of the human race. People are the lifeblood of journalism. Not just names and titles and addresses but also details about what those in the news look and sound like, how they behave, what they dream for. Sociologist Herbert Gans found that fewer than 10 percent of all the stories he studied were about abstractions, objects and animals. News is primarily about people, Gans observed, what they say and do.

■ News has a sense of PLACE. Of the five W's that are the essential elements of most news stories—who, what, when, why and where—the last one "is the least explored and most poorly executed in American journalism," says Jeff Klinkenberg of the *St. Petersburg Times,* one of the nation's best outdoors writers. News stories all too often deliver quotes from disembodied "talking heads" interviewed by telephone instead of sprinkling specific details that allow the reader to see the story as well as read it.

WHERE NEWS COMES FROM

The front page of any newspaper or Web site or the lead stories on a television or radio news broadcast give clear signals about some of the sources of news:

■ Official records
■ News conferences

- Press releases
- Decisions and other actions by government bodies: courts, police, legislatures from the local to the federal level
- Events

That partial list is drawn from traditional sentinel posts for journalists. Sentinel posts are traditionally those places, such as the police station, where journalists take up positions to chronicle the events and developments of interest and importance to a community. They represent a focus that dates back to the days when the government action "was one of the few sources of what little was new and different," according to journalist Max Ways. "Journalism still clings to the legislative act and the presidential decision because they are relatively easy to get into focus." Public officials do much of the legwork. But the good reporter doesn't rely solely on the legwork of police officers and politicians.

Good journalism means moving beyond the traditional gathering spots for news. Reporters have to go where news is happening—from the suburban neighborhood where a series of daytime burglaries has left people angry and vulnerable to the housing project where families struggle with poverty and its stigma. The traditional sentinel posts are the starting point, not the last stop. All too often, student journalists think they have gotten the story when they have the press release or have attended the press conference or finished the interview with the official.

News is the chronicle of our lives. If your police stories rely entirely on what patrol officers and detectives write in their incident reports, without also containing the experiences of crime victims, what you're doing is rewriting police reports instead of reporting what it means to be the victim of a crime and how that affects life in a neighborhood. If your school coverage is based on what you hear at school board meetings and not also what you see and hear in classrooms, at school bus stops or PTA meetings, then you aren't adequately reporting education news.

It's the reporter's job to decide what the news is. Some journalists let public relations specialists direct their reporting and frame their stories for them. Press releases can be a starting point for a story, but never the last stop. It's your job to decide what happened and to convey its significance.

Vanessa Bauzá, a student in the Poynter Institute's summer fellowship program in news reporting and writing, learned the value of going where the action is in St. Petersburg when she was reporting on a program to stem lead poisoning in children. From her interviews with health officials at the local children's hospital, she had the statistics, the scientific and medical background. What she didn't have was any children with lead poisoning. She wasn't likely to find any in the newsroom where she was sitting, and even at the hospital the chances that a mother would bring her child in at that particular moment for an examination seemed slim. Bauzá went to Jordan Park, a public housing project that had been the focus of the lead poisoning alert program. In a few hours she had just the details she needed.

Here's the lead Bauzá was able to write:

Getting Rid of Lead

Housing Authority Struggles to Remove Threat to City's Southside Children

By Vanessa Bauzá
Points South Staff Writer
June 27, 1996

ST. PETERSBURG—Last month, Tonvia Davis' sons, Eric, 4, and Donald, 2, tested positive for lead poisoning at more than double the acceptable blood lead level following a routine screening at the Health Department. Davis has since moved to a lead-safe apartment in the Jordan Park housing complex, but she says that for two years she lived in one of the older units, where chipping paint was "all over the house" and often accumulated around the doorway within easy reach of her children.

Davis feels that Jordan Park officials were slow to address the lead problem. "The whole project needs to do something about it. If my kids have lead there's a lot more kids out there got lead," said Davis.

HOW TO FIND NEWS

As a young reporter in the early 1970s, I began my day at 7 a.m. in the police station in Milford, Conn., a suburb of New Haven, leafing through the desk log—a huge ledger with handwritten entries—where officers kept track of the calls and arrests made the day before. I took notes and asked for more information from the desk sergeant, who made no secret of his disdain for this young pup wearing a hand-me-down suit. If the incident was serious enough, I had to go upstairs and solicit more details from the captain of detectives. From there I walked a few blocks to the fire station, where I copied into my notebook all the calls made by the city's firefighters and ambulance crews. My notebook full, I headed to the newspaper and spent the next two hours feverishly trying to transform my scribbled handwriting into stories about crime and emergencies in the town. After deadline and lunch, I attended meetings of the conservation commission and library board and worked on feature stories about interesting local figures like the police rescue team who made practice dives in the freezing Long Island Sound on New Year's Day. I often worried that they were mundane stories based on scant information, little knowledge and even less understanding. But the fact is they communicated the essentials to readers who wanted to know about crime in their community, introduced them to interesting people in their midst, and alerted them to news that affected their pocketbooks, their children's education and their family's health. In many ways not much has changed for reporters.

The police department and other public agencies remain a major source of news. As a reporter, you will need to be out on your beats: checking the daily police and fire logs, checking the agendas of meetings, talking with city officials and police officers, people on the street, kids in playgrounds, parents in the supermarket parking lot, the elderly, minorities, workers, crime victims. Reporters train a radar screen on their world, sweeping it constantly for the blips that signal a change that people need to know about. Reporters are on a constant quest for news. Covering Treasure Island, Fla., a quiet beach community, one summer as a Poynter Institute reporting fellow, Diana Peña was repeatedly told, "There's nothing going on here." But Peña kept asking questions until she heard that a new utility bill was going out in the mail from City Hall. She wrote a story explaining the charge.

Reporters must look beyond traditional sentinel posts to find stories in places that haven't been visited. "There is news in everything if you know where to look for it," John Hohenberg used to tell his students at the Columbia Graduate School of Journalism. I've found stories in the living room of a smoker's widow; on a park bench, where an elderly man reminisced about his dead wife and the pain of living alone; at the gate to a state fair, where a boy hoping to make it into the *Guinness Book of World Records* stood shaking hands with all who passed.

This is perhaps the most amorphous side of news gathering. When they get experience, reporters don't need to ask, "What's the news?" They know it when they see it. Reporters see the world through a unique lens.

So how do you, a beginning reporter, develop the reflexive skill of the veteran, able to pick out the relevant, interesting, important information from the mountains of data in your notebook?

News doesn't occur in a vacuum. Although a newspaper is one day's version of events, good journalism brings to its chronicling of the present a sense of the past and an appreciation for the future.

The reporter sizes up the situation, doesn't wait for the public relations official to dictate the story, and asks, "What do I think the news is?" Start early trying to figure out your story. At the Knight Ridder Washington Bureau, my colleagues and I had to identify the news quickly because hours before writing the stories we had to file four- to five-line descriptions of our stories— called budget lines—that were transmitted to the 29 Knight Ridder papers and the 250 other publications that subscribed to our news service. We were competing with a variety of other news organizations from *The New York Times* and *The Washington Post* to the wire services. Editors who subscribed to our service made decisions based on those budget lines. I had to learn to zero in on the news, to focus on the most important elements and to crystallize the story in a single paragraph. Very often the budget line became the lead of the story. I was forced to target the essential elements—what happened and what does it mean?—that captured the news.

You do this by bringing background knowledge and understanding and an appreciation of your responsibility to make sense out of the events, incidents, developments and actions that occur every day. "We're awash in information. Yet at the same time there is less understanding and more difficulty in gaining that understanding," says journalism scholar James Carey.

There will be times, especially at the start of your journalism career, when you will come into a story stone cold, with little or no background. It can be a terrifying experience: walking into a courtroom where you don't understand any of the procedures, can sometimes barely make out what's being said and yet have to figure out what's happening and what it means. Or you are sent to cover a meeting of a group you know nothing about, or a speech, or a strike where you don't know either side, the issues or what's at stake.

The only way to give yourself a head start is to begin thinking critically from the first moment, even if it's something you know nothing about.

Once you've found the news, how do you refine it? By asking the questions that place the news in context so your readers understand why they're

New technologies create new audiences, but fears that one will replace the other have proved groundless. To the newspaper and television watchers in this 1950 scene can be added a new generation who get their news from computer screens. (Courtesy of Library of Congress)

being told certain information. The best stories relate a specific incident or event to the larger community. They take the extra step to help readers understand what impact a news event or development might have on their lives. That's why, when you write a story about property taxes, you don't say just that the City Council increased the property tax rate by 10 percent. You describe what the bill of a typical homeowner would be after the rate hike takes effect.

KNOWING YOUR AUDIENCE

Audiences today can choose from a seemingly endless buffet of print, broadcast and online sources for news and information, many of which specialize in areas reflecting the interest of specific groups. The challenge for the 21st-century journalist is how to analyze audiences and to gather and present news and information that will attract and hold the attention of people chronically confronted with increasing choices.

Too often, as journalists, we ignore the audience—or we analyze and characterize its members without ever really talking to them, either as consumers or citizens with a vested interest in the news they receive from print, online and broadcast sources. We do so at our peril. Ned Barnett, metro editor of the Raleigh *News & Observer*, was talking about his segment of the industry, but his words resonate in television stations and online newsrooms as well: "For newspapers, locked in competition with an array of electronic rivals, every reader, even an angry one, is too precious to lose."

How can—and should—journalists think about audiences? You can think of them the way market researchers do, as audiences identified by their demographics—age, gender, race/ethnicity, income, education, occupation, location. Trevor R. Brown, dean of Indiana University's journalism school, advises his students to think of their audiences in light of the varying roles people play in their personal and social lives:

- As citizens who are part of "we, the people" on the one hand and as individuals with certain unalienable rights on the other, with responsibilities and interests, needs and wants, as they seek to enjoy their liberty and pursue happiness.
- As individuals who are children, siblings, parents, lovers, friends, workers, bosses, volunteers, consumers, fans, gamblers, and pleasure seekers, investors and on and on.

It may help to think of audience by thinking about how you read and react to stories you read or watch. Are you interested because you are a student, a fan of a particular team, a member of a racial or ethnic group, the child of an aging parent? Are you *not* interested because you are *not* a property owner, a registered voter, a member of the armed forces? How do your various roles and identities help determine what news and information you want? How well do your news sources reflect your needs and the needs of other audiences?

"To say that the audience is the most important part of the mass communication process is an understatement. Without the audience, there would be no mass communication."
—JOSEPH R. DOMINICK, THE DYNAMICS OF MASS COMMUNICATION

When Schwinn Bicycle Co. filed for bankruptcy in October 1992, it was a national story covered by newspapers and television news. In the four examples that follow, each news organization reflects, unconsciously or not, its sense of the audience it tries to reach.

The Wall Street Journal (1) aims at a national business and financial audience that likes its economic news played straight. The story's lead focuses on the cause and legal details of the company's bankruptcy and its long history. Note it attributes the story to the company.

USA Today (2) attracts a national audience of time-pressed travelers who want their news fast and lively. In 14 words, it sums up the cause of Schwinn's problems and uses wordplay ("rolling into") to tell the news with economy and a breezy style.

The New York Times (3) views itself as the nation's paper of record. Like *The Wall Street Journal*, it provides legal specifics, company history and causation, but blends attribution with its own analysis of Schwinn's market pressures.

The Washington Post (4) published the story in its feature section, where style, voice and an arch tone is aimed at an audience interested in attitude as well as information. It reports the news, but then the writer adds his own note of nostalgic sarcasm.

1. SCHWINN BICYCLE SEEKS CHAPTER 11 AS TALKS WITH BANKS BREAK OFF
Chicago—Schwinn Bicycle Co. said it filed a voluntary petition for relief under Chapter 11 of the U.S. Bankruptcy Code. The bicycle maker, founded in 1895, said the filing was prompted by a breakdown of negotiations with banks over payment of about $75 million in debts.
The Wall Street Journal

2. SCHWINN FILES FOR CHAPTER 11
Bicycle maker Schwinn, squeezed by competitors and poor management, is rolling into Chapter 11 bankruptcy-court protection.
USA Today

3. SCHWINN BICYCLE FILES
Under pressure from its creditors, the Schwinn Bicycle Company, America's oldest bicycle manufacturer, said yesterday that it had filed for protection under Chapter 11 of the United States Bankruptcy Code.
The New York Times

4. SCHWINN: IT WAS THE WHEEL THING
Schwinn Bicycle Co. filed for bankruptcy yesterday, thereby tolling the knell for the era when boys were boys and bikes were bikes and nobody went pedaling around wearing stupid little helmets.
The Washington Post

Talk to your friends, neighbors, classmates and others in your community or on your beat. Ask them what stories news organizations miss, what stories need to be told, what stories move and instruct them. Ask yourself: What stories do you want to read but don't find online, or in the newspaper or on television? Those are the stories that you will probably bring the most passionate interest to and that you will report and write with intensity and integrity. "People resent journalists not because we fail to understand, but because they think we don't try," says Judy Bolch, an editor at the Raleigh *News & Observer.* "Instead of news hounds anxious to learn it all, we're seen as lazy know-it-alls. They don't mind if we ask questions; they do object when we assume the answers."

SEEING NEWS AS CULTURE

What you think is news says as much about you as it does the story you are covering. In 1993, newly elected President Bill Clinton nominated lawyer Zoe Baird to be his attorney general. During the background investigation, it was learned that she and her husband had employed a nanny who was an undocumented immigrant. Michael Schudson, a journalism scholar, observed that the coverage of the case focused on the plight of Baird and her husband—well educated, affluent, a two-career couple, just like many of the reporters in Washington and New York who wrote the stories. But at Univision, the Spanish-language network, journalists concentrated on the domestics like the nanny who watched the Bairds' child. "When minorities and women and people who have known poverty or misfortune first-hand are authors of news as well as its readers, the social world represented in the news expands and changes," says Schudson.

"Who writes the stories matters," Schudson says, an observation that underscores the need for diversity in the news business. Your view of news also will reflect your background, your community and your sense of audience.

News judgment is often a subjective process, one that reflects the interests, prejudices and mind-sets of reporters and editors.

Your view of news also will reflect your assignment. To the investigative reporter, news is corruption in high places. To the health writer, it's the development of a new surgical technique or the hazards of a new drug. The political writer sees news in the strategies and techniques of campaign consultants. To the feature writer, news can be found in the lives of ordinary people as well as celebrity interviews. The police reporter finds news, as I did as a new reporter, in the human dramas that occupy law enforcement agencies

> "News is, in effect, what is on a society's mind. Has a bill been passed? Has anyone been hurt? Is a star in love? Through the news, groups of people glance at aspects of the world around them. Which of the infinite number of possible new occurrences these groups are able to see, and which they choose to look at, will help determine their politics and their philosophies."
> —MITCHELL STEPHENS, *A HISTORY OF NEWS*

NEWS IN THE INFORMATION AGE

Everybody's talking these days about how technology is changing the news business. But that's not new. More than 100 years ago, the invention of the telegraph changed the way news was reported, spawning the so-called "objective" style of reporting that replaced partisan politics with factual coverage of government and business affairs.

What has changed is the public's access to news. In the 1800s you needed a telegraph key and knowledge of Morse code to get instant access to news. Since 1994, when the World Wide Web appeared, you need only a computer,

"The infinite
volume of
unfocused
information
flooding up
from the
bottomless
computer
spring has
heightened the
value of the
guiding editor
who is
experienced
enough in
language and
judgment to
help us paddle
onto the shores
of meaning."

—EUGENE
PATTERSON,
RETIRED EDITOR
AND PRESIDENT
OF THE *St.
Petersburg
Times*, IN A
SPEECH
HONORING ELIJAH
PARISH LOVEJOY,
AN EDITOR KILLED
IN 1837
DEFENDING HIS
NEWSPAPER FROM
A PRO-SLAVERY
MOB

modem and telephone wire to download news feeds. Cable and satellite television offers dozens of 24-hour channels and even the live (and sometimes raw and unedited) feed of network news operations. More important, the personal computer gives the average citizen access to sources of information that once only journalists had.

The Internet eliminates the role of "middleman" between newsmakers and news consumers. After the April 19, 1995, bombing of the Alfred P. Murrah Federal Building in Oklahoma City, the Internet was scooping CNN as Oklahomans raced to their computers to file eyewitness accounts.

Electronic mailing lists and discussion groups have become a potent source of news. Word about a serious flaw in a new Intel Pentium computer-processing chip didn't emerge in a press release from the company or a leak from a disgruntled worker—two traditional sources of news. Rather, reporters found out about it from electronic bulletin boards on the Internet.

By giving direct access to government information, THOMAS, the congressional Web site, "does take the media out as the middleman interpreting the public process ... it gives the public the right to choose where they get their information," says Don Jones, the site's creator. And in the process, Jones argues,

The Internet published some of the earliest reports of the 1995 bombing of the Alfred P. Murrah Federal Building in Oklahoma City as citizens rushed to their computers to share eyewitness accounts. (AP/Wide World Photos)

NEWS THINKING: THE COACHING WAY

You can help a fellow student, colleague, even yourself, sharpen his or her news judgment by using two essential coaching skills: asking good questions and listening to the answers.

- What's new about this story?
- Why does it matter?
- To whom does it matter?
- Type the lead paragraphs of a half-dozen published news stories. What makes each one a news story? What elements—timeliness, importance, interest—does the writer consider most important?
- So what? Why should people want to read, listen or view this story?
- What headline would you put on the story?
- On your next story, keep asking yourself, "What's the news?" Sum up the news in a "budget line," that is, a single paragraph of no more than 25–30 words that can "sell" your story to an editor, teacher or reader.
- Have you considered whether your prejudices or other attitudes affect how you view what is news? Have you considered how others who are different from you might view the same story?
- Before you report and write your next story, ask yourself, "Who is the audience? How would you define and describe the audience? What information would be important to that audience?"
- Can you imagine a reader, viewer or browser you want to reach? Describe that person. Write the story for that person.

it redefines the word "news." "The technology empowers viewers to determine what they want to know, rather than have that packaged by someone else."

"Yesterday's editors decided what was important and made it so," says Doug Clifton, executive editor of *The Miami Herald*. "Today the consumer is at least an equal arbiter of what is important. In a world of dazzling choices the consumer holds power that once the editor held alone." Despite their increased power, consumers will still need someone to filter news and help make it coherent. Even fierce critics of the media like Michael Crichton—the novelist who created *Jurassic Park* and who predicted in 1993 that the media would be a dinosaur, extinct—see a role for reporters in the future. "They will give me high-quality information," Crichton says.

Technology changes news, the nature of it, how we get it, how we present it. Whether the task is writing for the newspaper, the television or the computer screen, the process of thinking about news remains the same. The tools the reporter may use to collect and deliver the information will undoubtedly differ. John Garcia, who created the online journalism program at New York University, predicts the 21st-century journalist will be armed with a video camera, tape recorder, digital camera. No matter what the tool, the reporter still has to figure out what the news is. That thought process is what editors demand and consumers need. Bombarded by information, society needs the journalist to help it make sense of the world. "We now have too much information to rationally deal with on a daily basis," says Beth Agnew in an essay titled "Writing for the Third Millennium." "We need skilled professional help to turn that information into the currency of the next millennium—knowledge."

GLOSSARY OF IMPORTANT TERMS

Audience. The people reading or viewing a news organization's print, broadcast or online product.

Critical thinking. The act of drawing inferences or conclusions from a body of information.

News. An ongoing, constantly updatable record of change.

News judgment. The ability to recognize and report news of interest and importance to an audience.

Ombudsman. A person appointed by a news organization to represent readers or viewers and to review the publication's fairness and accuracy.

Peg. Newsroom jargon for a reason to publish or broadcast news. Usually a time element event or development that makes the story newsworthy.

EXERCISES

1. Read Rhea Borja's essay, "Beginnings," on page 7 and, using it as a model, write a 250–500-word essay recounting your personal experience with news. When was the first time you were aware of news, either by reading a newspaper or by hearing a news or radio report? What was your reaction?

2. What is news? Borja ends her essay with her personal definition. Write your own definition of news, in no more than 25 words, based on your personal experience as a consumer of news and your personal sense of mission as an aspiring journalist.

3. Examine the front page of your local newspaper (it can be the campus newspaper, a local weekly or daily paper), watch the evening news (videotape it if you have access to a machine or make a list of the stories) or study an Internet news site. Review the contents, and decide what made the stories newsworthy. Try to figure out where the story originated. In a press release? A news conference? An action by a government body? An emergency? Study the story carefully, and identify the sources of the information contained in it.

4. Study news coverage as presented by different types of news-gathering operations—newspaper, radio or television news and online. For instance, compare the contents of the local newspaper with the stories reported on the local evening news broadcast—and compare their news judgments. Which stories have common appeal? Do some stories seem limited to a particular technology?

5. Make a survey of your news landscape. Identify and itemize all the news sources you're exposed to in a single day from radio, computer, television, newspapers and magazines. Which ones are your favorites and why? Which do you consider the most reliable or unreliable? What kind of news are you most interested in?

6. Evaluate the contents of a single newspaper, broadcast or Internet site, and list the stories under headings for "bad news" and "good news." Which side has more stories?

7. Pick a major story from the recent past: the 1996 presidential election, the 1995 death of Latina singer Selena, the July 1998 shooting of two police officers in the U.S. Capitol. Explain what made these stories newsworthy. Identify the common elements contained in all the stories, and discuss the different ways the stories were presented. Consider how cultural factors affected the selection and presentation of stories.

READINGS

Baker, Bob. *Newsthinking: The Secret of Great Newswriting.* Cincinnati, Ohio: Writer's Digest Books, 1981.

Boorstin, Daniel. "From News Gathering to News Making: A Flood of Pseudo-Events." Ch. 1, *The Image.* New York: Harper & Row, 1961.

Dominick, Joseph R. *The Dynamics of Mass Communication*, 4th ed. New York: McGraw-Hill, 1993.

Fallows, James. *Breaking the News: How the Media Undermine American Democracy.* New York: Pantheon, 1995.

Fuller, Jack. *News Values: Ideas for an Information Age.* Chicago: University of Chicago Press, 1996.

Manoff, Robert K., and Michael Schudson, eds. *Reading the News.* New York: Pantheon Books, 1987.

Oppel, Richard. "Personal Lives of Public Figures Are Not Automatically News." *The American Editor,* November 1995, p. 14.

Paul, Richard. *Critical Thinking: What Every Person Needs to Survive in a Rapidly Changing World.* Rohnert Park, Calif.: Center for Critical Thinking and Moral Critique, Sonoma State University, 1990.

Schudson, Michael. *Discovering the News: A Social History of American Newspapers.* New York: Basic Books, 1978.

Sneider, Daniel. "Redefining News in the Era of Internet." *The Christian Science Monitor,* June 26, 1996.

Stephens, Mitchell. *A History of News.* Fort Worth: Harcourt Brace, 1998.

Ways, Max. "What's Wrong With News: It Isn't New Enough." *Fortune,* October 1969, pp. 110–113, 155–161.

HOTLIST

http://www.cjr.org/year/96/2/tour.asp

"A Tour of Our Uncertain Future" by Katherine Fulton. A provocative look at the changing news environment—especially under the influence of technological changes—by a former newspaper editor and technology consultant. First published in *Columbia Journalism Review*, this online version includes a wide range of links to help illuminate the changes that technology is bringing to journalism.

http://www.journalism.org/lastudy.htm

"Changing Definition of News." Read how the definition of news has changed in the last 20 years in this online study produced by the Committee of Concerned Journalists.

http://www.wired.com/wired/archive/1.04/mediasaurus.html

"Mediasaurus." This 1993 speech, later reprinted in *Wired* magazine, by novelist Michael Crichton, fired a warning shot across the bow of a news industry struggling to stay afloat in the rough seas of technology. His message: Improve the quality of news, or it will meet the fate of the dinosaur.

http://www.newseum.org

Billed as "the world's only interactive museum of news," the Newseum is designed to let visitors experience "how and why news is made." It's a fascinating journalism attic loaded with objects and information about the people behind the news and the technology they've used since humanity's earliest history. Located across the Potomac River from Washington, D.C., the Newseum is also available in a "virtual" form online.

http://www.annenberg.nwu.edu/pubs/tabloids/

"Tabloids, Talk Radio and the Future of News Technology's Impact on Journalism" by Annenberg Senior Fellow Ellen Hume. A former *Wall Street Journal* reporter and executive director of the Public Broadcasting System's Democracy Project examines the differences between "old" and "new" media and the challenges that new communications technologies present journalists.

http://www.rtndf.org/rtndf/newtech.htm

"New Technology, Old Values ... And a New Definition of News" by Michael Schudson. An essay on the future of news and journalism. Includes links to related resources by a sociologist and journalism scholar.

http://mevard.www.media.mit.edu/people/mevard/papers/ what-is-news.html

"What Is 'News'? Children's Conceptions and Uses of News" by Michele Evard of the MIT Media Lab. Polls report that children don't care about news. A contrarian view—and, for those planning a career in news, a heartening one—is offered in this report of a study by a researcher in the Media Lab at the Massachusetts Institute of Technology, a think tank that combines passion for new technology with an abiding interest in news and communication. Evard says her research shows that "children are interested in particular aspects of news, and that the more a child feels that news is relevant to his or her life, the more interested he or she is in it."

See also:

http://www.almaden.ibm.com/journal/sj/mit/sectionb/evard.html

"Children's Interests in News: Online Opportunities." Examines online projects that try to interest young audiences in news.

http://sunsite.unc.edu/cmc/mag/1995/jul/lapham.html

"The Evolution of the Newspaper of the Future" by Chris Lapham, *Computer-Mediated Communication Magazine*, July 1, 1995. This link-rich hypertext essay examines the effect of two powerful forces that have altered mass communication: the use of computers to process, analyze and spread information, and "the constantly accelerating capacity of that technology to enhance communication so it is almost unbounded by time and space." The author argues for a model that combines the best of old and new: computerized access, delivery and packaging of information with insightful reporting and good writing.

http://www.kcmetro.cc.mo.us/longview/ctac/ENGLISH.HTM

"Critical Thinking Resources in English and Journalism."

As more teachers focus on the importance of critical thinking skills, sites like this one, produced by Dave Sharp of Maple Woods Community College, provide links to valuable resources.

http://www.unr.edu/unr/journalism/pro.home.html

The faculty members of the Reynolds School of Journalism at the University of Nevada at Reno spent a year refocusing their curriculum to integrate critical thinking skills into all their courses. The school's mission is "to teach students to think critically and to apply that thinking to the collection, organization and communication of information through the public media." Browse their course syllabi to see how they do it.

See also:

http://www.unr.edu/unr/journalism/pro.school.crit_think.html

"A Call to Reason" is an essay on how critical thinking applies to journalism. The Web page also includes a profile of a critical thinker and bibliography by Bill Dorman, a journalism and government teacher at Sacramento State University.

http://www.news-observer.com/daily/1997/08/10/tri00.html

"Are journalists and their readers on the same page? On the same planet?" The Raleigh *News & Observer* and some of its readers wrestled with those questions for four months in 1997. Link to this Web site to find out what they learned in essays by readers and articles by reporters and editors and an academic overview by a journalism professor.

THE REPORTER'S TOOLBOX

CHAPTER FOCUS

Today's journalists have more tools available than ever before, but the key to success is not mastering one over another, but rather gaining familiarity and practice with as many as possible.

CHAPTER LESSONS

- Reporting and writing tools
- Tips for working with photos and photojournalists
- Reporting and research tools for the wired journalist
- How to achieve accuracy
- Top ten tools for today's journalist
- Tool sharpening: The Coaching Way

INTRODUCTION

Every job has its tools: the carpenter's hammer and saw, the surgeon's scalpel and retractor, the painter's palette and brushes. Four centuries ago, in the time of Shakespeare, actors used to carry bags that contained implements of their art: makeup, props, scraps of costume, all the implements necessary to quickly change into a new character as they roamed from town to town. This chapter introduces you to the variety of tools reporters need to do an effective job. Some of them are **physical tools**—tangible objects that you will carry or keep on your desk.

Others are **electronic tools**—software, databases, search engines and other implements of the computerized age we live in. These new **reporting and research tools** for today's wired journalist will enable you to search for information in electronic databases, those limitless canyons of digitized information that expand your scope of knowledge, and organize and analyze data in ways that will make you a sophisticated analyst of government institutions, and help you to present interviews in audio and video as well as print.

A third and equally important category is what I would call **mental tools**—you can't hold them like a notebook or a laptop computer or wield them like a digital camera, but they are no less vital. They include your attitude and other characteristics of good journalists, such as persistence, commitment to accuracy, fairness and courage, that represent the reporter's mind-set.

PART 1: REPORTING AND WRITING TOOLS

WRITING INSTRUMENTS

Once a reporter needed nothing more than a pencil and paper to take notes and a typewriter to write the story. In some ways that's all some reporters still need. "Even in these days of high-tech weaponry, the writer's most effective research and interviewing tools remain the humble pen and low-tech notebook," says David Fryxell, a veteran newspaper and magazine editor. In his book *How to Write Fast (While Writing Well)*, Fryxell makes a persuasive case for leaving tape recorders and laptops for note-taking behind. There are countless reporters who bring nothing more than an empty notepad, a pen and an open mind to an assignment and produce compelling journalism. But many reporters today are attracted to using the available technology. Today's journalist has an array of tools to choose from. It's important to remember that it is not the tool but the way it is utilized that makes the difference.

First, you need something to write with. A pencil, a pen, a computer. Pencils are good in the rain. They never clog or run out of ink, but they can break, and then you're in trouble. I once took notes on a pad tucked inside a plastic bag when I was doing a "day in the life" story about a crab fisherman in Florida.

Tools for the 21st-century journalist include a notebook and pen, increasingly supplemented by a laptop computer, tape recorder and cellular phone. (Photo by Kenny Irby)

I could have used the waterproof notebooks that the *Anchorage Daily News* provides its reporters, who often have to brave the elements to get their stories. "They are expensive," notes reporter Lisa Demer, "but they have plastic paper. You can actually write on the paper during a rainstorm or snowstorm. Also good for writing on a boat." They're available from J. L. Darling Corporation at 2614 Pacific Highway East, Tacoma, WA 98424-1017; phone (206) 922-5000; fax (206) 922-5300; or online at **http://www.riteintherain.com**.

Reporters seem to collect pens the way Eagle Scouts collect merit badges. But you're not going to be able to take notes or write down what the fire chief—or the president—tells you if you don't have something to write with—and on. Reminder: Never leave the office without a writing instrument and something to record notes on.

The notebook is the reporter's basic tool. It's the repository of everything from quotes and descriptions to directions and phone numbers. In the old days reporters folded 8½-by-11-inch sheets of copy paper. Some reporters prefer a stenography pad; the pages divided in half by a vertical line allow you to write quotes and other notes on one side, with follow-up questions on the opposite side. Reporters covering courts often favor the long legal pads used by the lawyers they cover. But most of us use the classic reporter pad, 3 inches by 7 inches, lined paper, narrow enough to carry in a back pocket or slip into a purse and fit comfortably in the palm of your hand. When Claude Sitton, a legendary reporter for *The New York Times*, was covering the civil rights struggle in the Deep South in the early 1960s, he popularized the use of the narrow reporter's notebook. In places where carrying a notebook could be hazardous to a reporter's health, it fit easily in the inside pocket of a jacket. In warm weather, you could cut the bottom off and slip it in a pants pocket. "Invisible when properly worn," as a veteran of that coverage recalled, the unobtrusive notebook saved reporters from attacks by angry whites.

WRITING SURFACES

PAPER.   At my first job I banged out stories on low-grade copypaper using a manual typewriter. If I wanted to make changes I took a fresh sheet, typed a new sentence or paragraph, cut it into a strip and used a pastepot to glue it over the old version. You could add sections, even complete pages using this method, known as "shirt-tailing," which sometimes resulted in stories nearly as tall as I was.

When I finished the story, I went over it with a pencil to indicate any changes to the editors. Never satisfied with my writing, I was always making changes. Not surprisingly, an early job evaluation described my stories as "a copy editor's nightmare."

COMPUTER SCREEN.   Eventually I graduated to newspapers that could afford electric typewriters, but it wasn't until I arrived at *The*

Providence Journal in 1977 that I learned about the magic of computer-assisted writing. The newspaper was a beta, or test, site for a revolutionary dedicated word-processing system, called Atex. The computer was a godsend for newspaper writers and editors, putting an end to "shirttail" stories and copy paper covered with proofreading symbols like the tracks of a herd of deer on freshly fallen snow. With a few keystrokes, the computer allowed us to insert words, to copy, delete or move entire passages. I tell this story not to wax nostalgic about the "good old days." After I began to use a computer to write, I had even greater respect for the journalists who were able to write coherent stories on deadline with a typewriter.

Most of today's journalists take the computer for granted. In most newsrooms I've worked in or visited in the last five years you will be lucky if you can locate an electric typewriter, let alone a manual model. Word-processing skills are essential for today's reporter. If you don't know how to use word-processing software, such as Microsoft's Word or Corel's WordPerfect, learn immediately.

PREPARING COPY FOR THE PAGE. Every news organization will have its own rules for how it wants stories prepared for editing. Here are the basic elements for submitting news copy for newspapers: In Chapter 8 ("Reporting and Writing Broadcast News") you'll find similar guidelines for electronic news organizations.

1. SLUG. A slug is a word or two—"hearing," "clinton," "murder"—used to refer to a news story. The term comes from the word used for a line of type or a blank line set on a Linotype or "slug" machine, used in newspaper production until the mid-1970s. Think of your slug as a short title.

Accident (SLUG)
Brittingham (BYLINE)
500 words (LENGTH)
ART: Medevac helicopter takes off with injured victim (GRAPHICS)

    Police blamed a drunken driver for a Labor Day accident on Highway 50 outside Laramie that killed the mother of two children and severely injured her husband.

Every news organization has its own system for preparing news copy. Basic elements in print, broadcast and online include a one- or two-word title, called a "slug" or "slugline"; the reporter's byline; length or time of story; and information about graphics, photos or other visual elements.

2. **BYLINE.** Your name as you want it to appear over your story:

> By Stephanie Wilbur
> Staff Writer

3. **LENGTH.** An estimate of the story's length so the editor can gauge how much space the story will take on a page. Most word-processing programs include a "word count" feature that will give you the length in words. Dedicated word processors in many newsrooms compute the length in column inches.

4. **ART.** Information about any photos, charts or other informational graphics that accompany the story.

SHORTHAND SKILLS

Once you start your reporting career, chances are good you will wish you knew how to take shorthand. British journalists routinely learn to take down 100 words per minute, something that in this country has been traditionally considered a secretary's skill. Most reporters regret that they didn't learn shorthand. There have been many times in my career when I struggled vainly to record someone's comments during an interview, a trial or a public hearing and wished I had acquired shorthand, as Tom French of the *St. Petersburg Times* or Larry Gurwin of *Time* magazine's investigative unit did in high school.

It's never too late. When Mark Singer went to work as a staff writer for *The New Yorker* in 1974 after graduating from Yale University, he took a shorthand course "because I thought it was important to get dialogue as accurately as possible."

Even if you don't learn shorthand you can follow the example of countless reporters by developing your own speedwriting style. "The importance of developing a personal shorthand can't be stressed too much," says journalism teacher Sandra Combs Birdiett. She leads her Wayne State University classes in exercises, reading speeches aloud and playing songs as they struggle to get the words down, and encourages them to practice regularly until they have a workable and efficient shorthand. One quick way is to drop vowels from words and use phonetic spelling. For example, using phonetic spelling and eliminating vowels take a sentence such as:

> Because when they go out into the field, they need more tools than we can give. (63 characters)

and transform it into the much shorter:

> Bcz whn thy go out nto th fld thyl ned mor tls thn we cn gv. (44 characters)

Here is a small sample of common shorthand symbols reporters use:

w—with

w/o—without

&—and

Reporters who master shorthand can get down *every word* of an interview without relying on a tape recorder. Thomas French of the *St. Petersburg Times* used his high school shorthand skills on "Angels and Demons," which won the 1998 Pulitzer Prize for feature writing. (Photo by Kenny Irby)

pox—police

b & e—breaking and entering

adw—assault with a deadly weapon

hrg—hearing

mtg—meeting

Whatever "briefhand" system you employ, make sure that it enables you to "take detailed, accurate notes, while leaving accurate time for careful listening," as *The Oregonian* of Portland advises its reporters in its accuracy guidelines. Any system should:

1. Clearly indicate what is a direct quote and what is not. Use quotation marks " " for direct quotes and brackets [ ] or parentheses ( ) for indirect quotes or paraphrases.

2. Make clear the source of each fact and quotation in the notes.

3. Include citations to additional sources (such as a reference book, court record, or title of a government report quoted) that will help verify the accuracy of questionable items.

You can find books on shorthand and speedwriting in the library and at online booksellers such as **Amazon.com**. Easyscript, an inexpensive speedwriting program, can also be ordered online at **www.easyscript.com**. On its Web site, the company suggests these guidelines for speedwriting:

■ Practice listening and writing.

■ Learn to identify the pauses while following the speaker and to start a new sentence even though you did not complete the previous one. Keep in mind, if you try to "catch up" and write a previous sentence and the speaker already starts another, you'll lose the new sentence.

■ Use a notebook with pages divided in half. First, write in the left column all the way down and start writing in the right column. This approach will reduce the movement of your arm in half and will help you to write faster.

■ Don't print letters; write them out in script. It takes more time to print than to write.

■ Practice without listening to a speaker, for example, taking notes in a library while reading a book.

■ Write two- and three-character words in longhand.

■ Use a roller ball pen with a comfortable grip. Roller ball pens provide the smoothest writing with the least effort. Don't use a pencil.

NOTEPADS

Use your notebook as your first draft. Mark up the best quotes. Select possible endings. Jot a note about the possible theme or the lead paragraph of your piece. "Things become pieces as you're reporting, and you think, 'Ah, there's my lead,'" says Mark Fritz of the *Los Angeles Times*. The notion becomes "a scribble along the side" of his notebook. Or, "I'll circle something, or put an asterisk, or write a little note next to it. I'll underline it three times. I'll write in block letters **LEAD.**"

(A word of caution: Don't let your notes get in the way of the writing. Jane Harrigan, director of the journalism program at the University of New Hampshire, tells her students, "Notes are like Velcro. As you try to skim them, they ensnare you, and pretty soon you can't see the story for the details." Her advice? Repeat this mantra: The story is not in my notes; the story is in my head.)

Surgeons practice tying knots so they can suture quickly when it counts. Reporters should practice, too. Begin now taking notes at every event you attend. Keep a notebook handy at all times. As a student, you may not see the value of making it a habit, even a reflex action, to take notes. That's because note-taking as a journalist is different from note-taking as a student. "In a classroom setting," one of my reporting students observed, "where more abstract learning is involved, I have found that note-taking is more of a hindrance to me than a help. I almost never look back on class notes, and taking them distracts me from focusing on what is being discussed." Still another student argued that "excessive note-taking can turn people into human Dictaphones, rather than live participants and active listeners."

.Wendy Anderson, a former Poynter reporting fellow, expressed the difference this way:

"I have always taken notes in classes when there was something key that I thought I'd forget; hence, I wrote down the occasional date, formula, name, assignment, etc. I never took notes on my professor's hairdos, pants colors, or the details of the hockey game someone was discussing before class—not because I wasn't being tested on it (always a stupid motive) but because I was pretty well convinced that long-term knowledge of these facts would not serve me well."

———————————— ■ ————————————

A reporter is always making selections, however, and the act of note-taking can be viewed as part of the selection process. You won't write down every word someone says, but rather you must decide, usually in a split second, what is worth preserving in your notes. You're not taking dictation. You are taking notes selectively.

Behind each step of the reporting and writing process is a principle. The principle that underlies reporting is that we write from an abundance of information. In other words, reporters collect more than they need.

Journalists see the world differently. They have to. They aren't always sure what information will prove to be important, so they tend to fill the notebook with an overabundance of material. Much of it never will appear in the story, but often that realization doesn't come until they are back at the office writing the story. David Finkel, a prize-winning staff writer for *The Washington Post Magazine*, fills up lots of notebooks on stories "because I tend to write down everything I see, even if it's something like, '2 rocks off to left-sedimentary??-resemble poodle.' My hope is that as the reporting process continues, the significance of my notations will emerge. Usually, that doesn't happen. Out of a 50-page notebook, I'll have five pages of possibly usable quotes, ten pages of other possibly usable notes, and 35 pages of hieroglyphics." Finkel is an experienced feature writer and so has the luxury of more time than a reporter covering a meeting, say, or a speech, who has to file a story within an hour. (Finkel is also overly modest; many reporters who admire his work would be happy to find in their notes what he considers "hieroglyphics.") No matter what the deadline, the principle remains the same: When the time to write—or support what you've written to an editor—arrives, you will need to be able to refer to your notes. Your memory alone won't be sufficient.

Also, journalists use observations differently. Students taking notes are trying to absorb the lessons or get a good grade, maybe even impress the teacher with their diligence and interest. Reporters have a different goal: to report and write the most complete, accurate, fair and interesting story they can based on the information they have collected and analyzed. If you are one of those fortunate few who have a photographic memory, then turn the

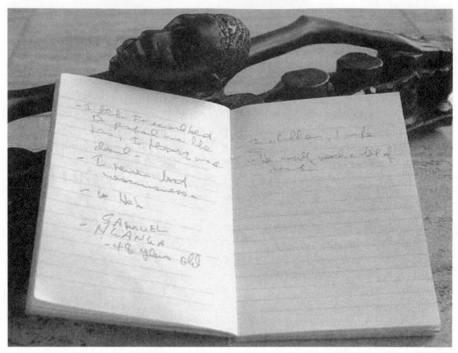

The notebook is where your reporting goes and the writing starts. Stephen Buckley of *The Washington Post* used his handwritten notes to write a survivor's tale after the 1998 terrorist bombing of the American Embassy in Nairobi, Kenya. (Photo by Kenny Irby)

page. For us mere mortals, the notebook is the place where the reporting goes and the writing starts.

Every story has what Melvin Mencher, who taught me reporting at Columbia University Graduate School of Journalism, calls **"nonnegotiable necessities."** These are facts, details and other information that must be included for a story to be complete and to answer the reader's questions. They vary from story to story; we'll treat them as individual cases in later chapters. But in general, reporters should always write down all names and addresses (with correct spelling), ages, figures, time and place of the interview, as well as verbatim quotes or paraphrases.

"Always get phone numbers," advises Erin Hemme Froslie, a Poynter reporting fellow who is now a reporter for the Fargo, N.D., *Forum.* "When you're writing under deadline it wastes too much time to flip through the phone book."

There are no hard-and-fast rules about note-taking. Every reporter devises his or her own system. Whatever system you choose, just be sure that it enables you to be accurate and record and recognize the critical information you will need to write your stories.

Note-Taking on the Screen

Many reporters use their computers as a sort of electronic notebook. A common sight in many newsrooms is a reporter with a telephone headset taking notes as she conducts an interview by phone. A keyboard and computer screen also make for easier access to computerized databases such as files of previous stories maintained by your newsroom library or a commercial service such as Lexis-Nexis and Dialog, Internet chats and e-mail exchanges with sources and readers. The advantages include speed, efficiency and access to other files on the computer.

Be sure to keep your notes organized by recording the source, date and time of your interview. Separate your interviews with line breaks or other devices so you don't confuse one person's remarks with another's.

A caution: Increasingly, reporters are tethering themselves to keyboards and telephone headsets. For many journalists, it has led to painful repetitive stress disorders, leaving them unable to type.

There's another hazard: Their stories betray the defects of not enough contact with the people, places and things that make news. As convenient as a telephone may be when a deadline is tight or when sources are too far away to see in person, it also can insulate you from the world you are covering. So can the Internet.

There's no substitute for face-to-face contact. Sometimes deadline pressures make that difficult, but you don't want all your stories to read as if they were reported from a desk, or from press releases and telephone interviews. Too often, I read stories about neighborhoods where there is nothing to indicate the reporter walked the area's streets and met with its residents, not just chatted on the phone with so-called "community leaders." There is a lifeless quality to much of today's journalism.

Don't buy into it when reporters and editors tell you time constraints make it impossible to leave the office as much as they would like. That often reflects a lack of will rather than lack of time. The fact is it takes effort—and sometimes courage—to leave the comfort of the newsroom. But the best editors will demand it by challenging reporters to bring back the sights, the sounds, the silences and the details that can come only from reporting in the field. That's why Joel Rawson, executive editor of *The Providence Journal*, used to say that he'd like to replace all the telephones in the newsroom with a single payphone "and I'd hand out the quarters." He wanted reporters where they belonged—on the street.

Cellular Telephone

Once a reporter is on the street, I doubt that even Joel Rawson would object to the communications tool—a cellular telephone—that is rapidly becoming standard issue. When TWA Flight 800 exploded on July 17, 1996, over the Atlantic Ocean off Long Island, killing all 229 people on board, editors at *Newsday* told reporter Steve Wick to charter a boat and get out to the crash scene as quickly as possible. Within a few hours, Wick was in the middle of a surreal scene: "For miles the ocean was covered with debris, seat cushions, insulation, big pieces of metal, a section of a wing, luggage, backpacks. An empty baby bottle floated by. The debris was so thick you could not see the water," he recalled. Normally, Wick would have had to wait until he returned to shore to file his story. Armed with a cell phone, however, he spent all night dictating what he saw and heard directly to a reporter back in the newsroom, who transformed his descriptions into a story in the next morning's paper. The cell phone, Wick says, "gives you the ability to be an eyewitness, as opposed to someone who takes just notes, then goes to a phone, and then calls in notes to rewrite. I just was dictating what I saw. It was literal deadline work, literally as close to the line as you can get. ... The value was that 600,000 people on Long Island awoke to an eyewitness account the next morning." Wick's on-scene reporting contributed to coverage that won the newspaper a Pulitzer Prize.

TAPE RECORDER

On May 6, 1937, Herb Morrison, a reporter for a Chicago radio station, was in a New Jersey field recording the arrival of the German dirigible Hindenburg, using a primitive machine that recorded voices on a wire coated with a magnetic substance. When the hydrogen gas-filled metal-frame airship exploded in flames, killing 36 people, the reporter's emotion-filled narration became the first recorded material broadcast on a radio network, according to historian Mitchell Stephens. In 1945, at the end of World War II, the victorious Allies discovered that the Germans had developed a machine that could record voices on a coated paper tape. That invention eventually replaced the wire recorder and led to the magnetic tape recorders used today. Before then, newspaper reporters could only scribble to record their observations, quotes and other information collected during their reporting. Many of today's reporters carry tape recorders as part of their basic reporting equipment. "Without a tape recorder, you really can't capture the full emotional breadth of what people are saying to you," says Mitch Albom, the *Detroit Free Press* sports columnist. "When you're talking to a grieving family, the way they say things, sometimes even a small little sentence, or the way their voice trails off is very important to re-create the mood and the spirit." In such sensitive reporting situations or when a verbatim transcript is essential, many reporters share Albom's fear: "I don't trust my penmanship to try to get it down." That fear of missing something important, especially in an electronic era when radio and television crews are recording news events, prompts many reporters to use the tape recorder as a backup to their handwritten notes. The advent of new media, and the convergence of news reporting technologies, also means that today's reporters may be asked to provide sound for their story.

LISTEN TO THE HISTORIC LIVE RECORDING OF THE HINDENBURG CRASH ONLINE AT http://www.historybuff.com/realaudio/hindenburg.html

Journalistic lore is rich with stories about reporters whose tape recorders failed or who couldn't take notes until after they had left the interview. In those cases, the reporters wrote down or dictated into a tape recorder everything they could remember from the interview. Reporters ask whether they can use verbatim quotes reconstructed from memory. Some reporters do it, but having used a tape recorder for much of my career I'm less likely to trust my memory. Bear in mind that working from memory is one of the most common causes of journalistic inaccuracy.

I've used a variety of tape recorders: Sony Walkman recorders, inexpensive Radio Shack models, even an expensive minicassette model with a clip-on microphone that supposedly was standard issue at the Central Intelligence Agency. It's not necessary to spend large amounts of money. Just make sure that whatever model you buy is equipped with a counter. That way if you hear something you know you may want to use, you can note the place on the counter and find it without having to listen to the whole tape. Remember to reset the counter to 000 when you turn the tape over or insert a new tape. The counter feature is especially important for broadcast and online journalists who need to locate quotes precisely.

Not everyone likes the tape recorder. "The machine, surprisingly, distorts the truth," argues Lillian Ross, a profile writer for *The New Yorker*. "The tape recorder is a fast and easy and lazy way of getting a lot of talk down. ... A lot of talk does not in itself make an interview." Ross and other critics say recorders encourage laziness in reporting. In Chapter 6, we'll cover the pros and cons of tape recorders in interviews in greater detail.

TYPING SKILLS

Fifty years ago, reporters were divided into two classes: legmen and rewritemen. (Literally. Few were women.) And a street reporter might not even have to know how to type. One of the last of that breed was immortalized in *All the President's Men*, the story of the 1972 Watergate investigation by Carl Bernstein and Bob Woodward of *The Washington Post*:

> The first details of the story had been phoned from inside the Watergate by Alfred E. Lewis, a veteran of 35 years of police reporting for the *Post*. Lewis was something of a legend in Washington journalism—half cop, half reporter, a man who often dressed in a blue regulation Metropolitan Police sweater buttoned at the bottom over a brass Star-of-David buckle. In 35 years, Lewis had never really "written" a story; he phoned the details in to a rewrite man, and for years *The Washington Post* did not even have a typewriter at police headquarters.

Those days are long gone, of course, although not in every newsroom in the world. Still, you must know how to type to be a reporter today. You don't have to be a star typist. Or even a 10-finger one. The fastest two-finger hunt-and-peck typist I know is my former Knight Ridder colleague Mark

COMPETENCE IN THE NEWSROOM: VISUAL LITERACY

Pegie Stark Adam, Ron Reason and Kenny Irby
The Poynter Institute

To become visually competent one must accept some basic principles: that visuals are vital elements in story telling; that visual decisions are as important as the choice of words, the style of writing, the proper grammar and the perfect edit.

When words and visuals work together in print—or when we marry language, sound and pictures for broadcast or new media—the reader, viewer or listener is the beneficiary. Information becomes more comprehensible and accessible; stories become more dramatic; news becomes more relevant.

Writing, reporting, editing and producing are creative endeavors. So are photography, design, art and graphics. To make words and visuals work together, journalists must seek common ground, seeing the world through the eyes of the colleague, finding similarities among the disciplines, searching for a common vocabulary.

That means understanding the inner workings of still and video photography—what makes good composition, lighting, balance, tension, mood. That means understanding the inner workings of design—the nuances of typography, organization, the grid and color. That means understanding the conceptualizing of an image in an illustration or graphic—the power of symbolism, the creation of texture, the beauty of composition. For broadcast and new media, it means understanding how to write with video and natural sound.

Thompson, who won a Pulitzer Prize at the *Fort Worth Star-Telegram* and now covers defense for *Time*. But quick typing skills will be an even greater advantage in the days of hyperspeed communication.

"To be able to type fast is an asset to writing a sports column these days," George Vecsey of *The New York Times* said when I interviewed him for *Best Newspaper Writing 1995*. He wrote his award-winning column about Ukrainian figure skater Oksana Baiul's victory in the 1994 Winter Olympics "literally in 25 minutes ... which is about as fast as you can type 800 words." Vecsey was grateful he took typing in junior high school.

This can be done through discussion, collaboration and participation. Go out on a photo shoot and experience what it's like to compose an image through the lens, learn how a scene is lighted, learn how to crop a photo. Read what artists, photographers and designers say about good art. Learn to be a visual critic by listening to visual journalists and incorporating their vocabulary into yours.

Assume that every decision a visual journalist makes is thoughtful, that decisions about content are guided by basic principles. For example, when a designer uses color, it can become a powerful tool that can enhance the meaning of a story by creating a certain mood. Color can create dimension on a flat two-dimensional surface by pushing some things forward and pulling other things back depending on the hue, the saturation and amount of it used. Color can "punctuate" a headline or a quote in a story, signaling the reader to stop, begin, pause or end a thought. In the hands of a designer, color creates mood, movement and dimension based on proven color theory.

Becoming competent, in whatever form—visual, aural or verbal—does not mean that a person needs to become a Jack or Jill of all trades, shooting photographs, designing pages and doing illustrations, writing stories and headlines, although such versatility may be valued when media converge.

Instead it means that each journalist engages in the journey to understand and appreciate another's craft, a process that results in a whole journalism that is excellent in all its parts.

VISUAL JOURNALISM TOOLS

"When words and visuals work together in print—or when we marry language, sound and pictures for broadcast or new media—the reader, viewer or listener is the beneficiary. Information becomes comprehensible and accessible; stories become more dramatic; news becomes more relevant." That idea is the foundation of visual literacy, a journalistic competency described on pp. 38–39 by the visual journalism faculty of The Poynter Institute.

WORKING WITH PHOTOS AND PHOTOJOURNALISTS

Two of my most important reporting teachers were photographers, Andy Dickerman of *The Providence Journal* and Ricardo Ferro of the *St. Petersburg Times*. From them, I learned how to be assertive without being aggressive, how to climb a tree to a roof to see a story from every possible angle and how to work as a member of a team. They taught me not only a different way to see the world, but also about courage, hard work and passion for excellence.

Unfortunately, many reporters don't think of their photographer colleagues as collaborators in the story process. Every photographer I've ever met remembers the sting of reporters introducing him or her as "my photographer," as if he or she was a servant rather than a collaborator.

Depending on the size or technical savvy of the news organization you work for, there is a good chance you may be expected to provide visual elements for your stories, including still photos or video. You may also be asked to provide information for a graphic or illustration. As reporter Jonathan Dube points out, the ability to think visually—identifying material for a chart or graphic, for example—can enhance your stories.

Whether or not you take photographs, you will undoubtedly work with photojournalists. As my visual journalism colleagues point out, appreciation of their craft is vital. "Photographs can be an important tool in these times of increasing divisiveness and separatism, to build a bridge of empathy. To show not only our diversities, but also the qualities that make us all part of the human family," says Carol Guzy of *The Washington Post,* who has won journalism's highest awards, including the Pulitzer Prize, for her stunning photography documenting the agonies and triumphs of humanity around the planet. "A photograph can be a powerful witness and an eloquent voice for those who have none. Pictures inform, educate, enlighten, captivate, spur governments into action. They are historical documents and poignant reminders of our human frailties."

Photography is a form of storytelling. Journalistic photography is crucial to educating, informing and entertaining audiences. "Reporters think that pictures and other visual elements are mere illustrations, window dressing to make their story more attractive," says Kenny Irby, who directs the photojournalism program at The Poynter Institute. "In fact, photographs, graphics and other visual elements are essential elements of the storytelling." To get a picture, you have to understand the issue and develop the idea, Irby believes. You have to be there. "The best writers I've ever worked with and learned from were people who were there, not behind a desk or a telephone but were there to actually see and experience where it unfolded," he says. The quality of your storytelling will depend on how successfully you communicate and collaborate with your visual journalist colleagues.

KENNY IRBY'S TIPS FOR REPORTERS TAKING PHOTOS

- Train yourself to see the world as photographers do: through the viewfinder of a camera.

- Turn around. Sometimes you get so focused on the action that you don't see how other people and aspects are acting or reacting. Focus on the crowd as well as the players.

- Get as close as you can. Fill the frame up. The closer you get to the photograph, the more pleased you're going to be.

- Get comfortable with verticals. Don't limit your photos to horizontal shots. Picture editors and Web page designers may want variety.

- It's the eye that counts, not the camera. At Poynter students in our college fellowship programs use disposable cameras, also known as PHD ("Push Here, Dummy") cameras.

- When using a flash move your subject away from the walls to avoid shadows.

"The ability to make technically excellent photographs is a shallow skill," says Rich Beckman, acclaimed wildlife photographer and professor of visual communication and new media technologies at the University of North Carolina at Chapel Hill's journalism school. "Photographs become important only when you add content and context and point of view."

PART 2: REPORTING AND RESEARCH TOOLS FOR TODAY'S WIRED JOURNALIST

Until the last few years when the **Internet** became widely available, a reporter trying to get background for a story on an unfamiliar topic had only a few options:

- CLIP FILES. Usually kept in bulging, dog-eared envelopes, these are collections of stories clipped from the paper by news librarians and kept in the aptly named "morgue."

  Although some reporters mourn the passing of **clip files** (and there was a special feel to reading the yellowing clip and realizing how much time had passed), progress has meant greater access to more information.

  According to Nora Paul, director of information research at The Poynter Institute, what caused the demise of the clip file in the late 1980s was not the revolution in information retrieval but rather one in the technology of newspaper publishing. It began in the 1970s, when most major newspapers switched from using "hot type"—so-called because it used molten lead poured into the typesetting machine to create the news page line by line—to "cold type," in which whole

"One of the most important things I learned early on in my first job was to think visually. Photographs and graphics can enhance the quality of a story and provide information you can't include in the article. Readers are more likely to be drawn to your story if photos or graphics are with it. Plus, editors are more likely to give your story good play if it has art elements."
—JONATHAN DUBE, PRODUCER ABCNEWS.com

Kenny Irby (Courtesy of The Poynter Institute)

columns of news on shiny paper are created by computers. Before that, Paul says, a news library's "only option for saving text was by clipping and storing the newspaper itself." Even though the switch to creating newspaper text on a computer became widespread, the development of software to store and retrieve the electronic text lagged behind. It was another decade before news libraries replaced clip files with online databases. Many newspapers now have in-house researchers and online clip files.

■ **CONSULTATIONS WITH EDITORS AND OTHER REPORTERS.** Newsroom colleagues are a rich source of background, sources and institutional memory for the new reporter. They remain an essential resource when you need to background yourself quickly on a subject, story or beat assignment.

■ **DATABASES.** Reporters who worked for major metropolitan papers with a well-funded library had indirect access to electronic **databases** through a librarian who knew how to access them and had the necessary passwords. Depending on your school library's resources, you may have access to one or more of these databases. Lexis-Nexis is the world's largest electronic source of full-text articles from newspapers, magazines and technical and industry journals. Other database services include Dialog and Dow Jones. Check with your librarian for availability and access.

```
JOURNALISM AND JOBS




Your search request has found 4 STORIES through Level 1.
To DISPLAY these STORIES press either the KWIC, FULL, CITE or SEGMTS key.
To MODIFY your search request, press the M key (for MODFY) and then the ENTER
key.

For further explanation, press the H key (for HELP) and then the ENTER key.
```

Databases, such as Lexis-Nexis, have transformed how reporters gather background for their stories. Smart journalists always double-check facts with original sources.

Today's journalists have the world at their fingertips: databases, newsgroups, e-mail, hypertext documents, literally millions of Web sites with access to story ideas, sources, reference materials. One of the most comprehensive guides to this world of information is *Computer-Assisted Research: A Guide to Tapping Online Information,* by Nora Paul, who was editor for information services at *The Miami Herald* before joining The Poynter Institute.

"Searching the Web is a lot like life. Some days you find all the answers, and some days you can't find a clue with a million dollars."
—Steven J. Vaughan-Nichols

E-Mail

As a student, you may be familiar with electronic mail. Perhaps your family has **e-mail** access through America Online, CompuServe or other commercial online services. That experience will come in handy as you begin your reporting career. The byline used to be the only way newspapers identified individuals who reported and wrote the news. Now they're adding tag lines to stories with e-mail addresses that give readers a way to respond instantly to reporters. Most reporters whose stories feature their e-mail addresses greet the development with enthusiasm. Among the rewards: story ideas, corrections, accessibility to new sources, sounding boards for stories a keystroke away, instantaneous communication, immediate response. Brad Goldstein, computer-assisted reporting editor at the *St. Petersburg Times,* says that e-mail responses to the reporters who investigated lucrative fire and police pensions in Florida let them know about other abusive pension practices. Now that more news organizations are providing journalists with Internet access, the ability to use e-mail is becoming a necessary basic skill.

Learn more about computer-assisted research online at http://www.poynter.org/car/CG_chome.htm

Exercise the same caution with e-mail correspondence as you would with any source. For a 1994 Knight Ridder Newspapers series of stories on the nation's child support crisis, I did several interviews via e-mail. However, I also telephoned the sources. No matter what the technology, good reporters confirm their sources; they go back to the original source or document. Apply the "How do I know this?" rule. No matter what you report in a story, you should be able to answer the question, "How do I know this?," and the more solid your documentation, the better off you will be.

What's the proper etiquette for journalists online? Professor Steven Ross of Columbia University Graduate School of Journalism conducts an annual survey of Internet use by journalists; he believes in four rules:

1. Identify yourself as a reporter.
2. Confirm the information independently.
3. Ask permission to quote from newsgroups and chat rooms.
4. Don't use anonymous quotes.

Watch your own behavior. E-mail doesn't have the same privacy protections as regular mail. You might find portions of your message posted on electronic mailing lists, so always behave in a professional manner. The Associated

Press advises its staffers who communicate on the Internet that much of what they do is public. Messages on a mailing list, for instance, may be archived and spread to hundreds of recipients. The Associated Press cautions that writing an e-mail as a reporter is just like "writing on company letterhead."

Find out your news organization's policy on Internet use, including e-mail. The AP and other news organizations have issued policy manuals and guidebooks.

THE WORLD WIDE WEB

You're not alone. That's the message the **Internet** gives journalists. Today, with a modem, an Internet account and a computer, you can pick the brains of the best and brightest reporters and editors around the world. You can let your own fingers do the searching. You don't need to reinvent the wheel. The Internet is loaded with pages containing hundreds of valuable links for journalists. New ones are added every day. In the "Hotlist" at the end of this chapter, you will find Web sites that are especially valuable for reporters.

SEARCH ENGINES

LEARN MORE ABOUT SEARCH EN-GINES ONLINE AT http://www. poynter.org/class/ L404/1998/ L404_yahoo.htm

Search engines are computer programs that allow you to search the **World Wide Web** and other Internet resources, such as newsgroups, using keywords. (Search engines are also known as robots, spiders, crawlers, wanderers and worms.) To use one, point your Web browser to the engine's address. You will see a dialogue box where you type in a word or phrase, known as a query—"calcium and osteoporosis" or "online journalism and jobs," for example—and receive in return a list of Web pages containing the search terms. Most search engines require quotes around a phrase. Click on the Web page's Internet addresses (known as URLs for "uniform resource locators"), and the computer will take you there to see if you found what you were looking for.

Because they search through millions of pages, with new ones added every day, search engines can be an indispensable way to find information on the Web. By November 1998 the All-in-One Search Web page listed more than 400 search engines, databases, indexes and directories that catalogue information on the Internet. New ones surface every day, and old-timers, such as AltaVista and Infoseek, regularly add new features that improve searching capabilities. The latest trend is the boom in so-called "metasearch engines," such as All-in-One, Dogpile and Mamma, that let you search multiple search engines with one query.

But a word of caution: The quality of any search a particular engine carries out varies depending on its features, so you will want to try more than one. One way to test search engines is to look for something you know about—a musical group, a favorite sport, a hobby. Familiarity with the subject matter will help you evaluate the value of the information located by different search engines. Experiment regularly to find the best ones.

Here is a table of some popular search engines:

SEARCH ENGINES

Name	Address
Alta Vista	http://Altavista.digital.com
All-in-One	http://www.allonesearch.com
Dogpile	http://www.dogpile.com
Excite	http://www.excite.com
HotBot	http://www.hotbot.com
Infoseek	http://www.infoseek.com
Look Smart	http://looksmart.com
Mamma	http://www.mamma.com
Northern Light	http://www.northernlight.com
Snap	http://snap.com
Yahoo!	http://www.yahoo.com

BOOLEAN BASICS: SPEAKING SEARCH ENGINE

"To be successful in searching, you also need to think about logic, or the way the computer is doing the search. One of the basic ways is through the use of Boolean logic," writes Lisa C. Miller in *Power Journalism: Computer-Assisted Journalism*. **Boolean logic** is a system of logic created by a mathematician named George Boole a century ago, B.C. (Before Computers, that is). It's the language that most search engines speak. Search engine help files generally say whether they use Boolean logic and which search terms (words or phrases called "operators") they require. Don't assume that all search engines use the same ones; they don't. There are five basic **Boolean operators:**

1. **AND** (the word is capitalized in bold here merely for emphasis; you can also type it in lowercase—**and**—as well.)
   The most important search term. Use AND to tell the search engine you want one word AND another word on the same Web page. Example: "Clinton and Starr" will return all pages with the words "Clinton" and "Starr."

2. **NOT**
   Use NOT to find one term but not another. Example: "Clinton not Starr" will return all pages that have "Clinton" but that don't have "Starr."

3. **NEAR**
   Use NEAR to find words close to each other in the same Web page. "Clinton near Starr" will return pages with "Clinton" close to "Starr."

4. **OR**
   Use OR when you want pages that contain either of two words.
   Some experts believe this is the least-useful search term. It's so broad,

returning hundreds of thousands of pages, that some search engines won't even recognize an OR request. "Clinton or Starr" will return pages with "Clinton" or "Starr."

5. **Quotation Marks (" ")**
Putting words in quotes normally means you want the search engine to find the exact phrase: "Storytelling on deadline" will return pages with that exact phrase.

SEARCH TIPS

1. Read the instructions. Every search engine is different. The minutes you take to read help files could save you hours of frustration.

2. Match your search with the right engine. Start a general search at a directory, such as Yahoo! or Snap or Look Smart, which is created by humans. It will take you to a list of topics. For a more specific hunt for a book title or a document such as the Bill of Rights, you're better off with a search engine, such as Infoseek or HotBot, that uses spiders to create indexes of keywords drawn from millions of computer-searched pages.

3. Don't go past the first page of results, experts advise. Search engines list their results in order of confidence or relevance, usually with a percentage (99 percent). The higher the percentage, supposedly the more likely your keyword is in the site, but it doesn't always work that way. Many searches generate dozens of pages with hundreds of Web sites. Although I often find interesting information by reading every page, a reporter on deadline may not have that luxury.

4. Refine your search. Don't use just one keyword. List several in a search string. If you want to find out about jobs in online journalism, try "online journalism news jobs openings" instead of "online jobs." Stay away from common words such as "and" or "the" because many engines ignore them.

5. Caution: Everything on the Internet looks so official that it's easy to assume it's fact. Often the information posted on the Web is incorrect. Smart reporters learn to double-check with another source.

A REPORTER'S BEST FRIEND: A LIBRARIAN

The Internet is a library that is open 24 hours a day, needs no library card and features no "Shhh" signs. But the wise reporter knows it's not the only re-search source. As a young reporter, I was fortunate to have a reference li-brarian in my family: my older brother, Jeff. For the first several years of my career, when I worked at small newspapers that didn't employ librarians, a call to him was one of my first steps. He introduced me to the *Encyclopedia of*

Associations, brainstormed ideas and searched card catalogues for books that met my information needs. In the years to come, other research professionals became invaluable collaborators on stories.

Remember: Always check in with a librarian. An information professional can save you time, help you avoid useless avenues of research and, in a moment's time, locate the fact that will help make your stories accurate. An informed, curious and patient mind is still the best search engine.

PART 3: THE REPORTER'S MIND-SET

ACCURACY ABOVE ALL

Surveys show that the public expects the news media to be accurate, even though people are less confident than they used to be that news organizations get the facts right. Accuracy is a mind-set, an attitude. The best reporters I know die a thousand deaths when they learn a story they wrote includes an error. Everyone makes mistakes, no one is perfect, but journalists must take great care to get it right. Otherwise they lose a news organization's greatest asset: credibility. Accuracy is the goal; fact-checking is the process.

The way to achieve accuracy is to develop a system and adhere to it religiously.

DURING THE REPORTING, take the extra second to read back the spelling of the source's name. Ask for the person's age. If you ask for birthdate and year, you'll always have the information needed to update an age.

DURING THE WRITING, consult your documentary sources—notebook, printed materials—as you're writing. If you don't want to interrupt the writing flow, make sure to put a mark reminding you to double-check it later. "CK" for "check" is the standard proofreader's mark. **"CQ"** is shorthand for "this has been checked for accuracy"; it is often used with unusual spellings, facts and figures.

AFTER THE WRITING, assemble all your source materials—notebooks, interview transcripts, tapes, books, studies, photographs, everything you've used to report and write your story. Then go over every single word in the story and compare it to the original source. It's time consuming, but you can sleep a little easier. On projects and even on daily stories, I made one printout just for names and titles, another for quotes, a third for other factual details.

Call your source back and double-check. If you're describing a financial transaction, a medical procedure or how a sewer bond works, there's nothing wrong with calling the source and asking him or her to listen to what you've written. Your obligation is to be clear and accurate.

Listen to the voice in your head. Whenever I made a mistake in a story, I could always go back to a moment where it happened. Usually it was an assumption I made or a question I failed to address. There is a moment of truth in writing where you can take either the accurate path or the inaccurate path.

I was obsessive about it, but in 22 years as a reporter, I wrote stories that had corrections appended only about a half-dozen times. That doesn't mean all my other stories were error-free. I don't think a story without some mistakes exists; Appalachian quiltmakers put mistakes in their work because, they say, the devil loves perfection, but the careful, responsible reporter tries hard to get it right.

Errors are the bane of journalists. As a new reporter, I used to keep my corrections in my top desk drawer; I wanted their presence to haunt me. Reporters who start their careers working for small-town papers learn an unforgettable lesson about accuracy when they make a mistake in an obituary and hear from the deceased's survivors. One of the disadvantages of the electronic newsroom is that reporters may not come into contact with the people they hurt with incorrect information.

After tracking errors in *The Oregonian* of Portland, editors concluded that the three most frequent sources of error are:

GET YOUR STORIES RIGHT BY STUDYING "44 TIPS FOR GREATER ACCURACY" AT http://oak.cats. ohiou.edu/~feef/ 44tips.htm

1. Working from memory

2. Making assumptions

3. Dealing with second-hand sources

Although teachers and editors preach the importance of accuracy, few provide students and reporters with useful tools to ensure it. Two noteworthy exceptions are "44 Tips for Greater Accuracy," a Web page written by Frank E. Fee Jr., a veteran editor who teaches journalism at Ohio University, and an accuracy checklist (which follows) created by Michele McLellan, an editor at *The Oregonian*, as part of a project to improve that paper's accuracy.

Some magazines employ fact-checkers. They verify names, titles, ages, addresses and the gist of quotations in the story. "Fact-checking is the stage in the editorial process where someone attempts independent confirmation of every fact in an author's manuscript before its publication," according to Richard Blow and Ari Posner, who described their adventures in fact-checking in *The New Republic*. It's a luxury that newspaper reporters rarely enjoy. Most professional reporters know they must act as their own fact-checkers. If you get small things wrong, you won't be trusted with big things. What news organizations have to sell, especially now with technology giving anyone the opportunity to report news electronically, is credibility.

GULP AND GO: ASSERTIVENESS IN REPORTING

Reporting and writing the news demand courage. What surprises many young reporters is the fact that reporting involves meeting strangers and persuading them to tell you things they may not want to tell you. There's only one way they learn that lesson. Here's how one student journalist, Steve Myers, described his assertiveness training: "I was surprised the most by the fact that I was able to get over my fears of doing the actual reporting. No matter how the writing of the story turned out, in my mind it was secondary to the fact that I knocked on all 18 doors on 56th Avenue S. I felt a little bit

AN ACCURACY CHECKLIST

■ **PROPER NAMES.** Did I check the spelling of a person's name directly with the person? Did I ask the person to spell it back to me? If the primary source isn't available, have I checked with two independent, knowledgeable sources? Have I applied similar scrutiny to other biographical details in my story such as age, family members, job title, educational background? Is all information up-to-date?

■ **TELEPHONE NUMBERS AND ADDRESSES.** Did I call any telephone number in my story, using the version I have typed into the computer? Have I verified related information such as addresses and locations?

■ **INFORMATION ABOUT EVENTS.** Have I double-checked the date, place and time provided and compared it to what I've typed in my story or listing? Does my editor have the information so he or she can double-check it, too?

■ **MATH AND NUMBERS.** Have I checked the calculations of my source? Is he or she using the correct method, and is the calculation free of math errors? If I am doing my own calculations, have I used the correct methods and double-checked my math? If I'm not a math whiz, have I run my calculations by a colleague who knows math? Have I provided my original numbers in clear

form to my editor and the graphics department for double-checking?

■ **PHOTOS, CAPTIONS, GRAPHICS.** Have I compared the information in my story to that provided in the captions or graphics that will accompany it? Does information match up?

■ **DIFFERENT VERSIONS.** Have I independently verified accounts of such things as historical events and records, legal situations and descriptions of problems with an authoritative source? For example, if I am quoting an opponent about the impact of a new law, have I looked up the law, and have I checked the opponent's version with legal experts? If there are different versions of the facts, have I done everything I can to resolve them, or does my story at least make clear that some information is in dispute? Does my story assert opinion as fact? Have I taken potentially out-of-date or incorrect information from old clips without verifying it? What additional verification do I need to do?

■ **ASSUMPTIONS.** Am I relying on assumption or memory that some information in my story is factual? Have I accepted information from a second hand source as correct? What must I do to verify the information?

Michele McLellan
The Oregonian

like an encyclopedia salesman, but I got over the nausea in the pit of my stomach by the fourth or fifth house."

What may help is knowing that many people are terrified of journalists. Although it may be hard to believe, most people will be more afraid of you and the power you wield as a reporter than you are of them. Consider what J. C. McKinnon, a burly, stern-faced St. Petersburg police officer, tells my reporting students:

> "I carry a can of pepper spray, a Glock pistol and 51 rounds of ammunition. But you've got something that can destroy me: a pen and a notepad."

If you're avoiding doing something—making the phone call, knocking on the door, visiting a part of your community you've never been to before—acknowledge that you're anxious and then go do it. I used to make a habit of writing in my journal whatever my fear was, what I expected would happen, and then reporting back the outcome. Invariably, the feared result never happened. On those rare occasions when it did, I found that I handled it. Even after 22 years' experience, I found I had to keep reminding myself that people usually want to talk.

Assertiveness reflects a belief in yourself. You have the right to ask questions, to approach someone for an interview, to request information. The flip side, of course, means that the person you're asking has the right to say no. Assertiveness also demands empathy. You have to understand that you wield power as a journalist. Your press pass will get you places the general public can't go. As a reporter, I've watched doctors try to impregnate a woman through in-vitro fertilization, sailed on a freighter, followed police on a drug bust. But freedom carries responsibility.

Don't be afraid. Or, rather, be afraid but do it anyway.

Gulp. And go.

TOP TEN TOOLS FOR TODAY'S JOURNALISTS

Here are the tools I think reporters need: a tightrope, a net, someone else's shoes, a loom, a bible, a zoom lens, six words, an accelerator pedal, scissors and a trash can. As you will see, these tools are mostly imaginary ones. They are metaphors for mental skills and attitudes that will help you achieve excellence.

1. A TIGHTROPE.   If you're going to be a writer, you need to take risks. You can always tell safe stories, and there are safe stories all over the paper and all over the broadcasts. The best advice I ever got as a journalism student was a throwaway line from my teacher, Melvin Mencher, who said, "You know, you have to be counterphobic." Meaning: Do what you're afraid to do.

Think of the tightrope, and every day walk across it. Walk across it as a reporter and writer. Who's the one person you're afraid to call? Where is the one place in town you've never been because you're afraid to go there? It may be a housing project, or it may be the top floor of the big bank. Force yourself to take risks as a reporter. And ask yourself every day, "Have I taken a risk?"

2. A NET.   The best writers cast trawler's nets on stories. They cast them wide and deep. They interview 10 people to get the one quote that sums up the theme. They spend half a day mining interviews for the anecdote that reveals the story. They hunt through records and reports, looking for the one specific thing that explains the universal. The detail that captures the person. Anne Hull of the *St. Petersburg Times* described a female police officer in

SACRED TEXTS: WHAT PRIZE-WINNING JOURNALISTS READ FOR INSPIRATION

- *Clockers* by Richard Price
- *There Are No Children Here* by Alex Kotlowitz
- "On the Pulse of Morning" by Maya Angelou, delivered at President Clinton's inauguration, 1993
- *The Writer's Art* by James Kilpatrick
- *The Elements of Style* by William Strunk Jr. and E. B. White
- *The Essays of E. B. White*
- *Writing for Your Readers* by Donald M. Murray
- *Writers at Work: The Paris Review Interviews*, edited by George Plimpton

- Works by:
  Ernest Hemingway
  Willa Cather
  Tom Wolfe
  John Updike
  Joan Didion
  Jimmy Breslin
  Mark Twain

—Suggested by Mitch Albom, Brian Dickinson, Michael Gartner, Anne Hull, Peter H. King, Susan Trausch and Ken Wells in *Best Newspaper Writing* 1994–1996

Tampa as "a brown-haired woman in a police uniform and size-4 steel-toe boots." A telling detail "can help explain the sum of a person," Hull says. In this case, it was "the Terminator meets a ballerina."

3. SOMEONE ELSE'S SHOES. Every journalist is equipped with this tool already, but it's surprising how few use it on a daily basis. I'm not just talking about shoe-leather reporting, but also about empathy. Empathy is the writer's greatest gift, and perhaps the most important tool: The ability to feel what another person feels, to walk in another's shoes. Richard Ben Cramer, talking about the reporting he did in the Middle East in the late '70s, says he tried to give readers a sense of what it is like to be living in a situation of terror, of life on the edge: "It's very hard to know what someone would feel in a situation unless you at least feel something of it yourself."

4. A LOOM. What do we journalists do? We make connections for people. We connect the police report at the station house to the red bungalow in the tree-lined neighborhood. We connect City Hall with the sewage project. Writing is a process of making connections, of discovering patterns. Are you weaving connections in your stories? In your reading? In your life? Turn your computer into a loom that weaves stories.

5. A BIBLE. Lowercase b. The sacred writing texts you read for guidance or inspiration.

Joan Beck of the *Chicago Tribune* actually was talking about Bible with an uppercase B: "I always read a couple of chapters in the Bible every morning. Whether I'm working or not. Those cadences get imprinted in your brain. When you write, you tend to write in those kinds of patterns and rhythms.

The cadences—but only in the King James Version—are so effective. You use them as sort of a touchstone."

Keep a collection of your sacred texts—books or stories that you keep nearby when you're getting ready to write and are trying to go to the next level of excellence. When stumped, take inspiration from writers you admire.

6. A ZOOM LENS.   David Finkel, staff writer for *The Washington Post Magazine,* says he tries "to look at any site that will be the focus of a narrative passage as if I were a photographer. I not only stand near something, I move away. For the long view. I crouch down, I move left and right. I try to view it from every angle possible to see what might be revealed."

Writers need to go in very close. There's a famous passage in a column by columnist Jimmy Breslin about the light coming in and glinting off a mobster's pinkie ring. Pay attention to the barely noticed details.

At the same time, we need to back up, see the whole scene, understand the context. We need to see the universal as well as the specific. Jewelers use a magnifying loupe to distinguish the true diamond from the cubic zirconium. We need to be like jewelers, looking for the quality and the flaws in our stories.

7. SIX WORDS.   "Tell your story in six words," is the advice that former AP feature writer, now syndicated columnist Tad Bartimus gives. Not eight. By reducing it to the single phrase, reducing it almost to a line of poetry, you can capture the tension of the story. You can capture the entire story. And make it six, not four or nine, for no other reason than because in discipline there is freedom.

One classic example, perhaps the shortest short story ever written: "For Sale: Baby shoes, never used." Six words.

8. AN ACCELERATOR PEDAL.   "There are some kinds of writing," William Faulkner said, "that you have to do very fast. Like riding a bicycle on a tightrope." Race past your internal censor. Novelist Gail Godwin called it "the watcher at the gates." This is the voice that says, "You're an incompetent. You can't write. That thing you did yesterday? You've lost it. You didn't do the reporting. You're an idiot." So you have to trick the watcher at the gates. And the way you do it is to speed. My colleague, Roy Peter Clark, put it in three words, "Write like hell."

9. SCISSORS.   Or its electronic equivalent: the delete key. Truman Capote said, "I believe more in the scissors than I do the pencil." In *The Elements of Style,* William Strunk Jr. said, "Vigorous writing is concise. A sentence should contain no unnecessary words, a paragraph no unnecessary sentences, for the same reason that a drawing should have no unnecessary lines and a machine no unnecessary parts. This requires not that the writer make all his sentences short, or that he avoid all detail and treat the subject only in outline, but that every word tell." Less is more. How many gallons of maple sap does it take to make a gallon of maple syrup? Forty. Boil away the sap.

10. A TRASH CAN. Isaac Bashevis Singer, the Nobel Prize–winning writer, once said, "The main rule of the writer is never to pity your manuscript. If you see something is no good, throw it away and begin again. A lot of writers have failed because they have too much pity."

It's funny—we journalists will have little pity for sources, but we will pity the weakest prose because it flows from our keyboard. "Hey!" a reporter will protest, "I spent two hours on that lead." We can't throw it away. Remember Singer: "I say that a wastepaper basket is a writer's best friend. My wastepaper basket is on a steady diet."

TOOL SHARPENING: THE COACHING WAY

- Study notes you have taken as a student or reporter and identify shorthand or speed-writing symbols you already use. Establish your own speedwriting system.
- Have you identified what Melvin Mencher calls your story's "nonnegotiable necessities"? Are you sure your story contains them?
- What surprises you about the reporting and writing tools you rely on? What have you learned from using them? What do you need to learn next to take your reporting and writing to the next level?
- Collect a variety of revealing physical details about someone: a friend, relative, roommate. Follow writing teacher Don Murray's advice: "Use all your senses— sight, hearing, smell, taste, touch—to pack your notebook, and your memory, with specifics you may need when writing." To the five senses add a few more: sense of place, sense of people, sense of drama, sense of time.
- Be honest: Are you spending too much time at your desk instead of being out in the community or the area covered by your beat? If you're not on deadline, get out of the office right now.
- Be counterphobic: Do something you fear.
- Is your story fair? How would you feel if the subject of the story was a member of your family or a close friend?
- Is your story accurate? Have you checked every name, address, title and fact against your notes or a document? Have you read sections with technical material to someone who is an expert on the subject?

GLOSSARY OF IMPORTANT TERMS

Boolean logic. A system of logic created by 19th-century mathematician George Boole, used to search databases.

Boolean operators. Terms, such as "and," "or," "not" and "near," that help narrow a search.

Clip files. Usually kept in bulging, dog-eared envelopes, these are collections of stories clipped from the paper by news librarians and kept in the aptly named "morgue." In many newsrooms clips have been replaced by electronic retrieval systems.

CQ. Shorthand for "This has been checked and double-checked." Often used with unusual names, figures, facts and numbers, such as John Smythe (CQ) or the score was 79–78 (CQ).

Database. A computerized collection of related information, usually arranged in a uniform format. Governments store public records in databases. Commercial databases offer full texts of news stories, statistics, reports, transcripts and other resources. Available, usually, for a fee. Charges vary.

E-mail. Electronic mail sent from one computer to another via a network.

Internet. Interconnected network of computers, first created by the government to guarantee communication in case of nuclear war, now linking public and private computer users worldwide.

Nonnegotiable necessities. Facts, details and other information that must be included for a story to be complete and answer the reader's questions.

Search engines. Computer programs that search the World Wide Web and other Internet resources, such as newsgroups, using keywords. Also known as robots, spiders, crawlers, wanderers and worms.

World Wide Web. The part of the Internet that lets a computer user move between linked documents—containing text, audio, video and animations that may be stored on computers anywhere in the world.

EXERCISES

1. Make an inventory of your reporting toolbox. If you've just started studying journalism, the list may be short: a notebook, pen, time-sharing on a news lab computer. Study the various tools cited in this chapter, and decide which ones you want to learn more about.

2. Use several search engines to research the history of the tape recorder. Who was the individual who brought back the technology to America after World War II? Who is credited with the invention of the wire recorder? Write a 250-word passage tracing the tape recorder's

history using the information you collected. List your sources, including Web site addresses, at the end.

3. Practice note-taking by transcribing dialogue from your favorite songs (country and western, rap, gospel, rhythm and blues, rock), recorded speeches and television shows. Compare your version with the original. Measure your speed *and* accuracy.

4. Go out on a photo assignment with a photographer and watch how he or she collects visual information. Better yet, take a camera yourself on your next story and experience for yourself what it's like to make pictures, use available light and crop a photo.

5. Hollywood has long turned to the newsroom for entertainment. Rent the movie *The Front Page* starring Jack Lemmon and Walter Matthau or *His Girl Friday* starring Rosalind Russell and Cary Grant to get a view of what journalism was like in the old days. Discuss what has changed since the 1920s and what is still the same. What were the "tools of the trade" back then? What has been lost and gained? Are journalists more ethical today than they used to be?

READINGS

Friedman, Bonnie. *Writing Past Dark: Envy, Fear, Distraction, and Other Dilemmas in the Writer's Life.* New York: Harper Perennial Library, 1994.

Houston, Brant. *Computer-Assisted Reporting: A Practical Guide,* 2d ed. New York: St. Martin's Press, 1999. Includes IBM disk. Mac version available.

Miller, Lisa C. *Power Journalism: Computer-Assisted Journalism.* Fort Worth: Harcourt Brace College Publishers, 1998. Includes Mac disk.

Paul, Nora. *Computer-Assisted Research: A Guide to Tapping Online Information,* 3rd ed. St. Petersburg, Fla.: The Poynter Institute for Media Studies, 1995, revised 1997. Online at **http://www.poynter.org/car/cg_chome.htm**.

Rosenbaum, Marcus D., and John Dinges, eds. *Sound Reporting: The National Public Radio Guide to Radio Journalism and Production.* Dubuque, Iowa: Kendall/Hunt, 1992.

Vaughan-Nichols, Steve J. "Find It Faster." *Internet World,* vol. 8, no. 6, June 1997. Online at **http://www.iw.com/1997/06/searchtips.html**.

Weinberg, Steve. *The Reporter's Handbook: An Investigator's Guide to Documents and Techniques,* 3rd ed. New York: St. Martin's Press, 1995.

Witt, Leonard, ed. *The Complete Book of Feature Writing.* Cincinnati, Ohio: Writer's Digest Books, 1991.

HOTLIST

http://www.poynter.org/research/research.htm

The staff of The Poynter Institute library maintains one of the most comprehensive collections of Web sites for journalists: links to news sites, bibliographies, current news, research files. It could keep you busy for years.

http://www.ksg.harvard.edu/ksgpress/opin/journpg.htm

A "One-Stop Journalist Shop" maintained by the Kennedy School of Government, Harvard University.

http://thorplus.lib.purdue.edu/reference/index.html

Purdue's Virtual Library is a gateway to census and other government data, maps and other information resources.

http://www.mediasource.com/intro.htm

The Media in Cyberspace: A National Survey. Every year, Middleberg & Associates, a public relations firm specializing in new media relations, polls working journalists about their Internet use.

http://oak.cats.ohiou.edu/~feef/accuracy.htm

"44 Tips for Greater Accuracy." Frank E. Fee Jr., a veteran editor-turned-journalism professor at Ohio University, draws on newsroom situations and analysis of errors to produce a list of reminders that helps journalists fulfill their obligation to readers and viewers.

http://www.isleuth.com/

The Internet Sleuth. Choose from more than 2,000 searchable databases. Unlike other search engines that try to index the entire Web, the Sleuth trains its sights on searchable databases, most of which can be searched directly without your having to surf over first.

http://www.editors-service.com/main.html

The Internet Newsroom. A limited online version of a twice-monthly newsletter that is a rich resource for journalists who want to use the Internet for information.

http://www.profnet.com/ped/

Profnet's Experts Database. Running on the World Wide Web, the PED offers capsule bios and contact numbers for more than 2,000 leading experts at hundreds of colleges. New contacts added steadily.

http://www.poynter.org/car/cg_cartrans.htm

This page on the Poynter Institute Web site describes the "where?," "how?," and "so what?" of full-text commercial databases. (Most of the services cited require a subscription or fee.)

http://www.poynter.org/research/pj/pj_photogloss.htm

Kenny Irby has devoted his career to taking news photos and inspiring photojournalists. As deputy director of photography at *Newsday*, he helped coordinate photo coverage on two Pulitzer Prize–winning projects. With this photojournalism glossary, "The Art and Language of Photography," his goal is to help reporters "understand the lingo of photojournalism and aid you when communicating with photographers."

http://searchenginewatch.com

Danny Sullivan maintains this site with almost everything you ever wanted to know about search engines, although some of the information is limited to subscribers.

http://www.nytimes.com/library/tech/98/09/circuits/articles/03sear.html

"Desperately Seeking Susan OR Suzie NOT Sushi" by Matt Lake. A *New York Times* "Cybertimes" article that provides one of the clearest explanations of how search engines work—and don't work—to find information. Includes a tip list for smart searching.

CHAPTER

A PROCESS APPROACH TO REPORTING AND WRITING

CHAPTER FOCUS

Good journalism is a process, a rational series of steps and decisions that can be studied and repeated.

CHAPTER LESSONS

- The process approach
- Brainstorming, branching and other idea-generating skills
- The ways reporters collect information
- Reporting by e-mail
- How to focus for story
- How to organize for story
- How to get the story written
- Techniques for revision
- Writers at work: The Coaching Way

A LIFE IN JOURNALISM

I came to journalism with virtually no experience. Not surprisingly, I didn't know what I was doing. For much of my early career, I was like a traveler without a map. I had an idea of where I wanted to be—I wanted to write the kind of stories that I admired—but I didn't know how to get there. Instead, I was flying by the seat of my pants.

As a boy, I figured that the way to be a better writer was to study how other writers did it. So I read every story and interview with writers I could find. I learned that writers had rituals: E. B. White, *The New Yorker* essayist, used to start with a martini. Thomas Wolfe, the North Carolina novelist who wrote *Look Homeward Angel*, was too tall to sit comfortably at a desk; he wrote standing up at a refrigerator. Gail Godwin, the novelist, lit two different kinds of incense before a writing session. My favorite was the writer who was so skeptical of his early **drafts** that he wouldn't even type them. Instead, he would write first drafts with pastel colored pens: rose, peach, and then move up to darker hues until finally he felt satisfied enough to type a draft. Then he would take the manuscript and tack it to a wall of his office. Back on his desk he kept a pair of binoculars. He sat down, picked them up and read his story word by word.

I used to think that if I copied some of these habits I could write like some of these greats. But it didn't work.

Then one day in 1981, a white-bearded man walked into the newsroom where I was working as a reporter. His name was Donald M. Murray. He was a Pulitzer Prize–winning journalist who taught journalism at the University of New Hampshire and was one of the first of a new breed of writing teachers in newsrooms dubbed "writing coaches."

What Murray taught us was the single most important element of my education as a writer. He taught us that writing may be magical, but it's not magic. Writing is a process, a rational series of steps and decisions that can be studied and repeated. Just like athletes who study films of the way they hit the ball, writers can study how they do their writing.

I know now that writing is a process—a series of decisions and actions that can be duplicated and repeated.

Essentially, the **process approach** presupposes that reporters follow a series of recognizable steps when they do their job. Follow those steps, and you can do the same.

Calling something a process does not mean the same as calling it a formula, a recipe that you must slavishly follow: Mix one part interview with two parts background material equals one story. A process is a description, rather than a prescription. It's not a formula. It describes the way reporters work. The process approach gives reporters and their editors a common language to discuss their craft. It also provides diagnostic tools that can help writers and editors discover the flaws in their stories and develop solutions to the problems that inevitably surface.

> "The single most important ingredient that a good reporter has is curiosity. And as long as you maintain that curiosity you will be a good reporter. The great reporters are those that never lose that curiosity."
> —BOB SCHIEFFER, *CBS NEWS*

Donald M. Murray

REPORTERS AT WORK: THE PROCESS APPROACH

Essentially, the process of **reporting** and writing the news involves six steps:

1. News thinking I: Getting ideas
2. Collect: Reporting the story
3. News thinking II—Focus: Thinking of stories
4. Order: Mapping the story
5. Draft: Writing the story
6. Revise: Rewriting for readers and viewers

In Chapter 1, you learned what news is and various ways to find it. The recognition of news is the first step in the process.

NEWS THINKING I: GETTING IDEAS

Reporters start with story ideas. Often and especially at the start of your career, these will be someone else's ideas, usually an editor's. Then they're called assignments.

Just as a flower begins as a seed, every story begins with an idea. The quality of your ideas will determine your success as a reporter. Editors are always looking for self-starters. They want to hire reporters who generate their own story ideas. The best editors are those who believe the reporters are the eyes and ears of the news organization; They are the ones out on the street. You must come up with your own story ideas. If you don't, you may find yourself saddled with stories you don't want to do. One of the keys to Bob Woodward's early success was his initiative. Although he was a new reporter on *The Washington Post* staff, he came in with his own story ideas.

WHERE DO IDEAS COME FROM?

YOUR PUBLICATION, BROADCAST OR ONLINE SITE.   If you don't have the newspaper-reading habit, start cultivating it now. There are ideas in every publication from the great dailies to the small-town weeklies, from the display ads to the obits to the legal ads. Watch the evening news and the 24-hour cable news channels. Watch educational television, and the History Channel, the Discovery Channel and the Learning Channel. Listen to National Public Radio. Browse online news sites; never before have

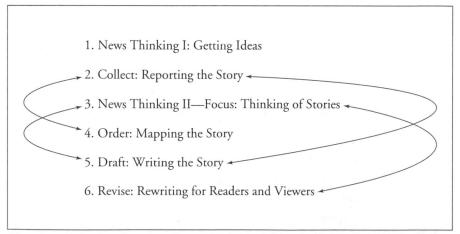

1. News Thinking I: Getting Ideas

2. Collect: Reporting the Story

3. News Thinking II—Focus: Thinking of Stories

4. Order: Mapping the Story

5. Draft: Writing the Story

6. Revise: Rewriting for Readers and Viewers

The writing process describes the steps writers follow from idea to revision. Writers often circle back through the steps to make the meaning of the story clear.

journalists had the ability to read the work of professionals from around the world without ever leaving their desk. Look for story ideas everywhere from the newspaper's front page to the classified ads, from the angles that a broadcast show overlooked to an interesting character who may be familiar to Internet browsers but unknown to the millions who still rely on print publications. Look for trends, stories that deserve follow-up, no matter what medium they appear in.

Go back two years and read a week's papers. Most stories are never followed up on. Journalists have very limited memory. I once produced a seven-part series, "The Burning of Rhode Island," that began essentially by pursuing the causes and impact of fires in abandoned buildings that normally rated no more than a few paragraphs in the paper. Steve Lovelady, a veteran editor at *The Wall Street Journal* and *The Philadelphia Inquirer*, who is now editor-at-large for *Time Inc.*, advises reporters to mine their paper for ideas.

VISIT ONLINE NEWS SITES AROUND THE WORLD THROUGH THIS SITE MAINTAINED BY THE AMERICAN JOURNALISM REVIEW AT http://ajr. newslink.org/

YOURSELF, FRIENDS, CLASSMATES, CO-WORKERS, NEIGHBORS, CHILDREN, TELEVISION, MOVIES, CHAT ROOMS, MAGAZINES, BOOKS. Eavesdrop, ask questions, observe, wonder. Ideas are everywhere if your mind is open to them. What's happening in your life? In your parents' lives? In your neighbors' lives? In your friends' lives? Use yourself as a resource. Because many students buy used cars, which are more likely to survive a crash? Are your friends consuming large quantities of calcium to "bank bone" and avoid the osteoporosis that plagues their mothers and grandmothers? What are the health, financial and consumer stories that matter to you and your peers?

When I arrived in Washington, D.C., in 1989 to work as a national correspondent for Knight Ridder Newspapers, my wife and I were the proud parents of a baby girl and expecting twins. For the first time in my life, issues such as the safety of minivans and cribs were of interest. I translated that personal interest into news stories based on interviews with federal agencies, consumer groups, businesses and parents that found a home in hundreds of newspapers. Eventually, I was named the bureau's first family beat reporter.

Reporters can use their own lives as a template for stories no matter what their beat. Kevin Merida of *The Washington Post* was a new parent, the father of a baby boy, when he was covering the presidential election campaign in 1996. One night, he was shopping for supplies in a baby superstore in suburban Washington, surrounded by new and expectant parents. He decided that he was in the midst of an ideal focus group, a group of voters who would probably have very definite opinions about the campaign. He returned to the store and spent part of an evening interviewing parents.

NEWS RELEASES. Corporations, public agencies and institutions are eager to get into the news. Their main tool is the news release, usually a printed document, increasingly a video or Web page, that is designed to attract the interest of a news organization. Press releases report upcoming events, announce the development of new products or programs, and profile people in the community who may be newsworthy. It's up to you to decide if the information in the release is really news or merely free advertising of more benefit to the person issuing the press release than to your readers or viewers. You still have to do your own reporting, but there's nothing wrong with using press releases as a tip sheet.

YOUR SOURCES.   Once you begin reporting, the people you meet and interview will be a steady source of story ideas: officials, residents, school administrators, teachers, lawyers, judges, doctors and so on.

OTHER PUBLICATIONS AND NEWS ORGANIZATIONS.   The competition is a rich source of ideas. What angles have they missed?

IDEA GENERATORS: CREATIVITY SKILLS FOR TODAY'S JOURNALISTS

BRAINSTORMING

When Susan Trausch, an editorial writer for *The Boston Globe,* sits down to write on deadline, she doesn't turn to her computer keyboard like most journalists. Instead, she picks up a pen and a legal pad. Before she can tell editorial page readers what to think on a given subject, she first has to find out what her own thoughts are. The notes she makes in those first moments make sense of the jumbled thoughts in her head. They will drive her reporting, plan her structure, make connections—all in rehearsal for the writing to come. "Then I turn to the screen, and somewhere in that list is a lead," she says.

With her legal pad and pen, Trausch is employing a basic creativity tool known as **brainstorming.** It has been seldom used in journalism, I believe, because one of its essential qualities—withholding judgment—is a foreign concept to many reporters and editors. They are often most comfortable in the role of critic or watchdog. If a watchdog doesn't bark, it's not doing its job. Brainstorming can be a solitary exercise or can be done with other reporters and editors. The key is to suspend critical judgment. Write down as quickly as possible all the ideas and related thoughts that surface on a particular topic. Don't stop to evaluate items. Don't worry if the ideas seem lame; don't cross out or ignore any idea. Don't worry about spelling or punctuation or fill in details. Write in your personal shorthand. Once the flow of ideas has petered out, then and only then do you review and evaluate, discard and organize, clarify and expand. Look for the information that surprises you or that connects with other information in an interesting, unexpected way.

Reporters often complain that the nature of the news they cover is boring. Government meetings, budgetary matters, legislation aren't the stuff that gets their creative juices flowing. Maybe that's why newspapers are so boring. Brainstorming requires you to apply creativity. Brainstorming is simple: You simply choose a topic and make a list of everything that comes to mind. Here's an example:

BRAINSTORMING THE SCHOOL BUDGET STORY

Next week, the School Board meets to vote on the school budget. The superintendent of schools has proposed a 140-page budget for the next school year with proposals for 5- and 10-year spending.

Without even looking at the budget, you can brainstorm ideas:

The making of a budget
1. How many people participate?
2. Who participates? Teachers? Principals? Students? Parents?
3. Is it top secret or an open process?
4. When does the process begin?

Mr. Holland's Opus
1. Are there any teachers whose programs are being cut in the budget?
2. Which programs are getting the biggest bite of the budgetary pie: computer science or the arts? Football or girls basketball? Why?

Inflation and the "three R's"
1. What does it cost to run a school in the 21st century?
2. How have school supplies changed—from chalk to computers—and how does that affect the budget?

Choose a topic and make a list of everything that comes to mind. There are no bad ideas in a brainstorming session.

That list took about seven minutes. It's sketchy, but it got me thinking about a budget in a variety of ways: It not only unearthed questions that I need to answer but introduced, via the popular movie *Mr. Holland's Opus*, a possible angle to explore.

Now try brainstorming with a buddy. Two heads can be better than one, especially in a brainstorming session. Ideas spark other ideas. Remember the first rule of brainstorming: There is no such thing as a bad idea.

MAPPING

Brainstorming is a linear process. You write down ideas, usually in list form, that march from top to bottom. But the brain processes ideas in other ways. Some people think in nonlinear fashion. **Mapping** and **branching** are techniques that accommodate that way of thinking. By letting you start in the middle, return to the start and go on to the end, and then go back to the middle and start over, these techniques allow you to retrace your thoughts and add afterthoughts, says Henriette Anne Klauser, author of *Writing on Both Sides of the Brain.* "And often the afterthoughts," she says, "are the most valuable aspects."

This time, instead of making a list about a story idea, put the topic or subject in the center of a page. When you get an idea, draw a line out from the center and write the idea at the end. If that idea triggers a new one, draw a new line from that word or return to the center and draw new lines for each idea. Continuing with the school budget, draw a map that encompasses the school budget idea and tracks your mind's journey.

Klauser and others interested in left brain-right brain activities believe that mapping and branching more accurately reflect the way the mind works. Our mind doesn't work in a straight line, but rather more like a pinball machine, bouncing ideas off one another helter-skelter. I like to think of it as drawing a map of your neural synapses firing.

Here's how mapping a story on a proposal to change a bus route might look:

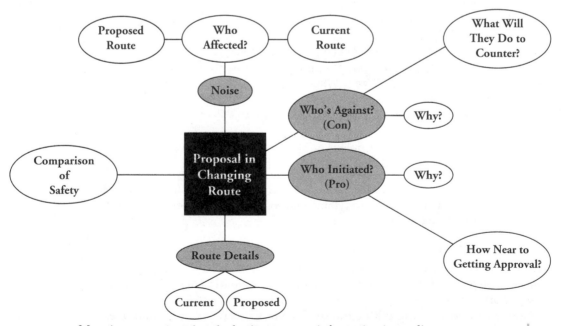

Mapping recognizes that the brain processes information in nonlinear ways.

Now try the same exercise using the branches of a tree.

Here's how it worked for me on a different topic: The crisis in child support enforcement.

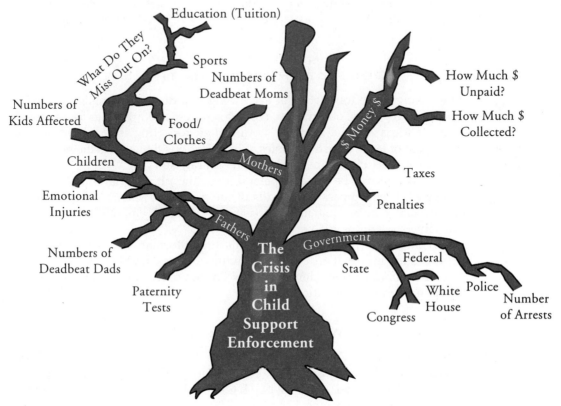

Branching provides another graphical alternative to the simple list technique of brainstorming.

Notice how nonlinear thinking takes you into new areas.

SCENARIO BUILDING

Trying to imagine the future is big business today. Corporations the world over employ futurists to help them envision markets, products and structures that will respond to future needs. Journalists can borrow their techniques to help stay abreast and ahead of the news.

Here's an example: Imagine it's the year 2025, a quarter of a century from now. You are 25 years older. If you are a college student today, you will be in your early to mid-40s. Sketch a scenario that describes where you live and work. Where do your parents live? What are their needs?

Now that you have built the scenario, consider what news stories you could write.

DAYBOOK. A daybook, or journal, can be a seedbed for ideas. Use it to record your observations, ideas, memories, imaginings, details, overheard conversations and lines of writing that pop into your head but that will evaporate if not recorded. Keep it with you and write down your ideas as they come to you. Set aside part of the day, when you get up or before you go to sleep, to fill out the fragmentary thoughts you've jotted down during the day.

COLLECT: REPORTING THE STORY

Reporting is the foundation of everything you do as a journalist. It encompasses interviews, observation, reading, analysis, computer-assisted reporting. If ideas are the seeds of stories, then reporting is the fertilizer, the compost of facts, statistics, quotes, interpretations that allows the reporter to produce a factual, complete, clear and accurate story.

Reporting can be done in person, over the phone, via e-mail over the Internet. It encompasses the skills of the detective, scientist, the confessor, analyst. It requires initiative, persistence, patience, empathy, courage, creativity, intelligence and nerve.

What is reporting? It's the act of collecting information. It's the act of communicating information. The two activities are inextricably linked. You can't do one without having done the other. For now, let's concentrate on the first step: gathering information.

WHAT REPORTING INVOLVES

OBSERVING. Rick Bragg of *The New York Times* walked through the bombed-out Alfred P. Murrah Federal Building in Oklahoma City on April 19, 1995, just hours after a terrorist bomb tore off the building's face, killing hundreds. "I did not stay long," he recalled, "but I just wanted to see the inside of the building. That's my job, you know, my job is to report it." In his Pulitzer Prize–winning story he used the details that he collected with his eyes, ears and heart to convey the immensity of the horror:

The destruction was almost concave in nature, shattering the building from the center, almost front to back, the blast apparently weakening as it spread to both sides of the structure. Blood-stained glass littered the inside. So complete was the destruction that panels and signs from offices several stories up were shattered on the ground floor.

People could not stop looking at it, particularly the second floor, where a child care center had been. ...

Everywhere observers looked, there were the discarded gloves, some blood-stained, of the medical workers.

There seemed to be very little whole inside the lower floors of the building, only pieces—pieces of desks, desktop computers and in one place what appeared to be the pieces of plastic toy animals, perhaps from the child care center, perhaps just some of those goofy little things grown-ups keep on their desks.

The New York Times
April 20, 1995

INTERVIEWING—GOING THE EXTRA MILE. When the big dailies in the Twin Cities had a brief about a missing teen in Farmington, Minn., Erin Hemme Froslie, a reporter for the town's weekly, was assigned to follow it up. She noticed that the brief didn't include any comment from family members. "The police weren't releasing family names. I went into one of Farmington's businesses where a poster of the missing girl was hanging, and asked if they knew who her mother was. Once I got the mother's name I left a message on her answering machine, giving her the option to call back. She did. P.S. This story does have a happy ending. The girl was found in Florida shortly before Christmas."

READING. The ability to read quickly and absorb the meaning of a text is vital for today's reporter. Our society generates an enormous amount of words—reports, studies, statements, speeches, and most of it, or so it sometimes seems to anyone standing in a newsroom, ends up on reporters' desks. Much of it has little news value, generated by public relations staffs hoping for some attention for their product, politician or cause. Your job will be to separate the wheat from the chaff, to determine what is significant information for your readers.

ANALYZING WHAT YOU READ. Reading as a journalist is not a passive behavior. Good reporters question and challenge the information they collect. Some of the best stories come from debunking conventional wisdom. The journalist is not a stenographer but rather a watchdog, an analyst of events and information. Journalism is an intellectual act. It's using the mind to analyze what the senses receive and then organizing and presenting the information with words, images and sounds to inform the reader or viewer.

Journalists play a vital role in keeping the world informed. They do it by going places and witnessing events that their readers can't see. They are a bridge between government and citizens, the link that connects neighbors and people who live on the other side of the globe. Reporters collect information by phone, by fax, by e-mail, from radio and television and the Internet. They collect information from government officials and public relations spokespersons, from police officers and firefighters. They are eyewitnesses to public events—parades, inaugurations, strikes, demonstrations—that make up life in a democracy. They attend meetings. They cover events. They cover cops and fires. They write stories about people and their struggles, the joys and costs of being human.

In Washington, I covered Congress, the federal bureaucracy and the satellites that circle the major national institutions: lobbyists, interest groups and citizens. As the bureau's first family reporter I made it my job to cover how decisions made in Washington affect America's families.

THE WAYS REPORTERS COLLECT

- Interview
- Observe
- Research
- Study
- Experience
- Beat reporting

Some reporters have beats: specific institutions and subject areas they are responsible for. In Chapter 13, we'll take a closer look at beat reporting. For now, it's enough to know that beats are one of the major sources of news. Reporters covering beats regularly make rounds on their beat. The police reporter will check the daily log of arrests and crime incidents. The state house reporter will make the rounds of committee sessions and legislative meetings. Often beat reporters work the phone regularly. Of critical importance for a beat reporter is the development of sources who can be counted on to provide information, context and advance word of upcoming stories and who, in special cases, will also provide information without their identities being disclosed.

- General assignment

Not all reporters have a specific beat. Instead, they are called on to do a variety of reporting tasks every day. In many newsrooms, this job is called "general assignment." You walk into the newsroom every day without a clue about what you will be working on. You may be sent to a meeting or to interview a newsmaker, perhaps write a feature story on an interesting person. General assignment reporters are at the beck and call of their editors. Some reporters like the assignment. They like not knowing what awaits them every day. Others like the benefits of a beat assignment: regularity, familiarity with sources and subjects, the chance to develop enterprise story ideas.

Journalism, as veteran editor Robert Haiman likes to say, is "a timed sport." In the all-too-brief moments you have on every story you must be enormously demanding:

- Do I have enough people?
- Do I know what my story is about?
- Do I have the evidence to support my theme?
- Do I have the "micro"—the people, anecdotes, details—that bring a story to life and the "macro"—can I sum up, in a paragraph, the significance of the story? Do I have the statistics or other figures that put the anecdotal evidence into context?

PUBLIC RECORDS

For the journalist, who must rely on the collection of facts, public records are one of the greatest gifts a democracy offers. I first learned the power of public records at *The Providence Journal* when I was assigned to cover the monthly meeting of the city's housing authority, which oversaw public housing projects. The people who lived in the projects complained bitterly about inadequate maintenance. I was surprised to learn that the authority didn't meet at the projects, where its members might get a glimpse of the living conditions. Instead, they gathered at local restaurants. My next stop was the housing authority office, where I asked to see the vouchers that recorded the authority's spending. I spent an afternoon sifting through restaurant checks, copying down dollar amounts and even the eggplant Parmesan and names of other entrees that authority members selected. In recent months, the authority had spent more than $3,000 to feed its members. "The restaurant tabs were paid from authority funds, the majority of which are derived from rents paid by low-income tenants at the city's 14 public housing projects and from federal subsidies," my story reported. After it appeared, the authority's members decided to forgo their dinner meetings and meet instead at the housing projects they were supposed to manage.

Mining public records should be an essential element of your reporting process. Here, based on a guide prepared for The Poynter Institute by Jeff Good and Frank Marquardt, is a sampling of the resources available in public records—where to go and what you will find there:

- Newspapers: Facts, obituaries, birth notices, legal notices.
- Telephone directories: Name, address, phone number, spouse's name.
- City directories: Job, spouse, neighbors.
- Courthouses: Lawsuits, marriage and divorce records, criminal records, wills, guardianships, property records.
- City and county government offices: Auto and boat licenses, voter registration, occupational licenses, hunting and fishing licenses, water and sewer service records, trash collection, even dog licenses. Local agencies, such as the fire department, health department and building inspection department, have records on housing code violations, arson fires and restaurant inspections.
- Local government records: Financial disclosure reports reveal the business holdings, savings and debts of elected officials. Campaign finance reports show who contributed to political candidates. Memos and meetings' minutes provide a record of official actions and are often a rich source for quotes.
- State government records:
  - Department of Motor Vehicles: Information from drivers' licenses, license plates and driving records. Good source for addresses, ages and traffic violations.
  - Department of Professional Regulation: Information about the qualifications and disciplinary history of doctors, lawyers, engineers, nurses, realtors and other licensed professionals.

"Public records document practically every human activity. They follow us from birth to death, from school graduation to retirement. They shadow our movements in business, politics and crime. They capture on paper the transfer of wealth, whether it be a motor home or a 5,000-acre ranch. They remember those who pollute the air and water, those who run fire-trap hotels, those who cheat employees out of wages."
—RONALD P. LOVELL,
REPORTING PUBLIC AFFAIRS: PROBLEMS AND SOLUTIONS

- ■ Department of Environmental Protection: Records of pollution, toxic waste spills and other environmental hazards.
- ■ Secretary of State: Records track officers of corporations and can reveal conflicts of interest involving public officials.
- ■ Federal records:
  - ■ Internal Revenue Service: Individual tax records are private, but private foundations and tax-exempt organizations must file forms that list income, expenses and salaries of highest-paid employees.
  - ■ Nuclear Regulatory Commission: Inspection reports and other details about nuclear power plants.
  - ■ Federal Aviation Administration: Airline inspection records, pilot records.

As the authors point out, this is not a complete list but gives an idea of the vast reporting opportunities available in file cabinets, dusty storage rooms and, increasingly, on computers. To expand your knowledge and understanding, visit the Web site maintained by Investigative Reporters and Editors at **http://www.ire.org**.

REPORTING BY E-MAIL

LISTSERVS

A **listserv** is a computerized mailing list that allows one person to send the same message to all the other members of a particular group. You join a listserv by filling out and e-mailing a subscription form to a listserv computer. In many cases, the computer will do all the work, although there are others, known as moderated listservs, which are supervised, as well as unmoderated automated lists. Once your subscription is accepted, messages from other subscribers are sent automatically to your e-mail address. Depending on the list, that can mean finding a few messages a day or hundreds. Some lists offer a choice between continuous or once-a-day delivery. The benefits for reporters who subscribe to such lists range from having an efficient way to stay current on a topic to meeting new sources from around the world.

FINDING A LISTSERV

Listservs are usually organized around a discussion topic or a common interest. Listservs are a convenient way to tap into communities of people without ever having to leave your desk. There are tens of thousands of listservs with more than 35 million members. To surf this maze of information, you'll find Web sites that index listservs by name, subject, description, host country and sponsoring organization.

Listservs are maintained by software programs, such as Listserv, Listproc and Majordomo, that run by slightly different rules. Because you are communicating with a computer, you must follow the rules for subscribing literally (the computer can't read your mind, after all). Remember: Listservs generally have two addresses: (1) the list address, which sends messages to every member of the list, and (2) the list manager or "subscription" address, which is the address of the computer program you send your request to subscribe or unsubscribe. *Do not send* requests to subscribe or unsubscribe to the list unless you like reading lots of nasty comments about your IQ.

Fortunately, many mailing lists make it easy to subscribe with a simple e-mail message.

TileNet is the guide to lists that use the oldest and most popular program, Listserv. Find it online at http://www.tile.net/tile/listserv/index.html

Subscribing

To subscribe to a list, send an e-mail message to the list manager address with one line in the body of the message:

> Subscribe MUCKRAKE-L Ida Tarbell
> Command Mailing List Name Your Name

Unsubscribing

To have your name removed from a mailing list, send an e-mail message to the list manager address with one line in the body of the letter:

> Signoff MUCKRAKE-L

Posting a Message

If you have an article (comments, questions, etc.) that you wish to distribute to all members of a list, send it as e-mail to the list address for that list. Please note that the list address is different from the list manager address.

Story Example

When I was researching my series on child support for Knight Ridder Newspapers in 1993, I subscribed to FREE-L, which describes itself as "an electronic conference for the free exchange of information regarding the issues of fathers' rights. These issues arise in the context of divorce, custody disputes and visitation and child-support arrangements." From my desk in Washington, D.C., I was able to learn about the attitudes and experiences of parents around the country, most of them fathers, who were divorced and did not have custody of their children. Although I did interviews with individual fathers and others familiar with the topic, the listserv enabled me to get a quick overview of the range of issues and opinions of a group.

Here's the story that ran as a sidebar:

Some Fathers Won't Pay, on Principle

by Christopher Scanlan
Knight Ridder Newspapers

WASHINGTON—John Hedin doesn't pay child support for his 6-year-old son, and he doesn't care who knows it.

"Call me a deadbeat dad," says Hedin. "I'll stand up to the scrutiny."

Hedin, a divorced father from Burlington, Vt., is one of a growing number of fathers who say they are fed up with the child-support system.

They're not deadbeats, they say, but victims of an unfair stereotype, unrealistic support orders, harsh laws and ex-spouses who interfere with visitation and custody or spend support money on themselves.

"Current policy makes the simplistic assumption that all noncustodians are 'runaway' parents when in fact, many noncustodians are 'thrown away' parents who are victims of a court order that assumed children needed only a custodian and a check," says one of their advocates, Washington attorney Ronald K. Henry.

As Hedin puts it, "I want to be a parent to my son, not a pocketbook to his mother."

Divorced twice, Hedin regularly pays support to the mother of two older children who live on the East Coast. But his 6-year-old son's mother, who has custody, has remarried and moved to California.

If forced to pay child support to her, Hedin argues, he has only painful choices: give up his job and move west or stay where he is and give up seeing his son. Instead, he's waging a court battle for a more acceptable support arrangement and spending thousands of dollars in travel expenses, clothes, gifts and phone calls for "meaningful contact" with his son, Hedin says.

It's an attitude shared by many absent fathers, says Frank Furstenberg, a University of Pennsylvania sociologist who has studied nonpaying fathers. "They're angry with their former partners and are not about to supply money that seems to contribute to that household."

The Clinton administration's welfare-reform task force vows to get tougher but concedes that "the needs and concerns of noncustodial parents are often ignored."

"The system needs to ... send the message that fathers matter," the group says in a draft of its welfare-reform proposal. Fathers' rights activists say greater use of joint custody arrangements and mandatory divorce mediation to give both spouses a voice in shaping life after divorce would solve many support battles. Men with joint custody and visitation rights have a much better record of paying child support than those who don't, census figures show.

"How many mothers tear children away from fathers, deny contact and use a prejudiced legal system to destroy that man's life?" Hedin wrote in a letter last year. "Isn't the real criminal a mother who takes a boy away and makes his father pay?"

Stephen Granucci, who is married to the mother of Hedin's 6-year-old boy, doesn't buy it. "We support his relationship with his son because he's his father. It's hard to do when a guy's not paying.

"The guy should just pay it, then if he has other issues, you deal with those," Granucci says. "You can quote me. He's a deadbeat. Very simple."

DEVELOPING A REPORTING PLAN

On a sultry August afternoon, Jeremy Schwartz walked around a St. Petersburg neighborhood that was to be his beat for the next six weeks. This was his first day on the job. His assignment: a shoe-leather tour to learn the area and interview residents about life in their community. Talking with an elderly woman, Jeremy noticed that part of her green lawn was white. The woman told him that boys in the neighborhood had sprayed her lawn with bleach fired from an oversized water gun. It was a problem all over the neighborhood, she said. Jeremy took notes and moved on.

He knew about the toy water guns, known as Super Soakers. In Boston, where he was from, they'd been a problem a few years back; police had mistaken them for real guns. Maybe, he thought, he could do a story about the Super Soaker in St. Pete.

That's how many stories begin, with a seed of information, nourished by a reporter's background and curiosity. But that's not enough. Reporting takes planning.

It can begin with sources or questions or a combination of both.

BEGINNING WITH SOURCES

A reporting plan can begin with a list of sources, people and resources that are likely avenues to pursue for the specific information that effective writing requires.

To pursue the Super Soaker story, Jeremy brainstormed and decided on a list of sources he wanted to try to reach:

- Victims: Neighbors targeted by kids with Super Soakers
- Law enforcement officials
- Toy manufacturers
- Kids

BEGINNING WITH QUESTIONS

Stories raise questions and answer them.

Jeremy and his editor talked and raised a number of questions about the Super Soaker problem:

- What do I know?
- What do I need to know?
- Where can I go to get it?
- Who can answer my questions?
- What's the problem?
- How serious is it?
- Why is it a problem?

- Who's to blame?
- What's the cause?
- Who makes Super Soakers, and what do they say about the problem?
- Have any kids been arrested for attacking people with Super Soakers?
- Why do kids use the Super Soaker toy?
- Why would they use it as a weapon?

If Jeremy wanted, he could draw lines linking questions with sources. He could add new sources and questions to his list and update it. That way, he could keep track of what he knew and what he still needed to know to collect the necessary information for his story. In the next chapter, you can see how Jeremy's reporting plan produced a well-reported story about a neighborhood problem.

News Thinking II—Focus: Thinking of Stories

The reason journalism is one of the most challenging and exciting professions is that it requires its practitioners to think fast, to think on their feet, to think clearly and logically and soberly at moments of intense chaos. Journalists draw connections between disparate events and developments. They fashion a mosaic from an overwhelming number of bits of information, detail and facts. And they must do it sometimes in a matter of minutes. To do it well demands great and quick intelligence, just the kind of critical thinking skills you read about in Chapter 1. Reporting and writing are all about thinking. If you can't think, you can't report well, and you certainly can't write well.

The question is the reporter's ally, the tool that enables you to find your way through the confusion of events and narrow them down to a single paragraph. Reporters are constantly probing, testing, questioning, all in a continuing effort to understand. Here's an example:

It was a great story—a feature about Jed Barton, a 7-year-old boy blinded at birth but attending public school, swimming at the YMCA, even riding a bicycle. I turned it in to the desk and waited for the raves to pour in.

Instead, Joel Rawson, my editor at *The Providence Journal*, wanted to know if I had spent a day with the kid and his family. You bet, I said. Several, in fact. I had gone to camp with him. Hung out at his school. Watched him bike, dive in the pool. Ate dinner with his family.

No, Rawson said. Have you ever spent an entire day with him from the time he wakes up until he goes to bed?

Well, nooo. But as I said, I went to camp, school, "the whole nine yards." Then Rawson leaned in close. "Look, do you know what this story is about?"

"Yeah, it's about a blind kid whose parents are mainstreaming him, who goes to school and camp and rides a bike."

"But what is it really about?" Rawson repeated.

"Well, he's living a normal life and ..."

My editor leaned in even closer, eyes aglitter. "I'll tell you what it's really about. It's about not being able to see from the moment you wake up until you fall asleep. For every parent, it's your worst nightmare; the perfect baby you prayed for isn't perfect. So what do you do about it? That's what it's really about!"

I went back to the Barton house and spent from morning until night there. The story I rewrote followed Jed from the moment when a bird's cry woke him from a dream until his mother hugged him goodnight, walked out of his room, and without turning around said for the 10th time that day, "Put your thumb down"—part of her campaign to break him of the eye-rubbing that is a blind child's bad habit.

I learned many lessons about reporting and writing over the eight years I worked with Joel Rawson, who is now the *Journal's* executive editor. But that day, when he demanded to know what my story was "really about," I learned the most important one. That day I learned the importance of thinking about stories. (The complete story about Jed Barton appears on pp. 78–86.)

At a time when readers can get information from a variety of sources, the thinking we do as reporters and editors is the way we transform information into an exceedingly more valuable commodity—knowledge. "Thinking is the great underappreciated and understated part of being a newspaper person," says David Maraniss, whose stories for *The Washington Post* won the Jesse Laventhol Award for deadline reporting in 1997. "Think hard. Think long," advises N. Don Wycliff, whose editorials for the *Chicago Tribune* won the American Society of Newspaper Editors' Distinguished Writing Prize for editorial writing.

As Maraniss points out, "The one ingredient that's often left out of the whole process is not the writing or the reporting, but the thinking."

Like their professional counterparts, student journalists often shy away from the hard work of focusing. "It is much easier to attempt simply to write a lead and try to write the story from there," Ken Thomas, a Poynter reporting fellow, observed one day after struggling with a story. Trying to write your way through a story without figuring out what you're trying to say is like hacking your way through a jungle with a butter knife: frustrating and fruitless. Thomas said he learned that "although focusing on a theme may take up precious time in a deadline situation, it is essential to building a good story."

For David Waters, the thinking began even before he wrote his first stories on the religion beat for *The Commercial Appeal* in Memphis. "I started thinking religion wasn't like any other beat I'd ever had," he recalls. "I'd had

"A good reporter is someone who can ask tough questions in a matter-of-fact way, is fair-minded but not soft, straightforward but not coy, and able to shift gears if the story is not what he or she thought it was."

—Bob Mong,
THE DALLAS
MORNING NEWS

government beats and the education beat, the legislative beat, politics. Every other beat I've had had a focal point. There was an agency or a board or a person, someone who seemed to be in charge, where you could go to find the center of that beat. And then I realized God is at the center of this beat. So I decided that my job was to cover God. ... And in every story I write, whether or not it's set in a church, I look for God. And it seems to work."

Waters learned that thinking is the way writers, whatever the genre, medium or deadline, make sense of the material they collect during the reporting. It's the compass that leads the reporter out of the tangled woods of reporting. It's the focusing ring on a camera lens that is turned back and forth until the image is clear.

Critical thinking was essential to the success of *Newsday's* coverage of the still-unresolved mystery of the crash of TWA Flight 800 in July 1996. Confronted with conflicting theories posed by warring bureaucratic factions, the paper's editors and reporters had to continually separate rumor from fact and decide which elements deserved their readers' attention. The paper's efforts were rewarded with the Pulitzer Prize.

Thinking about stories frightens some reporters and concerns some editors, who fear it sounds too much like a call to inject opinions into news stories. I'd argue that the best stories help readers understand how and why the news has meaning and relevance to their lives, which is a vital part of the journalist's job in a democracy. The way to achieve that is by reporters applying intelligence and critical thinking skills to every story, by reporters using themselves as a resource, as *Boston Globe* columnist Eileen McNamara learned when an editor gave her this piece of advice after she had turned in a story:

"You know more about this topic than anybody, and this is a good piece of journalism," she recalls Al Larkin saying. "But run it through the typewriter one more time, and this time, write it like you know it better than anybody else. Write it like you respect the fact that you have spent three weeks living this story. Don't report about it. Write out of the experience of reporting it."

The prospect terrified McNamara, but less than an hour later, her story was "stunningly different." It had, she says, "a voice of authority" missing from the first version. "I thought I couldn't do it. I thought I had handed him the best work I could do. And I'll always be grateful to him because he taught me that there was more in there than I knew."

Tom Hallman's ability to write evocative stories for *The Oregonian* of Portland draws from that same inner resource that McNamara's editor helped her tap. Hallman says, "I view myself as a guide, taking a reader by the hand and saying, 'Come, enter my world for a while and let me show you around.' When I'm reporting, I'm very aware of how I feel, and I've learned to trust my voice. As I'm reporting, I think, 'This scene makes me feel that way. Why am I feeling that way?' And then I look for the details I can use to make someone who's not there feel the same way I did."

Thinking about stories helps the writer create the voice—that unmistakable sense of one writer talking to one reader—that takes journalism beyond information into a richer level of communication. "Information also should educate, information also should enlighten and edify and even inspire people," religion writer Waters argues. "That's why people will get up every day and buy that newspaper. They want to be more than informed."

To provide that kind of story, writers need to "think hard, think long" and trust themselves more. Editors need to encourage reporters to apply critical thinking skills to their stories, to force them to dig deeper, to keep asking, as Joel Rawson once did, "What's this story really about?" Thinking about stories will enable journalists to help readers make sense of the news and their own lives.

A reporter's tape recorder fascinated Jed Barton, blind since birth. When it appeared in print, I read the story into a recorder so he could hear it. (Courtesy of Bob Thayer)

Mainstreaming a Blind Child:

"The Question Is Not 'Why Me?' The Question Is 'What Do I Do About It?'"

By Christopher Scanlan
The Providence Journal

BARRINGTON—The little boy sleeps on Star Wars sheets, the blanket kicked back. About 6:30, a bird's cry draws him from a dream he won't remember. From an open window, the October air feels cool on his face. But it takes the hissing drum roll of his father's shower to bring Jed Barton fully awake this Monday morning.

Sliding off the bed, he walks out the door and turns left into the bathroom. He knows the way without feeling. Moments later, still groggy with sleep, Jed walks into his parents' room across the hall, crawls into the big bed and cuddles under the warm blanket beside his mother.

Even before the diagnosis, Debby and Ned Barton knew.

A few days after they brought Jed home from the hospital seven years ago, Debby put the baby on the bed. She turned off the lights. Drew the curtains. Switched on the flashlight. Pointed the beam deep into Jed's blue eyes.

He didn't blink.

She didn't tell Ned.

Ned didn't tell her—until later—that he had lifted Jed up to a window bright with sunlight.

Not a flicker.

"We knew we were going to have a great beautiful, wonderful child," Ned said. "We never considered having a kid with any problems. ... It was something that happened to the next family."

Jed is pulling sneakers over bare feet when his mother walks into his bedroom a little after 7 a.m.

"Okay, how's this going?" she says. "Uh, where are the socks? Oh, twerp city. Get your sneakers off. Get your socks on. Let's move here."

"Where are they?" Jed asks.

"On the rocking chair where they were supposed to be."

"Well, they weren't there the last time I saw."

His hand probes the chair until he finds them on the seat. He laughs. "I got 'em."

On Nov. 21, 1974, Debby was barely six months pregnant with her first child and certain she was headed for miscarriage as Ned drove to Women and Infants Hospital in Providence.

They had been married five years. Ned helped run the family manufacturing company in Bristol. Debby was a substitute teacher in Warren.

On the delivery table, she heard a voice say, "Oh, my God. It's twins."

Jed was born first. He and his brother weighed 5.3 pounds—together.

That night, they woke her to sign a surgical release for the younger one. He died the next day. Jed hung on.

"Jed was in crisis constantly," Debby said. Heart murmur; jaundiced liver; infections; anemia; apnea that stopped his breathing; lungs too immature for the essential exchange of oxygen and carbon dioxide.

For weeks he lay in an incubator in the special care nursery, heart and respiratory monitors taped to his chest, a plastic hood over his head feeding him the oxygen he needed to live.

"My pediatrician called me every day ... ," Debby said.

"He would say the oxygen was 50 percent or 60 percent. If it went from 60 to 50, I would say, 'Well, that's good.' And he would say, 'No, that's not good. ... When it's up that high, it's dangerous ... [He] used the words retrolental fibroplasia. ...'"

It wasn't until three months later, when Jed came home, that she read about the disease. How an epidemic of blindness struck thousand of babies kept alive in incubators in the 1940s, and every year still blinds 500 premature babies who weigh under four pounds at birth. Doctors discovered that the oxygen that "preemies" need to prevent brain damage also withers blood vessels in their retinas.

The vessels hemorrhage, leaving scar tissue that in severe cases detaches the retina, snuffing vision forever. Without oxygen, certain death. With it, life—and the risk of blindness. The damage doesn't show up immediately.

Two weeks after Jed came home in February 1975, an ophthalmologist made the diagnosis. By then, Ned and Debby had made their own secret tests. "It was not anything that came out of nowhere," Debby said.

"He's blind in both eyes," the doctor said.

At 7:30 A.M., the Barton boys—Jed, 7, Bradford, 5, and Curtis, 3, are seated at the kitchen table, juice, bananas and toasted muffins before them. Jed is rubbing his right eye with his knuckles.

"Jed," his mother says sharply, "put your hand down and start eating." The hand drops.

Jed never has to be told to stop sucking his thumb; eye-rubbing is the blind child's bad habit.

Debby isn't sure why Jed does it.

"Does your eye hurt, Jed?"

"No," he will say.

"Does it feel good to rub it?"

"Yeah."

"Whatever the reason, I have to constantly tell Jed to get his hands down because it's unpleasant to look at. It makes him appear different."

His breakfast waits, but he has to feel for it.

He lifts his right hand off his lap. Fingers straight out, palm down. He starts at the edge of the table and makes a pass over the Formica. Slow and deliberate until it is over the muffin. The hand hovers like a spaceship and then descends. The fingers make a circle, pick up the bread, bring it to his mouth. He puts it down, and the hand reaches out again, looking for the cup. It stops when he feels the plastic.

"Is this mine?"

Continued

"Yes," his mother says, "that's yours."

Whenever Debby felt depressed those first days, she went into Jed's room and held him. Today, the center of Jed's eyes are milky white. As an infant, his pupils were gray. The retina hadn't detached completely yet.

"It was like the dot was set back," Debby said. "It wasn't horrible, it was a curious thing."

Jed didn't look at her, but when he moved his head, she moved with it, needing the eye contact even if her baby couldn't look back.

"He was adorable ... and really happy. ... That just jolted me out of it. That's when I decided I'm not going to feel sorry for myself. ... It's not me that's blind, it's him. If anybody is going to cry, he should do it."

The Bartons were assigned a social worker from State Services for the Blind. "My boss is blind," he told them, "and no, we don't have to spoon-feed him lunch."

"That made a tremendous impact," Debby said. "To know there were regular-type people holding regular-type jobs that we could think of in terms of our son's future."

"I'll be damned if I'm going to raise a pencil-seller," she told Ned. "The question is not 'Why me?' The question is 'What do I do about it?'"

"We decided we were going to do the most creative thing we could possibly do with this situation ... ," Debby said. "And we had to go out and find how to do it. That was the tricky part."

She read *If You Could See What I Hear,* the autobiography of Tom Sullivan, a blind actor and musician from Massachusetts.

"People forced him to function as a human being, not as a blind human being. That made a lot of sense to me."

"You want to help a blind child," she read in Sullivan's book. "Then start by teaching him the common courtesies: how to turn his face toward the person addressing him, how to dress well, to brush his hair, to mix with sighted children, not as a freak, not as someone to be pitied, but as a person, an individual with feelings and hopes, little hells and talents too."

Debby and Jed's grandmother began to learn Braille.

Until Jed was three, he was enrolled at Meeting Street School in East Providence, which treats handicapped children. Therapists worked with him in an airy room lined with cushioned mats, dotted with gym apparatus and toys designed to stimulate his other senses. They gave Debby exercises for Jed at home.

"I felt like I was solving the problem," she said. "You're not only dealing with it, you're working on it."

Jed's blindness wasn't apparent to casual observers until he was about a year and a half old.

"I can remember going up to New Hampshire skiing one weekend." Debby recalled. "We stopped at a Howard Johnson's. Ned was paying, and Jed was asking a hundred questions. Ned said to the lady: 'He's blind. That's why he's asking all these questions.' And the lady said, 'I know.' It was the first time anybody said, 'I know.' They had always said, 'He is?' It was such a jolt. Suddenly they knew he was blind. ... And as he became older it was more and more obvious."

When Jed turned three in 1977, his parents and the Meeting Street staff wanted him to go to regular nursery school for the play and social skills all 3-year-olds need.

"I was starting to be aware that he could not make social contacts easily," Debby said. "He might not know if there was another child standing next to him to say 'Hi' or 'Give me that toy.' He had to be put in situations to meet kids."

By then, however, Jed was the responsibility of the Barrington School Department. They recommended a preschool program run by the Rhode Island Association for the Blind and Visually Impaired or their own Child-Find class, which targets kids with learning problems.

"I can only assume they were uncomfortable with a blind child not being officially supervised for a whole year when they were legally responsible for him. ... But they didn't know him as well as Meeting Street or as I did. ... So we pushed it." Debby recalled.

They enrolled Jed in the Red Church Nursery School in town. "It was my first assertive act against the system," she said.

The following September, the Bartons went along with the School Department. If Jed were ever to attend regular school, he needed first to take advantage of the professionals at the Association for the Blind.

At the school in Providence, Jed learned how to be independent—to dress on his own, to eat without help—and to see with his fingertips and his ears and his nose.

During "mobility" lessons, he learned to "trail a wall"—holding a hand in front of him to anticipate obstacles. But there were only four children in Jed's class, not enough to keep the program going.

In June of 1979, the association shut the school down. The next September, Jed entered the Child-Find class at Sowams Elementary School. It was a small group, with several graduates of Meeting Street School.

The School Department still wasn't sure if Jed could handle a regular class with 25 kids. The Bartons didn't argue.

A few weeks after school began, they went to parents night.

Ned looked at the strings of beads, the puzzles the kids assembled, the boxes they stacked.

"Debby, this is the same stuff he's been doing for the last three years," he said.

"Oh, please, don't rock the boat," she said. "I feel so lucky they're taking him into the school system. Let's not start saying. 'He's too smart for this.'"

On Nov. 29, 1975, eight days after Jed's first birthday, President Ford had signed the Education for All Handicapped Children Act. No longer could schools dump handicapped children, regardless of their disability, into "special education" classes: They had to learn with "normal" kids, to join the mainstream.

Two years later, Rhode Island rewrote state law to get in step. Today, regulations that once were written in a couple of paragraphs fill a booklet 38 pages long.

"If I had to have a child who is blind. it's a good time," Debby said. "I think of what our family would have been like 20 years ago. I would have had to pack him up and send him off to boarding school by now. What would that have done to him and to us? But now we're together as we should be.

"I would love to have all those legislators in one room and be able to say to them:

Continued

'You were right. This is the kid you wrote that law for.'"

Debby knew Ned was right about the Child-Find class, but it took a couple of days for her to overcome her misgivings and go back to the school to talk with Jed's teacher.

She did not make demands; she asked a question. "We're wondering," she asked, "if this is challenging enough for him?"

The woman nodded her head but did not answer. Debby went home not knowing what she thought. The phone rang later that day.

"They had taken it up the chain of command at the school," Debby said. "Apparently everybody had been thinking the same thing, that he was very well prepared in the skills they were teaching in that class. They thought he was ready for kindergarten."

The change took about two weeks. "They'd bring him in for snack and story and then for snack and story and recess. The other kids were used to him, and he was used to it. It was handled very well," Debby said.

He was a month shy of his fifth birthday when he entered Mrs. Dwyer's kindergarten class. The mainstreaming of Jed Barton had begun.

At 8:05 A.M. Debby sits with her boys on the flagstone front step waiting for the school bus.

"All right," she says, "who has a green sweater on?"

"I don't know," Jed answers. "Who does? Me?"

"Yeah, you do. Who has green pants on?"

"Me?" Jed asks.

"No. Bradford."

"Who has a white shirt?"

"Me?"

"Yeah, you do. Who has sneakers on?"

"Me. Me," both boys say.

"Okay. Who has blue pants?"

"Me?" Jed says.

"Yes, you do All right, so you have blue pants, green sweater, white shirt, sneakers. Bradford, you have what?"

"Blue sweater, green pants and sneaks," Bradford says.

She goes through this drill every day, in case Jed's teacher says, "Everyone with blue pants stand up."

"I don't know everything there is to know about blind kids," Debby says. "I know absolutely everything there is to know about this particular 7-year-old blind child, but I don't know him as an 8-year-old yet. I don't know where it's going to go. I just keep trying things."

She put Braille labels on Jed's Crayons and his Rubik's Cube. She wrote story books that emphasize his other senses: "Did you ever take a train ride? Did you ever touch the engine or hear it toot? It's lots of fun," she wrote after the family visited Edaville Railroad on the Cape.

Instead of soccer and baseball, Jed took tap dancing. "He loved it. He loves to make noise." He takes piano lessons—the Suzuki method that trains children to play by ear instead of sheet music. He writes his Valentine cards in Braille.

"Every single step of the way," Debby said, "I felt there has to be a way he can be part of the mainstream."

At 8:40 A.M. Jane Long is waiting for Jed when he steps off the school bus in front of Nayatt Elementary School. He is in the third grade.

Mrs. Long, who taught herself Braille after she became Jed's aide in first grade, stays by his side all day. She Brailles Jed's lessons and checks his work on the Braille machine he uses instead of pencil and paper. She translates the Braille for his teachers.

"We treat him as any other kid. And that's the key," said Principal Robert V. Hassan. "He's a regular child. That's it." He watched Jed walk down the hall, one hand tracking the tile walls and door jambs to his homeroom.

A little after 9 A.M. Jed picks up his Brailler and walks by himself to an empty classroom in the adjoining wing for his Braille lesson with Miss Clarke.

It's the only time all day he is apart from his classmates.

For 23 years, Mary J. Clarke has traveled around the state teaching blind children, one of two "itinerant teachers of the visually handicapped" employed by the state Department of Education.

For an hour three times a week, she teaches Jed the Braille system. She also taught him how to skip. She works with seven other children in Rhode Island.

"They're not all Braille students," she says. "Some use large print, some have special eyeglasses." There are about 150 children in Rhode Island with severe vision problems, but only a few are totally blind like Jed.

One morning last June, Miss Clarke showed up at school with Jed's Thorndike-Barnhart Junior Dictionary in the trunk of her car. "It's 22 volumes," she told Mr. Hassan. It took five kids to carry it inside.

Educating a child in Barrington costs about $2,500. The cost rises for the town's 450 disabled children because they usually need special attention—aides, materials, transportation.

Mainstreaming Jed costs an extra $6,500 a year, said Chris Kendall, the town's director of special education. That is still cheaper than the old way.

If Jed went to Perkins School for the Blind in Watertown, Mass., tuition, room and board would cost the state and town more than twice the mainstreaming price: $15,480 a year.

Debby Barton worries people will resent the extra money taxpayers pay to mainstream handicapped children. But she says, "We can pay for 75 years of institutionalizing these kids or 75 years of Social Security payments. Or we can invest a lot of money in them between 3 and 21 and make them self-supporting. I think that's the far better thing to do."

At recess the other third-grade boys run off to play soccer.

"The older they get, the more they go off and play by themselves," Mrs. Long said. "But he makes his own fun."

"Let's go over and watch the cars," Jed tells her. "You can tell me what goes by."

They stand at the fence in front of school, cars whizzing by.

"What kind of car was that?"

"A Volkswagen bug," Mrs. Long says.

"And that?"

"A big truck."

"Well, what kind?"

Continued

"A furniture truck."

"You have to concede something to the blindness," Debby said. "He can't have the same experience of everyone else all the time. He is different ... but the only thing that's different about him is his blindness."

At 12:57 P.M., Jed leaves Mrs. Vern Kempf's classroom carrying his Brailler and walks next door for math.

The "Math Stars" of the day are posted on the bulletin board. Jed's arithmetic, Brailled on brown paper, hangs alongside his classmates' penciled work.

Math class, Jed's favorite, will be the scene of another triumph today.

Class starts with a game of "around the world," a flashcard drill.

In 10 minutes, it is a sudden-death face-off between Jed and Jonathan. The class is at a fever pitch.

"Look at the eyes. Everyone is paying close attention," Miss Jane Redfern says. "Jed is thinking, too. I can tell. ... Okay. Subtraction."

She holds up a flashcard and reads aloud for Jed's benefit. "Thirteen minus 8."

"Four," Jed screams. Jonathan chews his fingers. "Six," Jed shouts.

"No," the teacher says. Jonathan is paralyzed. The process of elimination is at work now. "Five," Jed says. The champion is offered a choice between a lollipop and a pencil. Jed chooses the pencil.

He returns to his seat, smiling and saying over and over in a low voice, "I won around the world. I won around the world."

Jed was about 5 when he began to ask questions about his blindness.

"How come other kids can see and I can't see?" he wanted to know. "How come they can do this and I can't do it?"

"We told him exactly what happened," his father said. "We told him that he was born very early and was in the hospital for three months and had a lot of problems and became blind. We just told him the truth. There's no sense in covering it up."

"He's pretty good about it. ... And we don't have those questions anymore really. ... Sometimes he says, 'Why can't I do that?' And I say, 'Jed, 'cause you can't see. And he just says, 'Okay,' and that's the end of that."

Jed doesn't have photo albums. He has an album of sounds made with a tape recorder.

Daddy starting the car. Daddy driving off to work. Beeping the horn. The lawn mower. The boat. The mailman's Jeep. Playing the piano. His birthday parties. Christmas.

"When Curtis was getting eye drops, he ran into the room to record him screaming. Once he recorded Bradford getting yelled at. He likes that," his mother said.

At 3:25 P.M., Jed stands in the shallow end of the Barrington YMCA pool, the afternoon sun bathing his face. He is playing an imaginary keyboard on the tiled edge as the instructor tries to coax a terrified little girl away from the ladder.

On a bench nearby, Lori Newcomb, the Y's aquatic director, recalls the first time she worked with Jed at summer camp.

"The kids were climbing up something and jumping off ... he asked if he could go up there, and I hesitated. But then I thought, why hold him back, if he wants to. ... He jumped and wanted to do it again. And from that time on, I knew he could do most anything ... because he just wants to."

There is a free swim when the lesson ends. "Jed, wanna go off the board?" says Pam Goglia, who was Jed's counselor at summer camp.

He slides almost the full length of the diving board on his bottom before he stands and feels the way to the edge with his toes.

"Should I jump to the right?"

"Straight ahead," Pam says.

"Ready?" Jed flexes his knees, bouncing lightly and then leaps off. He hits the water feet first, eyes squeezed shut, and disappears. A few seconds pass before his head pops through a circle of bubbles. Blond hair plastered on his forehead, he paddles to the edge, bursting with triumph.

"I — TOUCHED — THE — BOTTOM!"

"I still get a big kick out of it when he does something, and people don't realize that he's blind," Debby said. "I think that's the big success. He's so capable that he doesn't look like a pathetic, dependent kid. He plays the piano, and he rides a two-wheeler, and he swims. ... He's an usher in Sunday School, and he's in the Cub Scouts.

"We are forcing people to think of him as a regular person. ... They deal with him in the boys' room, in the cafeteria, in recess, on the school bus, and they cease to think of him as that blind kid after a while.

"Everybody responds the way that we do. They find a way for him to be a part of it. He's being a normal kid, and everyone else around him is being, I think, extraordinary people. ...

"I keep holding my breath and crossing my fingers right along. But now I know that it can work. Somewhere along the line, we're apt to bump into someone who says, 'Whoa, I can't handle this,' and then we just swing into action and say, 'Sure you can. Look at all the people before you who have.'"

At the dinner table the conversation turns to the theft of a relative's car stereo. Debby asks Jed to tell the story of an adventure with the next-door neighbor's car.

"Listen, this is the story," he says. "I was running to get the lemonade man. I didn't know Peter's car was there. I bumped into it and guess what? The burglar alarm went off, and it scared me to death. So I said, 'My gosh, I'm never going to do that again.'"

"So, Jed," Ned says, "how did you do in swimming? Did you go off the board today?" "Yep ... the last time I did a bellyflop."

His father guffaws, and Jed laughs, too, imitating his father's deep laughter. "Did you touch the bottom of the pool?"

"I touched the bottom of the pool at the deep end."

Since before Jed was born, Ned has dreamed of the day he and his son would go duck hunting together. Jed will never handle a gun, but there are moments he and his father can share.

There is a quiet time before sunrise, Ned says. "You hear the wingbeat of ducks going over you. ... Kind of a whistling sound. ... It's early in the morning ... still somewhat dark, you hear the ducks, and you look around. You can't see them, but you hear 'em."

"I still meet people who when they hear that he's blind, feel like disaster has struck ... ," Debby says. "Most people think

Continued

living with a blind kid must be the absolute ultimate disaster that could ever happen, but it isn't. It's an extremely manageable problem. I don't even think about him being blind."

One day last summer, she was working in her garden when she realized she didn't know where Jed was.

"He was out playing in the neighborhood somewhere, but I had no idea where. I think that would be a jolt to a lot of people, that I am comfortable letting him go off and play, that I don't even know where he is."

A little after 8, Jed lies on his Star Wars sheets, the blankets pulled up. His mother pounces, smothering him with kisses and tickling him.

"Mom!"

"Say Uncle."

"Mom!" He tries to squirm away. She won't give in. "Mom ... Uncle!"

"Now say Auntie."

"Mom! ... Auntie."

Debby gives him another kiss and walks out. She switches off the light. In the shadows, Jed's hand shoots up to his right eye and begins to rub.

"Good night, Jed." Without looking back, she says, "Put your hand down."

CHECKLIST: FINDING A FOCUS

THE PROBLEM

The reporting is done, but what do all these notes mean? How do I find the **focus** of the story?

SOLUTIONS

- Back off. Put aside your notebooks and interview transcripts and reports, the whole pile. What you need to know you will remember. What you forget probably wasn't worth remembering. You're the expert. Take a blank pad or put a fresh sheet in the typewriter or create a new computer file and start interviewing yourself:
- What's the news?
- What's the story?
- What information surprised me the most?
- What will surprise my reader?
- What one thing does my reader need to know?
- What one thing have I learned that I didn't expect to learn?

- What can't be left out of what I have to write?
- What one thing do I need to know more about?
- What can I say in one sentence that tells me the meaning of my story?
- Write a headline for your story.
- Write a title. In six words. (Not seven or eight or four.)
- What one thing, person, place, event, detail, fact, quotation have I found that contains the essential meaning of the subject?
- How will my story help the reader?
- What image sticks in my mind and seems to symbolize the entire subject?
- What person, or face, do I remember from my reporting?
- What is the most important single fact I have learned?
- What is the most significant quotation I heard or read?
- What statistic sticks in my head?

- Tell an editor, a colleague, your roommate about the story, to hear for yourself what you say about it.
- How would the reader describe my story to a friend?
- Draft a lead to reveal the direction and voice of your story.
- Using subject-verb-object (Who said or did what? What happened?) draft a skeleton summary.
- Identify the five W's and an H (Who, what, when, why, where and how).
  - Who is character.
  - What is plot.
  - When is chronology.
  - Where is place.
  - Why is motive.
  - How is circumstances.
- Draft an end to give yourself a sense of destination.
- Write a theme paragraph (also known as a "nut graf") that tells readers why they are reading the story.
- Freewrite a discovery draft or discovery paragraphs as fast as possible without stopping to revise to reveal the meaning and the voice of the story. Write about any part of the story as long as it reveals tone, mood, voice. Am I sad, joyous, incredulous, de-tached, outraged? Do I smell earth or engine oil or chalk dust?
- Listen to what your voice is telling you about the meaning of the story. The intensity, rhythm, tone of voice often reveal the meaning.
- Form is meaning. Try on different approaches to the story. Is it a narrative, hourglass, nut graf story or one of the other forms presented in Chapter 5?
- Look at the story from different points of view. The fireman on the ladder. The horrified parent watching her child trapped in a house.
- Rehearse the story in your head and on paper to hear what the story means.
- Find a frame that limits your subject to one single dominant meaning. Is your story about police stress or one cop's life-and-death struggle?
- Role-play your reader. Ask tough questions of your story.
- Discover the problem to be solved by the writing of your story. How can I communicate a bond proposal without putting the reader to sleep?
- Find the tension in your story. Who is in conflict? How can they be drawn together or forced apart?

FOCUSING YOUR STORY

John Silcox, a participant in the Poynter summer fellowship program in reporting and writing, demonstrates the value of focusing and organizing a story. On the following pages, you will find the "front-end" work he did before he wrote his story about the therapeutic benefits of physical exercise. You'll see John's draft and then the revisions he makes before the story is published.

Notice how John uses focusing questions—What's the news? What's the story?—and the technique of stating the story in six words, as well as asking the "So what?" question that forces him to state explicitly why his story is worth writing—and reading.

STUDENT EXAMPLE

What's the news?

Aerobic exercise not only keeps you fit but also can speed up the body's healing process.

What's the story?

Campbell Park aerobics instructor Alvina Miller doesn't let a knee injury keep her from exercise.

What's the image?

Alvina Miller leading an exercise class wearing a knee support.

Six words?

Aerobics can help body heal faster.

So what?

Another benefit of living an active lifestyle.

ORDER: MAPPING YOUR STORY

After the thinking and reporting and focusing, the reporter still isn't ready to write. Generals wouldn't go into battle without a plan. Builders wouldn't lay a foundation without a blueprint in hand. Yet planning news stories, organizing information into coherent, appropriate structures, is an overlooked activity for all too many journalists.

The smartest journalists plan every step of the process. They plan their reporting. They plan their writing, they plan their revision.

Finding your focus will give you a destination. Now you need a map to get there. Some writers make a formal outline. Others jot down a list of the points they want to cover. One way is to draw a map of your story. Where does your story begin? Where does it end? And what belongs in the middle? Don't confuse this map with the brainstorming map you did earlier in the chapter. Although that may look like a connect-the-dot picture, think of this as a road map that takes you from a starting point to a destination with clearly marked stops along the way.

Writers are always looking for a new way to tell their story, to stretch the traditional forms, to experiment. Writing the lead often helps writers devise their plan of attack. Effective leads "shine a flashlight into the story," as John McPhee of *The New Yorker* puts it. It is the first step of a journey. Just as important, if not more, is the last step, the ending. Create your own form, remembering that form follows content.

As David Zucchino of *The Philadelphia Inquirer* says, deadline stories are "totally determined by the facts on hand, the amount of time I have, and the space. ... The form is determined by the situation."

CHECKLIST: MAPPING YOUR STORY

THE PROBLEM

I know what my story's about now. I just don't know where I should put everything. How do I *map* my story?

SOLUTIONS

- Make a list of what you want to say.
- What piece of information should be at the beginning?
- What piece of information should be at the end?
- What belongs in the middle?
- Ask the questions the reader will ask and put them in the order they will be asked.
- Assign values to quotations.
- Think of "chapters."
- Identify the material in blocks. Organize them in sequence.
- Give the reader information in the lead that makes the reader ask a question. Answer it with information that sparks a new question. Continue until all the questions are answered.
- Write a headline and subheads for your story.
- Pick a starting point as near the end as you can. Look for the moment:
  - When things change.
  - When things will never be the same.
  - When we learn lessons.
  - When things hang in the balance.
  - When you don't know how things will turn out.
- Draft many possible leads—a dozen, two dozen, three dozen—as quickly as possible.
- Write with the clock. Begin at a moment in time. End at a moment in time.
- Seek a natural order for the story: narrative, chronology, pyramid, problem-solution, follow-up, a visit with, a walk-through, a day in the life.
- Draft a lead, list three to five main points and an ending. Consult an editor.
- Draft many endings as quickly as possible. Once you know where you're going you may see how to get there.
- Diagram the pattern of the story.
- Write an outline.
- Clip the notes on each part of the subject together. Move the piles around until you discover a working order.
- Use time lines.
- Organize your story by the high points. Organize it by scenes.

Armed with his focus, Silcox now moves on to mapping his story. He uses an outline form. But even though it looks set in stone, an outline is not the story, simply a vision of it. Study how the structure of John's published article differs from his outline.

STUDENT EXAMPLE

MAPPING

I. Lead
   A. women at aerobics
II. Introduction of Alvina
   A. aerobics
   B. accident
III. Nut graf

    IV. Background on Alvina

        A. car wreck

        B. knee injury

        C. rehabilitation

            1. nurses at Bayfront

            2. Dr. Rodriguez

    V. Expertise on issue

        A. Dr. Brown

            1. athletes

            2. smoking

        B. physical therapist

    VI. Countermoves

        A. mitigating factors

        B. lifestyle

    VII. Aerobics class

        A. Alvina at work

        B. encouraging/inspiring women

    VIII. Ending

DRAFT: WRITING THE STORY

Now comes the writing. Everything that has come before is preparation. You know your focus. You know what you want to say. You know what you want to include. You can set out on the journey.

The writer is ready to draft the story, almost like an artist with a sketch-pad. It may start with a line, a paragraph, perhaps even several pages. The writer is discovering the story by writing it. Writers use the draft to teach themselves what they know and don't know about their subject. Saul Pett, a veteran feature writer for The Associated Press, said, "Before it's finished, good writing always involves a sense of discipline, but good writing begins in a sense of freedom, of elbow room, of space, of a challenge to grope and find the heart of the matter."

Once you've settled on the focus and a plan, the time has come to write what some writing teachers call a "discovery draft." I was always envious of reporters who insist they must have their lead written and polished before they can move to the second paragraph and so on. It took me years to realize that I needed to discover my story by writing it. I took comfort when I learned that newspaper writers I admired followed the same uncertain path.

"The way I start is always the same," Cynthia Gorney of *The Washington Post* said. "I sit down at my typewriter and start typing. I start to babble, sometimes starting in the middle of the story, and usually fairly quickly I see how it's going to start. It just starts shaping itself."

Next time you can't come up with the perfect lead, follow Gorney's lead and start babbling. Eventually, you will begin to make sense or at least find something on the screen you can begin to work with.

DRAFTING TECHNIQUES

- Put your notes aside before you start to write. Remember Jane Harrigan's advice: "Notes are like Velcro. As you try to skim them, they ensnare you, and pretty soon you can't see the story for the details." Repeat over and over, "The story is not in my notes. The story is in my head."

- Follow the advice that Gene Roberts, legendary editor of *The Philadelphia Inquirer*, retired managing editor of *The New York Times* and now a professor at the University of Maryland, got from his first newspaper editor, a blind man named Henry Belk. "Make me see."

- Lower your standards. Of course, you and your editor must apply rigorous standards—of accuracy and clarity, among others—but ignoring the voice that says, "This stinks" is the first step to producing copy on deadline in time for revision. The wisest advice on the subject of writer's block comes from poet William Stafford:

"I believe that the so-called 'writer's block' is a product of some kind of disproportion between your standards and your performance. ... One should lower his standards until there is no felt threshold to go over in writing. It's easy to write. You just shouldn't have standards that inhibit you from writing."

That's not as paradoxical as it seems. With 35 years' experience at deadline writing, AP correspondent Saul Pett said he stopped spending as much time on leads as he used to. "We make a mistake when we're younger. We feel compelled to hit a home run in the very first sentence. So we spend a lot of time staring at the typewriter. I'll settle for a quiet single, or even a long foul, anything that gets me started."

Drafting isn't just a step in the writing process. It's a tool at every stage:

BEFORE THE REPORTING: As a Washington reporter, I once drafted the lead of a story on the Senate vote on the nomination of Joycelyn Elders as surgeon general as I rode in a taxi on the way to the Capitol building. How could I write before I reported? I already had some background from a quickie profile I'd written, but it was mid-afternoon, my deadline was four hours away, and I was nervous. Getting something in the notebook calmed me down and focused my reporting and, on deadline later, my writing.

DURING THE REPORTING: A draft can teach you what you already know and what you need to know. Often reporters go overboard on reporting because they are afraid they can't write with authority. A draft can teach you the extent of your knowledge and the holes you need to plug.

ORDER: Even though you may have done an outline for your story, drafting can show you a new beginning or end or middle.

DRAFTING A STORY

Silcox has his focus and his map. Now it's time for him to discover his story by writing it. As with any draft, there may be awkward spots, style errors or grammatical lapses that should be caught and fixed during revision.

FIRST DRAFT

John Silcox
Points South *Staff Writer*

The paramedics on the scene couldn't help but admire her shapely, well-defined legs. Alvina Miller was just worried she might lose one.

The 26-year-old aerobics instructor couldn't bear the thought of not being able to run, as she looked down at the left leg that was severely broken in a car crash that could have killed her.

Since graduating from Florida A&M University in 1995, exercise has been her passion. When not working as a marketing representative for Air Quality Control, chances are she's running laps, lifting weights or doing whatever it takes to slip into her size-three skirts. The accident on April 19 left her with a broken leg above her left knee, but that didn't stop Miller from maintaining her daily exercise regime, even doubling her efforts. Within a couple of months, she was back at Campbell Park leading her faithful flock of women in a chorus of scissors kicks.

Everyone knows that exercise gets rid of the lovehandles, but it can also help you heal faster. Doctors say that a healthy and active lifestyle can speed up recovery and spare injury patients months of painful rehabilitation. Although healthy living is not the only factor in recovery, physical therapists agree that aerobic exercise and proper nutrition can not only keep you fit but also can speed up the body's healing process.

Miller's Best Bud

Miller's story begins with a brown collie named Bud, which she describes as "Lassie with smaller eyes." Technically Bud belongs to Miller's neighbor Mrs. Arlie Jones, but over the years he has become a constant companion, accompanying her on evening runs around Tropicana Field.

Miller was on her way back from the store to give Bud a shampoo on the day of the accident. While making a left hand turn just a block from her house, Bud jumped in front of the wheel and blocked her view. Miller jammed her brakes, but the car's momentum carried her into the oncoming lane, where she smacked into a Toyota Corolla and then rolled her own Grand Am three times before slamming into a stop sign along the curb.

"I didn't feel anything for about three minutes," she said. "I didn't even hear what happened."

Miller crawled out through an open window, with the chivalrous but shaken collie following patiently behind her. Based on the status of the car, the paramedics on the scene presumed she was dead. They were surprised to find Miller alive and well, except for the bone above her left knee, which had broken through the skin. Miller was rushed to Bayfront Hospital. Bud walked home.

Miller suffered a broken leg above her left knee that required a 20 mm stainless steel rod to be inserted into the bone to help the knee heal properly. Miller spent her four-day stay chatting with nurses about nutrition and exercise, swallowing painkillers and doing leg lifts and crunches from her hospital bed. Dr. Jorge Rodriguez, a physician at All Florida Orthopedic Associates, said that it typically takes patients 8 to 12 weeks just to get off crutches. Miller was back in aerobics after two months.

"Before you know it, you'll be running like a gazelle," said Rodriguez, at a recent checkup.

Rodriguez said that because Miller was in such good shape to begin with, she didn't need to develop the muscle strength necessary to begin rehabilitation.

"People who are aerobically fit and in good health are in the best possible position to heal," he said.

Happy Healthy Healing

The reason is simple. Exercise strengthens the bones and joints by circulating the blood, according to Dr. Mark D. Brown,

Continued

professor and chairman for the department of orthopedic and rehabilitation at the University of Miami school of medicine. Doctors have observed for years that athletes with injuries heal faster than unconditioned individuals of the same age. Brown even recalls a conditioned young dancer who fractured her thigh bone and femur and lost one leg below the knee. She was dancing in a recital in New York four months after the accident.

Studies show that heavy smokers, drinkers and people with poor eating habits are slow healers. Even back pain can be exacerbated by smoking. Brown cited studies that show that smokers who undergo spinal fusions have only a 50 percent success rate, compared to 95 percent for nonsmokers.

"In a good happy person, the pain doesn't bother you as much," said Neil Spielholz, a research professor in the division of physical therapy at University of Miami.

But when it comes to bone healing, exercise is not the only thing that makes it or "breaks it." Brown said that family genetics, disease history and age are also important factors in recovery.

"Of course, when you are young, younger people heal much faster than older people," he said. "But it doesn't make any difference how old you are if you are in good health."

Miller stays healthy by sticking to a diet of fruits and vegetables, wheat bread and baked chicken, occasionally splurging for a vanilla milkshake at Dairy Queen or a slice of Grandma's sweet potato pie. But even that demands a penance of push-ups.

Leader of the Pack

Fifteen woman have turned out for Miller's Monday class. Some have even brought their children, who mimic Mom's movements on the leftover blue mats in the back of the room.

Pat Crumb, 47, comes because of her high blood pressure and cholesterol. "441V s down to 200," she beams proudly. Dorothy Daniels, 48, relieves the stress of teaching 25 first-graders at Eisenhower Elementary in Clearwater. Both are inspired by their instructor's determination.

Miller, limping slightly with her left knee wrapped in brown gauze, fires up the women with words of encouragement that get more intense as the night wears on. One flash of her toothy smile is always good for an extra set of sit-ups.

During an intense round of knee-bends, Miller scolds 38-year-old Deborah Wynn for not going down far enough. Wynn's winded reply:

"It's Monday."

CHECKLIST: DISCOVER BY DRAFTING

THE PROBLEM

How do I write and keep writing to *draft* the story into publishable shape?

SOLUTIONS

- Write fast without notes. What is remembered probably should be, what is forgotten probably should be. And you can go back to your notes when the draft is done.
- Write "TK" ("To Come") or place a blank underlined space in the text for details that you have forgotten and that can be checked later. Keep writing.
- Write early to discover what you know and what you need to know.
- Select the important points and take the time to develop them adequately. Brevity is achieved by selection, not compression.
- Write with your ear. Listen to what you are saying and how you are saying it. (If stuck, dictate to a tape recorder.)
- When possible, reveal the story to the reader. Show, don't tell. Use scene and anecdote. Let the reader experience the story and discover its meaning.
- Let action or the natural order of the story carry the exposition and description.
- If there is a serious problem in organization that hasn't been solved during the order stage of the process, write a paragraph and put six spaces between it and the next para-

graph. Make a printout, cut the paragraphs and play solitaire with them until you find their natural sequence.
- Write the easy parts first, the parts you want to write.
- If blocked, follow poet William Stafford's advice: Lower your standards. Or heed William Faulkner: "Get it down. Take chances. It may be bad, but that's the only way you can do anything really good." Writer's block often comes when the writer has set impossible standards.
- Provide the reader with the evidence an intelligent but uninformed person will need to believe the story.
- Vary the documentation. Pick the material and the form of that material (quotation, anecdote, statistic, action, description) that is appropriate for the point being made.
- Answer the questions the reader will ask. The story is a conversation with an individual reader, with only the answers to the reader's questions printed.
- Stop in the middle of a sentence.
- Write down the reasons you're not writing. Define the problems. Devise solutions: more reporting, lower standards, refocus story, new organization.
- Switch writing tools. Turn off the computer, pick up a pad and pen.
- Take a break.

A WORD ABOUT VOICE

Voice, says Don Murray, "is the most important, the most magical and powerful element in writing."

Writers talk about "finding their voice." The way to do that is to write, of course, but also to use your powers of speech and hearing to discover your voice by listening and tuning the words until they say what you want them to say in just the way you want them to say it. Read your words aloud, whether they are in your notebook or on the screen. If the sound of your story puts you to sleep, imagine how the reader will respond. Broadcast

writers are trained to strive for a conversational voice; print and online writers should follow their lead. Just as you have a voice, so does your story. Listen to what it says and how it says it.

REVISE: REWRITING THE STORY

Journalism has been called the "first rough draft of history." For many reporters, that seems to absolve them of the need to rewrite. **Revising** is the final but most critical step of the process of reporting. It's the last chance to
plug holes in your reporting, to verify your facts, to make sure your story is
the most complete, fair, accurate, clear job it can be.

Good writers are rarely satisfied. They write a word, then scratch it out or,
in this computer age, tap the delete key and try again. "Nonwriters think of
writing as a matter of tinkering, touching up, making presentable, but writers know it is central to the act of discovering," says Don Murray. The
writing process isn't a straight line. Often the writer circles back to rereport,
refocus, reorganize. Good writers are never content. They're always trying to
find better details, a sharper focus, a beginning that captivates and an ending that leaves a lasting impression on the reader.

Writers need distance from their stories. Use the technology: Make a
printout. Mark it up. Make the changes. Then read it aloud. Take a walk.
Give it to someone else to read. Take it back and see how you can make it
better.

Imagination happens here; take advantage of the opportunity to experience what novelist Bernard Malamud called the "flowers of afterthought."

Be the toughest reader of your own copy. Ask it tough questions, like the
ones *Washington Post* columnist Donna Britt poses as she revises. "I question
everything. Can I say this better? Can I be more direct? Can I make this
tighter? Can I clarify this point? Is this insensitive? Is it funny? What can I do
to make it jump off the page? What's going to make somebody go with me
to the end, ride with me the whole way?"

Don't be misled, as I was, by the myth that published writing is what the
writer began with. Too many reporters think that, because they are writing
journalism, they must be content with the first words that come to mind. In
my case, what comes first are cliches and stereotypes. It's only by being willing to accept the flaws of the first draft that you can find the promise of the
final one.

"I do not know anybody who writes well who writes easily," said the late
Chicago Tribune columnist Joan Beck, who continued to win awards and
readers after nearly 50 years in journalism. "And I think that is important for
people to know. Because, after I had been through journalism school and
graduate school and was working at the *Tribune*, I was still surprised to see
that people whose bylines I had admired for a long time were still sitting
there, head in hand, trying to write. It was a great revelation to me that it did
not come easily to anybody that I know."

Writing *is* hard work. It takes patience and, above all, faith. The best writers are never satisfied. The best writers know, as poet John Ciardi said, that "the last act of the writing must be to become one's own reader."

Chris Hall, a Poynter reporting fellow now working as a reporter in Pennsylvania, knows the value of the final step of the process. "I learned to really go over my copy better, even in a rush, to catch all the major copy errors. I also learned that editors don't take too kindly to reporters who cannot edit their own copy before sending it to them. The better a reporter is in the grammar, punctuation, spelling, accuracy and style departments, the more likely an editor won't mind reading the copy. This could aid editors in making the piece better by not needing to correct so many simple copy mistakes."

The writing process isn't a straight line. The idea and focus change during the reporting—the crowd of cars on the side of the road isn't an accident; it's a flea market. The reporter makes another phone call during the drafting. The writer organizes during the reporting by marking up the notes—this quote as a lead, this detail as a kicker. Often the writer circles back to re-report, refocus, reorganize.

That aspect of the process—the need to circle back to earlier stages—surprises many student journalists. They think that once they've done their interviews and other reporting, all that's left to do is the writing. Ken Thomas, a student journalist at The Poynter Institute, learned differently while working on a story about a local shopping center. "I thought after I had done the majority of my reporting, that I had the information that I needed," Thomas said. But that changed when he began drafting his story. "I found that I really needed to return to my community and find out more information—whether it was making the right phone calls or simply talking to more owners."

Good writers are never content. They're always trying to find better details, a sharper focus, a beginning that captivates, an ending that leaves a lasting impression on the reader. And they're always thinking—What's the news? What's the story? Focus is not only a step in the process. It's an essential ingredient of every step from idea to final revision.

STUDENT EXAMPLE

REVISING THE STORY

Notice how Silcox changed his story before it was published in the weekly newspaper produced by our students. He deleted some parts, added new ones. The computer-edited version follows; the published story is on p. 105.

Stories don't emerge whole with just some fine-tuning. Writing can be pretty messy. Like refinishing an old, paint-encrusted piece of furniture. You start by laying on stripper that gets it all gunky. Then you wipe it off and start again. You scrape and peel, and finally you start sanding it down, starting with a coarse grade and working down, layer by layer, until there's nothing but tiny blemishes.

For one aerobics instructor, an active lifestyle saved months
of rehabilitation
BY JOHN SILCOX
Staff Writer

The paramedics ~~on the scene couldn't~~couldn't help but admire her shapely~~, well defined~~ legs. Alvina Miller was worried
she might lose~~one.~~

~~one.~~ ~~The 26-year-old aerobics instructor couldn't bear the
thought of not being able to run, as~~As she looked ~~down at the
left leg that was~~at her left leg, severely broken in a car crash
that could have killer~~her.~~

her, the 26-year-old aerobics instructor couldn't bear the
thought of not being able to run.

"I was afraid they were going to have to amputate," said
Miller. "But the paramedics told me, 'They can do anything in
hospitals now; don't worry, we'll save your leg.'"

Since graduating from Florida A&M University in 1995, exercise has been her passion. When not ~~working as a marketing
representative for Air Quality Control, chances are she's running
laps, lifting weights or doing~~writing letters to customers of Air
Quality at 30th Avenue North, she's running laps, lifting weights
or whatever it takes to slip into her size ~~3~~three skirts. Her diet
of vegetables, wheat bread and baked chicken is interrupted
only by an occasional Dairy Queen vanilla shake or slice of
Grandma's sweet potato pie. Afterwards, a penance of pushups.

The accident on April 19 left her with a leg broken above her
left knee, but that ~~didn't~~didn't stop Miller from maintaining her
daily exercise regime—even doubling her efforts. Within a couple of months, she was back at Campbell Park, leading her
~~faithful~~ flock of women in a chorus of scissors kicks.

Everyone knows that exercise gets rid of~~the love handles,
but it can also help you heal faster. Doctors say that a healthy
and~~love handles. Miller now knows it does more. One benefit
often ignored is that an active lifestyle can help injuries heal
faster. More than 61 million injuries wee reported in the united
States in 1994 alone, the fifth-leading cause of death, according to the National Center for Health ~~speed up recovery and
spare injury patients months of painful rehabilitation. While~~Sta-
tistics. And although healthy living is not the only factor in recovery, ~~physical therapists agree that aerobic exercise and
proper nutrition can not~~ doctors say that Miller's physical condition spared her months of rehabilitation.

~~only keep you fit but can speed up the body's healing
process.~~

~~Miller's Best Bud~~

~~Miller's story begins with a brown collie named Bud, which she describes as "Lassie with smaller eyes." Technically Bud belongs to Miller's neighbor Mrs. Arlie Jones, but over the years he has become a constant companion, accompanying her on evening runs around Tropicana Field.~~

~~Miller was on her way back from the store to give Bud a shampoo on the day of the accident. While making a left hand turn just a block from her house, Bud jumped in front of the wheel and blocked her view. Miller jammed her brakes but the car's momentum carried her into the oncoming lane where she smacked into a Toyota Corolla and then rolled her own Grand Am three times before slamming into a stop sign along the curb.~~

~~"I didn't feel anything for about three minutes," she said. "I didn't even hear what happened."~~

~~Miller crawled out through an open window, with the chivalrous but shaken collie following patiently behind her. Based on the status of the car, the paramedics on the scene presumed she was dead. They were surprised to find Miller alive and well, except for the bone above her left knee which had broken through the skin. Miller was rushed to Bayfront hospital. Bud walked home.~~

"People who are aerobically fit and in good health are in the best possible position to ~~Miller suffered a broken leg above her left knee that required a 20 mm stainless stell rod to be inserted into the bone to help the knee heal properly. Miller spent her four day stay chatting with nurses about nutrition and exercise, swallowing painkillers and doing leg lifts and crunches from her hospital bed.~~heal," said Dr. Jorge Rodriguez, a~~Miller's~~ physician at All Florida Orthopedic Associates, ~~said that it typically takes patients 8 to 12 weeks just to get off crutches. Miller was back in aerobics after two months.~~

~~"Before you know it, you'll be running like a gazelle," said Rodriguez, at a recent checkup.~~

~~Rodriguez said that because Miller was in such good shape to begin with, she didn't need to develop the muscle strength necessary to begin rehabilitation.~~

~~"People who are aerobically fit and in good health are in the best possible position to heal," he said.~~

~~Happy Healthy Healing~~

~~The reason is simple.~~ Exercise ~~strengthens~~circulates the blood to the bones and ~~joints by circulating the blood, according to~~joints, said Dr. Mark D. Brown, ~~professor and chairman~~

Continued

for the department of orthopedic and rehabilitation chairman of the Department of Orthopedic and Rehabilitation at the University of Miami of Miami school of medicine. Better blood supply to the tissue allows for faster healing.

Doctors have observed known for years that athletes with injuries heal faster than unconditioned individuals of the same age. Brown recalls a conditioned young dancer who fractured her thigh bone and femur and lost one leg below the knee. She was dancing in a recital in New York four months after the accident, he said.

Rodriguez said it typically takes patients with Miller's injuries eight to 12 weeks just to get off crutches. She was in aerobics after two months.

Miller's Best Bud

Miller's road to recovery begins with a neighbor's brown collie named Bud, a faithful companion on her evening jogs around Tropicana Field.

Miller, driving with her left leg tucked under her body as she often does, was on her way back from the store to give Bud a shampoo on the day of the accident. While she was making a left turn a block from her house, Bud jumped in front of the wheel and blocked her view. She jammed her brakes, but the Grand Am slid into the oncoming lane and smacked into a Toyota Corolla, rolled three times and slammed into a stop sign. "I didn't feel anything for about three minutes," she said. "I didn't even hear what happened."

Miller crawled out an open window with a shaken collie behind her. The woman in the Toyota was not injured, but based on the looks of Miller's car, the paramedics on the scene presumed she was dead. They were surprised to find Miller alive and well, except for the bone that had broken through the skin behind her left knee. Miller was rushed to Bayfront Medical Center. Bud walked home.

Surgeons inserted a 20 mm stainless steel rod into the bone to help the knee heal properly. She spent her four-day hospital stay chatting with nurses about nutrition and exercise, swallowing painkillers and sweating out leg lifts and crunches in her hospital bed. "Before you know it, you'll be running like a gazelle," said Rodriguez, during a recent checkup.

Happy Healthy Healing

Studies show that heavy smokers, drinkers and people with poor eating habits are slow healers. Even back pain can be exacerbated by smoking. Brown cited studies that show that smokers who undergo spinal fusions have only a 50 percent success rate, compared to 95 percent for nonsmokers. In good

~~happy person, the pain doesn't bother you as~~ Brown said elderly patients with poor diets who have hip fractures suffer more infections and complications in healing. But physical therapist Sherie Wynn has seen active senior citizens, because of their endurance and muscle strength, bounce back from hip and knee replacements in six months. Wynn, who works at Bayfront, said people who aren't used to exercise get tired during recovery.

"The body expends so much energy trying to heal that there is nothing left over for functional activities," said Wynn, who compares it with someone being extremely sore after taking up jogging. "Somebody who runs 26 miles a day, if you add an extra mile, they won't feel it very much," she said.

And it helps to have a healthy outlook like Emily Peck.

A speeding car hit Peck as she crossed Fourth Street South at 13th Avenue in St. Petersburg on June 10, leaving her with two broken legs, a broken arm, a pair of cracked ribs and a collapsed lung.

"You just have to think, I'm going to do the best I can and not be beaten by this," said Peck, who was to be certified in scuba diving the weekend after the accident.

~~much," said~~ Mental attitude is a catalyst to healing faster, according to Neil Spielholz, a research professor in the division of physical therapy at the University of Miami. "If you are a happy person, the pain doesn't bother you as much," he said, adding that exercise releases endorphins, opiate-like substances that create a sense of well-being in the body.

Peck, a 34-year-old television producer from Alabama, was out of the hospital faster than expected, and doctors told her that because she was young and healthy she would bounce back quickly.

But when it comes to bone healing, exercise is not the only thing that ~~makes it or "breaks it."~~ "makes it or breaks it." Brown said that family genetics, disease history and age are also important factors in recovery.

"~~Of~~ "Of course when you are young, younger people heal much faster than older ~~people," he said. "But it doesn't~~ people," he said. "But it doesn't make any difference how old you are if you are in good ~~health."~~ health."

~~Miller stays healthy by sticking to a diet of fruits and vegetables, wheat bread and baked chicken—occasionally splurging for a vanilla milkshake at Dairy Queen or a slice of grandma's sweet potato pie. But even that demands a penance of pushups.~~

Continued

Leader of the Pack

Fifteen women have turned out for ~~Miller's Monday class. Some have even brought there~~Miller's aerobics class on a night just 12 weeks after her accident. Some have brought children, who mimic ~~mom's~~Mom's movements on the blue mats in the back of the ~~room.~~rec room at Campbell Park.

Pat Crumb, 47, comes because of her high blood pressure and cholesterol. ~~"It's down to 200," she beams proudly.~~"It's down to 200," she beams. Dorothy Daniels, 48, relieves the stress of teaching 25 ~~first graders~~first-graders at Eisenhower Elementary in Clearwater. ~~Both are inspired by their instructor's determination.~~

Miller, limping slightly with her left knee wrapped in brown gauze, fires up the women with words of ~~encouragement that get more intense as the night wears on.~~encouragement. ~~One flash of her toothy smile is always good for an extra, set of sit-ups.~~

During an intense round of knee bends, ~~Miller scolds 38-year-old~~she scolds 38-year-old Deborah Wynn for ~~not going down far enough. Wynn's winded reply:~~dogging it. Then Miller laughs to let her know it's all in fun.

~~"Its Monday."~~

One flash of her toothy smile is always good for an extra rep.

GUIDELINES FOR REVISION

Journalists traffic in words. You must be able to speak and write correct English. Your stories will make an indelible impression on your editors, readers and viewers. They expect you to be accurate and to know and follow the rules of grammar, spelling, punctuation and style. Here are some guidelines to help you convince them.

1. Master your organization's style. A stylebook sets forth the guides to capitalization, abbreviation, punctuation, spelling, numbers and usage. *The Associated Press Stylebook* is the "bible of style" for most news organizations. (It's also the stylebook followed in this book.) Other organizations produce their own. *Wired* magazine decided it needed to create an online style. By their very nature, stylebooks are arbitrary. Often it's not a question of what is right, but rather of what's been agreed upon. Like it or not, stylebooks set forth rules about language, word usage, punctuation and spelling that news organizations adhere to. You have to learn and follow them. You should have a copy of the stylebook that your organization follows beside your dictionary, thesaurus and sacred texts.

2. Never turn in copy before you've run it past the spell-checker, which is a standard feature of word-processing software. But don't assume that it will catch all your errors. If you trusted spell-check of the name Oksana Baiul, you'd identify the Olympic skater as "Osaka Bail."

"Bad spelling makes you look lazy," says Melinda McAdams, a veteran copy editor and new media consultant. "It's true that some geniuses can't spell, but some geniuses walk around with gravy stains on their shirts. That's what bad spelling seems like to me: a big, obvious gravy stain in the middle of your writing. If you wouldn't wear stained, smelly clothing, you shouldn't be content to have misspelled words all over your letters, articles, stories or Web pages."

3. Always proofread your copy, checking it against the notes and documents you have collected during your reporting and researching. I've never forgotten what a journalism teacher said to me when I turned in an error-filled story: "Whenever you hand in copy with errors that you should have discovered and fixed, you're sending a message to your editor that you think you're too important to take care of the little stuff." The less time editors must spend checking spelling, addresses and titles, the more time they will have to read, assess and edit in a substantive way.

> Try your skill with 50 commonly misspelled words posted on the Internet by McAdams at http://www.sentex.net/%7Emmcadams/spelling.html/

4. Diagnose your stories for common spelling, grammar and style errors. Post the list near your computer and double-check your story before you send it in. My list of common errors includes subject–verb agreement and split infinitives. I try to catch all of them and rely on a platoon of generous, careful readers to help me.

5. Make friends with the copy desk. Copy editors are the people in a newsroom whose job is to know and enforce the rules of grammar, usage, taste and the other issues that govern a publication's style. Copy editors are a newsroom's "last line of defense" against embarrassment, corrections, libel and other misfortunes. Listen to what they say about your stories. Ask them for help (off deadline, of course). Fortunately, a number of excellent Web sites maintained by copy editors offer a wealth of information for reporters and anyone interested in clarity, accuracy and fairness in newswriting. Check the "Hotlist" at the end of the chapter.

6. Punctuation matters. Punctuation marks are the traffic signals of written language. The AP stylebook contains a detailed guide to punctuation that you should be familiar with. Here is a list of the most important punctuation marks:

. Period

EXAMPLE: This sentence is finished.

"There's not much to be said about the period except that most writers don't reach it soon enough," says William Zinnser in *On Writing Well*. Use the period to keep your thoughts confined to single statements. You can improve most long sentences, which often confuse readers, by cutting them into two or even three sentences.

? Question Mark

EXAMPLE: This is a question, isn't it?

, Comma

EXAMPLE: Take a breath, please.

"Punctuation helps readers identify clusters of words," writes Laurie E. Rozakis in *The Complete Idiot's Guide to Grammar and Style*. Whereas the period is the most common mark of punctuation between sentences, the comma is the most common mark within sentences. Commas help us read and understand sentences by indicating where we should pause.

: Colon

EXAMPLE: Pay attention to what comes next: rules, tips, guidelines.

Use the colon before a list or a quotation, especially a long quotation.

; Semicolon

EXAMPLE: Mr. Period leaves three daughters, Comma, of Biloxi, Miss.; Ellipsis, of Los Angeles; and Parentheses, of Chicago.

The semicolon terrifies many writers. It's more than a comma but less than a period. Most commonly, it's used to separate elements of a series when individual elements must be set off by commas, as in an obituary.

" " Quotation Marks

EXAMPLE: "Quiet. Somebody's talking," she said.

... Ellipsis

Stylebooks vary on the treatment of ellipses. AP style calls for a 3-dot ellipsis treated as a single word, with no internal spacing.

EXAMPLE: I left something important out of this ... sentence.

Quotation marks and ellipses both contribute to the liveliness and integrity of the news. Words within quotation marks indicate that these are the *exact* words someone spoke. An ellipsis means that something has been deleted from a quote or a document. In an age when electronic recording is commonplace and the public's distrust of the news media perhaps never greater, the integrity of quotes has never been more important. (The use of quotes is treated extensively in Chapter 6.)

! Exclamation Point

EXAMPLE: I'm really worked up about punctuation. I love it!

This is the grammatical equivalent of a strong spice: If you overdo it, you'll ruin the dish. Exclamation points are used to indicate strong emotion, such as passion, violence or shock. But smart writers let their words convey the emotion.

Why does this stuff matter?

Primarily, because journalists work with words and people expect us to know the rules. Of course, someone else's mistake may be another's standard way of talking. "But if your standard usage causes other people to consider you stupid or ignorant, you may want to consider changing it," says Paul Brians, a professor of English at Washington State University, who maintains a Web site devoted to "Common Errors in English." It's your right to, he says, "express yourself in any manner you please, but if you wish to communicate effectively, you should use nonstandard English only when you intend to rather than falling into it because you don't know any better."

If English is not your first language, it's likely the mistakes you make reflect the rules of your first language. Check out Curricular Resources in English as a Second Language at **http://www.cln.org/subjects/esl_cur.html**.

STUDENT EXAMPLE

Back in Step

Exercise speeds up the road to recovery, experts say. For one aerobics instructor, an active lifestyle saved months of rehabilitation.

By John Silcox
Points South Staff Writer

The paramedics couldn't help but admire her shapely legs. Alvina Miller was worried she might lose one. As she looked at her left leg, severely broken in a car crash that could have killed her, the 26-year-old aerobics instructor couldn't bear the thought of not being able to run.

"I was afraid they were going to have to amputate," said Miller. "But the paramedics told me, 'They can do anything in hospitals now; don't worry, we'll save your leg.'"

Since graduating from Florida A&M University in 1995, exercise has been her passion. When not writing letters to customers of Air Quality Control at 30th Avenue North, she's running laps, lifting weights or whatever it takes to slip into her size three skirts. Her diet of vegetables, wheat bread and baked chicken is interrupted only by an occasional Dairy Queen vanilla shake or slice of Grandma's sweet potato pie. Afterwards, a penance of push-ups.

The accident on April 19 left her with a leg broken above her left knee, but that didn't stop Miller from maintaining her daily exercise regime—even doubling her efforts. Within a couple of months, she was back at Campbell Park, leading her flock of women in a chorus of scissors kicks.

Everyone knows that exercise gets rid of love handles. Miller now knows it does more. One benefit often ignored is that an active

Continued

lifestyle can help injuries heal faster. More than 61 million injuries were reported in the United States in 1994 alone, the fifth leading cause of death according to the National Center for Health Statistics. And while healthy living is not the only factor in recovery, doctors say that Miller's physical condition spared her months of rehabilitation.

"People who are aerobically fit and in good health are in the best possible position to heal," said Dr. Jorge Rodriguez, Miller's physician at All Florida Orthopedic Associates.

Exercise circulates the blood to the bones and joints, said Dr. Mark D. Brown, chairman of the Department of Orthopaedics and Rehabilitation at the University of Miami School of Medicine. Better blood supply to the tissue allows for faster healing.

Doctors have known for years that athletes with injuries heal faster than unconditioned individuals of the same age. Brown recalls a young dancer who fractured her femur and lost one leg below the knee. She was dancing in a recital in New York four months after the accident, he said.

Rodriguez said it typically takes patients with Miller's injuries eight to 12 weeks just to get off crutches. She was in aerobics after two months.

Miller's road to recovery begins with a neighbor's brown collie named Bud, a faithful companion on her evening jogs around Tropicana Field.

Miller, driving with her left leg tucked under her body as she often does, was on her way back from the store to give Bud a shampoo on the day of the accident. While she was making a left turn a block from her house,

Bud jumped in front of the wheel and blocked her view. She jammed her brakes but the Grand Am slid into the oncoming lane and smacked into a Toyota Corolla, rolled three times and slammed into a stop sign.

"I didn't feel anything for about three minutes," she said. "I didn't even hear what happened."

Miller crawled out an open window with a shaken collie behind her. The woman in the Toyota was not injured, but based on the looks of Miller's car, the paramedics on the scene presumed she was dead. They were surprised to find Miller alive and well, except for the bone that had broken through the skin behind her left knee. Miller was rushed to Bayfront Medical Center. Bud walked home.

Surgeons inserted a 20 mm stainless steel rod into the bone to help the knee heal properly. She spent her four-day hospital stay chatting with nurses about nutrition and exercise, swallowing painkillers and sweating out leg lifts and crunches in her hospital bed. "Before you know it, you'll be running like a gazelle," said Rodriguez, during a recent checkup.

Studies show that heavy smokers, drinkers and people with poor eating habits are slow healers. Brown said elderly patients with poor diets who have hip fractures suffer more infections and complications in healing.

But physical therapist Sherie Wynn has seen active senior citizens, because of their endurance and muscle strength, bounce back from hip and knee replacements in six months. Wynn, who works at Bayfront, said people who aren't used to exercise get tired during recovery.

"The body expends so much energy trying to heal that there is nothing left over for functional activities," said Wynn, who compares it with someone extremely sore after taking up jogging. "Somebody who runs 26 miles a day, if you add an extra mile, they won't feel it very much," she said.

And it helps to have a healthy outlook like Emily Peck.

A speeding car hit Peck as she crossed Fourth Street South at 13th Avenue in St. Petersburg on June 10, leaving her with two broken legs, a broken arm, a pair of cracked ribs and a collapsed lung.

"You just have to think, I'm going to do the best I can and not be beaten by this," said Peck, who was to be certified in scuba diving the weekend after the accident.

Mental attitude is a catalyst to healing faster, according to Neil Spielholz, a research professor in the division of physical therapy at the University of Miami.

"If you are a happy person, the pain doesn't bother you as much," he said, adding that exercise releases endorphins, opiate-like substances that create a sense of well-being in the body.

Peck, a 34-year-old television producer form Alabama, was out of the hospital faster than expected, and doctors told her that because she was young and healthy she would bounce back quickly.

But when it comes to bone healing, exercise is not the only thing that "makes it or breaks it." Brown said that family genetics, disease history and age are also important factors in recovery.

"Of course when you are young, younger people heal much faster than older people," he said. "But it doesn't make any difference how old you are if you are in good health."

Fifteen women have turned out for Miller's aerobics class on a night just 12 weeks after her accident. Some have brought children, who mimic Mom's movements on the blue mats in the back of the rec room at Campbell Park.

Pat Crumb, 47, comes because of her high blood pressure and cholesterol. "It's down to 200," she beams. Dorothy Daniels, 48, relieves the stress of teaching 25 first-graders at Eisenhower Elementary in Clearwater.

Miller, limping slightly with her left knee wrapped in brown gauze, fires up the women with words of encouragement. During an intense round of knee bends, she scolds 38-year-old Deborah Wynn for dogging it. Then Miller laughs to let her know it's all in fun.

One flash of her toothy smile is always good for an extra rep.

CHECKLIST: REWRITING FOR READERS

THE PROBLEM

My story is drafted. How do I *clarify* the meaning and keep the story tight and interesting?

SOLUTIONS

- Make a printout to "see" your story.
- Read your story aloud.
- Read in three stages:
  1. Like a reader
  2. Like a writer
  3. Like an editor
- Be patient, even on deadline. Take a breath and read it again.
- Interview yourself. What works? What needs work?
- Find a co-reader, someone who makes you want to keep writing. Avoid destructive types.
- Remember that shorter is better. What can be left out should be left out. A good piece of writing may be judged by the amount of good material that isn't used. Everything left in develops the single dominant meaning of the story.

- Does your story employ the senses: hearing, sight, smell, touch, taste?
- Does your story also have a sense of:
  People?
  Time?
  Place?
  Drama?
- Build in rewriting time. Write early. Print out early.
- Is there another way to write this story? Try it.
- Do I need more reporting?
- Are all the facts checked?
- Is there anything else I can do to make the story:
  Simple?
  Clear?
  Graceful?
  Accurate?
  Fair?
  Shorter?

RIDING THE ROLLER COASTER: THE UPS AND DOWNS OF REPORTING AND WRITING

Few endeavors are lonelier than being a reporter, standing on the sidelines watching events and going back to sit alone in front of a blank screen and make sense of it all. I like the description offered by the late sports columnist Red Smith: "There's nothing to writing. All you do is sit down at the typewriter and open a vein." To me, writing has always seemed like a roller-coaster ride: dizzying heights of excitement and dips into valleys of despair. Let's pick a point, arbitrarily, right after I've published a story. Let's say it was a good story, and people have said they liked it. I'm elated. That lasts a few seconds, replaced immediately by despair. "The story was a fluke," a little voice whispers. "Just a lucky break. You'll never be able to match it again. In fact, you'll probably never get another story idea again, and your bosses will realize you were just a flash in the pan." I've felt this way all my career.

But then another story idea appears: Either my editor comes up with one or an idea occurs to me. I'm high again, and as I launch into the reporting I start on a roll. Then an interview falls through, or I can't get to somebody, or I cover a meeting, and it makes no sense, and I'm back in the pits. The only solution is to keep slogging. Have I got a story? That's what I'm asking my-self as I come back to the office. I realize I can't let my boss know this. So I start pitching the story to myself and slowly start climbing again, convinced maybe there is a story after all. Then I sit down to write, and I realize it was a mirage. I sweat, the clock is ticking. Suddenly, at the very point of disaster, when I have hit what mountain climbers and runners call "the wall," I get a second wind and push ahead and finish the piece. I am at once elated but soon terrified. What if I got everything wrong? Are my notes accurate? Have I checked everything? At 4 that morning, I wake up. "Oh, no," the little voice says. "His middle initial isn't C." I race to my briefcase, fish out my notes. Yes, it is C. I go back to bed and spend the rest of the night picking apart each paragraph. The paper appears in the driveway at 6 a.m. This time, I vow, I won't get it. Or if I do, I won't look at my story. At 6:01 I'm outside, paper in hand. But, no, I won't look. I look. It's great. Then, "Oh, no, is he really the assistant town manager or the deputy town manager?" I go to work hoping no one notices me. I hope they crowd around my desk and cheer. I hope they forget I'm here. I hope they lift me on their shoulders. "Good story," a friend says. Maybe it was okay after all. Maybe my wife was right after all. I re-assess. "Hey, it's a damn fine story. One of my best. Hey, maybe it will win a prize. Oh, God, what am I going to do tomorrow?"

Such is the emotional roller coaster you've chosen to ride.

It's vital to understand the emotional highs and lows and to find ways to take advantage of them. To find comfort in despair, knowing, for instance, that sometimes you have to hit bottom before you can write your way out, and to learn to stop hating rough drafts because they contain the promise of the final one.

There are qualities, some of them contradictory, that can help writers deal more effectively with the emotions of what we do:

TENACITY to hold on and not give up, no matter how hard it is.

HUMILITY in the face of an activity that always leaves room for improvement.

CONCEIT to tell myself that what I think is worth recording.

CURIOSITY to ask "What am I interested in?" "What do other people seem to be interested in?" "What kind of stories do I want to write, do I wish I had written?" If you don't have a story file, start one. Use your-self as a resource. I once did a series on children who commit burglaries. My editor said she had no idea that this could be so interesting: How did I think it would be a story? Now, she may have been just flattering me—if so, it worked—but I got the idea because a neighbor's house was broken into three times, and my neighbor decided to stake out his own house. Sure enough, he caught the burglar: an 8-year-old boy. "What's an 8-year-old doing breaking into a house?" I wanted to know. "Why isn't he at school?" And I was off and running.

THE ABILITY TO LOWER YOUR STANDARDS: Clearly, at some point, you and your editor will apply rigid standards—of accuracy and clarity, among others—but ignoring the voice that says "This stinks" is the first step to producing copy that can be rewritten. Accept yourself and what you're capable of doing at that moment.

THE ABILITY TO LEARN FROM OTHERS: Newsrooms can be very competitive places. There's only so much room on the front page. It may not seem overt, but ask yourself this question: How many people in your newsroom would you, or do you, ask to look at a lead? Oh, sure, you may ask somebody for a phone number or the name of a source, but sadly, it's still rare for reporters to seek out help with writing a story from other reporters, unless they're friends. That's natural. A friend, you assume, isn't going to look at a story and say, "That really sucks." Lillian Ross of *The New Yorker* said it best:

"Do not be afraid to acknowledge that you have learned from other writers. Do not spend your time trying to kill off other writers and reporters. The more talented you are, the more you can learn from other writers and the freer you are to admit that you have learned."

■

What does that mean? At *The Providence Journal,* it meant a weekly writing contest in which the winner wrote an essay called "How I Wrote the Story" that was shared via bulletin boards and ultimately in a book with the paper's staff. It means reading other writers and trying to understand how they achieved effects you admire. It means seeking out writers in your newsroom or beyond and asking them how they do it. One of the best sources is the annual collection of work by winners of the ASNE Writing Awards, published in the *Best Newspaper Writing* series. Start a writing group. Note I don't say "writers' group" because editors, photographers and artists belong in it, too. It also means learning from yourself. If you're not keeping a daily log, a diary or what some people call a daybook, where you can write ideas and snatches of writing or just talk to yourself about your writing, you're missing a perfect opportunity to teach yourself.

PERSISTENCE: There was once a reporter who desperately wanted to work for *The Washington Post,* but the best he could do was get a job at a paper in suburban Maryland. He kept in touch with an editor at the *Post,* sending him clips and calling regularly. He even called him at home when the editor was on vacation, at which point the editor got very annoyed with this young man, until his wife asked, "Isn't that the kind of reporter you've always said you wanted?" And that is how Bob Woodward got his job. Persistence means making one more phone call, doing one more interview, knocking on one more door, trying one more lead, hanging around to read the page proof or look at the videotape one more time.

COURAGE: Most of all, what reporters do takes guts. It takes guts to ride a roller coaster, and it takes guts to get up every day and talk to people who don't want to talk to us and to intrude on people's lives at moments of distress, to ask questions people don't want to answer. It takes guts, as the clock ticks, to try to make sense of it, knowing that for the price of a quarter people are free to use our stories to line their cat litter box. Dan Rather doesn't say it anymore, but I think it is still a good way to sign off, especially to a group of reporters: Courage.

WRITERS AT WORK: THE COACHING WAY

- Ask yourself what your story is about. Say it in a single sentence.
- Plan your story. Use the outline method John Silcox employed for his exercise story as a model.
- Write down a list of possible sources.
- Remember Jane Harrigan's advice: "The story is not in your notes. The story is in your head." Write the first draft of your story without notes.
- Are you blocked, even after you've settled on a focus and drawn a map for your story? Freewrite a discovery draft or discovery paragraphs as fast as possible without stopping to revise in order to reveal the meaning and the voice of the story. Write about any part of the story as long as it reveals tone, mood, voice. Am I sad, joyous, incredulous, detached, outraged? Do I smell earth or engine oil or chalk dust?
- Read your story aloud. Keep a pad by your side and note possible changes.
- Write accounts that explore the conditions behind your reporting and writing successes.
- Answer these three questions: What surprised me? What did I learn? What do I need to learn next?

GLOSSARY OF IMPORTANT TERMS

Brainstorming. Requires you to apply creativity. Brainstorming is simple: You choose a topic and make a list of everything that comes to mind.

Draft. A version of a story. Verb: to discover a story by writing a draft.

Focus. The central point, or theme, of a story.

Listserv. An online discussion group, usually focused on a specific topic, such as vintage fountain pen collecting or computer-assisted reporting. Also known as a mailing list. You join by subscribing via e-mail.

Mapping and **branching.** Nonlinear brainstorming. Put a topic in the center of a page or on the trunk of a tree, and as quickly as possible, draw lines or branches to connected ideas.

Process approach. A way to describe and understand how successful writing is made, as a series of decisions and steps writers make from the story idea to publication or broadcast.

Reporting. Interviewing, observing, note-taking, researching, analyzing and other ways by which reporters collect information.

Revising. Making changes to a draft to improve the clarity, fairness and accuracy. The key to writing quality.

EXERCISES

1. Take one edition of your local paper and study every page for story ideas.

2. Select an issue that is news in your community: tuition increases, crime, inadequate student parking. Brainstorm a list of questions and possible story ideas.

3. Take the same issue and draw a map to produce the same questions and idea list. Which approach is more useful for you?

4. Select an issue and build a scenario about it. A water main break results in the collapse of the largest student parking lot. Date rapes increase dramatically on campus. Outline the possible developments, actions and reactions that might result. Identify four or five possible story ideas suggested by your scenario.

READINGS

de Bono, Edward. *Serious Creativity.* New York: Harper Business, 1992.

Downie, Leonard Jr. *The New Muckrackers.* New York: New American Library, 1976.

Goldstein, Norm, ed. *The Associated Press Stylebook and Libel Manual.* Reading, Mass.: Perseus, 1998.

Klauser, Henriette Anne. *Writing on Both Sides of the Brain*. San Francisco: Harper & Row, 1986.

Murray, Donald M. *Writing for Your Readers: Notes on the Writer's Craft From The Boston Globe*. Chester, Conn.: Globe Pequot Press, 1983.

Murray, Donald M. *Write to Learn*. Fort Worth: Harcourt Brace Jovanovich, 1993.

Scanlan, Christopher, ed. *How I Wrote the Story*. Providence, R.I.: Providence Journal Co., 1985.

Strunk, William Jr., and E. B. White. *The Elements of Style*, 3rd ed. New York: Macmillan, 1979.

Woodruff, Jay. *A Piece of Work: Five Writers Discuss Their Revisions*. Iowa City: University of Iowa Press, 1993.

Zinsser, William. *Speaking of Journalism: 12 Writers and Editors Talk About Their Work*. New York: HarperCollins, 1994.

HOTLIST

http://www.mindtools.com/brainstm.html

A Web page that gives an overview of the technique and suggestions for individual and group brainstorming.

http://www.wired.com/wired/scenarios/

Wired magazine's Web page devoted to the techniques of scenario building, including examples and essays by futurists.

http://www.copydesk.org/

The American Copy Editors Society (ACES), a professional organization of copy editors, "is dedicated to improving the quality of journalism and the working lives of journalists. Our main purpose is to educate our members—and others in the news business—in ways of improving the standards of copy editing and increasing the value the news industry places on our craft." The group's primary focus is on newspaper editing, but it has cast a wide net for colleagues from other media, as well as teachers and students. Check out its list of commonly misused and trite words. (It seems that I'm not the only one who uses "leafy" to describe a suburb. I won't do it anymore.) And if you need practice, take the editing tests from Pam Robinson of the Los Angeles Times–Washington Post News Service. Also, copy desk discussion boards reflect current newsroom debates.

http://www.theslot.com/

Bill Walsh, a copy editor at *The Washington Post*, spices grammar and style lessons with wit. His *Curmudgeon's Stylebook* on this site is an opinionated and useful supplement to the newsroom bible, the AP stylebook. It should be bookmarked on every reporter's desktop.

http://www.copyeditor.com/Links.html

Impress your editors by bookmarking this page of links for copy editors, maintained by the newsletter *Copy Editor*: *Language News for the Publishing Profession*. It will take you to online dictionaries and guides for print and online style.

http://www.wsu.edu:8080/~brians/errors/index.html

"Common Errors in English." Paul Brians, a professor of English at Washington State University, maintains this link-rich site, which is a treasure for anyone working with words.

CHAPTER

4

FINDING AND WRITING A LEAD

CHAPTER FOCUS

Whether you're reporting news or telling a story, the opening of a story dictates all that follows. Make sure your story delivers the promise made in the lead.

CHAPTER LESSONS

- The five W's, an H and an SW
- "Tell me the news" and "tell me a story" leads
- A lexicon of leads
- How to write a lead
- Choosing the right lead
- Clichés of lead writing
- Techniques for revising leads
- Lead writing: The Coaching Way

INTRODUCTION

When journalists talk about beginnings of stories the word they use is **lead.** Sometimes it's spelled "lede," a throwback to the precomputer age when the word for first paragraphs had to be distinguished from the word for the molten lead used to print newspapers. Leads are the foundation of every news story, no matter what the medium.

An effective lead makes a promise to the reader: I have something important, something interesting, to tell you. A good lead beckons and invites. It attracts and entices. If there's any poetry in journalism, it's most often found in the lead, as in the classic opening of what could have been a mundane weather forecast:

Snow, followed by small boys on sleds.

The examples in this chapter are drawn from newspapers. Later, in Chapters 8 and 9, which focus on broadcasting and online writing, we'll look at the special demands each places on leads. But this chapter's lessons are

> "Do not ever underestimate the importance of a lead to what we do each day. It is the way in. It is the greeting at the doorway that determines the tenor of the rest of the visit. As important as any first impression, it can be gotten past, but not easily."
> —JACQUI BANASZYNSKI, *THE SEATTLE TIMES*

applicable to all journalists. The ability to sift through the material you've collected in your reporting to discover the most newsworthy elements is fundamental to journalism. Whether you're a new reporter or a veteran writing for a newspaper, an online news site, radio or television news, you must be able to deliver the lead of a story quickly and accurately, with economy and power.

MASTERING THE FIVE W'S, AN H AND SW

In *Teacher's Pet*, a 1958 film about the newspaper business, a grizzled city editor, played by Clark Gable, teaches a cub reporter one of the enduring lessons of the craft. In rapid-fire dialogue, he doles out facts about a shooting, just enough information to spark a question from the green reporter. "Have you heard?" "What?" Barney demands. "Found dead," his editor replies. Intrigued, Barney responds to each new fact with another question. Who? When? Where? How? Why?

The reporter posed six crucial questions, his editor tells him: WHO, WHAT, WHERE, WHEN, WHY and HOW. "Make sure," the editor says, "you answer them in every news story. End of lesson."

It's a brief, entertaining scene that captures one of the enduring paradigms of newswriting.

Who. What. Where. When. Why. How.—**Five W's.** One H. They are the questions the journalist uses to gather information and to analyze, organize and present a news story. The five W's and one H represent an important paradigm of news reporting and writing. More than a hundred years ago, a young reporter named Theodore Dreiser heard about them from his editor, who had seen the words on a sign at a rival paper. "Over there in the *Tribune* office they have a sign which reads, 'Who or what? How? When? Where?' All those things have to be answered in the first paragraph, do you hear?—not in the last paragraph or the middle paragraph or anywhere but in the first paragraph."

Like Dreiser, you would be well served by keeping them in mind. This classic device of journalism remains a useful tool for the news writer, whatever the genre or medium. (As we will see in later chapters, the five W's can be used to test your effectiveness in news writing, diversity and ethics.) For the last 100 years, editors, reporters and journalism teachers have used them as the essential questions the reporter asks and answers, especially in the beginning, or lead, of a news story. Also known as a "hard news" lead or approach, its idea is to deliver the essential elements of the story in the first paragraph. The effective news lead captures the essence of the story, focusing on the most important, compelling or otherwise attention-getting aspect.

The five W's will continue to be useful in the 21st century. Online services rely on summary leads that pack a story into a single clear, concise, vivid, accurate paragraph. Even if you choose a career in corporate communications, you will need these skills to attract the attention of busy editors. Here are three examples of news leads that reflect the way reporters continue to

BREAKING DOWN THE LEAD

Gunmen Make Getaway on City Bus

Filed at 6:11 a.m. EDT

The Associated Press
May 10, 1997
NEW YORK—Heavily armed gunmen ambushed a payroll delivery and got away with $50,000 after spraying a quiet street with bullets, critically wounding a moonlighting off-duty detective and a retired police officer.

WHO
- Heavily armed gunmen
- Moonlighting off-duty detective
- Retired police officer

WHAT
- Ambushed payroll delivery
- Critically wounding

WHERE
- Quiet New York City street

WHEN
- Not in lead

WHY
- $50,000

HOW
- Spraying with bullets

Analysis: Aimed at a nationwide audience, this wire service story focuses on the event and players (cops, robbers). Characterizes place ("quiet") but doesn't give precise location.
Length: 30 words
Grade: A. Vivid, clear, economical

use the five W's and one H to organize and present information in a single, information-packed paragraph.

Although I've never been a big fan of the five W's—they always seemed formulaic and clichéd—I now realize that they have lasted so long because they do represent an effective paradigm—a description of the way news is structured. This is one way, but not the only one, as you will see. They can be used most effectively to help you formulate news judgment. Use them as a guide to a series of questions that will help you understand even the most foreign story. It's what working reporters do. When Mark Fritz was in Rwanda in 1994 reporting for The Associated Press, he found himself covering an ethnic massacre of a magnitude that seemed incomprehensible. The

BREAKING DOWN THE LEAD

2 Guards Delivering Cash Are Ambushed in Queens

The New York Times
May 10, 1997

NEW YORK—A frenzied crossfire broke the morning calm of a quiet Queens neighborhood Friday as masked robbers ambushed the two guards of a payroll shipment, leaving the security men—a retired police officer and an off-duty detective—bleeding on the sidewalk with more than a dozen bullet wounds, the authorities said.

WHO

- Masked robbers
- Two guards, retired police officer and off-duty detective, bleeding on sidewalk
- Authorities

WHAT

- Ambush
- Frenzied crossfire

WHERE

- Quiet Queens, N.Y., neighborhood sidewalk

WHEN

- Friday morning

WHY

- Payroll shipment

HOW

- Dozen bullet wounds

Highlights: Aimed at metropolitan audience, lead is detailed but gives general description of location (Queens).
Length: 50 words
Grade: B. Detail rich but too long

way he got through it was to keep peppering himself with questions, the five W's, an H as well as: "Why are you writing this story? What's it about?"

Reporters often fail to recognize that they themselves are the best single resource they have at every stage of the journalistic process. Start interviewing yourself, as well as others, as soon as you get an assignment. Begin, from this moment on, by evaluating every situation you face through the lens of the reporter. This will make it possible for you to answer the questions your readers have about a story. You are a surrogate for your readers. In a democracy, you are their representative.

BREAKING DOWN THE LEAD

Ambush and a Miracle

2 Survive Hail of Bullets From Masked Men

Newsday
May 10, 1997

Masked gunmen spraying a hail of bullets from submachine guns ambushed and seriously wounded a moonlighting detective and a retired police officer in a brazen morning payroll robbery in Flushing Friday.

WHO
- Masked gunmen
- Moonlighting detective and a retired police officer

WHAT
- Ambush
- Seriously wounded

WHERE
- Flushing

WHEN
- Friday morning

WHY
- Payroll robbery

HOW
- Brazen

Analysis: Aimed at a suburban Long Island audience familiar with local geography, lead focuses on drama and gives more precise location (Flushing).

Compare way *Newsday* and *Times* leads characterize event ("brazen") with *New York Times* ("frenzied crossfire broke the morning calm") with AP, which merely describes the event.

Length: 31 words

Grade: B-plus. Cliché ("hail of bullets") and redundancy ("gunmen," "guns") instead of more detail lowered grade.

WHO?

News is the record of human activity, what people say and do. Focus on the people in every story; ask yourself:

- Who's involved?
- Who are the stakeholders?
- Who are the major players?
- Who supports the issue? Who opposes it?

- Who is closest to the action?
- Who is affected?
- Who typifies the situation?
- Who are the most knowledgeable sources?

WHAT?

News is about actions, reactions, events, tangible things and intangibles like revenge, loyalty, power, weakness.

- What are the forces in support? In opposition?
- What's going on?
- What happened?
- What could happen?
- What are the key moments?

WHEN?

News is timely and a sense of time is an essential element of news reporting.

- When did the story begin?
- When did it end?
- When did the key moments occur?

WHERE?

News happens in specific places. Take your audience there.

- Where is this story taking place?
- Where is the main action or event happening?
- What does it look like? Sound like? Taste like?
- How can I make my reader see where the story is happening?

HOW?

In a complex society, reporters help people understand how things work. Their stories trace the evolution of events and issues that make the news. Good reporters go beyond the five W's so they can answer the readers' need to understand not just what happened but also how.

- How did it happen?
- How does it work?
- How did things go wrong?
- How was the story revealed?

WHY?

News is about causes, what makes events happen, what causes things to occur. Reporters are in a way like doctors diagnosing the society. Your job is to ask why. Always ask why.

- Why did this event occur?
- Why are people behaving this way?
- Why do the forces care so deeply?

SO WHAT?

In a world overloaded with information, people are hungry for news stories that help them understand why the news matters. The reporter provides context and background and analysis that let readers and viewers understand why they should care about the news. If they don't, people simply won't tune in. People have busy lives. News has to pierce what journalist and writer Susan Cheever aptly calls a "fog of personal concern." News can easily take second place behind the demands of work, school, family and a culture where there's never enough time in the day. The challenge for the journalist, whether reporting for print, broadcast or online, is to produce stories that lift that fog with stories that matter to people's lives and to do it with writing that makes that meaning clear. The question "So what?" is one that your readers and viewers are always asking, and so should you if you hope to reach them with news, information and stories you think are important. You have to convince them it's important, too. After you've answered those two vital questions, "What's the news?" and "What's the story?," always follow them up with questions that address the most challenging issue of all: "So what?" Ask yourself:

- Why should readers or viewers care about this story?
- How does this story relate to readers' and viewers' lives?
- Does this story reflect any larger themes? What are they?
- Why do people need to know this? What might it mean to their lives?
- Why does this story matter?

> "Can you remember five things you read in the paper today? I never can. News has to filter in to me through this fog of personal concern, and not much of it— I have the feeling—gets there. ... I do read *The Times* every day, and sometimes the tabs or *The Wall Street Journal*. I watch the news almost every night. Still, my principal concerns seem to be bologna sandwiches ... the holes in my kids' clothes, the puppy's whining. ..."
>
> —SUSAN CHEEVER, TEACHER, COLUMNIST, WRITER

THE TWO TYPES OF LEADS: "TELL ME THE NEWS," "TELL ME A STORY"

At *The Oregonian*, a paper with a long and dedicated history to good writing, team leaders met to talk about a problem: Too many stories were beginning with anecdotal leads. This wasn't the first newsroom staff to confront the debate over hard vs. soft leads. In 1982, Mitchell Stephens and Gerald Lanson gave a catchy name to leads that took too long to get to the point. They called them a symptom of "Jell-O journalism." Rightly, they complained that readers had to wait too long to find out the point of the story.

What set *The Oregonian*'s discussion apart was the way Jack Hart, the paper's staff development editor, framed the problem. "Newsrooms lack an adequate writing lexicon," Hart wrote in *Second Takes*, his monthly newsletter. "That shortcoming cripples conversation between writers and editors, limits creativity and restricts us all to a few tired story forms."

At *The Oregonian*, what seemed to be an overreliance on anecdotal leads actually highlighted a lack of precision in the way the paper's staff members described their writing, "calling everything other than a straight news lead an anecdotal lead," as one team leader put it.

To remedy the situation, Hart assembled a useful "Lexicon of Leads"— 14 types, illustrated by examples from the paper and grouped under the headings "Straight Leads," "Feature Leads" and "Dangerous Leads." (A lexicon is a collection of terms that applies to a particular skill or field of study.)

THE LEXICON

OF LEADS

BY JACK HART
The Oregonian

STRAIGHT LEADS

1. Summary leads

> The University of Oregon must move more women into higher-level faculty jobs or face federal sanctions.

This is the spring from which all journalistic waters flow. Summary leads summarize (what else?) the most important idea in the story. They often top inverted pyramid news stories, the most traditional form. Because a good summary lead makes meaning instantly clear, it's often the preferred form for breaking news and issue stories.

2. Blind leads

> The state's land-use planning agency on Friday chose a former city planner from Eugene to be its new director.

A blind lead is a summary lead that leaves out potentially confusing detail. The lead cited here omits the name of the planning agency (the Department of Land Conservation and Development) and the city planner, who was relatively unknown statewide.

A "catchall graf" immediately follows a blind lead. The catchall includes the specific detail omitted from the lead.

3. Wraps

> Thursday's storm caused the deaths of a Salem woman who broke her neck in a fall, a Bend man who had a heart attack while shoveling snow and a Eugene teen-ager struck by a skidding car.

An editor's order to "wrap it" means to combine several items. The reporter usually packages the items under a lead that refers to all of them.

SHIRTTAIL LEADS

A man taking photographs of Portland's skyline about 2:15 a.m. Sunday apparently was struck by a car and knocked into the Willamette River off the Interstate 5 ramp to Interstate 84. ...

Another accident Friday, this one involving a hit-and-run driver in Southwest Washington, left a Lynnwood, Wash., man in serious condition. ...

The shirttail is the alternative to the wrap lead. The reporter writes a summary lead focusing on the most newsworthy element in the wrap. Then he hangs the remaining items, each with its own lead, from the first element's "shirttails." Shirttail leads are traditional on meeting stories. The first lead targets the most important item on the agenda. The remaining items are introduced with an "in other business" transition.

FEATURE LEADS

1. Anecdotal leads

Richard Leakey likes to tell about the day in 1950 when he was a 6-year-old whining for his parents' attention. Louis and Mary Leakey were digging for ancient bones on the shores of Lake Victoria, but their little boy wanted to play. He wanted lunch. He wanted his mother to cuddle him. He wanted something to do.

"Go find your own bone," said his exasperated father, waving Richard off toward scraps of fossils lying around the site.

What the little boy found was the jawbone—the best ever unearthed—of an extinct giant pig. As he worked away at it with the dental picks and brushes that served for toys in the paleontologists' camp, he experienced for the first time the passion of discovery.

Kathleen Merryman
Tacoma News Tribune

Here's a true **anecdotal lead,** as opposed to all the other kinds of feature leads. As an anecdote, the lead takes the form of a short narrative with a beginning, middle and end. The end is particularly important. It's analogous to the punch line in a joke; it wraps up the story with a flourish that brings things to an apt conclusion. An anecdotal lead should illustrate the story's central theme. Kathleen Merryman's anecdote, for example, explains something central about her subject, Richard Leakey.

2. Narrative leads

They pulled the car to the side of the road, turned off the motor and waited silently as the memories washed over them in a series of gentle waves. ...

A narrative lead simply launches an action line. It's not part of an anecdote, necessarily. But it puts central characters into a scene and begins telling the story that pits those characters against some kind of complication. Narrative leads are—surprise!—most appropriate to narrative

Continued

stories. But they work on other kinds of stories, too. The bookend narrative, for example, begins with some relevant action, turns to standard newsfeature style for the middle of the story and completes the narrative for the story kicker.

3. Scene-setter leads

A woman with tormented eyes talks to herself as she plays a battered piano in Ward D's dayroom. Other psychiatric patients shuffle on the beige linoleum or stare from red-and-green vinyl chairs.

A bank of windows opens to a fenced courtyard. Outside. ...

Scene-setters open with description. They may contain some action, as is the case here. But the main point is to create a stage on which action can unfold or to give a sense of place important to the focus of the story. Brian Meehan's story concerned conditions at Dammasch State Hospital. So a description of those conditions was an appropriate way to begin.

4. Scene-wrap or gallery leads

A man claiming to be a Catholic priest sits in a Santa Claus suit in a wheelchair outside a Southeast Portland supermarket, collecting money for the "Holy Order of Mary Inc."

Across town, a supposed South African visitor asks a holiday-spirited shopper for directions to a local church. The South African then launches into a complicated tale that

soon has the Portlander withdrawing $2,000 from the bank. ...

Elsewhere, a boiler-room telephone sales company. ...

Scene-wraps illustrate trend stories. They show that the same thing is happening in a variety of places. Because they consist of a series of pictures, they're also called "galleries."

5. Significant detail leads

Hidden beneath a heap of inner-tubes in a tiny storeroom on an island in the middle of the Vistula River is the statue of Lenin that stood for decades inside the Gdansk Shipyard.

As you might expect, this story explored the operation of the shipyard and the economy of Poland. The statue of Lenin hidden, but still in the neighborhood, perfectly symbolized the story's central theme. And it perfectly illustrates the use of a significant detail to craft a lead.

6. The single-instance lead

For five days, Alice's husband, high on drugs, threatened to kill her. He hit her and abused her. Terrified, Alice fled the house when she finally got the chance and ran to a local business to call the police.

"He would kill me. He's very scary," Alice said. "He would walk through walls if he had to."

> The police advised her to contact the Domestic Violence Resource Center in Hillsboro, and Alice found her way there.

The single-instance lead uses one example to illustrate a larger topic. For that reason, single-instance leads are also called "microcosm leads." In this case, Alice's story was a gateway to a larger story on the Domestic Violence Resource Center.

Single-instance leads are a mainstay of magazine writing. In fact, they're almost required for stories in the most popular women's magazines. They've spread rapidly into newspaper writing, to the point that some critics now complain about their overuse.

7. Wordplay leads

> In Michael Crichton's previous novel, *Jurassic Park*, a tropical island has been transformed into a zoo whose denizens are dinosaurs brought to life by a group of greedy, irresponsible scientists who have been cloning around.

Wordplay is essentially lighthearted. Wordplay leads therefore work best on less-than-serious stories. They're popular in sports and entertainment, but they can succeed at grabbing and delighting readers in other forms as well.

DANGEROUS LEADS

1. Question leads

> What's black and orange and the worst nightmare for teams headed to the state football playoffs?

Some editors simply ban question leads, reasoning that readers want answers, not questions.

But George Orwell assures us that the only rule in writing is that there are no rules. So let's concede that question leads occasionally work, for all the right reasons.

Nevertheless, question leads often fail because they seldom perform the basic function of a lead—stating the central theme that organizes and explains the entire story. Furthermore, they can be irritating. Readers probably do resent frivolous questions when what they really want is news. Yes, some stories deal with fundamental questions. So a question lead can be appropriate.

Nonetheless, question leads seldom represent the best solution. It pays to be especially cautious when using them.

2. Quote leads

Quote leads are banned in some newsrooms, too. The rationale is similar to the rationale used for banning question leads: The chances that a quote was the best way to express the story's theme were awfully slim.

But quote leads can work wonderfully, too.

> Michael H. Walsh calls it "teaching the elephant to dance."
>
> That's his term for making the enormous, historic Union Pacific Railroad Co. competitive and profitable in the 20th century.

Continued

3. Topic leads

More than 40 environmentalists and developers debated before the Portland City Council on Wednesday on the future of wetlands areas in the Columbia South Shore area.

BOARDMAN—The prospect of tripling this town's population with a 3,000-inmate prison was the subject of a hot debate Tuesday.

Orwell notwithstanding, topic leads probably should be banned. The point of a news story is to tell us what happened, what the outcome was. In the case of a meeting story, the important thing is not that the meeting took place, but rather the consequence of the meeting. What was the key decision? Why is that important? Where do we go from here?

Topic leads, in other words, should be restricted to information. It's hard to imagine that they can ever be an appropriate way to introduce news.

Hart's "Lexicon of Leads" is the latest and, to my mind, one of the best examples of a continuing effort by journalists and teachers to improve news writing by better understanding what reporters do with language and why.

One of my journalism professors, Melvin Mencher, argues that there are only two types of leads: direct and delayed. I'd expand that notion. I believe that there are just two kinds of leads, both of which respond to a demand from a reader:

1. "Tell me the news" leads, what Hart's lexicon calls "straight" leads
2. "Tell me a story" leads, "feature" leads in Hart's list

"TELL ME THE NEWS" LEADS: SUMMARY AND ANALYSIS LEADS

SUMMARY LEADS

The ability to sum up a story in a single paragraph is one of journalism's most basic skills. News that delivers the news goes by various names: hard or breaking news, direct, summary. This type of lead generally answers the five W's—"Who?" "What?" "Where?" "When?" and "Why?" The best ones also answer "How?" and "So what?"

Barton Gellman of *The Washington Post* delivered understanding as well as information in his breaking news summary lead that reported the assassination of Prime Minister Yitzhak Rabin.

> JERUSALEM, Nov. 4—A right-wing Jewish extremist shot and killed Prime Minister Yitzhak Rabin tonight as he departed a peace rally attended by more than 100,000 in Tel Aviv, throwing Israel's government and the Middle East peace process into turmoil.
>
> *The Washington Post*

"Tell me the news" leads focus on the news, the breaking developments. They summarize the story in a single paragraph. Wire services and newspapers that see their role as newspaper of record favor this approach, as do online services and radio and television news. The idea behind it is to communicate the news—what is most important—as quickly as possible by compressing into a single paragraph the most newsworthy aspect of the story. Two more examples:

> The nation recorded a tragic new milestone Tuesday: Guns are killing U.S. teen-agers at the highest rate since the government began keeping count 30 years ago.
>
> Knight Ridder

> Dr. Joycelyn Elders, a former Arkansas health director controversial for her outspoken support of abortion rights and contraceptives for teens, won Senate confirmation as U.S. surgeon general Tuesday.
>
> Knight Ridder

ANALYSIS LEADS

Increasingly, readers are looking to the news media for stories that analyze the events and issues of the day, that put the news into perspective. That's where the analysis lead comes in:

> WASHINGTON—There's just one problem with the television networks' plan to put warning labels on violent prime-time shows to help parents protect their children. It won't cover daytime children's programming, which includes some of the medium's most violent shows.
>
> Knight Ridder

"TELL ME A STORY" LEADS: ANECDOTAL, SIGNIFICANT DETAIL, ROUND-UP AND EMBLEM LEADS

Editors and reporters know that by the time the reader picks up the morning paper, he or she has probably already heard the top stories of the day, from the radio, television or an online news source. When that happens the decision is made, consciously, to take a different approach.

That was the dilemma that faced *The Miami Herald* in 1995 when a deranged man hijacked a school bus carrying disabled schoolchildren. "We had a problem here that newspapers have more and more these days," said *Herald* senior writer Martin Merzer when I interviewed him for *Best Newspaper Writing 1996*. Merzer wrote the paper's award-winning story drawing on reports from more than a dozen of his colleagues. "This thing happened at 8:30, 9 o'clock in the morning. We couldn't get it in the paper for another 24 hours. All the local TV stations were already on it full-time. ... Local news was on it, it was on CNN live, and we still had 24 hours to go."

There was no sense in writing a hard news lead—**Police shot and killed a man who hijacked a bus and held 13 disabled children hostage Tuesday morning after a tense low-speed chase through rush hour traffic.** Merzer and his editors reasoned: "No one's going to read into the third paragraph because they figure they know that." The *Herald's* only hope, Merzer said, was "to try to tell it better, in more detail, so that people who think they know a lot about this story figure out real soon that there's more to know, and we're going to tell it to them. I figured our best contribution would be to tell the story in a different fashion with compelling detail."

Rather than summing up what readers already knew, Merzer gambled on writing a vivid, edgy reconstruction. The gamble paid off. The *Herald's* story, which won the $10,000 Jesse Laventhol Award for Deadline Reporting, began in this irresistible fashion:

A waiter fond of poet Ralph Waldo Emerson attends morning prayers at his church, steps across the street and hijacks a school bus. Owing $15,639.39 in back taxes, wielding what he says is a bomb, Catalino Sang shields himself with disabled children.

Follow my orders, he says, or I will kill the kids. "No problem, I will," says driver Alicia Chapman, crafty and calm. "But please don't hurt the children."

The saga of Dade County school bus No. CX-17, bound for Blue Lakes Elementary, begins.

The Miami Herald

The *Herald's* dilemma that day is shared by news organizations every day. Your responsibility as a reporter is to help decide—or defend—how you tell your story. Knowing the range of possibilities open to a reporter trying to write a lead that will attract readers and entice them to read on is the first step.

"Tell me the story" leads often begin with an anecdote, a scene or a quote that illustrates the story without saying explicitly what the story is about. An **anecdotal lead** begins with a compressed story that illustrates the story's theme or situation. It usually includes characters, dialogue and setting, almost like a movie scene. "The anecdote is a ministory, three grafs unto itself, that is a microscopic representation of the entire story," says Jacqui Banaszynski, who won a Pulitzer Prize for feature writing and now is a top editor at *The Seattle Times*. "It hits the note and tone and core of the greater piece. That is what the anecdote must do to work: Otherwise it is a faulty hinge."

Storytelling leads use suspense to grab readers' attention without giving away the ending. "This lead seeks to inspire and intensify curiosity rather than to satisfy it," James Stewart says in *Follow the Story*, his book on writing nonfiction. "It invites readers on a journey, but only hints at the destination. It must never give the ending away." Consider the approach I took in the following story:

STORY EXAMPLE: AN ANECDOTAL APPROACH

FORT LAUDERDALE—The lunchtime special is a grilled cheese sandwich with a side of potato salad for just 99 cents, but at Thee Doll House III the drawing card is definitely not the food. Young women in skimpy lingerie are the attractions here, such as the skinny blonde, who approaches a man at the bar and whispers in his ear: "This is Ladies Choice, and I'm going to dance for you whether you like it or not."

With that, she unhooks her lacy red and black brassiere and climbs up on the bar. To the deafening rhythm of heavy metal music, she peels off her Day-Glo G-string. Nude except for high heels, she begins a slow, grinding dance, her eyes locked on the man below her who sips a glass of cola that cost $2.25. The dancer's name is "Denise." She's been dancing here for three weeks. "I like it most of the time," she says.

Tina Mancini called herself "Zena" when she danced nude for men at this Pompano Beach "Las Vegas Style Adult Show Club."

Unlike Denise, Tina found the job degrading, so much so, the Broward County State Attorney's Office says, that rather than keep dancing, she killed herself 19 months ago. She was 17.

Today, in a paneled Fort Lauderdale courtroom a half-hour drive from Thee Doll House III, closing arguments are expected in the child-abuse trial of Tina Mancini's mother. A Circuit Court jury of five women and one man must then decide whether Theresa Jackson caused her daughter's suicide by forcing her to work as a nude dancer and living off her earnings, which sometimes reached $1,000 a week.

In what Mrs. Jackson's lawyer calls "landmark proceedings," the state of Florida is taking the unprecedented step of seeking to hold a parent responsible for a child's suicide.

St. Petersburg Times

HOW I WROTE THE STORY

News is local, as we learned in Chapter 1. Readers and viewers want to know what's happening in their communities. But the boundaries of their interest can stretch beyond city limits.

Although it happened in Miami, five hours away, the trial of stripper Tina Mancini's mother interested my editors. It was unusual, to be sure, but also raised significant legal and social issues in an era of latchkey children and child abuse. Had it happened in St. Petersburg, the trial would have received ongoing coverage from us, but its out-of-town status merited just one staff-written story. The paper could rely on wire service coverage for the verdict. We were more interested in the story—and larger issues—behind the case than routine trial coverage. In short, perfect conditions for an anecdotal, or storytelling, lead: Use one when the story is the news.

With just one day to report, I flew to Fort Lauderdale and spent the day racing from the courtroom, where the trial was winding up, to the clerk's office, where I read the case file. But the heart of the story, I knew, was at the strip club where Tina had worked. When the judge recessed for lunch, I raced in a cab to Thee Doll House. Tina Mancini was dead, but at least I could describe where she worked.

I told the cabby to wait outside. I was at the bar, sipping my overpriced soda and jotting notes on the napkin when a dancer approached and said she was going to dance for me. I didn't stay long—the meter was running—and on the way out I identified myself as a reporter to a hostess and asked if I could talk to the manager or owner about Tina. No one was available, she said. Walking out, I jotted down the lunch special. Driving back to court, I realized I had my lead: The vivid scene in the bar conveyed Tina's life as a stripper and seemed an ideal way to draw readers into the story. To keep the pace moving, I used active verbs and concrete nouns. The description "skinny blonde" struck me as a vivid, if vague, description.

Readers are impatient, however; I didn't think they would wait more than two paragraphs to discover the context of the scene. So in paragraph 3, I made the shift from the stripper in the bar to Tina, using her stage name, "Zena," as a transition to report her fate. (Notice how the verb tense shifted as well. In the first two paragraphs, I used the present tense—"approaches," "unhooks"—as a device of dramatic narrative because I wanted readers to envision the scene.)

In paragraph 4, I introduced the news peg, the time element of the opening arguments starting "today," to emphasize the story's timeliness. Finally, in paragraph 5, the time had come to give my readers the context that would, I hoped, convince them that this story was not only interesting but also important and newsworthy.

There were other options, of course. I could have opened the story with the defendant, Tina's mother, or with court testimony. To me, the story's focus was ultimately about a girl's life and death, and because I couldn't interview Tina, I wanted to use her place of work as an entry point. By any measure, the lead is long and violates other traditions, such as including the reporter (without directly revealing my presence at the bar) and using past tense. Storytelling leads—and editors who trust the reporting behind them—allow for such departures.

Narrative leads can also be short.

Through the rush hour gridlock of weary commuters headed home, a vanload of noisy boys inches along U.S. 19. It's a Friday evening, and the Jordan Park Midgets are bound, they hope, for glory.

St. Petersburg Times

SIGNIFICANT DETAIL LEADS

They can also begin with a close-up of a significant or interesting detail.

WASHINGTON—In an Information Age first, the White House on Wednesday gave reporters its hefty 1,300-page health-care reform plan on a pair of computer disks weighing less than two ounces.

Knight Ridder

ROUND-UP LEADS

Stories that report trends often rely on leads that round up anecdotes, illustrations or examples to demonstrate a trend, as in this example about the role firearms play in teen suicides.

In the basement of his Lemont, Ill., home, 14-year-old Paul Hoffman puts the barrel of a .22-caliber rifle under his chin and pulls the trigger. The gun had been kept in his parents' bedroom closet. Paul's last words: "My father doesn't love me."

In rural Philadelphia, Miss., a 16-year-old girl shoots herself in the head after an argument with her boyfriend. She got the gun from her mother's car.

In suburban San Diego, Calif., a 15-year-old girl runs into her parents' bedroom after fighting with her mother. Minutes later, a shot rings out.

"I didn't think she knew where the gun was," her grief-stricken father said. "I didn't think she knew where I hid the bullets. I didn't think she knew we even had a gun."

Knight Ridder

EMBLEM LEADS

Using a single instance or individual to illustrate the theme of a story is a popular approach to putting a human face on a social problem. The problem of eating disorders among pre-teen girls is dramatized by a troubled child whose case is emblematic of the problem.

Worried about her weight, Sarah swore off dessert and cut back on meal portions. Eventually, she began skipping breakfast and was just nibbling at lunch and dinner. Within six months, she dropped 13 pounds.

A weight-loss success story? Not at all. Sarah is only 10 years old. Her diet cost her 20 percent of her weight.

Knight Ridder

EXPLODING THE MYTHS OF LEAD WRITING

Lead writing may be the writing activity most shrouded in myth—long-standing, often-unspoken rules that govern the way journalists write and edit the news. Among the reigning myths that you will undoubtedly confront:

- Leads must never begin with a quote. Try one in some newsrooms, and it will be sent back immediately for a rewrite.

- Leads must always contain attribution. Without identifying the source of the information, many editors will throw such a lead back with a snarl: "Oh, yeah, who says?"

- A good lead is never more than three or four lines long. Today's time-pressed readers won't sit still for anything longer than that. "Trim it," your editor will say.

- A lead must sum up the story in a paragraph. "This is a newspaper, Kid, not a novel," your editor will growl. "Give me the news, and do it in a paragraph."

There are often good reasons for these old rules. Remember: Every editor is also a reader and can pinpoint problems in your lead that confuse your audience. Most of these rules apply to the **summary lead,** which is a more rigid form. Storytelling leads can take more chances. Beginning reporters may do better being asked to stick to some rules. As your news judgment and writing skills grow, so will the confidence that allows you to write leads that set their own standards of excellence.

There are rules, of course: Leads must be accurate, logical, fair and syntactically correct. Few would disagree that a news lead should contain the most newsworthy elements. But when you begin reading successful leads, ones that make you want to keep on reading, which is the lead's most important function, you find that the best ones often seem not to follow rules, but rather to defy them, break them, make new rules. The central myth about the lead is that there are strict rules governing its construction, rules that can never be broken. Let's take another look at some of the myths:

Leads must never begin with a quote. A good guideline, but had Saul Pett of The Associated Press followed it, his readers would have been cheated of this revealing, in more than one way, opening to a 1963 profile of Dorothy Parker, the legendary tart-tongued writer of the 1930s:

"Are you married, my dear?"

"Yes, I am."

"Then you won't mind zipping me up."

Zipped up, Dorothy Parker turned to face her interviewer, and the world.

Leads must always contain attribution. Although it's important to let readers know where information in a story comes from, slavish allegiance to the principle can bog readers down with unnecessary clutter. In 1981, Patrick Sloyan of *Newsday* delivered "instant history" without resorting to attribution that would bog the reader down.

CAIRO—Egyptian President Anwar Sadat, a modern-day pharaoh who attempted to lead the Arab world toward a permanent Mideast peace with Israel, was assassinated yesterday by a band of soldiers who attacked a military parade reviewing stand with automatic rifles and hand grenades.

Newsday

In the very next paragraph, Sloyan quotes an "official medical bulletin" describing Sadat's mortal wounds, leaving no mystery about the source of his information.

A good lead is never more than three or four lines long. Keep it short is always a good prescription for the news writer, but readers would have been cheated of an insight into the voyeuristic role of the audience at freak shows had David Finkel heeded it in his profile of T. J. Albert Jackson, a carnival performer billed as "The World's Biggest Man."

COCOA—Behold the fat man. Go ahead. Everybody does. He doesn't mind, honestly. That's how he makes his living. Walk right up to him. Stand there and look. Stand there and look. Stand there and gape. Gape at the layers of fat, the astonishing girth, the incredible bulk. Imagine him in a bathtub. Or better, on a bike. Or better yet, on one of those flimsy antique chairs. *Boom!* If you're lucky, maybe he'll lift his shirt. If you're real lucky, maybe he'll rub his belly. Don't be shy. Ask him a question.

St. Petersburg Times

A lead must sum up the story in a paragraph. Readers won't wait, proponents of this rule insist. They want the entire story, compressed like sardines in a can, in the lead. In many instances, that's true. I knew I was taking a gamble with a deliberately suspenseful lead on the following story about the traumatic birth of a baby. But I figured readers would want, would need, to know what was going to happen, and I could make them read until the end to find out. Positive feedback from readers and a first-place feature-writing award convinced me the gamble paid off.

In the labor room at Kent County Memorial Hospital, Jackie Rushton rose from the stretcher, her face pale and smeared with tears. A nurse pressed the fetal pulse detector against her abdomen, a taut mound stretched by seven months of pregnancy. The detector was blue, the size and shape of a pocket flashlight with earphones attached, and Jackie Rushton's eyes fixed on the nurse who strained to hear the bird-like beating of her baby's heart.

"Here's the heartbeat," the nurse said after several moments of silence. "It's 126, and it's fine."

If there's a heartbeat, why isn't she giving me the earphones so I can listen? Jackie thought. That's what the doctor always does when I have my check-ups. First he listens, and then he says, "Here's the heartbeat. Listen." She didn't say, "Here's the heartbeat. Listen."

I've lost the baby. The baby's gone.

The Providence Evening Bulletin

DISCOVERING THE POINT: HOW TO WRITE A LEAD

Lead writing is hard work. Jack Cappon of The Associated Press called it, rightly, "the agony of square one." To write an effective lead you have to know, first and foremost, what the story is about. That's where critical thinking comes in.

Start with the five W's and an H:

1. What happened?
2. Who did it happen to?
3. Where did it happen?
4. When did it happen? When is it going to happen?
5. Why did it happen?
6. How did it happen?

Equipped with that knowledge, you next logically zero in on the two basic focusing questions:

1. What's the news?
2. What's this story about?

Here are some suggestions that experienced reporters find helpful in their quest for a lead:

- Write your lead before you do your reporting. Earlier in this chapter, you read a lead about the nomination of Dr. Joycelyn Elders as surgeon general. That lead began in a cab as I rode toward the U.S. Capitol before the Senate had even voted. It was already mid-afternoon; I wouldn't have much time to make the early evening deadlines of our papers across the country. I scribbled a tentative lead in my notebook. I wasn't writing fiction but rather drawing on background from my regular reading of the news and an earlier story I had written about Elders. And, of course, I still had to sit through the debate on the Senate floor and wait for the votes to be tallied, but even before the final vote was cast, I had a lead that focused my thinking, reporting and writing. Most important, I had a lead I could revise.

- Don't spend all your time on the lead. Get on base, as Saul Pett of The Associated Press said. To find your lead, interview your best source: yourself. You've reported the story; you are the best authority you have.

- Try to put yourself in the role of the reader or viewer. What is the most important information the reader needs to know? Why does this news matter?

- Look for the tension in a lead. Effective leads provoke a question.

FINDING THE TENSION

"Many stories are best told by depicting tension between forces," Don Murray says in *Writing for Your Readers.* As you read in Chapter 1, the news media are widely criticized, often justifiably so, for their preoccupation with conflict. But tension, when two forces compete with each other, is not the same as conflict, when two forces attack each other. One way to inject tension is to introduce competing elements in the lead. The juxtaposition raises a question, an element of suspense, that is the key to draw the reader in.

To find the tension, ask yourself whether there is anything you've witnessed or heard about in your reporting that illustrates the core of the problem. In Chapter 3, you learned the importance of finding a focus to organize and develop your story. Notice how often tension is present in successful leads that you read.

In the following lead, reporting student Steve Myers used the natural tension between two kinds of objects swimming in the canal behind a waterside community.

BROADWATER—On any given morning, residents can look out over their backyard docks and see dolphins, tarpon and manatees swimming in the channels that lead out to Boca Ciega Bay. If it's high tide, they can also see floating aluminum cans, plastic bags and yard clippings.

Because dolphins, tarpon and manatees don't mix well with floating garbage, the reader understandably wants to know what is bringing them together. Steve could have written a lead that told readers about the problem: *Broadwater residents are complaining about yard clippings and litter collecting in the canals behind their homes.* Instead, he followed the classic "show, don't tell, rule," which allowed readers to visualize the problem and compelled them to read on to learn more about it.

Mystery novelists—and smart journalists—know the value of tension. When Jonathan Dube of *The Charlotte Observer* put this lead on top of a crime story, an editor nominated it for an in-house writing award with this comment: "You could have seen this sentence as the opening of a mystery novel."

Three bodies, two counties, one case, no suspects.

Just eight words, but each one so familiar, especially in these pairs, that this lead has the intrigue of a mind-twister. In addition, note the tension in the descending order of numbers: 3-2-1-0. But the professional knows that the news consumer, however fascinated, doesn't have the patience of a mystery reader. In the very next paragraph, Dube lets the reader in on the secret:

Tuesday morning, investigators found two burned bodies in the trunk of a smoldering car in southern York County and a 17-year-old boy shot to death in northern Lancaster County.

"The next big question would be how these murders are related to each other," said York County Sheriff Bruce Bryant. "We can't say. We don't know yet. But we believe there's a connection, and that connection would be their affiliation with each other. They were acquaintances."

But, he added, "We don't believe they did this to each other."

The Charlotte Observer

Choosing the Right Lead

But which lead is the right one for your story?

It depends on your news organization, the news and the timing of publication. When Merriman Smith of United Press International was riding in a press car with President John F. Kennedy's motorcade in Dallas on Nov. 22, 1963, and heard shots ring out, he didn't begin his story with a description of Jacqueline Kennedy's pink suit and pillbox hat. He had news to report. Grabbing the one phone in the car and dodging punches from his Associated Press competitor, he dictated these words:

> **"Three shots were fired at President Kennedy's motorcade today in downtown Dallas, Texas. ..."**

■

But in an age when technology gives the ability to transmit the outbreak of war live on television, newspaper editors are changing their opinions about which leads to use. Here are guidelines you can use to make your decision:

- **TIME:** Did the story just happen? Are you the first to report it, or will most people in your audience already know about it from another news source? Is the time element crucial?

- **READERS' NEEDS:** Will your readers get the news first from you? If they already know the news, would they be better served with a lead that anticipates their knowledge?

- **EXCLUSIVITY:** Are you the only news organization that has the story? Scoops once counted for a lot more in the days when several newspapers published in a city. Now the competition is from television and online. But there may be stories only you have, and you might want to tell the reader this is an exclusive. Three days after terrorist bombs exploded outside the U.S. Embassy in Nairobi, Kenya, on Aug. 7, 1998, killing hundreds and injuring thousands, *Washington Post* foreign correspondent Stephen Buckley was the first reporter to disclose details about events that preceded the attack. That exclusive information became his lead:

NAIROBI, Aug. 9—The vehicle that apparently contained the bomb that exploded here Friday morning was driven first to the main entrance of the compound, but guards refused to let it pass and sent it to the rear of the building, an embassy official said today.

The Washington Post
Aug. 10, 1998

"A lead is like your face. It's what stirs up further interest. Step out with a blob of tapioca pudding on your cheek, and you won't have to worry about conversation. A cheapjack lead is the blob of tapioca pudding: a clue that the person behind it isn't trying very hard."

—Mitch Broder, staff writer, Gannett Suburban Newspapers

Read the story behind Merriman Smith's scoop online at http://ajr.newslink.org/ajrsloyanMay98.html

Another image of terror, this one from Nairobi, Kenya, where a bomb that exploded outside the American Embassy on Aug. 7, 1998, killed more than 200 and wounded thousands. (AP/Wide World Photos)

"There is no one way to do leads. It is difficult—and perhaps dangerous—to set out a list of rules for the right and wrong way of leads. Leads need to be both creative and functional, but creativity should not undermine functional, and functionality should not undermine creativity."

—JACQUI BANASZYNSKI, *THE SEATTLE TIMES*

AVOIDING CLICHÉS OF LEAD WRITING

Have you made sure you're avoiding the pitfalls of lead writing, leads that make editors groan, teachers wince and readers turn the page? Is your newspaper lead better suited as a tease for a television report (*Tragedy occurs when car hits school bus.*)? Are you relying on a gimmick, such as fakeout leads (*It's just a dream.* or *Bill is an elephant.*)?

Mitch Broder, a staff writer for Gannett Suburban Newspapers, identified 10 clichés of lead writing and suggested three ways to avoid them in *Write On*, a newsletter produced by the group's writing coach, Jean Patman. Broder says: "Even a great lead can't guarantee that a reader won't stop reading. But when I come upon one of these, I usually won't even start."

1. The "move over" lead

Move over, Steven Spielberg, here comes Larry Bulansky of Shrub Oak.

2. The "came early" lead

Easter came early for Irma Blumkin, when gang members pelted her with nine dozen eggs.

3. The "one word as paragraph" lead

Springtime.
Baseball.
Lentils.
Herpes.

4. The "one word and 'ah'" lead

Ah, springtime.
Ah, baseball.
Ah, lentils.
Ah, herpes.

5. The "eating Baked Alaska in his posh hotel suite" lead

Elvis Presley is eating Baked Alaska in his posh hotel suite.

6. The quote lead

"Let's get a few more Baked Alaskas up here," Elvis Presley hollers from his posh hotel suite.

7. The question lead

So, just what is a Baked Alaska?

8. The recipe lead

Take a heaping helping of Fairbanks.

9. The "times, they are a-changin'" lead

This week in Purdys, the times they are a-changin'.

10. The "'tis the season" lead

'Tis the season to think for half a minute or until we come up with something original.

THREE WAYS TO AVOID CLICHÉD LEADS

1. **LOOK AROUND.** I was just starting out in 1978. I soon discovered that the "move over" lead appears somewhere daily. It's off-the-rack journalese, like "the end of an era." Which, as I recall, I also made up.

2. **THINK AGAIN.** Even if you've never seen a story start with "The times, they are a-changin'," consider whether some other story somewhere might have. When something is the first thing that pops into your head, yours is probably not the first head it popped into.

3. **BOYCOTT GENERICS.** Every story could start with a quote. Or a word. Or an "Ah." But very few stories, if any, should.

Broder's final word on leads: "Write something that could be written only for what you are writing. It may still turn out rotten. But you'll have only yourself to blame."

REVISING YOUR LEAD

In the introduction to his collection of classic first paragraphs by the likes of Tolstoy, J. D. Salinger and Carson McCullers, novelist Donald Newlove writes, "Genius or not, no writer in this book struck off a perfect opening at first try."

Look at manuscripts by the great writers, and you find pages "tattooed with second thoughts ... slashed pages, gutted paragraphs and scratched-in revisions right up to deadline."

So it should be for you. Some leads, a few miraculous ones, will fly off your fingers and appear, as if by magic, on the computer screen before you. But most are the product of hard work, of cutting and moving and pasting, asking tough questions, searching for the right word. Don't assume that once you've written a lead, you have a lead, whether it works or not—it's there, stuck on top of the story like a great hunk of cement. Think instead of leads like a piece of clay that you can play with and refine.

TESTING THE ANECDOTAL LEAD

Anecdotal leads have come in for lots of criticism over the years. Done poorly, the anecdotal lead can be a self-indulgent device for the writer and a confusing bore for the reader. Bait-and-switch is a common failing of storytelling leads. The story begins with an anecdote that may be lively, vivid and eminently readable, but just as it engages the reader, the tone shifts into a completely different approach. In stories like this, the person introduced in the lead never appears again. The result: reader confusion and disappointment.

Jacqui Banaszynski, a Pulitzer Prize–winning news storyteller and editor who has high standards for her own and others' writing, recommends three tests for an anecdotal lead:

1. Can you easily write from the anecdote to the story's nut graf? If not, if you keep getting stuck there and struggling to transit into the story, it's likely the anecdote doesn't serve as the lead. It might be fine and purposeful, but possibly it belongs somewhere else in the body of the copy.
2. Write the story with the anecdote, then excise the anecdote and read the story without it. Does the story suffer? If not, if you don't miss it, it's probably not serving much purpose. Because we are all wedded to our words, get an independent read for this test.
3. Show that independent reader (your editor or another reporter) your anecdote as a stand-alone item, without the story hanging below it. Then ask that person what he or she thinks the story is going to be about. If that person captures the essence, you're home free. If not, rethink your approach.

TIPS FOR REVISING LEADS

- **FOLLOW THE "READ ALOUD" RULE.** Always read your lead aloud. Give your lead a "breath test," that is, can you say it in a single breath? Do you stumble over words? Does it sound like something you'd tell a friend over the phone? Does it put you to sleep or confuse you? It will do the same for your reader.

- **PLAY THE REVISION GAME.** Count the words and see how many you can eliminate from the lead.

There are many good ways to enter a story. Just because a lead appears in print, even in the best newspapers, doesn't mean it can't be revised. In fact, it may build your confidence to rewrite a published lead. To demonstrate, let me take a shot at *The New York Times* lead about the early morning robbery that appeared earlier in this chapter.

NEW YORK—A frenzied crossfire broke the morning calm of a quiet Queens neighborhood Friday as masked robbers ambushed the two guards of a payroll shipment, leaving the security men—a retired police officer and an off-duty detective—bleeding on the sidewalk with more than a dozen bullet wounds, the authorities said.

As noted earlier, this lead is 50 words long and takes three breaths to read aloud. First, let's try knocking out some of the adjectives.

NEW YORK—A crossfire [Have you ever heard of a relaxed crossfire? Cut "frenzied."] broke the calm of a quiet Queens neighborhood Friday [Does the reader have to know it happened in the morning in the lead? Put the exact time in the second graf.] as masked robbers ambushed a payroll shipment, leaving the two guards—a retired police officer and an off-duty detective [Lead gives three descriptions of the guards. Two is enough.]—bleeding on the sidewalk with multiple ["More than a dozen bullet wounds" is more precise, but it takes six words.] bullet wounds, the authorities said.

This version eliminated nine words. Now you take a whack at it.

- **IS IT ACCURATE?** In the attempt to make leads brighter, stronger and clearer, writers and editors have been known to inject errors into the story. Refer to the accuracy checklist in Chapter 3.
- **PUT YOUR LEADS ON A "TO BE"-FREE DIET.** Replace all forms of passive verbs—"is planning," "are hoping"—with active verbs—"plan," "hope."

Vigorous sentences follow subject-verb-object format. "Passive voice twists sentences out of their normal shape," says *Oregonian* editor and writing coach Jack Hart. "That flabby form of English, more than anything else, chains newspapers to a dull and plodding style." Thus, the lead *The West Hills home of a prominent business executive **was destroyed** in a fire Monday morning* is stronger and actually more precise written as *A Monday morning fire **destroyed** a prominent business executive's West Hills home.* The fire is the subject, the actor, whereas the house is the object, which receives the action.

- **ELIMINATE JARGON AND CLICHÉS.** Strive for fresh language. Lawyers, politicians and bureaucrats thrive on arcane language. **Jargon** bewilders and distances readers. **Clichés** bore them. Read William Zinsser's *On Writing Well* for sound advice on ways to avoid both.
- **REDUCE REDUNDANCIES AND UNNECESSARY WORDS.** Which of these two is stronger?

Stricken by a nameless grief, Jesus grew very sad, and sitting in the garden he wept copious tears.

Or:

Jesus wept.

Tell Me the News, Tell Me a Story: A Lead Writing Workshop

To prepare you for the challenges of writing leads on deadline, here is a writing workshop that will enable you to put into practice the strategies and techniques covered in this chapter.

Following you will find details on the story as well as notes taken at the scene and the transcript of an interview. Use these real-life reporting materials to practice your lead writing skills. For further help, consult the checklists on focusing, mapping, drafting and revising stories found in Chapter 3. Your assignment is to read the following material and then craft a series of "Tell me the news" and "Tell me a story" leads.

The Assignment

It's a dead Saturday in June. Everybody else in the world is at the beach; you're stuck on the early cops beat, the 3–11 p.m. shift monitoring arrests, accidents and other police news. You're taking advantage of the lull to work on a Monday City Page feature when the city desk gets a call: There's a jumper on the police station roof. You and a photographer run out the door. It's 2 p.m.

At the Scene

You run into a stonewall at the stationhouse. The desk sergeant isn't talking and won't let you near the roof. But you luck out. The photographer's aunt lives in the high-rise apartment building right next door to the police station. You spend the next 90 minutes watching the drama from a window that looks directly onto the roof; however, you can't hear anything being said. Eventually, the jumper is talked out of leaping and is led back inside the stationhouse.

Interviews

The stonewall at the front desk is even higher now. A cop you know says the jumper is a former cop, but the brass isn't talking. You head back to the newsroom, hoping the one ace up your sleeve works out. You recognized the cop who seemed to be doing most of the talking to the jumper, and you place a call to him at the cop shop. It's definitely your day. You reach him before his bosses tell him to shut up, and he tells you what happened on the roof. All you have to do is write it for the next morning's paper.

Notes From the Scene

From a Reporter's Notebook

Saturday June 30 2:05 p.m. Jumper on police station roof.
Cop shop. Front desk. Sgt. R. Tamburini: "No comment."
Can't go up to roof.
2:08 p.m.

Continued

Watching from apartment at Regency Apartments opposite Providence police headquarters.

400 Fountain Street, Providence.

On roof: Man, alone, sitting on cornice overlooking Fountain Street.

Holding pistol, chrome-plated, in hand. Caliber?

Sturdy looking, about 30, brown hair, drooping mustache.

Brown pants, western-style calico shirt.

Building five stories high.

Roof gravel covered.

Radar screen and antenna on roof.

Sunny day. Puffy clouds in blue sky.

One level below, a uniform cop stands by a green metal ladder leading to roof.

2:10 p.m. Another cop approaches: Lt. William Lawton, personnel director, wearing brown uniform pants, white shirt. Climbs ladder, starts talking to man with gun.

2:40 p.m.

More cops arrive. Top brass, chaplain. In civilian clothes. They stand to the side.

Lt. Lawton is doing most of the talking with another cop, Det. Richard Solgot.

3:05 p.m.

Cop arrives with a soda. Solgot rolls the can to jumper. It stops several feet away. Jumper stands up to get it, puts barrel of pistol against his temple and holds it there until he gets soda in his hand and returns to edge of roof.

3:10 p.m.

Jumper seems to be taking pills. Tranquilizers???

Lawton still talking, arguing with jumper.

3:37 p.m.

Jumper throws gun at Lawton. Other cops leap at him.

3:40 p.m.

Cops help him away from edge of roof. Man is unsteady on feet. They hold his arms. Cop climbs down ladder, holds man's waistband, backs him down steps. They disappear through roof door.

3:42 p.m.

Lawton alone on roof. Empty Coke can on gravel. He's holding pistol. Shakes bullets out into his palm. Walks to edge of roof and climbs down ladder.

3:50 p.m.
Police station. Front desk. Sgt. Tamburini.
ID of jumper. No comment.
Former cop? No comment.
How get to roof? No comment.
Statement from chief? No comment.

INTERVIEW TRANSCRIPT

4 P.M. TELEPHONE INTERVIEW WITH LT. DONALD W. LAWTON
Man on roof was George L. Gregoire, used to be one of my men. Taught him ropes.
Gregoire's age? 31.
"I helped him with regards to writing out reports, police procedures. You may learn the basic knowledge in the academy, but when you get out in the street it's a little different."
Gregoire on force for 10 years. Patrolman. 1982, assigned to locate parking tag scofflaws, get them to court to pay back tickets.
Retired on disability about 7 months ago. Back injury.
Lawton on duty today? No.
Spent morning leading department color guard in Gaspee Days Parade. Hot and sweaty in dress uniform.
Got back to station a little before 2 p.m. Heading out door. Heading home to get wife and drive to Cornwall, small town outside Hartford, Conn., for weekend with married daughter Nancy.
Just walked out door of police garage on Broadway when Lt. Devine in Traffic stopped me.
"You better get inside. We just received a call. Gregoire, the retired officer, is on the top of the roof with a gun."
About 10 years ago, I was patrol sergeant in charge of half a dozen patrolmen on city's East Side. "I was their steady sergeant." (police lingo) Gregoire worked for me.
"As soon as I found out it was George, I couldn't get there fast enough because I had a lot of respect for him. When he

Continued

worked for me he gave me 100 percent. I just didn't want him to do harm to himself, that's all. I thought I could help."

I ran up stairs, ran up to roof. Found Lt. Higgins (James) waiting on level below where Gregoire sat.

I told Higgins, "Let me go first, I know him."

Lawton climbed ladder to the roof.

Gregoire had gun. .38 chrome-plated special.

Gun loaded? Yes. Six bullets.

Got about 30 feet away, started talking to him. Put hands over my head. Show unarmed.

"I'm coming to you. You can shoot me if you want, George."

He said, "I'm not going to shoot you. I'm going to shoot myself."

I said, "George, this is not you. I know you. I'm your friend."

He said, "I have no friends."

"You forgot me. You forgot me," Gregoire yelled.

"He was all fouled up. He was sick. He was going to jump off the building first but he didn't like the height."

He had decided instead to shoot himself. He swallowed several pills from a bottle he carried.

We started talking. Gregoire said he had money problems, marriage problems. Missed police work. Thought friends on force forgot about him.

Said he planned to go to church this morning and shoot himself in front of the congregation, but decided against it because he didn't want to upset any children who would be there. Instead, he climbed to the police station roof "because people over here don't like him."

"I talked to him. Solgot talked to him." Det. Richard Solgot, Juvenile Division. He was in F Troop too.

F Troop? Nickname for East Side patrol.

Cajoled. Coaxed. Pleaded. Give us gun. Give up.

Talked about the old times. Patrols. Arrests.

"You know, little things, even the way he shined his shoes. Anything to keep his mind off jumping or shooting himself."

Gregoire has kids. Talked about them. How embarrassed they would be if their father did anything bad.

"That helped."

He used the soda to take pills. Pills started taking toll.

Kind of pills? Some sort of tranquilizer.

"The more pills he took, the slower he got in his reactions. He got relaxed and he gave up, changed his mind. Who knows what goes on in people's minds."

Lawton: Ever talk anybody out of jumping before?

Once, long time ago, when rookie, helped talk a man off the roof at the Veterans Administration Hospital.

Another time, helped talk a father who had a gun trained on two of his children into surrendering.

Ever had special training? No.

"They teach us in the academy how to deal with different experiences and you get experience as you go along, how to talk to people. I think you just need common sense, a feeling toward another person."

What happened to Gregoire?

Examined by doctor at station. Taken by rescue to Rhode Island Hospital. Doctors there alerted about situation. Condition stable.

How did Gregoire get to roof? Don't know.

"He was a good policeman, no doubt about it, but he got fouled up."

ID: LT. DONALD W. LAWTON

Bureau of Personnel and Public Relations

Acting Personnel Director 25-year veteran

LEAD WRITING: THE COACHING WAY

- What do you want to do: Tell the news or tell a story? Why? What do your readers or viewers need to know?
- How fresh is the news you're reporting? Will your news organization be the first to report it, or will people already have read or heard about it?
- Have you scanned other news media: competing publications, online sites, television and radio news outlets?
- Talk about your leads. Tell someone your story and listen to his or her reaction. Do you answer his or her first question in the lead? Shouldn't you? Follow Jacqui Banaszynski's advice: "Learn to *summarize* what you really want to say, then say it directly and gracefully and with some passion."
- Reread "Avoiding Clichés of Lead Writing" by Mitch Broder on pp. 139–42. Trade stories with a classmate or colleague and go on a cliché hunt. Collect them and promise yourself you'll take the extra step to go beyond clichés in your own writing.

GLOSSARY OF IMPORTANT TERMS

Anecdotal lead. A lead that begins with an anecdote, a compressed story that illustrates the story theme or situation. May include narrative elements, such as characters, dialogue and setting. Usually one to three paragraphs long. Longer than that may lose reader interest. Also known as feature, soft or delayed lead.

Cliché. A descriptive term or phrase that has been used so much it has lost its power.

Emblem lead. Lead that uses a single instance or person to illustrate story's theme.

Five W's. Who, what, where, when, why. Asks questions that are typically, but not always, answered in a lead. May also include an H (how?) and SW (so what?).

Jargon. The specialized vocabulary of a group, such as a profession.

Lead (also spelled "lede"). The beginning of a news report and story. Usually the first paragraph, although can be more.

Round-up lead. Lead that brings together two or three anecdotes, illustrations or examples that demonstrate a trend.

Summary lead. Lead that sums up major news elements, often answering several of the five W's, usually in a single paragraph. Also known as straight, hard or wire service lead.

EXERCISES

1. Take today's issue of your local newspaper and identify the types of leads being used.

2. Take a national story and compare the various approaches used by different news organizations.

3. Is your cliché meter running? Are rescue workers sifting through debris? Must police dodge a "hail of bullets"? Study your work and the work you read for clichés.

4. Look at the last five leads you wrote and put a label on them. Experiment with other types.

5. Collect favorite leads. Copy them into your daybook. (Make sure you include the source and byline so you avoid the risk of plagiarism.) Deconstruct them: What did the writer include, leave out?

6. Pick a major story and collect as many leads as possible. Compare and contrast the different approaches. Discuss which is more successful and why. Write your own version.

READINGS

Cappon, Rene J. *The Word: An Associated Press Guide to Good News Writing.* New York: The Associated Press, 1982.

Clark, Roy Peter. *The American Conversation and the Language of Journalism.* St. Petersburg, Fla.: The Poynter Institute for Media Studies, 1995.

Hart, Jack. "The Lexicon of Leads." *Second Takes—Monthly Reflections on The Oregonian,* vol. 8, no. 11, March 1997, pp. 1–3, 7.

Newlove, Donald. *First Paragraphs: Inspired Openings for Writers and Readers.* New York: Henry Holt, 1992.

HOTLIST

http://www.newslink.org

Newspapers on the World Wide Web. Journalism students have the world's leads at their fingertips every day. Point your browser to any newspaper, broadcast or online news site and study the leads written by professionals. *American Journalism Review* offers a comprehensive list of news links in all media.

http://ajr.newslink.org/ajrsloyanmay98.html

"Total Domination" by Patrick Sloyan. An insider's account of Merriman Smith's scoop for UPI on the day President John F. Kennedy was assassinated. Gives insight into the relationship between competition and deadline writing.

http://www.scripps.ohiou.edu/mediahistory/mhmjour.htm

"The Evolution of the Summary News Lead." An interesting exploration of the societal forces that helped shape newswriting style 100 years ago. It also challenges historian David Mindich's theory of the inverted pyramid's history described in Chapter 5.

CHAPTER

5

STORY FORM: SHAPING THE NEWS

CHAPTER FOCUS

Like an architect, an effective news writer knows that form follows content.

CHAPTER LESSONS

- Story forms
- Writing the inverted pyramid
- Writing the hourglass
- Writing the nut graf story
- Writing the narrative
- The "five boxes" approach
- Writing the serial narrative
- A serial narrative glossary
- The inverted pyramid: past, present, future
- Shaping the news: The Coaching Way

INTRODUCTION

Stories need a shape, a structure, in the same way a building needs a frame and our bodies a skeleton. Ernest Hemingway, a one-time reporter who became one of America's most influential novelists, had this in mind when he said, "Prose is architecture, not interior decoration." Effective writers understand this and make sure their toolbox contains a variety of story shapes. This chapter introduces traditional story forms widely used by news writers—inverted pyramid, hourglass, nut graf and narratives—and describes the late 20th-century renaissance of a popular 19th-century form: the **serial narrative.**

STORY FORMS

Architects and writers follow the same rule: Form follows content. That means before you design a container you determine what you need to put inside. You wouldn't try to ship an elephant in a shoebox.

The best stories create their own shape; writers consider their material, determine what they want the story to say and then decide on the best way to say it. But journalists, like all writers, sometimes rely on tried-and-true forms and formulas. You need to be familiar with these forms whether or not you decide to write your story in a completely new way. Depending on the news organization you work for, you may be expected to report the news following one or more journalistic conventions of story form. The forms described in this chapter have been used for a long time, the oldest ever since humans began telling stories. But they remain relevant even to those on the cutting edge of new media.

Bill Mitchell

"It's difficult to overestimate the importance of Hemingway's point about stories being written in established forms," says Bill Mitchell, a veteran journalist and pioneer in online journalism who puts great faith in the importance of story forms. After more than 20 years as a reporter and foreign correspondent for the *Detroit Free Press*, he launched an interactive service at the *Detroit Free Press*, directed the online service of the *San Jose Mercury News*, and was editor and director of development for Universal New Media, before joining The Poynter Institute in 1999 as editor of its Web site. "Formulaic writing," he argues, "has gotten a bad name. Done right, it diverts creatively from formula in ways that serve the needs of the story at hand. Tying the reporting, as well as the writing, to the form lends a discipline and focus that produce better stories."

Mitchell's point is an important one for 21st-century journalists: All story forms evolve from previous forms. If you're intent on breaking new ground, or work for a news organization where the forms are changing, your knowledge of tried-and-true story forms will be of great use.

INVERTED PYRAMID: FROM THE TOP DOWN

Developed more than a century ago to take advantage of a new communications technology, the **inverted pyramid** remains a controversial yet widely used method of reporting news and will have a future in the 21st century, journalists in all media agree.

The inverted pyramid puts the most newsworthy information at the top, and then the remaining information follows in order of importance, with the least important at the bottom.

Historians argue over when the form was created. But they agree that the invention of the telegraph sparked its development so that it had entered into common use by newspapers and the newly formed wire service organizations by the beginning of the 20th century.

One of the first inverted pyramid leads was written by an Associated Press reporter after Abraham Lincoln was assassinated in April 1865:

To The Associated Press
Washington, Friday, April 14, 1865

> The President was shot in a theater to-night
> and perhaps mortally wounded.

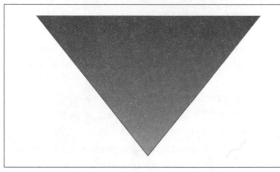

The information is presented to the reader in descending levels of importance.

Traditional wire service style. Useful for breaking news. Editors can cut from the bottom.

Popularized by newspapers during the 20th century, the inverted pyramid is a mainstay of online news reporting. The most newsworthy information goes at the top of the story.

The pyramid has to be big at the top because it must answer all the questions that readers have. Remaining information is arranged in diminishing order of importance. The conventions of the inverted pyramid require the reporter to summarize the story, to get to the heart, to the point, to sum up quickly and concisely the answer to the question: What's the news? The pyramid approach addresses the most important questions at the top of the story. It states the thesis and then provides supporting material.

Journalism has a love-hate relationship with the inverted pyramid. Its supporters consider it a useful form, especially good for breaking news. The inverted pyramid, or at least its most substantial element—the summary lead—is used widely and is one of the most recognizable shapes in communications today. You'll find it on the front and inside pages of most newspapers as well as in stories distributed worldwide by The Associated Press, Reuters and other news services. The inverted pyramid is also the dominant form in the news sections of America Online and on news sites elsewhere on the Internet.

"The inverted pyramid organizes stories not around ideas or chronologies but around facts," says journalism historian Mitchell Stephens in *A History of News*. "It weighs and shuffles the various pieces of information, focusing with remarkable single-mindedness on their relative news value."

Critics of the inverted pyramid say it's outdated, unnatural, boring, artless and a factor in the declining readership that newspapers have been grappling with for decades. The inverted pyramid, its critics say, tells the story backward and is at odds with the storytelling tradition that features a beginning, middle and end. Rather than rewarding a reader with a satisfying conclusion, the pyramid loses steam and peters out, in a sense defying readers to stay awake, let alone read on. Despite the criticism, the pyramid survives.

B-1 Bomber Explodes in Kentucky

The Associated Press
Filed at 4:14 p.m. EST
February 18, 1998

MARION, Ky.—An Air Force bomber on a routine training mission crashed Wednesday in a rural section of western Kentucky and exploded. All four crew members survived.

The B-1B bomber was flying out of Dyess Air Force Base near Abilene, Texas, said First Lt. Eric Elliott of Langley Air Force Base in Virginia.

The bomber had four aboard, its usual load, and all were found alive after the crash, state police dispatcher Jason Pelfrey said. Their conditions were not immediately known.

Witnesses said the craft burst into a ball of fire with debris raining down in the vicinity of Mattoon, a community five miles northeast of Marion.

"I saw a big mushroom fireball come up," said Billy Hinchee, who lives nearby.

The bomber was not one of the additional warplanes being dispatched to the Persian Gulf, Air Force officials said. T. J. Gibson, an Air Force spokeswoman, said officials were trying to determine if the bomber was carrying any live weapons.

Military police from Fort Campbell, Ky., were securing the scene of the crash. There was no immediate word as to its cause.

The B-1B "Lancer" bomber is one of three long-range heavy bombers in the Air Force arsenal, in addition to the B-2 Stealth bomber and the venerable B-52. With its adjustable, swept-back wings, it can fly intercontinental bombing missions without refueling.

Designed in the 1970s as a nuclear bomb-dropper, the plane has been converted since then for conventional missions and is being deployed to the Mideast for the first time in a potential combat role.

Last September, a pilot's attempt to perform an uncommon but permissible maneuver led to a crash of a B-1B bomber that killed all four people aboard.

The Air Force reported in December that the pilot of the $200-million plane was making a sharp right turn during a Sept. 19 training mission on the Montana prairie when the plane neared stall speed and crashed. The technique is uncommon, but not forbidden.

That crash was the sixth military air disaster in a seven-day period, and it prompted an unprecedented 24-hour grounding of military planes for safety training.

However, at 1.37 crashes per 100,000 flying hours in the fiscal year ending Sept. 30, the Air Force reported it had its fourth safest year ever.

In the memorable phrase of Bruce DeSilva of The Associated Press, "The inverted pyramid remains the Dracula of journalism. It keeps rising from its coffin and sneaking into the paper."

There are good reasons for this staying power. Many readers are impatient and want stories to get to the point immediately. In fast-breaking news situations, when events and circumstances may change rapidly, the pyramid allows the news writer to rewrite the top of the story continually, keeping it up-to-date. It's also an extremely useful tool for thinking and organizing because it forces the reporter to sum up the point of the story in a single paragraph. Journalism students who master it and then go on to other fields say it comes in handy for writing everything from legal briefs to grant applications.

The inverted pyramid can be a challenging form for some journalists, at least it was for me when I began reporting. Summing up three hours of a school board meeting or trying to answer the five W's about a fatal car accident in a single paragraph, then deciding what other information belonged in the story—and in what order—was arduous and frustrating, especially with the clock ticking to deadline. Also as a beginner, I usually didn't have the knowledge of the subjects I covered to easily answer the central question posed by the event: What was newsworthy about it, and in what order? I resisted the disciplined thinking the pyramid demands, and like many reporters, scorned the form as uncreative and stilted. I preferred the storytelling approach of the fiction writer to the "just the facts" style of the reporter. Over time it became easier, and I came to see that the form helps develop the powers of critical thinking, analysis and synthesis that are the foundation of clarity in thinking and writing. The inverted pyramid is a basic building block of journalistic style.

In the days of "hot type" printing, when stories had to be trimmed to fit a finite space, the inverted pyramid allowed editors, even the compositors who made up the pages in the back shop, to cut stories from the bottom up: no news judgment required. Technology continues to wield its influence. With studies showing that those who get their news from computers don't want to look at more than a screen at a time, it's not surprising that the inverted pyramid is widely used by online news organizations. Like it or not, the reporter of the 21st century must master this form.

THE HOURGLASS: SERVING THE NEWS, SERVING THE READER

In 1983, Roy Peter Clark began to notice something new as he read his morning paper. It wasn't the news; it was the way the news was being told. In their stories, reporters seemed to be combining two forms: the inverted pyramid and the **narrative.** Clark was a likely discoverer. A college English literature professor-turned-newspaper writing coach and reporter, he used his skills as a literary scholar and his experience in the newsroom to deconstruct the form. In an article published in the *Washington Journalism Review* (since renamed *American Journalism Review*), he described this form and gave it a distinctive name: the **hourglass.** News writers who adopted the hourglass were combining narrative elements that contained the power of storytelling with the inverted pyramid. It provided an alternative, Clark said, "that respects traditional news values, considers the needs of the reader, takes advantage of narrative, and spurs the writer to new levels of reporting."

The hourglass story can be broken into three parts:

THE TOP. Here you deliver the news in a summary lead, followed by three or four paragraphs that answer the reader's most pressing questions. In the top you give the basic news, enough to satisfy a time-pressed reader. You report the story in its most concise form. If all that is read is the top, the reader is still informed. Because it's limited to four to six paragraphs, the top of the story should contain only the most significant information.

THE TURN. Here you signal the reader that a narrative, usually chronological, is beginning. Usually, the turn is a transitional phrase that contains attribution for the narrative that follows—"according to police," "eyewitnesses described the event this way," "the shooting unfolded this way, law enforcement sources and neighbors agree."

THE NARRATIVE. The story has three elements: a beginning, middle and end. The bottom allows the writer to tell a chronological narrative complete with detail, dialogue and background information.

The hourglass is a form that satisfies editors who prefer a traditional approach to news writing as well as impatient readers who tire easily of leisurely approaches to stories that take forever to get to the point. Readers who want a more complete story, who like to see a story unfold as they read it, are happy as well. The hourglass serves readers' need for news and their natural desire for story.

The hourglass can be used in all kinds of stories: crime, business, government, even to report meetings. It's best suited, however, for dramatic stories that can be told in chronological fashion. In the right hands, as the following from *The Miami Herald* illustrates, the hourglass is a virtuoso form that provides the news-conscious discipline of the inverted pyramid and the story-telling qualities of the classic narrative.

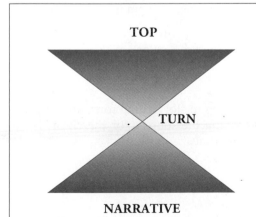

TOP

TURN

NARRATIVE

The important information appears high in the story. Then the story turns in the middle, and events are retold chronologically.

An important form, not new, but more relevant than ever. Combines news reporting and narrative. Excellent for police stories and other dramatic events.

The hourglass form summarizes the news, then shifts to a narrative. The top delivers the news, the turn acts as a transition, the narrative tells the story.

In the first five paragraphs, the story conveys all the information the time-pressed reader needs to know: Police shoot to death a man who refuses their commands to drop his knife and stabs his ex-wife instead. The top answers several of the five W's: who, what, where, when, why, as well as how. A special feature of this lead is the first paragraph, which departs from the usual summary lead: Police shot and killed a 37-year-old Davie man after he disregarded their orders to drop his knife. Instead the writer draws in the reader with an indirect approach that sums up the situation with chilling finality.

Hourglass Example

Shots Fired While He Stabbed Ex-wife

It wasn't the first time that Dennis Leach had violently terrorized his ex-wife. But it will be the last.

Leach, 37, was shot by Davie police Saturday afternoon after he disregarded their orders to drop his knife and instead plunged it repeatedly into Joyce Leach outside her duplex at 6110 SW 41st Ct.

Dennis Leach was pronounced dead at the scene. His ex-wife, who asked police, "Why did you shoot him?" as she was loaded into the ambulance, was taken to Memorial Regional Hospital in Hollywood, where she was listed in stable condition.

The mayhem was witnessed by Dennis Leach's parents and some neighbors. The neighbors said turmoil at the Leach home was nothing new.

In May, Dennis Leach was charged with aggravated assault when, according to police, he showed up with a hammer, broke a window and chased his ex-wife around the duplex, shouting, "I'm going to kill you!"

2. The Turn

The transition is short, alerting the reader that the news report is shifting to storytelling form and indicating the sources for the chronicle to come.

Police and neighbors gave this account of the latest domestic violence.

3. THE NARRATIVE

Now it's time to tell the story of what transpired the night Dennis Leach died. The writer tells the story chronologically, drawing together information gleaned from interviews with the sources identified in the turn. As with all stories, the narrative section has a beginning, a middle that describes the main action and an end, with the climactic cry of the abused ex-wife, "Why did you shoot him?" The conclusion wraps up the story with background about the couple's troubles and then, like many good stories, ends on a note that echoes back to the beginning. Note how the writer uses dramatic quotations and vivid details, such as the yellow tarp that covers Dennis Leach's body, to show the narrative scene that the reader is merely told about in the top.

Dennis Leach became angry with his 37-year-old ex-wife after he went to a neighborhood bar Friday night. He stormed into her duplex Saturday afternoon and threatened her with a butcher knife.

A terrified Joyce Leach dashed next door to the adjoining home of Leach's parents.

"He's got a knife, and he's gonna kill me!" Leach's mother, Reba Leach, said her daughter-in-law screamed.

At the same time, 15-year-old April Leach, one of their six children, called from a convenience store blocks away.

"Your father is going to kill me!" Joyce Leach yelled.

April Leach hung up and dialed 911.

When officers arrived at the duplex, Dennis Leach was chasing his ex-wife with a knife.

Police ordered him to drop the weapon, said Davie Capt. John George.

Instead, Leach started stabbing her.

An officer fired at Dennis Leach, striking him around a knee, but he wouldn't stop plunging the knife into his ex-wife, neighbors said.

An officer or officers fired again, this time hitting Leach in the chest. He collapsed and died on the side of the road. His parents were watching from inside their home.

Davie police would not say whether more than one officer fired at Dennis Leach, nor would they identify the officer or officers.

Neighbors say they heard at least five shots.

As police carried Joyce Leach to an ambulance, the knife still stuck in her right shoulder, she turned to police and said: "Is he dead, is he dead. ... Why did you shoot him?" said next-door neighbor Shannon Schmitzer.

As Joyce was hoisted into the ambulance and police placed a yellow tarp over Dennis Leach's body, April Leach and a brother arrived.

The two siblings cried and tried to run to their mother and father but were escorted away.

Police later drove them to Memorial Regional Hospital to be with their mother.

Dennis and Joyce Leach lived for years in the duplex owned by Leach's parents.

"They've had a lot of trouble in the past," Schmitzer said.

As the couple's problems escalated, the Department of Children and Family Services stepped in. The state took custody of

Continued

the children for a while, placing them in foster homes, neighbors said.

Joyce Leach got a job at Dunkin Donuts, just blocks away, but Dennis Leach couldn't stay out of trouble.

In May, Davie police charged him with domestic violence and aggravated assault after the incident with the hammer. He was convicted and jailed for 90 days.

He got out Tuesday night and returned to his family's house, his mother said.

"We weren't supposed to let him stay here," his mother said. "But he just showed up."

The Miami Herald
August 9, 1998

THE NUT GRAF: GIVING READERS A REASON TO CARE

Barney Kilgore was tired of *today*. He was sick of *yesterday*. And in 1941, he had the power to do something about it. "It doesn't have to have happened today to be news," he declared. "If a date is essential, use the exact date." From now on, he decreed, *The Wall Street Journal* would no longer use the words "today" and "yesterday" in the leads of stories.

With that single act, Kilgore, the new managing editor of *The Wall Street Journal*, paved the way for a revolutionary treatment of news. Journalistic story forms, like many creative ideas, are often linked with the places where they originated or where they reached their zenith. That's why the inverted pyramid, popularized by the newspaper wire services started before the U.S. Civil War, is often referred to as an "AP story" or a "wire service approach." In the same way, *The Wall Street Journal* is home to a form best known as the **"nut graf"** story, although it is also identified as the "news feature" and the "analytical feature." This genre's hallmarks include anecdotal leads that hook the reader, followed by alternating sections that amplify the story's thesis and provide balance with evidence that presents a counterthesis. But its chief hallmark is the use of a context section, the "nut graf" in newsroom lingo. Now newspapers and magazines around the world publish stories following the form that emphasizes explanation over information and understanding over knowledge. Online news sites also rely on this form.

The nut graf tells the reader what the writer is up to; it delivers a promise of the story's content and message. It's called the nut graf because, like a nut, it contains the "kernel," or essential theme, of the story. At *The Philadelphia*

Inquirer, reporters and editors called it the "You may have wondered why we invited you to this party?" section.

Nut Graf

The lead is an anecdote or scene or portrait. The news value is communicated in the third or fourth graph. The rest of the story delivers the promise in the nut graf.

Wall Street Journal style. Excellent for news analysis or trend stories. Forces writer to consider the most interesting information and the essential news value.

The "nut graf" story invites readers into a story, often with an anecdote or scene, and then by the third or fourth paragraph provides context by summarizing the essence, or "nut," of the story's theme.

The nut graf has several purposes:

- It justifies the story by telling readers why they should care.
- It provides a transition from the lead and explains the lead and its connection to the rest of the story.
- It often tells readers why the story is timely.
- It often includes supporting material that helps readers see why the story is important.

Ken Wells, a writer and editor at *The Wall Street Journal*, described the nut graf as "a paragraph that says what this whole story is about and why you should read it. It's a flag to the reader, high up in the story: You can decide to proceed or not, but if you read no farther, you know what that story's about."

As the name implies, most nut grafs are a single paragraph long. In the following example, Julia Malone, a national correspondent for Cox Newspapers' Washington Bureau, begins her story about pork barrel politics with a specific case that illustrates how politicians use tax dollars for pet projects that have dubious value.

> Blacksburg, Va.—High on a mountain overlook, construction crews blast through solid rock on a 20-hours-a-day rush schedule to build the first two miles of an expressway that, for the next few years, will lead only to a turn-around.

Malone then immediately provides the context for this scene and solves the puzzle of a two-mile-long expressway.

> But for promoters in this Appalachian university town, that's of little concern. Dubbed the "Smart Road" and designed to double as a high-technology research site, this federal-state project shows how a little "pork" tucked into a federal transportation bill can buy a whole hog for a community.
>
> *The Atlanta Journal-Constitution*

Wisely, Malone doesn't make her intrigued readers wait any longer to find out what the story is about and why they should bother reading it. The nut graf has done its job: given readers enough information early on to see where the story is heading so they can decide whether they want to keep reading.

STUDENT EXAMPLE

Rookie reporters can use the nut graf form to good effect, too. Jeremy Schwartz, a reporting student at The Poynter Institute, used two short vignettes to begin his story about the problem elderly residents in a St. Petersburg neighborhood were having with Super Soakers, oversized water guns wielded by local kids. In his lead, Schwartz described how Avita Berry, 62, watched as the occupants of a car "let loose with thick streams of water, soaking anyone unlucky enough to be in range," and Annie Lee, 72, saw a group of pre-teens open fire with massive water guns filled with bleach, "strong enough to turn her grass white."

Then it was time to step back from the specific cases and clue the reader in on the whole story:

> Berry and Lee are victims of a new urban weapon in South St. Petersburg: Super Soaker water guns—high-powered, bubble-shaped, neon water guns that can extend to three feet and hold up to two gallons of water. They tell stories of guns filled with bleach, hot pepper and even garlic and say that neighborhood youths have taken the game too far. This summer has seen an explosion of Super Soaker use on the South Side, say residents, local retailers and police.

First, Schwartz identifies the women in the lead as representatives of a larger group: neighborhood residents victimized by Super Soaker water guns. Then, he anticipates the readers' question by immediately describing the weapons, using details that paint a vivid picture. Nut grafs often use summary language to bring together disparate events to reveal trends or long-running situations. "They tell stories of" specific examples—"guns filled with bleach, pepper and even garlic"—to convey a fad gone out of control.

The nut graf can be longer than one paragraph but never more than two or three. Longer than that, and the story can bog down. In Chapter 4, you read this emblem lead on a story about pre-teen dieting:

NUT GRAF EXAMPLE

> Worried about her weight, Sarah swore off dessert and cut back on meal portions. Eventually, she began skipping breakfast and was just nibbling at lunch and dinner. Within six months, she dropped 13 pounds.
>
> A weight-loss success story? Not at all. Sarah is only 10 years old. Her diet cost her 20 percent of her weight.

By now, the reader is sufficiently intrigued: *"Hey, when I started reading I thought it was a story about a woman dieting, but actually, it's about a kid who lost an alarming amount of weight. What's going on here?"* At this point, unfortunately, too many writers might continue on with the story about Sarah, either by providing biographical details—Sarah lives in Philadelphia with her mother. Her dieting began three years ago when her parents divorced.—or a quote—"I wanted to look like Kate Moss," says Sarah. "The only way I could do it was to stop eating."

What the writer needs to do instead is anticipate the reader's reaction, every step of the way. That's where the nut graf comes in, stepping back from the individual case or scene or person to show where it fits into a larger picture. As Jack Hart, editor and writing coach at *The Oregonian*, described it so well, the nut graf is "a core statement that answers the basic question lurking in the mind of every reader: 'Why should I bother with this story?'"

In this dieting story, the two-paragraph anecdotal lead is followed by three paragraphs designed to answer questions raised by the lead and provoke further interest:

Children such as Sarah, a Philadelphia fourth-grader who's too embarrassed to let her real name be used, are at the forefront of a disturbing new trend affecting the health of U.S. children: dieting.

Around the country, children as young as 6 are shedding pounds, afraid of being fat and increasingly being treated for eating disorders that threaten their health and growth, health specialists report.

In trying to correct one problem—one in five children is now overweight—doctors, parents, schools and the media have unwittingly caused another.

BEHIND THE NUT GRAF

The first paragraph identifies Sarah further and discloses that her identity is being concealed and the reason why. Normally, news organizations identify subjects of stories, so it's important to explain when and why you depart from the norm. It also foreshadows a key theme explored later in the story: the stigma that being overweight carries in our society. The sentence then connects Sarah to a larger problem—dieting by children. Nut grafs must be economical. Notice how one word—*new*—conveys the story's timeliness.

Paragraph 2 anticipates the reader's reaction: *"Kids are dieting! Really? What do you mean?"* It answers it by amplifying the description of the trend: specifying the age of the youngest weight-conscious children and telling of an increase in children under treatment for eating disorders. Attribution of this conclusion, to health specialists, is an important feature of this paragraph, anticipating the reader's question: *"Oh, yeah? Says who?"*

Paragraph 3 concludes the nut graf section by building to a strong conclusion. Using the dash allows for insertion of a telling statistic that communicates the extent of the problem.

Using parallel construction—"correct one problem ... caused another"—creates ironic tension that the writer hopes will prompt the reader to now say: *"That's interesting. I want to know more."*

After the lead and the nut graf, this story form now consists of alternating sections, all designed to support the story's focus.

Section 1: Quotes from experts support the story's thesis.

"This whole pressure to be thin has backfired on children," said Joanne Ikeda, a dietitian at the University of California at Berkeley who counsels parents and health professionals about children and weight issues.

"It's a national crisis," said Frances Berg, editor of *Obesity and Health,* a North Dakota journal that reports the latest scientific research on obesity.

Section 2: The story now provides balance by introducing a section that contrasts the problem of dieting children with the very real problem of obesity among America's youth.

No one denies that many American children, like adults, have a problem with weight. American children are fatter than ever before, experts agree. Among children 6 to 11, obesity increased 54 percent in the past two decades, according to a 1987 review of four national nutrition and health surveys. The number of obese youths rose 39 percent in the 12–17 group.

Obesity a Health Risk

Obesity poses serious health risks for children. The condition is linked with high blood pressure and future problems with diabetes, heart disease and colon and breast cancer, said Dr. Gilman Grave of the National Institute of Child Health and Development.

In recent years, public health officials, doctors and the nation's schools have preached the importance of reduced fat and cholesterol and more exercise for children as well as adults.

Section 3: This chunk returns to the main theme of the story. It buttresses the thesis by citing medical evidence and experts. The last sentence provides a transition to the next section.

But now many health professionals are sounding a new warning: Children should never diet.

Dieting can lead to anorexia nervosa, bulimia and other eating disorders that cause death, serious illness, stunted growth and other health problems at a vulnerable stage when extra protein is needed for a child's healthy development.

It can also affect a child's learning, ability to concentrate and performance in school.

"Even with fat children you can stunt their growth so that instead of ending up with a slender child you end up with a short fat child," dietitian Ikeda said.

Children go through stages when they are heavier, especially during puberty, and often grow into their weight, dietitians say.

Children, whatever their size, need a healthy diet low in fats and sugars and high in fiber and an active life, health professionals say. Exercise is the key to preventing and controlling obesity, experts agree.

But that message apparently has not reached many children, recent surveys show.

Section 4: The following section amplifies the nut graf. With statistics drawn from a medical study, it tells the reader about widespread dieting among young people.

Pre-Teen Dieting

In a study published last summer, researchers at the Medical University of South Carolina reported dramatic evidence about the problem of pre-teen dieting. In the largest study of middle school children to date, they surveyed 3,175 boys and girls between 10 and 13. More than half the girls in the fifth to eighth grades who were surveyed felt they looked fat and wanted to lose weight.

One-fourth of the boys had similar attitudes. Among all the students, one out of three had dieted, and almost 5 percent said they had vomited to lose weight.

"The heavier the kids were, the more anxiety they expressed about their weight," said Elizabeth Hodges, who treats children with eating disorders and is one of the study's authors. "But even normal weight kids were dieting."

Unhealthy dieting is even more widespread among teen-agers. More than two-thirds of high school girls are dieting, one in five has taken diet pills, and many girls as well as boys are using laxatives, diuretics, fasting and vomiting in a desperate effort to become slim, according to a 1992 study of students in 10 Cleveland high schools.

Section 5: The next section shows another face behind the numbers. Nut graf stories should never rely on one example.

"If you want to look pretty, if you want to be popular, if you want to stand out, you have to be thin," said Katie, 13, who lives in a Chicago suburb.

Katie's ordeal began at 7 when she looked at the girl sitting next to her on the school bus. "I just thought my thighs were a lot bigger than hers. I was shocked because I thought I was fat." Her parents were dieting, and Katie said she was "afraid I was going to be like my mom."

What followed was a typical pattern, experts say. The 75-pound third-grader cut out fat from her diet and began refusing food. She began spending hours exercising to lose weight, often waking at 4:30 a.m. to jog in place in her bedroom.

42 Pounds at 11

By 11, when she was admitted to a psychiatric hospital for treatment of anorexia nervosa, she weighed 42 pounds.

Section 6: In the following two sections, the story alternates between the close-up and the wide shot. Specific examples are always related to the larger context.

Today's children face a cruel dilemma. They are growing up in a society that condones eating too much of the wrong foods and exercising too little, while at the same time clinging to unreasonable ideals of thinness and beauty. Fat children are often shunned and taunted by their classmates, who reflect society's prejudice against obesity.

Children today are merely reflecting a national obsession about diet and weight among adults, Hodges said. They are, in effect, the post-Weight Watcher generation.

"These children have always been exposed to the diet culture," said Hodges.

"It's a fact of life. Everyone's running and exercising and doing Nordic Track and step machines and watching their weight and what they eat. Kids get the message that to be thin is what's most important."

Section 7: The story comes full circle, returning to Sarah, the child in the lead. It avoids a common flaw: introducing a character in the lead who is never seen or heard from again.

That message is so overpowering, doctors say, that even children of normal size, like Sarah, who weighed 66 pounds when she began dieting, are driven to lose weight. "I couldn't control it," she said.

Sarah's mother recalls her daughter "starting to read labels, counting the calories, reading about the fat content. I thought it was a stage."

But her daughter quickly moved from avoiding snacks to skipping entire meals.

"She was beginning to look like a concentration camp victim. You could see her ribs. She had lost so much on her thighs there was a big gap between her legs.

"It was heartbreaking," her mother said.

Under therapy, Sarah and Katie both regained weight.

Section 8: Now that the problem has been fully explored, the story concludes with a section designed to answer the question on the reader's mind: What can be done?"

Therapist Ellyn Satter, author of *How to Get Your Kid to Eat ... But Not Too Much,* advises "carefully indirect" methods of weight control that divide responsibility for eating between parent and child. "Parents are responsible for what, where and when [the child eats]; the child is responsible for how much and whether," she said. She advises against allowing children to "panhandle" for food between mealtimes and recommends drinking water, rather than juice or soda, between meals.

Besides fostering good eating and exercising habits, what's needed most is acceptance of a child's weight, experts say.

The emphasis on being thin "sets up a dilemma for kids who are normally heavier

to try to diet themselves down to a biologically impossible state," Hodges said.

"The question should not be how do we make fat kids thin. It should be how do we make fat kids healthy," said Sally Smith, executive director of the National Association to Advance Fat Acceptance in Sacramento, Calif.

Attitudes that parents hold about obesity must change, Berg said. "They're conveying the message: There's something wrong with your body, and we've got to fix it. They need to give the message that you're great the way you are, and we love you."

Knight Ridder
February 18, 1994

Many reporters, both students and professionals, have a hard time writing a nut graf. The nut graf requires the writer to summarize the story in a way that may seem like editorializing. It's not. The critical thinking and analysis that the form demands must be supported by rigorous reporting. The nut graf makes a case, but it must be supported by evidence. The story about pre-teen dieting is based on numerous interviews with children, parents, doctors, nutritionists, psychiatrists and other health professionals and on extensive research of medical literature.

Magazine editors like Evelynne Kramer at *The Boston Globe Magazine* describe the paragraph as "opening the aperture." As members of a video generation, you may find it helpful to think of this form's lead as a close-up. The nut graf is a wide-angle shot. Theme has been defined as "meaning in a word." In a nut graf story, it's the meaning in a paragraph. William E. Blundell, a former *Wall Street Journal* writer who coaches writers, and whose stories illustrated the approach in its finest form, calls "the main theme statement the single most important bit of writing I do on any story."

The Wall Street Journal's approach redefined news, transforming it from events or actions that happened today or the day before to trends or situations that had been developing over time but that had not been noticed by a news media focused on the now. Most important, *The Wall Street Journal*'s reporters were following a new rule: Write a story that keeps readers reading rather than provides a built-in excuse to stop, a complaint made by the inverted pyramid's critics.

At the same time, the nut graf required in every story served the function of the inverted pyramid's summary lead: providing readers with the gist of the story up high. If they chose to stop then, they at least knew the broad outlines of the story. If they chose to continue, however, they knew they would be rewarded with even greater understanding and enjoyment.

Although the nut graf approach is most often associated with trend stories, analytical pieces and news features, reporters also employ it to bring drama and context to breaking news. An example of this approach is this prize-winning deadline story by Mark Fritz of The Associated Press.

KARUBAMBA, Rwanda (AP)—Nobody lives here any more.

Not the expectant mothers huddled outside the maternity clinic, not the families squeezed into the church, not the man who lies rotting in a schoolroom beneath a chalkboard map of Africa.

Everybody here is dead. Karubamba is a vision from hell, a flesh-and-bone junkyard of human wreckage, an obscene slaughterhouse that has fallen silent save for the roaring buzz of flies the size of honeybees.

With silent shrieks of agony locked on decaying faces, hundreds of bodies line the streets and fill the tidy brick buildings of this village, most of them in the sprawling Roman Catholic complex of classrooms and clinics at Karubamba's stilled heart.

In those first four paragraphs, Fritz sets a horrific scene, bringing the reader face-to-face with the massacred victims in an African village. The vivid details answer the questions "Where?" and "What?" and "Who?" in a powerful fashion that draws the reader into the story. Fritz's lead leaves unaddressed the "How?" and "Why?" Had he continued to describe the massacre there's a good chance the reader would become frustrated. That's where the nut graf comes in.

Karubamba is just one breathtakingly awful example of the mayhem that has made little Rwanda the world's most ghastly killing ground.

Karubamba, 30 miles northeast of Kigali, the capital, died April 11, six days after Rwanda President Juvenal Habyarimana, a member of the Hutu tribe, was killed in a plane crash whose cause is still undetermined.

The paranoia and suspicion surrounding the crash blew the lid off decades of complex ethnic, social and political hatreds. It ignited a murderous spree by extremists from the majority Hutus against rival Tutsis and those Hutus who had opposed the government.

This awesome wave of remorseless mayhem has claimed 100,000 to 200,000 lives, say U.N. and other relief groups. Many were cut down while cowering in places traditionally thought safe havens: churches, schools, relief agencies.

The Associated Press
May 12, 1994

Here, Fritz backs up to provide context for the scene in the lead, like a filmmaker drawing back from a close-up to a wide-angle shot. This is the "nut section" that provides the background by addressing "How?" and "Why?" the scene described in the lead came to be.

Without context the reader who is hooked by an arresting lead may feel left dangling. The image of the nut works whether we think of it as plant life or an industrial device. Consider what happens, for example, if you leave a lug nut off a car wheel; you run the risk of the car careening off the road. In the same way, a story that intrigues without providing context can quickly leave a reader feeling derailed.

When the nut graf became popular in the 1970s, many reporters and editors believed that a nut graf had to include a phrase that indicates the source of the conclusion—"officials say" or "neighbors and friends of the victim agreed." Although the paragraph provided context and meaning for a story, it needed to rely on some authority other than the reporter to do so. Otherwise, they argued, the story read more like an editorial. Although that mindset still lingers in some newsrooms, by the 1990s even The Associated Press permitted its reporters to draw conclusions when it was based on their reporting and expertise. Thus, Mark Fritz delivers his interpretation of the Rwandan massacre in the nut graf without attribution but for one exception—the casualty estimates that he, appropriately, attributes to relief workers. Because the nut graf is designed to provide context for the story and then should always be followed by the evidence supporting the conclusion, attribution is often unnecessary.

A word of caution about nut grafs from James B. Stewart, a former *Wall Street Journal* front page editor and successful nonfiction writer: Don't let nut grafs tell the reader so much about the story that they have no incentive to keep reading. In his book, *Follow the Story: How to Write Successful Nonfiction,* Stewart argues for nut grafs that accomplish the goals of the device, including "selling" the story to the reader by conveying its timeliness and importance while "preserving every bit of the suspense and curiosity so carefully cultivated in the lead." Stewart's guidelines to enhance rather than crush the story you want to tell include:

- Never give away the ending of the story.
- Anticipate the questions that readers might be asking early in a story, and address them.
- Give readers a concrete reason or reasons to move on.

Here's a quick way to produce a nut graf for your next story: Make up your mind what the story is about and why people should read it—and then type that conclusion in one or two sentences. Experienced reporters say they find it helpful to constantly write and rewrite the nut graf through the course of reporting the story. Doing so tends to reveal holes earlier in the process and helps you avoid too many intriguing but tangential side trips.

THE NARRATIVE: THE WAY WE TELL STORIES

Most of us learned about stories as children. I like to ask the best students in Poynter's summer reporting and writing program how they got started; invariably, the answer is, "My Mom [or Dad] read to me." That early reading experience stimulated a lifelong appreciation for stories. That certainly was the case for me, and that made it especially difficult to learn journalistic forms, such as the inverted pyramid, that turn the traditional story form on its head. What are the lessons about stories we learned as children?

Stories have characters, settings, themes, conflicts, plots with climaxes and resolutions. Storytellers don't give away the story in the first paragraph the way news writers do. Instead they set up a situation, using suspense or the introduction of a compelling character to keep the reader turning pages. Rather than put the least important information at the end the way an inverted pyramid writer might, the storyteller waits until the end to give the reader a "big payoff"—a surprise, a twist, a consummation.

As a writer I always found the hard news story to be the most challenging to write. It felt unnatural. I realized that as a writer I wanted to create the dramatic tension that I found as a young reader. I wanted to be caught up in the suspense of fiction that swept me away.

Narratives are often long stories. (In Chapter 12, "Storytelling on Deadline," we'll look at shorter narratives.) Readers find long stories off-putting. They will read them when the subject matters to them or the presentation is compelling. But for the most part, readers find a long story hard to take. I do, too. If a block of gray stares me in the face, it's possible I will give up. So if you're going to write a long story, you'd better have a good reason.

No matter what the length, the rules are the same. The story has to be clear and compelling. The reader should not be allowed to stumble. Don't put all your work into the lead and then start flinging stuff around in the middle. As with a short story, a long story should say one thing, convey one dominant impression.

Even the most fervent champions of narrative journalism are cautious about its use. "Not every story merits it, nor can every reporter be trusted with it," said Jon Franklin, a two-time Pulitzer Prize winner whose book *Writing for Story* continues to influence long-form writers. "Most stories should be short, to the point and written in traditional journalistic style. A cop round-up, written in fake Joan Didion, makes the reader wonder if the journalistic world is asleep at the switch." Franklin believes most stories would be "better handled as inverted pyramid stories or at most, delayed lead features. What could have been good stories come off instead as under-reported and overwritten fluff."

If you want to write long stories that people are unable to stop reading, ask yourself: Have I got the material, the scenes, some dialogue, details about lives? Narratives must grab readers' attention quickly, intrigue them, then satisfy their natural curiosity. Storytellers reveal story with dialogue and images.

To me, the story endings that are most satisfying reverberate like a Chinese gong. They conjure up images from throughout the story, then take you back to the beginning. In a story about the Navy's insensitive handling of a young seaman's unexplained death, I ended with a scene of a grief-stricken mother getting a letter sent to her son from the recruiting station a few days after he died. Unaware that the young man was dead, the recruiters wrote, "We liked your stuff, shipmate. We'd like to have you back." Most reporters might have used that as the lead. When I get something that is powerful and reinforces the story's theme, my impulse is to save it for the end.

The importance of reporting for a long story is critical. Look for details. Use the best. Here is an example of a narrative followed by an account of the writing.

NARRATIVE EXAMPLE

Having a Baby: "In Sorrow Thou Shalt Bring Forth Children"

By Christopher Scanlan
Providence Evening Bulletin
March 25, 1981

In the labor room at Kent County Memorial Hospital, Jackie Rushton rose from the stretcher, her face pale and smeared with tears. A nurse pressed the fetal pulse detector against her abdomen, a taut mound stretched by seven months of pregnancy. The detector was blue, the size and shape of a pocket flashlight with earphones attached, and Jackie Rushton's eyes fixed on the nurse, who strained to hear the birdlike beating of her baby's heart.

"Here's the heartbeat," the nurse said after several moments of silence, "It's 126, and it's fine."

If there's a heartbeat, why isn't she giving me the earphones so I can listen? Jackie thought. *That's what the doctor always does when I have my check-ups. First he listens, and then he says, "Here's the heartbeat. Listen."* She didn't say, *"Here's the heartbeat. Listen."*

I've lost the baby. The baby's gone.

Jackie and Rob Rushton's daughter, Lola, was 18 months old when they decided to have another child. Jackie went off the Pill. Nothing happened. By the time Lola started kindergarten in September 1979, her parents were convinced she would be their only child.

Then last June, Jackie, 25, missed her period. "Don't be silly," Rob said, "you're not pregnant." But one day early in July, Jackie went to the drugstore and bought one of those home pregnancy tests, and when Rob came home for lunch she was waiting with champagne.

The first three months Jackie was tired all the time. She dragged herself around during the day. She went to bed immediately after dinner. She woke up tired. Her parents visited from England, and she drove them to the beach often. She lay on the warm sand at Bonnet Shores in Narragansett and slept.

Autumn came to Pawtuxet Village, the neighborhood where the Rushtons have lived since they emigrated from England in 1978. Breezes carried the leathery smell of dying leaves. The air turned colder. Jackie felt fine again.

In November, the Rushtons bought their first house, a summer cottage on Warwick Neck that needed work. Rob, 31, is a building contractor, and he began spending all his free time getting the house in shape. In the meantime, they moved out of their apartment on Post Road to stay with their friend, Marge O'Hara, who lived a few blocks away on Spring Garden Street.

Winter arrived. The air in the village was tangy with wood smoke. The baby began to kick.

Shortly before Christmas, the temperatures dove below freezing. In the Rushtons' new house, the pipes burst. At the time it seemed like bad luck. A few weeks later, it turned out to be very good luck that they were still living with Marge, a delivery room nurse at Kent County Memorial Hospital.

In the early hours of Jan. 22, six weeks before her March 4 due date, Jackie's water broke, a normal beginning of labor. A doctor at Kent County Memorial told Jackie that morning that labor might still be a week away. He advised her to go home and wait.

That afternoon, Marge drove to the Zayres on Warwick Avenue with Dawn, her 13-year-old daughter. They bought a turquoise nightgown for Jackie and a yellow quilt with ducks and teddy bears for the baby. That night, they held an impromptu shower. They didn't have time to wrap anything, so they let Jackie open the bags. They talked about names. Joel for a boy. Zoë or Leah, if it was a girl. Maybe Hannah. Marge, who had to work the next day, went to sleep around 9.

At 10:15 that night, Jackie went upstairs to the bathroom. When she pulled down her pants, she saw the blood. She yelled for Rob, who came running with Dawn behind him. Dawn took one look and ran into her mother's bedroom.

Continued

"Mommy, Mommy," Dawn cried, "You've got to help. Jackie's bleeding." Marge shook herself awake and went into the bathroom. Jackie held a blood-soaked towel.

The bleeding, Marge knew immediately, meant one of two abnormal prenatal conditions: placenta praevia, in which the placenta comes out before the baby, causing loss of large quantities of blood; or placenta abruption, in which the placenta separates from the uterus. Either way, Marge knew, Jackie and the baby were in serious trouble. The placenta is the source of a baby's oxygen. If the infant wasn't delivered quickly by Caesarean section probably it could die. It might be too late already. Marge didn't tell any of this to Jackie or Rob.

"Get your bag, Jackie," she said. "We're going to the hospital. Get the car, Rob. I'll call the doctor."

Rob's tools filled the back seat of the station wagon. The three of them squeezed in front, with Jackie in the middle.

Rob speeded up when they turned onto Post Road. There were only a few cars on the road. He wished a policeman would pull them over and give them an escort to the hospital.

"What's going to happen?" Jackie said. She began to sob.

In the blackness of the winter night, the streetlamps shone like moons. Marge shivered with cold and fear. Should she just make small talk or try to prepare Jackie for what to expect at the hospital? Once they arrived, she knew, things would happen fast.

She tried to sound breezy. "Well, you've missed your shower, Jackie, but that's all right. We'll have one later. And don't worry about not having any baby clothes. I'll see to that."

"What's going to happen?" Jackie said.

Rob glanced at Marge. She looked worried, and that made him even more afraid. He had never seen so much blood. He thought about Susan Gilbert, a friend from England. She had started to hemorrhage before her second baby was born. The doctors couldn't stop the bleeding. Susan died. Rob gripped the steering wheel with both hands, grateful he had to concentrate on the driving. He wanted to scream.

"Everything will be all right," he told Jackie. "Keep yourself calm. If you're calm, the baby will be all right." *Come on God*, he thought, *You've got to be with us now.*

The light at Warwick Avenue was about to turn red. Rob slowed, looked both ways and shot through the empty intersection, horn blaring. "Be careful," Marge cried, "We've got to get there in one piece."

They passed a shopping plaza, a string of one-story shops. Behind the plate-glass windows, the night lights shimmered.

They turned onto Route 95.

"Rob, the petrol tank is on empty," Jackie cried.

"It's all right. There'll be enough to get us there."

We're going to stop in a minute, and I'm going to be stuck on 95. I'm bleeding, and I'm going to be on 95 flagging down cars.

Off the highway now, turning up a long, straight road lined with tall trees. Doctor's shingles hung from signposts in front of several houses. They climbed a slope and saw the hospital. Rob slowed by a cluster of signs and followed an arrow marked "Emergency Room Entrance."

"Don't worry," Marge said. "We're just going to get out here."

"Don't even tell me where you're going," Rob said. "I'll find you."

"Marge," Jackie said, "I'm frightened."

Marge took Jackie's arm and led her up the ramp to the emergency room. They walked through the first of two sets of glass doors. Marge hurried ahead to grab a wheelchair.

Suddenly, at the door to the waiting room, Jackie felt intense pressure in her abdomen. Then it passed. "Marge, help me," she cried. "I've delivered the baby. I've had the baby."

Marge let the wheelchair go and ran back into the doorway, grabbed Jackie and pulled her inside.

Jackie was dimly aware of the crowd in the waiting room, a large airy room with vinyl couches and chairs set in rows. A gray-haired man in a leather coat turned and stared at her.

Fay Masterson, Marge's supervisor in the obstetrics ward, appeared. Like an angel, Marge thought. She and Fay picked Jackie up and laid her on a stretcher.

Above her, Jackie saw only the white ceiling and fluorescent lights. She felt disconnected, unable to see what was happening: She sobbed hysterically. Everything had gone horribly, horribly wrong. She could feel herself bleeding. She felt exposed and alone, aware of people around her but not really caring. There could have been a crowd of 10,000, and it wouldn't have mattered.

Marge heard the squeak of screens being placed around the stretcher, blocking the view as she and Fay pulled Jackie's red corduroys off.

"It's all right, Jackie. It's not the baby," Marge said. "It's just a blood clot."

She's lying, Jackie thought. *I felt something come out of me. I've had a baby. They're just telling me that to keep me calm so they can get me to a room and try and get the baby breathing.*

Rob hurried into the emergency room and saw Jackie on a stretcher, crying hysterically. Before Marge whipped a white sheet over her legs, he saw the blood between them, a splash of scarlet. Marge and the other nurse pushed the stretcher through a set of swinging wooden doors and disappeared. He dashed after them. They were racing the stretcher down a narrow passageway with green walls and round convex mirrors high up in the corner.

"I've had the baby," Jackie was crying.

"No, you haven't," Marge said. "It's all right."

Rob tried to catch up. *This is really serious,* he thought. Susan Gilbert's face rose before him. *No, she's not going to die. Don't think negatively. Just go, man.*

"Get out of the way, Rob," Marge cried. "We've got to get her upstairs."

They took a sharp right, pushing the stretcher through another set of doors.

As the doors slapped back and forth, Jackie saw Rob's bearded face, framed by a small square window of netted glass.

They rode up in the service elevator to the maternity ward on the third floor. Marge held Jackie's hand and rubbed her head. She thought of Dawn and of Jonathan, her 9-year-old son. They had been so excited about the baby.

In the labor room, Fay Masterson and the other delivery room nurses alerted by Marge's call converged on Jackie, inserting an intra-

Continued

venous needle in one arm, taking her blood pressure. They wore sea green and flowered surgical clothes. A mobile of one-dimensional red apples hung from the ceiling.

Dr. Thomas A. Vest, an obstetrician, came in. He drew Rob aside and told him he would try to deliver the baby normally. If that was impossible, he would perform a Caesarean section.

The nurses were having trouble getting Jackie's sweater off. She lifted herself up so they could pull it over her head. She felt blood pump furiously from her body. There was blood everywhere.

Now they couldn't get her bra off.

"Let me do this," Rob said, stepping in. He tried to make a joke. "I can do it with one hand." Nervously, he struggled with the clasp. "I've lost my knack," he said, and then worked it open. They put a gown on her.

Jackie didn't understand. Everyone seemed so calm. Rob was managing to crack a joke. It was like he worked there, like he'd done this every day of his life. *Marge is so cool and confident. I'm the only one who's feeling this hysteria.*

The heavy bleeding, Marge knew, posed a serious threat to the baby. She took the fetal detector and pressed it against Jackie's abdomen, listening intently through the earphones. She was silent for several moments.

"I don't hear it, Jackie," she said.

Marge tried to make her voice carefree. "But I'm not too good at it. Let me get Beth." She walked out of the labor room into a small office used by the delivery team and stood there, taking deep breaths. *What are you going to say: "There's no heartbeat"?*

She's lying, Jackie thought. *I know she's good at this.*

Another nurse, Beth Graziano, took the detector and listened.

"Here's the heartbeat," she said finally. "It's 126, and it's fine."

Rob looked at Jackie. She was still bleeding. "Just think of yourself," he said. "Pull yourself through."

Jackie didn't say anything. *I can't. I can't just say, "Oh, well, you know, the baby's gone, but I'm going to try to fight to live." I don't want to.*

"You've got to keep calm," Rob told her. "Because the baby's still inside you."

For the first time, Jackie was afraid of dying. She remembered Susan Gilbert's sister telling her how much blood the doctors gave her. The more they gave her, the more it poured out. *Please, God, let the baby be alive. Let the baby be alive.*

"Say a prayer," Rob said. "Say a prayer."

Dr. Vest returned. He told Jackie and Rob that they were going to take her into the operating room now. Because of the bleeding, he was going to wait until then to examine her.

"Right," Rob said. "I'm ready then."

"No," the doctor said, "you're going to have to sit this one out."

Jackie spoke up. "Could you give me something to put me under?" she asked the doctor.

I want to be put out cold and not wake up for three days. They're going to wheel me in there, they're going to take a dead baby from me, and I'm going to be awake the whole time, and I'm going to know all about it, and I don't want to know. I want to be unconscious. I don't want to know anymore. I don't want to face it.

"Give me a kiss," Rob said, leaning down to kiss her.

The nurses wheeled the stretcher out of the labor room into the corridor. Jackie turned around and looked at her husband.

"Goodbye, Rob," she said. *Why did I say that? It's so final, so flat, so ending. Not like I'll be back in a minute. Like I'm leaving him.*

"Say a prayer," Marge told Rob. The nurses pushed the stretcher through a door marked "Delivery Room." "Take good care of her, Marge," Rob said.

Rob sank into a chair in the hallway. The floor was black and speckled tile. In the next room, a young woman in labor screamed. On the wall facing him, the bulletin board was crowded with hospital memos, an ad for a childbirth class and a large photo of a nurse cradling a naked baby. *Hey, man, grab hold of yourself. Nothing's happened. You've just got to say a prayer. Just shut up and say a prayer.* "Please, Jesus, don't let either of them. ... Please let them both live."

Jackie found herself in a large, blue room. Freshly washed surgical clothes were stacked on cabinets lining the wall. The nurses pushed the stretcher into another room. It had green walls. She saw the operating table, a narrow black cushion wrapped in white sheets. They lifted her off the stretcher and onto the table. The sheets were cool.

Above her hung two immense lights, like huge ice cream scoops. She could see her reflection in the shiny metal. She wanted to ask them to move the lights. But then the lights went on, and her image disappeared in the brightness.

They gave her a shot, and she could feel her legs tingle, and then she couldn't feel them anymore.

The anesthesiologist was asking her about England. She looked up at his masked face. She knew he was trying to take her mind off the situation, but what she really wanted to say was, "Why are you talking about that?"

A nurse attached the bottom of Jackie's gown to a metal stand in the center of the table, blocking her view of the operation.

Both of her hands were strapped down. *I feel like I'm crucified. I can't feel my legs.* She stared into Marge's eyes and gripped her hand. Marge looked so calm.

But Marge felt helpless and scared.

Dr. Vest made an incision in Jackie's abdomen and began to cut through the layers of skin and muscle. He took bandage scissors, with one blunt end, and cut into the uterus. Marge held her breath. *Please, God, please.*

In the hallway, Rob was praying. In his mind, he could see the operating table. The doctors and nurses in their gowns and masks stood over Jackie. Then something strange happened. Rob isn't a churchgoer, but he believes in God. And now he imagined he saw Jesus standing in the operating room. Rob watched Him move His hands over the table. A blessing. Rob let out his breath in a long, deep sigh, suddenly calm.

In the delivery room, Marge saw the little head emerge. It was pink. Marge looked at the clock on the wall for the precise time of birth. "Eleven eleven," she called out.

The doctor lifted the baby out. He could see that the placenta was in the path of the birth canal, placenta praevia. They had gotten to the baby just in time. Another few minutes, and the baby would have suffocated without the placenta's source of oxygen.

"We're all right, Jackie," Marge said. "You've got a daughter, and she's fine."

She can't be normal. It's still not all right.

Continued

"I've got to tell Rob," Marge said and ran out of the room.

Rob saw a nurse running toward him. "Rob, you've got a daughter, and she's fine," Marge said. "Jackie's fine. I've got to get back." Marge's face was half-hidden by the surgical mask. It would be a week before he realized it was she who had given him the news. He jumped out of the chair and then sat down again.

Jackie felt as if she had been lying on the operating table forever. A nurse walked to the head of the table. She held the baby in her arms. Jackie could see only the top of her head. She was tiny and wrinkled. When Lola was born, she felt so high, a "Wow, look at what I've done" feeling. She didn't feel that way now. Somehow it still wasn't right. *The baby's alive now, but in five minutes she's not going to be all right.*

The nurse took the baby away to be weighed and measured, to have her footprints taken.

Rob thought of Dawn, waiting back at the house. He lifted the phone at a desk in the hallway to call her. He heard the dial tone and then put it back down. His head was too fogged to dial.

A nurse walked by him, pushing a metal incubator with a glass top and side. The baby was inside. *She's pretty, but so small. Everything's all right.*

In the delivery room, Marge also was thinking of Dawn. She didn't want her daughter to remember only the frightening part: Jackie bleeding, rushing out of the house. She went to a phone outside the operating room.

"Dawn," she said, "it's a little girl, and she's fine."

"Mommy, I've never prayed harder in my whole life."

In the recovery room, Jackie drifted in and out of sleep. In the middle of a sentence she would doze off. Rob sat beside her bed and held her hand.

"I'm sorry you lost your sleep, Rob."

"Don't be silly."

She fell asleep again. When she woke, Rob said: "How do you like 'Hannah' for a name?"

"Yeah, that's nice."

"Well, let's call her Hannah."

"Okay. I really like 'Hannah' for a name."

It was almost midnight. Marge had to work in the morning. She went into one of the small bedrooms set aside for doctors and lay down on the narrow bed. She wanted to cry, but tears wouldn't come.

Rob kept nodding off as he sat by Jackie's bed.

"Why don't you go home?"

"No, I'm fine here." His head slumped.

"Please, Rob, go. I'm fine. Go home and get some sleep and come back tomorrow."

The doors were locked when he got home at 3 a.m. Normally, he would have been upset, but he didn't have an ounce of anger in him. He stood on the porch, calling for one of the kids. He waited almost a half-hour before Lola came to the back door.

"You've got a sister," he said, hugging and kissing her.

At 10 a.m., Marge came back into the recovery room, carrying a pink bundle.

She placed the baby in Jackie's arms. Hannah was asleep, nestled in a blanket. Around her neck was a blue and white necklace with her last name. She wore a diaper, and the soles of her feet were still smudged with ink used to take her footprints.

Jackie looked down at her daughter. She was so tiny. She looked at her face. *How pretty she is ... and how normal. Maybe everything will be all right after all.* She counted the baby's fingers and toes. There were 10 of each.

"Marge, look at her," Jackie said. "How beautiful she is." Jackie didn't feel a great surge of joy. That would come later. Now, she was in awe. She didn't touch Hannah. She didn't want to wake her. She could have held her forever, just looking at her.

HOW I WROTE THE STORY

By Christopher Scanlan

For much of 1980 and on into 1981, my beat on the *Bulletin* was not City Hall or courts or the economy, but a single Rhode Island neighborhood.

Pawtuxet Village, straddling Warwick and Cranston, was to serve as a sounding board for what was going on in the state and nation that election year. Photographer Anestis Diakopoulos and I did stories about people's attitudes toward the coming presidential primary, the 1980 census and pollution in the Pawtuxet River.

Joel Rawson, managing editor of the *Bulletin* at the time, was also interested in stories on people's daily lives. So Anestis and I reported on the first day of school from the point of view of the mother who must let go. We did a piece on loneliness and how a women's center in the neighborhood tried to cope with it, another on the courtship and wedding of a young couple. There was some resistance in the newsroom when these stories began to run: the "Is this news?" debate that always seems to arise when a story has no obvious peg.

One day, Mark Patinkin handed me a piece of paper with a quote on it from philosopher Will Durant:

"Civilization is a stream with banks. The stream is sometimes filled with blood from people killing, stealing, shouting and doing the things historians usually record; while on the banks, unnoticed, people build homes, make love, raise children, sing songs, write poetry and even whittle statues. The story of civilization is the story of what happened on the banks. Historians are pessimists because they ignore the banks for the river."

Continued

So are journalists, I decided, and stopped worrying about the criticism about the Pawtuxet stories.

Using the "banks vs. river" as a guidepost, I think the most effective story in the Pawtuxet series was "Having a Baby: 'In Sorrow Thou Shalt Bring Forth Children.'" It's about people's lives, and it's also what Rawson, who wants news writers to return to the storyteller's art, likes to call a "story story"—it had a beginning, a middle and an end. The New England Associated Press News Executives Association named it Best Written Feature for 1981 in a paper of more than 60,000 circulation.

The story began in February 1981 when *Bulletin* city editor Merrill Bailey, who lives in Pawtuxet and gave me many good tips, came up and said there was a hell of a story in the village. He told me about his friends and neighbors Jackie and Rob Rushton and Marge O'Hara and their mad rush to Kent County Memorial Hospital for the emergency birth of the Rushtons' daughter Hannah.

Merrill's description of it—the race to the hospital, the nearly tragic outcome—sold me in a minute. It was such a good story, and it even had a happy ending.

A few nights later, I sat in the living room of Marge O'Hara's house, where the Rushtons were staying. Jackie fed the baby, and then the three of them told me the story of that night as my tape recorder whirred.

I tried to get them to tell it in chronological order. I knew I was going to reconstruct the night, and I wanted to hear how it happened. I knew I could come back for details, but I wanted to have the story told to me as I knew it had been told to Merrill and how it had spread around the neighborhood.

The Rushtons and Marge O'Hara were very open. The baby had come home just a few days before, and their memories of the night she was born were fresh and vivid. They remembered every moment, it seemed, and I was able to stop them and ask what each had said at a particular moment, and even what they were thinking. To describe her interviewing technique, Barbara Carton uses the metaphor of a portrait painting: You have to get people to sit still long enough to get every wrinkle. That's what I was trying to do, and I pumped them for specifics: What happened then, what did it look like, what did you see, what did you say, how did you feel, what were you thinking at that moment?

I stayed for almost three hours that night. The next morning I began transcribing my tapes, which took me a couple of days. Although editors sometimes get annoyed by reporters plugged into earphones for days on end, there are times when the machine can't be beat. For someone like myself who can't take shorthand, it means getting every word, accurately, and all the nuances, as well as being free to take notes of a different sort: what people look like, their gestures, their setting, and to jot questions that pop up.

Actually, I think the tape recorder can be a time saver. If you've done the interview right, and you've asked all the questions, the answers are on the tape, and you don't have to keep going back.

I began by separating the material chronologically and then by setting. Breaking down the night into scenes: the ride to the hospital, the labor room, the delivery room, the hallway where Rob waited.

I realized I couldn't reconstruct the night solely on the basis of interviews so I arranged to visit the maternity ward at Kent County Memorial Hospital. In the labor room, I saw the fetal detector and noticed that it looked like a pocket flashlight. I got a lot of good details, the color of the room, the wall decorations, although I would use only a few, but this visit was crucial. Once I saw the setting, I felt I could convey it. I could also ask Jackie questions about what I had seen. Were the sheets cool? Could she see herself in the overhead light?

I had a lot more to do:

I drove along the route they took that night and noted what stores they drove by and the doctor's shingles on the road to the hospital.

I wrote a draft that showed me what I still needed to know. I went back for more details to Marge O'Hara's house one weekend morning when Anestis went to take a family portrait.

For facts on the medical problems that night, I borrowed a book on pregnancy from Peter and Nina Perl, who were the parents of two babies. I questioned Marge, the nurse, closely.

I knew I had the whole story there; the question was how to tell it.

Joel Rawson had taught me several stories before that there has to be a "spine," something to drag the reader along to the end. I decided that the question I wanted to set up immediately in the reader's mind was the one that keeps every storyteller going: What next?

Don Murray advises that stories should start as near the end as possible. I asked myself: What was the moment when the story could have gone either way, when the baby could have lived or died? I realized it was when Jackie thought the

Continued

baby had died and the nurse was lying about hearing the heart beat. That was my lead because I figured readers would want—need—to know what was going to happen, and I could make them read until the end to find out.

But how to write that lead? At the time, I was studying my colleague Carol McCabe's stories because I was really impressed with the way she immediately gets you into the dramatic action of a story.

In 1976 she wrote a series, based on visits to the 13 original colonies, that won the Ernie Pyle Award. I noticed that in most of these stories, she begins with a scene and an action. Her verbs are always active and vivid: "Cold rain spattered on the sand outside the gray house where Worthe Sutherland and his wife Channie P. Sutherland live. ..." "The Bicentennial tourists flowed through Paul Revere's Mall. ..." "Three trailer trucks growled impatiently as a frail black buggy turned onto Route 340. ..."

The lead-off scene then was the labor room, and the action was Jackie lifting herself up as the nurse listened to the baby's heart beat. That set up the tension I wanted, and I felt I could step away to give the necessary background and still keep people reading.

I switched immediately to the day Jackie learned she was pregnant. Then the pregnancy. But this had to be dealt with quickly; I used the weather to convey the passage of time. Other details like wood smoke in the cold night air told a story about the neighborhood I'd come to know.

My big problem was cutting, because the participants had given me a wealth of detail. The story was so powerful that I tried to understate as much as possible. Short sentences. Dialogue is action. Keep it moving.

Using the viewpoints of Jackie, Rob and Marge kept the perspective changing. Marge's job allowed me to talk about the medical problem without having to change to an intrusive reporter's voice. The different characters also bring a different tension to the piece. Marge tells the reader that the situation looks bad, something Rob and Jackie could only wonder about.

(There's a question about reconstructing dialogue. I think if everybody agrees on the dialogue, that's the memory they have. And because all agreed, I accepted it. I also let them read the final draft. Some people might be aghast at this tactic, tantamount to letting your sources edit you, but I thought it only fair because I was going to reveal some very intimate details. As it was, I made a few minor errors, which they caught.)

Once Jackie's water broke and the mad dash to the hospital began, I just followed the night through. I used italics for interior dialogue, making a point to use the words "Jackie thought" the first time I used this device. I jumped from my three characters. A major question was where to end it. I had material about their return home with Hannah, but Joel said cut it when Jackie has the baby in her arms and sees that everything is all right.

Merrill Bailey gave it a close reading and showed me that every editor is a reader and vice versa. He liked the dying leaves image but thought it wasn't precise enough. Okay, what do autumn leaves smell like? "They've always smelled like leather to me," he said. Perfect.

Joel taught me another lesson I won't ever forget. The story was almost finished, and I was pretty pleased with it, but he had a problem. There was something missing, he said. "You've got to paste some wafers in there," he said.

Huh?

The *Red Badge of Courage*, he said. Stephen Crane ends Chapter 9 with this line: "The red sun was pasted in the sky like a fierce wafer." Immediately, the reader is on that battlefield, staring up at the sky. You are there, in that place, in that time.

I had to find "wafers" in my story and paste them onto the narrative to give that sense of place, to make people "see." I had to go back for some, like the description of the shower gifts. Others were already in my notes, and some came from my own experience. I think that streetlights hang like moons and that the overhead lights in the operating room looked like ice cream scoops. Just little things, but they are the details that I like the best because they make me feel I was there the night Hannah Rushton was born.

FIVE BOXES STORY

Good writing comes from an overabundance of information. But collecting notebooks full of observations and computer screens of interview notes can pose another problem: where to put it all. Faced with that problem, many reporters and students swear by the **"five boxes" story approach.** I first learned about it when I interviewed Rick Bragg of *The New York Times* in 1996 when he won the Pulitzer Prize for feature writing and the American Society of Newspaper Editors' Distinguished Writing Award for nondeadline writing. "I've never outlined anything in my life," Bragg said. "But I do have a good plan for outlining that I sometimes share with young reporters who kind of get stuck on a story."

Several years earlier, when Bragg was reporting for the *St. Petersburg Times*, he was stuck on a story when Pat Farnan, a city editor, introduced him to the five boxes approach. Here's how it works:

1. LEAD. The first box contains the lead, the image, the detail that draws the reader into the story. It can be a single paragraph or several.

2. NUT GRAF. A paragraph (or paragraphs) that sums up the story and provides the reader with context and background is the second box.

3. RETELLING. This box is almost a second lead, based on a new scene, detail or strong image, which allows the writer to begin retelling the story that began in the lead and draws the reader into the bulk of the story. Length can vary.

4. BBI. Shorthand for "boring but important," this box contains less compelling material, such as quotes from experts or data bolstering the main theme. It rounds out the story and provides balance.

5. KICKER. The story ends in this box. It may be a quote, an image, a comment; whatever you choose, the best endings resonate. Says Bragg: "I'm a strong believer that you can't have a decent story if it doesn't leave you with a strong feeling or sense or image."

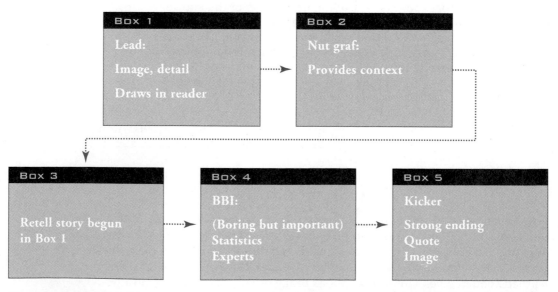

Dividing material into "Five Boxes" is an efficient and graceful way to organize information, especially on a deadline.

The five boxes approach is the easiest method for quick organization of material. Using the boxes you can select and arrange information, settle on the beginning and ending of the story and decide what the story is about. Armed with this rudimentary outline, you can flesh out your story. It breaks the story into components that can be developed and refined.

Although Bragg doesn't outline, it's interesting to see how prominently the five boxes approach figures in his work, as the following story, which was part of his Pulitzer Prize and Best Newspaper Writing Award-winning package, demonstrates.

READ MORE OF RICK BRAGG'S PULITZER PRIZE-WINNING STORIES ONLINE AT http://www.pulitzer.org/year/1996/feature-writing/

Another Battle of New Orleans: Mardi Gras

By Rick Bragg

NEW ORLEANS, Feb. 18—The little shotgun house is peeling, and the Oldsmobile in front is missing a rear bumper, but Larry Bannock can glimpse glory through the eye of his needle.

For almost a year he has hunkered over his sewing table, joining beads, velvet, rhinestones, sequins, feathers and ostrich plumes into a Mardi Gras costume that is part African, part Native American.

"I'm pretty," said Mr. Bannock, who is 6 feet tall and weighs 300 pounds. "And, baby, when I walk out that door there ain't nothing cheap on me."

Most days, this 46-year-old black man is a carpenter, welder and handyman, but on Mardi Gras morning he is a Big Chief, one of the celebrated—if incongruous—black Indians of Carnival. He is an important man.

Sometime around 11 a.m. on Feb. 28, Mr. Bannock will step from his house in a resplendent, flamboyant turquoise costume complete with a towering headdress, and people in the largely black and poor 16th and 17th Wards, the area known as Gert Town, will shout, cheer and follow him through the streets, dancing, drumming and singing.

"That's my glory," he said. Like the other Big Chiefs, he calls it his "mornin' glory."

BOX 1: LEAD

The first box contains the lead, the image, the detail that draws the reader into the story. It can be a single paragraph or several. Bragg focuses on Larry Bannock and the contrast between his shabby surroundings and the glory of his role as a black Indian of Mardi Gras. The section concludes with a brief-but-vivid quote. Note how Bragg separates the quotation with a description of Bannock: a technique that provides pacing and a vivid counterpoint.

He is one of the standard-bearers of a uniquely New Orleans tradition. The Big Chiefs dance, sing and stage mock battles—wars of words and rhymes—to honor American Indians who once gave sanctuary to escaped slaves. It is an intense but elegant posturing, a street theater that some black men devote a lifetime to.

But this ceremony is also self-affirmation, the way poor blacks in New Orleans honor their own culture in a Carnival season that might otherwise pass them by, said the Big Chiefs who carry on the tradition, and the academics who study it.

These Indians march mostly in neighborhoods where the tourists do not go, ride on the hoods of dented Chevrolets instead of floats, and face off on street corners where poverty and violence grip the people most of the rest of the year. The escape is temporary, but it is escape.

"They say Rex is ruler," said Mr. Bannock, referring to the honorary title given to the king of Carnival, often a celebrity, who will glide through crowds of tourists and local revelers astride an elaborate float. "But not in the 17th Ward. 'Cause I'm the king here. This is our thing.

"The drums will be beating and everybody will be hollering and"—he paused to stab the needle through a mosaic of beads and canvas—"and it sounds like all my people's walking straight through hell."

BOX 2: NUT GRAF

A paragraph (or paragraphs) that sums up the story and provides the reader with context and background is the second box. Bragg steps back now from the close-up scene of Bannock working in his house to place him in the larger context. The phrase "He is one of the ..." is a signal that the nut section is beginning. Here the writer provides an analysis, which he attributes to the Big Chiefs and academics. The section ends on a dramatic quote, a useful method of narrative as punctuation.

A man does not need an Oldsmobile, with or without a bumper, if he can walk on air. Lifted there by the spirit of his neighborhood, it is his duty to face down the other Big Chiefs, to cut them down with words instead of bullets and straight razors, the way the Indians used to settle their disagreements in Mardi Gras in the early 1900s. Mr. Bannock, shot in the thigh by a jealous old chief in 1981, appears to be the last to have been wounded in battle.

"I forgave him," Mr. Bannock said.

The tribes have names like the Yellow Pocahontas, White Eagles, the Golden Star Hunters and the Wild Magnolias. The Big Chiefs are not born, but work their way up through the ranks. Only the best sewers and singers become Big Chiefs.

By tradition, the chiefs must sew their own costumes and must do a new costume from scratch each year. Mr. Bannock's fingers are scarred from a lifetime of it.

His right index finger is a mass of old punctures. Some men cripple themselves, through puncture wounds or repetitive motion, and have to retire. The costumes can cost $5,000 or more, a lot of cash in Gert Town.

The rhythms of their celebration, despite their feathered headdresses, seem more West African or Haitian than Indian, and the words are from the bad streets of the Deep South. Mr. Bannock said that no matter what the ceremony's origins, it belongs to New Orleans now. The battle chants have made their way into popular New Orleans music. The costumes hang in museums.

"Maybe it don't make no sense, and it ain't worth anything," said Mr. Bannock. But one day a year he leads his neighborhood on a hard, forced march to respect, doing battle at every turn with other chiefs who are out trying to do the same.

Jimmy Ricks is a 34-year-old concrete finisher most of the year, but on Mardi Gras morning he is a Spy Boy, the man who goes out ahead of the Big Chief searching for other chiefs. He is in love with the tradition, he said, because of what it means to people here.

"It still amazes me," he said, how on Mardi Gras mornings the people from the neighborhood drift over to Mr. Bannock's little house on Edinburgh Street and wait for a handyman to lead them.

"To understand it, you got to let your heart wander," said Mr. Bannock, who leads the Golden Star Hunters. "All I got to do is peek through my needle."

I'm 52 inches across my chest
And I don't bow to nothin'
'Cept God and death
—from a battle chant by
Larry Bannock

BOX 3: RETELLING

This box is almost a second lead, based on a new scene, detail or strong image, which allows the writer to begin retelling the story that began in the lead and draws the reader into the bulk of the story. Length can vary. In this section Bragg's reference to an Oldsmobile is an echo of the lead. It is a clever technique that acts as a transition from the nut section to a new one that continues with the story of Bannock and the Big Chiefs.

The more exclusive party within the party—the grand balls and societies that underlie the reeling, alcohol-soaked celebration that is Carnival—have always been By Invitation Only.

The origins of Carnival, which climaxes with Mardi Gras, or Fat Tuesday, are found in the Christian season of celebration before Lent. In New Orleans the celebration reaches back more than 150 years, to loosely

Continued

organized parades in the 1830s. One of the oldest Carnival organizations, the Mystick Krewe of Comus, staged the first organized parade. Today, Mardi Gras is not one parade but several, including that of the traditional Zulus, a black organization. But Comus, on Fat Tuesday, is still king.

The krewes were—some still are—secret societies. The wealthier whites and Creoles, many of whom are descendants of people of color who were free generations before the Civil War, had balls and parades, while poorer black men and women cooked the food and parked the cars.

Mardi Gras had no other place for them, said Dr. Frederick Stielow, director of Tulane University's Amistad Research Center, the largest minority archive in the nation. And many of these poorer blacks still are not part of the party, he said.

"These are people who were systematically denigrated," said Dr. Stielow, who has studied the Mardi Gras Indians for years. So they made their own party, "a separate reality," he said, to the hard work, racism and stark poverty.

It might have been a Buffalo Bill Wild West Show that gave them the idea to dress as Indians, Dr. Stielow said, but either way the first "Indian tribes" appeared in the late 1800s. They said they wore feathers as a show of affinity from one oppressed group to another, and to thank the Louisiana Indians for sanctuary in the slave days.

By the Great Depression these tribes, or "gangs" as they are now called, used Mardi Gras as an excuse to seek revenge on enemies and fought bloody battles, said the man who might be the biggest chief of all, 72-year-old Tootie Montana. He has been one for 46 years.

Mr. Bannock said, "They used to have a saying, 'Kiss your wife, hug your momma, sharpen your knife, and load your pistol.'"

Even after the violence faded into posturing, the New Orleans Police Department continued to break up the Indian gatherings. Mr. Bannock said New Orleans formally recognized the Indians' right to a tiny piece of Mardi Gras just two years ago.

Shoo fly, don't bother me
Shoo fly, don't bother me
If it wasn't for the warden and them low-down hounds
I'd be in New Orleans 'fore the sun go down
—Big Chief's battle chant, written by a chief while in the state prison in Angola

They speak a language as mysterious as any white man's krewe.

In addition to Spy Boys, there are Flag Boys—the flag bearers—and Second Line, the people, sometimes numbering in the hundreds, who follow the chiefs from confrontation to confrontation.

They march—more of a dance, really—from Downtown, Uptown, even across the river in the poor black sections of Algiers—until the Big Chiefs meet at the corner of Claiborne and Orleans Avenues and, inside a madhouse circle of onlookers, lash each other with words. Sometimes people almost faint from the strain.

But it is mainly with the costume itself that a man does battle, said Mr. Montana. The breastplates are covered with intricate pictures of Indian scenes, painstakingly beaded by hand. The feathers are brilliant yellows, blues, reds and greens.

The winner is often "the prettiest," Mr. Montana said, and that is usually him.

"I am the oldest, I am the best, and I am the prettiest," he said.

A few are well-off businessmen, at least one has served time in prison, but most are people who sweat for a living, like him.

Some chiefs do not make their own costumes, but pay to have them made—what Mr. Bannock calls "drugstore Indians." Of the 20 or so people who call themselves Big Chiefs, only a few remain true to tradition.

Box 4: BBI

Shorthand for "boring but important," this box contains less compelling material, such as quotes from experts or data bolstering the main theme. It rounds out the story and provides balance. Here Bragg includes material from an academic expert, hoping that by this time the reader is sufficiently engaged and interested to care about the event's history. Writers often make the mistake of including this kind of information earlier in the story before the reader is ready for it.

Mr. Bannock sits and sweats in his house, working day and night with his needle. He has never had time for a family. He lives for Fat Tuesday.

"I need my mornin' glory," he said.

A few years ago he had a heart attack but did not have time to die. He had 40 yards of velvet to cut and sew.

The New York Times
February 19, 1995

Box 5: Kicker

The story ends in this box. It may be a quote, an image, a comment; whatever you choose, the best endings resonate. Now Bragg comes full circle, returning to the scene in the lead. Many writers might end with the "mornin' glory" quote, but Bragg chooses to end the story with a detail that strikes the chord of his theme: one man's devotion to a tradition larger than himself.

THE SERIAL NARRATIVE:
"TO BE CONTINUED ..."

Newspapers have been home to serial narratives since a young reporter for London's *Morning Chronicle* named Charles Dickens published the first one in 1836. A serial narrative is "any story, whether told with words, visual images or drawings, that is broken up into segments and is revealed gradually," says Tom French, who has written several award-winning serial narratives for the *St. Petersburg Times*.

A serial narrative can run for a few days to several weeks. It can range in length from 200-inch installments about a murder investigation and trial to stories about life along the 45th parallel in Oregon. Ranging from short installments designed to be read in five minutes to segments consuming several newsprint pages and large chunks of a reader's time, this form provides what one writer called a "drip-feed of narrative satisfaction."

Newspaper writers such as Tom French and Donald Drake at *The Philadelphia Inquirer* have been writing book chapter-length serial narratives for two decades, and there has been a revival of the form in a briefer version.

Hoping to repeat the 19th-century success of Charles Dickens, newspapers in the mid-1990s embraced the serial narrative, with more than 25 series published around the country.

Installments of these serial narratives are designed to be short—800 to 1,000 words long. "That's a five-minute read. Your breakfast serial," notes Roy Peter Clark, senior scholar at The Poynter Institute. In 1996, Clark published two serial narratives, "Three Little Words," a 29-day series about a family's struggle with AIDS, and "Sadie's Ring: A Journey of the Spirit," a poignant 11-part chronicle about his experience as a young Catholic man experiencing his family's Jewish roots.

Greg Lampman, a reporter for the *Norfolk Virginian-Pilot* who is credited with writing some of the first serial narratives in the 1980s, turned to the form when editors stopped making room for his long feature stories. He researched the form by studying microfilmed copies of stories published in Norfolk at the turn of the century, when the city had 11 daily papers and when luring readers "wasn't a matter of increasing circulation; it was a matter of survival." The absence of international copyright laws gave newspaper publishers license to pirate serial narratives written by Europeans such as Dickens, Thackeray and de Maupassant. (Interestingly, because the papers could get these fiction serials free, many American writers turned to factual reporting, the only writing they could get paid for.)

Lampman wondered, "could we use these techniques in modern newspapers? What about taking dramatic stories I'd been writing at 300 inches and doing them as a serial?" He realized that the common thread of the 19th-century serial was not curiosity but rather something stronger—"suspense"—that created a need in readers—"you had to know." For Lampman, the serial was "born of necessity because it was the day of the designer. With newspapers choosing shorter stories as a way to stem readership decline, I couldn't get a long story into my paper." But, Lampman adds, "Writing these stories is a lot more than cutting them into pieces."

Boosters of the serial narrative point to immense reader response—thousands of Web site "hits" as modern readers exhibit the same intense interest as did readers of Dickens' serials.

Jan Winburn, who edits serial narratives at *The Baltimore Sun*, identified four elements needed for a successful serial:

1. THE ENGINE. The unanswered question that drives the story—and the reader—forward. In *Wizard of Oz*, the question is whether Dorothy will get home to Kansas. In *Jurassic Park*, it's who will end up in the digestive tract of the dinosaur. In mysteries, it's whodunit.

    Although every narrative needs an engine—a narrative thread that drives the story and pulls the reader along—the serial narrative imposes extra burdens. If the narrative is a mountain that the reader is climbing, a serial requires what Winburn calls "switchbacks," things you didn't expect, lots of twists and turns, which give you the opportunity for cliffhangers.

    In the opening section of his award-winning serial, "A Stage in Their Lives," Ken Fuson of *The Baltimore Sun* introduces the story's engine—the suspense surrounding the mounting of a high school play—and its theme—a rite of passage:

Spellbound she sits, her mother on one side, her boyfriend on the other, as another young woman performs the role that will someday be hers.

Since she was little, Angie Guido has dreamed of standing on stage, playing the Puerto Rican girl who falls in love with the Polish boy named Tony.

Maria.

She will be Maria in *West Side Story*.

Say it loud and there's music playing.

"That's me, Mom," she said.

Say it soft and it's almost like praying.

It won't be long, Angie thinks as she delights in a touring company production of *West Side Story* at the Lyric Opera House in Baltimore. She and 20 members of the Drama Club from North County High School in Anne Arundel County attend the December show with a few parents. This is a prelude; there is expectant talk they will stage the same show for their spring musical.

Someday soon, Angie hopes, she will own the role that is rightfully hers. She has been a loyal drama club soldier, serving on committees, singing in the chorus when she yearned for a solo, watching lead roles slip away because she didn't look the part. But Maria is short, as she is, and dark, as she is, and more than that, Angie is a senior. This will be her last spring musical. Her last chance to shine.

Continued

But on the very next night, in that very same theater, another girl from North County High sits spellbound, her mother on one side, her best friend on the other.

She, too, is captivated by the Puerto Rican girl with the pretty voice.

She, too, wonders: What if that were me?

Two months later, in the middle of February, two dozen students gather in a dark and cavernous auditorium at North County High School to plan the spring musical.

You don't know them. Not yet.

Find a seat—there, in the middle, close to the stage—and watch.

You will meet two girls. One will have her dream come true, the other won't, and the experience will change them both.

You will meet a boy who can't sing but refuses to quit trying.

You will meet another boy, the leading man, who falls for one of the leading ladies. But so will someone else.

You will meet a girl who wants to be a star, then chooses a new destiny.

Come to the practices. Laugh at their goofy jokes. Encourage them when they flub their lines.

Soon you will know them.

And you will know this:

The high school musical is a rite of passage that will shape—and reveal—the adults they will soon be.

And nothing ever produced on stage can possibly match the drama of growing up.

By Ken Fuson
The Baltimore Sun
June 1, 1997

2. **ACCESS.** You need good access for any narrative story, but you can't have any reluctant sources for a serial narrative. When Fuson wrote his serial narrative, he attended scores of rehearsals, interviewed the students, teachers, their parents. Tom French of the *St. Petersburg Times* dressed up in a toga to follow the high schoolers he profiled in his serial narrative "South of Heaven."

3. A **"GOLD MINE" SOURCE.** Someone who knows all the answers, has all the details the reporter needs to craft a believable, dramatic story. Usually it's the subject of the narrative, but it can also be a detective or prosecutor privy to workings of a criminal case or a doctor overseeing the care of a cancer patient. Of course, the reporter should make every effort to verify the source's account with documents and interviews.

4. **THE BIG PAYOFF.** A resonant ending.

The unifying feature of a serial narrative is not length. Rather, "the serial forces the reader to wait, and that quality, that sense of enforced waiting, is what makes serial narratives different," says French.

Serial narratives have focused on a variety of subjects: ordinary life, crime, personal crisis, quests, and rites of passage, including the first year in the life of a widow and the making of a high school play.

A SERIAL NARRATIVE GLOSSARY

At a 1998 conference on serial narratives at The Poynter Institute, reporters and editors responsible for producing the more than two dozen narratives published since 1996 created a glossary of terms:

THE THREE DRAGONS. The main character in a serial narrative needs to face a series of challenges, just as medieval knights had to slay not just one but three dragons before reaching their goal. In a news serial, the main character can't kill all the dragons in the first chapter. He or she must kill one, then another, then another, in an increasingly more dramatic way.

CLIFFHANGER. A dramatic point at which to conclude a chapter, encouraging the reader to come back tomorrow. "At the end of each chapter, there has to be that, 'I want to go on.'" Example: Study how Fuson accomplishes that goal at the end of the first installment of "A Stage in Their Lives" by returning to the question posed in the lead: Who will get the part of Maria?

Casting Maria is just as easy. When the choice is finally made, there is no discussion about who has her heart set on the role, or who will be crushed with disappointment, or who has dreamed of playing Maria since that December night when she saw it on stage.

Only one question matters: Who can do it best?

Mr. Shipley writes the winner's name on a piece of paper.

NARRATIVE ARC. The curved line that connects the beginning of the story to the end. In *Romeo and Juliet* it is a boy and girl from feuding families falling in love, their deaths showing their families the cost of such hatred. In "Angels and Demons," Tom French tracks a murder from the crime to the killer's conviction.

SWITCHBACKS. Surprising reversals of fortune, plot twists that shock the reader.

GOLD MINE SOURCE. Court records, a diary, a willing source with a great memory, a trunk of letters.

STAKEHOLDER. A key character with something important at stake.

BIG PAYOFF. A satisfying ending to a long series: a resolution, revelation or exaltation.

CONCLUSION

"Can you imagine Hemingway or Steinbeck or Mark Twain—journalists all—sitting down to figure out whether an inverted pyramid or an hourglass structure would be the best formula for one of their stories?" asks writing coach Richard Andersen. "Good writers let their stories determine their own structures, but each course brings with it a new set of formulas."

Avoid formulas by reading widely. Andersen continues, "Reporters have to read more—not just the best writers in their field, for they, too, are often limited by preconceived ideas of what constitutes good writing—but our world's best writers, the ones who write what we call literature. They are the writers whose narrative techniques are as multiple and various as life itself—the way newspaper writing should be—and they are also the people who, at least in their writing, refuse to compromise their human integrity."

I agree with Andersen. But I also believe that to break the rules you need to know them and that on deadline even a creative, uncompromising reporter may need to rely on a formula. So which shape should the reporter select?

The accompanying table provides some guidelines.

STORY FORM GUIDELINES

Story Structure	Story Type
Inverted pyramid	Breaking news: police and crime news, accidents, meeting coverage, elections
Hourglass	Breaking news: stories with strong dramatic appeal that can best be told with a chronological narrative
Nut graf	Breaking news: news analysis, opinion pieces, news features, features, trend stories
Narrative	Stories that rely on characterizations, action line, rising action, climax and resolution
Five boxes	News features, trend stories, profiles, breaking news

Whichever form you choose, remember Associated Press Enterprise Editor Bruce DeSilva's point that none of journalism's forms "inherently requires a writer to sound pompous and dull." The most important thing to remember is "don't report a form; report a story." The more and better reporting you do through interviews, research, observation and analysis, the more likely you are to write a story that conveys more than just the five W's, no matter what shape the story assumes.

BIRTH OF THE INVERTED PYRAMID: A CHILD OF TECHNOLOGY, COMMERCE AND HISTORY

Before the end of the 19th century, journalist historians agree, stories were almost always told in the traditional, slow-paced (some might say long-winded) way. Whether they were fairy tales or newspaper accounts, they began with a signal that something important, useful, inspiring or entertaining was about to begin ("Once upon a time"). The narrator, or storyteller, started at the beginning and continued to the end, leaving the outcome until the last ("And they lived happily ever after").

Consider the leisurely style of British correspondent William Howard Russell in his coverage of the Battle of Balaklava in 1854.

If the exhibition of the most brilliant valor, of the excess of courage, and of a daring which would have reflected luster on the best days of chivalry can afford full consolation for the disaster of today, we can have no reason to regret the melancholy loss which we sustained in a contest with a savage and barbarian enemy.

Not until the end of the story does Russell get to the news: Because of a mix-up in orders a 650-man cavalry brigade charged head-on into enemy guns. In a few minutes more than 100 were dead. But Russell had no reason to write an urgent story because it would take nearly three weeks for his dispatch to reach his readers by boat and train and spread news of "The Charge of the Light Brigade."

That all changed with worldwide adoption of the telegraph, invented in 1845 by a portrait painter named Samuel Morse. A new and radically different story form—dubbed the inverted pyramid—emerged, a product of new technology and a changing intellectual environment that embraced realism in art, science and literature.

The inverted pyramid might not have happened were it not for the invention of the telegraph. The thing to know about the telegraph is that in its day it was as revolutionary as the Internet. In this age of instantaneous communication and "live late-breaking news," it's hard to imagine the reality of communications technology 150 years ago when it took two days for a letter to travel from Washington to New York, and a letter to the West Coast took a month by stagecoach or steamer via Panama.

But the telegraph had a drawback. It was expensive to use. One of the first charges was a penny a character. Newspapers spent hundreds of thousands of dollars in telegraph costs to report the Civil War. That economic pressure more than anything else influenced a new kind of writing that departed from the flowery language of the 19th century—it was concise, stripped of opinion and detail. Fueling the shift in writing style was a new type of news organization, named the "wire service" after the technology used to transmit the news. The fledgling Associated Press at one of its first meetings established the trend with an agreement that stories would be brief, tailored for a national audience and deliberately stripped of the partisanship that characterized American newspapers until that time. This technology—the telegraph and

Continued

the lingo of its transoceanic partner, the cable—provided, as journalism scholar James Carey said, "the underlying structure for one of the most influential literary styles of the 20th century."

By creating the "wire services," Carey says, the telegraph "led to a fundamental change in news. It snapped the tradition of partisan journalism by forcing the wire services to generate 'objective' news, news that could be used by papers of any political stripe." It eliminated the letter-writing correspondent, who announced an event and described it in rich detail as well as analyzing its substance, "and replaced him with a stringer who supplied the bare facts."

A popular myth about the inverted pyramid holds that it came about during the American Civil War (1861–1865) when reporters in the field who relied on the telegraph had to make sure they sent the most important news first in case the wires were cut. It's a romantic idea—and not a bad way for journalists to think of their own stories. If you had to send your story by telegraph, and the line was cut after the 1st or 2nd or 15th paragraph, would people at the other end know what the story is about?

The problem with that myth is that researchers who have studied leading American papers in the Civil War find numerous examples of stories written in the chronological style of the day rather than the "first news first" style of the inverted pyramid. It came later than that, and a young journalism historian named David T. Z. Mindich makes a persuasive case that "the inverted pyramid was born with the coverage of Lincoln's death."

Early in the morning on April 15, 1865, as President Abraham Lincoln lay dying from an assassin's bullet, newspapers received a copy of a telegram written by Secretary of War Edwin Stanton to the commanding general in New York City.

Although he was a government official and not a journalist, many editors chose his official account to run on the front page of their newspapers. Here's how it appeared in the *New York Herald* on April 15, 1865:

This evening at about 9:30 p.m. at Ford's Theatre, the President, while sitting in his private box with Mrs. Lincoln, Mrs. Harris and Major Rathburn, was shot by an assassin, who suddenly entered the box and approached behind the President.

The assassin then leaped upon the stage, brandishing a large dagger or knife, and made his escape in the rear of the theatre.

The pistol ball entered the back of the President's head and penetrated nearly through the head. The wound is mortal.

The President has been insensible ever since it was inflicted, and is now dying.

About the same hour an assassin, whether the same or not, entered Mr. Seward's apartment and under pretense of having a prescription was shown to the Secretary's sick chamber. The assassin immediately rushed to the bed and inflicted two or three stabs on the chest and two on the face.

It is hoped the wounds may not be mortal. My apprehension is that they will prove fatal.

The nurse alarmed Mr. Frederick Seward, who was in an adjoining room, and he hastened to the door of his father's room, when he met the assassin, who inflicted upon him one or more dangerous wounds. The recovery of Frederick Seward is doubtful.

It is not probable that the President will live through the night.

General Grant and his wife were advertised to be at the theatre this evening, but he started to Burlington at six o'clock this evening.

By today's standards, that story probably seems pretty old-fashioned, nothing at all like the "live, late-breaking" style of today's multimedia news delivery. But in 1865 it represented a revolutionary departure from the way news was normally presented.

Researchers have been unable to find examples of the inverted pyramid in coverage of the Civil War published by leading American papers. Stanton's telegram about the Lincoln assassination, Mindich argues, was the first significant example of a new way to write the news. Unlike the leisurely, ornate prose that filled most newspapers, Stanton's got right to the point: Someone shot the president of the United States, and he wasn't going to survive. "On or about April 15, 1865," Mindich says, "the character of news writing changed."

During the U.S. Civil War (1861–65) soldiers as well as civilians relied on newspapers, like these sold by a traveling dealer, to keep track of wartime news. (Courtesy of The Library of Congress)

SHAPING THE NEWS: THE COACHING WAY

- Make a list of everything you think belongs in your story. Number the list in terms of importance.
- Every story, no matter what form, has a beginning, middle and end. Make three piles, labeled *B*, *M* and *E*, and separate your list of separate elements by the part they belong in.
- Put yourself in your readers' or viewers' place. What questions do you have about the story? Can you organize your story so that each paragraph answers the readers' or viewers' questions in the order they ask them?
- Plan your ending first. What do you want your readers or viewers to do when they finish your story? Register to vote? Get an AIDS test? Open an individual retirement account? Rethink their opinions on an important issue? What do you have in your notes—a detail, a statistic, a quote—that might provoke such a response? Write it and show it to someone and ask his or her reaction.
- Plan your beginning. What's the news? What's the story?
- The next time you're stuck on a story, employ the "five boxes" method of story organization suggested by Rick Bragg of *The New York Times*. But don't feel bound to stick with it. "Even if you just completely scramble it later on," Bragg says, "at least it got you going."

GLOSSARY OF IMPORTANT TERMS

"Five boxes" story approach. A way of organizing a story in five parts: a lead, nut graf, a retelling of the story, background and kicker.

Hourglass. A story form that delivers the news value of the inverted pyramid and the storytelling power of the narrative. Composed of three parts: a four- to five-paragraph "top" that reports the most important news elements; a transition paragraph called the "turn" that shifts the story from a report to a story and contains attribution indicating the source of the information to come; and the "narrative," usually a chronological retelling of the story reported in the top using dialogue and scenes.

Inverted pyramid. A story form that puts the most newsworthy information at the top, and then the remaining information follows in order of importance, with the least important at the bottom.

Kicker. Newsroom jargon for a story ending that delivers a resonant conclusion with a detail, example or, most often but often least effective, a quote.

Narrative. The classic story form, featuring a beginning, middle and end, characters, theme, plot, climax and resolution. Scenes are the building blocks of narrative.

Nut graf (sometimes spelled "graph"). One to three paragraphs that summarize the theme of a story and tell the reader what the story is about and offer a reason to read it. Usually follows an anecdotal lead.

Serial narrative. A narrative broken up into segments that unfolds in installments.

EXERCISES

1. Study 10 news stories and determine what form they follow: inverted pyramid, hourglass, nut graf, narrative, serial narrative.

2. To determine whether your story needs a nut graf, follow the advice of Jack Hart, staff development director at *The Oregonian*: "Try putting yourself in the reader's place. Forget what you know about the story, read the first three paragraphs and ask yourself what the entire story's about. If you can't answer with reasonable accuracy, you need a nut paragraph."

3. Using the analysis of Rick Bragg's "Mardi Gras" story as a model, do the same exercise with one of your own stories. Break the story into "five boxes" by selecting the paragraphs or sections that make up the lead, the nut graf, the retelling of the story, the boring but important information and the kicker. Explain your choices.

4. Discuss how Ken Fuson creates suspense in the opening to "A Stage in Their Lives."

READINGS

Blundell, William E. *The Art and Craft of Feature Writing.* New York: New American Library, 1988.

Carey, James. "Technology and Ideology: The Case of the Telegraph." *Communication as Culture.* Boston: Unwin Hyman, 1989.

Clark, Roy Peter. "A New Shape for the News." *Best Newspaper Writing 1997*, pp. 255–258.

Hart, Jack. "Nut Graf." *Second Takes*, vol. 5, no. 4, August 1993.

Lindley, William R. *20th-Century American Newspapers in Content and Production.* Manhattan, Kan.: Sunflower University Press, 1993.

Stewart, James B. *Follow the Story: How to Write Successful Nonfiction.* New York: Simon and Schuster, 1998.

HOTLIST

http://interactive.wsj.com

The Wall Street Journal interactive edition. You have to pay to subscribe to this site, unlike the vast majority of online newspapers. But you can log on free for a 30-day trial subscription and read a month's worth of stories that illustrate the continuing power of this national newspaper's influence on writing and style.

http://www.ap.org

The Associated Press continues to set the standard for coverage of breaking news. In recent years, under enterprise editor Bruce DeSilva, AP writers have also been experimenting with narrative forms.

http://www.nytimes.com

The New York Times continues to rely on the inverted pyramid for much of its news coverage. The power and pitfalls of the form are on daily display. Of course, it also publishes compelling narratives regularly.

http://www.asne.org/kiosk/editor/december/clark.htm

"Serial Form Can Draw Readers in for Weeks." In this article on the American Society of Newspaper Editors' Web site, Roy Peter Clark describes his experience writing serial narratives and explains why the form is popular with newspaper readers and a growing number of journalists.

http://www.poynter.org/3LittleWords/3lw_intro.htm

http://www.poynter.org/SRing/sr_intro.htm

You can read Clark's serial narratives, "Three Little Words" and "Sadie's Ring," on the Poynter Institute Web site.

http://www.asne.org/kiosk/writingawards/98writingawards.htm#Fuson

"A Stage in Their Lives" is Ken Fuson's 1998 Best Newspaper Writing Award–winning serial narrative about a group of high school students staging *West Side Story*.

http://www2.sptimes.com/Angels_Demons/default.html

Read two of Tom French's narratives, including his 1998 Pulitzer Prize–winning series, "Angels & Demons," and its successor, "The Girl Whose Mother Lives in the Sky." Other serial narratives by Anne Hull, Bill Adair and other writers of the *St. Petersburg Times* can be found at **http://www.sptimes.com/web_specials.htm**.

CHAPTER

6

LEARNING TO LISTEN: BUILDING INTERVIEWING SKILLS

CHAPTER FOCUS

Interviewing requires more than a good ear for quotes; it's a process, like writing, that involves a series of decisions and actions designed to get the best possible information.

CHAPTER LESSONS

- The process of interviewing
- How telephone interviews become stories
- Questions that start and stop interviews
- Learning to listen
- Advice for interviewers
- Note-taking skills for interviews
- Pros and cons of taping interviews
- How to get and use quotes
- On and off the record: Guidelines for sourcing stories
- Interviewing: The Coaching Way

INTRODUCTION

Effective interviewing is a pillar of good reporting and writing. The ability to talk comfortably with people and to persuade them to give you information will be one of your most important skills. Yet journalists get little or no training in this vital aspect of their job. Most learn by painful trial and error. This chapter is designed to help you become an effective interviewer, a valuable skill whether you report for newspapers, radio or television, online news or advertising and public relations. How do you get strangers—tight-lipped cops, jargon-spouting experts, everyday folks who aren't accustomed to being interviewed—to talk to you? How do you make certain you've gotten down correctly what they said? How do you use what you get from an interview in your story? The ability to ask good questions and listen to the answers lies at the heart of the interviewer's craft—and of this chapter. We'll cover the range of issues that interviewing raises: types of interviews, types of questions and their purposes, the tools of interviewing, note-taking techniques, the attributes of a good interview and interviewer, the pros and cons of tape recorders, interview ground rules, and interviewing by e-mail.

Interviewers at Work: The Process of Interviewing

Reporting is the practice of gathering current information. The interview—whether face-to-face, over the telephone or, increasingly, by e-mail—is the way reporters get most of that information. The most current information—although not necessarily the most accurate—is usually what comes out of someone's mouth.

A good interview is wonderful, but not magical. Like good reporting and writing, interviewing is a process: a series of steps and actions that can be analyzed, described and repeated. You can apply the same process approach to interviewing that you apply to produce good writing. With some modifications, of course.

Compare the writing process with the interviewing process:

Writers at Work	Interviewers at Work
Idea	Idea
Collect	Plan-Focus/Arrange
Focus	Collect
Order	Order
Draft	Draft
Revise	Revise

Idea

This is the launching point. An interview can be prompted by a variety of things: an event such as an accident or fire, a public meeting, an issue of importance to your community, a newsmaker. The unifying element is *the need for information provided by another person*. The quality of the interview—and the information collected—depends on the thought and care the reporter puts into the rest of the steps in the process. Some ideas for interviews are obvious. A house fire breaks out in your community, so you must interview the firefighters, victims and neighbors. It's Election Day, so you interview politicians, campaign workers, winners, losers, voters. But whom should you interview when a new chain store arrives in town, or when you're trying to do a story about cheating on campus?

Every story idea generates its own unique list of interviewing possibilities. As a beginner, you may get some of your assignments from an editor. Spend a few minutes with her going over a list of possible interviewees. If it's your own idea, say, for a feature story, generate your own list of potential interview subjects. Use an approach Don Murray used in his long career as a reporter and magazine writer: In front of your notebook write a list of the five or six questions that readers would ask about your story and number them in the order that readers would ask them. Imagine that you had the assignment to interview former astronaut and now U.S. Sen. John Glenn about his plans to return to space in 1999, more than three decades after he became the first American to orbit the Earth. Here's a list of potential questions:

1. Isn't he too old?
2. Why does he want to do it?
3. Does he need special attention, equipment, training?
4. What if he dies up there?
5. Will this mean that all of the old astronauts will want to do it?
6. What surprised him the most in the training?
7. What's the biggest difference in the technology since he first orbited in space?
8. What do his wife and children think of the idea?

PLAN-FOCUS

As with all reporting and writing, *thinking* is the most important thing you can do to make the most out of every interview. It's important to stay alert at every stage of the interview, but the time you take at the beginning of the process is among the most crucial. This is the time to develop a strategy or plan, a series of maneuvers to ensure you reach your goal of a productive interview. Two important factors will aid in your planning:

1. Goal setting. First, identify your goal. The effective interviewer knows what she wants from her interview. She's like a chess player, in the view of John Brady, author of *The Craft of Interviewing*, never moving a piece or asking a question without a purpose. When somebody asks you a question, don't you sometimes wonder, "Why does she want to know?" It's the same for people you interview, so be clear in your own mind. Here are the types of questions you may want to ask yourself at this point:

   • What do I want to know? What does my audience need to know?
   • Who is most likely to give me what I need? Who is closest to the action or issue—the city councilwoman or the neighborhood resident, the police spokeswoman or the crime victim's spouse?
   • What's the quickest and most efficient way to reach my goal?

2. Type of interview. Now is the time to determine the type of interview you plan to conduct. Interviews can be in person, by telephone or even via e-mail. The face-to-face interview should be your first

choice. It's easier to ignore a phone call than a person standing in front of you. In person you have a better chance of persuading someone that you are a professional with an important job to do. Over the phone, you can get only a person's words; face-to-face you can gather details about that person's appearance, where that person lives or works or plays.

That holds especially true for broadcast journalists, although a tight deadline may mean settling for a taped telephone interview. There are drawbacks still, says veteran radio and television reporter Deborah Potter. "Obviously you don't get the kind of quality recording you would get in person. You can't make eye contact."

Regardless of medium, the face-to-face interview lets the reporter "look for the meaning behind the answer, the body language that says this is not really how I feel; it's what I have been told to say." Potter says, "Follow those clues with follow-up questions."

"You can get more accomplished by leaving the office than waiting for phone calls," agrees John Silcox, one of Poynter's summer reporting fellows. Instead of hanging around the newsroom waiting for people to call him back for a story he was working on, Silcox headed for City Hall and then the neighborhood he was covering and got what he needed for his story. "It might not always work," he says, "but you have a better chance of getting the interview if you go on the offensive."

DEADLINE REPORTING: How TELEPHONE INTERVIEWS BECOME STORIES

The day after a jetliner bound for Paris exploded and crashed over the Atlantic Ocean off Long Island on July 17, 1996, reporters for *Newsday* scrambled to find out information about the tragedy's 230 victims. Reporters fanned out over the region, while some, like Deborah Barfield, a social issues reporter, stayed behind in the newsroom, doing multiple interviews by telephone and crafting a story from the information she and her colleagues gathered. Alongside her story you can read her account of the reporting, including the search for sources and her interviewing method. Her questions are basic, simple and open-ended: "Tell me a little bit about him. What did he wear? What did he do? How often did he come in? And what was he doing when he came in?"

Like many reporters, Barfield is self-conscious, knowing she is intruding on another person's grief. But she has a mission—"to let folks know about this person they cared about"—and that helps her ask questions she worries are "stupid or personal" in a way that is respectful and effective. On deadline at a desk hundreds of miles away, she is able to write a story that transforms a name, an accident statistic, into a person.

Deadlines and distance often make personal interviews impossible. Enter the telephone—which some reporters consider their most important tool. "Phones connect reporters to sources, to facts, to information and verification," says National Public Radio host Susan Stamberg. In the hands of a curious, sympathetic and professional reporter, the telephone can be an indispensable device for gathering information about people in the news.

Friends, relatives and co-workers honor the memory of the victims of TWA Flight 800. (AP/Wide World Photos)

The Story

Newsday
July 19, 1996

Only days ago, TWA Capt. Steven Snyder stopped by a small airport in Bridgeport to check on the single-engine plane he loved to fly over the Connecticut countryside.

"He called it his pet," corporate pilot Stanley Logan, one of Snyder's flying bud-

dies for 15 years, said yesterday at the airport. "It was his pride and joy. He got more of a kick out of flying the small one than the big one."

Snyder was a captain aboard the TWA jumbo jet that exploded and crashed off Long Island Wednesday, killing him and 229 others aboard the flight. ...

When Snyder wasn't flying TWA planes to Europe, he was checking his plane or flying it across the state, Logan said. "He loved TWA and he loved to fly."

When he wasn't flying, he could be found on the golf course at the Oronoque Country Club. Pro shop manager Dawn Kusznir remembers him with pipe in hand, leaning across the glass at the pro shop.

"I was terrified of flying. He would reassure me about how safe the planes were. He said he was never afraid," Kusznir said. "He said these planes were so well taken care of. ... He would say, 'I wouldn't be flying if I thought something was wrong with my plane.'"

HOW I WROTE THE STORY
THE INTERVIEWS

A Conversation with Deborah Barfield

I was supposed to try to find out as much as I could about the TWA pilots. The library was working with us, especially with names and addresses and phone numbers to call neighbors. I knew somebody who used to work at TWA. He told me that one of the pilots had a license for a small plane, and he was able to give me the name of the airport and the number. They connected me with somebody who had just seen him the other day. I found out that he was a golfer. Some of his neighbors didn't want to talk on the record, but they led me to the golf course. I called there, and the manager was able to give us a lot more color. I learned to tell people that I just wanted to let folks know about this person they cared about. Simply asking, "Tell me a little bit about him. What did he wear? What did he do? How often did he come in? And what was he doing when he came in?" People wanted to share that, especially with somebody they liked. As one person was talking about it you could tell she was smiling. And I smiled and laughed along with her and got her to open up. By the time I was asking stupid questions like, "What color?" or "What kind of pipe?" it wasn't like I was asking a stupid or personal question. By then she was telling you about somebody that meant something to her."

Deborah
Barfield (Cour-
tesy of
Newsday)

ARRANGE

In the case of breaking news, arrangements may be limited to finding out the address of the fire or motor vehicle accident, or looking up a telephone number. If you're setting up an interview with an official or a neighborhood resident, you can call ahead and make an appointment, get directions, describe the purpose of the interview. If the interview subject is media-shy or a celebrity, find out who might be able to help you get the interview. A go-between may be needed.

Approaching a complete stranger sounds terrifying, doesn't it? My students usually find that task to be one of the most daunting until they've done a few interviews, and then they say it's easier if they keep a few thoughts in mind:

1. Most people love to talk, especially about themselves. Over and over, students discover how readily people are willing to share their lives with a reporter, especially one who appears professional, mature and interested.

2. Often the people you're interviewing are more afraid of the reporter. The more you can do to stay as relaxed as possible, the more comfortable you can make them and the better interview you will get.

PREPARE

A good interview requires preparation. Once you've identified what you want to accomplish, you should draw up a tentative list of questions designed to help you reach that goal. Even after two decades' experience doing interviews for radio and television, former CBS and CNN correspondent Deborah Potter admits: "I actually make a list of questions. I find it helps me remember to ask the questions I came in with, because an interview is almost a living thing. It can go off in unexpected directions."

Brainstorm a list of questions, either in a notepad or on your computer screen. Consult with your editor or colleagues: What do they want to know about this subject or issue?

Off deadline, develop a checklist of questions for recurring stories: fires, accidents, election results. You can use the examples of checklists that appear in this book. Keep these questions on file. Eventually, they'll become second nature, although it's a good idea to refresh yourself occasionally by consulting the checklist and revising it.

Before you head for the interview or pick up the phone ask yourself: What's the best-case—and worst-case—scenario? The best might be that the mayor admits he's embezzled city funds to support families in six other cities. The worst case: "no comment." If I'm expecting a refusal, I might even write a script: "Hi. I'm so and so, and I'm writing an article about such and such." This forces you to make clear what you're after as well as allowing you to present a coherent pitch. (If possible, I like to be able to say "So-and-So suggested I talk to you"; it makes me less of a stranger.)

Of course, as investigative reporters well know, not everyone will want to talk with you. That's why Stephen Kurkjian, a Pulitzer Prize–winning journalist for *The Boston Globe*, adopted the practice of preparing what he called "a long list, a short list and a 'hello-goodbye'" list of questions that he used depending on the person's reaction.

Make sure your equipment—notebook, pen, laptop—is ready and in working order. If you're using a tape recorder, check the batteries and make sure you have spares for an emergency. Bring extra tapes and, even if you're recording the interview, bring along a notebook in case the machine fails.

Always have a notebook and a pen. Don't ever be caught without one.

Get smart. "The best questions are informed questions," says Eric Nalder of *The Seattle Times*. Make your first stop the file, paper or electronic, of previous stories or books on the subject. Learn the background so you don't have to waste the subject's time—or your own—with unnecessary, uninformed questions.

No matter how hard you prepare or how well educated you are, there will always be stories where your knowledge is limited. That brings us to one of the cardinal rules of interviewing: *In reporting there is no such thing as a stupid question.*

In fact, you might as well start right now thinking that you are in the business of asking questions that other people might consider stupid. Your job as a reporter is to ask questions that seem obvious, personal and sometimes stupid. Journalism is a learning profession, a job that has inquiry at its core.

COLLECT

The heart of the interview process is the collecting of information. You do this, principally, by asking questions, listening to and recording the answers either in a notebook or electronically. Interviewers also collect non-oral information, such as details about the appearance of an interview subject, the person's surroundings, actions and reactions.

Radio journalist Susan Stamberg conducted about 7,000 interviews in the first 10 years of National Public Radio's *All Things Considered*. She says:

"My best interviews are the ones in which I listen most carefully: for new ideas, new perspectives, but also for slips of the tongue, slips of logic; for contradictions, enthusiasm, tension; for what's not being said; for silences, too, and what they reveal."

LISTEN TO NPR INTERVIEWS ONLINE AT http://www.npr.org

The effective interviewer does more than listen. We'll pay close attention to listening later in this chapter. You collect observations, and the richest ones usually come in a person's surroundings. "I always try to see people at home, no matter where else I may see them," says Carol McCabe, one of the most gifted writers at *The Providence Journal*. "In their own surroundings, you can see them much more naturally, watch them interact with others, and, most important, see the choices they have made: pictures, books, music, tools, toys, kids' rooms, formal or informal approach to home life. I can learn something from where the TV is, whether the set of encyclopedias or bowling trophies is prominently displayed, whether the guy hugs his wife or touches his kids, what clothes he or she wears at home, what's on the refrigerator door."

All interviews have to begin somewhere, and where most of them begin is with the question.

RED LIGHT, GREEN LIGHT: ASKING QUESTIONS THAT START AND STOP CONVERSATION

The dictionary defines a question as "a sentence in an interrogative form, addressed to someone in order to get information in reply." Notice that the root of the word is *quest*, which is a "search or pursuit made in order to find or obtain something." As a reporter you will be constantly in pursuit of the most timely, compelling and accurate information. Posed by a sincere, curious and open mind, the question is the most important tool you can use to reach that goal. Questions can be keys that open a door to a person's life or beliefs. Or they can act as padlocks, barring you from discovering the information and stories you need to do your job.

"Questions are precise instruments," says John Sawatsky, a Canadian journalist and teacher who knows how to ask questions that get rich answers. Used carefully, questions can make the difference between an answer and a quotable answer.

READ MORE ABOUT JOHN SAWATSKY'S INTERVIEWING THEORIES ONLINE AT http://www. algonet.se/ ~journal/ arteng.htm

I first met John Sawatsky, a, soft-spoken man who is the author of the definitive biography of Canadian Prime Minister Brian Mulroney, when he came to The Poynter Institute to teach interviewing to college reporting and writing students. After 20 years and thousands of interviews, I figured I knew what I was doing, but his interviewing workshop opened my eyes and ears. Interviewing isn't an art or a science, he told us. It's something in between, closer to a social science. You can make some predictions about an interview but not absolute ones because interviewing involves human beings who don't always behave in predictable ways. Ask the wrong question, and even a cooperative interview subject may not be able to give you the information you need. The question is the interviewer's most useful tool, but reporters ask too many questions (one-third to one-half, Sawatsky estimates) that suppress, rather than produce, information.

There's nothing more frustrating than trying to interview someone and getting one- or two-word answers ("Yes," "No," "Maybe," "I dunno"). Beginning reporters often blame their sources—the police are stonewalling, lawyers are tight-lipped, neighborhood residents are paranoid—but the fault often lies in the kind of questions they ask.

Many reporters confuse interviewing with interrogating, which involves questioning people about things they may consider personal or want to keep secret. I've listened as colleagues machine-gunned sources with queries, firing one after another. They're surprised when the sources hang up on them or answer in monosyllables. The most productive interviews are conversations, informal exchanges that encourage a flow of thoughts and information.

There are two basic categories of questions: questions that encourage conversation and questions that stifle it. Some interviewing experts refer to these types as open-ended and closed-ended. The most effective are open-ended, encouraging the person you're interviewing to respond fully. They are the opposite of closed-ended questions, questions that demand a brief, unequivocal response: "Yes," "No," "I don't know" or "No comment." I prefer the terms "conversation starters" and "conversation stoppers," or **"green light"** and **"red light,"** because that's what they can do. Whatever you call them, the one you choose to ask may end up suppressing rather than inviting answers.

CONVERSATION STARTERS: GREEN LIGHT	CONVERSATION STOPPERS: RED LIGHT
What was it like to be the only woman astronaut on the space shuttle?	Were you glad to be the only woman astronaut on the space shuttle?
How would you describe the treatment you underwent for AIDS?	Is AIDS treatment difficult?
Why did you decide to go to Pakistan for your junior year abroad?	Are you proud that you went to Pakistan for your junior year abroad?

CONVERSATION STARTERS are questions that send a clear message: Tell me your story. By asking such questions as "How did ... ?" "Why do ... ?" and "What is ...?" the reporter encourages subjects to tell anecdotes, opinions, the kind of complete answers that shed light on personality and attitudes. They keep the current of conversation flowing. Open-ended questions— "How did ... ?" "Why do ... ?" and "What is ... ?"—produce anecdotes, quotations and opinion and give the interviewee more control over content.

"Open-ended questions let the subject tell you what their thoughts are instead of simply responding to the narrow focus of yours," says Deb Nelson of the *Chicago Sun-Times.* Ira Berkow, a sports columnist for *The New York Times,* says that a successful interview can be conducted with just two questions: "What are your greatest hopes?" and "What are your greatest fears?"

Tough questions rarely get answers; they get defenses or denials. Tough questions are those that make the person you're interviewing work. Sawatsky compares the interview to a canoeing trip: The reporter steers, the source does the paddling. Asking, "Why do you believe that?" requires an explanation; "How did you arrive at the conclusion?" requires a description.

Sophisticated news sources will take advantage of a badly asked question: Said one press secretary, "I never lied to a reporter. But I more than once sought refuge in a badly worded explanation."

CONVERSATION STOPPERS are questions that stop conversation because they offer an interview subject a limited range of possible answers. "Did you kill your wife?" "Will you run for re-election?" "Do you deny ...?" "Any big arrests today?" These questions all close off rather than open the flow of conversation. "Are folks in the neighborhood upset about the nuclear power plant?" Sawatsky calls such close-ended questions "multiple choice questions with two options: yes or no."

Conversation stoppers confirm or deny, affirm or negate. They often sound tough—as when ABC TV's Diane Sawyer asks Cincinnati Reds owner Marge Schott, "Are you a racist?"—but actually are softballs easily batted away. Schott's reply: "Not at all. ... I look at my guys all alike." The exchange may make for dramatic television, but Sawatsky argues, it's not effective interviewing. Questions that are truly tough produce answers, not platitudes. Consider how Schott might have answered had she been asked a green light question, such as "How would you describe your attitude toward blacks?"

To be sure, closed-ended questions have a place in an interview. Shirley Biagi, author of *Interviews That Work: A Practical Guide for Journalists*, says closed-ended questions are good for obtaining facts, such as confirmation of an outcome, statistics or other quantifiable information. "Did the shooting victim die?" "Who won the game?" "How much money will the lottery winner receive?" "How many protesters gathered for the rally?"

Whatever kind of questions you ask, it's the way you listen to the answers that will determine the success of any interview.

THE CRAFT OF INTERVIEWING: LEARNING TO LISTEN

To be a good interviewer you must learn to listen—both to others and to yourself. What kind of questions are you asking people? Are you listening to the answers or merely waiting for the people to take a breath so you can interrupt with a comment?

"A lot of times we beat ourselves," says Pat Stith, investigative reporter for the Raleigh *News & Observer*. "We don't listen. We don't ask simple, direct, follow-up questions. We just talk, and we talk, and we talk. We forget why we're there. (We're there to acquire information.) When we're talking, we're not acquiring anything."

Prepare your questions. Write them down. Train yourself to ask them as you wrote them. Don't stumble. Ask the question and then stop. Don't apologize for asking it. Don't be afraid to ask the question again and again. Broadcast journalists know they may have to ask the question more than once to get an answer on tape that conveys meaning.

Ligia Carvalho, a Poynter reporting fellow, interviews St. Petersburg Police Chief Goliath Davis for a story. (Courtesy of The Poynter Institute)

Using a tape recorder, as I have for the last 15 years, has taught me my most important lesson of interviewing: to shut up. It was a painful learning experience, having to listen to myself stepping on people's words, cutting them off just as they were getting enthusiastic or appeared about to make a revealing statement. There were far too many times I heard myself asking overly long and leading questions, instead of simply saying, "Why?" or "How did it happen?" or "When did all this begin?" or "What do you mean?" and then closing my mouth and letting people answer.

"Learning to listen has been the great lesson of my life," David Ritz wrote in *The Writer*. "You can't capture a subject or render someone life-like, you can't create a living voice, with all its unique twists and turns, without listening. Now there are those who listen while waiting breathlessly to break in. For years, that was me. But I'm talking about patient listening, deep-down listening, listening with the heart as well as the head, listening in a way that lets the person know you care, that you want to hear what she has to say, that you're enjoying the sound of her voice."

There's a scene in *All the President's Men* when Robert Redford, as *Washington Post* reporter Bob Woodward, is asking a Republican how his $25,000 check ended up in the Watergate money trail. It's a dangerous question, and you see Woodward ask it and then hang there, not saying a word, until the man on the other end of the phone finally blurts out another piece of the puzzle. The moral here: To get people to talk, we need to learn the power of silence and master the art of listening.

ADVICE FOR INTERVIEWERS

Getting people to open up is your primary goal as an interviewer. It's not as difficult as it seems if you remember a few basic principles:

BE A PERSON

READ A PSYCHOLOGIST'S TAKE ON INTERVIEWING ONLINE AT http://www.freep.com/jobspage/academy/psych.htm

If there is a trick to persuading strangers to reveal intimate secrets, it is a simple one: Be human. At *The Providence Journal,* I once worked on a story about a controversial businessman who owned several properties hit by suspicious fires. I couldn't get past his lawyer. The man felt unfairly treated by the press and hadn't given an interview in six years. Trying to plead my case with his lawyer, I mentioned talking with my wife about the story. It seemed to me, I had told her, that if somebody were saying all these bad things about me, I'd at least want to have a chance to respond. The lawyer didn't seem impressed, but a few days later, he called back and said his man had decided to talk. Anybody who talks with his wife, he told his lawyer, sounds okay to me.

All too often, reporters take the tough guy approach. I think a softer, more human one is more effective. "Interviewing is the modest immediate science of gaining trust, then gaining information," says interviewing expert John Brady.

I've never forgotten an assignment to write a story about the accidental killing of a young woman caught in crossfire between a prison parolee and police. I had knocked on her parents' door, apologized for bothering them but said my paper was going to write a story about the incident. "I just didn't want you to pick up the paper and say, 'Couldn't they at least have asked us if we wanted to say anything?'" They opened the door and ushered me into their daughter's bedroom. On the bed was a package that had just come in the mail: pots and pans for the hope chest she was filling for her upcoming marriage.

DON'T JUDGE

My editors wanted a magazine profile of the city's police chief, a man who had a reputation as a racist, head-busting goon. In the course of a day I spent with him with my tape recorder going (even while we jogged the snowy streets of Providence) he made a series of outrageous statements that he later had to apologize for and that contributed to his firing months later. I think the reason he said all these things was that although I found them repugnant attitudes, I never once gave him that impression. I didn't judge him while I was talking. I nodded. I looked interested or sympathetic or most of the time looked at him with what I hope was an impartial face. I think if I had started a debate with him, he would have clammed up. I was following John Brady's rule: "Listen politely, almost naively. ... You get more information that way."

The police chief took my silence for agreement. I think this interview proves another maxim, attributed to Arnold Gingrich, the former editor of *Esquire,* who said that the cruelest thing you can do to people is to quote them directly.

PEOPLE LIKE TO TALK

Ask beginning reporters the biggest surprise about their job, and they often say something like, "I was so scared about talking to strangers. But, people really are willing to talk with me. Even eager."

A confession: It's only in the last few years that I haven't been scared to death every time I asked for an interview. Starting out as a reporter, I was so convinced people would hang up on me or slam the door that I often went to interviews with a chip on my shoulder or so nerve-wracked I couldn't re-lax enough to have a comfortable conversation. Finally, it began to sink in through my thick skull: People like to talk. Even in situations where you think they never would. "Most of us are shy about interviewing someone else," says veteran writing coach Don Murray, "but we have to remember that the person who is being interviewed is being put in the position of be-ing an authority, and most of us like to be an authority, to tell someone what we know. It is an ego trip for the interviewee."

Of course, not everybody will be happy about talking with you. But ques-tion the assumption that strangers won't. Be counterphobic. Show a genuine interest in people and their lives, and most will open up.

GETTING IT DOWN, GETTING IT RIGHT: THE IMPORTANCE OF NOTE-TAKING

Great quotes, vivid details and insightful observations won't do you any good if you don't record them, either in a notebook or with an audio or video recorder.

A reporter's notes, as you read earlier, serve at least two purposes: cap-turing details about the interview subject, surroundings or action, and recording quotes, either verbatim or paraphrased. Beginning reporters, and even some veterans, knock themselves out trying to write down every word. They'd do better concentrating less on the dialogue and more on the scenery.

"Even experienced reporters use too many verbatim quotes, which is bad writing," argues Gerald M. Carbone, a prize-winning feature writer for *The*

Providence Journal. "In theater, actors rarely stop and speak directly to the audience; characters do it all the time in newspaper stories, and it distracts readers." Freed from the need to scribble frantically to record every word like a stenographer, writers are able to look around and use their other senses to collect the richness of life. Carbone offers a sampling: dogs barking, sirens blaring, a plane droning overhead, the fragrance of spruce, the blend of stale cigarette smoke and cooking grease, sharp blades of dune grass or soft sand underfoot.

"All of these are details that jog your memory when you get back into the office and try to re-create a scene," Carbone says. "If you get back to your office and find that you've absolutely got to have that perfect quote, you can try again over the phone; but the details must be in the notebook to make it into the story."

Some journalists say they can rely on memory alone. Many reporters, editors and readers are understandably suspicious of such claims. Says Matt Schudel, who writes for the *Fort Lauderdale Sun-Sentinel* magazine: "People who claim they have perfect memories for conversation are either freaks or liars—probably the latter. I don't care what anyone says: No one can remember an entire conversation or interview word for word. At best, you will remember bits and pieces and filter the rest through your own wishes and expectations. Sometimes, when it's been awhile since I've interviewed, I'm amazed at how different my recollections are from the actual notes. Nothing can substitute for accurate, on-the-scene note-taking."

Some journalists advise learning how to take notes without seeming to do so. Once people see you scribbling away, this line of thinking goes, they will clam up. This is the "listen carefully, then run to the bathroom and write down what you remember" school of note-taking. In some cases, I suppose, a reporter might have no alternative. But it strikes me as a form of deception. It also furthers the mystification of what reporters do. Interviewing, especially in a democracy, should be a free exchange of information, not a surreptitious recording of things other people want to keep secret. Journalists play a vital role in informing citizens accurately about the world they live in; taking notes whether on paper, or on video or audiotape, is the method we use to record people's words and actions. The notebook, pen and tape recorder are your tools. Don't wield them like weapons, and people won't fear them.

"Put yourself in the interviewee's place," says Kris Gilger, managing editor of *The Statesman Journal* in Salem, Oregon. "People are not afraid of giving you information. They are afraid of looking stupid." Convey that you are a professional intent on recording information accurately, without badgering them or judging what they say, and most people—not all, of course—will cooperate. "Though some subjects may be a little awkward with my hurried note-taking at first, they usually grow comfortable with it," says Schudel, who offers this explanation: "I think there is something deep in the human psyche that responds to someone writing down the words you speak. It may sound mystical or atavistic, but we journalists are following the ancient tradition of the scribe. There is something timeless and honorable about this exchange of human ideas."

So if you're taking notes, and someone starts talking too fast, don't be afraid to ask the person to stop, slow down or repeat what he or she said. Imagine how you'd feel if a reporter said to you, "That's a really good point. I want to make sure I get it down in my notes." If you don't understand something, how are you going to make your readers understand? If a source is spouting technospeak or professional jargon, interrupt politely and say, "My readers don't have your scientific [or economic or medical or legal] knowledge and training. Could you put it in terms a layperson could easily understand?"

Accuracy counts. Make sure you double-check details for accuracy: names, titles, ages, addresses. Again, you're giving a strong signal that you're a professional who cares that the story is right. When you're interviewing several people, at a meeting or sporting event, use a separate page for each source to keep people's comments from getting mixed up with each other.

Transcribe your handwritten notes immediately or as soon as you can after the interview. Memory deteriorates over time, and that scribbled phrase that makes perfect sense when an interview is finished can look like hieroglyphics even a few hours later.

To Tape or Not to Tape

Reporters who don't want to use a tape recorder don't have to, although they often feel compelled to justify why using a machine for an interview is a bad idea. Tape recorders break, tapes and batteries run out, a siren goes by, drowning out all sound just as the subject whispers, "Yes, I did it. I embezzled the animal shelter's cash fund." Even if you get all the quotes, the tape still takes forever to transcribe. Of course, all these arguments are valid.

Still, there are few technology-averse reporters who don't wish they had a tape recorder going during some interviews, especially when the pace is fast or the content compelling. It's estimated that even a speedy note-taker can get down only 25 to 30 words a minute, a fraction of the 100 words a minute of a normal conversation. Magazine writer Matt Schudel prefers a notebook, but when he interviewed Southern writer Reynolds Price, "I was glad I had a tape recorder to convey the beauty of his spoken words." Even so, Schudel believes he listens more attentively when he takes notes. "I have to be an active listener. I ask better questions and participate more fully in the conversation."

But proponents of audio recorders make equally compelling arguments, such as those voiced in Chapter 2 by award-winning sports columnist Mitch Albom of the *Detroit Free Press*. Even tape recorder fans know better than to put all their notes in one medium, however. Albom notes that "I work with a notepad even with the tape recorder, because I don't trust technology."

It can be equally dangerous to trust the human ear. I once covered a speech by journalist and grammarian Edwin Newman along with a reporter for the local university campus daily. I had a tape recorder. The student reporter, I assume, did not.

Compare the two versions of the same speech:

RECORDED VERSION	UNRECORDED VERSION
People like Edwin Newman because he makes them laugh. He does that by making fun of **"the jargon, the mush, the smog, the dull pompous, boneless, gassy language"** that afflicts the world today.	"We have no hope of dealing with things unless we dig ourselves out of **the smog, the bog, the hash and the jargon. ..."**

The bottom line: Smart reporters learn how to take accurate, detailed notes by hand and use the tape recorder in those instances where a verbatim record is valued (such as press conferences or other events where electronic media are present). As a 21st-century journalist, you may also be required to collect audio to post on your online Web site.

ORDER

While you're interviewing, your notes can serve as a blueprint for the story you will write. Set off important quotes. You might use slash marks—//—or an asterisk—*—or giant parentheses—( ).

If it's an exact quote, use quotation marks; otherwise you might quote your own words or a paraphrase as a **quotation.**

Organizing your notes into a rough table of contents before you write deepens your familiarity with the material. It can save crucial time, especially on deadline. Number each page of your notes. Make a list of the pages, scan your notes and jot down the most important item or two on each page next to its corresponding number. Writers who use this method say it cuts down on deadline panic. Says Gerald M. Carbone: "It makes me more familiar with my material, and it saves time by preventing frantic flipping through the notebook in search of that detail that I need now."

DRAFT

The writer discovers a story by interviewing as well as writing. Carbone continues, "When you are taking notes, you are editing as well as writing; you are listening for that which will make a good story and omitting that which is superfluous. Actually, I can't overstate the importance of note-taking. Note-taking is writing. While you are scribbling those notes, you are writing the story, literally and figuratively; you are making the sacred connection of pen to paper and writing the story in your head. You are thinking: "How can

A tape recorder is essential for some interviews, especially when the subject is controversial. Providence Police Chief Angelo P. Ricci had to apologize for comments he made about minorities in a newspaper profile. (Courtesy of Andy Dickerman)

I use this? If I use this, what more will I need to know?" Answering these questions allows you to frame your next question, to walk with the interview down its most logical path. This is why I insist on taking notes even as I acknowledge the superior accuracy of tape, because ultimately interviewing is writing." Carbone's view is important because it reinforces the idea that the process of reporting and writing is fluid. Even when you think you're not writing, you are.

How People Talk: Getting Quotes, Using Them Effectively

Getting quotes is one thing. Using them effectively is another. Many reporters use quotations as a crutch. They forget that they, not their sources, are writing the story. It's the writer's job to make meaning with the materials collected during the reporting. You decide which quotes convey the information and which are better paraphrased. Quotations, as Kevin Maney of *USA Today* puts it, should occupy a "place of honor" in a story. Use quotes as punctuation: to drive home a point at the end of a paragraph—as I did in a story for Knight Ridder Newspapers about the impact on children when parents fail to pay child support:

220 CHAPTER 6 ■ LEARNING TO LISTEN: BUILDING INTERVIEWING SKILLS

> When friends ask Brian Lesefske what his father does, the teen-ager has a simple answer: "He runs from the law."

REVISE

People rarely speak in complete sentences. They stumble, stammer, circle around a subject. Consider the hypothetical but hardly unusual conversation that follows and how the quotation might appear in print.

Reporter: "Will you run for re-election, Congresswoman?"

Congresswoman: "Um, well, that's a ... I'm still ... If the voters want me ... I mean, that's what it all boils down to, doesn't it? Who am I to say no?

Rep. Mary Foghorn wants to try for a sixth term in Congress.

"If the voters want me ... who am I to say 'No?'" Foghorn said yesterday.

Revision is the last and probably the most important step in the writing and interviewing process. The journalist's job is to make meaning clear. But there's not a consensus among journalists on how much, if any, tampering with direct quotes is permitted. In some minds, changing a quote should be a firing offense. Others maintain that changing grammar or syntax to clarify a statement is allowed. Some go even further. "Play with the 'quotes' by all means—selecting, rejecting, thinning, transposing their order, saving a good one for the end," says William Zinsser, author of *On Writing Well.* "Just make sure that the play is fair. Don't change any words or let the cutting of a sentence distort the proper context of what remains."

Zinsser's attitude is a little too relaxed for most newspaper journalists who would never think of altering a quote. But it's not far in spirit from the philosophy eloquently expressed by James B. Stewart, the Pulitzer Prize–winning reporter, formerly with *The Wall Street Journal,* who now contributes to *The New Yorker.* Almost no quotation represents precisely what a speaker said because note-taking is "naturally subject to human error and spontaneous editing," Stewart argues.

"Even writers who record and transcribe their interviews correct sentence fragments and delete the 'uhs' and 'ahs' and other sounds so common in everyday speech," Stewart says in *Follow the Story.* "Publications use different standards, but all that I have worked for edit quotations for grammar and usage and simply to make sense of what was said. In fiction, too, no one actually speaks the way dialogue is written, in neat sentences and paragraphs. I believe that readers understand and accept this implicitly.

The important thing is that the substance of what was said be conveyed accurately."

The next time you want to alter a person's words, remember that the final word on the subject may come from a judge, as it did in the case of Jeffrey Masson, a psychoanalyst who sued *New Yorker* writer Janet Malcolm. Masson claimed that Malcolm libeled him by quoting several statements he said he never made. Masson lost his suit, although more than one court agreed that Malcolm apparently made up some of Masson's quotes. In the court's 1991 opinion, U.S. Supreme Court Justice Donald Kennedy established this standard for quote marks, the inverted twins—" "—that indicate a person is speaking:

> "In general, quotation marks around a passage indicate to the reader that the passage reproduces the speaker's words verbatim. They inform the reader that he or she is reading the statement of the speaker, not a paraphrase or other indirect interpretation by an author. By providing this information, quotations add authority to the statement and credibility to the author's work. Quotations allow the reader to form his or her own conclusions and to assess the conclusions of the author, instead of relying entirely upon the author's characterization of her subject."

What about ellipses, the three little dots ... that indicate that one or more words are omitted? Some older journalists say they were told to never use them because the average reader wouldn't know that an **ellipsis** is a punctuation device that alerts a reader that there are words missing from the sentence—words that the writer has left out for space or clarity but whose omission does not alter the meaning. That makes sense to me, but editors I respect disagree. The AP stylebook, followed by most news organizations, advises using an ellipsis "to indicate the deletion of one or more words in condensing, quotes, texts and documents" and cautions against deleting words that distort the meaning. Following AP style, I inserted an ellipsis in Rep. Foghorn's quote on the previous page. You should ask an editor about your news organization's policy.

Notice how many stories contain quotes that echo what you've already written:

> The mayor said he's pleased with the election results, noting that his victory demonstrates his popularity with the voters. "I'm pleased with the results," said Mayor Boggs. "It proves my popularity with the voters."

"Echo quotes" often mean the writer isn't giving readers enough credit. Readers don't need a paraphrase *and* a quote to understand. One or the other will suffice. Avoid repetitious quotes by always reading your story aloud as you make final revisions. Reserve quotation marks for words that reveal character, advance the narrative or drive home a controversial point. Use a blend of quotation and paraphrase. Don't use every quote in your notebook to prove you did the interviews. That's not writing; It's dictation.

To get the most out of your interviews, follow the guidelines in the next section. They are illustrated by student examples, drawn from *Points South,* the weekly paper produced by reporting students at The Poynter Institute.

USING QUOTES: DO'S AND DON'TS

Do use quotes for emphasis and authority, to breathe life into a story, when someone says something better than you can paraphrase it.

> No African American has ever been elected to the Pinellas County school board. Waller says his decision to run for school board is part of the struggle for community control of schools. "Black residents must have the power to control their own education," he said.

Do follow the correct style for quotes:

■ Begin a quotation with open quote marks—"—and end a quotation with close quote marks—".

■ Periods and commas go inside the close quotation mark.

Jason Myron, a freckle-faced 8-year-old, grows pensive at the mention of Mama Gert's name. "She was one of my most favoritest people," he says.

■ When quoting dialogue or conversation, use separate paragraphs, with quotation marks at the start and end of each person's quote.

"We paint on the first day?" asked 12-year-old Sharese Bowens.
"You're going to be exhibiting before you know it," answered art teacher Patsi Aguero.

Do use quotes that are complete statements. Avoid partial quotes, especially to report ordinary expressions. There's no need to say the student government president said she was "going home for the holidays."

If using a partial quote, put quote marks around only the words the speaker actually said.

GULFPORT—Stetson College of Law student Charles Behm was studying for July's bar exam in his dorm room last Monday afternoon when it happened.

The first time it happened, he checked with security and the dean's office. He found no answers. The power was out more than two hours. He said he was left to "fuss and fume" on his own.

Place attribution and speaker identification at the end of a single-sentence quote. Otherwise break up a longer quote by placing attribution and speaker identification in the middle of a quote for effective pacing.

"Nobody comes down here. They stop at Fifth," says Thinh Nguyen, owner of the Crab House restaurant on Ninth and Ninth. "When there are games, the whole street is quiet."

Lead into a quotation with attribution.

Two blocks to the south, Calvin Baker, owner of the Hogley Wogley Barbecue, says, "There's no extra business on this side. People go to the games and leave. They don't stick around."

Lead into a quotation with a paraphrase that explains the context of the speaker's comment.

> Berthelot acknowledges there are drugs in the Roser Park area. "See those people?" he says from his cruiser, pointing to a yard full of people huddled around a checkerboard in nearby Campbell Park. "They're selling dope. I know exactly what they're doing, but I have to be able to legally articulate what they're doing. I have to have a legitimate reason to search them."

Combine physical action with quotes, as in this story about a playground at All Children's Hospital. It not only lets the reader hear the sound of someone talking, but also shows the scene.

> "It's a safe place for Taylor to play," said Gilroy as she gazed at the playground through the hospital waiting room's half-open window blinds. "It's full of appropriate things for her—little cars, toys without small parts, big balls—and toys she uses in physical therapy."

You can use ellipses to show you have deleted words or sentences from a passage you are quoting.

> "For a parent, bringing a well child to the hospital feels terrible," says David. "Janet was not in pain or sick. Then she was given the chemotherapy. Ten days later she lost her hair. She became sort of lethargic, she lost her appetite ... she started vomiting."

Or to show a pause or interruption.

> Sitting in the living room, Bryant and Vaarkova talk about the language barrier. Bryant says, "Sometimes we don't exactly ..."
> "Understand exactly," Vaarkova says, filling in her host mother's sentence.

Use single-quote marks to indicate a quote within a quote. Alternate between double quote marks (" ") and single quote marks (' ').

> Today, Smith gets strength from his religious faith and his music. He writes for everyday people, like his 10-year-old son, Darius. He dreams of becoming the first St. Petersburg rapper to make it big—really big.
> And when he does, maybe he'll inspire a new rapper in his hometown. "When I do rise," says Smith, "people will say, 'If he can make it, I can make it.'"

KEEPING CONFIDENCES: ON OR OFF THE RECORD

We've all seen trials on television. "Strike that," a lawyer will say. Or a judge will tell the jury, "Disregard that answer." Soon after you start reporting, a police officer or a politician will say, "That's off the record." If you're not prepared, you may find yourself in trouble with your editor. In general, the guideline for most American journalists is that information provided by a source during an interview will be attributed to that source by name. For example: "The impeachment trial will begin tomorrow," said Senate Majority Leader Trent Lott.

Sources aren't always willing to be identified. In that case, the reporter can agree that the interview, or portions of it, will be used only if the source isn't identified. "If Saddam Hussein doesn't comply with the weapons inspectors," a top State Department official said, "we'll have no choice but go to war."

"The use of unnamed sources is among American newspapers' most damaging habits," argues newspaper ombudsman Geneva Overholser. "People allowed to say things without having to be responsible for them say things they wouldn't otherwise say. Misinformation, cheap shots—all is possible when no one is accountable. We rob readers of their ability to judge what is said. How well placed is the speaker? What motivates him? Finally, unnamed sources undermine confidence in candor and the value of sharing one's views and taking responsibility for them."

Defenders of the practice counter that, in some cases, they have no choice but to print information without revealing the source. "We realize many readers are infuriated by anonymous sourcing. Many journalists are, too," said Robert Kaiser, a former managing editor at *The Washington Post*. "But we also think our readers should know that sometimes granting anonymity to sources is the only way to acquire publishable information on matters of interest and importance to them. So, if we have confidence in our information, we will print it."

News organizations should have a policy about attribution, but some do not. As a 1994 *Air Force Media Guide* warns service members facing the news media: "Be absolutely sure everyone understands your definitions and agrees to the conditions in advance. There are no universally agreed on or standard definitions for interview terms."

Make sure you—and your sources—know the ground rules. And remember: There is no rule unless you agree on the rule with the source. Politicians and other supposedly media-savvy sources may have their own understanding of what "off the record" means, and it may be different from the policy set by your editors. Some sources may rely on a dim memory of how a reporter acted in a movie or television show they saw. When a source says he wants to go off the record (he might say something like, "But you can't use that" or "Between you and me ...") stop and ask, "What do you mean?" Some reporters will let a source go off the record but before the interview is over go back to their notes and review what the source said off the record. Often the source allows them to use the information on the record.

INTERVIEW GROUND RULES

"On the record" implies that anything said can be used in a story with complete **attribution** (name, title, address, etc.) so the reader knows precisely where the information came from. Once you've identified yourself as a reporter, you should operate under the assumption that everything said can be used in your story. You may need to educate your sources about this, especially if they have never been interviewed before. Never assume that an interview subject knows the ground rules.

"Not for attribution" is also sometimes referred to as "on background." Information can be used but without attributing it to the source, or with the source identified in only a general way, such as "a company spokesperson" or "a law enforcement official."

Essentially, you're promising sources that no one—including their boss, competitors, enemies, friends—will be able to identify them.

"Off the record" means that nothing—that's right, nothing—said by the source can be used in the story. If the same information is provided by an independent source **on the record,** the information can be used.

A variation on "off the record" is "deep background." This was the arrangement Bob Woodward had with "Deep Throat," an important high-level source in the Watergate investigation that led to the resignation of President Richard Nixon. Woodward "had agreed never to quote the man, even as an anonymous source. Their discussions would be only to confirm information that had been obtained elsewhere and to add some perspective."

Others believe that "deep background" means that information obtained in an interview can be published without attribution, as a conclusion drawn by the reporter. This confusion highlights one of the biggest dangers of conducting interviews in any way other than completely on the record. Such arrangements can blow up in a reporter's face if the source has a different understanding of these terms.

Sources may get cold feet during an interview and say, after they've told you something, "But that's off the record." Of course, you're within your rights to accept such a request, but you don't have to. Politicians, law enforcement officers and other media-savvy types try this, especially with a beginning or new reporter. It's important that you make it clear that this kind of behavior is unacceptable.

Consider this statement from a media guide published on the Internet by the United States Information Agency. "'On the record' is by far the best way to work. The other guidelines are nothing more than convenient shorthand for journalists and officials dealing with sensitive political, economic and law enforcement concerns. The best advice is to avoid relying on these shorthand terms. Understanding may vary from culture to culture and journalist to journalist. If you cannot go on the record, talk to the journalist and reach a specific understanding regarding attribution before the interview begins."

Obviously, these agreements with sources can be flexible. First of all, be wary of taking information off the record or deep background. You can't use it, so what's the point of having it? Your job is to get stuff into the paper, online or on the news broadcast. And once you make an agreement with a source, you must keep it. Remember that any agreement you make is not between just you and your source but also with your news organization. Reporters have gone to jail to protect the confidentiality of sources, so you had better be sure that the next time you offer confidentiality you are prepared to accept the consequences. If you have any doubts, make sure you call your editor before you make a promise that may be painful to keep.

Here are the agreements between reporter and source, in order of reference:

1. **ON THE RECORD.** Reporter can use all information provided during the interview both to gather further information and to include in the published story. Preferred agreement.

2. **NOT FOR ATTRIBUTION.** Reporter can use information but promises to protect the source's identity during reporting and in the published story. Second choice.

3. **OFF THE RECORD.** Information cannot be used in a story, even if the source is not identified. (Some reporters take "off the record" to mean that they can use the information, without indicating its source, to gather information.) Last resort.

TIPS FOR E-MAIL INTERVIEWS

Computers and the Internet give reporters another reporting tool: e-mail that allows them to interview potential sources around the globe at the click of a mouse. The advantages of e-mail are obvious to anyone who has played "phone tag" for hours waiting for a return call. E-mail interview queries are efficient. The reporter can provide a complete introduction and a list of questions and, if the source cooperates, get back a digital file with information, quotes and other story material.

But the disadvantages should make any reporter pause before replacing a face-to-face, or even a phone interview, with an e-mail interview. The authors of *The Internet Handbook for Writers, Researchers and Journalists* point out the major disadvantages:

- A reporter doesn't know who is replying. That executive's e-mail may have been carefully crafted by public relations advisers.

- E-mail denies the reporter the chance to ask spontaneous questions, to immediately follow up on an answer. "An online interview may get you a useable quote," the authors say, "but it's unlikely to produce a revealing interview."

Follow these commonsense guidelines: E-mail may last forever. Once sent, it can be forwarded to strangers. So keep it professional at all times. Identify yourself as a reporter. Apply the same critical thinking and fact-checking skills that you would to any other information source.

INTERVIEWING: THE COACHING WAY

- As you approach your next interview, write in the front of your notebook the five or six questions you think readers would ask and number them in the order readers would ask them.
- Read your quotes aloud. Do they occupy a place of honor in your story? Can you say it better? If so, don't be afraid to paraphrase.

- Promise yourself that the next time you hear something you don't understand during an interview, you will stop and ask for an explanation, no matter how stupid you feel.
- Before you publish material obtained from an online interview, follow the AP's guideline: Ask yourself: "Could this be a hoax?"

GLOSSARY OF IMPORTANT TERMS

Attribution. Identifying information about the source of material in a story, such as name and title.

Ellipsis. Punctuation mark—three dots (...)—indicating words or sentences deleted from a quoted passage.

Green light questions. Open-ended questions—"How did ... ?" "Why do ... ?" "What is ... ?"—that produce anecdotes, quotations and opinion and give the interviewee more control over content. They are conversation starters.

Off the record. Agreement between reporter and source that nothing the source says will be used in the story. (Some reporters believe that off-the-record information can be used to gather information if the source is not identified in any way. If the same information is provided by an independent source on the record, the information can be used.)

On the record. Agreement between reporter and source that anything the source says can be used in a story with complete attribution (name, title, address, etc.) so the reader knows precisely where the information came from.

Not for attribution. Agreement between reporter and source that information can be used but without being attributed to the source or with the source being identified in a general way, such as "a company spokesperson" or "a law enforcement official." Sometimes referred to as "on background." Essentially, you're promising sources that no one—including their boss, competitors, enemies, friends—will be able to identify them.

Quotation. A person's spoken or written words enclosed between open and close quotation marks.

Red light questions. Closed-ended questions, such as "Did you kill your husband?," that can be answered "yes" or "no." They are conversation stoppers.

EXERCISES

1. Diagnose your interviewing style. What are your strengths: empathy, note-taking, good eye for detail? What do you need to work on: setting ground rules, listening more closely, preparing more thoroughly?

2. Tape record one of your interviews. Transcribe the questions verbatim. How many are conversation starters? How many are conversation stoppers? Transcribe the answers. Compare the length of the answers.

3. Ask a dozen classmates, relatives and friends to define these terms: "on the record" and "off the record," "not for attribution,"

"background" and "deep background." Compare their answers. What are the differences and similarities? Discuss how your findings will affect how you set ground rules for interviews.

4. Identify an interview subject who you think might be difficult or reluctant—the quietest person in one of your classes, a teacher known as a taskmaster, a campus police official. By yourself or with a colleague or editor, consider the problems. Conduct the interview and write about the experience. What surprised you? What did you learn? What do you need to learn next?

5. Reporters agree that interviewing children is especially difficult. Tom Hallman, a feature writer for *The Oregonian* who has a knack for getting kids to open up, says it helps if he has tried to connect personally to that time in his own life. Write an essay about an important time in your childhood, such as attending the first day of school or trying out for a team. Follow that up by interviewing a child about that experience. How did writing about yourself first influence the questions you asked and the way the interview went?

6. Study how writers use quotations in their stories. Where do the quotes appear? How long are the quotes?

7. Watch *All the President's Men* and discuss Woodward and Bernstein's interviewing techniques. Do you think they always acted ethically?

READINGS

Arico, Santo L. "Breaking the Ice: An In-Depth Look at Oriana Fallaci's Interview Techniques." *Journalism Quarterly*, Autumn 1986, pp. 587–593.

Biagi, Shirley. *Interviews That Work: A Practical Guide for Journalists,* 2nd ed. Belmont, Calif.: Wadsworth, 1992.

Brady, John Joseph. *The Craft of Interviewing.* New York: Vintage Books, 1977.

Cohen, Akiba A. *The Television News Interview.* Newbury Park, Calif.: Sage Publications, 1987.

Chadwick, Alex. "NPR's Alex Chadwick Offers Interviewing Tips." *PRNDI Newsletter,* October 1994, p. 3.

Hudson, Berkley. "Talk Talk: Notes on the Art of Interviewing." In *How I Wrote the Story,* 2nd ed., ed. Christopher Scanlan. Providence, R.I.: *The Providence Journal,* 1986.

Killenberg, George M., and Rob Anderson. *Before the Story: Interviewing and Communication Skills for Journalists.* New York: St. Martin's Press, 1989.

McGuire, Mary, et al. *The Internet Handbook for Writers, Researchers and Journalists.* Toronto: Trifolium Books, 1997.

McManus, Kevin. "If You Absolutely, Positively Have to Talk to Real People—Here Are Some Tips on Coaxing Out Good 'Person in the Street' Interviews." *ASNE Bulletin*, November 1992, pp. 18–19.

Metzler, Ken. *Creative Interviewing*. Englewood Cliffs, N.J.: Prentice-Hall, 1989.

Morris, Susan. "Interviewing: How to Do It and Get the Information You Need." *Communicator*, October 1989, pp. 22–24.

Nalder, Eric. "The Not-So-Gentle Art of Interviewing." *The IRE Journal*, November/December 1992, pp. 4–6.

Nelson, Deb. "It's Time to Retire the Classic Confrontational Interview— Most of the Time. There Are Better Alternatives." *The IRE Journal*, July/August 1995, pp. 5–7.

Presson, Hazel. *The Student Journalist and Interviewing*. New York: R. Rosen Press, 1979.

Ritz, David. "Inside Interviewing." *The Writer*, March 1993, pp. 15–17.

Selcraig, Bruce. "Some Random Thoughts on the Art of Interviewing." *The IRE Journal*, Spring 1987, p. 4.

Silvester, Christopher, ed. *The Penguin Book of Interviews: An Anthology From 1859 to the Present Day*. London: Viking, 1993.

Stamberg, Susan. *Every Night at Five: Susan Stamberg's All Things Considered Book*. New York: Pantheon, 1982.

HOTLIST

http://www.december.com/cmc/mag/1997/jul/chang.html

Interviewing and Information in a Digital Age by I-chin Chang. Walking and talking isn't the only way to get an interview. This site explores the use of e-mail interviews.

http://www.algonet.se/~journali/arteng.htm

A Swedish site that focuses (in English) on the interviewing methodology of John Sawatsky, a Canadian journalist who has made a science of how to ask questions that get rich answers.

http://www.poynter.org/research/biblio/bib_int.htm

A comprehensive Poynter Institute bibliography of books and articles on the subject of interviewing.

http://www.cjr.org/html/95-01-02-interviewing.html

January/February 1995. "Yakety-Yak: The Lost Art of Interviewing" by Tom Rosenstiel. This article in the *Columbia Journalism Review* traces the interview as a journalistic form from its beginnings in the mid-1800s to today's explosions of interviews on network and cable.

http://www.freep.com/jobspage/academy/interv.htm

Interviewing tips for beginners from The Freep, the *Detroit Free Press'* excellent site for journalists and students.

http://www.bc.edu/bc_org/avp/cas/comm/free_speech/masson.html

The complete text of the U.S. Supreme Court decision in *Masson vs. New Yorker, Inc.* et al., the 1991 case that pitted an interview subject against a writer over the use of quotations.

http://www.mtn.org/~newscncl/fall95/Quotes.html

How sacred are the words found within quotation marks? A round-up of journalists' responses from the Minnesota News Council.

http://www.newslink.org/ajrtalk.html

This article from *American Journalism Review* explores the pride and pratfalls of journalists when the tables are turned and they become the interviewee. Author Chip Rowe's most useful observation: "Editors and reporters who have been interviewed for publication say that seeing their words compressed into print is humbling and has taught them to listen more carefully when sources complain about being quoted out of context or incorrectly."

http://ballmer.uoregon.edu/ponder/j202s/

Stephen Ponder, a journalism professor at the University of Oregon, specializes in teaching information gathering. Browsing this site isn't as good as taking his challenging course, but it will provide a range of materials and insights.

http://www.usia.gov/vitalvoices/media.htm

"A Media Guidebook for Women." An online publication produced by the United States Information Agency for women in foreign countries who deal with journalists. It's a valuable look at how government officials view the reporter, a view from the other side of the notebook, tape recorder or video camera.

http://slate.com

"For the Record, What 'Off the Record' Really Means." Washington journalist and *Slate* columnist Timothy Noah dissects the problems of imprecise arrangements between journalists and their sources in this June 1999 "Chatterbox" column. Use the *Slate* archives to find its current home.

CHAPTER

MAKING CONNECTIONS:
DIVERSITY AND THE NEWS

CHAPTER FOCUS

When journalists ignore the need for a multitude of voices, faces and viewpoints that reveal the diverse society we live in, they cheat their readers and viewers. They cheat society. And they cheat themselves.

CHAPTER LESSONS

- Minorities in the newsroom and the news
- Tips for better news coverage of minorities
- Stereotypes and other clichés of vision
- The case for cultural competence in journalism
- The five W's of diversity
- Connecting with diverse communities
- Reporting and writing about difference
- Guidelines for racial identification in stories
- Making connections: The Coaching Way

INTRODUCTION

For more than a year, I shared a cubicle in the news features department of the *St. Petersburg Times* with a reporter named Diane Mason. We compared leads and story ideas and traded family stories and newsroom gossip. One day, she taught me the value of diversity.

For several days, I had been working on the first installment of a series on ethics. "Choices" asked readers and a panel of experts to consider a range of ethical dilemmas in the fields of law, medicine, business and journalism. First we published the case studies, based on real-life examples, and asked our readers to respond. We promised a follow-up story that would report their answers and give comments from a panel of experts in each field. While we tabulated the results, I set about giving the test to the experts.

The first installment was about medical ethics. I told Diane about the doctors and medical school professors I was considering for my panel of experts.

"What?" she said. "There aren't any women doctors? There aren't any black doctors? No Hispanic doctors?"

My list of sources, read so proudly, consisted exclusively of middle-aged white men. Until Diane's question and the heated discussion that followed, it hadn't even occurred to me that anything was wrong. If communication is not so much what's said, but what's heard, then what was the message that my story would convey? That men and whites are the only experts on medicine and ethics? That women and people of color don't have the qualifications? If the news media hold up a mirror to society, didn't my sources present an incomplete picture? To be honest, I didn't really want to hear any of this. I'd already done a lot of work, and it would have been a lot simpler to dismiss my colleague's questions as just another example of politically correct thinking. But I knew she was right, that my reporting was incomplete. I went back to work and found that, with a little extra effort, I could find a wider range of sources—women and people of color—whose inclusion made the series richer and more reflective of social and cultural reality.

I thought about Diane Mason on a recent Sunday morning as I watched *Meet the Press*, NBC's long-standing public affairs program. The topic was the impeachment trial of President Clinton, and on hand to discuss it with moderator Tim Russert were Clinton's former press secretary Mike McCurry, Sen. Daniel Patrick Moynihan and conservatives William Bennett and the Rev. Pat Robertson. Four white men, middle-aged and older. I listened to them voice their opinions until finally, in frustration, I switched off the set. Couldn't they find anybody other than four white guys?

But what could I do about it? Phone *Meet the Press* or leave an angry e-mail message? Then I realized I could write about it. I could write about the lesson I learned from Diane Mason the day she pointed out the monochromatic sources I had assembled for my ethics story. The lesson she taught me: When journalists ignore the need for diversity, they cheat their readers and viewers. They cheat society. And they cheat themselves.

This chapter explores ways to avoid that trap with a series of checklists, strategies and practical tips from journalists and teachers who specialize in improving the way the media portray diversity in print, broadcast and online news.

MINORITIES IN THE NEWSROOM AND THE NEWS

If we could shrink the Earth's population to a tiny village of exactly 100 people, and if we kept existing population ratios the same, our village would look like this:

- Fifty-seven people would be from Asia, 21 from Europe, 14 from North and South America and 8 from Africa.
- Fifty-one would be female; 49 would be male.
- Seventy would be nonwhite; 30 would be white.
- Seventy would be non-Christian; 30 would be Christian.
- Half of the entire wealth would be in the hands of only six people, and all six people would be from the United States.
- Eighty would live in substandard housing.
- Seventy would be unable to read.
- Fifty would suffer from malnutrition.
- One would be near death, and one would be near birth.
- One would have a college education.
- No one would own a computer.

A poster with that statistical snapshot, which widely circulated on the Internet and elsewhere, but not independently verified, belongs in every newsroom; a laminated card with its message should be carried in every reporter's wallet.

We are a diverse world, but the world of news is dominated by white males—in its newsrooms and in its news stories. As a business we have done a poor job of diversifying our workplace. In our stories, we cover race, gender, ethnicity and sexual orientation badly when at all.

After America erupted in urban riots in the 1960s, a presidential commission appointed to investigate the causes concluded that there were two Americas: one white, one black. In 1996, the Associated Press Managing Editors Association drew a similar portrait of the news business: America's newsrooms are two different worlds: one white, one minority.

There has been some progress. Nearly two decades earlier, in 1978, people of color constituted only 4 percent of daily newspaper staffs. Since then, the number of minority employees at daily newspapers has nearly tripled, and African American and other people of color are top editors at several, mostly large metropolitan, newspapers. Still, as Creed Black, former president of the Knight Foundation, noted, nearly half of American daily papers (mostly smaller ones) still have no minority staff members.

In 1978, the American Society of Newspaper Editors (ASNE) adopted a goal to match minority employment in newsrooms with the U.S. minority population by the year 2000, when the group expect that number to be 15 percent. As it turned out, by the late 1990s, people of color made up 26 percent of the American population and the minority population was growing half a percentage point a year, observed ASNE President Edward L. Seaton in 1998. Yet the percentage of people of color in American newsrooms was far lower: Surveys found 20 percent in television stations, 16 percent in radio newsrooms and 11.5 percent in daily newspapers (which had grown "a total of 1.21 percentage points in the last five years," Seaton said). The statistics may look better in broadcast news, but higher numbers obscure the fact that although local anchors are diverse, far too few producers, editors and executives are people of color. The once-rapid growth in numbers of minority employees has slowed. In 1998, ASNE conceded that newspapers would fall "far short" of matching minority employment ratios with the U.S. population by 2000. Instead, it delayed the target date for newsrooms to reflect America's racial diversity to "2025 or sooner."

Most in the news industry agree there's a problem with who's in—and who's running—the country's newsrooms. But diversity goes beyond just having different races, genders and ethnic groups represented. A multicultural mix does little good if the culture of the newsroom quashes discussion of difference or doesn't encourage people to speak up when they see problems or different ways of looking at a story.

Diversity is a component of effective reporting. It reflects an understanding that everyone is different and unique, although certain groups do share attitudes, beliefs and customs. That understanding is absent in much news coverage, however.

When the three main broadcast networks—ABC, CBS and NBC—give experts the opportunity to speak on their early evening newscasts, the speakers are almost exclusively white and male, according to the 1998 annual Women, Men and Media Study, conducted by ADT Research in conjunction with the Freedom Forum.

SEE HOW THE NEWS MEDIA FAIL AND SUCCEED AT PORTRAYING DIVERSITY IN THEIR COVERAGE ONLINE AT THE NEWS WATCH PROJECT http:// newswatch. sfsu.edu/text/ Default.html

For more than a year, members of the nation's four largest organizations of professional journalists of color—the Asian American Journalists Association, National Association of Black Journalists, National Association of Hispanic Journalists and Native American Journalists Association—monitored the way newspapers, magazines and television broadcasts reported on African Americans, Asian Americans, Latinos, Native Americans and other ethnic minorities. When they published their findings in 1994, the journalists concluded that "News pages and news broadcasts are riddled with stereotypical portrayals, culturally biased and offensive reporting and a generally skewed presentation of people of color. ...

"Imagine picking up the newspaper and tuning into the news each day without expecting to see yourself or people like you there. ... That is a reality that readers and viewers of media in communities of color continue to confront."

Reporters and editors at *The Baltimore Sun* conducted a "content audit," an analysis of the way people of color are portrayed in its pages, in a single week in December 1996. As David Shipler later reported in the *Columbia Journalism Review*, "They noted that blacks and other minorities were usually portrayed as needy or in conflict ... features and business sections practically ignored nonwhites."

"On first glance," an auditor wrote, "it would appear that minorities rarely travel, eat or get married."

It's not just minority journalists who lose out, but also the news media as a credible institution. "The more diverse our work force is, the better we're going to cover our diverse society," says Norman Pearlstine, editor-in-chief of Time Inc., who has begun to link his news managers' bonuses to their success in hiring and promoting people of color. Mark Willes, the publisher of the *Los Angeles Times*, said in May 1998 that he would set specific goals for raising the number of women and minorities quoted in stories and tie editors' salaries to how well reporters meet the quotas, *The Wall Street Journal* reported.

Karen Lincoln Michel (Photo by Beatríz Terrázas)

An African American reporter for an alternative weekly paper interviewed for a diversity study predicted a dire future for newspapers, but his forecast holds true for all news media. Without diversity, this reporter argued, "Papers aren't going survive. ... They'll survive in terms of ad revenues and having papers to distribute, but not as relevant vessels of information."

Karen Lincoln Michel, a Native American who has worked as a reporter in Wisconsin and Texas, told a group of minority job seekers and news recruiters in 1996 that she and other minorities know what it's like when the only coverage their people get comes during holidays: Black History Month, Chinese New Year, Cinco de Mayo.

Her byline in the *LaCrosse Tribune* made it possible for her and the paper to break a story about bribes offered to members of a tribal council. She wondered later whether the story "would have been covered as hard if there hadn't been someone on the staff who understood the community."

"The news industry needs journalists of color to better reflect the diverse communities that it covers," Michel said. "Newspapers need to keep in mind that America is changing. It is becoming multicultural, multiracial and multiethnic. The 21st century will bring an America where diversity will be the norm and a way of life."

TIPS FOR BETTER NEWS COVERAGE OF MINORITIES

News organizations often fail to recognize the differences between people. Lillian R. Dunlap, a professor in the broadcast news department of the University of Missouri School of Journalism, uses the following list to teach her students how to better report stories involving women and members of America's ethnic minorities:

- Identify race only when necessary to understanding the story.
- Include minorities as sources in stories not focused on traditionally minority issues.
- Avoid direct or implied stereotypes of women and minorities (women and minorities are not always victims or criminals).
- Provide context for people and ideas in the story. (This may mean interviewing people in their offices instead of on the street or asking for a family photo instead of using the mug shot police provide.)

LEARN MORE ABOUT THE "FAULT LINES" OF RACE, CLASS, GENDER AND GEOGRAPHY THAT DIVIDE PEOPLE, FROM THE MAYNARD INSTITUTE FOR JOURNALISM EDUCATION ONLINE AT http://www.maynardije.org/faultlines/index.html

- Avoid using euphemisms such as "inner city" or "bad part of town" to describe places where ethnic minority members live or "escape" from.

- Identify people in photos by correct name and title.

- Consider a variety of perspectives. (Avoid exclusively making minority members the problem and majority members the solution.)

- Acknowledge only "leaders" who have been chosen or elected by "followers."

- Make technical preparation to photograph nonwhites. Pay attention to such issues as lighting to get as detailed and clear an image as possible.

- Provide context for understanding data and graphs about women and minorities.

- Resist making race an issue simply because minorities are part of a particular story.

- Avoid making gender an issue simply because women are in the story. Use relevant documents and human sources for stories.

- Show the variety and diversity within ethnic groups and women.

STEREOTYPES AND OTHER CLICHÉS OF VISION

LISTEN TO A PANEL DISCUSSION ON "STEREOTYPES IN THE MEDIA" ONLINE AT http://www.wiesenthal.com/audio/antis.html

"Clichés of language are significant misdemeanors, but clichés of vision are felonies," writing teacher Donald Murray says in *Writing for Your Readers*. "Too often editors punish each misdemeanor but advocate the commission of felonies. ... In journalism we too often leave the city room knowing what we'll find, and then, of course, we'll find it."

Stereotypes, generalizations about a person or group of persons, are clichés of vision. Although they usually reflect prejudice, in journalists they are often the product of laziness and can be countered by the hard work of reporting. That's how *Los Angeles Times* columnist Peter King responded when the mayor of San Francisco declared that a pregnant, unmarried African American woman on welfare who died saving her children from a fire in her apartment was the "real hero." The public had reacted to the mayor's comment "with letters, calls, faxes, all bubbling with pure white hatred and self-righteous indignation," King wrote in his column. Wrote one: "Where do you get the idea of Nina Davis as a hero? Her act of saving three of her seven illegitimate kids may be taken as a small token of repayment for all those tens of thousands of $$$$$ society, the federal government and California taxpayers have put forward." As talk shows took up the racist cry, King decided he had to write about the case. Using his training as a reporter, he first went to two places: the housing projects where the story happened and Nina Davis' funeral. In an interview for *Best News-paper Writing*, King explained why:

"It would be one thing to sit in there and say, 'What a bunch of ya-hoos, criticizing this poor woman—who, all she did was save her chil-dren—simply because she was on welfare has therefore forfeited her right to basic human dignity,'" King says. "It's another thing to go out there and see the lie of it all with your own eyes. When you see with your own eyes the reality of their dismal situation, then I think it not only in-forms the art, but it powers it."

Here is an excerpt from King's column that demonstrates how those basic reporting skills can enhance understanding for a writer and his readers:

> Where were the Cadillacs? This was Hunters Point, the projects. This was San Francisco's contribution to that part of the country known as "inner-city" Amer-ica, where the fear and the stereotypes play. Welfare Queens luxuriate in such places. They drive Cadillacs, crank out children, buy good whiskey with food stamps. It's a swell life, underwritten by taxpayers who have fallen prey to the Compassion Crowd and who themselves can no longer afford good whiskey, not to mention Cadillacs.
>
> I know these things.
> I listen to talk radio.
> And yet, somehow, standing beneath the burned-out unit where Nina Davis lived, it all didn't seem so swell. The cars were junkers, some stripped, tires flat. The housing units were sagging, dilapidated, the pastel paint chipped and scarred with graffiti. Faded orange bed sheets hung in the windows, blocking out the sun and everything else.

Los Angeles Times
Feb. 26, 1995

Balanced, fair and insightful reporting can also counter stereotypes. Dur-ing the 1998 Winter Olympics in Nagano, Japan, *San Francisco Examiner* sports writer Gwen Knapp wrote about the pressures faced by Shannon Miller, a coach on the Canadian women's hockey team. In the opening sec-tion, Knapp introduces the theme—homophobia in women's sports—and provides her readers with facts, context and refreshing candor.

Shannon Miller says she has been the target of gunfire twice. She was a police officer in Calgary, Alberta, for eight years, and a sniper once shot the lights off the top of her cruiser. The other time, a teen-age boy—drunk and suicidal after wrecking his fa-ther's car—locked himself in the family bathroom and started firing at her through the door.

Both incidents make her laugh now.

Miller left the beat two years ago to de-vote more time to coaching hockey, another job traditionally held by men. She has been

Continued

a coach on the Canadian women's team since 1991, and she is the only female head coach among the six hockey teams at the Winter Olympics. Some things haven't changed since she left the police force. She is still in a minority, and she is still a target.

Rumors that she was having an affair with one of her players, and cutting other women in favor of her alleged lover, have persisted for almost three years. The rumors, apparently spread by unsuccessful candidates for the national team, were investigated by Canadian Hockey and declared unfounded.

"We took it through our lawyers, had them investigate it," says Bob Nicholson, president-elect of Canadian Hockey. "We got very clearly from them that there was no substance to the allegations. But we took it one step further and we met with the team and talked about it, and talked with each individual player."

Yet the stories keep appearing in Canadian newspapers, years later. Whenever Miller has to make team cuts, she knows there is a chance someone will try to revive the story. At this point, she says, the whispering bothers her about as much as the armed teen-ager in the bathroom.

A player released three years ago "tried to make an issue of the fact that there are some gay players on the team. And that didn't go anywhere, so she tried to make up a story that I was having a relationship with one of the players," Miller says. "At first, [the coaching staff] felt bad about it, we felt betrayed and 'Oh, my God.' And now we just kill ourselves laughing about it."

It's not unusual for people to make enormous leaps of judgment and connect women's team sports, lesbianism and unethical behavior. What is unusual is for a team to acknowledge candidly, and without apology, that there are lesbians on its roster. Most teams dodge the issue or dismiss it as irrelevant. Ultimately, they are implying that heterosexuality prevails and, by extension, that sexual diversity threatens a team or a sport.

The Canadian team is braver than that. Miller does not discuss her own sexual orientation publicly. She considers that an entirely private matter. But because part of her job is to bring different people together and make them work in unison, she does not pretend that all of her players came from the same mold.

"We eat, breathe and sleep hockey together," Miller says. "We know so much about each other. It's amazing how much we know about each other. And you know what? Are there some gay women on our hockey team? Yes, there are. Do the straight women care? No, they don't. Is it an issue on our team? No, it is not. And I give you my word on that."

Sexual orientation, she says, had been a potential source of conflict when the national team first came together. But so had the division between French and English speakers, an ever-lurking tension for all Canadian teams.

San Francisco Examiner
Feb. 15, 1998

THE CASE FOR CULTURAL COMPETENCE IN JOURNALISM

Columnist Peter King was simply checking out a story with his own eyes and ears, doing the kind of fact gathering and critical thinking that any good reporter should do. That is especially important when the story involves a subject or people who seem different from you.

"Coverage that springs from ignorance or is inhibited by fear of the unfamiliar falls short of the basic tenets of ethical journalism; that is, journalism that is fair, complete, balanced, clear and, above all, true," according to Keith Woods and Aly Colón, former journalists who specialize in diversity training for journalists and news organizations at The Poynter Institute. Woods is African American. Colón is Latino. Here and in the following sections, they present the case for cultural competence in today's and tomorrow's journalists and ways for journalists to achieve that goal:

> Who should journalists address first when they want to interview an Asian family? Where can photojournalists turn when they want to know how to take pictures at a mosque, the temple for followers of Islam, one of the fastest growing religions in the United States? What's the difference between a Cuban American, a Puerto Rican, a Dominican and a Mexican American?
>
> The increasing cultural diversity of the United States, coupled with global interdependence, presents journalists today with a need to become culturally competent.
>
> Not only has the United States experienced a wave of immigration unmatched since the turn of the century, but also the makeup of those immigrants represents a far more varied cultural, religious and racial landscape. And the growing number of economic linkages within the international community requires us to understand and communicate across barriers of language and customs.
>
> In addition to the growing numbers of new U.S. residents, there has been a need to reacquaint ourselves with those who have been here all along but too often ignored: African Americans, Latinos, Native Americans, Asian Americans. Once seemingly invisible to the white population, these cultural groups occupy increasingly significant and visible places in the American mosaic.
>
> The mythological American melting pot idea allowed journalists to approach news and communities as if everyone shared the same news values. The reality today resembles a boiling stew. Dip into it in the wrong way, and journalists can get burned. And what they report will misrepresent the flavor of the community.
>
> Journalists who want to reflect the reality of the world around them need to be able to connect to the multicultural communities in their midst. They must relate to them not simply as outsiders looking in, but seek ways to see them as an insider would looking out.

"I try to cover life as it is, not as we would wish it to be. There is a tendency among white liberal editors and reporters to revert to what I call gee-whiz stories about minorities, stories that have a message, hidden or blatant, that says 'they are real people, just like us.' Conversely, there is sometimes a tendency among minority journalists to do 'advocacy' types of stories, stories that paint a particular underrepresented group in a purely positive light: Gee, aren't black people great, etc. I simply try to do what I think is honest journalism—truth-telling. If that means that I write about the dirty little secrets in a community— for instance, the fact that Puerto Ricans and Dominicans hate each other—then that is what I do. If it means writing a great story about an Anglo who is doing something terrific, I do that. I try to deal with all people as people, and I take their stories seriously, and research them to the best of my ability."

—ALISA VALDES, REPORTER, *The Boston Globe*

A journalist who wants to be culturally competent leaves the familiar behind and approaches the unfamiliar with curiosity, sensitivity and respect. Such a journalist creates a multicultural reading list; looks for "listening posts" where the authentic sounds of the community can be heard; seeks out cultural guides; visits those communities regularly and off deadline in an effort to become better educated.

Cultural competence creates opportunities to pursue excellence in journalism. It encourages explanations. It enhances understanding. It provides greater access to individuals. It develops more knowledgeable sources. It reflects a more accurate, complete and authentic picture of communities. It builds bridges between different groups. It captures the whole as well as it does the sum of its parts.

REPORTER'S TOOLBOX: THE FIVE W'S OF DIVERSITY

Before joining the Poynter faculty, Aly Colón covered the diversity beat for *The Seattle Times* and advised his colleagues as the paper's diversity coach. He suggests that reporters searching for diversity in their work can profit from using the journalistic tradition of the five W's:

- *Who's* missing from the story?
- *What's* the context for the story?
- *Where* can we go for more information?
- *When* do we use racial or ethnic identification?
- *Why* are we including or excluding certain information?

As diversity reporter for *The Seattle Times,* Colón brought a fresh perspective to stories.

What might have been a routine crime story about a shooting at a Vietnamese nightclub that left two dead and several wounded became an exploration of the clash of cultures and the criminal justice system. "There were language problems," he wrote. "Confusion about names. Many of the young Vietnamese didn't understand the police or trust them." The investigation, as one police official put it, "ended up being a hell of a mess."

In "Speechless in Seattle," which appears later in this chapter, Colón, a native of Puerto Rico, chronicled his experiences traveling throughout Seattle speaking only Spanish.

In the following example, notice how Colón takes a routine story—about an athletic event for wheelchair athletes—and lets readers see the challenges and triumphs of the world through the athletes' eyes. His tools are empathy, careful reporting and evocative writing.

Aly Colón (Courtesy of The Poynter Institute)

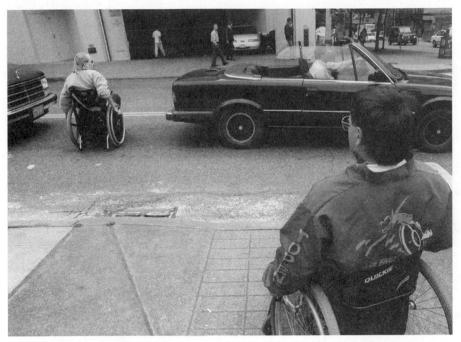

Aly Colón, diversity reporter for *The Seattle Times,* used a story about wheelchair athletes to gauge the city's accessibility for the disabled. Photo by Jimi Lott. (Courtesy of *The Seattle Times*)

Wheelchair Athletes Do More Than Roll Along; Visiting Veterans Rate City High on Accessibility

By Aly Colón
Staff Writer
The Seattle Times
July 4, 1996

SEATTLE—Thomas Reid shot down the curb cut on Pike Street and Seventh Avenue, his ponytail bouncing as he hit the downtown Seattle street.

He rolled a sharp left, then right, and wheeled between two cars. His friend Kent Brown followed, their wheelchairs navigating the rise and fall of the asphalt and the steep sidewalk grades.

Continued

Despite such corners, where the curb openings sit far from the crosswalks, and even in spite of the hills, Reid and Brown said they found Seattle relatively accessible. And for Reid, a 27-year-old Boston man who is partially paralyzed from the neck down, and Brown, a 43-year-old West Virginia man paralyzed from the waist down, that's important. As participants in the 16th National Veterans Wheelchair Games this week in the Seattle area, they and their fellow 548 wheelchair athletes know what it takes to get around in a variety of cities.

Seattle, many of them say, ranks highly when it comes to accessibility. They also cite the friendliness of people and places like Steve's Grill, where tables were moved about to make it more comfortable for them.

Tom Brown, one of the event's co-founders, said he would rate Seattle as one of the two best sites among the 14 cities that have hosted the games. He identified his hometown of San Antonio as the other. Miami and New Orleans also got high marks from other wheelchair athletes.

Brown pointed to the many accommodations Seattle has made:

—The Kenmore bowling alley that took out seats and put in ramps for the bowling competition.

—The Westin Hotel for manning elevators and programming them to stay open longer, taking doors off to make more room for wheelchairs, the use of service elevators, additional ramps for access.

—City transit with its tie-down system that enables wheelchairs to be strapped and hooked into place, the 20 reconfigured buses designed to transport 20 athletes at a time and wheelchair-access maps.

That's not to say it's all easy.

Steve Judd, 45, had nothing but complaints about the elevators at the Westin, noting half-hour waits were not uncommon and only two could usually squeeze in at a time. Quadriplegics assigned rooms with couch beds miss the mattress firmness their bodies need. And "all the carpeting makes it a bitch to push on," he said.

Larry Glenn, 49, from Erie, Pa., complained about his inability to get into the bathroom. Even though the hotel pulled off the door, the 26-inch width falls short of the 27 inches the wheelchair requires to get through.

He still hasn't gotten in. So what does he do? He doesn't, he said. A friend suggested he throw himself in the pool. "After a few days of this, I don't think they'll want me there," Glenn snapped back.

Others worry about the rain. There's no traction when surfaces get wet, and it can get very messy.

But the wheelchair athletes don't sit around feeling sorry for themselves. They roll down the hotel lobbies, brace themselves as they push up inclines and grab what they need.

John Reed, born in Princeton, Mo., the town that gave birth to Calamity Jane, plans to compete in bowling, basketball, discus throwing and his specialty—air rifles.

"There hasn't been any place I haven't been able to get to," said the 42-year-old veteran, who wheeled past the lunch table at the Convention Center, his left arm pushing one wheel as his right arm deftly snagged the smoked-turkey lunch bag and sped to his table to eat.

REPORTER'S TOOLBOX: TALKING ACROSS DIFFERENCE

As city editor of the *New Orleans Times Picayune,* Keith Woods led the paper's efforts to explore the issues of race in a six-month series, "Together Apart: The Myth of Race." He offers this advice to journalists trying to better understand and communicate with the differences among people they work with and report on:

BE HONEST. Be aware that cross-difference conversations pass through filters that interpret, analyze and sometimes bend the message. When you're clear and honest about what you mean, you build trust.

SEEK CLARIFICATION BEFORE CONFUSION AND CONFLICT. Be willing to extend the benefit of the doubt. Ask questions before reacting. "What do you mean?" "Can you explain that a little more?"

CHALLENGE WITH PASSION, NOT POISON. Keep the conversation going through rough spots by letting the other person know that your passion is born of a desire to get past misunderstanding.

BE WILLING TO CHANGE YOUR POINT OF VIEW. Practice the skill of truly considering the other's way of seeing things. You don't always have to change your mind. Just make sure it's possible.

STAY IN THE ROOM. The toughest thing to do when something is uncomfortable or painful is to keep doing it. The challenge here is to have faith that there is gain on the other side of the pain.

REPORTER'S TOOLBOX: GUIDELINES FOR RACIAL IDENTIFIERS IN NEWS STORIES

"The use of racial identifiers in the media was for decades a means of singling out those who were not white," says diversity expert Keith Woods. "The practice helped form and fuel stereotypes and continues today to push a wedge between people." Racial and ethnic identification remains a sensitive topic in many newsrooms. Journalists can handle this delicate material better, Woods says, if they examine every racial reference in a story before publication or broadcast, and ask these questions:

1. IS IT RELEVANT? Race is relevant when the story is about race. Just because people in conflict are of different races does not mean that is the source of their dispute. A story about interracial dating, however, is a story about race.

2. HAVE I EXPLAINED THE RELEVANCE? Journalists too frequently assume readers will know the significance of race in stories. The result is radically different interpretations. That is imprecise journalism, and harm may be magnified by the lens of race.

"As a lesbian, I can assure you that while I walk with privilege as white and middle class, I experience my share of discrimination and oppression. As a lesbian journalist— working in broadcast—I , for many years, feared coming out in my newsroom. I wondered if I'd be demoted, shunned aside in the kinds of assignments, reduced in airtime or even fired."

—KAREN-LOUISE BOOTHE, PRESIDENT, NATIONAL LESBIAN AND GAY JOURNALISTS ASSOCIATION

Keith Woods
(Courtesy of
The Poynter
Institute)

3. IS IT FREE OF CODES? Be careful not to use "welfare," "inner city," "underprivileged," "blue collar," "conservative," "suburban," "exotic," "middle class," "Uptown," "South Side" or "wealthy" as euphemisms for racial groups. By definition, the White House is in the inner city. Say what you mean.

4. ARE RACIAL IDENTIFIERS USED EVENLY? If the race of a person charging discrimination is important, then so is the race of the person being charged.

5. SHOULD I CONSULT SOMEONE OF ANOTHER RACE/ETHNICITY? Consider another question: Do I have expertise on other races/cultures? If not, broaden your perspective by asking someone who knows more about your subject. Why should we treat reporting on racial issues any differently from reporting on an area of science or religion that we do not know well?

REPORTER'S TOOLBOX: RESOURCES AND STRATEGIES FOR CONNECTING WITH DIVERSE COMMUNITIES

In the 1990 census, the U.S. Census Bureau listed 215 ancestry groups. Journalists can better connect with diverse communities. Colón offers these resources and approaches:

1. SPECIALISTS. Contact local diversity and/or race relations specialists. Check universities, institutes, diversity consulting firms, companies known for diversity efforts. Meet with diverse people in your own organization.

2. ORGANIZATIONS. Contact local organizations that represent diverse groups, i.e., Hispanic Chamber of Commerce, African American Coalition, Asian American Association, the Deaf Center, etc.

3. PUBLICATIONS AND BROADCASTS. Meet with publishers/editors of locally based publications (newspapers, magazines, newsletters) that focus on race, ethnicity, sexual orientation, gender, disabilities. Subscribe to the publications. Also check with television, radio and cable stations owned by, or oriented toward, diverse groups.

4. LEADERS. Ask people you meet whom they respect as knowledgeable people in their communities. Seek out unofficial leaders.

5. LIST. Create a list of people you can turn to in diverse communities who represent different perspectives within their groups.

6. VISITS. Visit communities different from your own. Eat at ethnic restaurants. Shop at ethnic stores. Meet the owners.

7. CONTACT. Remain in regular contact with people on your diversity list. Meet them for coffee, tea, breakfast or lunch, *in their communities*.

REPORTING AND WRITING ABOUT DIFFERENCE: STORY EXAMPLES

Felix Gutierrez is director of the Pacific Coast Center of the Freedom Forum and co-author of *Race, Multiculturalism and the Media.* With no single ethnic group holding the majority in some cities, Gutierrez advises students to deal with this reality by talking with people who have been in the minority all their lives. "Practice being in places where you're different, and not particularly welcome," he says, "and you'll be able to deal with that situation better in your reporting."

One way to do that is to write about a time in your life when you were "The Other," that is, the minority. Following are three examples, the first two by student journalists at The Poynter Institute, Linah Mathabane and Karin Fischer, and the third by diversity expert Aly Colón.

STUDENT EXAMPLE 1

Separate Scars, Equal Pain; A Feeling of Loneliness

By Linah Mathabane
Points South Staff Writer

I was born and raised in a two-room shack on 16th Avenue in Alexandra, South Africa. As one of seven children, I shared my cold floor bed with my four sisters and often my cousins. My schooling was constantly interrupted by riots or boycotts. My world was pure black with the exception of white policemen roaming the dusty, unpaved roads exercising their authority over my people. The white policemen represented the white world I was prohibited to enter.

I went in. I was chased away.

The system of apartheid, with its cruel and brutal practices, did not prepare me for the racial tensions poisoning the towns, cities and the nation of America. As a reporter, I covered an exclusively African American neighborhood. My skin color made me accepted in the community.

After five weeks reporting on the neighborhood, I decided to test the racial tensions in my community, especially after learning about the previous riots when a white cop shot an 18-year-old young African American male. I brought another reporter, Todd, white and Jewish, to a gathering held each Sunday at Bartlett Park.

At the gathering some 3,000 African American youth chilled, hung out and scoped each other. Boys dressed in baggy Bugle Boy jeans with name brand T-shirts such as Reebok showed off their well-polished, colorful BMWs, Jettas and '72 Chevrolet cars.

Continued

The girls, fat, slender, short and tall in their cheekiest hairdos, walked the avenues dressed in their latest polyester, flowery, spaghetti-tight dresses, '60s bell-bottoms. The shortest skirts and shorts showed flirtatious flashes of skin. Young mothers brought their toddlers. Drug addicts came to deal and share. Young, naive and innocent girls bloomed as they took on their newfound goddess positions.

I consider myself a fair person. An understanding person. An open-minded person. A nonjudgmental person. Growing up in the ghettos of Alexandra, I really believed that I would never encounter anything that beat the system of apartheid. Where I was hated because of the color of my skin. Where my tribes, Shanganis and the Vendas, viewed me as nothing more than a child bearer. Where my sex determined my course in life. Where an educated woman is viewed as stupid and corrupted by Western minds. Nothing could top that for me. Nothing came close to that. Nothing could ever be like that.

I was wrong.

My heart pounded. It beat like a tribal drum. "You have to be strong. You have to be strong," I kept telling myself as we approached the park. The pace of my heartbeat quickened, and my nerves tightened.

Todd and I strolled the spacious walkway leading to the center of the gathering. Eyes were glued on us. We seemed ridiculously out of place. At least that's one thing we both agreed on.

I came to watch and be watched. I came to judge and be judged. As I smiled nervously and pretended to be striking a conversation with Todd, I tuned my ear to the silent looks and the obvious comments.

"Oreos," one woman said as we passed by.

"Did you hear that?" I asked Todd. "They called us Oreos."

I sensed the vibrations. The killer looks with eyes bulging out. The intense distant coldness. I heard whispers, but I could not make out the words. I could imagine.

"How dare you. How dare you flaunt yourself with a white guy. Who do you think you are?" the imaginary voices said.

"Traitor, sell-out, Uncle Tom," more echoed.

I felt uncomfortable. I felt threatened. I wanted to disappear. I wanted to die. I longed to be invisible. My body was tense. I was stiff. I was sweating badly. Florida's humid weather was no help. I was reluctant to roam around. I wanted to just stand where I was and stop torturing myself. Enduring the comments and cold treatment I received. Women rudely told me to make way for them and laughed afterward as they walked in front of me.

"Ex...cuse me," the voice said, cold and irritated.

I had attended the gathering at Bartlett Park before. Alone. Then people received me well. They smiled. They asked me questions about my home country. Today it was different. Today some ignored me. Some looked at me with distant and frozen eyes. I had brought the enemy. I was roaming with a white guy in their neighborhood. It did not matter if Todd was Jewish or not. He was white. That's what mattered. Their cold looks and comments tore me apart—limb by limb. I slowly suffered inside.

I intruded. I sinned.

I decided that Todd should walk around the park by himself and that I should remain in the same spot. I was not intending to move in a million years. Going toward the car and home was the only move I was going to make. I remained standing. Staring across at two handsome young men, I badly wanted them to come talk to me. I longed for their company. Their manly approach, voice and touch.

I wanted to scream, "We are just friends. There is really nothing going on between us. Please, someone talk to me. Talk to me like you talk to the rest of the girls around. Just pay attention to me. Acknowledge me for Christ sakes."

To my dismay, no one approached me.

Todd returned. We continued talking. Stupid things. I do not really remember. I recall only how often I checked my watch.

"Let's leave now," I said.

"Let's leave at 8:30 p.m.," Todd said.

"Another torturous hour. Is he insane? Have I gone crazy, or I can't take it any-more? I just want to melt down," I mumbled to myself.

Two little girls approached me, smiling.

I opened a 20-ounce bottle of Sprite—the cap in my hand.

"Is that a winning cap?" they excitedly wondered.

"No. I am sorry," I replied, happy to have someone talk to me. To have someone make me revisit my childhood. A lonely and secluded childhood where racial segregation was law.

I glanced at my watch again. An hour of waiting felt like a century. I never wanted time to move as fast as I did that day at Bartlett Park. The two and a half hours I spent feeling worthless and nonexistent. The erasable scar in my life.

A permanent wound.

STUDENT EXAMPLE 2

A Short Ride, a Long Journey, a Courageous Trip

By Karin Fischer
Points South Staff Writer

Phil Struckman drives the people who can't walk.

The entire campus of Westminster Shores Retirement Community is only 27 acres, and the farthest point from the dining room is less than a quarter of a mile. But the residents need Phil—who is, at 82, the same age as many of his passengers—to drive them where their legs or the Florida weather prevent them from going.

There's something a little funny and a little sad about a bespectacled woman who takes the tram to Mansfield, an assisted living building. Mansfield actually is connected by a long, carpeted hall to the main building that houses the dining room, our point of departure, but the woman chooses to ride. "It's faster and easier," she says quietly, as she

Continued

inches snail-like toward the door. "It's faster to take the tram with Phil than to walk down the hall to my room."

The people who ride the tram are regulars. Phil knows every face and every address. He can't tell me every name, but he does know every ailment: strokes, pneumonia, survivors of heart surgery. The man on the second floor of Allen, in the independent living section, is recovering from a hip operation and uses a cane. The woman on the first floor has a walker and oxygen, 24 hours a day.

When I think about what disturbs me most that afternoon of driving in circles—from the main building to Allen, from Allen to the Villas, from the Villas down Calamondian Street to the water, back to the main building—it is the woman with the oxygen tank. She is on the tram, an oversized electric golf cart that courses along sidewalks instead of fairways, for less than five minutes. It is 12:30, the lunchtime rush, and the seven-person cart is full for the return trip from the dining room. The woman behind me is talking about my fair complexion and how nice and generous and what a truly great person Phil is, and so I pretend not to hear the woman with the oxygen tank that she wheels in front of her.

"I'll have the oxygen until the day I die," she says. "I'll always have this burden."

I could say to her, "I know what you mean." But I don't.

At Westminster Shores, it is always the people with the walkers and oxygen tanks and broken bones and fine hair downing their heads after chemotherapy treatments who stay in my mind. In my six weeks covering Westminster Shores as a novice reporter, I write stories about elderly romance and tell my friends about the vitality of the senior volunteers. But at night when I can't sleep, I get out of bed and run on the beach and think about the wheelchair- and bed-bound patients in the corridors of the health center. When I go to Westminster Shores, I don't see it as a foreign place, an other-world of old age and death. Instead, I think about how much we have in common, these 80-year-olds and I. Despite my generation, I am an insider. We deal in the same currency: sickness.

It is difficult for me to admit this shared knowledge. It's difficult for me to admit having been ill at all or my fears that one day, any day, I could be ill again. I thought if I didn't talk about it, then it wouldn't happen, it didn't happen. I remained silent through biopsies and X-rays, chemo and more chemo. I went to the doctor's office and the oncologist's office and the hospital by myself. In my dorm room I would look at my scar and cry and cry and cry. Then I'd button my shirt back up and tell no one. Ill health at 20 means only two things to people: pity or fear. I am not a martyr. Ill health at 80? That's life.

The women—there's a man or two every trip, but the tram is dominated by women—gossip casually about the heat and the lunch menu of soup and salad, beef burgundy with noodles, herbed chicken, royal flounder. And they talk about physical therapy and who is in the hospital now, the way my friends and I talk about movies or boys or mutual friends. There's no sense of stigma in the discussion of mending limbs and surgeries, an openness about ill health. In my home, we talk all the time, but we never speak of bad news. We, my family and I, are masters of the euphemism; we're never sick, just not well. My mother phoned me after the first wrenching chemo treatment. "How are you?" she asked. I told her I was fine. She wouldn't have expected anything less.

I can't decide if I welcome the freedom, the let-it-all-hang-out attitude toward sickness and death. Does the ability to talk about illness, to say its name, to speak it, make the betrayal of oneself by one's body any more tolerable? Does talking about mortality make death less frightening?

After the rush slows to an occasional trickle—a ride to physical therapy or a visit to the club house for the Monday afternoon movie—Phil lets me drive the tram, a Textron Ez-Go. We putt-putt ahead, down Bahama Shores Drive at 10 miles an hour. I wonder if the six batteries, lying lengthwise beneath the back seat, are running low. I gun the right pedal—the "Go" pedal, Phil calls it, versus the "Whoa" pedal—and we lurch ahead to 11 miles an hour.

As I drive, Phil tells me about his own health. He laments the fact that he can't windsurf or boat like he used to, 15 years ago when his wife was alive. But he's able to get around, to hold a job, to practice his pool game, to run to the grocery store for one of the Westminster Shores residents who recently came home from the hospital. Her husband is still in the health center. She has cancer.

Phil rolls the word around on his tongue. Cancer, he says, like he's speaking in a foreign language. I want to tell him that I need no translation. It's a word I know—people said it to me daily during my senior year of college. They said it clinically and stiffly and coldly. They said it in phosphorescent rooms, not out here in the bright Florida sun. Cancer. Lumpectomy. Lymph nodes. Cyclophosphamide. Doxorubicin. Cancer.

Phil looks at me. "Don't ever grow old," he says. "Don't ever get sick. You won't like it."

He's right, but that's no revelation. As a reporter, I demand honesty, candor, truth from the people about whom I write. I want to know their lives. Yet, I don't want to examine my own. Westminster Shores has prevented me from looking away. The residents are the embodiment of my fears. They broadcast their hurts; I no longer can hide my scars.

PROFESSIONAL EXAMPLE

Speechless in Seattle

By Aly Colón
The Seattle Times Staff Reporter

One night, in a restaurant in Prague, I experienced great frustration over a small thing: butter. I spoke no Czech, the waiter no English. When he placed bread on the table I held it up and said "Bbuutttteerr."

Continued

He smiled, repeated the word, then went away. But he brought no butter. When he came with our meals, I said "buuuuttterrr" hoping a slightly different pronunciation would help. He repeated what I said. I thought I'd gotten through this time. But again no butter. I tried a few more times. Raising my eyebrows to ask if he understood. Smiling to ingratiate myself.

Nothing.

I ate the bread dry.

Getting around in a country where you don't speak the local language can be frustrating for visitor and local alike. Ordering food or asking for directions can be a challenge.

But what about our country? Our city? Seattle? What kind of experience would someone who doesn't speak English have here?

I decided to find out.

One Person's Experience

I chose downtown areas that tourists might visit: the waterfront, hotels, department stores, cafes, buses and so forth. I dressed casually, as a tourist might:

Slacks, cotton shirt with an open collar.

Every place I went, I spoke only Spanish. No English.

The reactions surprised me. Sometimes, after getting over their initial shock, people attempted linguistic and physical contortions to help me understand what they thought I needed. Other times, their quick, cool dismissal made me feel lost, unimportant, almost invisible.

Foreigners unable to speak English may have had better or worse experiences during visits here. But I tried to put myself in their shoes, and these experiences and reflections stand as one example of what can happen to travelers who speak a language other than English in Seattle.

First Things First

First, I went to the central tourist-information office, buried in a back corner of the Washington State Convention Center. The place offers walls of information, from maps to brochures to bus schedules, rather like tourist centers throughout Europe. I felt confident they'd be able to help. The woman behind the counter wore a navy blue outfit with a red and white collar. *"Buenos dias. Hablas Español?"*

She looked at me with a surprised expression. Then she said slowly: *"No hablo Español."* She paused. A thin smile crossed her lips. "I speak Chinese," she said. I felt slightly ridiculous. There I was speaking to her in Spanish. She's telling me in English that she speaks Chinese. I decided to plow on in the hopes that something I'd say might trigger her to find someone else who spoke Spanish. I asked if she could recommend any interesting places for me to visit. She stared at me blankly: "I don't understand a thing you're saying." Now I felt stymied. I stood there with a "Please, can you help me?" expression on my face. She stared back for a few moments, I think hoping I'd just leave. Then she went to the center of the counter and looked around the room and blurted out loudly: "DOES ANYONE HERE SPEAK SPANISH?" A young woman, visiting from another state for a professional conference in the center, walked up and told her she spoke Portuguese and some Spanish.

"Wonderful," the information woman said, beaming. I told the young woman that I'd like to see some interesting places in

Seattle. She translated. The woman behind the counter pulled out a Seattle tour map, unfolded it and circled the visitor's center first. Then she pointed to the Pike Place Market, the waterfront, Pioneer Square, Westlake Center and Seattle Center. The younger woman explained it all to me. The information center woman looked at me and then at the map and then pointed to Pike Place Market and said "One," holding up one finger to show the best place to start. Then she pointed to the other attractions in order. When she finished she seemed quite pleased. But if the young woman hadn't happened to be there, I sensed I would have left just as lost as I'd been walking in. I smiled and thanked both women and walked west on Pike, toward Westlake Center.

If the Shoe Fits ...

I stopped at Nordstroms. A tall young man came over to me in the men's shoe department. I asked if he spoke Spanish. He leaned over, smiled weakly and said he didn't. Did anyone speak Spanish? He lifted his right index finger and motioned for me to wait. A couple of minutes later, he came back and said somebody who spoke *Español* would be available. Within a few minutes, a salesperson from women's jewelry approached me smiling. She asked in fluent Spanish how she could serve me. I told her I'd like to try on some shoes. During the next 20 minutes she chatted amiably in Spanish and translated all my questions and the salesman's responses in a friendly fashion. When I said I needed to think about the shoes before buying them, the salesman wrote down the shoes' name and size for me. He even said he'd hold them for me for a couple of days since they might run out of the style. Throughout my time there, I felt as comfortable speaking Spanish

as I have at other times when I went to Nordstrom and spoke English. Both the non-Spanish-speaking clerk and the one who spoke Spanish acted as if this was normal, everyday experience.

Helping Hands

I asked the woman at the Westlake Center information counter if she spoke Spanish. She smiled and shook her head. She did speak French. I said I wanted information about tourist sites. She picked up on the words *información* and *tourista* and figured she'd give it a try. She pulled out a Seattle tour map and pointed to Westlake Center to let me know where we were. Then she indicated the Pike Place Market. She pointed with her pen to the hill climb leading toward the waterfront. She could tell I looked a bit confused so she began moving her hands up and down to imitate feet going up and down steps. Her hands became the language of connection, darting from map to midair, doing aerodynamic maneuvers as she tried to convey visually some thoughts that might help me understand the sights of the city. She pointed to the Seattle Aquarium. She waved her hands back and forth, simulating swimming fish. When she pointed to the Omnidome, with a film depicting the Mount St. Helens explosion, she tossed her hands skyward. Although she couldn't speak a lick of Spanish, I appreciated her energetic efforts to help me. In fact, she seemed fatigued by the time I left.

No Bon Mots

I crossed the street to the Bon Marché. I went to the men's suits section. A salesman approached me. I asked if he spoke Spanish.

Continued

He smiled and said, "*No Español,*" then motioned for me to wait. He picked up a phone and said loudly, "HEY, RALEIGH, DO YOU SPEAK SPANISH?" He hung up and said with a contrite face, "No, no Español." I felt disappointed that he made no further effort to help. He might have shown me some suits, and I, through hand signals, could have indicated whether I liked them or not. As I walked away a couple came in. The salesman asked them if they needed any help "in English." He laughed. So did the couple. It was obvious, even to someone who didn't speak English, that the laughter was at my expense.

It felt demeaning, alienating. I thought I should try another part of the store. When I spotted a young man sitting at the "At Your Service" counter I asked him if he spoke Spanish, figuring that he probably didn't but might hook me up with somebody who did. But he gave me a quick, if polite, brush-off. He smiled and said no. When I asked if there was anyone who spoke Spanish, he just repeated that he didn't and then went back to reading his catalogue. I stood there for a minute, wondering if I should try another department. But then I figured I'd been blown off enough.

Extra Effort

At the Westin Hotel, I asked a young man at the registration desk for room rates. He looked lost. I asked if he spoke Spanish. He said no. I asked if anyone could provide me with information. He asked me to wait. He came back with another hotel official, a Latino who spoke Spanish. The Latino politely provided me with information and said to call him if I needed anything else. His professionalism and friendliness more than made up for the discomfort I'd been feeling. I proceeded down the hill toward the Pike Place Market, strolling past the crafts and food stalls that line the main level. I stopped to examine flowers framed in glass. The stall owner said he didn't speak Spanish but began trying what Spanish he did know. He pointed to the price tags on the items when I asked how much the items cost. He showed how the glass frames reflected in the light. He listened attentively, trying to make sure he understood what I was saying. His friendly attention seemed genuine.

Food and Water

Since it was lunchtime, I went to the Athenian Cafe. A blond-haired waiter greeted me right after I sat down. Although he said he spoke no Spanish, when I asked about the *especialidades* he pointed to the specialties of the house. I pointed to the pastrami on rye sandwich on the menu. He asked what I wanted to drink by using his right hand to form the shape of a glass and raising it toward his lips. "*Agua,*" I said.

He smiled, repeating the word. When he came back with the glass of water, he placed it on the table and said, "*Agua.*" Later when he dropped off the check he said, "*Muchas gracias.*" The waiter's attempt to use a word or two in Spanish made me feel he wanted to connect on some basic level. At the Seattle Aquarium, the experience turned out to be awkward for both me and the women who worked there. When I asked for information in Spanish, the cashier looked shocked, as if I'd just slapped her in the face. I kept talking in even tones. After several minutes, she left the register, walked behind some double doors and came out moments later with two brochures. One described the aquarium in German, French and Spanish. The other was in English and had a map. So, I'd received something for my efforts and decided to see if she could help me more. The brochures said nothing about hours or days of operation. So I asked. She didn't understand. Her colleague at the other register started giggling nervously. Obviously, neither knew what I was talking about or what they should do. But tourists who want to see certain sites need to be persistent. I asked again about the aquarium's hours. I pointed to my watch. The cashier said I could go in at anytime. She smiled with relief when I said *"gracias"* and left.

Helpful Enthusiasm

As I walked down the waterfront sidewalk, I paused at the Cruise the Locks stand. How much is the boat tour? I asked the woman at the kiosk. "Excuse me?" she said. Smiling I asked again. She looked at me, rubbed the fingers of her left hand and asked: "How much?" I nodded, also rubbing my fingers, grateful that she had picked up on what I wanted so quickly. She said, "$21.50." It was nice to get the right answer even if it was in the wrong language. A small rectangular sign, blue with white letters, pointed out the entrance to the state ferry terminal from the sidewalk level. ... Inside, a petite woman had just come on duty and immediately came over to ask me how she could help. I asked for information on the ferry rides and fares and if she spoke Spanish. She said, *"Un poquito,"* holding her thumb and forefinger very close together. She told her co-worker that she wished the Mexican janitor had taught her more than Spanish words having to do with cleaning and trash. I asked about the fare to Victoria.

She looked at me with an expression that sought to please, but she had no idea what I was saying. I asked again, slowly. She strained to hear the words. *"Cuesta?* Cost?" she said and began telling me the prices. Then she paused and asked if I would like her to write it down, moving her hands as if she were writing something. She wanted to be as helpful as she could. Her enthusiasm was contagious. She made me feel the ferry schedules could be made understandable even to a foreigner: She got a sheet of paper, wrote down the prices for passengers and car, individuals and kids, even writing some words in Spanish like *"niños."* She smiled and told her co-worker, "I think I'm getting the hang of this."

Curt Brush-Off

The man at the booth at the Seattle Harbor Tours for Tillicum Village was the complete opposite of the ferry employee. When I asked him if he could speak Spanish, he barely smiled as he said a curt "No." I asked if there was any information, times, prices. No. No. No. End of conversation. I'd just been told to "get lost." At the Space Needle, I went to the ticket window for the observation deck. How much time could I spend at the top? The woman smiled, saying she spoke just a little Spanish and what I had just said was way beyond her. What was the price to go up? The way she leaned back, away from the ticket window, made me realize that I was making her feel very uncomfortable. I felt uncomfortable myself, since there were people in line behind me who seemed eager to get their tickets. I heard someone shout from farther back in line, "He wants to know how much a ticket

Continued

is." She quickly pointed to a sign above the counter. From the worried expression on her face, I figured it was time to move on. I went over to the restaurant reservation desk for the Needle's restaurant. I asked a young man in a dark suit about making a reservation. As he heard me in Spanish, he tilted his head back and turned it from side to side, as if he were scanning the sky. "What you just said went right over me," he said. When I asked him if anyone there spoke Spanish, he apparently thought I wanted a menu and pulled one out for me to look at. I asked again how I could make a reservation. I could tell he felt he had to do something. So he did. He pointed to the items in the menu and said the prices would vary. I became increasingly frustrated in my attempts to figure out a way to make a reservation. When I asked if anyone in the restaurant spoke Spanish, he listened carefully to the words and seemed to pick up on the words *restaurante* and *Español* and said he thought someone might. But he just

stood there and did nothing to find out. As I left I said *"gracias,"* and he replied *"de nada* ["you're welcome"], that's about all the Spanish I know."

A Grateful Tourist

Having traveled throughout much of Europe, in countries where I couldn't understand or speak the language, I knew how it felt to be an outsider, ignorant of where I was and where to go. Many places in Europe, however, seem accustomed to having a variety of people traveling through who need help. And a number of them, through their tourist offices, and locals, do a good job of helping out. Throughout my Spanish-speaking odyssey in Seattle, it seemed more people made an effort to help than didn't. Those who didn't reminded me of some of my encounters in East Berlin before the wall came down: aloof and chilly. The ones who made that extra effort demonstrated a kindness and generosity that many believe come naturally to Americans.

MAKING CONNECTIONS: THE COACHING WAY

- Practice empathy. If you're white, try to put yourself in Latino shoes. If you're African American, practice the skill of truly considering the Asian American way of seeing things. If you're heterosexual, consider how a gay or lesbian might react.
- During the reporting, ask yourself: Have I tried to find diverse sources that reflect a range of experiences and viewpoints?
- Explore your own attitudes about people of color, the disabled, gays and lesbians. Do you let your own prejudices limit your efforts to include diversity in your reporting and writing?

- Watch out for "tokenism" in your stories, letting one minority represent an entire group.
- During the writing, ask yourself: Am I perpetuating stereotypes and clichés of vision? Do I use language to describe people with accuracy and care or with insensitivity?
- Have I checked with a colleague to test whether the story's subject or the way it's presented is offensive? Could I defend it against charges of insensitivity or bias?

GLOSSARY OF IMPORTANT TERMS

In the appendix you will find the complete "News Watch Project Style Guide," a diversity glossary compiled and edited by Judy Gerber, the program's co-director, using style guides of the Asian American Journalists Association, National Lesbian and Gay Journalists Association, The Associated Press and the *Los Angeles Times*.

EXERCISES

1. News organizations have established formal systems to increase representations of people of color. Discuss the advantages and disadvantages of such an approach. Are "quotas" the answer?

2. Using Lillian Dunlap's list of tips for better coverage of people of color, grade the news publications and broadcasts you read or view. Grade your own stories.

3. Do a content audit measuring how people of color and women are portrayed in pictures and print in the newspapers, newscasts and online news sites that you frequent.

4. Write an essay titled "When I Was 'The Other'" that explores a time in your life when you felt like a minority.

READINGS

Astor, David. "A Diverse Wire for a Diverse Country." *Editor & Publisher*, March 9, 1996, pp. 38–39.

Bailon, Gilbert. "Gulf Between Minority, White Journalists Wide." *The American Editor*, October 1996, p. 16.

Case, Tony. "Remember Newsroom Diversity?" *Editor & Publisher*, Feb. 22, 1997, pp. 15–18, 42–43.

"Cuban Americans, Latinos, and the Print Media." *The Harvard International Journal of Press/Politics*, Summer 1997, pp. 52–70.

Dennis, Everette E., and Edward C. Pease, eds. *The Media in Black and White*. New York: Columbia University Press, 1996.

Favre, Gregory. "An Essential Part of Our Culture." *The American Editor*, July/August 1997, p. 13.

Flander, Judy. "Tales From the Trenches." *Communicator*, October 1997, pp. 34–37.

Jennings, Veronica T. "Minorities Steady in a Shrinking Work Force." *The American Editor*, March/May 1997, pp. 10–12.

Michel, Karen Lincoln. "Where the First Amendment Doesn't Apply: The Native American Press." *The American Editor*, March/May 1997, pp. 4–7.

Moyer, Keith. "Improve Minority Representation, Panel Says." *The American Editor,* June 1996, p. 31.

Papper, Bob, and Michael Gerhard. "Moving Forward, Falling Back." *Communicator,* October 1997, pp. 24–30.

Papper, Bob, Michael Gerhard, and Andre Sharma. "More Women and Minorities in Broadcast News." *Communicator,* August 1996, pp. 8–15.

Powers, Angela, Shirley Serini, and Susan Johnson. "How Gender and Ethnicity Affected Primary Coverage." *Newspaper Research Journal,* Winter/Spring 1996, pp. 105–112.

Stainback, Sheila. "Broadcast vs. Print Minority Hiring." *Communicator,* November 1996, p. 56.

Stein, M. L. "New Diversity." *Editor & Publisher,* June 14, 1997, pp. 24, 26.

Tan, Alexis, Yuki Fujioka, and Nancy Lucht. "Native American Stereotypes, TV Portrayals, and Personal Contact." *J&MC Quarterly,* Summer 1997, pp. 265–284.

Walsh-Childers, Kim, Jean Chance, and Kristin Herzog. "Sexual Harassment of Women Journalists." *Journalism & Mass Communication Quarterly,* Autumn 1996, pp. 559–581.

Williams, Don. "People and Product: The Business of Diversity in the Newspaper Industry." Supplement to *Presstime,* July 1996.

Wilson, Clint C. II, and Gutierrez, Felix. *Race, Multiculturalism and the Media.* Thousand Oaks, Calif.: Sage Publications, 1995.

Woods, Keith. "Facing Race." *Presstime,* October 1996, p. 61.

Woods, Keith. "Improving Diversity in Employment, Coverage Discussed in Special Session." *News Photographer,* November 1997, pp. 58, 63.

Zacchino, Narda. "Newsroom Must Manage Diversity Better." *The American Editor,* October 1996, p. 17.

HOTLIST

http://www.aaja.org

Asian American Journalists Association.

http://www.nabj.org

National Association of Black Journalists.

http://www.nahj.org

National Association of Hispanic Journalists.

http://www.nlgja.org

National Lesbian and Gay Journalists Association.

http://www.naja.com

Native American Journalists Association.

http://moon.jrn.columbia.edu/SAJA/

South Asian Journalists Association.

http://newswatch.sfsu.edu/text/Default.html

News Watch. A news media monitoring and advocacy project of the Center for Integration and Improvement of Journalism at the San Francisco State Department of Journalism. Offers an online style guide, links to resources and regular reports on how the news media portray people of color and lesbians and gays.

http://www.cjr.org/year/98/3/diversity.asp

"Blacks in the Newsroom: Progress? Yes, But ..." by David K. Shipler explores the status of hiring, promotion and coverage. Shipler, a former *New York Times* correspondent and Pulitzer Prize winner, is the author of *A Country of Strangers: Blacks and Whites in America.*

http://www.naa.org/presstime/9803/read.html

In his article "Diversity Dissonance: Readership Numbers Confirm Disparate Perceptions" for *Presstime,* the Newspaper Association of America magazine, Poynter Institute teacher Keith Woods reviews current research and appraises newspaper readership among demographic groups.

http://webster.commnet.edu/hp/pages/darling/grammar/unbiased.htm

Using Unbiased Language. From the excellent *Guide to Grammar and Writing* by Professor Charles Darling and Capital Community-Technical College.

http://www.pomona.edu/repres/intro/intro.html

"Re/Presentation: Principles in Visual Literacy" is the Web site for a class taught at Pomona College that explores media stereotypes of blacks, black youth, women, Native Americans, gays and lesbians, and whites.

http://www.screen.com/mnet/eng/med/class/teamedia/cbc.htm

To make sure that the language used by on-air personnel treats men and women equally, the Canadian Broadcasting Corporation has developed these guidelines.

http://www.asne.org/kiosk/diversity/divdetl.htm

This Web page includes diversity resources from the American Society of Newspaper Editors.

http://www.alternet.org/diversity/

The Diversity Project. The Institute for Alternative Journalism initiated the Diversity Project to assess the state of racial diversity.

http://www.brad.ac.uk/research/eram/wwwsites.html

"Ethnicity, Racism and the Media." This list of Web resources comes from the ERaM Program, located at the University of Bradford in the United Kingdom.

http://www.poynter.org/king/begin.html

"A Family's Journey: On the Road to Civil Rights." Poynter faculty member Keith Woods takes his children on a weeklong pilgrimage to Montgomery, Selma, Birmingham, Memphis and other historic sites of the nation's struggle for racial equality.

http://www.iwmf.org/

International Women's Media Foundation. IWMF was founded to strengthen the role of women in the media around the world.

http://www.jaws.org/

Journalism and Women Symposium. JAWS supports the personal growth and professional empowerment of women in newsrooms.

http://www.latinolink.com/

LatinoLink contains stories and photographs by Latino journalists from the United States and Puerto Rico.

http://www.maynardije.org/

The Maynard Institute is dedicated to increasing racial and ethnic diversity in news coverage, staffing and business operations.

http://www.poynter.org/dsurvey/Firstscreen.html

Media Diversity Beyond 2000 is a Poynter Institute-Ford Foundation Project designed to help journalists improve the way they understand and cover people and communities typically underserved by the media.

http://www.webcom.com/mibtp/

The Broadcast Training Program. The mission of this organization is to provide training opportunities to minority college graduates in radio/television news reporting and news management.

http://www.rtndf.org/rtndf/diversity.htm

Newsroom Diversity Campaign is the Radio and Television News Directors Foundation effort to promote the hiring, training, promotion and retention of minority professionals in television and radio news.

http://www.rtndf.org/prodev/rtndf/minority.htm

RTNDF Minority Recruitment Directory provides news directors with names and contact information for 180 resources to help recruit women and minorities in the newsroom.

http://www.newsjobs.com

National Diversity Journalism Job Bank. A service developed to increase the participation of people of color and women in journalism.

http://www.fac.org/publicat/trahant/contents.htm

"Pictures of Our Nobler Selves: A History of Native American Contributions to News Media." A powerful history by Native American journalist Mark N. Trahant.

http://www.theatlantic.com/unbound/forum/race/intro.htm

"Race in America." An online roundtable sponsored by *Atlantic Monthly*.

http://www.cjr.org/year/97/5/reporting_race.asp

"Reporting on Race." *Columbia Journalism Review* article by Terry A. Dalton.

CHAPTER

REPORTING AND WRITING
BROADCAST NEWS

CHAPTER FOCUS

Broadcast news is written to be heard and/or seen rather than merely read. This distinction affects every stage of the reporting and writing of TV and radio news. The hallmarks of broadcast writing—short sentences, active verbs, conversational style written for the ear—can serve all news writers, no matter what their medium.

CHAPTER LESSONS

- Working fast
- Broadcast style
- Interviewing for broadcast
- Reporting and writing a package
- Writing for broadcast: Style, format and examples
- Teases and tags: Starting and ending right
- Making the shift from print to TV
- On-camera preparation and performance
- Broadcast quality: The Coaching Way

INTRODUCTION

When nightly television news began in 1948, newscasts were just 15 minutes long. Fifteen years later, in 1963, CBS broadcast the first 30-minute evening newscast. Today, CNN, MSNBC and other national and local cable networks broadcast news around the clock. Since then, television has become America's predominant source of news. In recent years, television cameras have begun appearing in an unlikely place—the newsrooms of some of America's largest newspapers. In the face of dwindling audiences, broadcast and print news organizations have decided that partnership may be wiser than competition. Print reporters are appearing on camera. Broadcast journalists are writing stories for their station's Web sites, even getting print bylines. The trend, known as **convergence,** is likely to continue with the advent of high-definition television and the growing ability to transmit video over the Internet and other technological breakthroughs. As the lines between media blur, the skills of the broadcast journalist are as vital as traditional print training to the 21st-century journalist. This chapter may be your first meeting with the broadcast side of news. Even if you think your future lies in print journalism, it would probably be wise to at least take an introductory course in broadcast journalism. A basic television news and production course will teach you how to write a television news script using words, video and audio and how to operate the video camera, set up the lighting for a video shot, shoot and edit video into proper sequence. Here you'll learn the basics of the TV reporter's craft from veteran broadcast journalists, teachers and beginning reporters. Surveys show that news directors who manage broadcast newsrooms value four characteristics: writing ability, good attitude and personality, knowledge and good work habits. And that quartet of skills and attributes, especially writing, is the focus of this chapter.

LEARN THE GOOD AND BAD NEWS ABOUT THE STATE OF LOCAL TV NEWS FROM THE PROJECT FOR EXCELLENCE IN JOURNALISM ONLINE AT http://www. journalism.org/ localtvnews/ default.htm

WORKING FAST

By its very nature, broadcast news has always been a culture where time is of the essence. But now in an age of 24-hour cable news stations and technology such as satellite trucks equipped with digital cameras and mobile editing systems, and gyro-stabilized cameras on news helicopters, the need to work faster has never been greater. As Tiffany Murri's account of a day in the life of a TV reporter shows (on p. 264), the TV reporter usually juggles several story assignments in a typical day. Unlike newspaper reporters, who may face just one deadline a day, broadcast reporters may face several: a live stand-up for the noon broadcast, sending in a tease for the early afternoon news and a complete package for the 6 p.m. newscast. Multiple deadlines are also a fact of life for online journalists.

So how do you get the job done when it feels like you don't have time even to think?

Remember the lessons of Chapter 3: All journalists, no matter their medium or deadline, follow the same process of generating story ideas, collecting information, focusing and ordering their story before writing and revising. Deborah Potter, a veteran broadcast journalist, teacher and now executive director of Washington, D.C.'s NewsLab, a group created to improve local news, offers a variety of practical suggestions to move through the process not only more quickly but also more thoroughly. Among her tips:

"Reporters and editors are, more than most workers, separate, different and proud individuals whose stock in trade is using their own eyes, their own ears, their own hearts and then—the last and most difficult task— translating what they see, hear and feel into words through which they can share their impressions."

—RICHARD SALANT, PRESIDENT, CBS NEWS, 1961–1979

PREPARE AND PLAN

- Know what you don't know and what you need to know. Make notes of questions you need to have answered.

A LIFE IN JOURNALISM

Tiffany Murri

As a television reporter my workday starts well before I actually go to work. It starts with catching up on what's going on in the world. First thing in the morning I listen to National Public Radio, as well as local radio news. I also read the newspaper. I'm trying to find national stories I can localize or local stories I can advance.

Our news meeting starts at nine o'clock every morning. Right off the news director turns to each reporter and asks, "What's your story today?" We all give our ideas. Then we ask questions like: "What are people talking about today?" "Who does this affect?" "Why do our viewers care?" The news director then assigns each reporter one big story and one or two smaller stories.

Next I make some phone calls to get my day set up. I try to leave the station with a photographer by ten o'clock. We go all over town, shooting video and interviews for our stories.

Our stories often change. Something exciting, or tragic, or unusual will happen somewhere, and we go check it out. That's one of the things I love most about my job: I never know what I'm going to see, or do, or learn.

We try to be back to the station by about two o'clock to start writing and editing our stories. First I "log" the tapes. That means I choose what soundbites, brief audio statements from my interviews, and video to include in each story. Next I write the scripts and get them approved by an editor. Our script deadline is 4:00 sharp. Finally I record the voice track for my story of the day, or package.

The photographer then goes to work editing the video. Everything has to be done when we go on the air at 5:30. I often have live shots in the field or live reports from our newsroom.

Again, my workday doesn't always end when I leave work. In the evening I stay tuned into the news, make phone calls, and work on story ideas for the next day. Well, I guess you could call that a typical day, if there's such a thing as a "typical day" in television news. Every day is different. Every day I meet interesting people, see amazing things and learn something new. At times my job is hectic, stressful and all-consuming. But I can't think of anything I'd rather do.

LEARN THE LANGUAGE OF BROADCAST ONLINE FROM THE MEDIALINK BROADCASTING GLOSSARY AT http://www.medialinkworldwide.com/glossary.htm#TOP

- Save information you may need later—not on your desk, but where you can find it. Use a system that works for you: subject files, three-ring binders, computer notes.
- Keep scripts *and* notes, and best tape—you may need them.
- File and update your phone list every day. (Note information about sources that may help you connect with them again.)

USE THE TECHNOLOGY

- Always tape interviews on a portable cassette recorder.
- Review tape and choose bites in transit: traveling to another interview, heading back to the station.

TAKE GOOD NOTES

- Always mark time-code and tape changes.
- Notes should be clear enough to read from, if you have to go live.
- Mark all good bites, then narrow the list.
- Type the bites you will use, word for word, and write to the exact words in the bites.

FIND OUT ON-LINE HOW TO MAKE DULL STORIES SHINE AND THE LATEST RESEARCH ABOUT HOW VIEWERS VIEW THE NEWS FROM NEWSLAB, A NONPROFIT TV NEWS LABORATORY AT http://www.newslab.org

FOCUS IN THE FIELD

- Be open to new angles, perspectives, points of view.
- Find the story within the assignment or topic you are covering.

THINK AS A TEAM

- Brainstorm with colleagues, especially reporters and photographers.
- Use time in the car to plan, not to complain. Find a way to care.
- Split up if you need to: Reporter collects facts; photographer shoots.

WRITE AS YOU GO

- Jot down descriptions, explanations that you can use almost verbatim.
- Make note of themes, connections. Put what you're thinking in brackets.
- Write fast. If you're stuck, go on, make a note and fix it later.

ORGANIZE

- Select elements that fit your focus. Ditch the rest.

"You give up something for breaking news. Sometimes you give up accuracy. ... The technology that lets us be instantaneous—it's a blessing and a curse. The blessing is you have it right now. The curse is the information may be wrong."
—BILL BERRA, NEWS DIRECTOR, WCPX-TV, ORLANDO

■ Choose sound for subjective information: opinion, reaction, experience, emotion.

■ Put the elements into blocks (what goes with what?), then organize them in sequence.

■ Make an outline, even if it's just a word or two on a line.

■ Find the thread that holds the story together, then string the pearls.

■ Know where you are going before you start. Have a strong ending.

BROADCAST STYLE

Broadcast news is written to be heard and seen rather than merely read. That is the essential difference between it and print journalism, and it affects every stage of the reporting and writing. The print journalist relies on words and still images to convey stories. The broadcast journalist has sound and moving pictures as well.

Broadcast writing features hallmarks—short sentences, active verbs, conversational style written for the ear—that can serve all news writers, no matter what their medium. Like all types of writing, effective broadcast journalism can be described, studied and repeated.

Broadcast stories have their own format as well, influenced by the technology used to gather and present information. Of course, each newsroom will have its own distinctive hallmarks, which you will learn when you begin work. In general, scripts are written in two columns: The left column contains information about what is shown on screen, such as graphics, audio and video on tape, which guides technical and production personnel, such as tape editors, **producers** and directors. The right column contains the narration, that is, the words spoken by the reporter, anchor or sources whose comments have been prerecorded.

Television news writers must follow other guidelines. (News writing for radio, also a medium written to be read aloud, follows many of the same guidelines. For tips on radio news writing online see Mike Meckler's Web site, Writing for Radio, at **http://www.newscript.com/.)** Among the most important:

■ LENGTH. Most broadcast stories range in length from 10 seconds for a brief to one minute and 30 seconds (1:30) for a package.

■ ATTRIBUTION. In broadcast news, attribution usually comes first. Otherwise the statement may sound like the reporter's opinion.

■ PUNCTUATION AND SPELLING. Nothing in a script should be difficult to read. Names should be spelled out phonetically or with hyphens. For example, in this story about a YMCA counselor:

Tonight, several children and a Y-M-C-A counselor are nursing wounds from yellowjacket stings they received during a field trip. Some youngsters were stung a dozen times.

In the past spelling wasn't as important in broadcast news. But convergence will change that. Television scripts that are rewritten in story form for a station's Web site will have to be spelled and punctuated correctly.

Broadcast copy differs dramatically from newspaper writing, as the following comparison demonstrates. Perhaps the biggest difference is the amount of detail, such as addresses and biographical information, which are provided by the newspaper account but lacking in the television account. Newspaper writers have a luxury of space that is rare in television, a medium where economic realities, such as the cost of airtime, make brevity essential. In many respects, television is a headline service with moving pictures. Like newspapers, it has its strengths and weaknesses. Compare the newspaper and broadcast versions of the same story.

NEWSPAPER VERSION

TAMPA—Sheriff's deputies arrested a 13-year-old Tuesday and charged him with killing a 61-year-old man who had been walking down the street with his wife.

Officials said Aaron T. Ashley, of 2032 Garden Lane, was charged with first-degree murder. He admitted Tuesday to participating in the killing and robbing of Donald Richard Rogers, of 1817 Winn Terr.

Rogers was shot after telling a man with a pistol that he had no money.

Deputies said the man with the pistol was Mario Preston, 26. Preston is wanted on a warrant charging him with first-degree murder.

"Preston shot the individual in cold blood," sheriff's Maj. Gary Terry said. He had not been arrested Tuesday night, and Terry said deputies believe "he is a very dangerous person" and may be hiding in the neighborhood where the shooting took place, near the University of South Florida.

While Preston pulled the trigger, deputies said, Ashley assisted in the killing and helped conceal it afterward.

As he was led to a sheriff deputy's cruiser Tuesday night, Ashley said, "I didn't shoot this man."

Rogers was killed Sunday night about 7:30 as he walked with his wife, Martha Rogers, to their son's apartment on N. 19th Street a few blocks away from their apartment.

An employee of a plumbing company and the father of two grown children, Rogers was planning to retire in a few months.

St. Petersburg Times
Dec. 30, 1998

A 13-year-old faces murder charges tonight after Hillsborough County detectives say he and a 26-year-old friend killed a man they were trying to rob. Deputies say this boy ... Aaron Ashley ... and Mario Preston confronted Donald Rogers on 19th Street and 137th Avenue near the University of South Florida Sunday night. The pair allegedly demanded cash. ... And when Rogers didn't give them any, they shot him several times. Tonight, detectives are still looking for Preston.

WFLA-TV
Dec. 29, 1998

Following is an example of a broadcast story reported and written by Tiffany Murri, a reporter for KIVI-TV, Channel 6, in Boise, Idaho, followed by her "How I Wrote the Story" account. Her story is called a **package** because it is a complete story told on tape with audio and video clips, plus graphics, animation and video effects. A package is usually divided into three parts:

1. **LEAD-IN.** The introduction read by the **anchor**. The reporter, who is most familiar with the story, typically writes the lead that sets up the story.

2. **PACKAGE.** The portion of the story narrated by the reporter. The package can be interspersed with live shots from the scene or in the newsroom.

3. **TAG.** The end of the story. May be read by the anchor or the reporter (although the reporter usually writes it).

Each portion of the script carries a title. As in newspapers, it's known as the "slug" or "slug line." Some slugs have the abbreviations *L, P* or *T* before or after them, indicating the segment.

News scripts are written in ALL CAPS to be easier to read, except for words spoken by persons interviewed, which appear in lowercase.

Many television stations now post their news scripts on their Web sites and include instructions on how to decipher the broadcast terms. Designed as a consumer service, such sites are an invaluable way for journalists to study their craft. WPLG, Channel 10, an ABC affiliate in Miami, offers viewers an online guide to reading a news script at **http://www.wplg.com/ script.htm**.

L-METH BUST_____
(Story slug, usually one word. L indicates lead-in, or intro by the

AND NOW A SIX ON YOUR SIDE
FOLLOW UP TO A NEIGHBOR-
HOOD PROBLEM WE

anchor. Reporter often writes the lead-in.)

—LIVE SPLIT—
CG:LIVESUPR\Tiffany
Murri\1600 blk Elder St
CG:LIVEBUG\
(Live split indicates split screen showing Anchor and reporter Murri in separate screens. CG indicates graphics, made by a character generator, that identify sources, location and station-specific logos, such as KIVI's Livebug.)

—LIVE FULL—
(Screen focuses on the reporter on scene.)

—VTR SOT—
:BANNER\Victory Party

"THOUGHT" WAS SOLVED ... THE NEIGHBORS "THOUGHT" WAS SOLVED ... BUT ISN'T.

A GROUP OF BOISE NEIGHBORS THOUGHT THEY HAD TAKEN THEIR STREETS BACK FROM A SUSPECTED DRUG DEALER.

TONIGHT THEY'RE NOT SO SURE.

{—LIVE SPLIT—}
TIFFANY MURRI JOINS US LIVE FROM THE NEIGHBORHOOD JUST OFF VISTA.

TIFFANY, A METH LAB WAS BUSTED IN A HOME JUST BEHIND YOU LAST NIGHT.

AND THIS IS THE "SECOND" METH BUST THERE IN "ONE" MONTH.

{—LIVE FULL—}
CLAUDIA ... THAT'S RIGHT AND WHAT'S DISTURBING IS NEIGHBORS HERE "THOUGHT" THEY'D WORKED WITH POLICE AND GOTTEN RID OF THE DRUG HOUSE.

BUT THE PERSON WHO LIVES IN THE HOME BONDED OUT OF JAIL AND IT LOOKS LIKE SHE'S SET UP SHOP AGAIN.

NEIGHBORS TELL ME THIS IS TERRIBLY DISCOURGAING.

THEY WORKED SO HARD TO CLEAN UP THEIR STREET.
{—SOT—-}

CG;3LINESPR\October
7\1600 blk Elder St\Boise
CG:NAMESUPR\Lt. Jim
Tibbs\Boise Police
TRT:
OUTQ: "get it done"
(VTR SOT "Video Tape Recorder
Sound On Tape" Indicates sound
will come from a source or reporter
on tape. The label SUPR, for "super"
shows characters shown on screen.
OUTQ, or out quote indicates the
end of the tape on quote.)

P-METH BUST _____

    LAST MONTH THIS WAS A
VICTORY PARTY FOR NEIGH-
BORS HERE.

(P indicates package, or main section, of the story.)

—VTR SOT—
57:40-:43
Length:0:03

    A HAZARDOUS MATERIALS
TEAM TAKING AWAY DANGER-
OUS CHEMICALS USED TO
MAKE METH.
    IT WAS SOMETHING PEOPLE
LIKE DENNIS BUNT HAD
WORKED FOR.
{—SOT—}
{License number and which house
they was stopping at}
    THE NEIGHBORS' HARD
WORK PAID OFF, THE DRUGS
WENT AWAY. AND THIS
WOMAN, JANICE MARSH, WAS
ARRESTED.
    FAST FORWARD TO NOW.
{NAT POP–FAST FORWARD
EFFECT}
{—SOT—}

—VTR SOT—
12:12-:13
Length:0:01

{They're back}
    BACK ALMOST BEFORE THEY
WERE GONE. NOW NEIGHBORS
HERE ARE FRUSTRATED ... AND
THEY'RE SCARED.

—VTR SOT—
18:38-:47
Length:0:09

{—SOT—}
{I'm tired of doing all this I want
to be comfortable in my own

—VTR SOT—
12:05-:07
Length:0:02

neighborhood I didn't go to sleep until 3:00 this morning}
{—SOT—}

—VTR SOT—
54:28-:32
Length:0:04

{Day by day it's the same old thing}
ONLY THIS TIME THE WOMAN WHO LIVES HERE WAS NOT ARRESTED.
SHE'LL REMAIN FREE UNTIL THE CHEMICALS TAKEN FROM HER HOME CAN BE TESTED IN A LAB.
{—SOT—} {It's a very frustrating issue for everyone in law enforcement}
BUT NOT A SURPRIZING ONE ACCORDING TO BOISE POLICE LIEUTENENT JIM TIBBS.
ONCE A PERSON BAILS THEMSELF OUT OF JAIL THERE'S NOT MUCH POLICE CAN DO TO CONTROL THAT PERSON'S ACTIONS UNTIL THEY GO TO TRIAL.
AND THAT CAN TAKE MONTHS.
{—SOT—}

—VTR SOT—
53:01-:07

Length : 0:06

{If they choose to set up another lab and start again that's a whole different investigation}
AND IF BOISE POLICE CAN'T SOLVE THE PROBLEM ... THIS NEIGHBOR IS READY TO TAKE IT TO A HIGHER LEVEL ... TO NEWLY ELECTED GOVERNOR DIRK KEMPTHORNE.
{—SOT—}

—VTR SOT—
19:51-:58
Length: 0:07

{If dirk is fired up on this drug thing then let's go to dirk, let's not cut corners, let's just get it done}

T-METH BUS _____
(T indicates Tag section.)

{—LIVE FULL—}
SO WHAT CAN THE NEW GOVERNOR DO?

—LIVE FULL—
CG:LIVESUPR\Tiffany
Murri\1600 blk Elder St
CG:LIVEBUG\

IN HIS CAMPAIGN
KEMPTHORNE TALKED ABOUT
BEEFING UP POLICE PROTEC-
TION AND GETTING TOUGH
ON DRUG DEALERS.
    BUT ONLY TIME WILL TELL IF
KEMPTHORNE'S CAMPAIGN
PROMISES COME TRUE FOR
NEIGHBORS HERE.

—LIVE SPLIT—
ANCHOR QUESTION

DON/CLAUDIA?
{—LIVE SPLIT—}
ANCHOR QUESTION
    TIFFANY IT SOUNDS LIKE
THE JUSTICE SYSTEM ISN'T
REALLY FAILING THE PEOPLE
THERE . . . IT MAY JUST NEED
TIME TO WORK.

—LIVE FULL—
C:LIVEBUG\

{—LIVE FULL—}
    THESE NEIGHBORS DID ALL
THE RIGHT THINGS TO HELP
POLICE . . . THE THINGS YOU
SHOULD DO TO PROTECT YOUR
NEIGHBORHOOD. BUT JUST UN-
DERSTAND THAT CHANGE
DOESN'T HAPPEN OVERNIGHT.

—LIVE SPLIT—

{—LIVE SPLIT—}
    THAT'S TIFFANY MURRI
REPORTING LIVE NEAR VISTA
AVENUE

Broadcast news organizations
have more than one newscast during the day, from early morning
and noon news shows to hourlong
evening broadcasts and late-night
news. Often the reporter will have
to provide a briefer version of the
package for a later broadcast. Notice how, in the following example,
Tiffany Murri trimmed her "Meth
Bust" package to a brief summary

of the story, featuring one sound-bite.

10-DRUG HOUSE _____
—VTR VO—
FOR: 20
CG:3LINESPR\October
7\1600 blk Elder St\Boise

—VTR SOT—
18:38-:47
CONCEAL IDENTITY!

TONIGHT A SIX ON YOUR SIDE FOLLOW TO A PROBLEM ONE BOISE NEIGHBORHOOD *THOUGHT* THEY HAD SOLVED.
{—VO—}
NEIGHBORS HERE FOUGHT FOR MONTHS TO SEND A SUSPECTED DRUG DEALER TO JAIL.
AND LAST MONTH THEY THOUGHT THEY HAD WON WHEN POLICE BUSTED THIS METH LAB.
BUT NOW THE WOMAN THEY ARRESTED, JANICE MARSH, IS OUT ON BAIL.
AND IT LOOKS LIKE SHE'S SET UP SHOP AGAIN.
LAST NIGHT POLICE TOOK *ANOTHER* METH LAB FROM HER HOUSE.
NEIGHBORS HERE SAY THEY'RE FRUSTRATED AND SCARED.
{—SOT—}
{(CONCEAL IDENTITY!)
I'm tired of doing all this I want to be comfortable in my own neighborhood I didn't go to sleep until 3:00 this morning}

Length:0:09
—VTR VO—

{—VO—}
THIS TIME THE WOMAN WHO LIVES HERE WAS NOT ARRESTED.
SHE'LL REMAIN FREE ON BOND UNTIL THE CHEMICALS TAKEN FROM HER HOME CAN BE TESTED IN A LAB.

"Unless a reporter has a personal vision, a strong personal vision of how creative, how wonderful, how meaningful, how powerful what we do is, they will begin to lose their competence. They will not have the passion that is the very foundation of competence. Their vision, by the way, must be held inside. It's got to be their own. It can be educated, it can be instilled, it can be nurtured, it can be helped along, it can be focused, but it has to be there inside, held close to the heart, firmly, because the demands of our industry, at least the part of it that I've seen so far, will chip at it relentlessly."
—JOHN LARSON, CORRESPONDENT, NBC's "DATELINE"

HOW I WROTE THE STORY
Tiffany Murri
KIVI-TV Channel 6

Walk around until you find a reason to care. My news director gave me that advice recently, and it worked on a drug bust story. Even in the small city of Boise, Idaho, there are methamphetamine labs busted almost every day. So there was just one reason a photographer and I went to this one: We didn't want to do the story we were assigned that day.

On the surface this bust seemed like all the others: yellow crime scene tape, a hazardous materials team dressed in silver "space suits," potentially explosive chemicals removed from your run-of-the-mill house. But as we started talking to on-lookers we discovered this bust was different. The neighbors had banded together to take back their streets from the suspected drug dealer. For months they wrote down license plate numbers of cars that came and went. They formed a Neighborhood Watch. They worked closely with police until the woman was arrested. The story led our newscasts that day: Ordinary citizens prove they can make a difference.

One month later, she's back. And she's set up shop again. But this time police couldn't arrest the woman because it was a holiday, and the lab that tests chemicals used to make meth was closed. Again, we led our news with a terrific follow-up story: Neighbors who thought they had solved the problem, only to find the legal system let them down.

After that I called the police department every day to find out if the woman had been arrested again. Six days later she went back to jail, and we did a third story. This time I tried to get an interview with her from jail, but she declined. So we talked to neighbors once again. They were glad her bond was set high enough that she wouldn't be going anywhere for a while.

The other stations ran just what we saw on the surface the first time we arrived at that crime scene. We found a reason to care.

TEASES AND TAGS: STARTING OFF, ENDING RIGHT

Like all stories, broadcast news stories have a beginning, middle and end. Beginnings are known as lead-ins, or **teasers.** They are designed to attract the viewer's attention. "Lead-ins hook the viewer," explains broadcast veteran Deborah Potter. "It's got to tell why you should care. But don't beat people over the head—'Now, a story you'll want to see.' And lead-ins must be honest (same with teases). Don't bait the hook with a promise on which the script cannot deliver."

Deborah Potter
(Courtesy of
The Poynter
Institute)

> He's just 13 years old. And charged with murder. But police say he didn't act alone. Today: another arrest. As cops try to close the case on a killing in Tampa.

Endings are known as **tags.** They sum up the story. Potter's advice: "Tags should be both useful and important. It is not an overflow valve for material that didn't fit the script. It is the final punch line, and it needs to be focused and tight. You can add background and context here—so you can stay focused on your characters in the package. It's the last thing people will experience, so it's what they will remember most."

> The state attorney will decide if Aaron will be charged as an adult and if both men are to face the death penalty for the crime.

ADVICE FROM A TELEVISION NEWSROOM

At KSTP-TV, the ABC affiliate in Minneapolis, the producers, reporters, photojournalists and managers behind the newscasts meet every morning to watch clips that worked from the previous 24 hours. "Even if it's just five minutes, to me it's a great investment in time," news director Scott Libin told *American Journalism Review* shortly after he joined the station in 1998. "We're going from examining what does work rather than rubbing their noses in what doesn't."

That attitude isn't surprising coming from Libin, my former colleague at The Poynter Institute. A former reporter and news director at WGHP-TV in Greensboro, N.C., Libin brings a special blend of energy, commitment and vision to broadcast news. He calls the following "Libin's List." It's a blend of practical tips, coaching strategies and inspirational guidance that lets you see what newsroom managers expect from today's broadcast journalists.

1. SELECT STORIES—NOT SUBJECTS, EVENTS OR ISSUES. Narrow your focus to something manageable but essential to a broader topic. Don't do "the plant-closing story." Do a *new* story about the closing's impact on one affected family. Or about the one most significant change in the economy that's making such plants close. Or about what employees' rights and options are when they lose their jobs under such circumstances.

Teamwork is essential in television newsgathering. Photojournalist Larry Phillips and reporter Amy Oshier edit their package on an Avid newscutter system for SNN 6, a 24-hour cable news channel operated by the *Sarasota* (Fla.) *Herald Tribune.*

Your newscasts' coverage might include all these elements, and more, but don't try to jam more than one story into a single package.

2. PRODUCE FOR THE VIEWER—NOT THE BOSS, THE COMPETITION OR THE CONTEST JUDGES. And don't mistake yourself for a viewer. Your concerns and interests might be quite different from those of your audience. Get to know your customers.

3. FIGHT FORMULAS. Don't get caught in the trap of believing that every newscast must have a certain number of packages, every package a certain number of soundbites, every **soundbite** a certain number of seconds. Viewers don't understand or care about format. They watch for information. Provide it in any way that will work best *for them.* Try something you *haven't* seen dozens of times.

4. CONTROL THE DRIVE FOR LIVE. A reporter standing in a dark parking lot in front of a locked building does nothing to enhance storytelling. Don't cut corners on content, writing or editing just to make time for a few seconds live on camera. Don't let "going **live**" mean more to you than it does to your viewers. If it's live, make it matter by interacting with what's going on at the moment. Make reference to time, weather, traffic, light and other current conditions.

5. DO STAND-UPS THAT STANDOUT. Don't just stand there, but *don't* do the "walk to nowhere." In real life, that's called "pacing." Talk, don't read or recite. Show, don't just tell. Don't act. Be real.

6. USE SOUND WITH REAL BITE. Use it to convey emotion, opinion or perspective—*not* factual information. Avoid officials; you might need to talk to them—maybe even on tape—but that doesn't mean you need to put them in your story. Say it yourself if you can do so more clearly. Use the bite if it carries impact you can't capture in your own words.

7. OVERCOME OVERWRITING. Let a good story tell itself. Complement what you have on tape; don't compete with it. Use short, declarative sentences. Use strong nouns and verbs. Ironically, avoid the shocking, tragic use of subjective, loaded language. (For example, "the *bizarre* story" uses a subjective or judgmental modifier; "the *50-pound* bag" uses an objective or descriptive modifier.)

8. RECOGNIZE THE POWER OF PICTURES. Write to the obtrusive and the unusual. Refer directly to what's on the screen. Don't make viewers choose between what they see and what they hear; they won't be able to pay full attention to either. In case of a tie between audio and visual, go to the video.

9. RETHINK, DON'T REINFORCE, STEREOTYPES. Find some new experts. Talk to people of color, other minorities and those with disabilities—even on stories that aren't about "their" issues. Introduce viewers to people they might not otherwise meet. Get some new voices into your work, on the air and off.

10. BE CLEAR. Don't be a mindless conduit. Translate. What does it mean? If you don't know, find out. Don't leave it to your viewers. It's your job. Never raise a question you don't answer, or at least acknowledge.

11. BE CONVERSATIONAL. Say nothing on the air you would not say in real life. *Avoid jargon. Resist clichés—especially "journalese." Use the active voice.*

12. BE CREDIBLE. Demonstrate that you are neither stupid nor oblivious. Address obvious gaps in information or odd elements in your stories. Anticipate your viewers' reaction to what they see and hear. Use language with precision.

BROADCAST INTERVIEW TIPS

Interviews provide the building blocks for nearly all news stories, in whatever medium they appear. In broadcast, "the aim of the interview is to elicit answers that will be news ... and soundbites/actualities," says Deborah Potter, who conducted thousands of interviews during her two decades in radio and television news, including CBS News and CNN. She offers these specific tips to broadcast interviewers.

TECHING IT

1. If you are running your own gear, be sure to check it before you go. Make sure your batteries aren't dead, your tape is rewound to the top, and your microphone and cable are in your bag. Hook everything up and do a test before you leave. It can save you time, trouble and embarrassment. And check tape very quickly before you leave. Glitches do happen. Better to find out while you and your subject are still together, and you can start again.

2. Listen! Any interview not done in a studio will have some kind of background sound. Make sure it is acceptable. Listen for the buzz of fluorescent lights, the hiss of air conditioners or heating systems. Ask if you can turn them off or move to another room. Make sure your mike is close enough to the person's mouth. Rule of thumb: about a fist away—that's less than six inches. Beware of people in chairs that swivel and rock. The movement is distracting on camera, and the sound will be all over the place. Try asking them to sit next to you on a sofa or in comfortable chairs (padding has the added effect of keeping sound from having too much echo) or leaning on a desk. Be quiet yourself. Don't agree audibly—many interviews have been ruined by the person doing it saying "ummhmm" in the middle of a bite!

CUTTING IT

1. Notes help. This does not mean you should take notes during an interview the way you would during a lecture. You need to pay attention to what is being said, maintain some eye contact, be responsive (silently, remember). But take a note or two when you hear something good. If possible, mark down your counter time or time code. Anything you can do to avoid listening to the whole thing over will help when you are on deadline.

2. If you are on deadline, start your selection process on the way back. Keep an earphone with you, and you can listen anywhere. This is called "logging." Cue tape to the beginning and zero the counter. Mark counter time where good bites begin, time them exactly and take a few notes. When you have selected what you want, go back

and transcribe every word. You may find at that point that your good bite has lots of "ums" and "ahs" in it. Or a stumble where you least expect it. You may have to find an alternative. Your notes, however, will give you information you can use in copy, even if the sound doesn't work.

3. Choose the strongest bites to tell your story. What makes a good soundbite?

- Context/opinion. How is the situation different? Why does this matter?

- Detail/color. Descriptive, eyewitness sound.

- Emotion. Deborah Amos of National Public Radio calls this "hot tape." It often comes in response to the question: "Can you give me an example?" You may not get this in every interview.

- Sound quality. It should be clear, understandable. And it should *add* something.

- Length. How long is this bite? Too short, and the audience won't catch it. Too long, and the audience may be lost.

4. Choose your tape first, then begin to write. Don't write an outline and then try to find something to plug in. The script should fit the sound, not the other way around. (Sure, sometimes when an interview is being done very late, right up against a deadline, you have to leave a gap for a bite and move on. It can work, but only if you have done a preinterview on the phone, and you have a very good idea what the person is going to say, and even then you can get fooled. It's a bad habit to get into.)

WRITING FOR BROADCAST

"Great broadcast writing is like poetry," says Potter, a gifted writer whose passion for the word shines through her own work and teaching. "It's written for the ear. It has rhythm and sound." She points to this sentence from a script by Edward R. Murrow, the famed radio and television journalist considered one of the medium's finest writers.

> The blackout stretches from Birmingham to Bethlehem, but tonight, over Britain, the skies are clear.

Say that sentence aloud, the way it's meant to be read. What makes it work? "Simple words, alliteration, sentence structure, a crisp ending," says Potter. "It follows the admonition of Charles Osgood, the radio commentator and host of *Sunday Morning* on CBS: 'Bloated words and phrases don't penetrate. Well-chosen, well-ordered ones do.'"

LISTEN TO WORLD WAR II RADIO REPORTS BY EDWARD R. MURROW, THE ERA'S TOP NEWS BROADCASTER, ONLINE AT http://www.otr.com/murrow.html

"Penetrating" writing is the term Potter uses to describe the goal of the broadcast writer. That quality "counts even more in radio and television than in print because consuming broadcast news is a secondary activity," she says. "Listeners and viewers are frequently involved in other activities—they may be driving in traffic, fixing dinner or taking a shower while the news plays on. So writers must compete for attention and avoid errors and language that can further distract the audience."

To win that competition, Potter suggests following these three guidelines, each buttressed with vivid examples.

1. WRITE THE WAY YOU SPEAK

Broadcast writing should be conversational. Write for your mom or your cousin Vinnie. Don't write for people who already understand the story. They're not the ones you have to explain it to. Use simple language and translate jargon.

Hint: Read your story out loud, beginning with: "Hey, Mom, guess what?" Or "You won't believe this, but ... " If you don't sound the way you normally talk, revise your copy until you do.

Example: "Mom, problems with critical landing controls likely will force the space shuttle Columbia to limp back to Earth today." Imagine your Mom's reaction to that stilted newspeak.

Avoid print-style phrases that make your copy awkward to read: "The ailing 76-year-old pontiff." If a person's age is relevant to the story, use it the way you would in conversation, in a separate sentence. "The pope is 76." Always read copy out loud, and ask yourself: "Do people talk like this?"

The lone female police officer ...

The coveted jingle-singing commercial role ...

A Belgian child-sex ring case ...

Reading copy aloud also will tip you off to double meanings. Reporting on a charity golf tournament, you don't want to say that someone "played a round with the president."

2. WRITE SEAMLESSLY

A strong story is woven so tightly there is no place to cut. Think of all sound—natural sound and soundbites—as part of the storytelling. The bites are not designed to break up narration. They're not about "pacing." They're about advancing the story.

Unlike writing, listening is a linear process. There is no opportunity to loop back to pick up what you missed. Broadcast stories must be structured so they are easy to follow. Answer questions as you raise them. And pay particular attention to writing in and out of sound.

To do this, you have to know *exactly* what the bite says. Leading in to a soundbite that begins with a personal pronoun, write narration that ends with the information needed to make clear what the bite is about.

Hint: Write so that the ear gets the information needed to decode what's coming next as late as possible.

Example: There's an outbreak of head lice in the Tampa public schools. You've got a school nurse on tape. She says, "They come in here scratching, and we just know what we've got. It's so obvious." "They" are children. You've got to set this up so it makes sense. So your lead-in might say: "Nurse Mary Smith at Polk Middle School says she's seeing a lot more children than usual today."

To keep the listener with you, pick up and reuse the words at the end of bites as you begin your next narration, as Judd Rose did in this report for ABC News about the sale of O. J. Simpson's house.

JUDD ROSE: (voice-over) There are still a few Lookie Lous, but in recent days, they've been coming for *one last look* before O. J. Simpson is evicted.

SIMPSON'S ATTORNEY: He is *looking* at various places to live. He wants to give a good environment for his children. He's looking at condominiums and private homes. And *he'll have to make do* on the pension that he's currently drawing from.

JUDD ROSE: (voice-over) *Having to make do* on his private pension, will that *change his lifestyle?*

O. J. SIMPSON: Well, if not owning a home and having no car isn't *a change of a lifetime—of lifestyle*, I don't know what is.

JUDD ROSE: (voice-over) *This change of lifestyle* was brought about by the $33.5 million judgment leveled against Simpson at the civil trial. All of his assets have been scooped up, and now the house goes on the auction block.

3. Write Backward

Bob Dotson of NBC News says he writes his close first, so he knows where he's going. It's like getting in the car with a destination in mind, as opposed to wandering around aimlessly. We waste so much time when we aren't sure where we are going. Planning for the end will help you avoid writing redundant copy. Lead-in, soundbite and tag are not three different things, but rather three parts of a whole. Be sure you save something for the end, so you don't repeat yourself.

Edit backward sentence by sentence as well. Make sure you have put the power words at the ends of sentences. Instead of writing: "Her dream died on March 23rd," reverse the sentence: "On March 23rd, her dream died."

A chrysanthemum show featured 51 varieties (of the flower).

A cancer patient died (of the disease).

Wasted words. Delete them.

"I am not the VP and editor of a newspaper, I am the manager of an information company. And what we do is we gather content, and we distribute content, and some of it goes in the traditional print medium, but it also goes out on cable, and it also goes out via the Internet. So the emphasis is not on shovelware; it's on gathering content and then having each of the media adapt it to their particular means of delivery."

—HOWARD TYNER, EDITOR, *Chicago Tribune*

Convergence means newspaper reporters such as business writer Jeff Zbar, may find themselves appearing on camera. Photo by Lou Toman. (Courtesy of the Fort Lauderdale *Sun-Sentinel*)

FROM PRINT TO TV: MAKING THE SHIFT

At the Fort Lauderdale *Sun-Sentinel* a reporter's work can be featured in three places: in the newspaper, on the World Wide Web and on television. Through its partnership with the CBS affiliate in Miami, the newspaper provides two weekly segments, one featuring its film reviewer and the other starring business reporters who provide previews of stories that will appear in the Monday business section. "We don't want to do just a promo," says Donna Rowlinson, a veteran broadcast producer who is the paper's liaison with the television station. "We want to give viewers information. What we're hoping is that they will see the story and want to read the rest of it."

Rowlinson helps print journalists make the shift from type to television. "There's been some wariness, some reluctance," she says, but many reporters are curious and aware that some form of convergence lies ahead. "This is something coming down the road, not only here, but in most big markets."

Rowlinson believes that all journalists need to know the basics of writing for television. Her advice:

■ Watch television news and study how stories are written. Many stations post their scripts on their Web sites.

- Take a course in broadcast writing.
- Read your work aloud.

Keep it short. The biggest problem that print reporters have in writing for broadcast is adjusting to the limitations of airtime. "When you write a story for a newspaper you can get in so much more than you can get in with a minute or two of television, so I try to stress just hit the main points. You're trying to give the viewer at hand the broad outline of the story."

Here is a script for one of the *Sun-Sentinel's* weekly business segments:

ON/CAM	THIS MORNING ON YOUR BUSINESS ... OUR WEEKLY SEGMENT WITH OUR NEWS PARTNERS ... THE *SUN-SENTINEL*
Sun-Sentinel over-the-shoulder graphic	
TWO BOX	FROM SIMPLE CARDS TO ELABORATE GIFTS ... BUSINESS OWNERS SHOW THEIR APPRECIATION IN MANY WAYS. BUT THAT DOESN'T MEAN DECEMBER IS THE ONLY TIME A COMPANY SHOULD REMEMBER ITS CLIENTS AND CUSTOMERS. TODAY, WE'RE GOING TO DISCUSS HOLIDAY—AND EVERY DAY—GIFT GIVING.
CC: Jeff Zbar	
Sun-Sentinel	
Full-screen CG	
Memorable Gifts to Give:	
Charity Donations	
Parties	
Books	
Personalized Cards	JOINING US IS *SUN-SENTINEL* BUSINESS REPORTER ... JEFF ZBAR ... TO TALK ABOUT GIFT GIVING AS A MARKETING STRATEGY.
	Q&A
	SO MANY CARDS AND GIFTS ARE SENT THIS TIME OF YEAR. HOW CAN A COMPANY BREAK THROUGH THE CLUTTER AND GET REMEMBERED?
	(Design a gift that reflects you or your client. Get something personalized.)
	WHAT'S A MEMORABLE OR PERTINENT GIFT TO GIVE?
	(Charity donations, parties, gift subscriptions, a book on a relevant topic, personalized cards w/pictures)

WHAT ARE SOME OF THE OTHER DATES PEOPLE SHOULD REMEMBER?

(Thanksgiving, Independence Day, New Year's Day, Z Day or a date from Chase's Calendar of Events)

CYNICS WOULD QUESTION THE MOTIVE OF "MARKETING" DURING THE HOLIDAYS. WHY DO SO?

(The intent is to show you care and appreciate your client's business. The goal is to get more business.)

THANKS, JEFF. FOR MORE ON HOLIDAY GIVING IN THE WORKPLACE AND FOR ALL YOUR BUSINESS NEWS ... PICK UP A COPY OF YOUR BUSINESS IN TODAY'S *SUN-SENTINEL.*

ON-CAMERA PREPARATION/PERFORMANCE TIPS

On camera. Of course, that's the most obvious and significant difference between newspapers and television. Print reporters must merely write their stories; broadcast reporters must deliver them before a camera and an unseen audience. Appearing on camera requires professional clothing (jacket and tie for men, dress or business suit for women) and makeup to avoid faces appearing shiny under studio lights. In some major markets, stations hire consultants to ensure positive on-air appearance and provide vocal training, hair and clothing tips, and other assistance. A more modest approach is this list of tips given to reporters at the Fort Lauderdale *Sun-Sentinel* to ease their transition to television news reporting.

PREPARATION

- Avoid open-ended questions ("Tell me about your story ...").
- Be prepared for anything—expect the unexpected.
- Find out what will be said about the story prior to your Q&A.
- "Warm up" (10–20 minutes prior to your appearance).
- Relax—especially your upper body (concentrate on your shoulders and stomach muscles).

- Take a few deep breaths (in through your nose, out through your mouth).
- Sit with good posture—it'll help your breathing and make you look more confident.

PERFORMANCE

- Focus on the camera, not on the activity near it or around you.
- Be conversational.
- Be brief and direct with your answers.
- "Humanize" your answers (how does your story affect the viewers?).
- Avoid fact overload.
- Avoid "legal" or "officialese" ("Officials say the alleged perpetrator was apprehended ...").
- If you don't know the answer to a question, say so.

CLOTHING

- Solid colors are best.
- Avoid white, thin stripes and checks (all unfriendly to the camera).

MISCELLANEOUS

- You are providing analysis and observation, not opinion.
- You're the "expert"—you have the information viewers need.
- Afterward, get feedback from your peers.
- Practice.

BROADCAST QUALITY: THE COACHING WAY

- What's your focus? What's your story about? Have you captured that focus on tape?
- Revise your writing by going over it backward. Take your script, cover up the close and work back, paragraph by paragraph. You may find that your story actually ended long before you finished writing.
- Call in to the newsroom often if the story is changing. Surprise the viewer, not the producer.
- Remember that preparation is the key to good on-camera performance.

Glossary of Important Terms

Anchor. The main narrator of a newscast.

Character generator. An electronic typewriter that creates letters and symbols that can be superimposed over video to identify sources and locations, and so forth.

Convergence. The blending of print, audio and video to create multimedia news products for television, newspapers and on the Internet.

Live. A script cue, or instruction, that indicates a report is being delivered live from the scene of the story, on the newsroom.

Name/title. Indicates that character generator identification of an individual should be placed on the screen.

NATSOT. "Natural sound on tape." A script cue that indicates videotape with audio running under the sound of the reporter or anchor speaking.

On camera. A script cue that tells the director to return to the anchor or reporter on set, usually from a VO.

Package. PKG. A complete story with all its elements on videotape.

Producer. The producer is responsible for all aspects of the newscast. The anchors, video producer, assistant producer, news and sports writers, reporters, video editors, videographers, etc., all report to the producer.

SOT. "Sound on tape." A script cue for videotape with audio.

Soundbite. A brief recorded statement from a radio or television interview.

Sweeps. Four month-long periods each year when television viewership is measured to set advertising rates.

Tag. The final element in a package. It wraps up the story.

Tease. The beginning of a broadcast story. Also known as a teaser.

TelePrompTer: A device, attached to a television camera, that displays a television script in large letters so anchors can look into the camera while reading. The name is a trademark.

VO. "Voice-over." The anchor or reporter doing a live shot continues to speak over videotape without audio.

Exercises

1. Using the notes provided for the writing workshop in Chapter 4 and the exercises in Chapter 10 (the suicidal ex-officer on the police station roof, and Jon and Lani) write the script for a 1:30 television package. You may assume that all the quotes were recorded on videotape.

2. Study the newspaper and television news stories about the murder suspects in this chapter. Write an analysis that compares their qualities (length, style, information) and strengths and weaknesses.

3. Write three news lead-ins and tags for Tiffany Murri's drug bust story.

4. Read online the report "Local News: What Works, What Flops, and Why" at **http://www.journalism.org/localtvnews/whatworks.htm**. If the report mentions a station you are familiar with, compare your own experiences as a news consumer with the study's findings. If not, study your local stations and see how they compare using some of the study's benchmarks.

READINGS

Buzenberg, Susan, and Bill Buzenberg, eds. *Salant, CBS, and the Battle for the Soul of Broadcast Journalism: The Memoirs of Richard S. Salant.* Boulder, Colo.: Westview, 1999.

Kisseloff, Jeff. *The Box: An Oral History of Television, 1920–1961.* New York: Viking, 1995.

Keith, Michael C. *Signals in the Air: Native Broadcasting in America.* Westport, Conn.: Praeger Publishers, 1995.

O'Dell, Cary. *Women Pioneers in Television: Biographies of Fifteen Industry Leaders.* Jefferson, N.C.: McFarland and Company, 1997.

Winerip, Michael. "Looking for an 11 O'Clock Fix." *The New York Times Magazine,* Jan. 11, 1998, pp. 30–36, 50, 54, 62–63.

Zettl, Herbert. *Television Production Handbook,* 6th ed. Belmont, Calif.: Wadsworth, 1996.

Looker, Tom. *The Sound and the Story: NPR and the Art of Radio.* Boston: Houghton Mifflin, 1995.

HOTLIST

http://www.journalism.org/localtvnews/default.htm

"Local TV. What Works, What Flops, and Why" Quality sells. That's the key finding of a new study of local television news, released in January 1999. The study by the Project for Excellence in Journalism ranks the quality of 61 stations in 20 cities and compares the results with ratings. Its conclusion: "The best stations as defined by local news professionals in the study were more likely to succeed commercially than fail."

http://www.tvrundown.com/index.html

The TV Rundown on the Web. A weekly newsletter focusing on local television news, programming and community service projects. Features current research and commentary on television news. For students and anyone trying to get better at their craft, the site is rich with story ideas, reporting and writing tips, and behind-the-story accounts. One example is:

http://www.tvrundown.com/writing.html

which is a how-to article about writing in a conversational style.

http://www.poynter.org

The Poynter Institute broadcast journalism program. In 1999, the broadcast journalism program celebrated its 10th anniversary under the leadership of Valerie Hyman, an award-winning television reporter. With online articles and resource files, Hyman and other broadcast faculty members offer expert guidance and coaching to broadcast journalists.

See also:

http://www.poynter.org/research/biblio/bib_bj.htm

A voluminous list of online and print articles and books compiled by David Shedden of the Poynter Institute library.

http://spj.org/reports/pauleytaskforce/index.htm

"Tomorrow's Broadcast Journalists." A report and recommendations from the Jane Pauley Task Force on Mass Communication Education originally published in September 1996. Funded by Pauley, the NBC anchor, this sobering report provides a candid assessment of how well broadcast journalism schools are preparing their students (not well enough, it concludes) and the gap between what news directors want in job candidates and what they often get. If you want to succeed as a broadcast journalist, use the task force curriculum recommendations to design your college career.

http://www.komu.com/354/html/survival_guide.html

"Producer Survival Guide." A useful primer from the University of Missouri Journalism School.

http://www.scripps.ohiou.edu/producer/thebook/

"The Producer Book." Do you want to know what life is *really* like in television news? Bookmark this site, and you'll find out. Edited by Alice Johnson Main, executive producer at WLS-TV in Chicago, its main purpose is "to provide a convenient source of information and advice to help producers improve the quality of the news programs they produce." It's a refreshing blend of advice and tales of glory and horror from the producers who do the behind-the-scenes work required to create newscasts. One of the best ways to stay current is to regularly check out its newsroom jargon page at:

http://www.scripps.ohiou.edu/producer/thebook/jargon.htm

http://www.nytimes.com/subscribe/help/apaudioindex.html

Broadcast News on the Web. Listen to AP Radio news.

http://www.npr.org/news/

Listen to National Public Radio (NPR) news.

http://www.cnn.com

CNN on the Web.

http://www.abcnews.com

ABC News on the Web.

http://msnbc.com

NBC News on the Web.

http://www.cbs.com

CBS News on the Web.

http://www.b-roll.net/

B Roll Online is devoted to TV news photography.

http://www.rtnda.org/pubs/index.htm

Communicator is a publication of the Radio-Television News Directors Association. The Web site lists printed articles going back to 1995. Topics include technological advances, innovative newsroom practices, and regular features on writing, legal issues and management.

http://www.webcom.com/mibtp/

The Minorities in Broadcasting Training Program's goal is to diversify the newsroom.

http://www.newscript.com/

"Writing for Radio." Mike Meckler, an experienced radio journalist, created this Web site to "provide creative suggestions and ideas" to radio news reporters, writers and anchors. Includes a useful glossary and practical tips.

http://metalab.unc.edu/nppa/sherer/sherer_tv.html

Making the Commitment: Achieving Excellence in Television Photojournalism. In some small stations and cable news operations, a reporter may double as photographer. In this online book, Michael D. Sherer, a professor at the University of Nebraska at Omaha, provides a vivid look at the past, present and future for television photojournalists.

http://www.scripps.ohiou.edu/actv-7/manual/

ACTV-7 News Manual. This is the manual that must be followed by broadcast students working in the television station run by Ohio University's E. W. Scripps School of Journalism. A useful introduction to the various roles and responsibilities of a television newsroom.

http://www.mbcnet.org

The Museum of Broadcast Communications examines popular culture and contemporary American history through the sights and sounds of television and radio.

http://www.mtr.org/

The Museum of Television and Radio collects and preserves television and radio programs and makes these programs available to the public.

http://www.nab.org

National Association of Broadcasters. For 75 years the NAB has represented the radio and television industries in Washington.

http://www.rtnda.org/rtnda/

Radio and Television News Directors Association. RTNDA represents local and network news executives in broadcast, cable and other electronic media.

http://www.rtndf.org/rtndf/

Radio and Television News Directors Foundation. RTNDF promotes electronic journalism through research, education and professional training. The site is rich with useful links and reports.

http://www.newstrench.com

"Thunder and Lightning News Service." This Web site offers online resources for TV news gathering.

http://www.ultimatetv.com/shoptalk/shop.html

Shoptalk is a daily newsletter about the television industry and a must-read in TV newsrooms. The last month of *Shoptalk* is available online.

CHAPTER

9

WRITING ONLINE NEWS
NEW TOOLS AND TECHNIQUES

CHAPTER FOCUS

Today's technologies offer journalists new ways to report, write and present stories. Use them or at least know what opportunities—and ethical pitfalls—they offer.

CHAPTER LESSONS

- Storytelling and news in the electronic age
- Hypertext and the future of writing
- A process approach to online writing
- Roads to "Way New Journalism"
- Multimedia: Reporting live on your computer
- Video: Pictures at 11 and anytime
- Audio: Adding the sound of news
- Graphics: Informational, animated
- Tips from an online newsroom
- New forms for a digital age
- Electronic ethics: Brave new world
- Online writing: The Coaching Way

INTRODUCTION

When I began reporting in the early 1970s, a reporter's tools were a pen and notebook, which I filled with information collected by being on the street or by talking on the telephone. Writing my stories required a manual typewriter and paper. Revising called for a pencil, scissors and a gluepot. As you've seen earlier, reporters today use most of those same tools, but increasingly rely on a whole new set—most of them electronic—that fill their journalism toolbox for entering the 21st century.

Stacked alongside the reporter's notebook today are computer disks and tapes filled with digitized information. On the reporter's computer desktop, the video screen and keyboard have replaced typewriters. The landscape is dotted with new technologies that would astound reporters of an earlier time: e-mail systems for conducting interviews with sources around the globe; spreadsheets that allow even the most math-phobic reporter to process with speed and accuracy calculations that once would have occupied mathematicians for hours; vast databases of information, much of it publicly available and free; database managers that can detect and analyze patterns and trends in these canyons of information—jobs that would have once required days and weeks in dusty backrooms. It's hard to fathom that I once spent several months combing through scores of cartons in courthouse basements to create my own database for five years of arson prosecutions in the state of Rhode Island. In addition to these reporting resources, there are new writing tools, principally **HTML**, that allow writers to tell stories using elements beyond words: audio, video, hyperlinks.

As newspapers surge onto the Internet (nearly 5,000 by early 1999), print journalists are also learning to make use of tools long familiar to their broadcast counterparts—tape recorders, video cameras, editing equipment for sound and video—as well as to master the knowledge of how to transmit such material over the Internet.

The need to know about some of these tools will obviously be greater if you work for an online news organization. But it's also important for every journalist entering the 21st century to have some understanding of these tools. These are exciting times for reporters in every area of the media. It's a new world out there, and it's changing every day. The journalists who will survive and succeed are those who are flexible and open to such change. Learn about these new tools. Try them out—either at school or through the Internet, which is the biggest and cheapest university ever witnessed on the planet.

STORYTELLING AND NEWS IN THE ELECTRONIC AGE

Leading journalism educators and futurists forecast a time where techno-savvy reporters will use "mobile journalist terminals" and omnidirectional cameras to regularly conduct electronic interviews. Reporters, they say, will become multimedia presentation teams. Someday. Perhaps.

But journalists need to bring a little skepticism to new media, as they would to any issue. There's no doubt that newsroom technology has changed dramatically, but at what cost? Sure, it sounds great that a reporter can interview sources by video conferencing without leaving the newsroom, but too many stories today are reported over the telephone, and, as a result, what they lack is the texture, completeness and accuracy that only person-to-person reporting can bring. Young reporters often find face-to-face contacts awkward and uncomfortable, but they are the lifeblood of good journalism. Although new technologies bring important advances, I'd be concerned if reporters used them as excuses to avoid the messy and sometimes difficult aspects of real life.

In Chapter 1 we learned how technology has changed the news in a variety of ways. Technology's impact on storytelling has always been profound since the days when reporters kept their stories short to save on telegraph charges. In much the same way, today's electronic technology—live, satellite-transmitted television, near instantaneous reporting over the Internet—is changing the way that reporters at America's newspapers tell stories. Electronic texts have already supplanted printed ones in our daily life and will continue to do so, presenting writers and their audiences with new ways to write and read. This new kind of text has special relevance to journalists who continue to struggle to create forms that demand to be read.

We are living in the "late age of print," as new media scholar Jay David Bolter describes it, a time when words printed on paper are being replaced by words flashed on computer screens. In this early stage of new media, we are still in the process of discovering the shape journalism will take in a new age.

One thing is clear: In this new world, the inverted pyramid is here to stay— for now at least. The pyramid is the story form of choice for most of the news on the Internet, which is a breaking news medium. In that way it follows the form of the first telegraph news transmissions— bulletins followed by constantly updated dispatches. The inverted pyramid can help the beginner—no matter the platform choice—to figure out the importance of facts available. Then, the writer chooses the other form he or she might use.

"On the Web, the inverted pyramid becomes even more important since we know from several studies that users don't scroll, so they will very frequently be left to read only the top part of an article," argues Jakob Nielsen, a former Sun Microsystems engineer turned consultant who specializes in Internet desktop design. "Very interested readers will scroll, and these few motivated souls will reach the foundation of the pyramid and get the full story in all its gory detail," he says. Those findings will prompt Web writers "to split their writing into smaller, coherent pieces to avoid long scrolling pages. Each page would be structured as an inverted pyramid, but the entire work would seem more like a set of pyramids floating in cyberspace than as a traditional 'article.'" Imagine that. Pyramids floating in cyberspace.

GET A NEW MEDIA JOURNALISM HISTORY LESSON FROM THE POYNTER INSTITUTE'S "NEW MEDIA TIMELINE" ONLINE AT http://www.poynter.org/research/nm/timeline/

A LIFE IN JOURNALISM

JONATHAN DUBE IS A SENIOR ASSOCIATE PRODUCER FOR ABCNEWS. COM AND A FORMER REPORTER FOR *THE CHARLOTTE OBSERVER* WHO

Jonathan Dube
(Courtesy of
*The Charlotte
Observer*)

SPECIALIZED IN ON-LINE REPORTING AT COLUMBIA UNIVERSITY GRADUATE SCHOOL OF JOURNALISM. HERE HE SHARES HIS EXPERIENCES AND INSIGHTS ABOUT THE WAYS PRINT REPORTERS CONTRIBUTE TO ONLINE VERSIONS OF THEIR NEWSPAPER. IN "HOW I WROTE THE STORY," DUBE RECOUNTS HOW HE CREATED AN ONLINE NEWS STORY FOR THE CHARLOTTE PAPER'S WEB SITE.

Jonathan Dube

The Charlotte Observer (**http://www.charlotte.com**) has been putting early versions of the major breaking local stories on the Web in the afternoon, the day before they're in the newspaper.

For example, one morning in the fall of 1997 we knew the local prosecutor was going to announce that day whether he would prosecute Charlotte Hornets owner George Shinn on sexual assault charges. So I wrote up about 12 inches of b-matter (background material) and a possible lead. The press conference went from 1:30 to 2 p.m. I called in the information, and it was on the Web by 2:15. Later in the day we added a complete transcript from the press conference and eventually the full story (but not until after the 11 p.m. TV news). Although the TV stations did get news bulletins on the air before we could publish on the Web, we still had a huge advantage over them—because our story stayed up all day. Many folks who missed the TV broadcast, or who wanted more information, could get it on our Web site. It was also valuable because people outside the TV station's range—such as NBA officials—wanted information immediately.

And as a reporter I found it surprisingly useful, too, because some people I needed to interview for the story hadn't been at the press conference. I referred them to the Web article, rather than waste valuable time summarizing the press conference for them.

In the year since then the newspaper's use of the Web has progressed well. When Hurricane Bonnie hit the Carolinas' coast in August 1998, the *Observer* sent a team of photographers and reporters—including myself—to cover the preparations and damage. No other news organization in the country devoted the resources we did to covering the storm, and it would have been a shame to use only the information we gathered for the newspaper. After all, by the time the next morning's paper went to press much of the information would be useless.

So several times each day reporters filed dispatches (one of which follows, and includes links to storm photos), and they were posted to the Web site along with information gathered by Charlotte-based reporters working the phones. We updated the Web every half-hour all week and broke previous records for page views. Our Web site also provided an outlet for many fine photos which never made the print edition and gave readers up-to-date county damage assessments, insurance contacts, useful weather links and the ability to print out a storm-tracking chart (see **http://www.charlotte.com/ special/bonnie**).

Posted at 12:05 p.m. Wednesday
By Jonathan Dube

PINE KNOLL SHORES—As Hurricane Bonnie approached, wind banged against plywood-boarded windows, as if hammering out a distress signal. On one board, someone wrote this message to Bonnie: "My Bonnie lies over the ocean, My Bonnie lies over the sea, When her rage kicks a—on this island, she'll go down in history."

Ray Churchill headed down to the beach with his 14-month-old yellow Labrador, **Judge**. The two usually take a four-mile walk along the beach every morning, but today, most of the beach had disappeared, and man and dog were alone. Churchill watched as Judge ran along the wet dunes, the wind rustling his short hairs as water splashed at his paws. "I got to walk my dog," said Churchill, 62, a retired dock builder. "He's been on this beach since he was 6 weeks old."

Continued

For breaking stories, such as the 1998 arrival of Hurricane Bonnie along the North Carolina shore, online journalists can instantly post stories and hyperlinked images, like this picture of Judge, that tell the story in words and pictures. Photo by Patrick Schneider. (Courtesy of *The Charlotte Observer*)

From the reporting end of things, everything went smoothly—well, as smoothly as possible when you're trapped on an island facing 100-mph winds!

I didn't have to do any extra work for the Web site that I wouldn't have had to do anyway. I took breaks from my reporting every few hours to write up my notes and file via modem, but I would have done that even if we weren't putting the information on the Web, for two reasons: first, so that the editors in Charlotte were kept up-to-date on the rapidly developing situation, and second, because at any moment we could have lost electricity and telephone connections on the island and thus the ability to communicate.

Just about the only effect our Web site had on my work was that it kept a lot of it from going to waste. Writing and reporting that didn't make the print edition because of space limitations found a home on the Web site. And there was the added benefit of knowing that my reporting would be published quickly and have an immediate impact.

We did not use audio or video, and that is the next step for many news organizations. For television stations audio and video come naturally, and many, such as MSNBC and CNN, are already incorporating such features into their Web stories. For newspapers to go down that road would require major training and equipment purchases.

All of the work—from reporting to writing to editing—was done by the newsroom's reporters, photographers and editors, with the same focus on quality as if we were putting it in the newspaper (albeit with never-ending deadlines). The only difference was that once the copy was ready, instead of giving it to layout we gave it to the Charlotte.com producers to upload. The producers also played a big role in creating a great site with useful links.

In my mind, this worked far better than it would have if we had separate reporters for the Web site—simply because the reporters already covering the story were the ones most knowledgeable about the subject. It's also exciting as a reporter, because it negates some of the frustration newspaper folk feel about TV always getting the story out first.

However, the caveat is that the way the system works now, reporters who are already overworked may eventually have to do even more work, under greater time constraints, for the same amount of money. If newspapers continue down this road—and most will—then they'll need to hire more reporters. Or else we won't be able to do our jobs as well.

Continued

EXPERIENCE "AMBIENT STORY-TELLING," THE NEW MEDIA PROGRAM AT COLUMBIA UNIVERSITY GRADUATE SCHOOL OF JOURNALISM ONLINE AT http://newmedia.jrn.columbia.edu/1997/projects/Project_2/Manners/

HOW I WROTE THE ONLINE STORY

Jonathan Dube

When I was assigned to produce an education story while at Columbia University Graduate School of Journalism, I thought the idea of New York City trying to teach subway passengers to be more polite was too good to pass up.

The subway story, for example, is a version of serial storytelling, combined with broadcast style effects.

What I tried to do with that site was what I call "ambient storytelling." I tried to re-create the experience of being on the subway platform, with the sights and sounds of people rushing onto the cars. Combining those features with the details in the story itself, I hoped to give readers a more

With photos, illustrations and audio, online stories can not only report on but also re-create experiences. This story about a program to teach manners to New York City passengers features the sounds of a subway door opening. (Courtesy Jon Dube)

complete experience, to bring them closer to the truth. That is, I think, the promise of multimedia. Not to dress up journalism with bells and whistles, but to use the new technology to bring our readers closer to the reality of the world.

I reported that story the same as I would a print story. The first thing I did was research the topic, using Lexis-Nexis. I then interviewed several key people with the city's transportation department. Once I had a good idea where my story was going and what I was looking for, I visited the subways. I brought a tape recorder, and my partner brought a camera. I interviewed conductors and passengers and listened to the sites and sounds (and tried to ignore the smells!).

Throughout this process, I was thinking not just of the reporting, but of how I could incorporate visual elements into the Web site to make it a more effective story. I knew from the beginning I wanted to re-create the ambiance of the subways. So when I went to the subway, I made sure I recorded all the sounds I would need, such as the opening and closing of train doors. I also asked my partner to take pictures of the walls and the doors.

When it came time to write the story and create the Web site, I had everything I needed. I structured the story so that it would have several natural breaks and put each section on a separate Web page, so that readers wouldn't have to scroll very far on a page and the pages would load fast. I incorporated photos and sound clips of interviews—but different ones from the quotes I used in the story. I added useful subway links and information. As a navigation device, I used icons from the different subway lines, which conveniently were numbers and letters. Navigation is one of the most important aspects of Web design. It's important to give people an easy way to move back and forth between the pages, ideally using some form of navigation bar that remains consistent on all the pages. Remember, many visitors to your sites may not be experienced Web users.

For the site's front page, I combined photos of the doors opening and closing to create an animated picture and timed that with the corresponding sounds. So the first thing readers see is the subway doors opening, and the first sound they hear is the bell ringing. In other words, the message I'm sending is: Welcome to my site, come on in.

Judging by the feedback I got, the site was a huge hit. Unfortunately, there are few news organizations now that

Continued

LEARN THE BASICS OF HTML ONLINE FROM THE BARE BONES GUIDE AT http://werbach.com/barebones/

would give a reporter the time or resources to do such a project. The focus on the Web appears to be breaking news, fast, faster and fastest.

As a result, many of the advantages the Web offers are being underutilized.

Getting Wired

I began by teaching myself. In 1994 I got a free starter kit for America Online and tried it out. After I got the basics down, I started reading some of the many Web sites on the Internet that tell you how to build Web pages (I recommend the Bare Bones Guide to HTML). Nearly everything you'd need to know is out there for free. I read some Internet books in the bookstore. Then, when I knew I was interested in the Internet, I enrolled in Columbia University's Journalism School, which has become an early leader in teaching new media.

You must know the basics first. Better to take a job in old media and learn new media skills on the side. I turned down a job as a producer on *The New York Times* Web site to be a reporter for *The Charlotte Observer* and have no regrets. Why? Because instead of learning more coding, I've become a better writer and reporter. And in the end, those are the skills that will make you stand out as a journalist. At least, I hope!

SINCE WRITING THIS ACCOUNT, DUBE HAS TAKEN A JOB AS A SENIOR ASSOCIATE PRODUCER FOR THE ONLINE EDITION OF ABC NEWS, ABCNEWS.com.

AS WE MAY WRITE: HYPERTEXT AND THE FUTURE OF WRITING

The biggest change in writing journalism, certainly for print journalists, will be adjusting to a new approach to the concept of text. Stories can accommodate a whole new range of materials that will demand a new form of electronic literacy—"E-Literacies," in hypertext scholar and designer Nancy Kaplan's phrase, "to mean those reading and writing processes specific to electronic texts (by 'texts' I mean a whole range of digitally encoded materials—words, sounds, pictures, video clips, simulations, etc.)."

The electronic age we live in has redefined the very concept of what makes a story. "Text" used to mean one thing: words on a page. More specifically, "text" meant "the main body of matter in a manuscript, book, newspaper." To printers and graphic artists, it meant "black letters," i.e., an "old style of typeface based on broad-nib script, also called Gothic and Old

English." Most simply, it differentiated type in a manuscript from illustrations and margins. For writers, it meant getting "black on white," as the French short-story writer Guy de Maupassant put it. With computers, that changed to "green on black" (the colors of the early monochrome monitors). There's another term that reporters and editors use that has changed: "document." When reporters see the word, they may think of court papers and other public records that support elements of their stories. They need to consider documents in a different way, one described by Microsoft founder Bill Gates in his book, *The Road Ahead*. "When you think of a document, you probably visualize pieces of information with something printed on them, but that is a narrow definition. A document can be any body of information. A newspaper article is a document, but the broadest definition also includes a television show, a song, or an interactive video game. Because all information can be stored in digital form, documents will be easy to find, store, and send on the highway. ... Future digitally stored documents will include pictures, audio, programming instructions for interactivity, and animation, or a combination of these and other elements."

HTML, which stands for "hypertext markup language," is the code that creates the text and graphic layouts known as Web pages, which are viewed over the Internet with Microsoft Internet Explorer, Netscape Navigator or another Web **browser**. HTML was developed by Tim Berners-Lee in the early 1990s. Some scholars believe the concept was used in ancient literature such as the Talmud, which includes commentary on commentary, annotations and references to passages within the Torach and Tenach. But its contemporary roots go back to right after World War II and a scientist named Vannevar Bush. In a 1945 landmark article in *Atlantic Monthly*, titled "As We May Think," Bush, who was one of President Roosevelt's top science advisers, proposed a system to deal with the deluge of information available (they were drowning in data even then!). A system was needed because the present one for organizing information wasn't up to the task.

Twenty years later, in 1965, a visionary named Ted Nelson gave the name "hypertext" to Bush's concept. **Hypertext** is the feature that made the World Wide Web possible by allowing users to move ("hyper" is a Greek word meaning "beyond") from place to place to place, whether it's inside the text itself or to another site on the Internet.

Hypertext is the heart of online news. The key to hypertext is the **link** that sends readers traveling through cyberspace with the click of a mouse to another page of text, a video or audio clip, or a Shockwave animation that allows you to plot the course of a hurricane or to calculate your tax bill, or to a computer on another continent or across the room.

But don't be misled or dazzled by the technology. Knowing HTML or **Photoshop** may get you a job coding pages or preparing photos for an online news site, but it won't make you a reporter. The people who run online sites are clear about this: They want journalists, not just coders.

So do you have to know HTML? You have to know what it is. "Applicants should have good HTML skills," one recent ad for an online editorial job says. "Although basic HTML skills are always a plus," says another, "the production design team handles the actual conversion chores."

HTML began with raw code. Now it's point and click, cut and paste with such dedicated HTML editing programs as Hot Dog and HotMetalPro and add-ins such as the HTML templates for Microsoft Word. As late as 1996, a national survey of webmasters and Internet content creators found that one out of three preferred to create Web pages by hand in raw HTML code, even though a variety of WYSIWYG (What You See Is What You Get) software packages did the job automatically. Raw code made it easier to find and correct mistakes, Webmasters said. "You can see everything that's going on and easily figure out what's going wrong," explained Kim McGalliard, webmaster of *Editor & Publisher's* Web site. Instead most used basic text editors such as WordPad or Notepad.

Like any other language, HTML has its own grammar, diction and syntax, a set of rules so elaborate and ever-changing that it has generated shelves of books, many with CD companions, and online sites devoted to tips and techniques. There's no shortage of resources for the student interested in learning HTML. This book will give you the basics and point you, in the "Hotlist" section of this and other chapters, to the best places to learn more.

HTML is ASCII text separated by paired tags enclosed in angle brackets. The first tag begins a formatting command, the second turns it off. ASCII means you can write HTML with any word processor. With about 10 commands, you can create a home page with links, graphics and a variety of text styles that can be viewed by every Web-connected computer on the planet.

HTML: BEHIND THE WORLD WIDE WEB

1. The Basics

   "HTML" stands for "hypertext markup language."

   HTML documents (also known as "pages") are written in plain text (ASCII) and contain two elements:

   a. The text of the document.

   b. HTML tags that determine what the document looks like when viewed with browser software such as Internet Explorer. Tags control structure, formatting and the hypertext links that propel the reader to other pages or other media (photographs, video, sounds, animations).

2. Anatomy of a Tag

<Tag Name> affected text </Tag Name> (for example: <bold> indicates that the browser will display the text in boldface).

Tags are enclosed in brackets: <Tag Name>

Most HTML tags have beginning and ending tags.

The beginning tag switches on the feature, such as italics, bold and center, and the ending tag shuts it off.

With closing tags, you need to precede the tag name with a slash: </Tag Name>

So let's say you wanted to have a line of your page centered:

<CENTER> PUT ME IN THE CENTER</CENTER>

PUT ME IN THE CENTER

It doesn't matter if HTML tags are upper or lowercase (that's called "case insensitive").

3. Links

To create a link, you need two things:

1. The name of the file you want to link to (or its Web address, known as a Uniform Resource Locator, or **URL,** such as **http://www.poynter.org)**.

2. The text that will serve as the "hot spot," that is, the text that will be highlighted in the browser (usually with underlined blue text), which readers can use to follow the links.

The link tag is also known as the "anchor" tag. It has several features:

The opening tag <A> includes both the name of the tag and extra information about the link. These extras are known as attributes. The most common attribute is HREF, which specifies the name of the link or URL of the file the link points to.

4. Anatomy of a Link

File to load when link selected

<A HREF = "http://www.poynter.org/summer/summer.html">

Text that will be highlighted

How I spent my summer vacation></A>

5. Images

HTML allows you to include images—photos, graphics, icons—on a Web page.

The tag for images is <IMG SRC="studentname.jpg">

The IMG SRC (image source) attribute indicates the filename of the image you want to display, in quotes.

BASIC HTML TAGS

Name	Tag	Result
Headings	<H#> . . . </H#>	Creates headline size
		# Header 1
		## Header 2
		### Header 3
		Header 4
		Header 5
		Header 6
Paragraph Break	<P>	Starts a new paragraph
Line Break	 	Breaks current line of text
Horizontal Rule	<HR>	Places horizontal line across screen
Unnumbered List	<UL>	Toyota
	<LI> Toyota	Chevrolet
	<LI> Chevrolet	
	</UL>	
Numbered List	<OL>	1. Toyota
	<LI> Toyota	2. Chevrolet
	<LI> Chevrolet	3. Volkswagen
	<LI> Volkswagen	
	</OL>	
Block Quote	Remember what Epictetus said: <BLOCKQUOTE> "If you wish to be a writer, write." </BLOCKQUOTE>"	Remember what Epictetus said: "If you wish to be a writer, write."
Italics	<I>Italics</I>	*Italics*
Boldface	<B>Boldface</B>	**Boldface**
Typewriter	<TT>Typewriter</TT>	Typewriter
Image	<img>	Creates and formats an image, such as a photograph, icon or other graphic element

---

TIPS FROM AN ONLINE NEWSROOM: Q&A WITH MICHAEL ROGERS, EDITOR AND GENERAL MANAGER, NEWSWEEK.COM

VISIT *NEWSWEEK* ONLINE AT http://newsweek.com

What does a reporter need to know about online news?

The fundamentals still apply and will even more so as we go forward and the Net becomes just another medium. If you can't analyze and communicate, you're not in the right ballpark.

What skills does a reporter need to survive/thrive in today's online news environment?

For the moment, a predilection or at least a tolerance for engineering. The print world, being highly evolved, lets you concentrate on writing and editing. Part of the online world is still engineering: How do we make this work given the resources and capabilities we have? Why is this broken? What's the best workaround? Or, on a more positive note: How does that other site get those great rollover pop-ups, and what could I do with the same ability?

If people don't enjoy, or at least tolerate, that stuff, they're going to be better off in print or television, where the technology has been thoroughly tamed.

What story forms are emerging in online news?

At the moment we all seem to be treating the Net as a wire service—indeed, it's the first time that Everyperson could have their own wire service, and when you have a new hammer, everything looks like a nail. But as time goes on and **bandwidth** increases, I think we'll see a rich variety of story types. What I emphasize in my own thinking about the future is this: The Web will ultimately be a metamedium in which storytellers have the freedom to choose exactly which medium is the best for telling a story at any given moment: text, audio, video, animation, still photography, simulations, etc.

The other thing we're going to have to learn is how to balance narration with exploration. On some level our audience still expects us to execute our old duties—tell a story that has a beginning, middle and end, or sum up what's important to know in the order you need to know it. But now they're also going to want to be able to click off and explore on their own. How do we provide both the narration and exploration—a coherent and orderly line of thought they can return to between forays out into the untamed wilderness of associated ideas?

What skills, both traditional and new media, do you think reporters need or will need?

We're going to have to learn to see in all media types. Unlike the TV reporter who looks for the movement or the radio reporter who looks for the actuality—or the print reporter who comes back to the office and when the photo editor asks, "What should we shoot?" replies, "How should I know?"—the next generation of reporters will need to be at least conversational in all media types. They will need to be able to look at a story and say, "Here's some great video, here's something we can do with stills, here's material that will make a great searchable database, and here's where I need to write 250 cogent words." Now, specialists may actually go and do the video or create the photo essays, but the reporter/writer will need to participate in the process. And that leads inevitably to a second skill: combined with the ability to see in all media must be the ability to collaborate. Interactive media is communal and iterative: You don't get to just phone your part in and walk away.

What advice would you give a newcomer? What should I know? Study? Learn?

We still look for strong reporting and writing skills, but it's a tremendous advantage—indeed by now a necessity—to have some basic HTML experience putting together your own home page, plus lots of time on the Web doing research and just poking around. A couple of years ago we might have hired someone who was a terrific writer/reporter who was very eager to learn online, and we'd take the time to teach them. That's pretty rare these days. In general, when we see someone who wants to work for wp.com or nw.com, yet they haven't done much online in their own lives, then probably they're going to be happier in traditional media.

Having worked in print, what do you see as the advantages/disadvantages of online news?

The disadvantage is that we're still spending so much time simply trying to get it to work—on every level from having our text display consistently in different browsers to fashioning a business model that will let us support serious journalism in the next century. As a result you don't get the time to do as much writing and reporting that you would in traditional media. The advantage—well, not to sound pretentious, we're inventing the future of news one day at a time, and if you can stand the uncertainty, frustration and constant change, then I don't see anything much more exciting to do for now.

ROADS TO "WAY NEW JOURNALISM"

READ ABOUT "THE BIRTH OF WAY NEW JOURNALISM" ONLINE AT http://www.hotwired.com/i-agent/95/29/waynew/waynew.html

An important place for journalists interested in new media writing is in the literary hypertext community. In the same way that literary writers influenced the "New Journalism" popularized in the late 1960s by Tom Wolfe, Joan Didion and Gay Talese, hypertext poets, novelists and literary scholars will leave their stamp on "Way New Journalism," a phrase coined by Joshua Quittner.

I first encountered the hypertext community in April 1995 at the National Writer's Workshop in Hartford, Conn. Robert Arellano of Brown University led a session, seated in front of a Macintosh computer from which he displayed on a screen behind him the world of hypertext.

Web pages represent what the scholars of print called "incunabula" (Latin for swaddling clothes)—the early products of Gutenberg's presses. It took about 100 years for the book as we know it and its trappings—chapters, table of contents, index—to emerge. We're still in the swaddling clothes stage.

LEARN MORE ABOUT THE HYPERTEXT COMMUNITY FROM EASTGATE SYSTEMS ONLINE AT http://www.eastgate.com

WRITING THE ONLINE STORY: A PROCESS APPROACH

In the online world, the search for the Holy Grail seems centered on identifying the electronic version of the inverted pyramid, that much-maligned but indestructible story form that remains a staple of communication in a time of immense technological change. What will be the inverted pyramid of the Internet? How will writers answer the question "How did I write the online story?" Whatever the form is called, it will be the result of a process, the decisions and steps that people take to successfully write for the electronic screen.

The process approach, as you learned in Chapter 3, gives writers and editors a common set of diagnostic tools and a language, enabling them to communicate and to highlight problems and discover solutions that serve the reader.

By now you have learned that although good writing may seem magical, it doesn't happen by magic. Behind every effective piece of writing is a rational series of decisions the writer makes. Study it, replicate it, and like an athlete scrutinizing film of a swing or a dive, you will see that the process and the successful stories can be repeated.

Donald Murray began to describe this process of writing in the late 1960s. He defined six steps:

1. Idea
2. Collect
3. Focus
4. Order
5. Develop
6. Revise

I want to propose a tentative model for online writing inspired by the work and techniques utilized by successful Web designers, especially Elizabeth Osder, a former content development editor at *The New York Times,* now an executive with the new media company, iXL.

THE PROCESS OF WRITING ONLINE

1. **IDEA/BRAINSTORM**: In traditional journalism, stories are either self-generated or assigned. Perhaps a photographer is involved, but generally the reporter is a one-person band. Collaboration is the hallmark of new media: Brainstorming involves everyone on the team from writer and producer to programmer and designer.

   "Good sites need a high concept or strong theme," Osder says.

2. **COLLECT/NET**: A site is nothing without depth of content. Think links. Collect graphics, sounds, video, annotative materials from the full text of a speech to the statistics behind a report's conclusion.

3. **FOCUS/FOCUS**: What is the purpose of the site? Say it in six words or less: Osder dubbed Cockroach World "The Yuckiest Site on the Internet." She calls it "editorial direction."

4. **ORDER/MAP**: Whatever the medium, a story is still a journey. The reader has more control, but the writer can and should make navigation simple and meaningful. Every page needs doorways, exits and entrances. "Navigation is an integral part of a site's narrative," says Osder.

5. **DEVELOP/ASSEMBLE**: The various elements (text, image, multimedia, interactivity) must be produced and assembled by the online team.

6. **REVISE/UPDATE**: Online stories are dynamic, not static. Information can be constantly changed/revised, features added, reader feedback incorporated, links added to earlier stories rather than churning out boilerplate summaries.

"Users are going to need what readers and viewers have always needed: someone to sort through developments and provide the latest version of a story, instead of 4,000 duplicates; someone to find the beautiful or unusual; someone to focus the wild maelstrom of the electronic net. You know, a journalist."
—DAVID M. COLE, EDITOR AND PUBLISHER, *THE COLE PAPERS*

The Process of Writing

1. Idea: Assignment
2. Collect: Report
3. Focus: What's the news? What's the story?
4. Order: Plan
5. Develop: Draft
6. Revise: Edit/Revise

The Process of Writing Online

1. Brainstorm
2. Net
3. Focus
4. Map
5. Assemble
6. Update

Collaboration is key, says Osder, developer of the Web site rockhall.com for the Rock and Roll Hall of Fame and of Cockroach World: The Yuckiest Site on the Internet: "Just like the best story packages, the best sites are tightly edited collaborative efforts of skilled journalists and technologists, reporters, photographers, artists and programmers." Osder lists six stages in a Web site's development.

OSDER'S STAGES OF SITE DEVELOPMENT

1. Brainstorm

2. Research

3. Editorial direction

4. Storyboarding/site map

5. Copy and design

6. HTML markup

7. Programming

Here are some tips to help you make the transition to new media writing:

THINK LINKS

At *The Providence Journal* in the 1970s–'80s, there was a push to make better use of photography in the paper. "Think pictures" was the motto. Stickers emblazoned with that motto were everywhere, even affixed to the wall above the toilet roll dispenser in the restroom of the suburban bureau where I worked. The byword for writing journalism online should be "Think links."

You can waste a lot of time looking for links in news stories on the Web. Instead what you find is **shovelware**, the indiscriminate dumping of full text that takes absolutely no advantage of the medium's most exciting attributes. Brainstorm links to your story. The first stories I wrote as a new police reporter were police briefs limited to a few paragraphs. From an item on an arrest for burglary, I can envision links to a page of criminal law terms and penalties (burglary in the first degree, class A felony, punishable by two years in prison) to an updatable neighborhood map imitating a pin map that police use to track crimes, a victims forum where people could exchange support and advice, an audio file of crime prevention tips.

The ability to find relevant links quickly will be a necessary skill. Nora Paul of The Poynter Institute recommends the following sites to make link-searching more effective.

How to Find Links

Directories and guides find Web sites:

Yahoo! **(http://www.yahoo.com)**

Magellan **(http://mckinley.netcom.com)**

Spiders and robots locate individual pages:

Infoseek **(http://www.infoseek.com)**

Indexes and databases:

Find newsgroups at **http://www.dejanews.com**

USE THE MEDIUM. On the next page, a Web page from the Minneapolis *Star Tribune's* investigative series on a legal publishing company's questionable relationships with top federal judges, including Supreme Court justices, provides a good example of effective use of this new medium. The page displays the letter from a justice concerning his thinly veiled pitch for a resort location to judge the company's contest, followed by a photograph of the luxurious location.

One newspaper site featured a link to a series of interviews using a nifty icon of a radio microphone. Must be a sound file, right? But click on it, and what you get are four paragraphs of text from a new media guru and a note that the guru "was interviewed by phone." That's not the most effective use of the available technology.

Compare this to the coverage of President Clinton's August 1998 speech to the nation when he admitted he had lied about his relationship with White House intern Monica Lewinsky. At CNN on the Web, computer users could click and view the speech on their desktops.

KEEP THEM COMING BACK FOR MORE. Osder's Farmer's Almanac site for Newhouse Newspapers New Media ensured repeat visits with its "Today in Weather History" feature. The *Houston Chronicle* site featured comprehensive coverage of the 1995 trial of the woman accused of killing Latina rock star Selena. But even

Visit CNN
on the Web at
http://www.
cnn.com

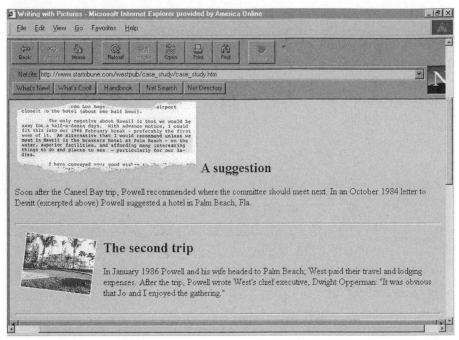

Graphics play as important a role in online publishing as they do in print and broadcast news. (Courtesy of the Minneapolis *Star Tribune*)

more compelling was the bulleted list of trial transcripts that allowed fans worldwide to follow the daily testimony.

STUDY THE CRAFT.   Where is the Tom Wolfe of the "Way New Journalism"? "I don't think *great* new media writers have emerged yet. That's because there aren't great new media editors at great new media publications to call attention to writers' work," says Osder. "What a wonderful time to bust through the pack and make a name for yourself." Until now, the pioneers of hypertext have come from the world of literature.

TEAM UP.   "Team work makes sites work," Osder says. "There have always been two kinds of journalists, word and picture. Learn your craft and respect the others.

IT'S THE CONTENT, STUPID!   Don't get too distracted by the technology. The fact is that people will put up with a lot for content they can't get anywhere else.

Tips From an Online Newsroom: Q&A With Glenn McLaren, Assistant Editor, Internet Edition, Fort Lauderdale Sun-Sentinel

How did you get started in journalism?

I started as a general reporter for a weekly paper in October 1989, then moved to a sports reporter/editor job with a small daily. I moved to the sports copy desk in Corpus Christi and then into the online world.

How did you learn online skills?

"Learn HTML in 7 Days" and a lot of on-the-job training. I also took several computer science classes on UNIX and Perl.

Are there books or Web sites that you'd point folks to to learn what they need to know?

Unless you are planning to go into site or systems administration or object programming, you don't need to know anything other than basic HTML. The above book and CNET's **www.builder.com** are great places to start.

What are the most important lessons you've learned about online news that you think reporters need to know if they want to survive/thrive in the future?

There is plenty of value in two paragraphs of text if (1) it is posted minutes after an event occurs, (2) it is clearly written, (3) it is factually correct.

Television has thrived for years on this formula, and it translates very closely to the Internet. The advantage of the Internet is that the reader doesn't have to wait through the commentary and filler of the talking heads if all they want is the news.

What do you think a reporter needs to know about online news?

Unlimited news hole does not suddenly change the attention span of the reader. Just because we have room for 30-inch stories doesn't mean people want to read past the first three paragraphs if the content does not interest them.

What skills does a reporter need to survive/thrive in today's online news environment?

More than ever, I think reporters need to have the ability to organize information into logical threads, thus allowing producers/editors to package information supplied by reporters more efficiently and effectively. Take the recent cruise ship fire off the coast of Miami. That story had numerous threads.

Rather than trying to piece them together into a traditional four- or five-story package, we should have gone online with information by threads (the fire, the ship, the passengers, the history, the people on shore, the scene, the rescue, the chaos on board, etc.). After a three- or four-paragraph overview, links to each of the threads could have followed.

Where can students learn these skills?

News organizations need to take the lead on training their employees. But the best way for reporters to learn these new skills is to use the Internet. As they become more familiar with the medium, they should begin to understand the unique and powerful potential it holds.

What story forms are emerging in online news?

Threading (as described earlier) is one ideal, but because most of us are consumers receiving information from a primary news provider, we frequently have to take what they give us. Threading would mean rewriting and reworking many stories.

Chunking is another emerging form. This basically calls for longer stories to be broken into chunks, with each chunk presented on its own page. A reader would click from the first chunk to the last, reading in a serial fashion familiar to traditional newspaper and magazine readers.

Bulleting is another practice we've adopted. This is done by summarizing a print story with a two-paragraph lead and several bullet points detailing key elements of the story. Our usage calls for the lead and bullets to be followed by the full version of the story or a link to the full version of the story.

Currently, we are planning for online staffers to prepare the summaries and bullet points, but I could foresee a time when the reporters would prepare all copy.

What advice would you give a newcomer? What should I know? Study? Learn?

First of all, know that the Internet is here to stay, but it is very likely to change drastically in the coming years. These changes will, for the most part, make the Internet a more robust medium.

Do not be intimidated by people with "years of Internet experience." In many cases, that means they just have bad habits and old ideas.

Learn basic HTML so that you can understand simple design structures. Learn as many "applications" as possible (FrontPage, Photoshop, Web Spinner, Freehand). Although these are often considered the tools of designers and imaging technicians, they are very useful for online producers/reporters/editors and relatively simple to learn.

How are online reporting and writing similar to or different from the traditions of the inverted pyramid, the feature and other story forms?

The inverted pyramid is a long, one-way road. Threading, what I consider the best format for the Internet, is a road that goes a few blocks and then forks into six different directions. And if you pick one direction, you can still see the other five alternatives quickly and easily.

Features and columns aren't impacted as greatly, but could certainly be adapted for the online environment.

Also, although not necessarily a form issue, reporters need to be aware they will more frequently come across situations where their sources and subjects will also be publishing "news" stories. Balance will continue to be critical, but reporters should be aware of information being published by agencies, activist groups, companies, nonprofit organizations, etc.

How should/can a reporter prepare himself or herself for the kind of newsroom environment that exists in Fort Lauderdale?

On a regular basis, read as many newspapers as you can get access to, either in print or online. Focus on a handful of key stories or content areas and see how they are affected by events. Whenever possible, read the competing papers in a market and try to determine the difference between each paper's coverage.

Finally, become as fully acquainted with the Internet as possible and don't even come to work if you don't have basic computer skills (Windows 95 at least).

Is Fort Lauderdale a model of the typical newsroom in years to come?

Yes and no. Yes in the sense that, in physical terms, we're moving toward an integrated environment where electronic publishing (Internet, radio and TV partners) are included in the traditional mix.

No in the sense that, even with the evolution, we are still a very traditional (some would say stuffy and conservative) news organization that overwhelmingly thinks "print first." Of course, time and tides can change this, but even with a full-time Internet staff in the room, we are often an afterthought when news breaks or projects are being formulated.

What will online news look like?

My son is 11 weeks old. How tall is he going to be? What will his first car be? The answers are very similar.

My best guesses are 6 feet 1, a Ford, and online news will look more like television, with increased use of audio and video as bandwidth restraints are minimized, and much less geared toward "the big story," instead relying on threads to be brought together around key events and ideas.

Is there an online format that reporters should know about?

Threading, chunking and bulleting are three that I think are worth becoming familiar with.

What about audio and video tools? Will the reporter need to carry a tape recorder to upload audio or a camcorder to feed video?

Although I don't foresee a day when reporters would need to process audio or video, I can easily see them being called upon to gather that type of information. Our sister paper in Orlando has already outfitted photographers with video cameras so that they can feed footage to their cable TV partner.

Do you think that there will be people who will always be print reporters or online or broadcast, or will the journalist of tomorrow be a blend of all three?

I strongly believe that single-platform journalists will be few and far between in the future. While the convergence brought on the Internet is a compelling reason, the marketing angles that are being more aggressively pursued will call for newspaper reporters to go on radio and television and TV folks to cross over to print more and more frequently.

Having worked in print, what do you see as the advantages/disadvantages of online news?

Advantages are up-to-the-minute timeliness, ability to provide depth with related links, ability to combine audio and video with print depth.

Disadvantages are the technological barriers inherent to getting online, the perceptions that an online newspaper is simply the print version on the Internet and the lack of clout that online departments have in most newsrooms.

As you can see, the disadvantages I mentioned could be viewed as temporary or rooted in print-centric traditions. I, along with many others, do view them that way, and I foresee a trend which brings a news organization's online presentation onto the same plateau with its primary outlet, whether it's newspaper, radio or television.

MULTIMEDIA: REPORTING LIVE ON YOUR COMPUTER

On Oct. 12, 1993, when computers connected to the Internet broadcast a speech by President Clinton—pictures and sound—the news landscape underwent a fundamental change. For the first time, people didn't have to rely on a broadcast network or television station to get pictures and sound. The shift creates new opportunities and challenges for reporters.

"Print journalists are trained to be sensitive to the words of the source, but also to the setting, the background noises, the smells and the gestures that give the words context and provide description so that the reader can 'see' the source and scene," write Nelle Nix and Michael Clapp, two journalists who chronicled their experiences creating a multimedia report on Bulgaria in "Interactive Multimedia as a Journalistic Tool."

"For the print journalist, moving into the multimedia realm means that all of the senses must be heightened," they wrote. "For in addition to jotting down notes about when that lone dog barks in the distance, it would also be nice to have that sound on tape. Where the print person might struggle to describe the odd gestures of an eccentric artist, the video camera can record the move so that the CD viewers interpret it for themselves."

VIDEO: PICTURES AT 11 AND ANYTIME

"There's a real hunger for video products—live animation, video downloads, pictures. People want to see those things; people will download them," John Smyntek, director of *Detroit Free Press* on CompuServe, said in 1995. Responding to that hunger, news organizations—first broadcast, followed by newspapers—have added video to their online news sites. What made it possible was the development of streaming video technology that brought the television and movie screen to the desktop computer.

AUDIO: ADDING THE SOUND OF NEWS

You've probably listened to music on your computer, but audio on the Web means you can hear the news, too. Since 1995, audio streaming technology has given journalists the ability to add the near-real-time sound of news, such as interviews, speeches and continuous broadcasts, to their stories on the Internet. Audio news also offers access for the 11 million visually impaired Americans, including 1.5 million who are blind.

Audio streaming technology allows listening to begin before the file arrives and to continue as long as you're hooked up to the source site. Before this was possible it was necessary to wait for the download of a usually very large sound file to your computer's hard drive, and then to play it back after a wait of a minute for a 10-second clip. "Anything from a pop song to a political convention can be recorded and made available on a Web site," *Internet Computing* said in November 1997. News organizations are behind the curve, except for those with ties to radio or television.

By the middle of 1996, National Public Radio had begun making portions of its broadcasts available on its Web site. Now CNN offers audio clips, as do most of the network news sites. *The Christian Science Monitor,* which has its own radio outlet, Monitor Radio, was one of the first newspapers to offer audio news.

KEEP UP WITH THE CURRENT STATE OF ONLINE NEWS BY READING STEVE OUTING'S COLUMN ONLINE AT http:// www.mediainfo. com/ephome/ news/news htm/stop/ stop.htm

This means that 21st-century journalists may need to add audio skills to their reporting toolbox. Says Steve Outing, the new media columnist for *Editor & Publisher Interactive:* "The Internet is beginning to change what skills are required of writers. Particularly for new media or online news organizations, writers may need to turn in more than just text to satisfy their employers." Depending on the news organization, a reporter may be asked to collect supplementary audio. In an illuminating 1997 column, Outing described the work habits of Reid Goldsborough and Alan Boyle, two free-lance writers who contribute to MSNBC, the cable-Internet collaboration between Microsoft and NBC News. Here are tips he gleaned from the pair:

- Either the audio interview can be separate from the print interview, or the standard interview can be interrupted to capture a soundbite.
- Sound clips are usually 30–60 seconds and are best when they don't repeat what's in the story.
- The technical side is handled by an audio technician at MSNBC headquarters.
- Interviewees sometimes get stage fright: Goldsborough tries to stem those concerns by telling interviewees they can start over.

"We're trying to recognize the best ways to tell elements of a story (some are best heard, some are best read, some perhaps are best experienced as an application)," Boyle told Outing. "Seems to me that marriage of sound, text, pictures and interactivity is what the medium's all about."

"The equipment required to get broadcast quality is inexpensive and readily available, and basic recording and interviewing skills are easily mastered," award-winning radio and television producer Jay Allison wrote in "HOT AIR: Tips for Citizen Storytellers," a 1991 article that appeared in *Whole Earth Review.*

"Audio ... can add actual weight and depth to the online experience, it can lead to intriguing new ways to provide information— and it's a lot more fun than the sound of one hand clicking."
—DOMINIQUE PAUL NOTH, EDITOR AND INTERNET COLUMNIST

INSTANT NEWSPAPER AUDIO

News organizations are using audio to add timely and rich additions to their online editions. During the 1998 Winter Olympics in Nagano, Japan, a *Los Angeles Times* sports columnist phoned in voice mail messages about the games. Online editors posted them on the paper's Web site, latimes.com, giving visitors "radio-like reports" from the newspaper columnist, *Editor & Publisher* reported.

SOUND EDITORS

LEARN THE BASICS OF AUDIO INTERVIEWING FROM BROADCAST VETERAN JAY ALLISON ONLINE AT http://www.well.com/user/jwa/tips/html

Once, providing audio required a sound studio equipped with expensive audio recording and playback equipment. Now, with sound editing software, you can use the cut-and-paste features familiar to word-processing reporters without ever leaving your computer. Sound delivery software can create, encode and broadcast sound. Several shareware versions of sound editing software can be downloaded from the Internet, tried out and then registered for about $50 or less. Windows users can use Cool Edit or GoldWave, whereas Mac users can use Sound Effects.

AUDIO EDITING

LEARN MORE ABOUT ONLINE GRAPHICS AND DESIGN AT THE POYNTER INSTITUTE'S VISUAL JOURNALISM PAGE ONLINE AT http://www.poynter.org/vj/index.html

You can cut and paste, record separate tracks and mix them into one sound and adjust volumes. But as news photographer Michael Clapp learned during production of his multimedia report, sound editing software "cannot do much to improve poor audio. You need a quality recording from the start."

Make the tape recorder part of your dress code. By doing that, Nelle Nix and Michael Clapp "succeeded in obtaining some incredible pieces of audio." "The chanting of Rila Monastery's museum director in the top of a now-closed 14th-century tower chapel created inspiring sound for our piece on the monastery. The love song strummed by an 87-year-old musician, the brother of Krum Dermendjiev, added depth to our piece on the sculptor," they said.

GRAPHICS: INFORMATIONAL, ANIMATED

Graphics—photographs, video, animations and illustrations—play a vital role in presenting information. As Hurricane Bonnie churned its way through the Caribbean, the Fort Lauderdale *Sun-Sentinel* offered pictures of the hurricane and a graphic that showed readers the course of the storm.

NEW FORMS FOR A DIGITAL AGE

Writing journalism online—electronic storytelling—is truly in its infancy. In the near future, online news is likely to become a blend of audio, video and

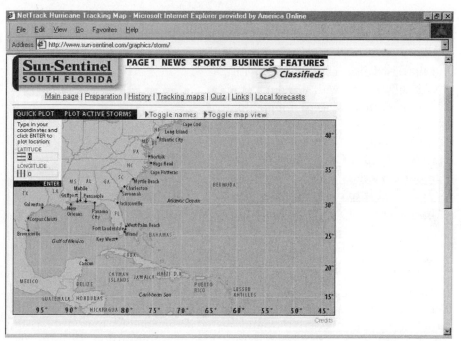

Animated graphics combine illustration, information and interactivity that represent one of online's greatest strengths: the ability to fully engage readers, as in this "Stormtracker" map that charts the path of tropical storms. (Courtesy of the Fort Lauderdale *Sun-Sentinel*)

text. The 21st-century equivalent of the inverted pyramid still waits to be developed. What will it be? Here are some possibilities:

AS WE MAY REPORT: THE POLICE BRIEF

A hyperlinked police brief could include these elements in addition to the news item:

- Crime Map. A Java applet updates a real-time map of crime incidents by city, neighborhood, street, and so on.
- Crime and Punishment. All references to criminal offenses and penalties are linked to a glossary of reader-friendly legal terms and penalties.
- Victims Chat. This is a bulletin board where readers can share experiences, sympathy and advice.
- Prevention Tips. These are crime prevention tips: animations (how to secure doors, windows), audio, video.
- Tell It to the Chief. This includes a mailform to contact the police chief.
- The Bottom Line. This is the costs of crime prevention, control, prosecution.

Here's how it might look on an online news site:

> Milford—Police charged a 17-year-old city youth with breaking and entering after officers found him trapped inside a chimney at a local seafood store.
> **Crime Map** | **Crime and Punishment** | **Victims Chat** | **Prevention Tips** | **Tell It to the Chief** | **The Bottom Line** |

INSIDE-OUT MATRYOSHKAS

An innovative suggestion by Ruth Gersh, editor of multimedia services at The Associated Press, is a new form that will retain the spirit but replace the structure of the inverted pyramid using an inside-out matryoshka, the Russian nesting dolls that open to reveal smaller dolls inside. Turn the idea inside-out: Each page can lead to a larger block of text. This is similar to a notion known as "stretch text," which allows the reader to choose from a variety of texts of different lengths.

SERIAL STORYTELLING

Kevin McKenna, editorial director of *New York Times* Electronic Media, says reporters using serial storytelling will tell their story in 400- to 500-word installments. "Readers can go back as deep as they want into the sequence, and along the way they will encounter sound and picture hyperlinks," he says.

MULTIPLE INVERTED PYRAMIDS

In this form, each element of the story is its own pyramid: a summary lead and supporting material arranged in descending order.

BROADCAST-STYLE WRITING

Web publishing may compel newspaper reporters to adapt a broadcast style, says the AP's Gersh.

In broadcast, you write to video and still images and to sound. You accompany, enhance and amplify what the viewer sees and hears from the screen. Words in broadcast complete the puzzle in the viewer's mind. The writer for print, by contrast, must use language to create in the reader's mind what the television screen provides.

The broadcast writer writes for the screen; the print writer tries to create a screen in the reader's mind that the memory and imagination can fill. Like the broadcast writer, the writer for the Web has additional electronic texts to work with ("e-texts" include video and still images, animation, sound, as well as words). But just like the print writer, the Web writer must use language that is specific, vivid and accurate. The challenge for the Web writer is to use words to provide multiple perspectives—not to repeat information, but to add new layers that deepen the understanding and impact of the story.

But technology also poses one of the great dangers of reporting/writing for the new media, online news pioneer Bill Mitchell believes. "Because of the additional tools at the reporter's disposal, there are at least a couple of dangers: (1) failure to focus hard enough at the reporting stage to get the details that might—or might not—be conveyed by the streaming video or audio accompanying the story and (2) an imprecision and incompleteness in the writing, based on the assumption that these other tools will deliver those parts of the story left out of the narrative."

Mitchell's concern is based on his experiences in print journalism as a foreign correspondent for the *Detroit Free Press* in the 1980s when he often had to double as photographer and reporter. "I remember sitting down to write an account of a dramatic scene of Polish riot police chasing people through Warsaw's old town. I found myself without the details I needed, in part because I'd been diverted from getting what I needed into my notebook by my work with the camera. Twofold problem: At its simplest level, it's hard to do more than one thing at once and do them well. But there's also the subconscious feeling that those other tools will convey those parts of the story. In both cases, the story suffers as a result. This will be a challenge for the journalist of the future, who will be expected to work simultaneously in several media. Not impossible and not necessarily detrimental to the story, but clearly an undertaking that will require extraordinary focus as well as skill."

Old forms will continue to influence the new ones. Landscape format monitors are favored over portrait format monitors, according to research by Kent State University's Information Design Laboratory. People prefer, by a wide margin, to read something that looks more horizontal than vertical. The front page feature stories of *The Wall Street Journal* are used as a model in the online world. Online practitioners design storyboards for their pages, just like film, television and advertising writers. In the online world, storyboards sketch content, graphics and hyperlinks, combining content with navigation. The first page may be an anecdote, something to hook the reader. The next page provides context (the nut graf described in Chapter 5). Subsequent pages link to content or segments that support or challenge the story's thesis.

Most importantly, the Web writer must inspire the user to scroll for further text or to click for additional information, just like writers in newspapers and magazines constantly try to make sure readers go beyond a jump line to an inside page. The challenge, to hold on to readers, is identical, even if the medium is different.

Links, which allow readers to jump around a story, or outside one, pose a particular challenge, especially when links lead readers to another site on the Internet. In that way, links may discourage readers from staying with a story.

My Poynter Institute colleague Mario Garcia, who has redesigned hundreds of newspapers and has now begun redesigning their Web sites, believes the new medium will enable the reader to choose among the "quick read, the substantial read and the encyclopedic read," something that print media have found difficult to accomplish.

VISIT WEB DESIGNER MARIO GARCIA ONLINE AT http://mariogarcia.com

Although writers worry whether there will be a place for them in the new media, I am heartened by the support that writers get from Garcia, a visual artist, and other observers. "It is in writing that I see the greatest possibilities for creativity, for pioneers to leave the legacy that historians will talk about," Garcia writes in *Redesigning Print for the Web.*

Doug Underwood echoes that sentiment in his book, *When MBAs Rule the Newsroom:* "But even as the computer comes more to dominate our lives, writing, I'm confident, will continue to be at the base of the unfolding Information Age. By that, I mean writing that is more than just conveying information. The written word has always provided the weave and fabric of our culture. When words rest in software, they don't necessarily lose their allure. In fact—given the flexibility of the word processor—writing becomes even easier. The medium changes the outcome somewhat, to be sure. But as long as there are real writers and real thinkers at the keyboard, I'm not worried."

TIPS FROM AN ONLINE NEWSROOM: Q&A WITH DAVID HO, *THE WALL STREET JOURNAL* INTERACTIVE EDITION

VISIT THE WALL STREET JOURNAL INTERACTIVE EDITION AT http://wsj.com

How did you learn your online skills?

The Web itself taught me. By its very nature, everything is interconnected. From portals to search engines to broken links, every connection or lack of a connection can tell you something, can bring you someplace new. There is a natural selection at work, useless links and sites are discarded, while the helpful ones are emphasized and expanded upon. If you really want to function and research online, you just have to surf. A lot. Surf with a purpose. Surf mindlessly like flipping channels. Before you know it, you'll know your way around.

What are the most important lessons you've learned about online news that you think reporters need to know if they want to survive/thrive in the future?

For the new media reporter: Even now, online news is still new. Much of it is just repurposed versions of print news. The exciting prospects of new media may dim for new journalists when they discover that most of their time is spent adding hyperlinks to stories that have already been extensively reported and edited by their print edition counterparts. Much of new media for major news organizations is just another extension of the print paper's printing press and delivery trucks.

For breaking news, reporters will have deadlines minutes long. Reporting directly for an online service will be much like working for a wire service. You would file immediately with whatever news was at hand and then send constant updates as things developed. It's a convergence of print media's depth with television's immediacy. This kind of reporting and reader inter-action already exists, for you can see the AP wire online and refresh every few minutes to see a story change before your eyes. People in newsrooms may be accustomed to watching a wire feed go by, but now that view of a changing story is accessible to the general public.

Reporters and editors will have to resist the temptation of the Internet's velocity. The competition to be the first to hit the Web with a story is and will be fierce. Mistakes can be made. Traditional news judgment may be sacri-ficed. And there is the temptation to publish first and fix later, simply be-cause on the Web you can correct your mistakes before anyone sees them (or too many see them). It's not like a newspaper whose typos and factual errors will be sitting around all day reminding you of how you screwed up.

At the smaller news organization, just as it has always been, it pays to wear many hats, some editorial, some production. Without a massive edit-ing system in place, the small town editor or reporter will have to be *more* computer literate than his counterpart at a larger organization. It is the same way now in that a reporter at a small organization may have to be a graphic designer, photographer and receptionist, while at a larger organization there is a greater stratification and specialization of responsibility. For the here and now, I don't think it unreasonable that reporters might carry digital cameras, which they could plug into their cell phones to upload pictures.

What story forms are emerging in online news?

Frankly, narrative style and structure don't seem to be changing that much. Much of online news is just regurgitated print news. What is different are the sidebars and boxes. The little additional information stuck into or around the story text. These are hyperlinks to other related stories, to Web sites relevant to the story, or video or audio clips.

I think the greatest change, one that must be embraced by reporters and editors, is seeing any one story in a greater context. Regardless of form, a story is riddled with branches that lead in all kinds of directions. The tradi-tional forms continue, but it's more like another dimension has been added. Imagine the inverted pyramid and its variations. It's still useful, and it still works, but it's self contained and flat. Now imagine layering, above and be-low it, stacks of different forms all bridged by words, ideas and names. The Web makes narrative structure three-dimensional. Reporters will have to ask themselves: What other stories are relevant to my story? How much infor-mation do I convey in my story, and how much do I link to through other news stories or third-party sites? Where do the links go? Should I avoid putting in links in certain places because they'll disrupt the flow of the nar-rative? Do I really want my reader linking out of my story? What if he or she doesn't come back? Should the link blow away my browser window or open a new one? Should it be a smaller, subordinate window? How much of the content remains my own? What exactly is plagiarism?

(David Ho was an interactive producer at *The Wall Street Journal Interactive Edition* from 1996–1999. He is now reporting for The Associated Press in Washington, D.C.)

ELECTRONIC ETHICS: BRAVE NEW WORLD

Every new tool raises its own ethical dilemma. Photoshop allows photographers and pictures editors to manipulate images. The availability of digitized information makes copying—and plagiarism—as easy as cut and paste. With desktop audio and video editing software, sound and images can be trimmed, enhanced, rearranged, even doctored. Miniature cameras allow undercover reporters access to situations they'd never be allowed to witness if they had to show their press pass.

Technology has made plagiarism easier to commit and, ironically, easier to detect. In 1998, *Boston Globe* columnist Mike Barnicle's defense was that the George Carlin jokes he used in his column had been posted all over the Internet. It's a question of intellectual honesty. Peel back most plagiarism incidents, past the excuses of stupidity and bad note-taking, and the common link is dishonesty.

As nature photographer and visual journalism professor Rich Beckman notes, since photography's beginnings in the mid-18th century, photographers have manipulated images, but the digital darkroom, with Photoshop, scanners and other electronic tools, provides a wide range of sophisticated accomplices. The result: "seamless manipulations that could pass as original images even to the eye of the trained professional."

Digital manipulation is defined by Beckman as changing the content or quality of a scanned image beyond what is needed to reproduce the image with the highest quality on a specific media. "Technology has spawned a new media with new challenges, new opportunities and new relationships, and consequently there is a need for new protocols and policies."

Beckman maintains that "perhaps no area of technological advancement in the history of photography has both advanced the careers of photojournalists and threatened the credibility of photojournalism as much as the digital darkroom. The ability to digitize photographs gave photographers, editors, scanners and designers the ability to consistently improve reproduction quality, improve work flow efficiency, and, most importantly, to move from the darkroom into the newsroom where they could become active advocates for the importance of strong visuals within daily news coverage. It also gave them the ability to alter every pixel in a seamless environment and made disappearing Coke cans, relocated pyramids and transposed figure skaters part of the national debate on the credibility of photojournalism."

Even professional photographers familiar with Photoshop, the most popular image editing software, actually have no more than "a solid grasp of one or two techniques that everyone at the paper uses, whether they are actually the best technique for a certain task or not," a survey by Beckman found.

Journalists and their news organizations, educators, and media leaders have begun to wrestle with these and other electronic dilemmas. If you take advantage of new technology to enhance your story, be upfront about it. Let your readers and viewers know what you've done. The best way to keep faith with your audience, says ethics expert Bob Steele, of The Poynter Institute, is to always disclose and explain.

READ MORE ABOUT THE MANIPULATION OF IMAGES IN AN ONLINE ESSAY BY JOURNALISM HISTORIAN MITCHELL STEPHENS, AT http://www.mediastudies.org/define/stephens.html

A FINAL WORD

I know from experience that it takes hours to become familiar with even the basic tools of complicated visual software. My best advice to a reporter: Make friends with visual journalists. Take a course. Surf the Internet. Know your strengths. I am a good reporter and writer. I don't have the interest to devote the time that mastery of these tools demands. Whether or not I have the talent or skills is another matter, but without the passion I'm not going to spend my time doing it.

"There are some clear ethical benefits to presenting news and information on the Web. With an endless news hole, we can be more complete, we can add more context, we can include more voices, and we can help people more fully understand complex issues," says Fred Mann, general manager of Philadelphia Online, the joint Web site of the *Philadelphia Inquirer* and *Daily News* at **http://www.philly.com**. "But, also, ... just because a news hole is endless doesn't mean that we can fill it properly. We still face those wonderful age-old issues of who's going to fill it. And with what? Resource and time pressures don't disappear just because we've moved to the Internet."

New media are evolving, and the rules are still in flux. You'll need a different set of skills, which may include HTML writing, which you should get in your college years—although not from journalism school necessarily. Just being open to learning new skills is the most important attitude you can bring to the professional world.

ONLINE WRITING: THE COACHING WAY

- Be open to learning new skills, no matter what you think your journalism path will be. Keep an open mind.
- Spend time on the Internet researching and writing. Learn basic HTML and construct your own home page. Don't be left behind.
- Team up on a new media project. Bring your own set of skills and interests and invite others with different ones to collaborate.
- As exciting as the Internet may be, promise yourself you'll spend part of each day in the world, interviewing, observing, listening and watching. No matter how news is presented, the best reporting involves collecting, analyzing and organizing.

GLOSSARY OF IMPORTANT TERMS

Bandwidth. Measurement of speed, in bits per second, that information travels on the Internet. Greater bandwidth allows more bits per second.

Browser. Software, such as Netscape Navigator and Microsoft Internet Explorer, that enables accessing and viewing pages on the World Wide Web.

Bulleting. An online story form. Story is summarized with a two-paragraph lead and several bullet points detailing key elements. Lead and bullets can be followed with full version or link to full version.

Chunking. Emerging online story form. Longer stories are broken into chunks of several paragraphs that fit on one Web page.

Digital manipulation. Alteration of the content or quality of a scanned image.

e-Text. Short for "electronic text." Digitally encoded materials such as words, sounds, pictures, video clips, animations.

HTML. The abbreviation for "hypertext markup language." The code that creates the text and graphic layouts known as Web pages that are viewed over the Internet with Microsoft Internet Explorer, Netscape Navigator or another Web browser.

Hypertext. A document that contains links to other documents, commonly seen in Web pages and help files. Hypertext is the feature that made the World Wide Web possible by allowing users to move ("hyper" is a Greek word meaning "beyond") from place to place to place, whether it's inside the text itself or to another site on the Internet. Hypertext is the heart of online news.

Link. Short for "hyperlink." Anything in a hypertext or hypermedia document that connects one document or section to another document or another section.

Photoshop. The most popular image editing software.

Shovelware. Derogatory term for material from print publications posted on the Web without enhancing to take advantage of Internet features.

Threading. An online story form. Topical information organized by links to form an interrelated story that allows a reader to pick one thread and also select other alternatives.

URL. Stands for "uniform resource locator." The address of an Internet site.

EXERCISES

1. Select a front-page feature story from *The Wall Street Journal* and storyboard it for online presentation. Use the first screen for the opening anecdote and the second screen for the nut graf. Divide the remaining

content into a series of Web pages that provides amplification of the story's theme, as well as illustrations, hyperlinks, graphics.

2. This chapter presents several online story forms. Choose a form—threading, bulleting, chunking—and use the notes provided for the writing workshop in Chapter 4 and the exercises in Chapter 12 (the suicidal ex-officer on the police station roof and Jon and Lani) to write the stories. Imagine that you have photos, audio and video, and provide links for each version.

3. Visit one of the sites mentioned in this chapter and study the ways it tells stories. Discuss which stories are most successful and why.

READINGS

Bolter, Jay David. *Writing Space: The Computer, Hypertext, and the History of Writing.* Hillsdale, N.J.: L. Erlbaum Associates, 1991.

Borden, Diane L., and Harvey Kerric, eds. *The Electronic Grapevine: Rumor, Reputation, and Reporting in the New Online Environment.* Mahwah, N.J.: Lawrence Erlbaum, 1998.

Byrd, Joann. "Online Journalism Ethics: A New Frontier." *The American Editor,* November 1996, pp. 6–7. Also available online: **http://www.poynter.org/research/me/nme/jvnm2.htm**

Clapp, Michael and Nelle Nix. "Interactive Multimedia as a Journalistic Tool." Master's Project. University of Missouri School of Journalism, 1996.

Demac, Donna A. "Is Any Use 'Fair' in a Digital World? Toward New Guidelines for Fair Use in the Educational Context." New York: Media Studies Center, 1996.

Fitzgerald, Mark. "The Effect of the Internet on Print Journalism." *Editor & Publisher,* April 13, 1996.

Fredin, Eric S. "Rethinking the News Story for the Internet: Hyperstory Prototypes and a Model of the User." *Journalism & Mass Communication Monographs,* 163, September 1997.

Garcia, Mario. *Redesigning Print for the Web.* Indianapolis: Hayden Books, 1997.

Gates, Bill. *The Road Ahead.* New York: Viking, 1995.

Harvey, David A. "Working on the Web: HTML Authoring Tools." *Computer Shopper,* November 1995.

Levins, Hoag. "Webmasters Prefer Raw Code, Surprising Find of New Survey." *Editor & Publisher Interactive,* Dec. 27, 1996.

Murray, Janet. *Hamlet on the Holodeck: The Future of Narrative in Cyberspace.* New York: The Free Press, 1997.

Rich, Carole. *Creating Online Media: A Guide to Research, Writing, and Design on the Internet.* New York: McGraw-Hill, 1998.

Rosenbaum, Marcus, and John Dinges, eds. *Sound Reporting: The National Public Radio Guide to Radio Journalism and Production.* Dubuque, Iowa: Kendall/Hunt, 1992.

Wendland, Mike. *Wired Journalist: Newsroom Guide to the Internet.* Washington, D.C.: Radio and Television News Directors Foundation, 1996.

HOTLIST

http://www.poynter.org/research/nm/timeline/

"New Media Timeline." A hypertext history of new media, from their beginning in the late 1960s to the newest features of the 1990s. Compiled by David Shedden, researcher at The Poynter Institute.

http://www.useit.com/alertbox/9606.html

"Inverted Pyramids in Cyberspace." Jakob Nielsen is an influential Internet desktop designer. He argues for the adoption of the inverted pyramid by Web writers.

See also:

http://www.useit.com/papers/webwriting/index.html

"Writing for the Web," a research project by Nielsen and John Morkes on how users read on the Web and how authors should write their Web pages. Includes case studies and Web writing guidelines.

http://www.poynter.org/car/cg_carlists.htm

Nora Paul, library director at The Poynter Institute and former editor of information services at *The Miami Herald*, shares her wealth of knowledge, tips and insight in this page devoted to listservs from her online guide to computer-assisted reporting. Includes tips for using listservs, valuable links and advice for reporters: "Anyone with a specific 'beat' (health or education or environment, for example) should subscribe to at least one listserv on that topic. This is a great way to keep up with what experts are talking about, solicit information, advice or contacts from them and to generally tap into a broad expert base."

http://www.journalismnet.com/column3.htm

"An AIDS conference is coming to your city? Why not talk to some of the world's leading experts of AIDS statistics or AIDS education?" "A debate has erupted in your city over police use of pepper spray? Why not ask police officers from across North America what their experience has been?" Those are just two of the many reporting resources available through electronic mailing lists cited by Canadian journalist Julian Sher in his comprehensive Web site **Journalism.Net**, which includes this excellent overview on mailing lists.

http://sunsite.unc.edu/cmc/mag/1995/dec/osderdonts.html

"The Vision of an Accomplished Webmaster: An Interview With *The New York Times'* New Content Development Editor Elizabeth Osder" by Chris Lapham in *CMC Magazine*, Dec. 1, 1995.

http://www.poynter.org/research/me/nme/jvmann.htm

"In the online world, the challenges to traditional journalistic values and ethics are major," concludes Fred Mann, general manager of Philadelphia Online, the online sites for *The Philadelphia Inquirer* and *Daily News*. In his thoughtful keynote speech at a new media conference at The Poynter Institute, Mann raises important questions about the ethics of links and the blurred boundaries between online news and advertising and offers provocative answers based on his editorial experience in print journalism and his new life as an online news executive.

See also:

http:/www.poynter.org/research/nm/nm_mann98.htm.
"New Media Brings a New Set of Problems."

http://www.contentious.com/

Contentious bills itself as "The Web-zine for writers, editors, and others who create content for online media."

http://www-personal/umich.edu/~froomkin/

Dan Froomkin's Home Page. Froomkin is senior producer for political news at Washingtonpost.com and teaches a course in online journalism. His site is rich with ideas and inspiration.

http://www.eastgate.com/

Eastgate Systems publishes hypertext fiction, poetry and nonfiction. Its site offers a hypertext bibliography that covers the past, present and future of this interactive writing medium.

CHAPTER

FIRST ASSIGNMENTS

CHAPTER FOCUS

Planning and having a sense of wonder are the keys to success for the new reporter.

CHAPTER LESSONS

- Succeeding with your first assignments
- Writing about accidents
- Writing about fires
- Writing about festivals, fairs, parades and more
- Writing about meetings and hearings
- Writing about speeches
- Writing obituaries
- Using news releases
- First assignments: The Coaching Way

INTRODUCTION

The day has finally come. It's your first day at work in a newsroom, and you're about to receive your first assignment. There's no predicting what it will be, but most likely it will be one of several possibilities covered in this chapter: writing an obituary, covering a meeting or rally, reporting an accident or a fire in your community. This chapter describes such stories and shows examples produced by beginning and veteran reporters who share the reporting and writing lessons they've learned. It details the basic information used to compile the stories. Most important, however, it describes the set of attitudes and behaviors that will make your first story—and every one after—a success, no matter what its topic.

TIPS FOR SUCCESS FOR BEGINNING JOURNALISTS

You're probably nervous as you get ready for your first day as a new reporter. What will your first assignment be? Will you do a good job or fall flat on your face? All sorts of doubts, questions and worries assail you. As uncomfortable as this may be, there's also a positive side. Your concerns demonstrate that you care, which is the most important characteristic you can bring as you go out on your first assignment. No matter what that assignment is, you'll have a better chance of success if you keep these points in mind:

1. **LET THE FIVE W'S, AN H, SW AND WN GUIDE YOUR REPORTING.** You've heard it before, but once again, the basic journalistic paradigm—"Who?" "What?" "Where?" "When?" "Why?" and "How?"—as well as "So what?" and "What next?"—will get your through almost any news story, whatever the assignment.

   - Who are the people involved in the story: victims, rescuers, speakers, opposing sides? Identify the people.
   - What is the story about: a car crash, a picket line, the death of a beloved figure? Describe the event.
   - Where did the story occur: a sun-dappled park, a crowded intersection, a trailer park, outside a small factory? Establish the place.
   - When did the story occur: the last day of school, 5 a.m., the dead of night, at the height of rush hour? Give the time.
   - How did the story happen: a driver lost control on a curve, children were playing with matches, management and labor were unable to agree about wages? Explain the circumstances.
   - Why did the story happen: speeding, carelessness, to raise funds, to celebrate a holiday? Explore the cause.
   - So what? An accident holds up traffic, a festival brings a community closer together, a strike affects customers. Assess the impact.
   - What next? Criminal charges, hospital treatment, funerals, a new traffic light, higher prices. Look ahead.

2. **HUMILITY.** Don't be afraid to admit your ignorance. Journalism is a lifetime of continuing education. People often say reporters are superficial, uninformed or downright ignorant. They don't realize how hard the job of reporting is—that on any given day, you may be thrust into a subject you know nothing about. That's why having basic information about how society operates is so critical. You need at least a rudimentary understanding of how things work. The only way you're going to get this is by studying, by asking questions, by keeping your eyes and ears open, by being curious, by being humble enough to admit what you don't know. People may criticize you for not knowing something, but they can't criticize you for trying to learn and wanting to get smarter.

3. **FRESH EYES.** A good reporter is forever astonished at the obvious. Bring a sense of wonder to your first story and every story after that, and your writing will have an energy and excitement that captivate readers and viewers.

4. **KNOW THE TURF.** For every story you work on there is a specific set of rules. Each constitutes a domain, with its own vocabulary and rules that govern fields of knowledge or activity concerning anything from law and medicine to sports. The challenge for the reporter is to master these other worlds—or at least be familiar enough with them to be able to communicate their meaning. The journalist is the bridge between such domains of modern life and the public.

Now let's take a look at the kinds of stories you will undoubtedly tackle as a beginning reporter.

FIRST ASSIGNMENT: WRITING ABOUT ACCIDENTS

Accidents—at home, on roads and highways, everywhere people work, play and travel—kill more than 90,000 Americans a year and cause nearly 20 million disabling injuries, according to the National Safety Council. The annual price tag in lost wages and productivity, property damage, and medical care totaled $478 billion in 1997.

There are more than 13 million motor vehicle accidents every year. In a society where the car is the principal means of transportation, motor vehicle accidents are news. But there are so many accidents that most news organizations limit coverage to those accidents that are fatal, affect large numbers of people or involve unusual circumstances.

Remember to stick with the basic information as you begin your coverage.

FIND OUT ABOUT ACCIDENTS NATIONWIDE FROM THE NATIONAL SAFETY COUNCIL ONLINE AT http://www.nsc.org

- Who are the drivers, passengers, dead and injured?
- What type of accident occurred: motor vehicle, airplane, boating, etc.?
- When and where (time and location) was the accident?
- How and why? What were the circumstances and cause of the accident?
- So what? What was the impact on traffic?
- What next? Condition of injured. Funeral arrangements for fatalities. Status of criminal charges.

What makes an accident newsworthy? Readers may drive by what looks like a terrible collision and wonder why they don't see anything about it in the next day's paper. The answer lies in the numbers: There are just too many accidents occurring daily to write about every one. Depending on the size of the community, news organizations generally use the following criteria to determine which accidents are story material:

1. Fatal accidents.
2. Multiple vehicle collisions resulting in severe injuries.

3. School bus accidents even when no injuries result.

News organizations generally don't cover accidents that end with vehicle damage and no injuries (unless a celebrity or prominent figure is involved). That's why the example in Chapter 1, a mall fender bender in Pleasantville, had little news value.

Many motor vehicle accidents, even fatal ones, rate little more than a few paragraphs in a metro brief. In many cases, coverage is limited to a photograph and caption. Browse most American newspapers, and you will find accident briefs like this one from a West Virginia daily:

Nitro Man Unhurt in Crash That Closed I-64

Charleston Daily Mail
July 13, 1998

A Nitro man whose car overturned today on Interstate 64 emerged from the accident unhurt.

Troy Miller, 49, "didn't have a scratch on him," said Putnam County Sheriff's Deputy S. I. Hamrick, who investigated the 6:10 a.m. crash.

The Sheriff's Department was forced to shut down both eastbound and westbound lanes of I-64 for about half an hour while crews cleared Miller's car from the road, Hamrick said.

Miller apparently fell asleep as his car crossed a highway bridge just outside of Nitro.

His car first rear-ended a motor home, then struck the concrete bridge barrier and flipped over.

Hamrick did not know the name of the motor home driver.

But many accidents merit fuller treatment. Notice how, in the following story, the reporter finds a focus that communicates the individual tragedy of an accident, its human dimension, and also conveys important public service information.

Take-Charge Effort Turns Deadly on I-65

By Carol Robinson
Birmingham News Staff Writer
June 2, 1998

As Birmingham's district manager for Waffle House, Michael Jerome McClellan was used to taking charge when a problem arose.

Continued

Monday his initiative cost him his life.

When he was involved in a fender bender on Interstate 65 during morning rush hour, McClellan, 36, got out of his car and started to direct traffic until police arrived.

"That's every bit like him," said David Rogers, manager of the Hoover restaurant. "He's been a manager for years. That's just the kind of guy he was. He was used to dealing with problems that popped up."

McClellan tried to route traffic around the two cars involved in the accident, both of which were in the left-hand lane of traffic on southbound I-65 near Fultondale. As he did so, a car swerved to avoid hitting another and instead hit McClellan.

LifeSaver helicopter was called to the scene, but McClellan died of multiple injuries before help arrived, said Jefferson County Chief Deputy Coroner Jay Glass.

"It probably could have been avoided if they had pulled over into the emergency lane," Glass said.

"It's deadly on the interstate."

McClellan, a native of Gordo who lived in Fultondale with his wife of only several months, had worked for the Waffle House franchise for six years. He was the district manager in charge of three Birmingham-area restaurants.

Friends described him as a hard worker with a good attitude. "He'll certainly be missed," said Jim Hutto, director of operations for the franchise.

McClellan's death hit co-workers hard, many of whom gathered at his Fultondale home Monday afternoon.

"It took the breath out of all of us," Rogers said. "I couldn't say enough about him. He was a tremendously great guy."

Birmingham police Capt. Hollis Crutchfield said McClellan's death was the city's 20th traffic fatality so far this year. The interstate, he said, is a dangerous place to get out of a car.

"Our officers who work up there would be the first to tell you that," Crutchfield said.

"In any situation, safety is the primary concern. The best thing to do is move (the cars) to the side, get out and don't stand close to the vehicles. Whatever you do, don't stand between the cars."

"We've had numerous police cars with their lights flashing rear-ended," he said. "Obviously cars on the side of the interstate are some kind of attraction."

FIRST ASSIGNMENT: WRITING ABOUT FIRES

LEARN THE EXTENT OF AMERICA'S FIRE PROBLEM ONLINE FROM THE U.S. FIRE ADMINISTRATION AT http://www.usfa.fema.gov/about/

More than 4,000 Americans die each year in fires, and more than 25,000 are injured. An overwhelming number of fires occur in the home, the U.S. Fire Administration reports. America's fire death rate is one of the highest per capita in the industrialized world. Firefighters pay a high price for this terrible fire record as well; approximately 100 firefighters die in the line of duty each year. Direct property losses due to fire approach $9 billion a year. Most of these deaths and losses can be prevented.

A reporter interviews a fire official in the ashy debris left from a building fire.

There are thousands of fires in America every day: car fires, kitchen fires, forest fires, grass fires, house fires, apartment fires, restaurant fires. Generally speaking, the news value of a fire story is governed by the number of deaths and injuries, property damage and visibility.

Again, it's important to use the five W's checklist when covering fire stories:

- Who are the people involved? List the names, ages, addresses of casualties. Who discovered the fire? Number of firefighters. Eyewitnesses. Heroes. Firesetter.

- What type of fire occurred: commercial building, home, apartment house, number of stories of building? Construction type (brick, wood frame, etc.), grass fire, forest fire. Fire equipment (ladder trucks, pumpers, rescue vehicles) responding. Damage estimate.

- Where and when did the fire happen? Give the address of the fire. Time when the fire was discovered. Time when alarm was turned in.

- How and why explain the cause of fire. Narrow escapes. Rescue efforts.

- So what? Describe the impact on families, neighborhood, loss to community tax base.

- What next? Will there be an arson investigation, treatment of injuries, commendations? Demolition of structure? Prevention efforts?

Like police officers, firefighters have a job to do at the scene. The journalist who recognizes and respects that is going to have an easier time getting the information needed to report the news. Don't go barging past fire lines. Ask for the officer in charge. Ask when information might be available. (Your phone list should have numbers for public information and other sources.) While the firefighters are occupied, keep busy yourself interviewing witnesses, recording quotes and facts. Before you leave make sure you've got all the facts you need to write your story. Back in the newsroom you may need to make a follow-up call.

WILDLAND FIRES: A GROWING PROBLEM

In the United States, tougher building codes and fire prevention programs have combined to cut structural fire losses. In fact, America's fire losses today represent a dramatic improvement from more than 20 years ago. In 1971, this nation lost more than 12,000 citizens and 250 firefighters to fire. But there's a new and growing problem as urban areas continue to expand in what was once rural and wilderness areas: wildland fires.

According to a National Park Service report, "In the 1980s, wildfires burned large tracts of land across the United States. More fires have damaged even larger tracts of land and personal property in the 1990s. A dream home built in an idealistic wildland setting can be razed by fire in a matter of minutes."

In 1991, the Oakland Hills, Calif., fire destroyed 3,000 structures and killed 25 people in one of the most densely populated metropolitan areas of the United States. The following year the Fountain fire in northern California burned 64,000 acres of forest land and destroyed 330 homes and 37 businesses.

"Reporters accustomed to urban structure fires that are extinguished in hours may have had difficulty understanding the inability of authorities to suppress wildfires with equal speed. Local residents who believed all fires could easily have been extinguished if only there had been more bulldozed firebreaks often succeeded in catching a reporter's attention. Never mind that wind-borne embers sometimes started spot fires a thousand bulldozer-widths away," says journalism professor Conrad Smith, of the University of Wyoming.

The problem with fire coverage is that fires are usually covered as separate events. Reporters cover fires the way firefighters do: They get there when the blaze is reported and leave when it's out, never to return. Rarely do they interpret the social or environmental cause of fires or go back to study the long-term impact. When reporters dig deeper, looking beyond today's news, they often find stories that are richer and more significant and enhance their readers' understanding of social forces. Whether it's an accident or a fire, there are powerful and important stories to be told about the long-lasting consequences of news events—on individuals, families and communities.

READ AN ANALYSIS OF NEWS COVERAGE OF A MAJOR WILDFIRE STORY IN WILDFIRE MAGAZINE ONLINE AT http://www.wildfiremagazine.com/smith.shtml

WRITING THE FIRE STORY

In the following example, from the *Austin American-Statesman*, notice how the writer uses an inverted pyramid structure to present the facts of the fire in an apartment complex. A summary lead covers the basic facts, which are amplified in the rest of the story.

Fire burned eight units at an East Austin housing complex early Wednesday, critically injuring an Austin man and forcing more than 100 residents from their apartments.

Investigators said the blaze at the Kensington Apartments, 3300 Manor Road, started shortly after 1 a.m. It burned for about 90 minutes before firefighters brought it under control. In addition to the eight units that were burned by the fire, eight more received water damage, for a total damage estimate of $250,000.

Joe Kropka, 37, was in critical condition in the burn unit at Brooke Army Medical Center in San Antonio on Wednesday, hospital officials said.

Kropka was burned as he attempted to put out the fire in a trash can under the kitchen sink of his second-floor apartment, according to Austin Fire Department spokeswoman Cathy Brandewie.

She said the fire in the trash can may have been started by a discarded cigarette. She said flames from the can ignited gas leaking from a utility connection behind Kropka's kitchen stove, causing an explosion.

Neighbors on the western wing of the complex, where the fire started, said the explosion forced Kropka to back out of the front door of his apartment.

"I heard this big boom, and then I could see him lying outside," said Jesse Miller, 46. "He was burned very bad. There was blood all over him."

A woman who lives two apartments down from Kropka said the victim then picked up one of her daughters and carried her down the stairs to get her away from fire.

"After he tried to fight the fire, he just picked up my 7-year-old and took her down the steps away from the fire," said the woman, who declined to give her name. "I don't know how he had the presence of mind to do anything, because he looked burned all over."

Red Cross officials estimated 89 people from the complex took refuge overnight

Continued

in the gymnasium of the World of Pentecost church several blocks away at 1504 E. 51st St.

Among those at the gym were Bobby Blevins, 34, and his fiancée, Carolyn White, 27, both telemarketing workers, whose apartment was next to Kropka's. They said they lost all their belongings in the fire.

"All we've got is what's on our bodies," said Blevins. "I heard an explosion and shattering glass and everyone running up and down knocking on doors telling people to get out."

The owner of the complex, Zahir Walji, said he has not had a problem with gas leaks at the units. "Most of the complaints we've had about gas have turned out to be pilot lights that went out on stoves," he said.

The Austin Fire Department is investigating whether the complex ever had any reported fire code violations, Brandewie said.

Walji said Wednesday afternoon that plumbers and other utility workers were working to restore gas and water to the apartment so that most of the residents could move back in by Wednesday night.

He said one wing of the complex where the fire occurred will be closed for several days until it can be cleaned up.

Austin American-Statesman
Jan. 29, 1998

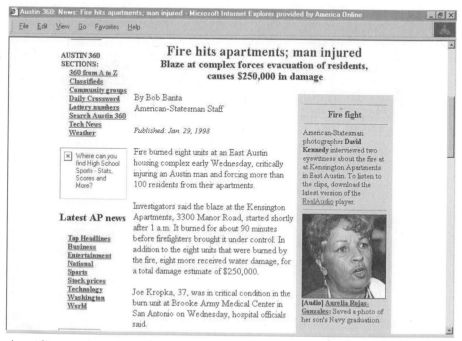

An online version of a traditional newspaper fire story includes dramatic audio interviews with survivors. (Courtesy of Cox Interactive Media)

When *Austin American-Statesman* photographer David Kennedy took photographs of the fire at an East Austin apartment complex, he also tape recorded interviews with residents who had to flee their burning home. The audio clips were posted on the paper's online news site on the same page with the story, giving an added dimension to the paper's coverage.

FIRST ASSIGNMENT: WRITING ABOUT FESTIVALS, FAIRS, PARADES AND MORE

Nearly every weekend, festivals, fairs, art and craft shows and a variety of other events sprout up in communities across America. Maybe it's not the most glamorous assignment in journalism, but when people gather to celebrate a holiday or share a common interest, the news media will be on hand.

Reporters often dismiss such stories as fluff, as assignments somehow beneath them. Ariel Sabar, a reporter for *The Providence Journal*, is more insightful about the professional challenge. "In some ways I dread these assignments," Sabar says. "The thought that always crosses my mind is 'What on earth am I going to find here that readers will care about?'" To counter that attitude and bring new dimensions to these assignments, a group of newsroom writing coaches assembled this list of tips and story ideas that goes beyond routine coverage of festivals and fairs:

- Begin reporting the story before you go, just as you would for any other news feature. By calling the art show coordinator, the dog show director, etc., you can find in advance the "story within the story" that makes the pieces work. As Ann Portal, assistant metro editor of the *Statesman Journal* in Salem, Ore., says: "It rarely works to show up and hope to stumble across a good human interest feature. But if that happens, at least find a focus. It's not enough to interview a handful of visitors about what they think of the stock car race or the new historical exhibit."

- Talk to organizers before and after but remember that they aren't the story and may never show up in your story.

- Be wary of crowd estimates.

- Don't treat it as a boring event. That shows up in your writing.

- Write about people different from you. Reflect the diversity of the event in ethnicity, background, sex and age.

- Have a sense of humor but not sarcasm. Have fun but don't make fun of people. When humor falls flat, it's deadly.

- Work with photographers. Get their cell phone number ahead of time so you can contact them if you're at different areas, but try to go together. Give them a good idea of whom you may write about. If that changes, let them know. It looks dumb to have a great photo of someone who's never mentioned.

READ HOW ARIEL SABAR HANDLED "THE EVENT STORY" ASSIGNMENT FOR *THE PROVIDENCE JOURNAL* ONLINE AT http://www.projo.com/words/tip513.htm

- With editors, figure out at the start of the season which events you'll cover. Brainstorm on what you can do differently. Look at past clips, talk with colleagues, readers and especially photographers who've covered the same event over and over. As Candy Page of *The Free Press* in Burlington, Utah, says: "It's important to have a diverse group of staff members at the brainstorming because a 20-year-old's interest in Lollapalooza or the county fair is very different from a 60-year-old's."

- Cover the news: balloon accidents, animal problems, crowd injuries. Check with the organizers and police afterward to see whether there's news that you missed.

- Choose a piece of the event, or a person, and write about that, not the whole thing. Take the approach of describing the overall pie by focusing on a single piece. As Adell Crowe of *USA Today* says, "Take a piece of the event and tell a story rather than describing the strawberry queen, the snowcones and quoting the kids."

- Have a structure, a theme, to your story, not just a collection of anecdotes. As Bill Luening of the *Kansas City Star* says, "I tend to believe that festival, weather, promotion stories succeed or fail not because of how we approach the event but how we write what we see."

- Don't overload your story with quotes and different people. Stick with your focus.

- Avoid numbers that tell nothing. For example, that fairgoers consumed 12,300 hot dogs, 8,427 snowcones, 6,000 gallons of Diet Pepsi. Do the math and put those in perspective: The average fairgoer ate two hot dogs and a snowcone.

STORY IDEAS FOR FAIRS, FESTIVALS, PARADES AND MORE

- Spend a day (or an hour) with a vendor. Cover how he or she does the job but also ask about weird and funny experiences.
- Spend time with the oldest people you can find at the fair or a young couple. Cover it through their eyes.
- Find the oldest person working at the event and do a story through his or her eyes about how it's changed over the decades.
- Ride in one seat of a popular carnival ride for a while and see who gets in with you.
- Volunteer to work a shift serving up strawberry shortcake or walking the grounds as McGruff the Crime Dog. Do a first-person story about your experience.

- Ask fairgoers to rate things, such as parents vs. kids rating the quality of the food.
- Look for stories that explain and teach, such as tips from a 4-H Club judge about how to tell what's a good cow or pig, etc.
- Have someone figure out how many calories you can consume at a concession for $15.
- Spend the night in an animal barn with a 4-H member; tell what it's like to prepare an animal for showing.
- Give kids' tips on adult things. For example, Soap Box Derby racers' tips for driving straight or avoiding potholes in the track.

Source: Newscoach-L

■ Arrange to get results for events and get them into the paper, broadcast or onto your online site promptly. But make sure organizers know what you want, such as just first-place winners or all the winners from your geographical area. Otherwise you may get way too much or too little.

Record-Seeker Wants a Fair Shake

Delaware State News

HARRINGTON—Tom Paswater says he isn't interested in a career in politics, although he would be a natural on the campaign trail. He has, as they say in basketball, the hands for it.

What Paswater, a 13-year-old from Greensboro, Md., is interested in doing is breaking a world record.

Any world record.

"I was going to try crawling seven miles. But that was too hard on my knees," he said.

So yesterday, he stationed himself at the rear gate of the Delaware State Fair and asked everybody who passed by him for a handshake.

Paswater said the world record for handshaking, according to the *Guinness Book of World Records,* is 8,513.

He wanted to shake 10,000 hands yesterday to break it, and he picked the right place to do it. Thousands had thronged the state fair every day since it opened last Friday, and on the last day things were no different.

Despite the dripping humidity and spotty rains that have hung around the fair for the past week like a little kid eyeing the Ferris wheel, the fairgrounds were blanketed with people.

When they left, clutching teddy bears or exhausted children, they were greeted by Tom Paswater, a skinny kid who looks like Woody Allen must have at 13. Sneakers, blue jeans, a T-shirt emblazoned with a motorcyclist bursting through a wall of flame, eyeglasses, a few pimples.

"Mind if I shake your hand for a world record?" he asked them.

Some people looked at him like he was asking for money and walked on.

"Come on. Just shake my hand. It's not *Candid Camera,*" Paswater told the reluctant.

But even though there were probably 10,000 people on the fairgrounds throughout the day, Paswater's chances for a new world record didn't look all that good.

For one thing, the notebook he had people autograph to prove he had shaken their hands had room for only 400 signatures. For another, he didn't have any witnesses, except a reporter.

Some of those signatures looked a bit doubtful, too.

"Somebody signed it 'Bing Crosby,' which might be his name, but somehow I don't think so," he confided.

Paswater had competition, too. At the main entrance to the fair, GOP congressional hopeful Tom Evans was pressing the

Continued

flesh, although he didn't seem to be counting the palms he shook.

Nevertheless, the teen-ager was determined to stay "until my Mom left or I get 10,000. Whichever comes first."

After an hour he had 83 signatures.

"Boy, you better get shaking," Pat Dean of Chestertown, Md., told him as she wrote her name in his book.

COVERING A STATE FAIR: LOOKING FOR AN EMBLEM

The sheer size of many events often overwhelms reporters and their stories. They jam them full of statistics and quotes but fail to capture the human spirit that motivates festivals, fairs and other gatherings. They should focus instead on a single person who can serve as an emblem for the news event. When my editors sent me to the closing day of the state fair, I chose to write about the skinny kid at the gate asking people to shake his hand. Had I thought of it, I should have gotten statistics (attendance, corn dogs sold, etc.) and used them for a sidebar or better yet, a graphic.

I like to think the memory of his quest lasted in some readers' minds long after the midway lights had dimmed.

FIRST ASSIGNMENT: WRITING ABOUT MEETINGS AND HEARINGS

As a reporter you will spend a lot of time at meetings. Meetings are the principal way public business is done in a democracy. Open to the public and the press, meetings are the forums where decisions are discussed, debated and voted on.

Here's a sampling of the kinds of meetings you may be assigned to cover:

- School board
- Planning and zoning commission
- City or town council
- Housing authority

Public officials meet to discuss policies and transact business, including taking votes, approving the spending of public money and deciding on personnel matters or how property owners use their land, homes or businesses.

In addition, the meetings of private groups also make news. Reporters attend meetings of neighborhood groups, companies and business organizations.

How Do You Cover a Meeting?

1. **Background.** Read previous stories to learn about the issues and people involved. If another reporter covered the beat before you, ask him or her for a briefing. If you have time, visit the meeting site first to get the lay of the land. Often you will be able to get a copy of the agenda and perhaps even talk with an official who can brief you and explain the issues. Follow this advice offered by reporters at *The Providence Journal:*

   Prereport the meeting. Determine what will be the key issues and talk to the main sources beforehand. Before the meeting, go with a photographer to the neighborhood that's going to get zapped by a zoning change, get some pictures and quotes and write the bottom of the story before the meeting. Get the decision in the lead and top off the story, and you'll look smart in the morning.

2. **Get close to the action.** Before I went to work as a Washington correspondent for Knight Ridder Newspapers, the best piece of advice I got came from a reporter who'd spent time working in the nation's capital: "Remember," this reporter told me, "nothing happens in Washington. It happens everywhere else in the country. They just come to Washington to fight about it." An exaggeration, of course, but the philosophy behind it stood me in good stead.

   Meetings are usually a lot of talk with very little action. (Cynics, often with good reason, believe that decision makers have already decided what they're going to do in private and put on a show of deliberation for the public.) If a group of neighbors comes before the city council to complain about sewage flooding in its neighborhood, that's where the real story is, where parents worry about their children getting sick from playing in contaminated puddles. To do the job of meeting coverage right, you need to be where the story is happening, not just where it's talked about. Reporters generally counter that they don't have time, that their editors overload them with assignments and story counts. I say you don't have time *not* to find out what the story is about by going to the place where it's happening if you are serious about informing your community.

3. **Get to the meeting early.** Introduce yourself. Ask people why they've come. Ask officials and clerks what to look out for. Get copies of statements and briefing papers.

4. **Hang around** after the meeting ends. Get reactions and explanations for issues you didn't understand during the meeting.

5. **Know the players.** It's your job to know the members of the public agency, their political affiliations, their positions. Make sure you have their office, home and cell phone numbers.

6. **Keep asking yourself:** What's the news, what's the point? What else do I need to know to write this story?

7. **HUMANIZE THE STORY.** People are the essential ingredient of any story, but reporters often forget that when they're writing a meeting story. Meeting stories are often dull because the writer has left out the people whose lives, concerns and interests are the reason for the meeting in the first place.

LET THE SUNSHINE IN: WHAT YOU NEED TO KNOW ABOUT OPEN MEETINGS

The First Amendment of the U.S. Constitution protects a journalist's right to publish information about the government without government interference. But it doesn't guarantee access to that information or to the meetings, hearings and other sessions where government officials make the decisions that affect the public (other than criminal trials). The people's right to know is protected, however, by state and federal laws, known as open meetings or "sunshine" laws, that require public officials to conduct public business in open meetings. Because those laws vary, reporters need to know the laws governing open meetings in their community. The Reporters Committee for Freedom of the Press, a nonprofit group that provides free legal help to reporters and news organizations, publishes *Tapping Officials' Secrets,* a complete reference to open meetings and open records statutes and cases in all 50 states and the District of Columbia, available in print and online at **http://www.rcfp.org/tapping/index.cgi**. Laws vary from state to state, but, according to the Reporters Committee, essential elements of open meetings laws generally include:

"At its core, participatory democracy decries locked files and closed doors. Good citizens study their governors, challenge the decisions they make and petition or vote for change when change is needed, but no citizen can carry out these responsibilities when government is secret."

—TAPPING

OFFICIALS'

SECRETS

■ Public agencies, such as city councils and planning and zoning commissions, give advance notice of all meetings, even emergency ones, and publish or post agendas in advance, listing items to be discussed.

■ Agencies must keep minutes and/or transcripts of all meetings, even the ones they can legally close to the public. Some agencies also record their meetings, and those audio and video tapes are available for review.

■ Every state allows agencies to conduct certain discussions in closed sessions, which they usually refer to as "executive" sessions. (They usually can't take formal action, such as vote, unless they are in public session.) These discussions may be held in secret:

1. Personnel matters, such as hiring, firing or disciplining an employee.

2. Collective bargaining sessions, with a teachers union, for instance.

3. Discussions with agency attorneys about a pending or imminent lawsuit.

4. Discussions about buying or selling public property.

If a meeting is closed in violation of open meetings law, the public and news media may complain to the courts. Inform your editor or news director if a public agency violates the public's right to see not just what decisions it makes, but also how and why.

Finding Stories in Meetings: How One Reporter Did It

You pick up the morning paper or log onto your favorite online news site. "Putnam commissioners get earful over abandoned house," the headline reads. You're not all that interested, but your eyes drift over the first paragraph:

A Putnam County resident warned county commissioners yesterday that a snake- and rat-infested abandoned house on her street poses a threat to children and threatened to prove it by presenting officials with a bounty of dead varmints she's shot at the place.

Would you keep reading? Perhaps. But what if the story began with the following?

Dodie Griffin sits on her concrete porch, aims her Mossburg shotgun across the way and blasts her target.

Over the last few years, she's bagged a slew of snakes and rats that take refuge most of the time in an abandoned house next door.

She told Putnam County commissioners Monday how she had thought of gathering up her dubious bounty and plopping it onto the desk in their chamber.

But she thought better of it and addressed the commission without visual aids. This time.

I wrote the first version as an example of a summary lead, which is the way many reporters would approach a story of this type. But I prefer the second, which appeared in the *Charleston Gazette* in West Virginia on Sept. 10, 1996. It was written by Heather Svokos, who covered the meeting where Dodie Griffin warned commissioners of the dangers posed by the abandoned house next door to her house. It's an excellent example of the way a good journalist can report the news and tell a story. The full story appears next followed by Heather Svokos' tips for writing about meetings.

Putnam Commissioners Get Earful Over Abandoned House

By Heather Svokos
Staff Writer
Charleston Gazette

Dodie Griffin sits on her concrete porch, aims her Mossburg shotgun across the way and blasts her target.

Over the last few years, she's bagged a slew of snakes and rats that take refuge most of the time in an abandoned house next door.

She told Putnam County commissioners Monday how she had thought of gathering up her dubious bounty and plopping it onto the desk in their chamber.

But she thought better of it and addressed the commission without visual aids. This time.

Griffin recalled creating a stir 20 years ago when she brought commissioners a dead dog. It had apparently been mistreated at the county's animal shelter.

"I'm gonna be nice about this in the beginning," she said after Monday's commission meeting. "But if something isn't done about this, then I'm gonna be nasty."

Griffin said the house on Scott Lane has been abandoned for three years, and it's not only driving the varmints into her yard, it's a dangerous hazard for the children who often play there.

The basement of the rickety house is half filled with water which floods it constantly, she said, because the lot used to be a swamp.

Children could easily fall through the floor and never be heard from again, Griffin told commissioners.

Another danger is the freezer and other appliances that sit on the porch with their doors open. "They should be removed or turned toward the wall," Griffin said.

And don't get her started on the cockroaches. "I can spray cockroaches all day and I've got a dozen to deal with the next morning," she said.

Griffin is demanding action from the commission. She says she has been to the Health Department and the Solid Waste Authority, with little result.

She figures a recent state law regarding abandoned buildings should force commissioners into action.

The law, enacted June 1, gives counties and municipalities the power to sue property owners who have let their structures or property become rundown.

Previously, the only avenue was to put a lien against the property, a lengthy and often ineffective recourse. Now the county or city would be able to recoup cleanup and legal fees from the owner.

But in order to enforce the law, the commission needs to adopt a building code. They haven't and have indicated they won't until they've studied the matter in great detail.

Commissioner Jim Caruthers said it would be difficult to track down the owner, but he agreed to talk with members of the Solid Waste Authority about the problem. Likewise, Commissioner Steve Hodges said he would discuss it with officials at the Health Department.

If the commission doesn't do something within 10 days, Griffin says she will be back. "If it's a danger, they're supposed to take care of it immediately," she said.

"I'll be back over here with a pack of rats. I'll kill 'em, bring 'em here and dump 'em on their desk. If it takes shock treatment to get them to do something to that place, I can give 'em shock treatment."

In other activity, commissioners:

- Signed off on a letter informing the Putnam County Development Authority that the commission would not contribute funds for an industrial park at Fraziers Bottom.
- Told Sen. Oshel Craigo that they would present him with a drawing and cost estimates for an access road that the Putnam County Board of Education may have to build before they're displaced by a courthouse construction project.

A LIFE IN JOURNALISM

HEATHER SVOKOS COVERS POPULAR CULTURE FOR THE *LEXINGTON HERALD-LEADER,*

Heather Svokos (Courtesy of *Lexington Herald-Leader*)

WHERE SHE WRITES A COLUMN CALLED "THE HEATHER CHANNEL." BEFORE THAT, SHE WAS A REPORTER FOR THE *CHARLESTON GAZETTE.*

Heather Svokos

I was the Putnam County reporter for the *Charleston Gazette* for a year and a half. The beat was lousy with meetings. County commission, school board, town councils, court hearings, sewage, transportation, solid waste, flooding—*you name it, they met about it, and I had to be there.*

I have to be up front, and I'm being as subtle as I can here—as a latent pop culture writer, that beat was not something I looked forward to every morning. Some days, I would rather have bled from every pore than come into work. Since I assume this isn't a therapy session for myself, I won't get into all the reasons. But a funny thing happened on the way to my next job. After I left the beat and the paper, editors and veteran reporters at the *Gazette* started coming out of the woodwork with praise for how I had covered Putnam County. Hmmm. I guess I had unwittingly made lemonade out of lemons. In the back of my mind, I was using some guidelines, and most of them were born out of a dual purpose: to inform my readers and entertain myself. Here they are, and do try them at home.

Continued

1. What I really want to do is direct.

Think in visuals, and then do what you have to do to paint that image like the opening scene of a movie. That's where Dodie Griffin and her Mossburg shotgun came into play. At first glance, her story was one I had told several times before: Angry resident comes to county commission to complain about an abandoned building: Children will fall through the floor to their death! Cut themselves on broken glass! And God knows what else! Sometimes, that's powerful enough. But like I said, it's been done so many times, I wanted a new twist. So when I heard her tell the commissioners about how she'd taken to shooting the rats that crawl out of the building, I knew I needed to hear more. After Dodie was done speaking, she started to take off, but I couldn't leave the meeting, so I got her phone number and called her when I got back to the office. I basically asked her to reconstruct the image of how she shot at the rats. Was she sitting, standing? Did her porch have wooden steps? It helped that she was a real live wire.

2. Have fun, take risks and steal from popular culture occasionally.

Think: What image or sentiment could I use that would not cause my eyelids to slam shut and little pockets of drool to form in the corners of my mouth? In one school board story, a certain theme kept coursing through that meeting. "We know everyone's request is legitimate. We want to help you all. We know you need desks and chairs and pencils and books, yadda yadda yadda." My ears just kept hearing a subtext of Bill Clinton's "I feel your pain." And fortunately, that phrase was still rumbling through our vernacular, so I went for it. Here's the lead I wrote:

> WINFIELD—It's not that the Putnam County School Board doesn't feel people's pain. They just don't have enough money to ease it all.

I also once wrote a court hearing story about this woman who worked with both the child welfare system and the police. This caused her to be embroiled in some pretty dicey situations—caught in the middle very often. So, I just kept thinking: Rock and a hard place, rock and a hard place. It didn't hurt that Chandler had just used the phrase awhile back on *Friends*. So I decided to test my crazy idea on my editors. My lead was:

> Rock. Susan McQuaide. Hard place.

It took my editors awhile to get it, but when they did, they thought I was brilliant. I didn't tell them I just watch too much TV. Then, to my surprise, they actually let it run. Woo-hoo!

Poca Water Project Gets off Ground

By Heather Svokos
Charleston Gazette Staff Writer
Nov. 1, 1996

Let the dirt fly, let the bulldozers roar.

Let the water company use Willard Beller's field as a parking lot for the backhoes.

"They can park them in my field if they have to, until they get done," Beller said. "I'm just happy to be getting it started. It's been a long time."

The residents of Heizer and Manilla creeks in Poca have been fighting for water for a decade. On Saturday, county and water company officials will crunch the first shovelful of earth that marks the first real promise of water.

The $2 million project is funded by West Virginia-American Water Co. and the state Office of Abandoned Mine Lands and Reclamation.

Continued

It will lay down 12 miles of water pipe that will serve 275 customers, or about 800 residents. The project has a 270-day completion time, which would have water flowing by July 30 or possibly sooner, said project engineer David Carovilano.

Some residents of Heizer and Manilla manage to pump good, clean well water. But for the second year in a row, both creeks have made the state Division of Environmental Protection's list of most polluted waterways. They are contaminated with mine drainage and, some fear, chemicals from companies that dumped drums of plant waste into a nearby hollow.

Residents are thrilled they'll no longer have to buy gallons of bottled water or cart their dirty laundry across the county for washing. "It should have been done before now, but it's just red tape," said Renae Bonnett, a Manilla Creek resident and longtime noisemaker in the struggle.

"If it could have just been handed to us, that would have been nice. But it's given people the opportunity to work together for a common good. They did not give up and they did not shut up. It's awful to have to torment people to get something, but in essence I think that's what it takes.

"If we accomplished that, there's probably a lot more we can do," she said.

In addition to the community activists who worked on the project, Bonnett also praises Putnam County Commissioner Jim Caruthers as instrumental.

New figures from the county's Office of Planning and Infrastructure indicate that the number of waterless families is shrinking. But in the increasingly affluent county about 21 percent of households still don't have water service.

"It's amazing to think we have all this progress going on and something this necessary isn't being done," Bonnett said.

"The shame of it is that the degradation was ever allowed to happen. Water is a natural resource. The problem is that it's just been ruined, through no fault of the people that live here. They're forced to live with it. They did the best they could for all these years."

The groundbreaking is scheduled for 10 a.m. Saturday at Heizer Creek Church Community Center in Poca.

3. Frustration rules.

The "Let the dirt fly ..." story is a prime example of a follow-up that could have been as boring as a retrospective of "The Single Guy." My editors weren't even sure I should do anything on it. About a month before this story, I did an in-depth piece about how this rural but vocal community had been trying to get safe, nonacid runoff water for years and years. I tapped into the frustration then, and people told me later it might have actually hastened the process of starting the project. So by the time the water company was ready to finally start digging, people were elated but jaded. Willard Beller, one of the early community movers and shakers on the water project, perfectly summed up his desire to get on with the show. When I interviewed him, he mentioned that he was so thrilled that he wouldn't mind if they parked the backhoes in his yard. I just pictured him throwing his hands up in the air, yelling, "Let's roll, people!"

4. Be an idiot.

My mentor, Christine Martin, constantly pounded this into our heads: Don't be afraid to ask the knucklehead questions. I often have the problem of not being able to relate to the whole bureaucratspeak thing. And believe it or not, sometimes these meetings are more formality than anything else— a lot of the hashing out has been done behind closed doors (which isn't always legal, but that's another chapter). So often, I would sit in the meeting, listening to this gobbledygook and these streams of seemingly meaningless numbers and think to myself: "Uh ... like ... this sucks." (Note: Uttering such statements out loud might make other reporters laugh, but sources don't tend to smile warmly upon it.)

So, two things help here: Find out the agenda and seek out a knowledgeable source before the meeting and make him or her give you all the layperson's background possible. (Example: "Yes, Mr. Hatling, this is Heather with the *Daily Grind*, can you tell me—and pretend you're talking to a second-grader here—what the words 'The Synergy of Implementing a Strategic Plan on the Paradigm Shift of Stormwater Runoff' mean to the average resident of East Overshoe County?")

And if you still have questions, don't be hesitant to ask them after the meeting. You might feel like an idiot in front of them, but (1) when they know you want to get the facts right, they'll be helpful and (2) it's always better to feel like an idiot in front of three county commissioners than in front of 120,000 readers.

Continued

> And, if you follow this knucklehead approach, most times you'll come up with explanations that are much more accessible to your readers.

FIRST ASSIGNMENT: WRITING ABOUT SPEECHES

In many communities speakers make news. One of your first stories will most likely be a speech. You'll be assigned to cover speeches at the local Rotary, Kiwanis or other civic groups. Campaign speeches. Lectures by visiting educators and authors.

Here are two typical examples: a speech at a Rotary Club meeting and a lecture by a visiting dignitary.

Creating a Quality of Life Checklist

Katie Rizer of Lake Erie Land Co. Offers a Unique Idea on How to Prioritize and Balance Hectic Daily Schedules

By Jerry Davich
The (Munster, Ind.) *Times* Staff Writer
June 3, 1998

CHESTERTON—Buying milk and bread, as well as making an important meeting, is usually put on a list to remind us of its importance. But how about penciling in when to spend quality time with your kids or squeezing in a rare meeting with yourself or jotting down a note to remind you to write a friend?

Many people say these are special moments during their day, but how often are they written down to ensure they get done, such as the milk, bread and meetings?

This was the point stressed Tuesday at the weekly Chesterton Rotary Club meeting, which is addressing the topic of community through the month of June.

"Do you keep track of your family life as well as you do your important business meetings and deadlines?" asked Katie Rizer of Lake Erie Land Co., as she hosted a presentation in front of 40 Rotarians. "Or do you come home late from work at night and say, 'Wow, I'm glad I have kids' as you just watch them sleep?

"That's the whole issue at hand here," she told the audience as they nodded in agreement.

"Choosing your priorities and finding the time to organize them. You have to respect your family and home as much as you do your workplace."

Rizer is in the process of writing a book called *Creating a Quality of Life,* which will include a comprehensive and adaptable checklist that can be copied and used on a weekly basis.

At Tuesday's meeting, she passed out samples of the multi-item checklist and briefly emphasized the importance of a "balanced" life and becoming a "pretty well-rounded human being."

The checklist includes topics such as health, family and friends, manners, career goals and spiritual concerns.

"It's important to find time to meditate or talk to yourself during the day," she said. "And it's also important to talk to your higher power, whatever that may be. Just finding time to stop and relax can really turn your day around."

Rizer, who encouraged audience members to copy her checklist, displayed numerous books at the meeting.

"The best gift to give a wife who usually cleans the house every day is to give the house a 10-minute clean-up," she said. "Involve the kids if possible and see what a difference it makes to her."

"The idea is to make it fun, and by being a better person it can help you make that happy little circle into contributing to a better community."

As the military launched missiles against Iraq, former Secretary of State Henry Kissinger fired off a few verbal attacks of his own against the Clinton administration's "shilly-shallying" policy toward dictator Saddam Hussein.

"I strongly oppose the wishy-washy way the Clinton administration handled Iraq," Kissinger told about 1,200 people at the Charleston Regional Chamber of Commerce's annual dinner Wednesday night.

But Americans need to rally around the military and support the attacks in the Persian Gulf, said Kissinger, who was secretary of state under Presidents Richard Nixon and Gerald Ford.

Kissinger opened his speech saying, "First, I want to congratulate the chamber for arranging a topic for this evening. It shows terrific planning."

Kissinger said the attack, ordered on the eve of a now-delayed impeachment vote in the U.S. House of Representatives, was "the right action taken too late."

"I've been in office when we undertook military action, and I think the only thing to do is to fundamentally support what the military is doing," Kissinger said.

"Whatever else we think about any other aspect (of the president's behavior), that is not the issue today."

Continued

Armchair strategists can't possibly understand the pressures and difficulties the president and major decision makers confront. All choices are important, urgent and can't be retracted, Kissinger pointed out.

"You only get one guess, and you can't say that you are going back to the drawing board," Kissinger said.

He added that, as president, "you're responsible not only for your brightest ideas but also the contingency of failure."

For that reason, Republican or Democrat, impeachment advocate or Clinton supporter, all Americans need to stand behind the president's decision, Kissinger said.

Even the timing of the attack shouldn't be in question—not now, he said.

"(Impeachment) is not the issue now," said Kissinger, who declined to offer an opinion on the impeachment proceedings. "I'm going to support the president's military action.

"I was secretary of state, and it's tough enough to take these actions. It's intolerable when you have the people against you."

As about 20 protesters and counterprotesters demonstrated about the Vietnam War outside the Charleston Civic Center, Kissinger defended some of the more controversial policies of his tenure as America's chief diplomat.

He said the problem with the country's military actions is that the United States doesn't know how to end wars.

"The United States is not good at ending wars," Kissinger said. "We're not good at synchronizing moves between the military and diplomats."

Eight years ago, in the Persian Gulf War, troops were pulled back 48 hours too soon. The military forces weren't able to finish their job, Kissinger said.

He also criticized the Clinton administration's hesitancy in attacking when United Nations weapons inspectors were denied access and national policy was threatened.

There are only two acceptable outcomes of the latest military action, Kissinger said. Either airtight inspections need to be ensured or Hussein must be overthrown.

"We're in it now. We've got to win," the Nobel Prize winner said. "They don't give any prizes for winning with moderation."

By Karin Fischer
Charleston Daily Mail Capitol Reporter
Dec. 17, 1998

Here are some guidelines to make your first speech assignment a success:

- **GET THERE EARLY.** Check in with the organizers; they may have biographical material or details about the speech, the sponsor or even an advance text that you can check against the speech that is actually delivered. Don't think you can leave or stop taking notes just because you have a text. Often speakers make dramatic and newsworthy departures from their prepared remarks.

- **FIND A GOOD LISTENING AND WATCHING POST.** Make sure you can hear the speaker and see the reaction of the crowd.

- **COUNT THE AUDIENCE MEMBERS.** If the meeting about the city budget draws only a handful of citizens, or if a hearing about a controversial coach has the audience members standing in the aisles, that's newsworthy.

- **KEEP ASKING: WHAT'S THE NEWS? WHAT'S THE POINT?**

- **ORGANIZE IN YOUR NOTEBOOK.** Highlight strong quotes, possible leads and endings.

- **MEET AND GREET.** Always speak to the speaker after the speech so you can clear up any questions or misconceptions you might have. If you've decided on your theme, try it out on the speaker. You may even get a stronger quote. Solicit reaction from audience members.

- **REMEMBER YOUR ROLE.** If the speaker or organizer requests "off the record," you need to object. You may be a guest of an organization, but you can make the argument that it will be difficult to keep a speech before a group of people a secret. Especially because you'll be interviewing those in attendance.

- **REPORT, DON'T TAKE DICTATION.** Bear in mind that you won't need the entire speech to write a story, just selected quotes, so don't waste your time writing down every quote. Many print reporters, aware they're competing with broadcast reporters who have the same material on tape, use tape recorders, too. Like them, they should remember to use the tape counter to make it easier to find quotes. On deadline there won't be time to transcribe a tape recording.

WRITING THE SPEECH STORY

The speech story focuses on three items: the speaker, the speech and the setting. Notice how the following ABCNews.com story on the earl of Spencer's eulogy at his sister's funeral focuses on the news in the lead, backs up to give reaction to the speech, then summarizes the main points from his speech. The story ends with a reference to earlier critical comments.

Sept. 6—Earl Spencer, Princess Diana's younger brother, delivered an outspoken funeral oration full of praise for his sister, bitterness at the media he blamed for her death—and a promise to her sons that they will be raised in the way she intended.

"I don't think she ever understood why her genuinely good intentions were sneered at by the media, why there appeared to be a permanent quest on their behalf to bring her down. It is baffling," Spencer said with undisguised contempt.

"My own and only explanation is that genuine goodness is threatening to those at the opposite end of the moral spectrum."

The massive crowd watching on giant TV screens in Hyde and Regents parks rose

Continued

in a standing ovation after the ninth Earl Spencer finished his oration.

Applause rolled through the streets of London and into Westminster Abbey, where the VIP audience joined in prolonged clapping as the earl left the pulpit.

"There was actually applause in Westminster Abbey," said ITV anchor Trevor McDonald, expressing surprise.

The remarks appeared to cheer many observers.

Claudette Lambert, assistant manager at a London shoe store, said the speech "brought tears to the eyes. He says what he wants—he doesn't worry about it."

Not everyone, however, was pleased by Spencer's sharp remarks.

"It injected a very sour note into what was a very solemn service," one commentator told ITV.

Noting the Irony in a Name

The earl spoke fondly of Diana's March visit to his South African home, when they succeeded in eluding the press for a few brief days.

"We managed to contrive to stop the ever-present paparazzi from getting a single picture of her," he said. "That meant a lot to her."

The visit, he said, reminded him of the many happy hours they spent together as children, before Diana embarked upon "the most bizarre life" and became the most hounded celebrity in the world.

The incessant media pressure was such that she often contemplated leaving her homeland for good, he said.

"She talked endlessly of getting away from England, mainly because of the treatment that she received at the hands of the newspapers," he said.

"It is a point to remember that of all the ironies about Diana, perhaps the greatest was this: A girl given the name of the ancient goddess of hunting was, in the end, the most hunted person of the modern age."

Vowing to Protect the Princes

The earl walked between Diana's two young sons, Prince William, 15, and Prince Harry, 12, behind her coffin for the last leg of her journey to Westminster Abbey.

And during his oration, the earl vowed to protect his nephews from their mother's misfortune—living a life relentlessly documented on the front pages of the world's newspapers.

"She would want us today to pledge ourselves to protecting her beloved boys, William and Harry, from a similar fate, and I do this here, Diana, on your behalf," he said.

"We will not allow them to suffer the anguish that used regularly to drive you to tearful despair."

Criticizing Intrusive Photos

Earlier this week, the earl exercised a blood-tie prerogative by banning from the funeral seven tabloid editors invited by the palace.

On Sunday, hours after learning that his sister was pursued literally to her death by paparazzi, Spencer delivered a harsh indictment of the media.

"I always believed that the press would kill her in the end. Not even I could imagine that they would take such a direct hand in her death, as seems to be the case," he said.

"It would appear that every proprietor and editor of every publication that has paid

for intrusive and exploitative photographs of her, encouraging greedy and ruthless individuals to risk everything in pursuit of Diana's image, has blood on his hands today," Spencer said.

ABCNEWS.com's Dorian Benkoil in London and Reuters contributed to this report.

By Jørgen Wouters
ABCNEWS.com
Sept. 6, 1997

Beginners often begin speech stories by confusing the fact that someone gave a speech with news. They will write a lead like this:

Joe Smith gave a speech about the political problems in Bosnia. ...

It's not news that someone gave a speech—unless, I suppose, it's an animal doing the talking. Your job is to decide the newsworthiness of what a person said and then convey that.

Avoid turning a speech story into a list:

Smith then talked about the peace effort in Bosnia. He then told the audience about the problems in reaching peace. Then he ...

It bears repeating that an effective story, no matter what the topic, has a single dominant message. Your job as the reporter is to listen carefully, analyze what you've heard, decide on the focus of your story and then assemble the material you've collected (in a speech story, that means the speaker's remarks and delivery, audience reaction and necessary background) into a coherent account.

FIRST ASSIGNMENT: WRITING OBITUARIES

"In community journalism, the writing of obits is one of the most important things we do," says James A. Raykie Jr., editor of *The Herald* in Sharon, Pa. The paper publishes about 2,000 obituaries a year, most written by a full-time obit writer assisted by other reporters and newsroom assistants on days when local deaths exceed an average of nine. Just how important obituaries are to readers the paper learned in 1988 when a redesign moved death records from the front to the back page. Reader complaints prompted the paper to go back to front-page death stories.

An **obituary** (the root of the word is "obit," the Latin word for "death") is a news report of someone's death, often with a biographical sketch of the deceased. Think of an obituary as a capsule biography published after a person dies.

Death has always been news, and obituaries are an important—and widely read—part of the newspaper. The obituary is by and large the

READ HOW
ONE NEWSPAPER
HANDLES OBITUARY
WRITING, ONLINE
AT http://www.
sharon-
herald.com/
localnews/
obituaries/
smsobits.html

province of the newspaper. Broadcast news outlets generally limit death reports to the passing of the famous or infamous, and their online sites mirror that tradition. Search for obituaries on MSNBC.com, and you get a page of hits about folk singer John Denver's death and the death of Princess Diana. Some textbooks devote many pages, even entire chapters, to the topic needlessly, I believe.

Fifty years ago, obituaries were a rite of passage for new reporters. Reporting and writing obits were the first journalistic task assigned to a new reporter. (Today that first assignment is more likely to be a meeting, a speech or a police brief.) Obits introduced neophytes to the basic story form, the absolute need for accuracy, the painful but necessary task of interviewing people at times of stress. Reporters who started after World War II remember their first days as journalists being consumed by the tedious but crucial job of reporting death with speed, accuracy and clarity. Obituaries illustrate the power of the definition of news as culture by marking the critical milestones of life.

Obituaries are one of the news industry's oldest conventions and have shown little change over the centuries they have appeared in print. Reporting and writing an obituary remain one of the journalist's basic skills. You need to be able to produce obituaries with speed (they typically are written for the next edition of the paper) and accuracy. Depending on your newsroom structure, obituaries may be assigned to new reporters or may be the exclusive responsibility of an obituary editor or writer.

Obituaries can be divided into three categories:

NEWS OBIT: The report of a death that is considered newsworthy because of the prominence of the individual or his or her place in the community.

FEATURE OBIT: The basic news report fleshed out with detailed biographical information, including anecdotes, descriptions, quotes, reminiscences. Although feature obits are usually limited to prominent, influential or famous people, a new form—dubbed the **"common man" feature obit**— emerged in the 1980s. At the *Philadelphia Daily News*, a former investigative reporter named Jim Nicholson brought the form to an art, winning prizes for his sensitive portrayals of the lives and deaths of ordinary men and women, in the process earning the nickname "Dr. Death."

APPRECIATION: An essay that explores the impact of a person's life—and death—often written by someone familiar with the person or the person's work.

OBITUARIES: A PROCESS APPROACH

IDEA. Deaths are usually reported by funeral homes, although word of accidental deaths, such as those occurring in motor vehicle and plane crashes, may come from police, fire or other public safety agencies. Editors

usually make the decision on treatment: whether the story will be a brief news obit or a **feature obituary.** Of course, an enterprising reporter can pitch a story about a local figure or an appreciation of a cultural icon, such as Kurt Cobain or Selena.

COLLECT. Funeral directors generally obtain and disseminate the basic facts for an obituary to the news media, but the reporter will have to do additional reporting to flesh the story out. Who will be your best source? Often closest relatives are too distraught to be of much help. But a co-worker or friend of the deceased can often provide rich details.

An obituary contains standard information. Here's a checklist:

- Name of deceased
- Age
- Address
- Occupation
- Cause of death
- Memberships
- Education
- Military history
- Survivors
- Names and addresses of family members
- Donation information
- Funeral information

FOCUS. Although death is the obvious news peg, an obituary, like any story, needs a central point. What is the most newsworthy aspect of this person's life—or death? Why is this person's death of interest to your audience?

ORDER. Obituaries follow a standard structure. The lead reports the identity of the person who died, the middle recaps his or her life in chronological order from birth to death and the ending provides information about survivors and the funeral.

DRAFT. The obituary lead includes:

- Name, a phrase that conveys the person's significance (i.e., "the inventor of the Slinky"), date of death (location, circumstances are optional)
- Age
- Cause of death

As the adjacent lead on a wire service obituary of singer John Denver shows, the traditional obituary lead is at home online. But an online site such as ABCNEWS. com, can also link to other stories and a Denver discography featuring song clips: http:// more.abcnews. go.com/ sections/us/ denverobit1013/ index.html

PACIFIC GROVE, Calif., Oct. 13—John Denver, whose '70s hits such as *Rocky Mountain High* and *Take Me Home, Country Roads* gained him millions of fans worldwide, was killed when his experimental plane crashed into Monterey Bay. He was 53.

Associated Press story on ABCNEWS.com Oct. 13, 1998

REVISE. Style is important, but accuracy is the top priority in an obituary. Obituaries are often the only time a person's name will appear in the newspaper. Obituaries, often laminated, become part of a family's permanent record. Mistakes can add lasting pain to already grieving survivors. Make sure you've got it right: spellings, ages. "I learned a lot when my father passed away," said John Nick, who edits obituaries at the *Daily News-Sun* in Sun City, Ariz. He keeps his dad's framed obituary, which he wrote, on a wall at home. "I learned the importance people put on reading the obituary. It's the last time a person's name will be in the paper. You have to get the facts right."

Generations of reporters have been raised on the journalistic bromide "If your mother says she loves you, check it out" and for good reason. The principle behind it—careful journalism requires a dose of skepticism— can keep you and your news organization from making embarrassing mistakes, as Greg Toppo learned on an obituary story during his first months as a reporter at the *Santa Fe New Mexican*.

A LIFE IN JOURNALISM

Greg Toppo

This past weekend I was the only reporter on duty at the paper. Well, Saturday afternoon I get a call from a very distraught woman, says she's calling from Washington, D.C.

Seems a family member, a certain doctor who lived for years in Santa Fe, died Thursday in D.C., and could we run a short obit for him in the Sunday paper? I said sure, just fax us the info, and we'll try to run it, I'm sorry to hear about your loss. She thanks me 100 times over, says she'll try to fax the stuff right away.

A few hours later a three-page handwritten fax comes in, detailing this guy's life. I ask the editor if he wants to run it, he says we've got no room, wait until Sunday to deal with it.

So Sunday rolls around, it's a madhouse. When things calm down, I go through the pile of stuff on my desk, about 8:30 p.m., and I find the fax. I ask the Sunday editor if she wants to run it. She says sure, so I type up six inches on the thing. At the end of the fax, it says that in lieu of flowers, donations should be sent to the New Mexico AIDS Center. Well, I've never heard of the place, so I look it up in the phone book. No New Mexico AIDS Center. I think, the woman is in D.C., probably doing all of it from memory, she must just have the details wrong. So I look at the fax to see if she's given us a number. No number, no name. She sent it from a Kinkos, but they don't give their number, either. I give it to the editor to look at. She says, "I know this guy! I just saw him a month ago! He looked great!" A bell should have gone off, but it didn't. I thought maybe it was a sudden illness. Still, the New Mexico AIDS Center thing is bugging me. I notice that there's a place called NM AIDS Services, but I'm reluctant to type that in, for fear of just plain getting it wrong.

Well, it seems this doctor was married twice and is survived by a longtime companion. The editor, it turns out, knows the longtime companion, leaves a message on her machine, so sorry to hear about it, please give me a call, etc. Meanwhile, she suggests, why don't I try to get the second wife on the phone—she lives in Santa Fe.

I call her, apologize for the inconvenience, but had she heard about the death of etc. and has she ever heard about New Mexico AIDS Center?

She says, "*What*?!"

Yes, I say, I'm awfully sorry. He died Thursday.

She says, "Well, I just talked to him this morning. His daughter got married today. *Who is this*?"

The long and short of it is that the second ex-wife tells me that the doctor had a girlfriend in Austin, Texas, with whom he just broke up, plus the longtime companion in Santa Fe:

Greg Toppo was a reporter for the *Santa Fe New Mexican* from 1995 to 1997. He is now a reporter in the Baltimore bureau of The Associated Press.

Continued

two girlfriends in long-distance relationships for months, and the Texas one just found out about the Santa Fe one. I called Austin info, and sure enough the fax was sent from Austin, not D.C. The jilted girlfriend made up the whole thing. We finally got the Santa Fe girlfriend on the phone, she verified it. The doctor called an hour later and did the same, with great embarrassment. It was then, of course, that I remembered "If your mother says she loves you, check it out." As it turns out, we have no policy on accepting obits from family members, but thanks to this, we will soon. I thank my stars that we made the calls. The editor thanks hers, too.

ETHICS CASE

It's a common newsroom dilemma. A person in your community has died, and a reporter pulls out the clips of past stories to obtain biographical background. Twenty years earlier, the person got in trouble. The details vary: a youthful indiscretion that lead to an arrest and conviction, accusations of political corruption that led to a resignation. Does this information go into the obituary? Certainly the family would say no, but what is the journalist's obligation? In general, editors and obituary writers agree that "obituaries are not eulogies and that newsworthy indiscretions, scandals, crimes or failures must be included to make obituaries fair and accurate."

WRITING THE FEATURE OBITUARY

Gerry Goldstein of *The Providence Journal* is a veteran reporter who relishes the obituary assignment. "I get excited because I'm about to face my favorite professional challenge: freeze-framing a lifetime in the newspaper version of tarpit amber—a column of type." Goldstein brings care and craft to the task. After you read the following obituary and his account of writing it, it may not surprise you that before they die, some readers ask him to write their obituaries.

Clifford E. 'Duby' Tucker, 101, Lifelong Resident of South County

By Gerald S. Goldstein
The Providence Journal Staff Writer
Jan. 20, 1998

SOUTH KINGSTOWN—Clifford E. "Duby" Tucker, 101, of 273 Pond St., a classic swamp Yankee who dined on fried eels and delighted in reminiscing beside his potbellied stove, died Sunday at the Westerly Health Center. He was the husband of the late Margaret (Holgate) Tucker.

A wiry figure who barely topped out at 5 feet, Mr. Tucker lived his entire life in the South County region, wringing a living from it by running a fish market, spearing eels, crabbing and laboring in textile mills.

Even at the age of 100, the elfin Mr. Tucker was a familiar sight behind the wheel of his Mercury station wagon.

On the road, his only concession to age was a refusal to make left turns across oncoming traffic, because "I don't trust the other guy." So whatever his destination, Mr. Tucker drove a circuitous route that would get him there with turns only to the right.

Born in 1896, when Grover Cleveland was president, Mr. Tucker delivered the old *Evening Bulletin* to earn enough for his first car, a used Ford that he bought for $15 in 1919.

Required as a boy to support six younger siblings when his father died suddenly, he learned early to be resourceful with a dollar. And true to his Yankee heritage, he was just as economical with words.

Mr. Tucker downplayed the observance of his 100th birthday in 1996, saying "birthdays are not good for you."

In providing his recipe for cooking eels, he said, "First you parboil 'em, then fry 'em. Never eat eels that's just plain boiled—a boiled fish is a spoiled fish."

Noting in his later years that eels had declined in popularity at dinner tables, he mused, "The world's gone daffy."

Asked about longevity, he advised: "Throw away those damn cigarettes." He attributed his long life to his avoidance of tobacco and liquor and to hard work.

Mr. Tucker, who lived with a niece, whiled away his hours in a rocking chair near the woodstove in his garage workshop, which was awash in dusty model ships, fish nets, eel spears and coffee cans brimming with nuts and bolts.

He loved to tell visitors about his beloved Boston Red Sox, recalling that he saw them play the New York Giants in the World Series of 1912—the year Fenway Park opened. Mr. Tucker, then 16, took the train from Peace Dale to Boston, then walked the remaining two miles to Fenway Park, where he bought a 50-cent ticket that gave him standing room on the perimeter of center field, patrolled by Boston's immortal Tris Speaker.

Explaining where he got the nickname Duby, Mr. Tucker said that he had been a cutup in school and "my teacher kept telling me, 'Clifford, do be quiet. Do be still. Do be this, do be that.'"

Continued

Asked once why he had never lived anywhere but South County, Mr. Tucker replied, "There ain't no better place."

Mr. Tucker was born in Wakefield, a son of the late William and Nancy (Whipple) Tucker.

He leaves two nephews, Arthur Malenfant of Cambridge, Mass., and Clifford Malenfant of Elpena, Mich.; and two nieces, Marjorie Stevens of Wakefield, with whom he made his home, and Nancy Maziarz of Hopedale, N.J.

The funeral will be Monday, Jan. 26, at 1 p.m. in the Avery-Storti Funeral Home, 88 Columbia St., Wakefield. Burial will be in Riverside Cemetery, Wakefield.

READ GERRY GOLDSTEIN'S PHILOSOPHY ON OBIT WRITING ONLINE AT http://www.projo.com/words/tip325.htm

HOW I WROTE THE STORY

Gerald S. Goldstein

Local character Clifford Tucker lived for 101 years and really didn't do anything. It was how he didn't do it that made him special.

He was a simple New England Yankee who loved a hearty supper of fried eels and got by in life shellfishing, running a little fish store and watching time and tide pass him by. In one of my favorite lines from the obit, he once mused in an interview—at age 95—that "The world's gone daffy." That's what most of us tend to think as we grow older and drift out of touch; I found his complaint touching and universal.

That's what I look for in reprising a life: what can we take from it that's both basic and cosmic—about values espoused or ignored; glories or failures and how they were abided; kindness or callousness; the impact of personality and character?

Anecdote is crucial; thus we read how Clifford Tucker refused to make left turns across traffic and drove to his destinations on routes that included only right turns because "I don't trust the other guy."

Tucker could have gotten three grafs as a nonentity. But it's satisfying to have given him his due because he was part of what makes this place special.

Most lives, in one way or another, are special; it's just that some so obviously telegraph what we can achieve, or have suffered, or have overcome, that they move us when crystallized in print.

I don't know how Saint Peter figures out what to write in his book, but I'm sure he's careful—after all, he has a judgment to make.

In our book it's easier; we take the rough diamond of a life as lived and rub away at it until facets emerge. Then the reader can hold it up and examine it—turn it around and around and cogitate on just how much light it reflects.

FIRST ASSIGNMENT: WRITING ABOUT NEWS RELEASES

Although you will often encounter people who don't want to have anything to do with you or your news organization, there are many others who want your attention. To get it they will inundate your desk with news releases: announcements of events, promotions, new products, services, developments and other activities that they hope will be treated as news.

A **news release** is a document, usually printed, but increasingly offered in video or electronic format, that provides information from a company or other organization interested in getting news coverage of the subject covered in the release. You may receive an e-mail release or a video news release, which is the video version of a printed news release and is distributed to television newsrooms nationwide without cost, to be used either full or in edited form. New media technology has created an updated version, online news columnist Steve Outing reported in early 1999. "Increasingly, reporters will see news releases that contain add-on components: photos (including high-resolution shots suitable for publication); audio clips; video clips; PowerPoint slide shows; and spreadsheets," Outing predicted.

Here's an example of a typical news release produced by a major auto manufacturer.

LEARN MORE ABOUT NEWS RELEASES AND PUBLIC RELATIONS FROM **PR**NEWSWIRE ONLINE AT http://www. prnewswire.com/

First Engine Celebration Held at New West Virginia Toyota Plant

BUFFALO, W.Va., Dec. 11—Less than three years after announcing the building of a new Toyota engine plant in Buffalo, W. Va., today a ceremony was held commemorating production of the first four-cylinder engine built at Toyota Motor Manufacturing, West Virginia, Inc. (TMMWV).

Dr. Shoichiro Toyoda, chairman of the Board of Directors of Toyota Motor Corporation (TMC), Akira Takahashi, executive vice president of TMC, Sen. Jay Rockefeller (D-WV), West Virginia Gov. Cecil Underwood and other officials joined TMMWV President Tomoya Toriumi in a ceremonial tightening of bolts on the first engine produced by TMMWV's team members.

The $900 million plant will employ some 800 employees when in full production. Initially, TMMWV will produce 300,000 four-cylinder engines annually. The engines will be used in Toyota Corollas manufactured in California and Canada.

"Production of the first engine is a symbol of the team spirit demonstrated by the state of West Virginia, the Putnam County community and TMMWV team members," said Dr. Toyoda. "While I know this plant is important to all of you here, it is also a vital part of Toyota's global efforts. Our global business plan involves increasing local investment in the countries where Toyota sells cars. The engines built here will power Toyota's best-selling products in North America."

Referring to the 1996 TMMWV groundbreaking where Toyota officials helped local school children plant maple trees to symbolize Toyota's new roots in West Virginia, Mr. Toriumi noted, "Due to the hard work of everyone in the plant and the tremendous support of Putnam County residents and all West Virginians, the TMMWV trees have begun to bear fruit."

Two expansion announcements for the Buffalo facility were made earlier this year. Construction already has begun on a V-6 engine plant that will produce 200,000 engines a year for models built at Georgetown, Ky. and Cambridge, Ontario. Production will begin in early 2000. The two engine plants will produce half the engines Toyota plans to make in North America.

In addition, a transmission facility will make 360,000 automatic transmissions annually for North American-built Camrys. The transmission has been the final high-dollar component still imported for Toyota's number one-selling car. Construction on the transmission plant will begin next year, with production slated to begin in 2001.

TMMWV is one of eight Toyota plants located in North America. Toyota now has capacity to build more than one million cars and trucks, as well as a million engines, in the United States and Canada and employs 20,000 Americans at its manufacturing facilities. Some 190 team members have been hired to date for engine production at the Buffalo plant.

Toyota Motor Manufacturing, West Virginia, Inc.

News releases are written in inverted pyramid style, with what the person writing the release considers the most important information in the lead. Your job is to read the entire release and use your own news judgment to determine what is most important to your audience.

Again, focusing is the most important part of the process.

What's the news? What's the point?

Don't ever write up a news release without also calling up the originator of the release to verify that it is genuine and accurate. Always do additional reporting, for balance and context, before you write a story based on a news release. Call the contact person identified on the release to double-check dates, telephone numbers. Ask if you can interview some of the key people involved in whatever is being promoted. As with any story, identify the most newsworthy elements for your audience and determine the story's focus. Don't be concerned if it doesn't match the headline of the release. Your job as a journalist is to evaluate information and events that others want to promote, not to serve as the promoters' assistant. Reporters always supplement the information in a news release with information they get through interviews, either by phone, e-mail or direct observation.

Compare the preceding Toyota news release with the story written about the event by George Hohmann, business editor for the *Charleston Daily Mail*. Hohmann attended the event, provided background information and kept his eyes open. Note the final paragraph about the feverish efforts to spruce up the plant before the ceremony. That's the kind of detail that a public relations person probably wouldn't point out, but the smart reporter sees it as an emblem supporting the story's theme. News releases rarely include the kind of human touches that bring news alive. That's the reporter's obligation.

Celebrating First Engine From Plant, Toyota Chairman, State Delegation Praise Effort to Bring Factory to W. Va.

By George Hohmann
Charleston Daily Mail Business Editor
Dec. 11, 1998

BUFFALO—Sen. Jay Rockefeller, D-W.Va., and Gov. Cecil Underwood joined Toyota Chairman Shoichiro Toyoda and other dignitaries this morning in a ceremonial bolt-tightening of the first engine produced at Toyota's new factory here.

"The day is fast approaching when these engines will be installed in Corollas that will be driven all over North America," Toyoda said. "Yes! It's something to be proud of.

Continued

Your energy and enthusiasm will be the spark that gets the motors running.

"Soon, when I drive a car with an engine made here, I will say to my colleagues, 'Listen! Can you hear the beating pulse of West Virginia?'"

Toyoda praised state officials and citizens for the support Toyota has received since the company announced it would build an engine factory in this rural area of Putnam County.

He said the two plant expansions announced this year present quite a challenge. The only way to fill "this tall order," he said, "is to advance one step at a time, with everyone working closely together as a team."

Toyoda promised that in return for the employees' hard work and the community's support, Toyota will be a good corporate citizen.

Rockefeller called Toyota's decision to build the $900 million plant "one of the most important things to ever happen to West Virginia." He said building the heart of a car in the state "will change the way we look at ourselves."

"But this is not about the past," Rockefeller said. "This is about the future. Today is a celebration of our state's potential."

Rockefeller said Toyota is known around the world for its long-term view. "That's why we in West Virginia are determined to live up to the high expectations Toyota has for us and we have for ourselves. We are going to show Toyota and the world we have the best people in West Virginia."

The senator said establishment of the plant represents the realization of "one of my most precious dreams," adding it took more than 10 years to turn the dream into reality.

The plant "holds out the promise of better lives for the 800 people who will work here and their families, and for the others in the community who will gain work because of your work. It has been estimated that this plant may create close to 5,000 jobs in West Virginia."

Underwood said, "We live in a world economy. The growth of international investment in West Virginia is a major building block for us as we enter the 21st century."

The governor said jobs are being created in West Virginia at a record-setting pace, with more than 10,000 created in the first 11 months of this year.

"I'm hoping Santa Claus has a few more under the Christmas tree," he added.

Although today's ceremony in the plant's final assembly area was originally scheduled to be a small gathering, more than 400 attended.

Team members cheered loudly when one of their own, Nancy Sadaro, told what the Toyota job means to her.

A year ago, she was working for the U.S. Postal Service. Sadaro said she knew when she applied for the Toyota job "getting in on the ground floor of this amazing facility would be the chance of a lifetime."

"When I got the call informing me I got the job, I felt I'd won the lottery," she said. "This year, instead of drowning in a sea of mail, I'll be with my family."

The ceremony occurred on a stage. A large sign behind the participants said, "Toyota and West Virginia—Manufacturing the World's Best Engines."

To one side was a spotless, silent assembly line filled with partially assembled engines.

Although the plant is still under construction, Toyota did everything possible to present the best impression. Less than two hours before the event, employees of Lawns Unlimited, Teays Valley, were working feverishly in a heavy fog, placing ferns in a planter at the main gate.

WRITING WORKSHOP: WRITING A POLICE BRIEF

Stephen Buckley, a foreign correspondent for *The Washington Post*, began his career at the paper as night police reporter. He wrote hundreds of briefs—100- to 200-word stories—often based on a single conversation with a police spokesman and about 20 minutes of total reporting and writing time. News organizations frequently learn about accidents, crime, fires and other public safety incidents close to deadline, which means the reporter has very little time to collect information and produce a story. The stories may be short, but they are no less important. "If you can't get a brief done," Buckley says, "nobody's going to trust you with anything bigger." To make his deadlines, Buckley followed these guidelines:

■ Rely on the five W's, "How?" "So what?" and "What next?"

■ Get the nonnegotiable necessities: names, ages, relationships, causes, circumstances, addresses, including city quadrants (was it Second Avenue North or South?), numbers killed or injured.

■ Always repeat the information back to the source to make sure you have understood it correctly. "Did you say the accident happened at the intersection of Interstate 95 and State Road 30?" "Let me make sure I got this correct: You said the mother died of head trauma?" Buckley says sources will be "surprised if you don't double-check. Often I had to call back three to four times to make sure I had everything right." If you have time after you've gotten the basic information, try to get as many details about the incident as you can.

FIRST ASSIGNMENTS: THE COACHING WAY

■ Focus your efforts on a festival, parade or community activity, on a piece of the action. It's a more effective approach than jamming a story with details from all corners of a festival.

■ Remember the tightrope strung across your desk. Don't be afraid to take a risk with your leads, especially on a parade or festival story that has been written a hundred times before. Ask a colleague to read it before you submit it. Don't spring it on your editor unawares: Tell her you want to try something different.

■ Whatever your first assignment, keep an eye out for the most interesting person at the event. Talk to that person and find a way to put him or her in your story.

The best tip yet is *still* to do the homework that shows the story behind the story. The second best is to remember to write about people who don't look like you.

GLOSSARY OF IMPORTANT TERMS

Executive session. Closed meeting of a public agency, permitted by law to conduct discussions on personnel matters, union negotiations, sale of property or pending legal action.

Feature obituary. Basic news report of a death fleshed out with detailed biographical information, including anecdotes, descriptions, quotes, reminiscences. Although feature obits are usually limited to prominent, influential or famous people, a new form—dubbed the **"common man" feature obit**—emerged in the 1980s.

News release. A document, usually printed, but increasingly offered in video or electronic format, that provides information from a company or other organization interested in news media attention on the subject covered in the release.

Obituary. A news report of someone's death, often with a biographical sketch of the deceased.

Open meeting laws. Also known as "sunshine laws." Federal and state laws that require public officials to conduct public business in open meetings.

EXERCISES

1. Here is a verbatim transcript of a conversation between a reporter and a police desk sergeant. Your assignment is to write a brief of 150–200 words based solely on the information provided here.

   POLICE: Westerly Police. Sgt. Johnson.

   REPORTER: Hi, Officer, this is Lois Lane of the *Daily Blatt*. Anything going on today?

   POLICE: No, pretty quiet.

   REPORTER: Any arrests?

   POLICE: Nope. Real quiet. Just the way we like it.

   REPORTER: That's great. Uh, well, anything go on over the weekend?

   POLICE: No, not really.

   REPORTER: How about accidents?

   POLICE: Accidents? Couple fender benders. Nothing serious.

   REPORTER: Okay. Well, thanks.

   POLICE: We had that train accident.

   REPORTER: What?! There was a train accident?

   POLICE: Yeah. Saturday about noon. You know, the one where the kid got hit.

   REPORTER: A kid got hit by a train!

POLICE: Yeah. I guess you could say she got hit. Hold on, let me get the report. Okay, here we go. Yeah, Lani Reynolds, white female, DOB 5-6-83. Address: 5546 Sylvan Oaks Lane, Westerly.

REPORTER: What time did this happen?

POLICE: Let's see. 12:10 p.m.

REPORTER: And where?

POLICE: On the trestle just outside town, where the tracks cross over the Westerly River.

REPORTER: Gosh, what happened?

POLICE: Hmm. Not much of a report. Let's see, the victim was on the trestle when an Amtrak train, the Colonial, en route to New York out of Boston, began to cross the trestle. She lay down on, next to the track, and the train severed her leg at the knee. Victim transported to Westerly Hospital.

REPORTER: What was she doing on the trestle?

POLICE: No idea. Doesn't say.

REPORTER: Do you know her condition?

POLICE: As of last night she was stable. This is one lucky kid.

REPORTER: Yeah, I guess.

POLICE: No, really. She'd probably be dead if it wasn't for another kid, what's his name, yeah Jon Tesseo, DOB 9-16-81. He works over at Toscano's Men Shop on Main Street, came upon the scene and gave her first aid until rescue showed up. Report says he's a Boy Scout. Guess he got his merit badge.

REPORTER: Yeah, I'll say. Wow, what a story. Have you got any more details?

POLICE: No, that's it. Just this incident report.

REPORTER: Who was the investigating officer? Can I talk to him?

POLICE: Steve Aspinall. He's off duty now. I can't give you anything else. Call back in the morning, and you can talk to the chief.

REPORTER: What was your name again?

POLICE: Johnson, but don't put that down. It just gets me in trouble. Just say a police spokesman.

REPORTER: Okay, well, thanks a lot.

READINGS

"Covering Crime: A Resource Guide." *Columbia Journalism Review*, January/February 1997, pp. 45–48.

Harrigan, Jane. *Read All About It!*, Chester, CT: Globe Pequot Press, 1987.

Nicholson, Jim. "Obituary Writing" in *Best Newspaper Writing 1987*. St. Petersburg, FL: The Poynter Institute and Bonus Books, 1987.

Selditch, Dianne, ed., *My First Year as a Journalist: Real-World Stories from American Newspaper and Magazine Journalists*, New York: Walker & Co., 1995.

HOTLIST

http://www.nsc.org/

The National Safety Council Web site is a valuable resource for reporters. Accident statistics and safety prevention material. The council's library is one of the world's largest sources of safety and health information with thousands of books, research studies and contemporary and historical documents. It also offers a comprehensive list of links to other Web sites with injury statistics or other useful information.

http://www.azcentral.com/news/scanner.shtml

"Listen to news as it happens by tuning into the Arizona Central Police and Fire Scanner!" Similar to a scanner used in *The Arizona Republic* newsroom by police reporters, the Arizona Central version tunes in the main Phoenix police and fire frequencies, then broadcasts the signal across the Internet using Real Audio.

Depending on when you tune in, you may not immediately hear any transmissions. That's because you're listening at a time when radio traffic is low. At other times, the dispatches will be nearly constant. Either way, you can keep the scanner running in the background as you explore other parts of Arizona Central.

http://www.usfa.fema.gov/nfdc/fius9th.htm

Fire in the United States: A Statistical Handbook. The United States continues to have one of the most severe fire problems in the world relative to its population size. Most Americans are not aware of this nor of the nature of the fire problem.

This 232-page report is a statistical portrait of the fire problem in the United States over the period 1985–1994. It is intended for use by a wide audience, including the fire service, the media, researchers, industry, government agencies and interested citizens. The report focuses on the national fire problem: The magnitude and trends of the fire problem, the causes of fires, where they occur and who gets hurt are topics that are emphasized. One specific focus is on firefighter casualties—causes, types of injuries, etc.

http://www.prnewswire.com/

PR Newswire. A leading source of full-text news releases distributed on the Internet to the news media. Includes links to public information officers around the country.

http://www.rcfp.org/

The Reporters Committee for Freedom of the Press provides free, and invaluable, legal help to reporters and news organizations. Online publications include *The First Amendment Handbook*, a state-by-state guide to the legality of tape recording phone calls and searchable archives of the group's biweekly newsletter.

CHAPTER

11

DOING THE RIGHT THING: LIBEL, PRIVACY AND ETHICS

CHAPTER FOCUS

Freedom of the press brings enormous power, but with it come enormous legal, ethical and moral responsibilities.

CHAPTER LESSONS

- The elements of libel
- *The New York Times vs. Sullivan* and public and private figures
- Avoiding libel
- Online libel: The new frontier
- Privacy: Guidelines for reporters
- A new trend: Reportorial conduct
- Broadcasters and the "Phone Rule"
- Hidden cameras
- Ethical decision making
- Copyright and the journalist
- Doing ethics: Ask good questions to make ethical decisions
- Avoiding conflicts of interest
- History of newsroom ethics
- Fabrication and "The Legend on the License"
- Ethics of reconstruction
- Avoiding plagiarism
- Doing the right thing: The Coaching Way

Congress shall make no law respecting an establishment of religion, or prohibiting the free exercise thereof; or abridging the freedom of speech, or of the press, or the right of the people peaceably to assemble, and to petition the Government for a redress of grievances.

—FIRST AMENDMENT TO THE U.S. CONSTITUTION

INTRODUCTION

Journalists possess enormous power in a democracy. The First Amendment's provisions give reporters the right to disseminate information to society without government interference.

But with that power and freedom comes a great responsibility: to report the news accurately and fairly. In some cases, your behavior is subject to legal action. That's where the laws of libel and privacy come in. In most of what you do, you'll be governed by the rules of your news organization and the decisions of your superiors, and even more by your conscience. Frequently, as a journalist, you'll encounter situations that trouble you. You'll wonder which way to turn, how to behave. This chapter is designed to help you make the right choices, ones that keep you and your news organization out of court while still informing your readers. It points you to helpful organizations such as the Reporters Committee for Freedom of the Press, which offers free advice and a wealth of knowledge on libel and privacy issues facing journalists. It will teach you how to avoid what Robert Steele, director of ethics at The Poynter Institute, calls the ethical "potholes and land mines" that confront today's journalists.

LIBEL

It's a moment every reporter dreads. Frank Greve, an investigative reporter for Knight Ridder Newspapers, was at home recovering from eye surgery when a process server knocked at his door and handed him a legal document that said he was being sued for libel for a newspaper story he had written. The subject of the story was asking for $150 million in damages.

Sometimes it's nothing more than a blustery threat—"If you print that, I'll sue!" or "Put that on TV, and I'll see you in court!" Sometimes it's a carefully worded warning letter from a lawyer—"If you proceed with publication, my client will have no choice but to seek legal redress." And sometimes, as Greve learned, the words are backed up with a lawsuit that can put any reporter and news organization on trial.

Libel is the publication of false statements that expose someone to public hatred, contempt or ridicule in writing or pictures. The word itself comes from the Latin "libellus" for a "little book." During the French Revolution, scandalous underground pamphlets, known as *libelles,* accused powerful figures of depravity and other offenses. Today, libel is a legal term that means the publication of a false or defamatory statement about a person, an institution or a company. In essence, it means that someone's reputation has been injured falsely.

Libel is serious stuff. Defame someone with something you write, photograph or say on the air, and it can cost plenty. In a six-year period in the 1990s, "juries awarded a quarter of a billion dollars in libel damages," journalism professor James Boylan reported in *Columbia Journalism Review* in

1997. Even when the damages are reduced or dropped by the ruling of an appeals judge—as they are in almost half the cases—big libel awards against news media have been a continual phenomenon of the 1980s and 1990s.

"Jury Awards Millions in Libel Case," the headlines read. Large libel judgments get a lot of attention. Conventional wisdom is that they occur only in highly publicized investigative pieces. In fact, many big libel judgments occur in "routine" stories that aren't thoroughly checked. It's the routine stories, the kind often written by beginners, that are vulnerable. Of course, veterans make mistakes, too. That's why knowledge of libel is important and why it should be the underpinnings of your behavior as a journalist.

News organizations have libel insurance, so it's unlikely, if you are a full-time employee and you wrote the story as part of your job, that you'd have to pay out of your own pocket if you libel someone. But the emotional and professional toll on reporters such as Frank Greve can be immense, as you'll read later in this chapter. Even though newsrooms have editors, news directors and lawyers whose job is to protect the news organizations from libel actions, that doesn't absolve the reporter from knowing the basics. Libel laws vary from state to state, but some general principles apply. Much of the information in this section is drawn from the *First Amendment Handbook* published by the Reporters Committee for Freedom of the Press.

READ JAMES BOYLAN'S ENTIRE ARTICLE, "PUNISHING THE PRESS," IN *COLUMBIA JOURNALISM REVIEW* ONLINE AT http://www.cjr. org/year/97/2/ punishing.asp

READ THE COMPLETE *FIRST AMENDMENT HANDBOOK* PUBLISHED BY THE REPORTERS COMMITTEE FOR FREEDOM OF THE PRESS ONLINE AT http://www.rcfp. org

THE ELEMENTS OF LIBEL

At the heart of libel law is the conflict between two important interests: freedom of speech and the importance of reputation. In America we cherish both, and so courts have over the years established rules that govern libel actions. In the last half-century the courts have placed the burden of proof on the plaintiff, that is, the person complaining of **defamation.**

Libel is the (1) **publication** of a (2) **statement of fact** (3) that is **substantially false** and (4) that reasonably **refers to the plaintiff** (5) in a manner **that tends to injure his or her reputation** or to discredit him or her in the estimation of the public (6) and that is published with the requisite degree of **fault.**

1. **PUBLICATION.** Publication occurs when information is negligently or intentionally communicated by newspapers, magazines, books, radio, online or television broadcasts to someone other than the person defamed. "It can be communicated through oral speech, too, as long as it is to a third party. Reporters have been sued for leading questions asked during an interview," says Jane E. Kirtley, executive director of the Reporters Committee. The full context of a publication is generally considered when determining whether a statement is libelous. Even a headline can be libelous, however. A week after a jury acquitted O. J. Simpson of murdering his ex-wife and a friend in October

1995, a front-page headline in the tabloid *National Examiner* said, "Kato Kaelin … Cops Think He Did It!" Even though the story did not support the headline, a federal appeals court in December 1998 ruled that headlines alone can be libelous and said Kaelin could sue the tabloid.

2. **A STATEMENT OF FACT.** The law holds that you can defame someone only with a fact that is "probably true," that is, that can be determined to be true or false. Reporting that someone was convicted of murder can be proven with a court document. In general, opinions— "I think John Doe is a bad guy"—cannot be libelous. However, the U.S. Supreme Court has ruled that an editorial or commentary can be libelous if it contains false assertions of fact to support that opinion.

3. **SUBSTANTIALLY FALSE.** The plaintiff must prove that the statement is false and substantially so. If your story reports that the mayor embezzled $25,000, but the actual figure was $30,000, the case would be dismissed because the sting of the statement is not substantially different from the truth.

4. **REFERS TO THE PLAINTIFF.** Someone reading or hearing the story must be able to reasonably identify the person being defamed. That doesn't mean that the story must actually name the person. Saying that the high school football coach molested students would identify him or her. Magazine photos or broadcast images that do not identify people in cutlines or scripts can still defame people if they can prove that other people could readily identify them.

5. **TENDS TO INJURE HIS OR HER REPUTATION.** It must lower the reputation of a person in the eyes of some other reasonable person. A Texas legislator who won a libel suit against a television station testified that, after the broadcast, strangers in the local mall asked him why he wasn't in jail.

6. **FAULT.** Constitutional law requires that plaintiffs prove fault before a news organization can be held liable for defamatory communications. Because of the importance of free speech, the law tolerates a margin of error. Although carelessness is not usually considered reckless disregard, ignoring obvious ways of substantiating allegations could be considered reckless.

The element of fault leads to another important principle, the distinction between **public officials** and **public figures** and private figures.

THE NEW YORK TIMES VS. SULLIVAN:
PUBLIC OFFICIALS AND PUBLIC FIGURES

It was an ordinary transaction: A committee paid a newspaper to take out an ad in support of its cause. But that exchange in March 1960 led to the most important protection journalists have in their effort to report the news.

The parties in the case were L. B. Sullivan, a city commissioner in Montgomery, Ala., and *The New York Times*, which published an ad from a group of civil rights activists who were protesting police brutality and retaliation against peaceful protests of segregation. Sullivan claimed the ad libeled him, even though it did not name him. In a landmark decision, the U.S. Supreme Court ruled in 1964 that the First Amendment protects the publication of all statements about the conduct of public officials. The statements are protected even if they are false, unless the plaintiff can prove the statements were made with "actual malice." "Actual malice" means that the reporter knew that the story was false, or should have known it was false, but published it anyway.

The Times vs. Sullivan decision provides a solid defense against libel of a public official. Later rulings expanded the definition to include so-called "public figures" and to "limited purpose public figures." A public figure may be an elected or appointed official (a politician) or someone who has stepped into a public controversy, such as a celebrity or star athlete. There is a third group, known as "limited purpose public figures." These are private individuals who have put themselves into the public limelight over a controversial issue. There are involuntary public figures who have become prominent through no purposeful action of their own. Because public officials and figures must prove actual malice, their chances of victory are slim.

Private figures have an easier time of it in a libel case. They have to prove only that the journalist was negligent and did not take the ordinary care a reporter should take in reporting and writing. In some states, even private figures have to prove actual malice. Actual malice is necessary for any plaintiff who wants punitive damages, which are designed to punish a defendant for grossly inappropriate actions and to deter others by signaling that the consequences for such action can be severe.

Although the First Amendment is a powerful shield, it doesn't mean a reporter can do anything to get a story.

DEFENSES AGAINST LIBEL

Even if a plaintiff can establish that all the elements are present, journalists do have defenses.

1. **TRUTH.** The best defense against libel is the truth. But the truth is often elusive and may be difficult to prove.

2. **STATEMENT OF OPINION.** As mentioned earlier, a statement of pure opinion can't be libelous, although it's vital that the story include the facts providing the basis for the opinion.

3. **PRIVILEGED INFORMATION.** Information obtained from an official proceeding, or record, is another crucial defense. Because informing the public about official proceedings or records is vital in a democracy, the law protects journalists who provide a fair and accurate account of them even if the charges are false. The degree of protection varies

from state to state. All "official" records aren't privileged, either. A police detective's notes that do not become part of the official police report may not be considered part of the public record.

4. **DEATH OF THE DEFAMED.** The dead can't be libeled, but their surviving relatives can be, depending on what the allegations are.

AVOIDING LIBEL: A CHECKLIST

The actions of professional, fair and careful journalists, like the ones in this checklist suggested by the Reporters Committee for Freedom of the Press, are the best protection.

- Check sources thoroughly. Get independent corroboration whenever possible. A source could have a vendetta against the subject and willfully or unintentionally misrepresent the facts for his or her own purposes. Confidential sources, such as government employees, may disappear or recant in the face of a lawsuit. Don't rely on someone else to be accurate.

- Do not let your opinion about whether someone is a public figure or official color your decision to verify the accuracy of a story. Juries do not respond favorably to reporters who fail to confront their subjects with defamatory information and to provide them with an opportunity to comment.

- If you cover the police or courthouse beat, make certain you understand criminal and civil procedure and terminology. (See "Covering Courts" section in Chapter 13.) Be especially careful to restate accurately any information obtained about arrests, investigations and judicial proceedings.

- Be cautious when editing. Make sure the story does not convey the wrong information because of a hasty rewrite.

- Watch for headlines and cutlines that might be defamatory even though the text explains the story.

- Make sure broadcast news promos used to stir audience interest are not misleading or defamatory.

- Do not use generic video footage or file photos when reporting on an activity that might be considered questionable.

- Just because someone else makes a defamatory statement does not mean that a news organization cannot be sued for republishing it. This includes letters to the editor. Check out any factual allegations contained in them as carefully as you would statements in a news story.

- Be sensitive about using words that connote dishonest behavior, immorality or other undesirable traits, whether in your published story or in marginal comments in your notes. Remember that a judge may order a news organization to produce reporters' notes, drafts and internal memoranda at a libel trial.

■ If contacted by someone threatening a libel suit, be polite, but do not admit error or fault. Talk the case over with your editor, supervisor or attorney immediately and follow procedures established by your news organization.

A LIFE IN JOURNALISM

FRANK GREVE IS AN INVESTIGATIVE REPORTER FOR KNIGHT RIDDER NEWSPAPERS IN WASHINGTON, D.C.

Frank Greve (Courtesy of Knight Ridder Newspapers)

HERE HE DESCRIBES WHAT IT'S LIKE TO GO THROUGH A REPORTER'S WORST NIGHTMARE, A LIBEL SUIT, AND OFFERS A SURVIVOR'S ADVICE.

DODGING THE LIBEL BULLET
Frank Greve

I was home alone one morning recovering from eye surgery when a process server rang the doorbell and delivered a libel suit seeking $150 million in damages.

It was a test I'd been expecting all my journalistic life. But the suit came out of the blue on an article 9 months old. So I raced down to the office to find my notes and assure myself that my story was solid. Reassure myself, to tell the truth.

The case involved a man I'd called a "charity entrepreneur." He'd devised a plan to deliver Christmas goodies to U.S. troops caught in the Middle East during the 1990–91 build-up for the Persian Gulf War. My story disputed his claim that the contents of his "GI Gift Pac" cost $15 and questioned his ability to deliver them to hundreds of thousands of soldiers by Christmas, as his ads promised donors.

The story noted that in a prior campaign to fight narcotics, he'd spent nearly all the money he raised on direct mail seeking more donations. The story even questioned his inclusion of dates from California in food caches bound for the Persian Gulf, date capital of the world.

Because the piece had run widely in the midst of his nationwide fundraising effort for the Gift Pac, there was no question that he'd been damaged by it. So the story's truth was my only defense.

In short order I found notes justifying virtually all of the 26 items in the article to which he'd taken offense. I told my bureau chief that. He assured me Knight Ridder would foot all legal bills, including an independent lawyer for me if I ever decided Knight Ridder's interests conflicted with my own.

The defense was neither easy nor efficient, however. Private investigators recommended by Knight Ridder's lawyers turned up nothing for $25,000. That I had supportive notes proved a mixed blessing and not just because I had to read my own handwriting. I also had to reconstruct from them the thinking—and to justify the wording—of each disputed point in the article. Because my notebooks (and tapes) were subject to discovery by the other side, I also had to justify omitting what they showed I'd left out.

This process raised lots of editorial questions unconsidered prior to publication. For example, because an entrepreneur intends to make a profit, didn't the term "charity entrepreneur" imply fraudulence? When I wrote that he was charging "hefty markups" on his wholesale costs, what exactly did I mean by "hefty"? And—a classic question—when I wrote that his costs "appear to be under $10," to whom did they so appear?

More than anything else, this hedged style ("appear to be") helped my case. That's because the plaintiff essentially conceded that my facts were right and argued that my consistently negative interpretation of them did the damage. His problem was that a vengeful writer wouldn't have hedged allegations or, as the story had done, quoted a staunch supporter at some length.

Nonetheless, over several months I spent about a third of my reporting life at my law firm's overheated offices. The task was turning a story that had raised questions about a charity into something else: an unassailable argument that it was a swindle. I was prepping for the first deposition of my life.

I found it unnerving to have my every "yeah" and "er" recorded but heeded the advice of counsel to pause long after every question from the plaintiff's lawyer, then answer concisely only the question asked. Instead of sputtering at insinuations, for example, I learned to defuse them. ("You mean you've never taken a course in journalistic ethics?" ... "No.")

Just as heart bypass survivors forget their postoperative pain, I've forgotten the 20 months of acute professional anxiety I endured before a three-judge court of appeals decided in our favor. The judges did it with these sweet words: "The truth may sting, but it is the truth nonetheless."

My advice to future libel defendants:

1. To the most obvious question, whether to keep notes or destroy them, there's no right answer. Sometimes

Continued

they help, sometimes not. Whatever you decide, be consistent.

2. The tougher the story, the more generous a reporter should be in allowing its target to have his or her say.

3. Reporting findings is more useful to readers than reporting conclusions. Distinguishing between findings and conclusions is libel insurance.

4. Check all numbers. Check them again. Then get someone else to check them.

5. After an investigation's target declines comment, but well before you publish, send him or her a list of the questions you'd intended to ask. It may not yield an interview or new information, but it's impressive evidence of a reporter's intent to be fair. Follow up with a phone call and report the target's response to the effort.

6. Do some reporting on your sources' motives.

7. Listen to your inner voice that asks incessantly: Is what I'm writing fair?

ONLINE LIBEL

STAY ON TOP OF ONLINE LEGAL ISSUES WITH THE ELECTRONIC FRONTIER FOUNDATION AT http://www.eff.org/

Three decades ago, the case of *The New York Times vs. Sullivan* was a watershed event in the history of press freedom. For the first time, the nation's highest court gave the press an extra measure of protection against public officials suing for libel. But how, legal observers wonder, will that precedent survive on the Internet, where anyone has the potential to be a publisher and a public figure?

Until now there have been few court cases involving libel on the Internet. One of the first and most closely watched cases illustrates the legal and journalistic challenges posed by new media. The case, which was pending in 1999, is *Blumenthal vs. Drudge*. It pits a former journalist and White House aide named Sidney Blumenthal against Matt Drudge, a controversial gossip columnist who maintains a Web site called the Drudge Report. By early 1999, the only significant decision has been that America Online, which posted Drudge's column on its Web site and paid him a monthly royalty fee, isn't liable for the content. Courts will have to address such questions as: In a world where anyone with a modem and a computer can be an online publisher, what is a journalist, and what sets a journalist apart from what some call "cyberspace citizens"?

PRIVACY

Samuel Warren and Louis Brandeis were upset. The media had been writing scandalous stories about the private lives of their friends. New technology and competitive pressures meant that people were losing their right to be left alone. "Instantaneous photographs and newspaper enterprise have invaded the sacred precincts of private and domestic life," the two lawyers complained in a law review article, "and numerous mechanical devices threaten to make good the prediction that 'what is whispered in the closet shall be proclaimed from the housetops.'"

That's how bad things had become in the '90s. Not the 1990s, the decade of Bill Clinton, Gennifer Flowers and Monica Lewinsky, Linda Tripp and Kenneth Starr. The 1890s.

The article that Warren and Brandeis wrote in 1890 proposed a new kind of legal theory that would allow people to sue the media for invading their privacy. **Privacy**, essentially, is the right to be left alone. The legal right to privacy is not nearly as clear as the legal right to reputation. As a result, it's harder to assess.

Essentially, a journalist invades privacy by:

1. **TRESPASSING OR OTHERWISE INTRUDING ON PEOPLE, PHYSICALLY OR OTHERWISE, IN A PLACE WHERE THEY HAVE A REASONABLE EXPECTATION OF PRIVACY.** Journalists are free to interview or photograph people in public places, such as a city street, park or city hall meeting room. But a press pass isn't a license to trespass on private property or climb a tree to see over a fence and photograph inside of a house.

2. **PUBLISHING TRUTHFUL BUT EMBARRASSING PRIVATE FACTS.** In one case, a reporter was held liable when a woman who had been in a car accident sued because the reporter disclosed she was living with a man who wasn't her husband. The defense to a **private facts** claim is that the information is newsworthy. The court said that the fact of her living arrangement wasn't pertinent to the story.

3. **PUBLISHING A STORY THAT PLACES PEOPLE IN A "FALSE LIGHT" BY PRINTING OR SHOWING THEM ACTING IN AN INACCURATE WAY THAT REASONABLE PEOPLE COULD CONSIDER OFFENSIVE.** "It isn't defamatory to say that someone is rich under most circumstances," Kirtley of the Reporters Committee notes. "But if you said it about Mother Theresa, while she was still alive, that might be false light." This claim has been rejected by many courts. One Indiana judge called it "libel lite."

4. **APPROPRIATING A PERSON'S NAME OR LIKENESS FOR TRADE PURPOSES.** This involves using a person's name or image to promote a product or service. Because news coverage provides information rather than promotion this doesn't usually apply to journalists.

LEARN THE CURRENT STATUS OF PRIVACY ISSUES IN "THE PRIVACY PARADOX" ONLINE AT http://www.rcfp.org/pp.html

Remember: Consent is a defense to most types of invasion of privacy. If a person waives the right to privacy by giving consent, then there can be no invasion of privacy. However, the reporter should be sure that the subject has not only consented to be interviewed, but also consented to the publishing or airing of the interview or photographs. When minors or incompetent people are involved, the consent of a parent or guardian may be necessary. Consent can be revoked by the subject.

REPORTER'S PRIVACY CHECKLIST

The Reporters Committee for Freedom of the Press advises journalists to follow these guidelines to avoid privacy lawsuits:

1. CONSENT FROM THE SUBJECT
   - Is the subject an adult?
   - If not, do you have parental consent?
   - Is the person mentally or emotionally disabled and unable to give consent? Have you obtained valid consent from a guardian or other responsible party?
   - Has that consent been revoked?
   - Is the subject currently a private or public figure? Has the person's status changed over time?

2. METHOD OF OBTAINING INFORMATION
   - Is it a public place?
   - If it is a private place, do you have permission to be on the premises and permission to interview or photograph?
   - Was the information contained in a public record? A semipublic record?

3. CONTENT
   - Would publication of the information offend community standards of decency?
   - Have the facts been embellished with information of questionable accuracy?
   - Is the information outdated and not obviously of current public interest, or has a current event revived its newsworthiness?
   - Is the information vital to the story?

A NEW TREND: REPORTORIAL CONDUCT

The First Amendment and a string of Supreme Court decisions have given journalists enormous protection over the years. Although the First Amendment prohibits any law abridging the freedom of the press, what people forget is that the First Amendment doesn't immunize journalists from being charged with and convicted of violating laws generally applied to anyone.

The First Amendment provides protection to journalists when they write tough but accurate stories, libel lawyers say, but journalists can't break the law to get a story or go someplace the public can't go—like a prison. In the past, most lawsuits against news organizations focused on libel—what was published; now the emphasis has shifted from the product to the process— how the story was reported, such as the use of hidden cameras or theft of voice mail. This is so because the courts have yet to define the First Amendment protections for newsgathering.

THE CINCINNATI ENQUIRER

An apology to Chiquita

Starting on May 3, 1998, the Enquirer published a series of articles regarding Chiquita Brands International. Many of the conclusions in these articles were based upon the contents of voice mail messages of employees of Chiquita. At the time, the Enquirer believed that the series' accusations against Chiquita were based upon what was thought to be factual information obtained in an ethical and lawful manner. Specifically, the Enquirer asserted that the voice mails were provided by "a high ranking Chiquita executive with authority over the Chiquita voice mail system."

The Enquirer has now become convinced that the above representations, accusations and conclusions are untrue and created a false and misleading impression of Chiquita's business practices. We have withdrawn the articles from continued display on the Enquirer's Internet web site and renounce the series of articles.

Information provided to the Enquirer makes it clear that not only was there never a person at Chiquita with authority to provide privileged, confidential and proprietary information, but the facts now indicate that an Enquirer employee was involved in the theft of this information in violation of the law.

The employee involved, lead reporter Mike Gallagher, has retained counsel and will not comment on his news gathering techniques. Despite his assurances to his editors prior to publication that he obtained his information in an ethical and lawful manner, we can no longer trust his word and have taken disciplinary action against him for violations of Enquirer standards. The Enquirer will continue to investigate whether others involved in the Chiquita articles also engaged in similar misconduct.

We want to send a strong message that deception and unlawful conduct has no place in legitimate news reporting at the Enquirer.

We apologize to Chiquita and its employees for this unethical and unlawful conduct and for the untrue conclusions in the Chiquita series of articles.

The Cincinnati Enquirer

Harry M. Whipple,
publisher

Lawrence K. Beaupre,
editor

The Cincinnati Enquirer published this extraordinary apology on the front page of its newspaper and online site. The paper apologized for "untrue conclusions" about the conduct of Chiquita Brands, but did not say its story was fabricated.

A string of high profile cases in the 1990s made it clear that reportorial conduct—how reporters get a story—is as important an issue as the story they publish. Plaintiffs are using laws that govern individual behavior of individuals and businesses, not just libel and defamation laws.

In a 1998 case, Chiquita Brands, the world's largest banana producer, accused a *Cincinnati Enquirer* reporter of stealing the voice mail of high level executives after the newspaper published a series questioning the firm's Central American business dealings, including accusations of bribery in Colombia, pesticide practices that endangered workers' health and the use of Chiquita ships to smuggle cocaine.

READ "BITTER FRUIT," *AMERICAN JOURNALISM REVIEW*'s ACCOUNT OF THE CHIQUITA CASE ONLINE AT http://ajr.news link.org/ ajrlisasept98a. html

Chiquita challenged the series, but even without its taking legal action against the paper, the *Enquirer* published a front-page apology that ran for three days, reportedly paid the company $10 million and fired the reporter who later pleaded guilty to illegally breaking into the company's voice-mail system. The reporter was trying to expose alleged wrongdoing on the part of the company, and although the newspaper apologized for what it called "untrue" conclusions in the Chiquita series and repudiated the way the story was gathered, it has not accused the reporter of fabricating the story.

The moral for reporters, says Kathy Pellegrino, an editor-turned-newsroom lawyer for the Fort Lauderdale *Sun-Sentinel,* is clear: Reporters should never steal to get a story or induce someone else to steal for them.

In 1994, "Prime Time Live," the ABC newsmagazine program, lost in court after the Food Lion grocery chain accused the program of lying to get producers undercover jobs in its stores. A jury found that two producers fabricated their backgrounds to get jobs at the store to do a story about alleged unsanitary conditions at Food Lion stores. From a legal standpoint, the case demonstrates that reporters are not immune to the laws that prohibit trespassing. Actively lying, as the network producers did by falsifying their résumés and failing to disclose their affiliations with a news organization, offends people, as one of the jurors in the case said later.

Lawyers for the news media see this as a new wave of legal attack that sidesteps the traditional First Amendment free press protection and focuses on reporting practices that lead to claims of invasion of privacy and intrusion upon seclusion, inflicting emotional distress, trespass, fraud and others. Plaintiffs, such as public figures or companies that would find it difficult to prove actual malice, are instead using these novel approaches, not previously applied to newsgathering, "to do an end-run around the constitutional protections that have not been recognized for libel and invasion of privacy," says Kirtley. The Chiquita and Food Lion cases provoke concern in news circles that the trend will make news organizations less likely to tackle sensitive topics.

A century after Samuel Warren and Louis Brandeis complained about newspapers prying into the lives of the rich and famous, the media have again come under attack for invasions of privacy. The death of Princess Diana and resulting outrage over media intrusions into her life inspired efforts in Congress and state legislatures to toughen privacy laws and restrict newsgathering. The Reporters Committee offers this advice: "Members of the news media must tread ever more lightly through an expanding field of privacy land mines. Because the law can and does change over time, it is wise to check with an attorney before embarking on newsgathering or reporting that could be considered to violate an individual's right to privacy."

TAPING PHONE CALLS

Secretly taping phone calls has been "standard practice" in many newsrooms, Tom Goldstein writes in *The News at Any Cost,* a comprehensive account of ethical practices in American journalism.

Depending on the law of the state in which you are working, or calling, and on the policy of your news organization, a call may be taped without informing the other party. According to the Reporters Committee, 37 states and the District of Columbia permit people to record a conversation to which they are a party without informing the other party that they are doing so. Federal laws allow taping with the consent of one party. These laws are referred to as "one-party consent" laws, and as long as you are a party to the conversation, it is legal for you to record it.

Thirteen states require, under most circumstances, the consent of all parties to a conversation. Those states are California, Connecticut, Delaware, Florida, Illinois, Maryland, Massachusetts, Michigan, Montana, Nevada, New Hampshire, Pennsylvania and Washington. Be aware that you will sometimes hear these referred to as "two-party consent" laws. If there are two or more people involved in the conversation, all must consent to the taping.

Given the differences by state, the Reporters Committee advises caution when making an interstate call.

A case in point: Linda Tripp taped her phone calls with Monica Lewinsky, the White House intern at the center of the 1998 impeachment of President Clinton. Even though Lewinsky lived in the District of Columbia, which, like federal law, permits one-party consent, Tripp lived in Maryland, a two-party consent state. A Maryland grand jury will decide whether to indict her under that state's law. "The safest strategy is to assume that the stricter law will apply," the reporters' group says.

Legal or not, is taping phone calls ethical? I've recorded my telephone interviews for years. I don't take shorthand, and there are times I want a verbatim record of a conversation, especially if the subject is unfamiliar or the story sensitive. There's no doubt it heightens the accuracy of my story, and not only because the quotes are accurate. Taping means I have the full context of an interview.

THE REPORTERS COMMITTEE FOR FREEDOM OF THE PRESS OFFERS "CAN WE TAPE": A PRACTICAL GUIDE TO TAPING CONVERSATIONS IN THE 50 STATES AND THE DISTRICT OF COLUMBIA ONLINE AT http://www.rcfp. org/taping/index. html

Many, if not most, complaints about misquotes, I believe, stem from a person's remarks being taken out of context. As a young reporter, I often didn't inform the people I was interviewing that my tape recorder was on. I confess I was afraid that if I told them they would refuse to let me tape and that my poor note-taking skills would lead me to make a mistake. I was also worried that they might hang up or clam up or just become overly cautious. But I never felt good about it and always worried that the person on the other end would ask, "Are you taping?" It was a relief when I went to work in Florida, where it was against the law to tape without telling the other person. What I found was that people didn't care, especially after I told them the reasons: I don't take good notes, and I want to make sure my story is accurate. I now believe that, regardless of the law, you should never tape record a conversation without informing the other person and obtaining his or her consent on tape.

As in most situations involving ethics, the decision of whether to tape secretly will probably be up to you, especially in a state where one-party consent is the law. In many newsrooms no one will be peeking over your shoulder or questioning the way you gather news. Always check with your newsroom supervisor about your news organization's policy about taping telephone conversations.

Broadcasters and the Phone Rule

Anyone who broadcasts a telephone conversation without notifying the other party involved in the conversation may be fined or chastised by the Federal Communications Commission.

Under the so-called "Phone Rule," anyone who intends to broadcast a conversation or record a conversation for later broadcast with another party on the telephone must, at the beginning of the telephone call, inform the party that the conversation will be broadcast. No consent from the party is required. The fine is up to $25,000 for a single offense and no more than $250,000 for continuing violations. The Reporters Committee for Freedom of the Press notes that, in recent times, the FCC has been issuing only admonitions to first offenders.

Read the complete article by Robert Steele on hidden cameras in *Communicator* online at http://www.rtndf.org/prodev/articles/hidden.htm

Hidden Cameras

As anyone who watches network television newsmagazines such as ABC's "20/20" or NBC's "Dateline" knows, hidden cameras have become a staple of modern investigative reporting.

"The best of hidden camera reporting has exposed systemic racial discrimination, critical weaknesses in airport security, gross incompetence by law enforcement officers, and abhorrent patient care in nursing homes and hospitals," Robert Steele, the Poynter Institute's ethics director, wrote in *Communicator*, a publication of the Radio and

Television News Directors Association. "Unfortunately, those moments are outweighed by the glut of hidden camera stories focusing on small-scale consumer problems, 'gotcha' pieces and weak investigative reports that don't justify deception."

Hidden cameras aren't new. In 1928, a *New York Daily News* photographer secretly snapped a picture of a woman being executed in the electric chair. States don't allow any cameras at executions, and some states have made use of hidden cameras illegal. Today's hidden cameras shoot video and are tiny. The TV producers who taped the Food Lion video concealed their cameras in wigs. The network also chose to tape in a state, North Carolina, where hidden cameras are not prohibited by law.

But as the Reporters Committee points out in *A Practical Guide to Taping Conversations*, "The use of hidden cameras or other forms of surreptitious filming can leave journalists vulnerable to a variety of legal charges, such as trespass and intrusion."

Steele advises journalists to consider the following checklist when contemplating using hidden cameras in news-gathering:

When might it be appropriate to use deception/misrepresentation/hidden cameras in newsgathering? (You must fulfill all of the criteria to justify your actions.)

- When the information obtained is of profound importance. It must be of vital public interest, such as revealing great "system failure" at the top levels, or it must prevent profound harm to individuals.

- When all other alternatives for obtaining the same information have been exhausted.

- When the journalists involved are willing to disclose the nature of the deception and the reason for it.

- When the individuals involved and their news organization apply excellence, through outstanding craftsmanship as well as the commitment of time and funding needed to pursue the story fully.

- When the harm prevented by the information revealed through deception outweighs any harm caused by the act of deception.

- When the journalists involved have conducted a meaningful, collaborative and deliberative decision-making process on the ethical and legal issues.

Criteria that do not justify deception:

- Winning a prize.
- Beating the competition.
- Getting the story with less expense of time and resources.
- Doing it because "others already did it."
- The subjects of the story are themselves unethical.

COPYRIGHT AND THE JOURNALIST

ON ITS WEB SITE, KLAS, THE CBS AFFILIATE IN LAS VEGAS, NEV., PROVIDES A GUIDE TO COPYRIGHT WRITTEN IN "READABLE ENGLISH." READ THE FULL VERSION AT http://Klas. cbsnow.com. AN EXCERPT APPEARS BESIDE THIS BOX:

"Assume that everything on the site is copyrighted [read: it's not yours] unless we say otherwise. So you can't use the stuff except how we say you can on this page or anywhere else on the site without our written permission. In fact, even if we wanted to, the lawyers are likely to veto any deal; so, it's better you don't even ask! There's also a lot of trademarks, logos and service marks on the site, including ones like CBS and the CBS Eye logo that either we own or we're using with someone else's permission. So don't think you have any kind of license or right to use them, because you don't, and we're not about to give you one."

Copyright, the right to own and control the copying of one's creative work, is one of America's basic freedoms, contained in the U.S. Constitution:

> The Congress shall have power ... To promote the progress of science and useful arts, by securing for limited times to authors and inventors the exclusive right to their respective writings and discoveries;
>
> —ARTICLE I, SECTION 8.8

■

The Founding Fathers recognized the importance of copyright to preserve the free flow of ideas and creativity. The law has long recognized another important right: to communicate, teach, comment or criticize creative works. That doctrine, embodied in the copyright act as "fair use," gives reporters, critics, teachers and others the right to copy limited portions of copyrighted materials without obtaining permission for noncommercial purposes. Note the word "limited."

Like so many things today copyright law is in flux because of the Internet, which has revolutionized the ability to make and distribute copies. Despite these technological advances, the basics of copyright protection have not changed. Just because you have the technology to copy doesn't mean you have the legal right to do so.

According to the U.S. Copyright Office, copyright is a form of protection provided by the laws of the United States to the authors of "original works of authorship" including literary, dramatic, musical, artistic and certain other intellectual works. This protection is available to both published and unpublished works. Copyright, which is a federal law, generally gives the owner of copyright the exclusive right to do and to authorize others to do the following:

- To reproduce the copyrighted work in copies or phonorecords.
- To prepare derivative works based upon the copyrighted work.

- To distribute copies or phonorecords of the copyrighted work to the public by sale or other transfer of ownership, or by rental, lease or lending.

- To perform the copyrighted work publicly, in the case of literary, musical, dramatic and choreographic works, pantomimes and motion pictures and other audio-visual works.

- To display the copyrighted work publicly, in the case of literary, musical, dramatic and choreographic works, pantomimes, and pictorial, graphic or sculptural works, including the individual images of a motion picture or other audio-visual work.

- In the case of sound recordings, to perform the work publicly by means of a digital audio transmission.

How to Avoid Copyright Infringement

As with many legal and ethical issues, the simplest strategy to avoid infringing on someone's copyright may be to ask how you would feel if it were your story or photograph or video that someone else was using without your permission.

The Reporters Committee for Freedom of the Press offers journalists these specific guidelines to avoid copyright infringement:

> READ JOURNALIST JAMES GLEICK'S TAKE ON COPYRIGHT ON THE INTERNET, ONLINE AT http://around.com/copyright.html

- The best way to avoid violating a copyright is simply to obtain the author's permission before using that person's expressions of ideas or facts. If you cannot get the author's permission, restate the ideas in your own words.

- Avoid using large segments of someone else's expression verbatim—this could be a blatant copyright infringement. The radio news announcer who broadcasts stories from the local newspaper word for word is asking to be sued.

- Not every unauthorized use of a copyrighted work is a copyright infringement. The statute considers some uses to be "fair uses," such as news reporting, commentary, criticism, research, teaching and scholarship. The Supreme Court recently found that the commercial parody of the classic rock 'n' roll song "Oh, Pretty Woman" by the rap group 2 Live Crew may be protected as a "fair use" under the copyright law.

- However, no use is presumptively "fair." Courts examine four factors in deciding whether a specific use is a "fair use":

1. THE PURPOSE AND CHARACTER OF THE USE, including whether the use is commercial or of a nonprofit, educational nature.

2. THE NATURE OF THE COPYRIGHTED WORK. Uses of expressive, as opposed to factual, works are less likely to be considered fair uses, as are uses of unpublished works.

3. **The amount and substantiality of the portion used in relation to the copyrighted work as a whole.** Here the court will consider the qualitative as well as the quantitative use. If the user excerpts 200 words from a 10,000-word book, but those 200 words constitute the heart of the book, this may not qualify as "fair use."

4. **The effect of the use upon the potential market for or value of the copyrighted work.** If the challenged use adversely affects the potential market for the copyrighted work, the use is not fair.

Ethical Decision Making

"Journalists travel through moral mine fields," my Poynter colleagues Bob Steele and Paul Pohlman have written. "Intense deadlines and competitive fervor weigh on reporters and photojournalists. ... Complex issues, convoluted information, and contradictory facts cloud logic, erode common sense and undermine good intentions. Yet many journalists admit to being unprepared and uncomfortable about making the ethical decisions that will improve their chances for getting through the mine field."

The results can be troubling and harmful for journalists and the public we serve. There have been many examples of unethical behavior by journalists, but 1998 was an especially bad year:

- Stephen Glass, a writer for *The New Republic,* was fired for fabricating stories.

- Patricia Smith, a columnist for *The Boston Globe,* resigned after admitting to making up people and quotes in her columns. Mike Barnicle, another *Globe* columnist, was forced to resign for fabrications in a column.

- CNN and *Time* were forced to retract a series alleging American military use of nerve gas during the Vietnam War.

- *The Cincinnati Enquirer* renounced a hard-hitting series on the multinational Chiquita Brands after one of its reporters stole voice-mail messages from the company.

In his book *The News at Any Cost,* Tom Goldstein, a former reporter for *The New York Times* and dean of the Columbia Graduate School of Journalism, quotes from a student essay written in the early 1980s at the University of Florida: "If you're too ethical and nice, you're never going to get anywhere in journalism, in my opinion. ... As a journalist you do whatever you have to for a story. That's your job."

Unfortunately, many reporters and editors believe that—whether or not they would admit it as openly as the student did. Journalists historically have been held in low esteem by the public. That comes with the territory.

Every day journalists report news that people don't like, and those people can confuse the message with the messenger.

Is it proper for reporters to pretend to be what they are not to get a story—posing as bar owners, for instance, to expose graft and corruption involving city officials? Should a television station broadcast details of an adoption because the child is the daughter of a convicted murderer and the man who wants to adopt her is the prosecutor who sent the child's mother to prison? If a newspaper has a policy against using unnamed sources, would it be ethical to abandon it in the case of a major story, especially if a competitor that has no such restrictions is scoring major scoops?

Ethical decision making is a craft and a skill. Good ethical decision making often means choosing alternatives that allow you to minimize harm and maximize truthtelling. Practice front-end ethics: What are the potential potholes? What are the potential land mines? Ask yourself: What do readers need to know, and when do they need to know it?

DOING ETHICS:

ASK GOOD

QUESTIONS TO

MAKE GOOD

ETHICAL

DECISIONS

Ethical decision making is a skill, just like reporting and writing and critical thinking. Front-end work is just as important in ethics as it is in reporting and writing a story. Bob Steele advises reporters to ask a series of questions when faced with an ethical dilemma:

1. What do I know? What do I need to know?
2. What is my journalistic purpose?
3. What are my ethical concerns?
4. What organizational policies and professional guidelines should I consider?
5. How can I include other people, with different perspectives and diverse ideas, in the decision-making process?
6. Who are the stakeholders—those affected by my decision? What are their motivations? Which are legitimate?
7. What if the roles were reversed? How would I feel if I were in the shoes of one of the stakeholders?
8. What are the possible consequences of my actions? Short term? Long term?
9. What are my alternatives to maximize my truthtelling responsibility and minimize harm?
10. Can I clearly and fully justify my thinking and my decision? To my colleagues? To the stakeholders? To the public?

READ MORE

OF BOB STEELE'S

ARTICLES ON

JOURNALISM ETHICS,

ONLINE AT

http://www.
poynter.org/
faculty/fac_rs.htm

GUIDING
PRINCIPLES
FOR THE
JOURNALIST

The news presents too many different ethical challenges for them to be covered by a blanket set of rules. It's more important, the authors of *Doing Ethics in Journalism* say, that journalists be guided by a set of principles that can aid them in making decisions. The principles are:

1. **SEEK TRUTH AND REPORT IT AS FULLY AS POSSIBLE.**

   ■ Inform yourself continuously so you in turn can inform, engage and educate the public in a clear and compelling way on significant issues.

   ■ Be honest, fair and courageous in gathering, reporting and interpreting accurate information.

   ■ Give voice to the voiceless.

   ■ Hold the powerful accountable.

2. **ACT INDEPENDENTLY.**

   ■ Guard vigorously the essential stewardship role a free press plays in an open society.

   ■ Seek out and disseminate competing perspectives without being unduly influenced by those who would use their power or position counter to the public interest.

   ■ Remain free of associations and activities that may compromise your integrity or damage your credibility.

   ■ Recognize that good ethical decisions require individual responsibility enriched by collaborative efforts.

3. **MINIMIZE HARM.**

   ■ Be compassionate for those affected by your actions.

   ■ Treat sources, subjects and colleagues as human beings deserving of respect, not merely as means to your journalistic ends.

   ■ Recognize that gathering and reporting information may cause harm or discomfort, but balance those negatives by choosing alternatives that maximize your goal of truthtelling.

PRIVACY CHECKLIST

Earlier in the chapter, you learned about the legal issues surrounding the right to privacy. The following list, which appears in *Doing Ethics in Journalism,* is designed to help journalists meet the challenge "to be courageous in seeking and reporting information, while being compassionate to those who are being covered."

■ How important is the information I am seeking? Does the public have a right to know? A need to know? Merely a desire to know?

■ What level of protection do individuals involved in the story deserve? How much harm might they receive? Are they involved in the news event by choice, or by happenstance?

■ How would I feel if I were being subjected to the same scrutiny?

- Do I know the facts of the story well enough? What else do I need to know?

- What can I do to minimize the privacy invasion and the harm? Can I broaden the focus of the story, thereby minimizing harm to a select few?

- Can I postpone the story without significantly jeopardizing information to the public?

- Do I need to include in the decision making other individuals to gain more perspective?

- Should I be focusing more on the system failure or the big issue picture, as opposed to focusing intensely on individuals?

- Can I clearly and fully justify my thinking and decision? To those directly affected? To the public?

CONFLICT OF INTEREST

For years, reporters covering the Tampa Bay Buccaneers bellied up to a buffet at the Florida stadium on game days. The team provided the food as a convenience to reporters who had to be at the game hours before it began and who were usually too busy watching the game and writing about it afterward to get anything to eat. But that all changed when Robert Haiman, executive editor of the *St. Petersburg Times*, decided the buffet was a conflict of interest for his paper's reporters. The *Times*, he said, could no longer accept the free food. Sportswriters argued that the buffet was the only way they could get any food during the 12-hour shift they worked on the day of a game. It was a convenience. Besides, they couldn't be bought off for the price of a sandwich and some potato salad. Haiman resolved the issue by estimating the cost of meals consumed by the paper's sportswriters and writing a check to the team. In the following section, Haiman, president emeritus and distinguished editor in residence at The Poynter Institute, provides necessary historical background for any discussion of journalism ethics.

ETHICS IN AMERICAN NEWSROOMS: A BRIEF HISTORY BY ROBERT HAIMAN

The notion of the journalist as an honest, ethical person, an impartial observer who brings to his or her assignment no bias other than to report an event or situation honestly, fully and fairly, is actually a relatively new idea. In fact, it dates back in the United States no more than 40 or 50 years.

The early U.S. papers were extremely partisan, starting with those edited by Ben Franklin, Tom Paine and others.

All through the 19th and early 20th centuries, the same pattern remained. If

Continued

you read Col. McCormick's *Chicago Tribune*, you knew the paper was going to be laced with his ideology, which was nationalistic, chauvinistic, isolationist, America-first, Republican and very antiunion. The same could be said for the old *Los Angeles Times* with an additional twist of California Republicanism, which made it anti-Mexican and anti-Asian. The same could be said for the old Hearst papers, with William Randolph Hearst generally credited with starting the Spanish–American War because he thought it would help sell papers. And the same for Joe Pulitzer's papers, which were virulently anticapitalist and proworker.

Moreover, in addition to being a time of blatantly partisan papers, it also was a time of highly sensational newspapers of unsavory techniques and of fairly corrupt reporters who probably deserved the lowlife reputation most of them had.

It was not uncommon, in fact it was close to general practice, for reporters then to accept bribes to publish or not publish something, for reporters to write nice things about their friends and to slam their enemies or the enemies of the paper.

Publishers in their way encouraged reporters to take free booze, clothes, shoes, watches, pens, train tickets and cash—by paying such miserable salaries.

A story is told about the Chicago lawyer visiting his friend the publisher in the publisher's office the week before Christmas and seeing cops delivering turkeys and bottles of booze right to the desks of reporters in the newsroom. The food and booze were being sent to the reporters by the mayor.

The lawyer said to the publisher, "Look, that isn't right; these reporters cover the mayor for your newspaper, and look at all the loot they are taking from him."

The publisher, according to the story, shrugged and said, "Hey, with what I'm paying them ... what choice do they have?"

So the reporters took the loot, and the publishers were no better, and in fact, worse. We tend to think of the Teapot Dome affair as a scandal of the Congress and of the Interior Department. But one of the key players was Fred Bonfils, publisher of the *Denver Post*.

When Gov. James Cox of Ohio, owner of the *Dayton Daily News* and later the *Atlanta Constitution*, was campaigning for the presidency, he shamelessly used his papers to support his campaign.

The Hobby family used its Houston paper the same way in Texas, and it's pretty clear that if it were not for the *Los Angeles Times* there would have been no Richard Nixon. It got to the point where reporters, and their papers, all over the country were on the take one way or another.

It got so bad that finally some publishers and editors decided to do something about it.

And so the American Society of Newspaper Editors began to write its first code of ethics in 1922. Sigma Delta Chi wrote its first code in 1923. ASNE rewrote its code in 1949. Associated Press Managing Editors (APME) started to work on its code in 1960. And there has been a great flurry of activity in the areas of prescribing ethics for journalists and avoiding conflicts of interests.

Some of the earliest motivation actually was quite commercial, as opposed to moral, in nature. Many publishers were heard to say:

"If people think we are liars, bums, drunks and crooks, they won't believe our newspapers, and that could be bad for business."

But soon at least some editors and a few publishers were beginning to try to take some higher ground, saying:

"Look, we in the newspaper business are constantly blowing the whistle on those in politics, government, business, law, education, medicine and other establishments for their conflicts of interest. So isn't it time that we take a searching look at our own ethical standards and clean up our own act? Moreover, isn't it time for us to start worrying about appearances of conflict as well as actual conflicts?"

From that point we began to enter what I'd call the "modern era" of newsroom ethics, an era in which many editors and other journalists began to work hard at transforming the old journalist with his free booze, free travel, many political entanglements and lax standards into a modern professional who was better trained, much better educated, much more highly paid, nonpartisan and ethical, someone who had a fairly firm base from which to say: I am an honest professional who does an honest job. I am not on the take, so you can believe what I say.

That is a foreshortened, rather simplified and quick tour of where we have been. It's also fair to say that the reform spirit has not found its way into every corner and every newsroom. There are still some abuses, and I hope you do not confront them because it is no fun when you do.

I came into the business thinking that there really was no need for editors and publishers to spell out what was ethical behavior for their staffs. I assumed in my youth and ignorance that it was a basic matter of right and wrong, that it was something you learned by the third grade from your parents, or in religious school, like "thou shalt not steal." I agreed in those days with a famous journalist named Penn Kimball, who once wrote about ethics codes: "We don't need to write any of this stuff down. It is a matter of professionalism. And professionalization is a natural human process, a feeling that comes over a person when he behaves in concert with his conscience."

But like most young editors and other young journalists, I was in for a rude awakening and a loss of innocence.

I became managing editor of the *St. Petersburg Times* in May 1966, just a day before my 30th birthday. The first month I was on the job, I had to fire a veteran reporter because he took a bottle of Scotch to keep out of the paper the name of a lawyer friend who had been arrested for drunken driving.

The next month, I was faced with one of the most prominent individuals in town offering to pay our society columnist a $50 monthly retainer to make sure his wife's parties were mentioned in the society column.

In the next year we discovered that the outdoors editor had been given free use of a fishing boat and an outboard motor for a whole year by a boat dealer.

And we had to fire a real estate writer because we discovered he was buying land on speculation in a redevelopment area about which he was writing.

And then we had to jump hard on a city hall reporter who had bought stock in a garbage incinerator company when the city was thinking about buying a multimillion-dollar incinerator from that company, and he was writing lots of stories about it.

And this—remember—was happening at the *St. Petersburg Times,* supposedly one of the most honest and ethical papers in the country!

So I had my rude awakening—and my loss of innocence. That notwithstanding, I still have some problems with omnibus codes, which try to cover every nit and jot of how a journalist should live. But I have come to believe that management does have an obligation to set some basic standards for those of us who work in a business where credibility really is all we have to sell.

FABRICATION: THE LEGEND
ON THE LICENSE

Ian Restil, a 15-year-old computer hacker who looks like an even more adolescent version of Bill Gates, is throwing a tantrum. "I want more money. I want a Miata. I want a trip to Disney World. I want *X-Man* comic [book] number one. I want a lifetime subscription to *Playboy,* and throw in *Penthouse.* Show me the money! Show me the money!" Over and over again, the boy, who is wearing a frayed Cal Ripken Jr. T-shirt, is shouting his demands. Across the table, executives from a California software firm called Jukt Micronics are listening—and trying ever so delicately to oblige. "Excuse me, sir," one of the suits says, tentatively, to the pimply teen-ager. "Excuse me. Pardon me for interrupting you, sir. We can arrange more money for you. ...."

The New Republic

Great lead, huh? Vivid, dramatic, rich with detail. It was written by Stephen Glass, who crafted the riveting scene of the youthful hacker Ian Restil's demands from executives at Jukt Micronics, in an article titled "Hack Haven" published on May 18, 1998, in *The New Republic* magazine.

There's just one problem. It never happened. When the article first came out, it struck a skeptical chord among staffers at Forbes Digital Tool, the Web site for *Fortune Magazine.* When they couldn't find any trace of either the characters, companies or government agencies mentioned in Glass' article, they contacted *The New Republic,* which launched its own probe.

"Hack Heaven," the New Republic's editors said later in a note to the magazine's readers, "was not the product of keen observation or intrepid reporting. The entire article was made up out of whole cloth."

In a follow-up story, *Washington Post* media critic Howard Kurtz quoted friends who painted a portrait of Glass as a young, ambitious writer who had overextended himself with free-lance assignments. Others, such as Scott Rosenberg, a columnist for the online magazine *Salon,* were less understanding:

"I can't say I feel much sympathy for poor Glass and his over-booked assignments for high-paying or prestigious publications like *Rolling Stone, Harper's* and *The New York Times Magazine*—where editors presumably fell in love with his great lead paragraphs. Fabricating stories for maximum 'juiciness' is a loathsome enterprise," Rosenberg wrote. "Beyond bamboozling the public, it also devalues the work of more diligent writers who actually depend on mundane reporting for their stories—but whose articles, forced to conform to the less-than-cinematic nature of reality, may come off as pallid next to such feverish concoctions."

When it's discovered, fabrication usually costs the writer his or her job and, in some cases, a career. In 1981, Janet Cooke, a young reporter for *The Washington Post,* was awarded the Pulitzer Prize for her graphic story, "Jimmy's World," which explored the life of an 8-year-old heroin addict. The paper was forced to return the prize when it was discovered that Cooke had invented the child, along with various facts on her own résumé. Not the first example of fabrication in the history of journalism, the incident still sparked a firestorm of criticism and soul-searching in the newspaper business. It also ended the career of a promising young writer.

But all journalists pay a price if readers wonder whether or not "this story is made up."

In May 1998, *The New Republic* fired Glass from his job as associate editor and began a search of previous stories it published by Glass that turned up numerous other fabrications. Of the 41 articles the magazine had published under his byline in the last few years, he had fabricated characters and quotes in 27. A string of other magazines that had him under free-lance contract also cut him loose.

The following month, *The Boston Globe* reported that it had asked for and received the resignation of one of its metro columnists, Patricia Smith, after she admitted fabricating people and quotations in four of her columns. An investigation by the newspaper later found more than 20 columns for which the paper's editors couldn't document the identities of individuals mentioned.

Earlier that year, Smith's work had been honored with the Distinguished Writing Award for commentary/column writing by the American Society of Newspaper Editors. She was also a finalist for the Pulitzer Prize and had won a national reputation as a powerful poet, writer and role model for writers of every kind. Subsequently, the *Globe* asked ASNE to rescind the award, and the editors' association agreed. "There is no place in journalism for fabrication of any kind," the society board said in a statement.

And just when it looked like things couldn't have gotten worse, *Globe* columnist Mike Barnicle was forced to resign when evidence pointed to his fabrication of people and events in at least one column.

In a 1980 essay, John Hersey, the reporter and novelist—his nonfiction classic *Hiroshima* is a skillful example of narrative reconstruction—drew an obvious but important distinction between journalism and fiction. "There is one sacred rule of journalism," Hersey said. "The writer must not invent. The legend on the license must read: NONE OF THIS WAS MADE UP."

Journalists who want to invent characters, dialogue or scenes can always write screenplays, short stories, novels or, in the case of Patricia Smith, compelling poetry. Those who choose journalism must always remember—and live by—what Hersey called "the legend on the license." When they ignore it, they betray not only themselves but also their readers, every other journalist and anyone who admires the power of journalism to inform, educate and inspire. If you choose journalism, remember: Don't make things up.

If there is a profile of the kind of writer who fabricates, it's an ambitious and desperate, often, but not always young reporter, anxious to succeed and often in over his or her head. If you're tempted to fudge a quote, to put a comment into an unnamed source's mouth for whatever reason—you procrastinated, you're hung over, you stayed up too late the night before—there is another option. Tell your editor you can't deliver the story. You may suffer consequences, but it's doubtful they will be as dire as those experienced by Mike Barnicle, Patricia Smith, Janet Cooke and Stephen Glass.

"As anyone who has ever touched a newspaper knows, that's one of the cardinal sins of journalism: Thou shall not fabricate. No exceptions. No excuses."

Those are Patricia Smith's words, written in her final column for *The Boston Globe*.

As a reporter who has written dozens of narrative reconstructions for newspapers and magazines, most recently in a 1992 cover story for *The Washington Post Magazine,* as a writer who also publishes fiction, and lastly and perhaps most importantly, as a reader, I have had numerous troubling conversations with editors and fellow writers, but mostly with myself, about the validity and accuracy of passages that attempt to reconstruct reality. "Reconstruction" was the term we used at *The Providence Journal* in the 1980s to describe stories that tried to re-create newsworthy and usually dramatic events for our readers. The story "Having a Baby" in Chapter 5 is an example of a narrative reconstruction.

Reconstructions trouble me when I am trying to write them because I know they depend on reporting that must go beyond the superficial stenography of quoting what official sources tell reporters and instead require multiple interviews, a search for independent verification and, above all, a consuming, sometimes obsessive, passion for accuracy.

They trouble me when I read one because I am full of questions: Wow, what a scene! I wonder how the writer got that? I can remember as a young writer being awestruck by *New Yorker* pieces that quoted people for columns at a time. As someone with no shorthand skills, I wondered how they got these long quotes, especially in situations where a tape recorder would seem unlikely. It pained me considerably in recent years when I discovered to my chagrin that *The New Yorker*'s standards of proof didn't seem as high as those of my newspaper editors.

But what is blurry, or at least not as clear to writers and their editors, is how you achieve that standard and still write prose that is dramatic, vivid, detailed, powerful, compelling and as true as humanly possible. That's where the rigor of journalistic and intellectual honesty comes in.

THE ETHICS OF RECONSTRUCTION

STANDARDS OF FACTUAL ACCURACY AND CONTEXTUAL AUTHENTICITY

To help reporters maintain accuracy and authenticity when reconstructing narratives, Bob Steele, ethics director at The Poynter Institute, and I formulated the following list of standards after the 1998 firings, for fabricating stories, of Stephen Glass, Patricia Smith and Mike Barnicle.

These standards are all about craft. They focus on the demands of rigorous reporting and vivid writing as well as the need for sound ethical decision making. They are not intended to inhibit dramatic storytelling but rather to reflect the need for writers and editors to meet a high threshold of accuracy and authenticity that serves the story and its readers. Of course, these standards can and should be applied to any story.

QUESTIONS TO ASK WHEN WRITING AND EDITING A NARRATIVE THAT RECONSTRUCTS EVENTS

- How do I know that what I have presented really happened the way I say it did?
- Is it true?
- According to whom?
- Do I not only have the facts right but also the right facts?
- How complete is my reconstruction?
- Is it based on one source, two or several?
- Have I tested it against the memory of other participants?
- Have I sought independent verification from documentary sources, such as historical accounts or public records? For example, my source describes a "dark and stormy night." Did I call the National Weather Service and get the weather report for that date?
- Do I have a high level of confidence in my sources?
- Could I have been fooled by an unreliable source or a source with a faulty memory or an ax to grind?
- Is my purpose legitimate? Am I trying to convey the reality of an event for my readers or simply trying to entertain or impress people with my writing ability?
- Does lack of attribution—a hallmark of reconstruction—diminish credibility?
- Does a reconstruction need an editor's note to help readers understand how the story was reported and sourced?
- Am I willing—and able—to fully disclose and explain my method to my editor? to my readers?

WHERE CREDIT IS DUE:
AVOIDING PLAGIARISM

As college students you already are aware of the seriousness of plagiarizing someone's work. You know the penalty—a failing grade, possible expulsion. In journalism, the rules are similarly strict.

DEFINITION OF ACADEMIC DISHONESTY

One of the clearest definitions of academic dishonesty is the one that puts journalism students on notice at Northwestern's Medill School of Journalism:

> The profession of journalism values the gathering of accurate information from a variety of sources and the presenting of such information in a way that clearly indicates its sources. The most profound transgressions of journalistic standards are fabricating information or sources, or representing the words or pictures of others as one's own. The profession traditionally responds to such transgressions with dispatch and severity.

> The following conduct violates the school's code of academic integrity:
> 1. **FABRICATION.** Fabrication consists of the intentional falsification or invention of information, data, quotations, or sources in an academic exercise or in a journalistic presentation. Fabrication also includes, but is not limited to, misattributing information or presenting information in an assignment that was not gathered in accordance with the course syllabus or other course outline.
> 2. **PLAGIARISM.** Plagiarism consists of intentionally or knowingly representing the words or ideas of another person as one's own. Plagiarism includes, but is not limited to, the knowing or intentional failure to attribute language or ideas to their original source, in the manner required by the academic discipline (such as by quotation marks, attribution in the text, and footnote citations in an academic exercise) or in the manner required by journalism practice (such as by quotation marks and attribution in a journalistic presentation).

Plagiarism is taking someone else's words or ideas and passing them off as your own. The first plagiarists stole not words but rather human beings. Using a net, called a "plaga," they were thieves who made off with another's child or slave. Now the word means the theft of someone's writing.

It's easier than ever to plagiarize. Before computers and scanners, you had to copy someone's words—by hand or with a typewriter. Now you can lift text verbatim by using the copy and paste functions of your word-processing software. If you're not careful when you're taking notes, you may find yourself accused of plagiarism. Like many writers caught using others' words, you will claim the defense of carelessness or sloppy note-taking. Still, you may get fired or, if you're lucky, suspended.

Plagiarism doesn't mean lifting entire stories. Michael Kramer of *Time* and his editors apologized after the writer took just a single sentence from a *Los*

Angeles Times article. Five paragraphs from *The Boston Globe,* slightly rewritten and reorganized, tripped up respected *New York Times* reporter Fox Butterfield.

Unfortunately, in too many newsrooms the punishment doesn't match the crime. "Punishment is uneven, ranging from severe to virtually nothing even for major offenses. The sin itself carries neither public humiliation nor the mark of Cain. Some editors will keep a plagiarist on staff or will knowingly hire one if talent outweighs the infraction," concluded Trudy Lieberman after a close examination of 20 newspapers and magazines for *Columbia Journalism Review.*

In her analysis, Lieberman blamed "the profession's inability to define exactly" what constitutes plagiarism. That's a big problem, especially in a deadline profession that relies on precision in the use of words. She also blamed "an evolving journalistic culture that has come to rely heavily on borrowing and quoting from other publications as a substitute for original research. Reporters also tend to use the same sources, who offer the same pithy quote or put the same spin on an issue." There's another word for that: laziness. Confronted with someone else's words, well-written or containing information or insights you don't possess, it takes little work to simply use them as your own.

READ COLUM-
BIA JOURNALISM
REVIEW'S COMPLETE
ARTICLE ON
PLAGIARISM ONLINE
AT http://www.
cjr.org/year/95/
4/plagiarize.asp

Some experts attribute plagiarism to a psychological problem. Although that may be valid, I think the real problem is that the industry has failed to address adequately the problem. In its Code of Ethics, the Society of Professional Journalists says only, "Never plagiarize." As a profession, journalism has not provided writers and editors with the specific guidelines and standards they need to avoid plagiarism. Writer Verlyn Klinkenborg of *The New York Times'* editorial board argues that attributing to texts, even those in the public domain, is the very foundation of intellectual honesty.

Part of the problem lies in the competitive nature of the news business. Reporters and editors don't want to admit they got scooped by another paper, or they don't want to—or don't know how to—conduct original research. The profession would rather perpetuate the myth of the journalist as the Lone Ranger, collecting information single-handedly and weaving a seamless web of prose without any help from anyone. The academic world has certainly had more than its share of plagiarism, but at least schools do a better job of trying to articulate what the offense entails.

The next time you **paraphrase** something for a news story you are writing, remember these words that Judy Hunter, a teacher at Grinnell College in Iowa, tells first-year students: "In a bad paraphrase, you merely substitute words, borrowing the sentence structure or the organization directly from the source. In a good paraphrase you offer your reader a wholesale revision, a new way of seeing the text you are paraphrasing. You summarize, you reconstruct, you tell your reader about what the source has said, but you do so entirely in your own words, your own voice, your own sentence structure, your own organization. As this definition reveals, paraphrase is a very difficult art."

TIPS FOR AVOIDING PLAGIARISM

- Give credit. Always attribute. Thomas Mallon, author of *Stolen Words*, an engaging history of plagiarism, says writers should follow a general rule: "If you think you should attribute it, then attribute it."

- The only way you can use a quote from another publication is if you attribute it. ("The mayor is crazy," Smith told the *Daily Blatt.*) The need for attribution should be enough to make you realize you should do the interview yourself, unless that is impossible. ("The mayor is crazy," Smith told the *Daily Blatt* the day before he disappeared.)

- Consider using a text box or online links. In some magazines, readers are pointed to source materials for the story if they wish to pursue the subject further.

- Always identify the sources of your information as you are gathering it. If you copy something verbatim be sure to put it in quotes and identify the page number and source, whether it's a book or magazine or page on the World Wide Web. If you are paraphrasing, be sure to include the source.

- Note your sources: book title, author, page number; address of a Web page (you'd be wise, given how often the link you read yesterday might be inactive today, to make a printout).

- Manage your time wisely. Plagiarism is a desperate act. Writers behind on a deadline, exhausted, anxious, may delude themselves into believing that what they're doing is nothing more than a shortcut.

- When in doubt, check with your editor.

- The bottom line: Be honest about where you got your information.

DOING THE RIGHT THING: THE COACHING WAY

- There are some rules that will tell you how you should act in certain situations. More often you will be working with loose standards and guidelines set by your organization. Perhaps most important, you can avoid the potholes and land mines by becoming collaborative in your ethical decision making. Asking good questions. Having meaningful conversations with colleagues and supervisors. These are all the hallmarks of the coaching that will lead you toward excellence and principled behavior.

- Remember that the best test to determine whether something you write or say may damage someone's reputation is to ask if you would be upset if the story were about you. If you answer "yes," then it's possible your story may be libelous, and you should check with your editor or supervisor.

- The best defenses against libel are the truth and documents that support your story. Have you attributed the information in your story to reliable sources who are willing to be identified by name? Are you relying on public records, transcripts, court papers and other "privileged" information? Have you summarized information fairly and accurately? Have you given subjects an opportunity to comment? Have you made sure that headlines, promos and artwork are fair and accurate reflections of your story?

■ Examine the methods you use to avoid plagiarism. Do you have a system for keeping track of citations and material from other sources? Do you always put quotation marks around any direct statements?

■ Could you write an editor's note explaining how and why you reported and wrote your story? What would you say if you were on the witness stand being cross-examined by a plaintiff's attorney about your reporting methods?

■ When you're troubled by something you have to do as a reporter, talk it over with someone: an editor, a colleague, a reader or viewer. Collect various opinions and use them to help you evaluate your actions.

GLOSSARY OF IMPORTANT TERMS

Copyright. The right to own and control the copying of one's creative work. The federal law that guarantees and protects those rights.

Defamation. Defamation, or "defamation of character," is spoken or written words that negatively and falsely reflect on a person's reputation. Libel and slander are two types of defamation.

Invasion of privacy. Privacy is invaded when one intentionally intrudes, physically or otherwise, on people in a place where they have a reasonable expectation of privacy.

Libel. Libel is the publication of false statements that expose someone to public hatred, contempt or ridicule in writing or pictures. Libel is written defamation, although since the emergence of radio and television, radio and television broadcasts are usually considered to be libel rather than slander.

Paraphrase. To restate what someone else wrote or said in your own words.

Plagiarism. Plagiarism consists of intentionally or knowingly representing the words or ideas of another person as one's own.

Privacy. The right to be left alone.

Private fact. Information about a person's sexual activity, health or economic status.

Privileged information. Information obtained from an official proceeding or record, such as a police report or court transcript.

Public figures. Celebrities, athletes, past and present government officials, political candidates, entertainers, sports figures and others who have prominence or power in a community or are involved in a public controversy.

Public officials. Politicians and high-ranking government personnel and public officials who have substantial responsibility for or control over the conduct of governmental affairs. Some courts have found that public school teachers and police officers are public officials.

Slander. A spoken defamation.

EXERCISES

1. *Absence of Malice* is a 1981 film, starring Sally Field and Paul Newman, about a businessman who finds that he is the innocent subject of a criminal investigation. But it's the power and ethics of the news media that are on trial in this powerful movie. Rent the film and write a 500-word essay describing your reactions to it as a reporter and consumer of news.

2. In *Make No Law: The Sullivan Case and the First Amendment*, columnist Anthony Lewis of *The New York Times* reconstructs the story behind

the 1960 libel suit that pitted *The New York Times* against a Montgomery, Ala., city official and redefined what journalists can print and say. Read the book and discuss how the practice of journalism today might be different if the Supreme Court had decided against the newspaper.

3. Visit the Web site of the Reporters Committee for Freedom of the Press at **http://www.rcfp.org** and read "The Privacy Paradox." Write a 250-word essay explaining how you as a journalist can justify disclosing information that people might want to keep private.

4. Read "The Bummer Beat: Covering Tragedy and Victims" on the Poynter Institute Web site at **http://poynter.org/research/me/et_ index.htm**. Discuss experiences you might have had as a victim or as a reporter covering a tragedy. What are the most troublesome aspects of such coverage? How can a reporter be best prepared? How would you articulate your purpose as a journalist to someone who criticized the intrusive role of the news media?

READINGS

Balough, Maggie. "Journalism's New Voices." *Quill*, July/August 1997, pp. 19–21.

Bezanson, Randall P., Gilbert Cranberg, and John Soloski. *Libel Law and the Press: Myth and Reality*. New York: Free Press, 1987.

Black, Jay. "Now That We Have the Ethics Code: How Do We Use It?" *Quill*, November 1996, pp. 24–25.

Black, Jay, and Ralph Barney. "Journalism Ethics Since Janet Cooke." *Newspaper Research Journal*, Fall 1992/Winter 1993, pp. 2–16.

Black, Jay, Bob Steele, and Ralph Barney. *Doing Ethics in Journalism: A Handbook With Case Studies*, 3rd ed. Boston: Allyn and Bacon, 1998.

Byrd, Joann. "Online Journalism Ethics: A New Frontier." *The American Editor*, November 1996, pp. 6–7.

Goldstein, Norm, ed. *The Associated Press Stylebook and Libel Manual*. Perseus Books, New York: 1998.

Goldstein, Tom. *The News at Any Cost: How Journalists Compromise Their Ethics to Shape the News*. New York: Simon and Schuster, 1985.

Lewis, Anthony. *Make No Law: The Sullivan Case and the First Amendment*. New York: Vintage, 1992.

Mallon, Thomas. *Stolen Words: Forays Into the Origins and Ravages of Plagiarism*. New York: Ticknor & Fields, 1989.

Steele, Robert. "Ethics Clinic: A 10-Step Approach to Good Decision-Making." *Quill*, March 1991, p. 36.

Steele, Robert. "Doing Ethics: How a Minneapolis Journalist Turned a Difficult Situation Into a Human Triumph." *Quill*, November/December 1992, pp. 28–30.

Steele, Robert. "ABC and Food Lion: The Ethics Question." *The Communicator*, April 1997, p. 56.

HOTLIST

LIBEL AND PRIVACY

http://www.rcfp.org

Organized in 1970, the Reporters Committee for Freedom of the Press is a nonprofit organization dedicated to providing free legal help to reporters and news organizations. Its Web site offers a wide range of publications and services on libel, privacy, freedom of information, reporter's privilege and access to court as well as searchable archives of its biweekly newsletter. The committee also offers a toll-free legal defense hotline at (800) 336-4243.

http://www.ldrc.com/

The Libel Defense Resource Center is a nonprofit information clearinghouse organized in 1980 by leading media groups to monitor and promote First Amendment rights in libel, privacy and related fields of law.

http://www.freedomforum.org/newsstand/reports/sofa/chap02.asp

"State of the First Amendment: Freedom of the Press." A study, sponsored by the Freedom Forum, written by Donna Demac, a lawyer, author and First Amendment advocate.

http://www.freedomforum.org/first/timeline97.asp

A time line of historical events, court cases and ideas that have shaped our current system of constitutional First Amendment jurisprudence.

http://www.creativeloafing.com/jewell/index.html

"Jewell Box." A multimedia presentation of the libel case involving security guard Richard Jewell, who was identified and later exonerated as a suspect in the 1996 Atlanta Olympic bombing case. It was produced by the Creative Loafing Network, which publishes alternative newspapers around the country.

ETHICS

http://www.spj.org/ethics/index.htm

The ethics site of the Society of Professional Journalists includes the full text of the SPJ ethics code as well as links to resources elsewhere on the Internet.

http://www2.hawaii.edu/~tbrislin/jethics.html/

"Web Resources for Studying Journalism Ethics," a site maintained by the Department of Journalism, University of Hawaii.

PLAGIARISM

http://cjr.org/year/95/4/plagiarize.asp

A comprehensive and disturbing report by Trudy Lieberman on how newspapers fail to discipline writers for plagiarism.

http://www.csmonitor.com/durable/1998/08/21/p3s1.htm

"Newspapers Hold Columnists to Rising Standard for Truth." Resignation of Boston writer raises debate over storytelling vs. accuracy and authenticity.

http://lcweb.loc.gov/copyright/

The U.S. Copyright Office Web site is one of the best sources for information about copyright issues, including current information about new legislation. It even has a sense of humor, with information about how to protect your sighting of Elvis. "Copyright law does not protect sightings. However, copyright law will protect your photo (or other depiction) of your sighting of Elvis. Just send it to us with a form VA application and the $20 filing fee. No one can lawfully use your photo of your sighting, although someone else may file his own photo of his sighting. Copyright law protects the original photograph, not the subject of the photograph." Sorry, Elvis.

CHAPTER

STORYTELLING ON DEADLINE

CHAPTER FOCUS

As technology shortens deadlines to seconds, the storyteller's craft is more crucial than ever.

CHAPTER LESSONS

- What's a story?
- The process of storytelling
- Enterprise: A broadcast storyteller's approach
- How to find stories in news
- Reporting for story
- Focusing in the field
- Planning on the fly
- Drafting on deadline
- Rewriting for readers
- Deadline storytelling: A Writing Workshop
- Deadline storytelling: The Coaching Way

A LIFE IN JOURNALISM

Christopher Scanlan

At the age of 22, I was the police, fire, library board and conservation commission reporter at *The Milford Citizen,* a small daily newspaper in a Connecticut suburb.

One weekend, I was sent to cover a drowning at a park outside town. It was a summer Sunday, and the park was crowded with families who had come to escape the heat and to frolic in the cool water of the lake.

There was no one in the water when I arrived, except for a fire department rowboat moving slowly across the smooth brown surface. Beneath the water, divers searched for the body of a teen-age boy who had disappeared.

On the banks, families stood around, talking in hushed tones, all their games and Frisbee throwing halted by the accident. Even the children played quietly in the dirt, as if they, too, were mindful of the tragedy unfolding before them. Off to one side, by the cluster of police cars and emergency vehicles, the boy's family waited.

It took about an hour for the divers to find the boy on the lake floor. A diver surfaced and signaled to the men in the boat, and then, suddenly, the boy's head and shoulders broke through the water.

I don't remember many details from that day, but the image of that dead boy is as clear as if I was still standing on the bank watching the rescuers carry his body onto the grassy shore. He was naked except for the long, sodden blue jeans he wore swimming. His chest was muscular and hairless and deathly white. He appeared to be sleeping. I scribbled observations in my notepad.

The boy's mother, a middle-aged woman who had waited, slack-jawed, chain-smoking, leaned on the hood of a police car now and beat a tattoo in the dust with her feet, an angry, futile rhythm. I followed the rescue procession out of the park. Back in the empty newsroom, I struggled for several hours to write a story for the next day's paper.

I wrote a lead, then a second graph and then as the minutes to deadline ticked away began throwing words on the page. This was in the days before word processors, and my desk sat beside a black Associated Press ticker. I was full of the experience, the images, the feelings, but I sat at my typewriter unable to capture them.

I wrote lead after lead. I tried to describe the bitter staccato the boy's mother beat in the ground. Nothing satisfied me, and I ripped the abortive attempts out of the machine. The pile of crumpled copy paper grew in the wastebasket at my feet.

Eventually, I gave up. I surrendered to the wire service standard that clattered incessantly over that machine next to

Continued

me. I don't have the clip, but I'm sure it came out something like this: "A 17-year-old Milford youth drowned yesterday at Lake ..."

I've never forgotten that experience because there was a story to tell that day, and I didn't know how to tell it. I didn't have the tools.

Today, as technology shortens deadlines to seconds, the storyteller's craft is more crucial than ever. This chapter describes the tools that can help you become a storyteller on deadline.

THE CLOCK IS TICKING

Learning to write well with the clock ticking may be the most important challenge that you will face as a journalist. Getting enough narrative information and being able to focus, organize, draft and revise it into a story, all in the space of a working day, is one of the toughest high-wire acts of the news business. But those are the kinds of stories that editors and consumers of news demand from today's reporters.

Far too often, reporters focus on process rather than people and on the policymakers rather than those whose lives are affected by policies. Instead, news stories often seem to be a grab bag of quotes from politicians, bureaucrats and other officials that merely skim the surface. And too many stories in every section are written with sources or subjects in mind. The best writing shows readers their world in new, sometimes startling ways.

The readers' interests and needs seem to be last. Not enough stories take readers anywhere. A story about a neighborhood's complaints about a quarry mentions dust and noise but conveys no sense of what it's like to live near a limestone quarry. What does it sound like? What does it smell like?

And don't stop there. What's it like for the owners to try to make a living when your neighbors and the state are constantly at your back? What's it like for the quarry's customers? This is a story about the tensions that exist in a modern society. It's not—and shouldn't be—a dry report about action taken by a government body. Stories should put people on the page rather than titles and give a greater sense of the human condition that lies just beneath the surface of all news.

A story about a proposed hike in water rates quotes officials, but what does the person who washes three cars a week or waters her lawn in August have to say? Faced with a summer drought, the *St. Petersburg Times* tracked water bills and put the spotlight on the biggest water users in its area.

By its definition, deadline storytelling doesn't mean conducting lengthy investigations, but rather encouraging reporters and their bosses, in all media, to demand that stories use people as the primary vehicle to make the news relevant and understandable to readers.

In an article in *Wired* magazine, provocatively titled, "On-line or Not, Newspapers Suck," media critic and former editor Jon Katz argues that "newspapers must begin to think about reversing their long-standing priorities, recognizing that everyone with electricity has access to more breaking news than they provide, faster than they provide it. They should, at last, accept that there is little of significance they get to tell us for the first time. They should stop hiding that fact and begin taking advantage of it. What they can do is explain news, analyze it, dig into the details and opinions, capture people and stories in vivid writing—all in greater depth than other media. They should get about the business of doing so."

FIND THE FULL TEXT OF THE JON KATZ ARTICLE ONLINE AT http://www.wired.com/wired/archive/2.09/news.suck_pr.html

Kelly Garbus of *The Kansas City Star* captured a person in a story about a new cellular phone system for a community's paramedics. The story featured Sharon Miller, an asthma sufferer aided by advance word about her condition conveyed by a friend as the ambulance was speeding to her home. In four paragraphs, the reporter conveyed what the change would mean in a way readers could readily understand.

Joel Rawson, my former editor at *The Providence Journal*, says that if a copy of his paper was placed in a time capsule and dug up a century later, a reader from the future should know from its pages what it was like to be alive in his community on that day.

All too often readers get a better sense of what life is like from classified advertising and agate reports of arrests than from the stories. From the news columns, you'd see a community where business development is an activity that dominates the community and crime is clearly a big problem, but what about the other ordinary activities of life, the stories of drama, pathos, suspense, joy that are buried inside news stories? You get only the barest hints of it in the Neighbors section and occasionally in high school sports coverage.

There are many opportunities for storytelling—journalism at the intersection of civic clarity and literary grace—that reporters and editors fail to take advantage of. Too many stories are devoid of flesh and blood that make stories interesting, but more importantly, that amplify the news. How can you do a story about overtime/housing projects/water rates/crime/business/you name it and never quote anybody who is closest to the story, the people whose lives are impacted by the policies/issues/events?

People should be at the heart of every story. The challenge is to discover them. Obviously, everyone you interview is a person. But there are official sources—police officials, public officials, spokespersons—who will provide all sorts of facts, statistics and analysis—and what I always think of as "real people." I don't mean to suggest here that police officers or politicians aren't real, but they are inevitably several steps removed from the action of a story. The councilwoman proposing cuts in the school budget won't feel the reductions as sharply as a teacher who must cope with larger class size or the music students whose practice time is cut in half.

Of course, examples of good news storytelling abound. Unfortunately, in too many newsrooms, storytelling has become the exclusive province of the feature or project writer who is given space and time denied to other writers. Good writers, those who care about the craft and want to get better at it, often chafe at the restrictions of daily deadlines.

They don't have enough time, they say, to gather the material they need—the telling quotes, the revealing details, the senses of people, place, time and drama—to write a story rather than an article.

Fortunately, there are examples that show clearly that storytelling can be done on deadline.

Often the best stories focus on a single character, as Matthew Purdy of *The New York Times* did in a short (556 words) but poignant story about the courtroom testimony of a young boy who witnessed the shooting death of his father.

New York, Oct. 14—Johnny Morales was all boy. His white shirt sleeves poked from the sleeves of his uncomfortable blue suit. He mumbled answers to questions from grown-ups. And when they weren't looking, he squirmed in his seat and yawned.

But when he was asked to, Johnny, 7, raised his right arm and brought a crowded Bronx courtroom to a commanding stillness yesterday as he pointed to the man he said he saw shoot and kill his father two years ago.

"He's right there," the boy said, pointing at Louis Bracero, a thin man with dark glasses sitting at the defense table.

The New York Times
Oct. 14, 1994

Stories are about people. Notice how Purdy begins by describing his main character, Johnny Morales. He uses vivid details—the color of his shirt, the ill-fitting suit and the squirming little boy—to put the reader in the courtroom. But just as quickly, the reporter gets to the news: Johnny's chilling eyewitness account of the shooting. Economy is the hallmark of the news storyteller. In just three paragraphs, five sentences, 99 words, Purdy has introduced all the necessary ingredients of a story: **characters, setting, plot, conflict, suspense** (see the glossary for definitions). Using the techniques and strategies employed by Purdy and other news storytellers outlined in this chapter, you will be able to produce stories that have the immediacy of good fiction and the authority of solid journalism.

WHAT'S A STORY?

Story. It's a word you'll hear echoing in a newsroom on an average working day. "I've got a great story." "Hey, Malika, great story!" "I'm working on a story about ..."

But what journalists mean when they say "story" is usually something else. We call them stories, but most of them are articles, and many are competent, complete, clear, accurate and convey vital information to readers. They may present information—about an accident, a public meeting, a speech—in clear, logical fashion. But they're not stories.

In Chapter 5, we examined a variety of journalism story types, ranging from the inverted pyramid to the narrative that "consists of a sequence of actions that occur when a sympathetic character encounters a complicating situation that he confronts and solves," as Jon Franklin describes it in *Writing for Story*. Franklin is the first to admit that although the formula sounds simple, its execution is far from it, especially on deadline.

READ AN IN-
TERVIEW ABOUT DEAD-
LINE STORYTELLING
WITH DAVID
MARANISS OF *THE
WASHINGTON POST*
ONLINE AT
http://www.
poynter.org/pub/
bnw97/
bnw97Con.htm

The traditional narrative, although increasingly popular at many newspapers and a few magazines, usually requires far too much reporting and writing time to produce in the kind of deadline atmosphere that you will face as a journalist. With the advent of new media, the ability to write fast and compelling copy has become even more necessary. A reporter may function as a wire service reporter, phoning or transmitting by wireless modem the barest outlines of a news flash, and then return to the newsroom to update the story for the next cycle—and do that more than once.

On deadline, you and your readers can be satisfied if your story meets the qualifications of this definition:

> A story features characters rather than sources, communicates experience
> through the five senses and a few others: a sense of people, sense of place, sense
> of time and, most important, a sense of drama, has a beginning that grabs a
> reader's attention, a middle that keeps the reader engaged and an ending that
> lingers in the reader's mind like the reverberations of a gong.

Let's take a closer, individual look at these easily recognizable—and with experience, diligence and practice, obtainable—features. Storytelling on deadline:

1. Features characters rather than sources.

In most news reports, people are little more than a name, a title, age and address. "Janice Richardson, 35, advertising account manager at Hathaway Communications" or "William Masterson, 22, of 568B Crowne Court Apartments." It takes a little more effort to zero in on the physical attributes that distinguish one person from another, but that's one of the writer's gifts that makes storytelling such a special experience.

Notice how Anne Hull of the *St. Petersburg Times* puts people on the page, not as sources or as talking heads, but as fully rounded characters:

> Carl's skin was black-gold, and his eye-
> lashes curled over his eyes, just like Eu-
> gene's. His beard needed trimming, and the
> T-shirt he wore was faded and too small,
> but there was something proud and impen-
> etrable about him.

A person can be sketched quickly and with powerful effect with a few brushstrokes, as Mitch Albom of the *Detroit Free Press* does with his portrait of a football player and convicted rapist:

> He is kind of thin for a football player, with
> a gangly walk, dark hair that falls onto his
> forehead, a thick neck, crooked teeth, a few
> pimples.

These examples may seem beyond the reach of beginning writers, but even they can inject humanity into their stories in small ways.

WITH JUST A WORD. In her story about Mama Gert, which you will read in Chapter 13, Rebecca Catalanello could have simply written, "Jason Myron, 8." Instead, she wrote, "Jason Myron, a freckle-faced 8-year-old," evoking a child's face.

IN A SENTENCE. Rhea Borja described a female minister this way: "She's a woman with a friendly and open air, more comfortable in Birkenstocks and summer dresses than the vestments of her trade."

2. **Communicates experience through the five senses and a few others: a sense of people, sense of place, sense of time and, most impor- tant, a sense of drama.**

The first storytellers, recounting the day's hunt as firelight flickered on cave walls, described action they had witnessed personally. Too often, to- day's news stories read as if they were reported from the end of a telephone, which isn't surprising because many of them are. To write a story built on sensory details, the reporter must use her senses: sight, sound, smell, touch.

Far too many stories read as if they're reported from a desk, from releases and from telephone interviews. I want to *see* the community, but in many stories those kinds of images are few and far between. Instead I read stories about troubled neighborhoods and housing projects where there was nothing to indicate that the reporter has walked its streets and talked, not just with its so-called "leaders," but also with the people living there. As a result, there is a flat, bloodless quality to much newswriting.

When a reporter is on the scene, the contrast is striking. Out in the field, Gerald M. Carbone of *The Providence Journal* records sensory details in his notebook. "I will always write down 'Sight,' and I'll look around and see what I'm seeing; and I'll write down 'Sound,' and then 'Smell' or 'Scent.'"

The habit enabled him to report and write an award-winning story in three days about a dramatic mountaintop rescue that contained this evocative passage, lifted directly from his notebook.

Below the treeline, the White Mountains in winter are a vision of heaven. Deep snow gives them the texture of whipping cream. Boulders become soft pillows. Sounds are muted by the snow. Wind in the frosted pines is a whisper, a caress.

The Providence Journal

You don't get writing like that by calling up the Weather Service.

While other reporters were getting their facts about massacres in the African nation of Rwanda in 1994 from embassy officials, Mark Fritz and photographer Jean-Marc Bouju of The Associated Press looked for their stories among the people most directly affected by the horrific events.

"Jean-Marc and I wanted to just hit the villages and the back roads, and stay away from the other reporters and just see if we could find out what was going on, on the real basic fundamental level. ... You really have to find out how the most typical person caught up in your story is living it," Fritz says. That approach enabled him to write the lead of this poignant story that was part of a package that won him a Pulitzer Prize for international reporting and the Jesse Laventhol Award for deadline reporting. (Fritz discusses his methods further later in this chapter.)

KIBUNGO, Rwanda (AP)—Dad was drowned in a cattle dip and mom was taken away by a man with a machete. But 14-year-old Donata Nyinshimiye was singing as she walked to get water with her new family.

Twelve kids from different towns and ethnic backgrounds clanged their containers and their voices together as they trooped down main street toward the water pump in the center of this town 70 miles southeast of Kigali.

Singing, they walked to a mass grave sealed over with red soil by a yellow bulldozer—a single left arm reaching out from the ground.

The Associated Press
May 25, 1994

3. Has a beginning that grabs a reader's attention.

Contrast these two leads on the same story:

> A 28-year-old Queens woman was stabbed to death early yesterday morning outside her apartment house in Kew Gardens.
>
> Neighbors who were awakened by her screams found the woman, Miss Catherine Genovese of 82070 Austin Street, shortly after 3 a.m. in front of the building three doors from her home.
>
> *The New York Times*

> The neighbors had grandstand seats for the slaying of Kitty Genovese. And yet, when the pretty, diminutive 28-year-old brunette called for help, she called in vain.
>
> *The New York Herald Tribune*

The case of Kitty Genovese and her callous neighbors became a symbol of a new generation of uncaring Americans. It's hard to imagine that the story would have been so deeply embedded in our country's history had it been based merely on *The New York Times* approach.

Like any good storyteller, the deadline writer searches for a way to draw the reader in. Anne Blackburn of *The Kansas City Star* captures your attention with an intriguing lead on her profile of the author of a book about a black baseball team:

> All she wanted was enough information to put together signs for a museum exhibit. An interview, a class project and she'd be done. But when Janet Bruce Campbell left the home of Hilton Smith, the famed pitcher of the Kansas City Monarchs, she knew the project wouldn't stop.
>
> *The Kansas City Star*

How might a reporter assemble a lead like this? I can envision Janet Campbell telling reporter Blackburn how she thought she was getting involved in just a simple project. We fashion stories out of the fabric of our lives, and the attentive journalist keeps her ear open for the threads of narrative woven into her sources' stories. The journalist may have to work on the pattern and do some of the stitching, however.

That's where reporting comes in, the observations, interviews and analysis that shape information into a recognizable pattern. Why did you think it would be a simple project? What did you think you'd have to do? When did you know it was going to be different? Finally, the writer steps in and weaves the information into an opening that is richly detailed and yet leaves enough out to create an irresistible sense of mystery.

4. A middle that keeps the reader engaged.

Like a runner who falls flat halfway through a race, reporters often use the middle of their story as a dumping ground for boring information. After a quick start, they bog the story down with extraneous information written in a clumsy fashion. The middle can be a useful spot for a telling anecdote, a vivid description of a process or other information that enlarges a reader's understanding in a painless way.

When Tony Conigliaro, a much-beloved former Boston Red Sox player, emerged from a four-month long coma after suffering a heart attack, I was assigned to cover a hospital press conference about his condition. I decided to use the middle of my story to convey details about his physical condition.

Reporters were not allowed to see Conigliaro, who had auditioned for a sportscasting job the day of his heart attack. What they would find in a second-floor hospital, Dr. Kaulbach said, is a 37-year-old man "in extraordinary condition. He is lean, he looks like an athlete, his muscles have not lost their tone."

It is a mirage.

"If you watched him for a while," the doctor said, "you would realize he does not behave like a person who is awake. He's sort of vague, he sort of stares. He is no longer truly comatose, but you cannot say he is conscious."

Conigliaro faces "many months" of physical therapy, and even after that, the doctor said, he could not predict a full recovery or a normal life.

"He will not recover to the point where he will go jogging or do anything that is within the realm of possibility for the average citizen."

The Providence Journal

The information about Conigliaro's medical condition was important but wasn't appropriate for a lead or an ending because my focus was on the devotion of his family and fans. Rather than slow the reader down, I used the line, "It is a mirage," set off as a paragraph, to heighten the surprise and maintain the story's interest.

5. An ending that lingers in the reader's mind like the reverberations of a gong.

Matt Purdy of *The New York Times* meets that standard in his story about the testimony of Johnny Morales, the little boy who saw his father murdered.

"You saw the shooting?"

"Yeah."

"You saw your Daddy get killed by the man you saw?"

"Yeah."

No further questions. For whatever it was worth, the 7-year-old had done his part in the adult version of justice.

Then he was hustled out of the courtroom, walking in a smart suit between two comforting women.

The door banged open and Johnny was a boy again. He quickly drew his hand up to his mouth as if it had been hit by the door, let out a big "Ah," and broke into a big, toothy smile.

The New York Times

With his description of the boy's reaction outside the courtroom, Purdy lets the reader share the boy's palpable sense of relief.

Choose your endings with care, drawing on vivid details that will resound in the reader's mind. When I wrote about two teen-agers who met on a railroad trestle one day in "From Jon to Lani, the Gift of Life," I wanted to convey the special qualities of Jon Tesseo, the 17-year-old Boy Scout who saved 15-year-old runaway Lani Reynolds' life after a train cut off her leg. The story could have ended a number of different ways—a quote from the girl's parents, Lani's condition in critical care, her chances for survival. Instead, I chose to end with a quote from Jon's boss that suggested how concerned and responsible Jon felt for this stranger who asked him to "stay with me." I ended the story of Jon and Lani this way:

After Lani Reynolds was taken away for surgery Saturday, Jon Tesseo called Paul Gencaralla, the owner of the men's shop, to ask for a few hours. He felt a little sick. Jon left the hospital and walked to a friend's house nearby. Before he got there, he was sick in the street.

"He didn't get sick because of the gore," Gencaralla said yesterday. "An ambulance attendant had told him he didn't think the girl would make it. She'd lost a lot of weight. Jon said, 'I should have made a tourniquet.' What made him sick was the thought he didn't do enough."

The Providence Journal

Of all the definitions of "story" I've seen, the one that strikes closest to the heart of the matter was given by Bill Buford, an editor at *The New Yorker* magazine.

"Of the many definitions of story, the simplest may be this," Buford says. "It is a piece of writing that makes the reader want to find out what happens next. Good writers, it is often said, have the ability to make you keep on reading them whether you want to or not—the milk boils over—the subway stop is missed. ... But stories also protect us from chaos, and maybe that's what we, unblinkered at the end of the 20th century, find ourselves craving. Implicit in the extraordinary revival of storytelling is the possibility that we need stories—that they are a fundamental unit of knowledge, the foundation of memory, essential to the way we make sense of our lives: the beginning, middle and end of our personal and collective trajectories. It is possible that narrative is as important to writing as the human body is to representational painting. We have returned to narratives—in many fields of knowledge—because it is impossible to live without them."

The Process of Storytelling on Deadline

Think back to the process approach covered in Chapter 3. Reporting and writing may be magical, but not magic; instead, they're a rational series of decisions. Those principles are even more important when the reporter is challenged to produce a story in a matter of minutes.

IDEA. News drives storytelling on deadline. The union's strike vote. The first day of school. An arson fire at the town's biggest employer. But news storytelling reveals truths that don't emerge in straight-ahead news reports. The compelling dramas they craft are the stuff of life. The reporting of meaningful information and developments is the primary responsibility of the journalist, but the principles of narrative—character, plot, writing with a sense of people, drama, time—are the engine of stories that will capture your audience.

COLLECT. Good writing demands excellent reporting. The deadline storyteller must report for story: collecting the details that convey the sense of story. As with any story, reporting is the foundation of deadline storytelling. The importance of reporting and techniques are covered in "Reporting for Story," which appears later in this chapter.

FOCUS. Critical and creative thinking fuel storytelling. The writer has a firm grasp of the story's theme—the central meaning—and can express it in a word or six, that is, with economy and verve.

ORGANIZE. Even though time is short, planning is vital. On deadline, reporters think they have no time to plan, to sketch out their approach to the story. Effective writers know differently, that a few minutes of planning at the outset will save them and their editors time in the final minutes when time is even shorter, pressure is higher and the chance for errors higher.

Remember the words of Rick Zahler, a prize-winning writer and inventive editor at *The Seattle Times* who crafted a powerful deadline narrative about the ruinous impact when a volcano on Mt. Saint Helens erupted: "The mistake that most people make when they are writing on deadline is that they think they can dispense with planning and organizing. I mean taking three or four minutes before you start to think about the material you have, what you want to cover." Try to follow his advice:

Make a quick list of the high points of the story and organize your thinking before you write.

DRAFT. This is the stage of the process when inexperienced and ineffective writers spend nearly all their time. As a young reporter, I flailed away at the keyboard on deadline, like the old joke about a thousand monkeys typing who would eventually produce prose if given time enough. I would begin with nothing more than a lead in mind and then type away, hoping that somehow the story would emerge on the page or screen in front of me. As I grew more experienced, I spent more of my drafting time on focusing and organizing. When I did draft I felt more in command of the material. Following the advice of my Poynter colleague Roy Peter Clark to "write like hell," deadline storytellers can use the draft as a means of discovering the best way to deliver on the promise of their planning.

CLARIFY. On deadline, reporters assume there is no time to revise, only to write. But if you want your stories to stand out, you must take time to clarify the meaning, structure and language before you hit the "send" button. That means making time, even when it is short, to print out your story, read it aloud, mark it up, cut, refine, reorganize to make it clear, accurate, fair and compelling. A magazine writer might take hours or days; the storyteller on deadline takes minutes. Three minutes to focus. Two minutes to plan. Fifteen minutes to write. Five minutes to revise.

ENTERPRISE: A BROADCAST STORYTELLER'S VIEW: JOHN LARSON, NBC'S "DATELINE"

John Larson
(Courtesy of
NBC News)

John Larson is one of the finest storytellers I've ever known. He is a correspondent for NBC's television newsmagazine "Dateline." He learned his craft at KTUU-TV in Anchorage, Alaska, and at KOMO, Seattle. He has won numerous awards, including 13 regional Emmys for his reporting and investigative stories. John Larson's report on the misuse of Louisiana's drug asset forfeiture law prompted the state's governor to introduce legislation that reformed the state's law. Just as powerful have been his stories that opened a window on America at the end of a century: following a homeless alcoholic struggle to regain his dignity with the help of high school buddies, tracking an endangered owl in the Pacific Northwest or sharing the whimsy of a country town whose mayor moves a lone parking meter around Main Street.

The key to all these stories is a quality that lies at the heart of much of the journalism in this book: a reporter's enterprise, "making something out of nothing," as Larson defines it, and "asking the question nobody else is asking."

Collaborating with talented photojournalists, Larson finds stories in the tiniest details, in the small things that represent universal themes. "It's looking for little things that echo," he says. "Like an owl talking about an ecosystem."

Larson's heroes and teachers are John McPhee, John Hart and other outstanding print and broadcast reporter-writers. He learned how to do it by being a reporter. He paid close attention to stories he admired, tried to figure out how the writer did it and then tried to repeat the lessons he learned. "You watch how people do it," Larson says. "Study it and make up rules of how you think it was done."

In the following list, Larson gives his own storytelling tips. Although a few relate specifically to broadcast, most are lessons that will help every writer.

- Storytelling is as old as language. The basic rules have not changed. You need story line, surprise, character and conclusion. You should have a sense of place. Is there tension? Release? Where have you placed your elements, and why? Think like a reporter or producer but move like a storyteller.

- Find a way to care. Your first mission on any story is to find a way to care. If you don't care, no one else will.

- Stories must have surprises. Anticipate them, allow them to happen. If your story is predictable, you don't have much of a story.

- Stories must have characters. Great stories begin and end with people. Even when they are not there.

- Remember that God is in the details. Listen. Pay attention. One detail can give you the world. Look and listen for small things. The way to bring character to life is with well-chosen detail: the forgotten birthday, the patron saint, a nickname, etc. Keep sifting details until you find a way to care, and then allow your viewer the same opportunity.

- Look for universal themes, "echoes." Is it the story about the love of a father, the loss of a dream, the pride of accomplishment? Or is it just another press release?

- The smallest, least powerful voice frequently holds the most powerful story. Think big, then search the smallest places.

- Do you have a plot, "quest"? What is it? Whose is it?

- Once you've found a reason to care, *focus!* You'll know your focus when you hear it, or see it. It will make you smile, shake your head in disgust or sense the "shared truth." It will make you think of your own neighborhood, school, father, etc. Be ruthless about your focus.

- Once you've focused, prove it with video. If you're talking about how hard someone had to work, then prove "hard work" *with your tape!* Don't just talk over your points, show them, experience them.

- Allow your viewers to experience the same surprise, alarm, joy you experienced when you first discovered your story.

- Sound is the heartbeat, the engine. Use sound as punctuation, cadence, beat. Remember, a great preacher uses rhythm to draw his congregation closer. Storytellers also do this.

- Follow the energy of what happens. Be ready to change directions.

- Frequently, the "juice" is in the raw tape. The offhand comment, the way in which someone moves through the frame can make a story. Look at raw tape with "new eyes."

- Play left field. Someone has to think outside the box. Have "What if ..." conversations with people you work with.

- Listen to your values. Find one story to make your own.

Finding Stories in the News

We are all storytellers. We tell stories to our families, our friends, our co-workers. What's the last story you told someone? Chances are if you look deep enough you'll see yours is a familiar tale whose reach extends far beyond your life.

Here are three examples of personal stories that mirror news on a larger scale:

1. Perhaps you described how painful it was to put your elderly grandfather in a nursing home. What's the news? As baby boomers age, they face the painful task of caring for their parents as well as their own children.

2. Or how your little brother came home from kindergarten singing an antidrug chant. The news? Loss of innocence comes earlier for children at a time when schools are trying to stem the rise in drug abuse.

3. Maybe you're worried about the new development near your house that will claim your favorite stream. The news? Environmental protection and community progress are often pitted against each other.

Look around at your own life for stories that need to be told.

Newspapers are full of stories waiting to be fleshed out. Police briefs, classified ads, obituaries, the last two paragraphs of a city council brief; all may hold the promise of a dramatic story. Mine the paper.

The newspaper is just one fountain of ideas. Traditionally, the story was the "news," the event or development considered significant and worthy of attention. The challenge for today's journalists is to go beyond bureaucracy, beyond meetings, and to write stories that reveal the joys and costs of being human.

TECHNIQUES

- Examine how the "news" affects people's lives: a burglary, a bankruptcy, marriage, death, accidents. "The point is to stress the importance of getting true stories in the paper," says Jack Hart, writing coach at *The Oregonian.* "Human dramas that go beyond the reports we usually run."
- Find the extraordinary in the ordinary stuff of life: graduations, reunions, burials, buying a car, putting Mom in a nursing home, or the day Dad comes to live with his children.
- See the story from a different perspective. After John F. Kennedy's assassination in November 1963, columnist Jimmy Breslin interviewed Clifton Pollard, the worker who dug the dead president's grave at Arlington National Cemetery. From that perspective, Breslin produced a haunting column that conveyed the nation's loss more poignantly than reams of eulogies from the high and mighty:

One of the last to serve John Fitzgerald Kennedy, who was the 35th president of this country, was a working man who earns $3.01 an hour and said it was an honor to dig the grave. ... At the bottom of the hill in front of the Tomb of the Unknown Soldier, Pollard started digging. Leaves covered the grass. ... When the bucket came up with its first scoop of dirt, Metzler, the cemetery superintendent, walked over and looked at it.

"That's nice soil," Metzler said.

"I'd like to save a little of it," Pollard said. "The machine made some tracks in the grass over here, and I'd like to sort of fill them in and get some good grass growing there. I'd like to have everything, you know, nice."

REPORTING FOR STORY

We don't write with words. We write with specific, accurate information. Deadline storytellers must bring back the sights and sounds of their communities, breathing new life into the answers reporters collect to the questions that are the engines of journalism: Who, what, when, where, why and how?

"You can't write writing," Melvin Mencher of Columbia Journalism School counseled his students. Instead, you must "report writing." The power of stories lies not just in their evocative use of language, but also in their compelling power of facts.

To report for story, the reporter finds out what the names of trees or flowers were, as Carol McCabe of *The Providence Journal* always did for her prize-winning stories about New Englanders that won the Ernie Pyle award for human interest reporting.

To report for story, the reporter uses the clock as an organizer, telling the story about the life-saving operation by zeroing in on what surgeons call "the Golden Hour," the 60 minutes immediately after an injury that often spell the difference between life and death.

To gather these facts the reporter should always try to be on the scene, not just at the meeting of the state environmental protection agency but also in the neighborhood where people live in fear of toxic chemicals in their groundwater and in the local chemical plant where workers and managers grapple with the dilemma of deciding which comes first—their livelihood or public safety. But even if the writer can't be present and must reconstruct the action, specific details are needed to bring the story alive in the reader's mind.

My father and grandfather were both salesmen. As a reporter, I used to think I had chosen a different life for myself. Now I know that reporting and writing are also a kind of sales job, one that requires you first to persuade your sources to give you information and second to write a story that engages readers.

As a reporter, I must convince the widow of the man who smoked for 50 years and died in six months, horribly, of lung cancer to open their life to me in one afternoon. Interviewing people at their home or office—what outdoors columnist Jeff Klinkenberg of the *St. Petersburg Times* refers to as "their natural habitat"—is an invaluable way to establish trust. "Never, ever, ever, let a story subject come to your office if you can help it," Klinkenberg says. "Every picture, every book, every piece of furniture, can tell a story."

Like my former colleague, I am a big believer in asking people for tours of their homes. When Marie DeMilio, the smoker's widow, led me through her house and stood in the bedroom she had shared with her husband, Pete, she gave me a powerful way to communicate her loss:

> "It feels like one big nightmare," she says. "Maybe I will wake up, and he will be in bed with me. But I know it's not going to be so. Would you believe it? I take his aftershave lotion and spray it on his pillow just so I can smell him. Just the smell of it makes me feel like he's with me."
>
> *St. Petersburg Times*

REPORTING TECHNIQUES

- Get out on the streets. Don't hang around the campus newsroom or your dorm. Storytellers aren't tied to their desks. They are out in the streets. They're the reporters who show up before the news conference and hang around after it's over, the ones who interview the victim two weeks after the shooting. They know that stories don't end after the arrest or the election.

- When Francis X. Clines was writing the "About New York" column for *The New York Times,* there were days he didn't know what he was going to write about. But, he said, if he could just go somewhere, he knew he'd be okay. "Reporters always want to witness when they write," Clines said after he won the American Society of Newspaper Editors award for best deadline writing in 1989. "And when you do witness, then you know there's no way the story won't be interesting."

- "You can't win the deadline writing contest unless you are where the story is," *Concord Monitor* editor Mike Pride noted when ASNE judges gave the top deadline writing award to Colin Nickerson of *The Boston Globe* for his Gulf War dispatches in 1992.

- Look for revealing details that put people on the page. "In a good story," says David Finkel, staff writer for *The Washington Post Magazine,* "a paranoid schizophrenic doesn't just hear imaginary voices, he hears them say, 'Go kill a policeman' and 'You can't tell Aretha Franklin how to sing a song.'"

- In your reporting use the five senses and a few others: sense of place, sense of people, sense of time, sense of drama.

- How did it look? Study how *Providence Journal* reporter Gayle Gertler's description of a wealthy murder defendant's daughter lets the reader see her studied attempts to maintain control.

> Miss von Bulow, tall and thin with short blond hair and blue eyes, sat with crossed legs and clasped hands. She sat motionless, except for an occasional effort to keep the collar of her pink shirt upright.
>
> *The Providence Journal*

- What sounds echoed? If music is playing, is it the lush strings of a classical piece or the head-banging clang of guitars? Is the wind whistling through the leaves? Are children's cries filling the air? Close your eyes and record in your notebook every sound you hear.

- What scents lingered in the air? Smells can trigger powerful emotional reactions. I still can't go into a flower shop without remembering the perfume of flowers that surrounded my father's coffin when I was 10 years old. Telling your readers that a nursing home smelled of disinfectant, stale urine and talcum powder or that the aroma of peanut butter filled the air in a grade-school cafeteria will connect them to the reality you are trying to convey in a much richer way.

- Consider how this lead by Michael Specter of *The New York Times* draws on several of those senses:

> Grozny, Russia, Jan. 3—This grim city was strewn today with scores of dead Russian soldiers, who lay in stacks along the broad, tree-lined boulevards. Wild dogs roamed among them on the streets. Old women locked out of darkened basements wailed in terror, shielding their eyes from the frightening skies above.
>
> *The New York Times*

- Write while you're reporting. Listen for quotes, find details, uncover information that you know will be in the story. Look at how Alan Bavley of *The Kansas City Star* uses details in his story about hospital security measures to prevent baby snatching from maternity wards:

> They tag newborns with the same kinds of sensors department stores tack on expensive clothing. They put babies behind doors equipped with combination locks. They scrutinize their nurseries with television cameras.
>
> *The Kansas City Star*

- Notice how Bavley works hard to connect with his readers. Even people who know nothing about security sensors probably remember combination locks from their school lockers and have seen cameras staring at them from their local convenience store.

FOCUSING IN THE FIELD

Reporting is where most reporters spend their time. Few focus or organize, even though that is the single most important part of the process.

The search for focus must be relentless. "What is this story about?" the news storyteller keeps asking. "Why does it matter?"

If I get to the end of a story wondering what it's about and then realize I was never told, I will be disgruntled. Readers may call with a complaint about errors; they won't call and say, "I wasn't sure what that story was about."

That's why the most effective writers recognize that the most important task is finding the central idea. "It's one thing to be given a topic, but you have to find the idea or the concept within that topic," says sports columnist Thomas Boswell of *The Washington Post*. "Once you find that idea or thread, all the other anecdotes, illustrations and quotes are pearls that hang on this thread. The thread may seem very humble, the pearls may seem very flashy, but it's still the thread that makes the necklace."

Boswell puts into words the experience I had many times trying to tell news stories on deadline, for example, my story about the girl rescued by a Boy Scout after her leg was cut off by a train. By the time I reached the home of victim Lani Reynolds, I had already obtained a police report rich with detail and gleaned other nuggets from a variety of witnesses, including Jon Tesseo, the shy Boy Scout hailed as a hero.

My notebook was filling up with quotes, facts and revealing details, but I was still hunting for the element that would elevate the piece beyond a clichéd rescue story ("Boy Scout Saves Girl"). Then Lani's mother, sitting on her living room couch, said this about the boy who came to her daughter's rescue—"He's a preppie, everything Lani disliked"—and I knew I had found the "north star" that leads a writer out of the tangled woods of reporting.

Like every step of the writing process, focus depends on the quality and rigor of the reporting.

If you think the story is about "x," and you don't have the facts, it's like a square peg in a round hole; it won't fit. You either must do more reporting or (especially on deadline) shift the focus to the information you have and be upfront with the reader about the holes. Inexperienced writers often feel thwarted by missing facts; I think readers prefer an acknowledgment of ambiguity to a story with a gaping hole that's never filled. "No one knows how the would-be suicide reached the roof of the police station" and "No one collects statistics on the number of Internet users who abuse caffeine" are quick and easy touches, unobtainable facts that don't interfere with the flow of a story.

FOCUSING TECHNIQUES

- Don't wait until you're back at your desk to figure out what your story is about. Find your focus in the field, award-winning journalist and author Richard Ben Cramer advises, so you can search for the details, scenes, quotes that support it. The deadline storyteller must be a radar screen, forever monitoring for information that is the heart of the story.

■ The more I work with reporters and editors, the more convinced I am that the problems with many stories lie not with the reporting and writing. It's the thinking that's missing. How much planning goes into your stories? How much hard thinking goes into even the most mundane story? Are reporters and editors constantly challenging themselves: What's the story about? What's the news here? Why should it matter? Why should I care to read this? What's the best way to tell this story? Who is missing from my reporting? Have I touched all the bases? Good journalism demands this kind of rigor.

■ Good writers know that a story should leave a single, dominant impression. On deadline, finding a focus quickly is even more crucial. An effective focusing strategy came to me one desperate afternoon in *The Providence Journal* newsroom as I battled to meet my deadline and the expectations of my editor for a newsy, well-written story.

■ The strategy is asking the two questions that help me keep track of the focus of my stories as I write and read and rewrite. To this day, I still write them at the top of my video display screen, even before the dateline. They are:

What's the news?

What's the story?

■ Answering the first question is usually easy. "Police credit the quick actions of a shy Boy Scout with saving the life of a 16-year-old runaway whose leg was cut off by a speeding freight train Saturday."

■ As a journalist, your first responsibility is the news, the information you are trying to convey. In this complicated age of ours, information without context is meaningless. If the Public Utility Commission approves a rate increase for the electric company, that is the news, but the context, the focus, the point of your story must take the news one step further to make it connect with your readers' lives.

■ The second question is often more difficult, but it is more crucial.

■ Forcing yourself to describe, concisely, what your story is about, its theme, not only may give you the focus, but also may let you hear the voice of your story.

■ What's the story about? Electric bills are going up.

■ What does the reader need to know? How much is my electric bill going up a month?

■ What's the dominant message? A government agency's decision hits you in the pocketbook.

- Rather than write a lead that says "The PUC approved a $13 million rate hike yesterday," the reporter who asks these kinds of focusing questions may start this way: "Your electric bills are going up. A rate increase approved by the PUC yesterday will add $45 to the average residential customer's monthly bill."

- In deadline writing, the biggest failure is not the writing; it's the thinking and the reporting. One can't overemphasize the importance of asking good questions, before and during the reporting and writing, before and during the editing. These are questions that editors need to ask reporters and that *reporters* need to ask themselves.

- When in doubt how to lead or end a story, always look to the focus—What's the news? What's the story?—as your guide.

PLANNING ON THE FLY

Finding your focus will give you a destination. Now you need a map to get there. Some writers make a formal outline. Others jot down a list of the points they want to cover.

As a young reporter I would drive back from assignments trying out leads in my head and sometimes even scribbled on my notepad against the steering wheel. "The Town Council last night voted to cut the school budget in half ..." That was as close to planning as I got. At the keyboard, I would often write the first paragraph and then a second, tear it up and start again. Then when my time was almost gone, I would frantically empty the contents of my notebook into the rest of the story and hope for the best. It was only after I began taking time to plan my stories, considering where I would end as well as begin and what shape the middle would take, that my stories became more coherent.

Writers are always looking for a new way to tell their story, to stretch the traditional forms, to experiment. Writing the lead often helps writers devise their plan of attack, they "shine a flashlight into the story," as John McPhee of *The New Yorker* puts it. It is the first step of a journey. Just as important, if not more, is the last step, the ending.

David Zucchino of *The Philadelphia Inquirer* says his deadline stories are "totally determined by the facts on hand, the amount of time I have, and the space. ... The form is determined by the situation."

Create your own form.

PLANNING TECHNIQUES

- Before you begin writing, make a list of the elements you know you want to include in your story. Number them in order of importance. Structure your story accordingly.

- Look for **pivotal moments** that make story beginnings dramatic and irresistible:

When things change.

When things will never be the same.

When things begin to fall apart.

When you don't know how things will turn out.

■ Think "short" from the beginning. That's a suggestion echoed in *The Elements of Style*, Strunk and White's indispensable guide: "You raise a pup tent from one sort of vision, a cathedral from another." Staying faithful to an 800-word length will help you jettison irrelevant information and avoid reporting detours that might be interesting but that will consume valuable time.

■ Once the writer accumulates a wealth of material—statistics, quotations, differing opinions—confusion often sets in. What does it all mean?

Here are other strategies for keeping on track:

■ Conceive and reconceive the story in your head. The story in the press release may be completely different after you've done some interviews. The profile about the new mayor may be a story about her husband, who has put his own career on hold.

■ Give yourself three minutes to write a five-step plan to structure the story. List your lead, ending and three main points you want to cover.

■ Dig deep. Keep asking yourself, "But what is this story *really* about? What makes it different from every other fire/meeting/budget story? Why will people care about it?"

DRAFTING ON DEADLINE

The writer continues the process of discovery by writing the story. For me, that means putting my head down and pecking away at the keyboard or scribbling in a daybook. Other writers tackle the lead or write an ending. Either way, the idea is to generate copy that you can work with.

Notice how Christine Vendel of *The Kansas City Star* got to the heart of her story with this lead on a story about teen-agers facing possible charges for Halloween candy thefts.

Halloween tricks are one thing. But knocking down children to steal their treats may be something else: a felony.

The Kansas City Star

Use the **scene**—action occurring in a definite place and time—as a building block of narrative. Study how Andale Gross of *The Kansas City Star* opened her story about an inspirational teacher with a precise rendering of a moment in a classroom.

Eleventh-graders in a Kansas School for the Deaf chemistry class swarmed around a lab table Monday. Time for a lesson in polymers.

Melissa Nix, 17, poured water into a measuring cup containing rock salt. She stirred the mix, scooped out a spoonful and placed the mush in her right palm.

"It feels cold," Melissa said, using sign language.

Teacher Becky Goodwin nodded. "It should feel like the absorbent inside of a baby's diaper," said Goodwin. "We have created a polymer of a different kind. Just like atoms connect, the water and salt connected."

Experiments like that one are common in classes taught by Goodwin, who last weekend was named Kansas Teacher of the Year for 1995.

The Kansas City Star

REWRITING FOR READERS AND VIEWERS

Writing is hard work. Even when you think you're finished, good writing requires you step back and ask tough questions: Is this clear? Is it accurate? Is it fair? Could I say it better?

REWRITING TECHNIQUES

- Role-play the reader. Step back and pretend you're reading your story for the first time. Does the lead make you want to keep reading? Does it take you too long to learn what the story is about and why it's important? If not, are you intrigued enough to keep reading anyway? What questions do you have about the story? Are they answered in the order you would logically ask them?

- Read your story with an eye for what is missing. When I wrote a story about a search my wife and I made during our honeymoon in France to find the grave of an American soldier killed in World War II—the relative of a newsroom colleague—I knew next to nothing about the man whose grave we hunted. But I knew the story had a big hole, and I set out to find more. After I interviewed the soldier's mother, I crafted this paragraph:

> John Juba was 18 years old when he was
> drafted out of trade school in 1942. Every-
> one called him Johnny. He loved to play
> football and baseball. He was engaged to a
> girl named Dorothy.
>
> *The Providence Journal Sunday Magazine*

With those details, he became a person rather than just a name on a mar-
ble headstone.

- Shoot for a draft and a half. Write your story once through and then
  go back to polish, to reorder, to refine. If your time is limited, I'd argue that it's best spent on your ending. That's the last thing readers
  will experience. Make it memorable.

- Too many news stories drift off at the end. Or seem to follow the principles of the inverted pyramid—least important newsworthy information at the end. That was fine in the Civil War when correspondents
  faced the threat of losing telegraph lines to enemy forces. In our computer age, there's no excuse for bottom-of-the-story amputations on
  the copy desk. Reporters should be encouraged to write—and copy
  editors to preserve—endings that resonate with the reader. After all,
  that's the last moment a reader will have with your story. Why would
  you make it the weakest element instead of the strongest?

STORY EXAMPLE

Many reporters equate storytelling with long stories. But vivid writing
that conveys drama, character and news can be done with brevity. Consider
the following story by Rhonda Cook, a reporter with *The Atlanta Journal-
Constitution*.

JACKSON—The room was deathly still.
The only sound was that of five reporters taking notes and the far-off rumble of a heater
warming the death chamber at the Georgia
Diagnostic and Classification Prison.

No one spoke as the witnesses filed into
three churchlike pews to witness the final
moments of the life of Larry Grant Lonchar, who killed three people a decade ago
and since has seesawed between saying he

wanted to die and challenging his death sentence.

For years following his 1987 conviction, Lonchar insisted that he preferred death in the chair to life in prison. Yet three times he decided at the eleventh hour to file appeals of his convictions. Twice he was successful and delayed his execution—once with 32 minutes to spare, and again with little more than an hour before his scheduled death. The third time—Wednesday night—he tried once more but ultimately failed.

With his appeals finally exhausted, Lonchar bounded into the death chamber, appearing almost eager. His eyes darted around the room as prison officials, all without any uniform markings that would tell their names, attached straps and electrodes to his body.

A leather strap forced his mouth closed, and the final electrode was attached to his shaved head and right leg.

As the straps were attached, the fingers on his right hand drummed against the chair arm. Then he lifted a finger on his left hand to wave goodbye.

As a brown leather mask was placed over his face, he closed his eyes.

As the powerful generators clicked on, sending 2,000 volts through the electrodes, witnesses flinched, and Lonchar's body tensed and then seemed to relax.

He moaned and his fists clenched. He seemed to gasp for air.

The current remained on for two minutes, then was cut on again for another cycle. Finally, doctors entered, listened for a heartbeat and heard none.

Nodding to the warden, they indicated that Lonchar—the 45-year-old killer of Margaret Sweat, Charles Smith and Steven Smith—was dead.

Warden Tony Turpin stepped in front of Lonchar and told the 34 witnesses on the other side of the glass window that the order of the court had been carried out at 12:39 a.m. Thursday, Nov. 14, and officers moved to draw the curtain across the window.

Lonchar's hands were still clenched into fists.

The Atlanta Journal-Constitution
Nov. 14, 1996

Cook's story was selected by her colleagues as the winner of a newsroom contest for best short writing. "From the lead to the final haunting image, this story demonstrates both the storyteller's art and Rhonda's superb powers of observation," one judge said. "She shows us not only the condemned man bounding into the death chamber, but also the observers flinching and the prison officials whose uniforms do not reveal their names. We see Lonchar's eyes darting around the room, and his fingers drumming against the arm of the electric chair. We see him lifting a finger to wave goodbye, and we see his hands clenched in death. Vivid stuff, powerfully written."

Another judge described the story's structure: "Effective lead. Then five grafs of the news. Then, the really good stuff—vivid, compelling but not gratuitous detail. The blow-by-blow account of Lonchar's execution walks the line between fine and overly fanciful writing. To pick up all the nuances proves Cook's sharp eye."

HOW I WROTE THE STORY

An Interview with Rhonda Cook

As part of its writing improvement program, directed by training editor Michael Schwartz, the winning writer discusses how the story was reported and written. Following are excerpts from Rhonda Cook's interview with Mike Tierney:

Q: How did you prepare for covering the execution, in terms of advance interviews and research as well as emotionally?

A: This was my first, and most likely my only, experience as a media witness to an execution. I didn't do any advance interviews or research. I had been covering the Larry Lonchar saga for a few years. All the information was already in my head. I did talk, however, with Elliot Minor from The Associated Press about what to expect emotionally. That week Elliot was a witness for his 12th and 13th executions, and he offered suggestions for getting through it emotionally. Mostly, I made sure to remain detached and keep it very impersonal.

Not only was I seeing a man die, but I was seeing a man I knew die. I had interviewed Lonchar many times on the telephone and in person, and he wrote me often. So I refused to think about what was actually happening. It was hard for a few days after the execution, but by then the story was done.

Q: Your story is structured with a lead that combines news and scene, followed by about five grafs of news. Then the rest is devoted to scene stuff. Why did you organize it that way?

A: I tried to limit the news in that story since there was another story devoted only to the carrying out of the execution. I wanted readers to see what I had seen and not maintain some romantic idea of capital punishment.

Q: In describing the scene, were you concerned about maintaining a balancing act between not enough detail versus overly vivid detail?

A: There was no problem with being overly vivid because the process is now so sterile. The state made changes in the process when executions resumed in 1983, so it's not as grotesque as it used to be. The condemned is strapped in so tight he can't move anything except his hands. It's quite benign compared to how it used to be.

Q: Was it difficult writing down notes during the execution? Did you take mental notes?

A: I wrote constantly. I thought that would be the best way to control my feelings. Also, as one of the pool reporters, I had to be able to describe the execution to the reporters who did not go inside, so I wrote down everything. It turned out the notes were not necessary because I remembered so much in detail.

Q: Was your description of the execution based entirely on your own notes and observations, or did you draw from someone else?

A: Virtually all of it was from my observations, though the five pool reporters compared notes during the bus ride back to the road where the other reporters were waiting. ... Dave Kindred went with me because he planned to write a column but also helped with my news story. He filled me in on things that happened while I was inside the prison and helped with interviews that occurred simultaneously.

Q: Do you think you could have used more space? If so, how did you meet the challenge of covering the event in the space allotted?

A: I could have used more space to get even more detail in there. While the whole process lasted only 10 minutes, it seemed to go on forever. I could have described the guards in the room with the witnesses. I could have written more about the witnesses and how they reacted. I could have written about the process of bringing the witnesses in and out of the execution chamber.

Q: Given the midnight-hour timing of the execution, what hurdles did you face in writing and filing the story?

A: Though I took very detailed notes, I wrote without looking at them. I was counting on my emotions, and that's the way it worked. Also, I was particularly proud of this story because of the circumstances. I had only 30 minutes to dictate two stories (my cell phone battery had died, so I couldn't transmit). Filing was complicated even more because I was getting very sick and had almost no voice. ... Dave Kindred drove while I wrote. I had written much of the news story before I went inside so all I had to do was fill it out. I filed that one first. The second story, the one based on events in the witness room, was written in 5 to 10 minutes as we drove north on Interstate 75. When it was finished, Dave pulled off at a truck stop, and I dictated the second story.

A CONVERSATION WITH MARK FRITZ
OF THE ASSOCIATED PRESS

This is one in a series of discussions with working journalists about the craft of reporting and writing.

When ethnic massacres broke out in the African nation of Rwanda in 1994, The Associated Press assigned correspondent Mark Fritz to cover the tragic story. The deadline dispatches Fritz wrote won a Pulitzer Prize for international reporting and a Jesse Laventhol Award for deadline reporting. On deadline, Fritz is part storyteller, part historian, part tour guide. Here he describes how he writes stories on deadline with speed, economy and power.

How do you write on deadline?

You learn little tricks: writing it in your head, jotting a transition. You break it down into its raw essentials. It may sound formulaic, but I don't think it really is. Things become pieces as you're reporting them, and you think, "Ah, there's my lead." I'll scribble along the side and I'll circle something, or put an asterisk, or write a little note next to it. I'll underline it three times. I'll write in block letters "LEAD." Sometimes after I've talked to somebody, maybe it's an element, or a particular person that is the best way to get the reader into the story, and I'll write the lead on the spot in the notebook or flip open the laptop and type it in.

Are there rules that guide you as you write?

Don't bury your lead. Get your lead up there with your nut graf.

How would you define your lead?

The hook, the thing that makes readers interested in reading the story. Hit them with the news, the peg. Why are you writing this story? What's it all about?

What advice would you give to the reporter who has 45 minutes to write the story?

I've been in the exact same position many, many times. And a little trick that seems to help is to put away your notes and try to write the story without consulting them, and sometimes the rudimentary framework will come together, and you won't have the technical detail getting in the way of the gist of your story.

Sometimes I've spent more time on the lead than the rest of the story. I'm one of the people who believes that if you get the lead right, if you nail your story in the first couple of graphs—maybe leading with an anecdote and then your nut graf—if you nail that, the rest just flows.

Get your lead—just put away your notes and try to think about what your story is about and what example you have that most compellingly explains your story. If I get the lead right, I can inch my way through the story. I can bring it to the end. And sometimes, if I don't have that lead, I'll just start throwing notes up on the screen, stuff I know is going to go in the story, and look at it and just wait for lightning to strike.

What advice would you give somebody facing a tough deadline story?

There's nothing wrong with preparing some material that you can put in your story. Graphs, boilerplate. I don't think there's anything wrong with thinking in advance. The best way to write a story is to report the hell out of it. Then you know before you write that you have a story, and it's just a short hop to actually beginning it. I have to do enough reporting that I know what the story is and how it's going to begin. If I have a deficiency putting those notes together from my notebook, I didn't do enough work on the story. If I'm going through my notes, and I'm trying to think about how to start the story, or what my nut graf is, then I haven't done enough reporting.

THE CLOCK TICKS: HOW A DEADLINE STORYTELLER WORKS

The clock ticks for the deadline storyteller. David Von Drehle of *The Washington Post* filed his story on the funeral of Richard M. Nixon about 90 minutes after the former president's coffin was lowered into the ground. Rich with insight and penetrating description, his story displays the graceful power of the elegy and the long-term memory of the obituary. "Men of Steel Are Melting With Age" is a cautionary tale for the powerful and a model of elegant writing for the deadline writer.

In the essay that follows his story, Von Drehle provides one of the best descriptions of the high-wire act that is deadline writing and the ways a consummate professional approaches the challenge with intelligence, courage and common sense.

Men of Steel Are Melting With Age

By David Von Drehle
The Washington Post
April 28, 1994

YORBA LINDA, Calif., April 27—When last the nation saw them all together, they were men of steel and bristling crew cuts, titans of their time—which was a time of pragmatism and ice water in the veins.

How boldly they talked. How fearless they seemed. They spoke of fixing their enemies, of running over their own grandmothers if it would give them an edge. Their goals were the goals of giants: control of a nation, victory in the nuclear age, strategic domination of the globe.

The titans of Nixon's age gathered again today, on an unseasonably cold and gray afternoon, and now they were white-haired or balding, their steel was rusting, their skin had begun to sag, their eyesight was failing. They were invited to contemplate where power leads.

Continued

"John Donne once said that there is a democracy about death," the Rev. Billy Graham told the mourners at Richard M. Nixon's funeral. Then, quoting the poet, he continued: "It comes equally to us all and makes us all equal when it comes."

And here, the great evangelist diverged for a moment from his text to make the point perfectly clear. "We, too, are going to die," Graham intoned, "and we are going to have to face Almighty God."

Coming from Graham, the words were especially poignant. He is the only American who claims the place of honor in our solemn national ceremonies, even above the sitting president. And once he was the vivid, virile lion of God, with a voice like Gabriel's trumpet. Now he is a frail old man who struggles to his feet.

The senior men of the Nixon administration looked quite old: George P. Shultz, the all-purpose Cabinet secretary; the disgraced vice president Spiro T. Agnew, who emerged from his long seclusion clearly stooped; the foreign policy guru Henry A. Kissinger, who seemed small and somehow vulnerable.

And the junior men looked very senior: Nixon chief of staff Alexander M. Haig Jr., resembling a retiree at the yacht club; political legman Lyn Nofziger, still looking like an unmade bed, but now your grandfather's unmade bed; muscle man Charles W. Colson, his crew cut replaced by a thinning gray thatch. G. Gordon Liddy, with his bullet head, looked the least changed of all.

"Let not your heart be troubled, neither let it be afraid," Graham said.

They arrived full of the old sangfroid, smiling and glad-handing for as much as an hour before the service began. Nixon's men and many of the other dignitaries worked the crowd like a precinct caucus; surely Nixon, the best pol of his era, would have approved. As a Marine band played Bach's ineffable hymn, "Jesu, Joy of Man's Desiring," Republican National Committee chairman Haley Barbour pumped hands with a broad grin on his face, and nearby David R. Gergen, the perennial presidential adviser, worked a row of mourners like a rope line.

And in the beginning, perhaps, the event reminded them of just another political event. A very small number of people attended, compared to the number who no doubt wished to honor Nixon, but even among the exclusive group, the crowd was separated by various shades of lapel pin. Purple was the best, the regal color-bearers of purple buttons could go right up to the front rows, where generals mixed with corporate titans and international arms dealers mingled with movie stars.

The band had shifted to "God of Our Fathers" when the congressional delegation arrived, and this ignited another flurry of politicking. A number of people had dusted off old Nixon campaign buttons, which they displayed proudly as they milled among old friends. Nixon speechwriter Patrick J. Buchanan caught sight of an old friend and stepped lively to meet him, while nearby White House Chief of Staff Thomas F. "Mack" McLarty chatted amiably with Colson. (They call McLarty "Mack the Nice." No one ever called Colson "nice" when he served Nixon; Colson was the one who offered to run down his grandmother. But that was a long time ago.)

It is possible to pinpoint to the instant when the mood of a political rally evaporated. It was when Kissinger, almost invisible behind the bulky presidential lectern, quoted Shakespeare in speaking of Nixon: "He was a man, take him for all in all, I shall not look upon his like again."

And that great rumbling Kissinger voice—which once spoke of war and nations and nuclear strategy as if all these things were mere entertainments, mere exercise to tone his Atlas-like muscles—cracked into a sob.

The sky darkened just then. The sun gave up its hours-long struggle to penetrate the clouds. The day turned cold, and after the shock of hearing Kissinger cry, moments later Senate Minority Leader Robert J. Dole (R-Kan.) was crying, too.

It was appropriate, perhaps, that the funeral of the first U.S. president from California should be held on a parking lot, across the street from a strip mall. The Nixon Library and Birthplace stands on the spot where Nixon's parents raised a mail-order house nearly a century ago.

This was the frontier then; now it is just another cookie-cutter suburb. Tough people settled this place—"Chinatown" tough. They diverted vast rivers, crushed powerful unions and made this remote land of dry winds, hard ground, earthquakes, fires, droughts into the great postwar city. Richard Nixon was one of them, and he went farther than any of them: He remade the country through his unstinting use and abuse of power; some say he remolded the world.

But none of that kept him from the leveling end that awaits even the most vigorous and clever wielders of power. The cannon boomed; the rifles popped; the polished wooden coffin sank into the wet ground. Chilled, the mourners hastened across the green grass to a gathering where canapés were served by uniformed staff.

And though their smiles returned, the end of power lay before them, down the path, beneath the trees, under the ground.

HOW I WROTE THE STORY

David Von Drehle

The day of Richard Nixon's funeral was unseasonably cold. The sky was overcast, and the air was damp. I don't know why a wet chill goes right to the bone, but it does. Sitting in the press tent, watching the minutes tick away toward deadline, I lost the feeling in my fingers.

Continued

But then deadline always makes me shiver.

My seat was next to the team from *The New York Times*. Earlier in the day, I watched them arrive with the same sick feeling pitchers experienced watching the '61 Yankees take the field. Maureen Dowd, Johnny Apple, David Margolick— they were so deep in talent they had a Pulitzer Prize winner, William Safire, shagging quotes. So I was cold, and I was scared.

At a time like that, you have to fall back on the basics: Sit down and tell a story.

What happened?

What did it look like, sound like, feel like? Who said what? Who did what?

And why does it matter?

What's the point? Why is this story being told? What does it say about life, about the world, about the times we live in?

Newspaper writing, especially on deadline, is so hectic and complicated—the fact-gathering, the phrase-finding, the inconvenience, the pressure—that it's easy to forget the basics of storytelling. Namely, what happened, and why does it matter?

I did this story the way I always work on deadline: I wandered and watched and listened and wrote down everything as I waited for the story to emerge. Until I figured out the what and the why, I had no way of knowing what details would prove important.

Then I saw Henry Kissinger, the cerebral Cold Warrior, and Bob Dole, the stoic veteran of World War II, each burst into genuine tears. And I heard Billy Graham speaking of the "democracy of death." It hit me that I was watching one of the oldest and most important stories there is: the leveling effect of death and the fear, the awe, it inspires. Thomas Gray wrote his famous "Elegy in a Country Churchyard" on just this theme:

> The boast of heraldry, the pomp of pow'r,
> And all that beauty, all that wealth e'er gave,
> Awaits alike th' inevitable hour,
> The paths of glory lead but to the grave.

Once I realized what the story was, I targeted my reporting to find details that would drive it home. The signs of time in the faces of the mourners. The ineffable music floating over the babble. The landscape remade in Nixon's lifetime, by once-powerful, now-forgotten men and women.

> I learned long ago: Don't get fancy on deadline. Keep the structure simple; start at the beginning, march through the middle, end at the end. That's what I did here. There are no flashbacks, no digressions, no interwoven story line. Just beginning, middle, end. Lead, chronology, kicker. What else? Lots of short sentences. Active verbs. Clear metaphors. Pithy quotes. Vivid details.
>
> That's about it.
>
> And that's the lesson I learned: Fall back on the basics. They'll get you through—even when you feel like you're going to freeze.

Six days after attending a National Writers' Workshop where I taught a "Storytelling on Deadline" seminar, reporter Erin Hoover put into practice the lessons of this chapter while covering the gunning death of a young man in a Portland neighborhood. Her story is followed by an account of how she wrote it.

Portlanders Grapple With Rising Violence

By Erin Hoover
The Oregonian Staff
April 30, 1994

Nathan stands alone near the yellow police tape, his hands shoved in the pockets of his black Raiders jacket, hood pulled over his short braids. The 17-year-old stares at the body.

It is a young man he knew. Not very well. But well enough.

He met him a couple of months ago while hanging out with friends. Nathan can still see the guy laughing at a joke they'd made. He had a nice laugh. Earlier this week, he had pedaled by Nathan's house on his bike. Nathan waved. The man smiled and nodded hello.

Leshon Denail Brown, better known as Corey Taylor, 22, was on that same bike Friday when he was gunned down on Northeast Beech Street just west of Cleveland Avenue. It was 2:20 p.m. Broad daylight.

Now Taylor is on his back, the left arm is flung across the chest. His close-shaved head is bleeding onto the word AHEAD printed

Continued

in large letters on the street—the last part of a warning for drivers to stop.

The police don't know why it happened. They don't know who did it. They know only that a group of youths was there, scattering when the shots were fired.

Police know that Taylor—under either name—is not on their gang list, said Lt. C. W. Jensen, police spokesman. He does have a criminal record, including several arrests for cocaine possession and delivery in 1991.

Taylor's mother apparently lives in California, Jensen said, but police are listing Taylor as a North Portland resident. He doesn't appear to have close family in town, Jensen said.

"He didn't like the police," said Sgt. Drew Kirkland, "but he was real easy for us to get along with. He knew it was necessary to get along with us."

Several gang outreach leaders say they've heard of him but don't know much about him.

"Certainly, he was known somewhere, but it wasn't that he had a real tie-in to the community at large," said Robert Richardson of Portland Youth Redirection, which works with troubled young men.

The body is left lying on the street for a long time. The arm and hand, folded into a fist, are all that is visible beneath the yellow tarp.

Men in T-shirts and jackets, sandal-footed women and quiet, wide-eyed children come by bike, car and on foot. They look at the body, they look at each other. They remark on the killing. They reflect on their own lives and wonder what this means.

Clemon Roach and two other men gather near a police car. They grew up together in this neighborhood. Roach said he's been there since 1962.

A man with graying hair, brown cap and glasses told Roach: "Remember? We used to have fun—chasing each other around. Yeah, we got in fights, but nothing like this."

"We had some fun," agreed Roach as he watched police mill around Taylor's body. "We didn't do this kind of stuff." Roach sizes up the problem. "No self-respect," he said.

Eleven-year-old Thomas Vicente eyes the body with his brother, Josue, 9. Book bags are slung over their shoulders. Thomas clutches a brown paper bag. Inside are chocolate bars he and Josue just bought at the corner store.

Thomas said they were walking home from Boise Eliot School when they saw all the people. "I thought it was a party," said Thomas quietly. Then he saw the police. And the yellow tape. "Then, the body."

A group of girls leans on a police car and talks about what's next. An angry-eyed young man in a letterman's jacket stares at the yellow tarp. His cellular phone rings. He steps away.

Suddenly, other teen-agers come out of nearby houses and stride down Cleveland toward the body. Johnny A. Gage, director of House of Umoja, and Richard Brown, co-chairman of the Black United Front, move toward them to soothe emotions. Nothing happens.

And Nathan, who didn't want to give his full name, stands alone trying to understand.

He was hanging out with some friends a few blocks away when a girl ran up and told him the news. It took a minute. But then he remembered Taylor.

"I flew down here," said Nathan, his face tense, his eyes moist. "I just kept looking (at his body). Then tears started coming down my eyes a little bit."

Nathan's tone changes. He talks with determination about his own life. He says he's stayed close to God, but many of the boys he grew up with have gone astray. He says he dropped out of school but now plans to go to Portland Community College for his General Educational Development certificate and then major in interior design.

He wishes he could change his world.

"I want us to wake up," he said, looking at Taylor's body. "How many more black people have to get killed?"

HOW I WROTE THE STORY

Erin Hoover

My swing shift had just begun that Friday when day cops reporter John Snell gave me the news. Homicide. Guy gunned down on his bike. Cleveland and Beech.

Just six days earlier, Chip Scanlan had taught us about "Storytelling on Deadline" at the National Writers' Workshop. This was the pop quiz.

My approach to the story began taking shape in the car on the way to the scene. Bracing myself to see my first dead body was part of it.

But I was more anxious about how to get people to talk. I was an outsider. Establishing trust would be key. Don't be a vulture. Be respectful.

Now, what did I want to know: Who was this guy? Why did this happen? How did it happen? What does it mean?

More important, though, I told myself to open my mind to the images. Scanlan told how he covered a drama-packed drowning one summer day, returned to the newsroom and wrote: "A 17-year-old boy drowned Sunday at 2:30 p.m. in Smith Lake, police said." That hit home. I tend to get caught up in the facts, appropriate attribution and the exact chronology of events. It was time to let all that go. Pulling up amid

Continued

the growing gathering of people at Cleveland and Beech, I met Lt. C. W. Jensen, police spokesman, at the yellow tape. He didn't have a lot of information. That was fortunate. It forced me to ask the neighbors. But I waited a little while, taking in the scene.

A young man named Nathan stood alone at the police tape. He looked scared. I knew he'd have something to say, and he looked vulnerable enough to say it.

"Did you know this guy?" I asked quietly.

He began talking haltingly. When I realized he knew the dead man, I started building his story, slowly and gently. When was the last time you saw him? What memories do you have of him? How did you hear of his death? Where were you when you heard? What did you think and do? How do you feel now?

After talking to Nathan, I relaxed a little. I knew I had something. That's when what was really happening at the scene started sinking in.

The longer the body lay there, the more it became a mirror for bystanders to reflect about their lives and their neighborhood.

I saw little Thomas Vicente. The 11-year-old was shorter than the police tape was high. He smiled shyly at me. I called him over. His little brother came, too. I saw the brown bag in his hand. I asked what was inside. It was candy bars they had just bought at the store on the corner.

I wanted one more vignette. When I overheard Clemon Roach reminiscing with his neighborhood buddies about how things and people had changed, the picture felt complete. I still had no idea who the dead guy was, but I knew I could get that later.

On the way back, I did what Scanlan suggested. I interviewed myself out loud. The first two questions: What's the news? "A guy got gunned down on his bike." What's the point? "Neighborhood reaction paints a picture of the victims left behind to deal with their shattered world."

And then: What information surprised me the most? What image sticks in my mind as a symbol for the event? What's the most significant quote I heard?

Anyone driving by would have thought I was talking to my sun visor.

Michael Rolling, night city editor, called Brian Meehan and me together. The march on violence and a conference on children and violence were happening the next day, and a meeting on the topic was that night. Michael wanted to package them. We talked about how to do that.

Then Michael asked me to tell him what I remembered from the street. No peeking at your notes, he told me. He said he wanted to see those images in my story. Make a list of them and see if they would create an outline, he told me.

"The story is not in your notes. The story is in your head," I told myself as I started writing, remembering what Scanlan said was Jane Harrigan's advice. He was telling us to trust ourselves.

I typed in my answers to Scanlan's questions and then made a list of the images I remembered. I toyed with some themes to tie together the key images—the body, Nathan, other teen-agers, moms and dads, Thomas and Josue, the older men.

Michael later trimmed the sentence describing the theme I chose—three generations of men react to a young man's death. I hadn't presented it well.

But the theme served its purpose. It helped create a structure for the story.

I had a rare luxury—time. My first homicide was a mid-afternoon shooting. I had about three hours to gather more information and write for the third edition. Once I got the victim's name, I had time to call gang outreach leaders to flesh out this guy's past.

Then I decided the key image I wanted to lead with—Nathan—and I just let my mind go and wrote as if I were back at the scene. "Nathan stands alone at the yellow police tape"—I put all the basic information high up but tried to fit it into the flow of the story rather than stringing "police said" graphs together. "The police don't know why it happened. They don't know who did it ..."

I also remembered Scanlan's advice to decide on an ending as well as a beginning and, if you use someone as a scene-setter in the lead, to come back to that person. I decided to begin and end with Nathan and his message.

STORYTELLING ON DEADLINE: A WRITING WORKSHOP

To prepare you for the challenges of storytelling on deadline, here is a writing workshop that puts into practice the strategies and techniques introduced in this chapter. Like the leads workshop in Chapter 4, it includes details about a real-life assignment and notes taken at the scene and transcripts of interviews. Use these materials to practice your storytelling skills. For further help, consult the checklists on focusing, mapping, drafting and revising stories found in Chapter 3. Your assignment is to read the following material and then focus, plan, draft and revise a story that applies the principles of this chapter.

THE ASSIGNMENT

Monday morning. You're reading the paper over your first cup of coffee when the city editor approaches with a clip. "Seen this?" she asks, pointing to an item in today's Metro briefs column. It's a two-paragraph police short about a teenage girl hit by a train over the weekend in the town of Westerly. The girl lost her leg, but survived, the cops say, thanks to quick attention from another teenager, a clerk in a nearby store who rushed to the scene and gave her first aid.

"This is definitely worth more than a Metro brief," your editor says. You agree and head out with a photographer.

THE REPORTING

The police station is your first stop. The chief provides details on the accident, including a report from the train crew. He also tells you where the accident occurred. You head there to check out the scene. From there you visit the men's store where the boy who rescued the girl works. You interview him and his boss and then head for the girl's house. The victim's parents are just back from the hospital. Their daughter is still in intensive care and can't be interviewed, but they give you lots of details. By now, it's late afternoon; deadline is a few hours away. On the following pages you will find the contents of your notebook.

Read the material as quickly as possible. Make it your story, which for the purposes of this exercise, it is. Employing the methods cited in this chapter, write a 750–800 word story in 2–3 hours.

NOTES

INTERVIEW WITH WESTERLY POLICE CHIEF NUNZIO CIMALORE
Accident occurred Sat. at 9:35 a.m.
Location: Railroad trestle south end of town.
Links Westerly and Pawcatuck. Kids use it as shortcut between the two towns.
Victim: Lani Reynolds, 15, 2306 Arlington Street

Admitted to Westerly Memorial Hospital. Good condition.

Girl was walking across trestle when train came.

Report from Amtrak officials:

Amtrak train—The Colonial—headed south to Washington from Boston.

Had just rounded curve past Westerly depot. Approaching trestle.

In engine compartment Jackson Wilson, fireman, spotted girl on tracks. Pointed out window. Shouted "Girl."

Engineer, Burke Hudson, said he immediately hit brakes and pulled train whistle.

Couldn't stop in time.

Hit girl.

Train took off her right leg just above knee.

Leg found up track. 61.5 feet away.

? How fast train going:

Don't know. But engineer said maximum speed along that section of track is 92–100 miles an hour.

It takes two miles to stop train at that speed, engineer said.

?Who reported accident:

Kids walking by saw girl. Ran for help. Saw kid—Jon Tesseo—on street.

Brave kid. He ran to help. Sent kids to call 911.

Police responded within five minutes.

By the time I got there, Tesseo kid was giving first aid. Holding girl's leg up. He was sweating. White as a ghost. But he stayed there. He prevented her from bleeding to death and going into shock.

AT ACCIDENT SCENE

Railroad trestle. Woods on all sides.

Below: Pawcatuck River. Fast-moving. 60-foot drop

INTERVIEW WITH JON TESSEO

Toscano's Mens Shop, 56 Canal Street

Age: 17

Tall, husky, black hair, neat cut, black shoes, polished

Stacking shirts

Saturday morning, I was at work by 8:30.

Continued

About 9:30 coming back from Fusaro's Tailors. Two boys ran out of parking lot beside railroad tracks screaming to get an ambulance. A train hit somebody.

I said Take me there.

I know first aid. I have Boy Scout merit badge in first aid.

I have 11 merit badges. You need 20 for Eagle Scout.

The girl was sitting up on the trestle when I got there. I didn't see anything wrong at first.

Then she said my leg hurts. Her leg was gone.

I sent the two kids to get help.

I told her Pretend you're in Bermuda. You're sitting on the beach soaking up the sun.

I tried to be careful. I lifted her thigh and kept it up to stop the bleeding.

Then the police came. And the ambulance. She said stay with me please.

So I went in the ambulance. She asked me to hold her hand until we got to the hospital. I did.

?After.

They took her away. For surgery. I didn't feel so good. I walked to a friend's house. Before I got there, I got sick. In the street.

Everything I did was all reflex.

INTERVIEW WITH PAUL GENCARELLA OWNER OF TOSCANO'S MEN'S SHOP

Re: Jon A great kid. Photographer for school yearbook. Boy Scout.

He called me from the hospital. Asked for a few hours off. Then he got sick.

He didn't get sick because of the gore. An ambulance attendant had told him he didn't think the girl would make it. She'd lost a lot of blood. Jon said, I should have made a tourniquet. What made him sick was the thought he didn't do enough.

INTERVIEW WITH OTEY AND CHERYL REYNOLDS, GIRL'S PARENTS

Arlington Street.

Ranch house.

Parents sitting in living room.

MOM:
This morning they brought Lani out of intensive care.
She's got a good attitude. She's faced the reality her
limb is gone.
Dad is engineer Electric Boat
DAD:
She's a mixed-up kid.
sort of the rebel in the family
We moved here from Maine last fall
Lani had trouble adjusting. She was fooling around with
drugs. We didn't like the crowd she was spending time
with.
She's taken off a couple of times before. Always came
back though.
She went out Friday night. Said she was going jogging.
Said she slept in the woods.
Saturday morning she was walking across the trestle.
There's a walkway, but she didn't take it. Hopped along
the ties. Westbound tracks on one side. River on the
other.
Got about a third of the way across. Heard the train.
She was going to jump into the river. But she thought
that would be dumb.
Instead, she lay face down on the ties next to the rail
and held on as tight as she could.
By rights she should have been safe.
But ...
Object moving at high rate of speed creates a vacuum.
Air rushes in to fill it. It makes a wind. And the wind
sucked heir leg under the train.
As train passed, wind picked Lani up and slammed her
back down on the wooden ties, facing the opposite way
?Did she know Jon Tesseo?
No. They go to same school—Westerly High. Different
classes.
MOM:
He's a preppie. Cleancut. Good student. Everything Lani
disliked.
I asked Lani if her friends would have done what he did.
They wouldn't know what to do, she said.

Deadline Storytelling: The Coaching Way

■ Follow Gerald Carbone's example and write the five senses—sight, sound, taste, touch, smell—in your notebook. Find examples of each in your interviews and observations.

■ Change your point of view. Not your opinion, but rather the spot from which you see the story. Write the council story through the eyes of the Asian American who asks for better police protection in his neighborhood. Tell the story of the foiled suicide attempt through the cop who talked the jumper down.

■ Always ask the two questions to find your focus: What's the news? What's the story?

■ Make a quick list of the high points of the story and organize your thinking before you write.

■ Look for the "pivotal moments" in your story: when things began to fall apart, the ordinary moment before the explosion.

■ The next time you read or see a story you admire, interview the reporter and ask him or her the lessons learned during the reporting and writing.

GLOSSARY OF IMPORTANT TERMS

(See also glossary in Chapter 5.)

Character. A figure in a story.

Conflict. Opposition between two characters or forces. Man against man. Man against himself. Man against nature.

Foreshadowing. A literary device that provides a hint of what is to come later in the story.

Pivotal moments. When things change. When things will never be the same. When things begin to fall apart. When you don't know how things will turn out.

Plot. The organization of incidents in a story.

Scene. Action occurring in a definite place and time.

Setting. Time and place in which the action of the story occurs.

Suspense. An uncertainty in a story, such as the fate of a character or outcome of the plot, that keeps the reader or viewer wondering what will happen.

READINGS

Atchity, Kenneth. *A Writer's Time: A Guide to the Creative Process, From Vision Through Revision.* New York: W. W. Norton & Co., 1996.

Blundell, William E. *The Art and Craft of Feature Writing: Based on The Wall Street Journal.* New York: New American Library, 1988.

Brande, Dorothea. *Becoming a Writer.* Los Angeles: J. P. Tarcher, 1981. (Reprint of 1934 edition published by Harcourt Brace.)

Brown, Karen, Roy Peter Clark, Don Fry, and Christopher Scanlan, eds. *Best Newspaper Writing.* St. Petersburg, Fla.: The Poynter Institute and Bonus Books, 1979–1999.

Clark, Roy Peter. "A New Shape for the News." *Washington Journalism Review,* March 1984, pp. 46–47.

Clark, Roy Peter, and Donald Fry. *Coaching Writers: The Essential Guide for Editors and Reporters.* New York: St. Martin's Press, 1992.

Clark, Roy Peter, and Donald Fry. "Return of the Narrative." *Quill,* May 1994, pp. 10–12.

Giblin, James Cross. "A Nonfiction Writer Is a Storyteller." *The Writer,* April 1988, pp. 13–15, 46.

Hart, Jack. "The Art of Storytelling." *The Coaches' Corner,* March 1992, pp. 1, 4, 6.

Harvey, Chris. "Tom Wolfe's Revenge." *American Journalism Review,* October 1994, pp. 40–46.

Kaye, Sanford. *Writing Under Pressure: The Quick Writing Process.* New York: Oxford University Press, 1989.

Klement, Alice and Carolyn Matalene, eds. *Telling Stories, Taking Risks: Journalism Writing at the Century's Edge.* Belmont, Calif.: Wadsworth, 1998.

Murray, Donald M. *Read to Write: A Writing Process Reader.* Fort Worth: Harcourt Brace Jovanovich, 1993.

Murray, Donald M. *Writing for Your Reader: Notes on the Writer's Craft From The Boston Globe.* Old Saybrook, Conn.: Globe Pequot Press, 1995.

Scanlan, Christopher, ed. *How I Wrote the Story.* Providence, R.I.: The Providence Journal Co., 1989.

Scanlan, Christopher. "Storytelling on Deadline." *Best Newspaper Writing 1995.* St. Petersburg, Fla.: The Poynter Institute and Bonus Books, 1995, pp. 355–365.

Snyder, Louis, ed. *A Treasury of Great Reporting.* New York: Simon and Schuster, 1949.

Witt, Leonard, ed. *The Complete Book of Feature Writing.* Cincinnati: Writer's Digest Books, 1991.

Hotlist

http://www.poynter.org/

The Poynter Institute for Media Studies. A collection of materials on storytelling on deadline can be found on the Poynter Web site.

writerL@telix.com

bylines is an online gallery of literary nonfiction created by Jon Franklin, journalist and author of the classic text, *Writing for Story.* It features, for extremely moderate prices, ranging from 39 cents to $2.50, digital copies of essays, stories and complete books by Franklin, Lynn Franklin, Jacques Leslie and other journalists.

Writer L is an electronic mailing list created and moderated by Jon Franklin. It has a $17 annual subscription fee with $5 origination cost. There is a $5 student membership available for one term or semester if an entire class subscribes. For more information contact Lynn Franklin at WriterL@telix.com.

http://www.wired.com/wired/archive/2.09/news.suck_pr.html

For anyone wondering what place newspapers have in the world of new media, read this now-classic rant by *Wired* magazine media critic Jon Katz. His prescription is a return to what newspapers have always done best: telling stories.

http://www.projo.com/words/main.htm

"The Power of Words." Storytelling is one of the pillars of this outstanding site maintained by Bob Wyss of *The Providence Journal*. Read examples of deadline, storytelling and insightful commentary from writers who are passionate about their craft at a paper recognized for its dedication to writing.

CHAPTER

13

ON THE BEAT

CHAPTER FOCUS

A beat is a series of relationships that the journalist establishes and cultivates to produce coverage that communities deserve and need.

CHAPTER LESSONS

- Ingredients of successful beat reporting
- Getting—and staying—organized
- The new beats
- Covering a community
- Covering the suburbs
- Covering government
- Covering law enforcement
- Essential terms for police reporters
- Covering courts
- Criminal and civil procedure: Step by step
- Essential terms for court reporters
- Covering schools
- Covering sports
- Working a beat: The Coaching Way

INGREDIENTS OF SUCCESSFUL BEAT REPORTING

Journalists have a language of their own. One of my favorite words is "beat," newsroom jargon for the place or subject area a reporter covers regularly, such as city hall or health. The word appeals to me because it evokes the image of the cop on the beat, a solitary figure watching over things while the world is asleep. Its associations of responsibility, solitude and a certain amount of bravery appeal, I admit, to my romantic side, which helps explain why I have spent most of my life in journalism.

In music, a beat is a space. In news, it's often a place, like a courthouse, or a subject area, like education or medicine, or geography, like a suburb. A beat is a reporter's assignment. The beat reporter's job is to make sure that all the news in a place or subject area is covered. Beats are the way most news organizations cover news. News managers use beats to divide work among the reporters and get stories they need to fill the paper or broadcast. As a new reporter you most likely will be assigned a beat. Reporting is usually divided among beat reporting, general assignment and projects.

The first beats, journalism historian Mitchell Stephens tells us, emerged in the early 1800s in England, where editors such as Thomas Barnes of the *Times of London* believed it was a newspaper's job not just to find news, but also not to miss it. For the first time, reporters were assigned to make the rounds of Parliament and the courts, seeking out news.

Today, we still name many news beats after the buildings where the sources work: city hall, the cop shop, the White House. But beats are not constructed of brick and fluorescent lighting or the glistening antiseptic of the hospital or the institutional dinge of the police station or prison. A beat is a series of relationships, and the reporter's job is to identify those ties and explore their impact on society. Covering a beat means getting to know people and their concerns, wishes, complaints, aspirations, challenges and triumphs. A good beat reporter, as John Keller, who was an award-winning telecommunications reporter for *The Wall Street Journal* says, is never off duty.

In this chapter we'll look at the variety of beats and their constant morphing as news organizations struggle to remain relevant and serve their audiences' needs and interests. In Part 1, you'll learn essentials of beat reporting from new reporters and experienced ones. Most important, you can use this chapter to learn how to cover a community beat, based on a model devised by newspaper writing coach and journalism teacher Christine M. Martin, the same model used to train student journalists at The Poynter Institute. Part 2 focuses on the basic beats: government, law enforcement, courts, education and sports. Essential principles are illustrated with examples and commentary from student and working journalists. Interspersed are glossaries of essential terms for beat reporters.

Responsibilities depend on the particular beat, of course, but generally speaking a beat reporter's main job is to stay on top of the news on the beat. That means breaking news, features and profiles of newsworthy people. Beat reporters sometimes get in a rut, always writing stories about meetings or focusing coverage on politicians instead of voters or writing horse-race stories about election campaigns instead of paying attention to the issues that matter to voters. Avoiding this limited view of news takes discipline, energy and imagination and a commitment to look beyond official sources to the people and communities whose lives are affected. Later in this chapter, you'll learn about specific approaches to beat reporting that can help you produce stories that give your audience a more complete picture.

Success as a beat reporter is a result of many factors:

- Knowing the territory, by being as familiar with your beat as a police officer is with a neighborhood.
- Developing sources.
- Becoming a recognizable presence.
- Using all the digital resources available to a reporter in the 21st century yet continuing to make people the foundation of your reporting.
- Knowing where to find public records.
- Knowing the participants.
- Understanding causes and effects as well as issues.
- Serving as the conscience, the town crier.
- Asking what people need to know and what's the most effective way to tell them.

In recent years news beats have undergone dramatic transformation in many newsrooms. A century ago, beats included city hall, the coroner's office, shipping offices and hotels. Then, it was news when a ship arrived and a famous person got off the gangplank. Many of these beats still survive: In most newsrooms, someone covers city government, politics, police and other law enforcement issues. But over time the news media expanded their vision of beats in response to community interest. After the urban riots of the '60s, many newspapers assigned reporters to cover race relations. After the Vietnam War, militant veterans prodded news organizations to cover veteran affairs. The recession of the mid-'70s sparked intense interest in consumer affairs; I was a consumer reporter for a newspaper and magazine. But by the time I arrived in Washington in 1989, consumer reporters were mostly a thing of the past.

The best beat reporters I've known are well organized, determined, with a clear sense of mission and a wide range of sources. They are constantly reading about the beat and striving to learn new things. They are well versed in the language, issues and events that matter. They are judged by the breadth of their knowledge and their success at communicating the important stories on their beats.

Beat reporters in the Knight Ridder Washington bureau faced a difficult challenge when I worked there in the early 1990s. We weren't on the top rung of the newsgathering ladder. "People here aren't going to answer your calls first," news editor Bob Shaw told me the day I started work. "At the end of the day, there may be a stack of messages from reporters. By the time they've finished calling *The New York Times*, *The Washington Post*, *The Wall Street Journal* and the networks, it's time for them to go home. So how do we get the stories, the information, the access we need?"

Reporters handled it differently, Shaw said. Owen Ullman and Ellen Warren, the White House reporters, did it with persistence by demanding that officials treat them with the same respect as more high-profile competitors. Ricardo Alonzo Zaldivar, Charles Green and David Hess did it in

Congress by being everywhere, from committee hearings and bill markups to news conferences, and by talking to as many people as they could. Mark Thompson at the Pentagon and investigative reporter Frank Greve did it by knowing the turf so well that often their sources wanted to talk with them to find out what *they* knew.

Probably the hardest part of being a beat reporter is staying on top of things and dealing with sources you have to return to every day even if you've written a story they don't like. Unlike other journalists, beat reporters every day face the challenge of encountering sources who may not be pleased with their reporting. That experience, although sometimes painful, helps instill the quality of persistence that defines good reporters. That's a lesson *New York Times* reporter George Judson learned early in his career. Judson's first job in newspapers had been in rewrite, turning other people's reporting into stories. Years later when he went to work as a reporter at *The Hartford Courant* in Connecticut, he saw what he had missed. At the Hartford paper, newcomers at the paper were assigned to cover a specific town— everything from police and fire news to zoning commission meetings.

"What they were learning (and that I was not learning as a rewrite man) is that they had to go back to the same people day after day and develop re-lationships that got beyond the superficial, to find out what was going on that wasn't quite public," Judson recalled in *My First Year as a Journalist*, a collection of insightful memoirs by reporters and editors looking back at the lessons of their first year. "They had to learn to be better reporters than I was required to be."

Beat reporting takes courage, discipline and judgment, knowing which story has to be written today and which can be put off. It requires teamwork with an editor and other reporters. Working quickly: getting to sources and obtaining information and then writing on deadline stories that give the news and why it matters. Not getting into a rut.

Covering a beat isn't easy. You often feel like an alien, especially during your first days on the job. You have to acknowledge your ignorance and learn the language, learn the process, learn the people. The best reporters know how the world works, whether it's the world of law enforcement, the laboratory or the corporate boardroom. That takes time, dedication, disci-pline and courage. It also takes a sense of mission. Your job is to inform your audience.

Some reporters take a limited view of their beat. The city hall reporter haunts the corridors of power but rarely visits the neighborhoods where the decisions take effect. The police reporter shoots the bull with the desk sergeant but spends little time talking with victims or suspects. Beat re-porters get comfortable with their sources, the jargon and the process, for-getting who they're working for.

Defining your beat is crucial, says Jane Mayer, who covered the White House for *The Wall Street Journal*. "Beats can be constricting. Some people think that if you cover city hall you should never talk to anyone outside city hall. But I urge anybody whose job is to cover a narrow assignment to interview everyone who touches your beat. Interview the caterers who come in with the food, interview the photographers who take the pictures. Talk to relatives. Talk to officials who come in contact with the person you're covering. Those things can lead to wonderful stories, and generally people who are on the periphery are looser with the details than those working directly for the person you're covering," she says in *Speaking of Journalism.*

Each beat has its own language, a vocabulary of terms, a collection of jargon, a way of describing things that you must master but not allow to be limiting. In fact, it's your job to translate the jargon of the beat, the shorthand, so that your readers understand the meaning and significance. Prosecutors may talk about a decision to "nolle prosse" a criminal case, but your story should say they chose to drop charges. Listen on your beat for the language that is unique to the people in it.

GETTING—AND STAYING—ORGANIZED

Beginning reporters often ask, "How do I stay on top of everything?"

You can't spend any time with journalists and not be aware of how time-pressed they are. Journalism, as Jack Hart, a managing editor at *The Oregonian,* says, is produced with state-of-the-art technology but with workers using what are essentially early 20th-century industrial methods. Reporters and their editors bemoan the lack of time, often without learning how to control more of it, how to use calendars or planners. There's no way you can keep track of everything if you're disorganized.

First, use a calendar to keep track of meetings, hearings and deadlines for reports. Keep an address and phone list, whether it's on a pad, notecards or a personal digital assistant. Develop a "futures file" where you can put notes, press releases and other reminders of coming events, deadlines, and issues and events that need regular follow-up. Don't leave work at night without making a list of what you need to do the following day.

- **USE THE CLOCK AS A TIME MANAGEMENT TOOL.** Divide your day into segments of time and fit the tasks to the time allotted. (Lawyers, who know that time is money, divide their day into "billable" periods; a journalist's time is just as valuable, especially on deadline.) When I'm having trouble on a story, I use a Radio Shack timer (they start at about $8 and cost up to $16 for a "talking model" that tells you how many minutes you have left) and set it to count down from 20 minutes. My goal isn't to write the best story ever written; all I want to do is write for 20 minutes. When I'm done I have a text I can revise, although very often I find what I've written is, surprisingly, better than I thought I could have produced. I've come to view the ticking clock as an important ally in my work.

- **KEEP FILES AND BINDERS.** On deadline the last thing a reporter needs is a time-consuming hunt for a fact or quote in a messy pile of notebooks, releases, reports and other materials. Some reporters use their computer to keep track. Others stay organized with low-tech manila folders and three-ring binders. (Whatever planning and organizational tools you employ, don't forget the importance of developing sources who will also let you know what's going on. When I was a Washington reporter, on more than one occasion a congressional staffer kept me from being scooped with a heads-up on a newsworthy development in a story I was covering.)

■ USE THE INTERNET. You can stay on top of your beat by subscribing to electronic mailing lists, known as listservs, that relate to your beat. If you're lucky enough to have a competing news organization, track what it reports. Keep your eyes and ears open. Ask yourself what's news, what's important, what is happening in town and how can you explain it. In your head constantly write or rewrite nut grafs that strive to explain the meaning behind things, why they matter, why people need to know these things. Be your most demanding boss. Keep setting goals for yourself. I resolved to be the best family issues reporter in Washington. That goal kept me striving. It also kept me interested. It's exciting to cover a beat: A landscape spreads out before you with people and rules and a culture to learn about, and as a journalist you get to look at it through a special lens—what people should know to be good citizens and perhaps to improve their lives.

THE NEW BEATS

As the 20th century began, reporters gathered news at places where information was assembled by officials. These places included police and fire stations, criminal and civil courts, town and city clerks' offices. "To get all the news that develops at each of these and many other places," Willard G. Bleyer wrote in a 1913 journalism textbook, "the city editor divides the news sources into 'runs' or 'beats' and details a reporter to each 'run.'" Whether the reporter had the city hall or the police "run," the term was apt nearly a century ago because, as Bleyer noted, the reporter was expected to visit each office on the beat one to six times a day, checking records, interviewing officials and chatting with secretaries and clerks.

Not much has changed in the last 100 years. In some ways, that's unfortunate. Too often, news coverage relies exclusively on visits, or worse, on telephone calls, to officials in the buildings that have always been the traditional sentinel posts of journalism. Editors complain that too many beats are heavy on bureaucracy and light on relevance and enterprise. They worry when reporters get too wrapped up in the process of government or politics and fail to provide the context that lets audiences understand the significance of news. The results are superficial stories that skim the surface. But faced with declining audiences, news organizations have been forced to change.

All my assignments throughout the 1970s and 1980s would have been familiar tasks for reporters during much of the 20th century. At my first job, my beat was police, fire, conservation commission and library board in Milford, Conn. At my second job, I covered three Hartford, Conn., suburbs where I was responsible for all the news in the community from crime to education. At my third job, I was a business reporter. At my fourth job, my beats included night cops, a suburb, the police beat and general assignment. At my next job I was a general assignment feature writer. But by the 1990s the nature of beats began to change dramatically.

At my last job I covered family issues as part of the "Close to Home" team in the Washington bureau of Knight Ridder Newspapers. That assignment was part of a nationwide effort by news organizations to find solutions to the growing problem of declining readership. Among the "keys to survival," as a 1991 report from the American Society of Newspaper Editors put it, were "hot topics" for building readership, such as stories on education, family and parenting. The problem with newspapers wasn't competition from television and the way it lured away so-called "time-starved readers" who preferred the nightly news or 24-hour cable news networks. Newspapers, critics said, just weren't giving readers what they wanted. Relevance, or the lack of it, became an industry buzzword.

LEARN MORE ABOUT THE WAYS THE "CIVIC" OR "PUBLIC" JOURNALISM MOVEMENT IS CHANGING HOW NEWS ORGANIZATIONS DEFINE AND REPORT NEWS ONLINE AT http://www. poynter.org/ research/biblio/ bib_pj.htm

In the 1990s, news organizations also looked to a controversial new approach known as "civic" or "public" journalism to make coverage more meaningful to audiences. Among its hallmarks: stories that propose solutions to societal problems, co-sponsoring reform efforts with government and nongovernmental organizations, engaging public officials and citizens with polls, town meetings and other dialogues about community problems and solutions. Proponents say that journalists must become more involved in civic life, not stand by while society crumbles. Some journalists contend that public journalism is just another name for good journalism, while critics argue that civic journalists end up reporting news they have helped create and may lose the independence good journalism demands. As many news organizations produce civic journalism projects, the debate continues.

At the Norfolk *Virginian-Pilot*, where the newsroom was organized by traditional core beats, such as education, city government, police, fire and courts, reporters and editors were designated to accommodate old and new definitions of news: public life, real life, global and women, family and children. Staffers at the *Orange County Register* in California brainstormed to define the "beats of the '90s."

"When the dust settled, dozens of new beats had been placed on the table," Richard Cheverton, the *Register's* managing editor for strategy and administration, recounted in a Poynter Institute case study. "The oldies-but-goodies survived: politics, courts, environment—some with suspicious new names, such as 'The Law and You.' " The paper even instituted a shopping mall beat. Although many journalists scorned such changes as "New Age"—thinking that had no place in a responsible newsroom—the proponents had evidence to support the need for change. Readership *was* down, especially among younger readers. As a consumer of news, I know I was not very interested in many stories in the newspaper. As a parent of young children, I wanted to read stories that helped me with my family's life. As a reporter I wanted to produce them. My interest dovetailed with my editor's demand for new approaches to news. The stories I produced—about minivan safety, deadly hazards posed by unsafe garage door openers, and juvenile gunshot victims—earned affirmation from editors who ran them on Page 1 or the front page of their lifestyle sections and were validated in positive reaction from readers.

The moral: Journalists need to be as flexible in defining news beats as they are in revising their stories.

FIRST BEAT: COVERING A COMMUNITY

Covering a community is the way many, if not most, reporters will begin their careers. Although the national media get most of the attention, the majority of journalists in America work for daily or weekly papers or local television or radio stations. Assigning a community beat is the way we train beginning reporters in Poynter's summer program. We have right outside our building a richly diverse collection of neighborhoods, and we use it to advantage. This approach is based on a course developed and taught at West Virginia University by Christine Martin, who co-directs Poynter's summer program. (Martin credits her curriculum to research by Professor Barbara Zang at the University of Missouri.) The goal is to discover a community by meeting and interviewing people and writing about them and the news, issues and events that affect them. Lessons learned in a community beat can be applied in every assignment you have.

In our program, each student is assigned, at random, to a neighborhood beat. Each beginner is given nothing more than a city map with the neighborhood highlighted in yellow and a city directory that lists the neighborhoods, its boundaries and the name of a person affiliated with the neighborhood association. The reporters immerse themselves and come to understand what residents, businesspeople and public officials consider important to their lives in that community. They uncover not just news, as Martin says, "but ... people—and their hopes, dreams, fears, plans, problems and solutions."

Like most newsrooms, ours practices the "sink or swim" approach. The first assignment: Take a three-hour shoe-leather tour of the neighborhood, including lunch at a local eatery; interview at least six people. When they return, reporters have to draw a map of their beat, indicating boundaries and landmarks and interesting spots they noticed. We post these on the walls and then ask each reporter to introduce the beat to his or her colleagues. This is on Friday. By Monday morning they must turn in a "beat at a glance" memo and story idea list. Over five subsequent weeks, they find all their stories for the weekly paper we publish. No stories are assigned by editors.

Our mandate for covering a beat is to go below the surface with stories that would be overlooked, not even noticed because they wouldn't generate a press release, or that fall between the cracks of traditional beats. The approach demands enterprise and trains reporters to be their own assignment editor. It reflects our belief that the reporter, not an editor tied to a desk or to the Internet, is the single best source for story ideas. This method of training requires bottom-up sourcing: those people whose lives are affected by events and trends inspire stories. But even more important, it incorporates the notion of giving voice to the voiceless, the poor, minorities, children, the elderly, among others. If you go out and talk to folks instead of just designated leaders, you're painting a more diverse, complete portrait of the world we live in.

Our students cover meetings, crime, education, business, environment, public safety, health and medicine, tree plantings, festivals, holidays, weather. But they approach each topic looking for relationships, stories that affect people in a community rather than information picked up from a police blotter.

The relationship between a reporter and her source lies at the heart of successful beat coverage. Carrie Sturrock, a Poynter reporting student, interviews a St. Petersburg resident for a story. Sturrock now reports for *The Concord* (N.H.) *Monitor.* (Courtesy of The Poynter Institute)

On the following pages you'll find two examples of stories reported and written by our summer students on their neighborhood beats. Each story is followed by the writer's answers to three questions about the "lessons learned": (1) what surprised me about reporting and writing this article, (2) what I learned from the experience and (3) what I need to learn next.

STUDENT EXAMPLE 1

During her first "shoe-leather" tour of her beat, Rebecca Catalanello heard that neighbors in her community still mourned an elderly woman who used to sell candy and sweet ice confections known as "flips." The result was a story that revealed a neighborhood's changing character and the timeless needs of children.

Memories of Mama

Gertie Coker Was an Inspiration to Many Adults, But Her Relationship to Children Was More Personal

By Rebecca Catalanello
Points South Staff Writer

ST. PETERSBURG —She was a secret only the children knew.

When Gertie Coker's obituary ran in the *St. Petersburg Times* it recounted her life as a highly visible member of St. Petersburg's African American community. She was a retired restaurateur who came to St. Petersburg in 1928. She was the grandmother of Doug Jamerson, Florida's labor secretary. She was an early feminist who kept her maiden name throughout her entire life. She was someone people wanted to be around, even after she retired.

But the obit left something out. When she died at 87 on April 22, she left a hole.

To the children of Old Southeast, that hole was "Mama Gert," the neighborhood fliplady.

"Every time we had money, we'd go over there," says Laquetta Jackson, 12, her short thin braids hitting her cheeks. "Sometimes we'd go two or three times in a day."

Across neighborhood lawns and streets and blocks, on Big Wheels or dirt bikes or foot, Jackson and other children pilgrimaged daily to Mama Gert's home, where the thick smell of simmering collard greens and hot fried chicken was an unwanted distraction on the way to the 25-cent, sticky-sweet cool-down treats called "flips" that she housed in her freezer.

Jason Myron, a freckle-faced 8-year-old, grows pensive at the mention of her name. "She was one of my most favoritest people," he says.

Parents knew who she was. They knew that if they ran out of laundry detergent or

Continued

sugar or bread, Mama Gert usually had it. But most of them never met her.

"She had everything anyone needed," says Mitzie Simmons, a 35-year-old mother of two who never saw Mama Gert's face. "The kids all knew her."

They knew the way her housecoat folded around her plump frame and how her glasses slid down her face when she looked at you. They knew the way she called your name when she sat at the table and gently chided you when you made your way through her screened-in porch to her kitchen. They knew how to avoid the stares of TV-watching men who crowded her single-story, blue-gray house and waited for plates of Mama Gert's lunch du jour.

Most of all, they knew that in her freezer was a world where shelves of sodas, candy, pickles and homemade frozen Popsicle treats called "flips" awaited sticky palms.

"She was sick a lot, but she was always there," says Brandi Morse, 17. "I couldn't believe it when she died."

Like many of the children, Morse had been there when, weeks before her death, an ambulance pulled up and worked to revive her from an earlier stroke. But none of them thought she would die—and not one of the children has forgotten how they learned she was gone.

"I went over there and knocked on the door, and no one answered," remembers 11-year-old Niam Lee. His legs dangle from the steps of his front porch.

Mama Gert gave the children lessons on what it means to be a good neighbor. When she was sick and in bed, children would carry her mail to her. When an earlier stroke

took her steam, children would give her bedside inspiration.

Jamerson, 50, remembers that his grandmother's connection with children was always a strong one. "The children were good therapy for her toward the end when she was sick. And she was always good therapy for them."

Today, children with a sweet tooth look elsewhere for treats. The older kids make their way down to Gita Food Store, a convenience store on Third Avenue South, a few blocks north of Mama Gert's. But the conversation isn't the same.

"You can't send the younger ones to the store," says Mitzie Simmons, whose youngest child is 8. "There are too many drunks and drugs. You can't afford to have your kids out of sight, and there's nowhere for the younger ones to go."

According to Sunny Patel, 17, a cashier at Gita for three years, the past few months have seen a boom in the sale of its 25-cent groceries—the quarter bags of chips, 25-cent snack cakes and the eight-ounce, multicolored fruit juices.

But the kids know what's missing.

"They don't have flips over there," says Jackson, her thin arm motioning toward the store. "Sometimes we just go there and fill them paper cups and get a drink ... but they don't know us. Miss Gert knew us all."

LESSONS LEARNED
Rebecca Catalanello

What Surprised Me

I was surprised by how difficult it was for me to let go of this story. For the past two nights, since I turned it in, I have tossed and turned at night over "what I didn't put in." Did I do it justice? Did I leave gaps? Would Mama Gert be the same woman I described in my story had I actually met her? Why has the story been on my mind so much?

What I Learned

I learned that journalism is not the same as poetry. When I first wrote the story, I guess I wrote it as though I were writing a poem. I jumped from line to line to describe what the kids saw when they saw Mama Gert. I was in love with the image I had of Mama Gert and was eager to get it all on the page at once. I learned that, though it may be all lovely and well, readers need to know right away what the story is about. I had to tame, restructure and reorganize the story to fit with a more newspapery format. I learned that self-indulgence during the writing process can be a detriment to the reader.

What I Need to Learn Next

I need to learn how to think about the reader more during the writing process. My first draft described the refrigerator door as Narnia (from C. S. Lewis' "The Lion, the Witch and the Wardrobe"). It wasn't until someone else read it that I realized that not everyone understands the reference. That "Narnia"—one word—would be confusing.

STUDENT EXAMPLE 2

On his beat, Richard Peacock spent a Saturday hanging out at a local barbershop and discovered an oasis of racial tolerance in a city that two years earlier had suffered through a riot.

The Barber of Civility

The Manager of Neighborhood Barbershop Says Her Shop Caters to the Needs of a Diverse, and Growing, Clientele

By Richard Peacock
Points South Staff Writer

At the Neighborhood Barbershop in the Skyway Plaza, three hair experts debate what it means to be a woman barber:

"Some people believe that a woman barber is like Delilah," says Benjamin "Doc" McAllister, 48, a barber. "If she cuts a man's head, he can lose his strength." Press-and-curl specialist Revear "Rita" Howard, 60, says that Samson lost his strength not because of Delilah but because he rebelled against God. Thinking the whole idea ridiculous, Deborah "Deb" Bevens Evans, 48, a master barber, says, "If a man wants to blame me for losing his strength, then he never had any to begin with."

Evans, an African American female barber and manager of Neighborhood Barbershop, actually represents a different sort of Delilah. Working with men daily, her expertise in barbering rejuvenated a once-all-white male establishment from critical decline.

John High, 35, the white owner of the barbershop that Evans manages, calls her "a knight in shining armor." Evans came to his rescue two years ago when she took over the management of Esquire Barbershop, located on Dr. Martin Luther King (Ninth) Street

South in the Skyway Plaza. Before she came, High says, this particular barbershop, one in a chain of five he owns, ranked near the bottom of his shops. High ranks the barbershop near the top now, crediting Evans' business acumen with a 110 percent increase in business.

Until five years ago, Evans worked full-time as an aviation equipment inspector for the Honeywell Corporation and did part-time barbering. When she arrived at High's barbershop she noticed that it did not reflect the surrounding community's multiracial and cultural makeup but looked more like an old segregated establishment reminiscent of the days of Jim Crow.

On the outside, she changed the name of the barbershop from Esquire Barbershop to Neighborhood Barbershop, a name, she says, that gives it a sense of community. Inside she added masks from Zaire and the Philippines to the walls where two murals of white men already exist. Gradually, she recruited barbers adept at cutting all grades of hair and skilled in hair and scalp treatment. And later she got Howard, an old friend who specializes in the nonchemical press-and-curl hairstyling technique that was popular among African American women in the 1950s and 1960s and, Evans says, is a rarity found in very few hairstyling sites today.

With these unique changes made, she envisioned a barbershop that could be like the Kash 'N Karry grocery store in its vicinity. "If people of different races and families can shop in one place, a grocery store, then why shouldn't they be able to get their hair cut in one place?" she said.

Despite friends and other barbers who said her experiment would not work, Evans prevailed. Neighborhood Barbershop has five barbers on staff—one African American woman, three African American men and one white man. According to Evans, each one averages 50 to 60 customers in a six-day workweek. Evans puts the client ratio at nearly 50-50 in terms of African Americans and whites who get haircuts, with a small sprinkling of Asian and Latin Americans.

Constantly attentive to her customers' needs, Evans knows they often want more than an attractive haircut. The other services that she and her colleagues offer range from doing repair work on damaged hair to counseling. Felix Busch, 41, travels more than 30 miles from Palmetto to have Evans cut his hair. "I come to her because she fixed my hairline once, and I've been coming back ever since," explained Busch.

Since 1968, Evans has defied traditionalists in the St. Petersburg hairstyling community by becoming one of the few African American female master barbers who cuts the hair of both genders as well as all races. And she finds joy in bringing diverse groups of people together and making them feel good about themselves.

Randall Mays, 21, a young white man, says he prefers going to African American barbers because they specialize in fades, a short-layered haircut blended in closely to the scalp. At other African American barbershops he visited, Mays felt awkward. According to him, "Deb was the first to make me feel welcome."

LESSONS LEARNED
Richard Peacock

What Surprised Me

I was surprised to discover there was no end to which I could stop reporting. My reporting started with women, and then it involved a barbershop, the owner of the barbershop, the history of barbershops, the legislation for the licensing of barbers, and it went on and on. Everything was news to me.

What I Learned

I need to know what my focus is, even if I have collected a mountain of information. I had trouble developing a focus because I didn't think about a focus throughout the whole reporting process.

Continued

What I Need to Learn Next

How to narrow my lens through which I look at the world. In doing so, I think I would better zoom in on what is central, what I should emphasize.

COVERING A NEW FRONTIER: THE SUBURBS

The Carrollwood bureau of the *St. Petersburg Times* sits nestled between Mel's Hot Dogs and Household Finance Corp. in a strip mall 30 miles north of the newspaper's city room. Reporters there covering the suburban boomtown are engaged in a revolutionary act: covering suburbia like it really matters. These reporters are struggling to report news in communities where traditional sentinel posts are absent. In the following memo to his editors, Bill Coats, a former *Times* editor who now reports, with gusto and imagination, from the suburb of Lutz ("as in 'boots,' not 'butts,'" he tells people), talks of writing about things "that are close to the soul" of a community.

A Prescription for Better Suburban Beat Coverage
Bill Coats

Newspapers for years have assigned reporters to cover the suburbs with little definition of a mission other than to write lots of "local" stories, "neighborhood" stories.

Left without a government complex, the reporters have sought out suburban institutions resembling government: neighborhood associations, chambers of commerce, sheriff's substations, special taxing districts and county government disputes that particularly affect suburbs, such as rezonings. These have tended to generate a smattering of ongoing stories that suburban reporters milked repeatedly for copy. Stories of universal reader appeal, with page-anchor potential, have been in short supply.

With some of the following ideas as cues, we should broaden our concept of news. We should recognize that nearly all our readers live in suburbs and most of them work there, so many of the most important factors in their lives are there.

The nerve center of the community no longer is Main Street or Courthouse Square. The community today is fragmented into many subcultures, each with its own less visible nerve center. We have to prowl around and discover where those communities and nerve centers are. Then we can write stories that touch the lives of thousands of suburbanites. Here are some coverage ideas:

- 911. Most 911 calls come from the suburbs, and they are recorded. Develop contacts among the operators and paramedics. Potential stories: dramatic situations and dramatic rescues that didn't make the police log because they didn't have a crime or catastrophe component.

- SCHOOL GUIDANCE COUNSELORS. They should be tapped into several communities: a generation of local kids, their parents and their teachers. Potential stories: newest influences, for better or worse, on kids' problems in the classrooms; social problems seeping onto campuses; individual cases of achievement, tragedy; the effects, for better or worse, of latest parenting trends.

- PREP SPORTS. Roam the stands during a game. The fan following of a prep sports team can be an eclectic community, crossing many cultural and class lines. Potential stories: the most rabid fan; a family or neighborhood makes a teen athlete its hero; how a community's mood can rise or fall with the fortunes of the team.

- DAY CARE. Develop sources among day-care providers, government regulators and parents, with an eye toward tapping into the community of working parents. Potential stories: parental coping problems (Mom works in one city, Dad in another; kid gets sick in a third); trends in care; substandard centers.

- WISDOM FIGURES. They don't have to be old; merely established and respected. Develop them as sources and tipsters. Potential stories: subsurface perspective on community issues; profiles; local initiatives that are afoot and have been broached with the wisdom figures.

Continued

- SCHOOL AND COMMUNITY THEATER. Tap into the community of amateur actors and theatergoers. Potential stories: features/advances on the productions; the little crises and triumphs behind the curtains.
- COMMON GROUND. Look for communities that have brought together disparate subcultures: teens working at nursing homes; ethnic mixtures in classrooms and workplaces. Potential stories: the processes by which they discover their differences and their common ground.
- VETERINARIANS. Plug into the community of pet owners. Potential stories: How bad is flea season this year? What is the latest fashionable pet? Cat becomes puppy's adopted mom; collie gets air-conditioned doghouse with TV.
- FITNESS CENTERS. Develop sources among the managers and the patrons. Potential stories: individual fitness and rehabilitation triumphs; health fads and new businesses catering to them; membership rip-offs.
- CHURCHES. Develop sources among pastors, activists and the community of worshippers. Potential stories: unusual community projects; thriving and dying churches; splits and mergers; fringe religions; triumphs and tragedies among members.
- THE RESTAURANT BUSINESS. Watch for grand openings and final closings. Cultivate sources at local favorites that have developed a community of patrons. Potential stories: neighborhood restaurant wars; health department crackdowns; trends in menus, marketing themes and customers' tastes.
- HOME SALES. Develop real estate agents as sources. Potential stories: neighborhoods changing in value or character.
- FRANCHISES. A suburban business beat. Develop sources among retail analysts. Potential stories: how chains are choosing the neighborhoods for locating stores. What market niche they are fighting to occupy. How the host communities are reacting.
- NEIGHBORHOOD WATCH. Develop sources among neighborhood watch organizers on the police force. Potential stories: latest neighborhood crime patterns and the latest crime fear patterns.

- CAMPUS POLICE. Develop sources among police officers assigned to high school, middle school and college campuses. Stories: trends in student misbehavior; tips about campus incidents.

- WILDLIFE RESCUE AGENCIES. Develop sources among their staffs. Potential stories: Python eats poodle; baby raccoons found in attic; trends in wildlife populations, migration and coping with human encroachment.

- COMMUTING. Talk to police and traffic planners about rush hour pressure points in your neighborhoods. Interview commuters at service stations and other stops near those points about how they cope. Potential stories: Suburbanites encounter what they moved there to avoid; neighborhoods suffer shortcutters; the price of having limited public transit; how participants in a carpool came to give up their individual independence.

- SUBURBAN LAWYERS. When any serious conflicts develop in your part of suburbia, these folks eventually will hear about them.

- KIDS' ATHLETICS. Drop in on some big games; develop sources among coaches and association directors. Potential stories: Girl all-stars beat boy all-stars; the priority conflict between winning and good sportsmanship; triumphs and tears among the kids; the problem of zealous parents; government support or lack thereof.

- BUSINESS ASSOCIATIONS. Attend chamber of commerce mixers and similar events. Potential stories: unusual businesses; innovative ones; competitions and shakeouts in various local industries.

- TENSION. Be alert for evolving collisions of different cultures, social classes or land uses and the friction those collisions cause.

- FLEA MARKETS. Tap into the communities of vendors and regular customers. Potential stories: profiles; the functioning of an offbeat economy (who are the vendors' wholesalers?).

- RIVALRIES. Ascertain from sports when the biggest high school football rivalries are about to be played and check in with those campuses. Potential stories: pranks, skits and

Continued

other shenanigans that may say a lot about each community's view of the other; anatomy and history of a rivalry (do the students even know why they're rivals?).

■ MINORITIES. Find ethnic subcultures in the suburbs via churches, the school system and the census. Potential stories: their special occasions; their experiences, for better or worse, of mainstreaming in the 'burbs. How suburban minorities are connected, or disconnected, to urban minorities.

■ CHARITIES. Meet the directors and die-hard activists. Potential stories: victims of injustice; NIMBY (not in my backyard) confrontations; do-gooder heroics.

■ MALLS. Develop contacts among managers and merchants. Good for ways in which the mall is replacing town square as focal point of a community. Potential stories: emerging local fashion fads; trends in consumer behavior; what people are doing, other than shopping, when they visit a mall.

■ HISTORY. Develop sources among local historians. Potential stories: Big news of today had its roots in situations years ago; what passes for historic structures in areas that were scrub 20 years ago and what people are doing with those structures.

■ ICE RINKS. Tap into the growing community of upscale families who are taking up ice skating. Potential stories: Olympic hopefuls; parental politics; the business of lessons, equipment and ice time.

Here's a light-hearted example of Coats' work reflecting his understanding of his community:

Anything Goes at Lutz Celebration

Bill Coats
St. Petersburg Times
July 3, 1998
LUTZ—The annual Fourth of July parade here doesn't celebrate just independence, it celebrates democracy: Anybody can be in the parade.

You don't even have to be human. Some of the most memorable parade units in recent years have included dogs, horses and even a dressed-up cow.

"You just don't know what you're going to get," marveled Jan Smith, who organizes the parade for the Lutz-Land O'Lakes Woman's Club, sponsor of the community's July Fourth celebration. "You don't know who's going to be in the parade and whether they're going to be in the right place in line."

As any politician will attest, democracy can be a messy system. So can judging the parade entries.

Therefore, Lutz this year is adding an uptown feature to its down-home parade: a judge's reviewing stand.

"We've had a few major complaints over the last few years," said Auralee Buckingham, who coordinates the day's events for the Woman's Club. "All these groups have become very competitive."

Most other aspects of the day will remain the same.

As usual, the big events are the one-mile and five kilometer foot races, beginning at 8 a.m.; the parade beginning at 10:30; the Lutz Volunteer Fire Department's barbecued chicken sales beginning at 11; and the inauguration of a new Guv'na at 12:30 p.m.

For the third year in a row, Ben Nevel will ride in the parade as a VIP. This year Nevel is grand marshal, a tribute to his work on behalf of the Old Lutz School. Last year he was Guv'na. The year before he was a Guv'na candidate, touting his campaign by firing blasts from the gondola of his hot-air balloon.

A second change this year affects the cake-baking contest. It is being moved to the conference room of the Lutz Branch Library. Last year, air conditioning was turned off in the Community Center, and the cake icings sagged.

So both cake judgings and parade judgings are being moved.

Traditionally, parade judges scanned the entries and awarded trophies at the point the parade was most orderly: just before it started moving. But that system has tended to catch paraders before they put on costumes, a practice they delay in the July heat until the final moment. Civil War reenactors, for example, wear wool battle uniforms.

So last year, judges toured the parade early, then watched it at the end and dispensed trophies. But many units, after an hour in the sun, promptly vanished.

"I have most of last year's trophies in the trunk of my car," said Smith.

The organizers hope to implement a numbering system this year to help the judges. But even that won't account for people who join as the parade rolls toward downtown Lutz.

"Last year, one of the funniest entries in the parade we didn't even know we were going to have," Smith said.

That entry was Kevin Waller and his dog Brady. Waller rode an antique motorcycle. Brady, wearing goggles, rode in a sidecar in front of a big American flag.

The parade's unpredictability also tends to cross up master of ceremonies Bob Moore, who announces the 60 to 80 entries from a list of sign-ups.

"I'm sorry, but the Little League 10-year-olds look an awful lot like the Little League 11-year-olds," Moore said. "I announce the 11-year-olds, and they all yell, 'We're the 10-year-olds!' I say, 'I'm sorry, dude.'"

BEGINNER'S BEATS: COVERING GOVERNMENT

Consider the typical beginning reporter: young, single, childless, owns no property, has never paid any property tax, may never have voted. Despite that profile, many, if not most, beginners will find themselves covering the institutions that decide how much taxes people will pay, what they can do with property they own, how their children will be taught and what laws the community will follow. In terms of impact on people's lives, local government is by far the most important news beat. City and town governments provide fire and police protection, maintain streets and sewers, libraries and parks, collect garbage, issue permits for everything from new home construction to sidewalk hot dog sales, and provide social services from welfare to cemetery maintenance. Despite its importance, government is the beat that most beginners are least prepared to cover and least interested in covering. It's soooooo boring. That was certainly my attitude when I found myself, in my 20s, sitting at meetings of the zoning review commission and the school board.

READ "THE LOCAL NEWS HANDBOOK" FROM THE AMERICAN SOCIETY OF NEWSPAPER EDITORS ONLINE AT http://www.asne.org/kiosk/reports/99reports/localnews.htm

Government is important because of the ways it affects people's lives. Government can seem boring because, by its very nature, it is legalistic and rooted in tedious process and ceremony that often seem irrelevant. The key to making it interesting, to you and your readers and viewers, is understanding the way government works—and doesn't work (but might work better)—and communicating that in your stories. Eventually, I came to realize that government is one of the most exciting and significant beats in journalism.

One of your first stops in a new community should be the town or city hall. Check in with the city manager or town clerk and ask for materials that outline and describe the way the local government operates. In most cities, city councils serve as the highest authority within local government in deciding issues of public policy. At open sessions, city councils pass laws, also known as ordinances, adopt resolutions and lead conversations about how their community will be governed and how to provide services for the citizens' welfare.

Generally, these are the various forms of city government that act as the administrator, implementing the policies voted on by the elected members of the city council.

1. COUNCIL/MANAGER OR COUNCIL/ADMINISTRATOR. The council hires a chief executive officer who, in effect, runs the community's day-to-day operations.

2. COMMISSION. An elected commission functions collectively as city council and serves as administrator of city departments.

3. MAYOR/COUNCIL. The legislative and policymaking body is a popularly elected council. There are two types:

A. **WEAK-MAYOR.** The mayor chairs the council, but other elected officials and council members share managerial duties.
B. **STRONG-MAYOR.** The mayor serves as chief executive officer, has the authority to appoint administrative personnel, is responsible for city administration and serves as the presiding officer at council meetings.

Below the mayor and council are the agencies responsible for the city's daily operations, such as the police and fire departments, public works, school, and parks and recreation departments. Depending on the size of the community and the news organization, a reporter may be responsible for news coming out of all government agencies in one, or even several, towns or cities.

BEGINNER'S BEATS: COVERING COUNCIL MEETINGS

Governments do their business at public meetings. In Chapter 10, you learned about meeting coverage. Here is a checklist of practical advice about meetings of government bodies, such as city council or county commission, that Kelly Ryan of the *St. Petersburg Times* gave to reporting students at The Poynter Institute. Ryan is a city hall reporter who recognizes the challenges that government coverage poses to the young journalist: "You've never owned property. You've never paid property taxes. You don't have any children. Everybody uses a lot of words that mean absolutely nothing to you. So how do you cover government?"

Here is Ryan's checklist for city council meetings:

- Before the meeting, get the agenda and use databases to report and write background. Governments generate reams of documents. Read everything you can.

- Remember creature comforts. Meetings can go on for hours without break. Bring gum or candy, such as Life Savers, to ward off distracting hunger pangs. Get a good night's sleep the night before.

- Dress professionally. Your youth can work against you; if you want to be treated like an adult don't dress like a kid.

- Keep track: How long do meetings last? How long do council members speak, argue, doze?

- Know the lay of the land: where the staff and council hang out.

- If math isn't your strong suit, check it with another reporter, an editor, an informed source.

- Remember a key lesson about government: Every issue, every person, has a history. Learn the background.

Breaks give reporters covering government meetings the opportunity to fill in gaps in their reporting. Anthony Hall and Teresa Rochester, two Poynter reporting students, get background from a city official. (Courtesy of The Poynter Institute)

- Government is of the people, by the people and for the people. The best government stories are about the people who run and are affected by it.
- Always keep asking: Why does this matter to people? Possible answers: The decision is racist. The vote means taxes are going to go up.
- Cultivate sources. Find at least one or two people you can ask the dumb questions.
- Think of every meeting as part of a larger picture.
- Keep good notes: Note times, dates, use initials to identify speakers. Go back and fill in as soon as you can, or else you may find you can't use a good quote because you can't decipher it a week after the meeting.
- Bring business cards to give to speakers and witnesses. Ask for theirs. See if they'll call you when the meeting is over.
- Write your first draft without your notebook. Ask yourself: How would I tell this story to my mother, my friends?

STUDENT EXAMPLE

DAVID HO

POINTS SOUTH

STAFF WRITER

The St. Petersburg City Council blocked conversion of an abandoned Central Avenue topless bar into a temporary labor office today, supporting the appeal of the Kenwood Neighborhood Association who feared the labor pool would be a blight on their community.

1. Lead: Summarizes the story, focusing on impact and the social forces behind the government action.

The unanimous vote came after nearly two hours of emotional testimony by Kenwood residents and business leaders, who cited repeated instances of vagrants drinking alcohol and urinating outside of similar nearby labor offices.

2. Second part of summary lead: Provides background that explains conditions that led to action in the hearing room and the neighborhood.

"This is not a landscape problem, this is a people-scape problem," said Pat Fulton for the Kenwood Association. "We're not concerned about trees and shrubs, but alcoholics who walk by killing the growth of the neighborhood."

She went on to describe their neighborhood as a formerly seedy area that had been revitalized in recent years through the hard work of community leaders.

3. Quote: Vivid and concise summing up of the neighborhood's position.

Mike Hanlon, owner of the Antique Exchange on Central Avenue, initiated the appeal to prevent the move, objecting to the type of clientele served by the labor office and the fact that they loitered outside. Hanlon noted that there are already three other labor offices in the Kenwood area and that already hurts local property values and the image of the neighborhood.

The labor office, Pinellas Personnel, is owned by James Britt, who wishes to move to the vacant building at 2451 Central Ave. It is currently located at 1742 Central Ave. but has been functioning under a Board of Adjustment grace period since Dec. 17, 1993, when it was decided that it did not qualify to operate in that area.

"We ask the city to look beyond fear, ignorance and paranoia," said William Davenport, Britt's attorney. "What Mr. Britt does is place blue-collar workers in jobs, those that want to work up a sweat rather than go on welfare."

Britt said that his company earned over $1.1 million in 1995 and employed over 1,400 workers who did such jobs as making key chains for Disney World and performing janitorial duties at the St. Petersburg pier.

"We want to be a productive member of the community, not a drain on it," said Britt.

4. More arguments against the change: Always good to keep related material together to avoid "ping pong" effect caused by alternating quotes from warring sides.

5. Now the other side gets to present its case: history, statistics and arguments.

The audience, filled with Kenwood residents, murmured and chuckled as Britt made his assertions.

District 6 council member David T. Welch said he lives near the area in question and vehemently told Britt, "You can't fool me about that place. I live by there and go by there every day. ... You don't have control over it."

In defense of his client, Davenport called Britt's business "an American success story," which was met by derisive laughter from the gallery.

6. Back-and-forth at hearing: Example of color—exchange between witness and council member and audience reaction—that conveys tenor of hearing.

When the vote came, the powerful feelings in the council chamber were made clear, as City Council Chairman Edward Cole cast his decision but prefaced it by saying, "I'm going to vote yes. I'm not sure I'm not betraying the needy. If I am, I hope God forgives me."

District 7 council member Ernest L. Fillyau, who earlier in the meeting read an emotional letter from one of the transient laborers employed in Kenwood, asked, "Where will these people go? These people are also in my neighborhood or in my district. I sit under trees and talk to them, and I get notes that they're about to lose their homes. ... It lay heavy on my heart, because I pledged to help the neighborhoods ... but you have to look at the facts and put the emotions aside."

7. Kicker: Ending uses two quotes from council members to help readers understand the vote.

David Ho wrote this meeting story as a Poynter reporting fellow in 1996. He now reports for The Associated Press in Washington, D.C.

BEGINNER'S BEATS: COVERING COPS

The police beat is one of the most important beats in a community. Often, it is given to beginners. "Covering the police is like any other beat," says Tim Roche, a veteran reporter who started out reporting police news in Texas at the age of 15. "Very seldom does a story come to you. The way you discover them is by making the rounds."

Chances are you'll be replacing another reporter who will introduce you to the chief and other officers. But you may have to do it yourself. Hand out your card. Offer your home phone and e-mail address. Let them see your face.

Some reporters think that the minute they arrive on the scene of a story, they're entitled to know everything. Professionals realize that the police and rescue personnel have their own responsibilities. Police officers say they can always spot amateurs: They're the ones who run up, out of breath, notebook open, demanding information so they can make their imminent deadline. Officers understand reporters have a job to do, but so do they. You'll get your facts faster if you stay cool, calm and collected.

Police are governed by laws, rules and regulations. Find out their press policy, their system for releasing reports, how court records are kept and where you can find information about prisoners. Police officers are often reluctant or downright fearful about talking to the media. They know that if they say the wrong thing or if you misquote them they can get in deep trouble. "There is a tremendous amount of peer pressure not to screw up in the paper, not to screw up an investigation," says William Doniel, who manages press information for the St. Petersburg Police Department.

As a police reporter for the *St. Petersburg Times,* Tim Roche always let other reporters ask all the basics and then came back afterward with questions that weren't asked or that would draw out a good quote. He was never afraid to play stupid because "they will be more eloquent the second time around."

A LIFE IN JOURNALISM

KARIN FISCHER'S FIRST NEWSPAPER JOB AFTER COLLEGE WAS THE POLICE BEAT AT THE *CHARLESTON DAILY MAIL.* SHE NOW COVERS THE STATEHOUSE FOR THE PAPER.

COVERING COPS: "THE BEST AND THE WORST"

Karin Fischer
Charleston Daily Mail

Three days on the job and I found myself, photographer by my side, tramping through mud and knocking on the doors of modest houses and mobile homes along a hollow known as Paint Creek, about 20 miles east of Charleston, W.Va.

I was in Paint Creek talking to these people because of what had happened to their neighbor and her two young children in the early morning hours. Two intruders allegedly had driven in from the interstate highway that runs within shouting distance of the woman's modest home, broken in, tied up her two sons (seriously cutting one on the arm) and robbed and repeatedly raped her.

This woman is a hero, although her name has never seen print. I knew it. Her neighbors knew it. She'd hung on for four hours before she escaped with her children, leading them on a run, through a creek in the early December morning, to safety.

That's what my beat is like: a mixture of the best of the best and the worst of the worst. Heroism and horror. Courage and cowardice. Learning how to distinguish between the two and how to balance the conflicting emotions they evoke has been one of my biggest challenges.

There's a fine line between being jaded—when I covered the crash of a West Virginia University charter plane on deadline, I had to combat the adrenaline rush by reminding myself, "Two men died; two families lost their sons"—and caring too much. My Page 1 story is someone's tragedy. But, ultimately, it is theirs. I shouldn't bring tragedies home from work.

Talking with the families and neighbors and friends of victims (and of suspects) often pulls me up short, and as much as I sometimes hate making the call I know it's necessary. I need people to talk with me. And, frequently, they do want to talk. They need to talk.

Once, I was working on a story—for an 8:15 a.m. deadline—about a woman who allegedly had badly beaten her daughter. The woman's own sister had turned her in to the police; she feared for the safety of her niece. I did not want to make a phone call to the suspect's sister. I did not want to call an unknown woman at 7 a.m. and ask her why she sent her sister to jail.

But when I called her, she was glad to talk. Her family was furious for what they believed was betrayal, and no one had bothered to ask her why she had done it. It turned out both women had suffered severe beatings at the hands of their father, and she was terrified that history was repeating itself. She really wanted to tell her story. She really wanted someone to listen.

Continued

Of course, many of the stories I cover lack both the drama and the tragedy of these articles. The variety within my beat can be enormous. Major breaking news on deadline is counteracted by the many days when I make 70 phone calls to State Police detachments and sheriff's departments around the state only to be told, "All's quiet here, Honey."

The daily crime is the foundation of my beat, but I like to think my other stories, offbeat and enterprise, comprise the walls and windows and ceiling, that they complete my beat.

I cover fire as part of my beat, but it isn't just alarm calls. I've gone on patrol with forest rangers at the start of forest fire season. I've traveled to an abandoned quarry with assistant state fire marshals to blow up unstable Civil War-era cannonballs.

On the police side of things, I've had the opportunity to cover murders, robberies and aggravated assaults. I've also covered pit bull fights, rampaging bulldozer drivers and tornadoes. I've written stories about police stress and physical fitness, manpower issues and possible police corruption.

Working on the beat has given me an appreciation of the breadth of the subject matter, of the potential for stories and of the poetry of the most basic, day-to-day minutiae.

When I come into work early every morning—too early for the local news to be broadcast on the radio or television—I don't know what the next two hours will bring. I approach each day with a combination of anticipation and dread. Chances are, I'll talk to dozens of police and fire dispatchers and come up with nothing more than a short story or a police brief or two.

Or maybe the minutes until deadline will be a mad rush, a string of phone calls to the police and hospital, a quick trip to the scene, a talk with neighbors.

If nothing else, I've learned more about reporting. My questions now are reflexes: "What are the descriptions of suspects?" "What kind of structure was the building that burned?" "Who notified authorities?" I don't agonize over a word or a line or a paragraph—I just write. And I know the phone numbers of half the police departments in the state by heart.

TIPS FOR COVERING COPS

Stephen Buckley
The Washington Post

STEPHEN BUCKLEY SPENT 11 MONTHS AS NIGHT POLICE REPORTER IN THE DISTRICT OF

Stephen Buckley

COLUMBIA FOR *THE WASHINGTON POST*. AFTER COVERING COPS, COURTS AND EDUCATION FOR THREE YEARS, HE JOINED THE PAPER'S FOREIGN SERVICE AND SERVED AS NAIROBI BUREAU CHIEF FROM 1995 TO 1998. HE PREPARED THESE TIPS FOR THE POYNTER INSTITUTE'S COLLEGE PROGRAM IN NEWS REPORTING AND WRITING.

Cops are human, **too**, **Part 1:** Get to know them. Like everyone, they respond to reporters they know. So if you're on the night cops beat, and things are deadly dull, go down to the police shop and hang out with the detectives. When you meet detectives you like, ask them out for a beer. Tell them a little about yourself. Ask them about their families. And of course, ask them about the work. Steve Aspinall, a detective from the St. Petersburg Police Department, said a reporter once called him in the hospital where he was a patient. After that, no matter what he was doing, he always returned that reporter's calls.

Always go to the scene, **Part 1:** This is where you get the details that the public information officer can't provide. The blood on the sidewalk. The howling, disconsolate mother. The stunned friends. Perhaps the eerie quiet that settles over the neighborhood. And most importantly, you sometimes find witnesses at the scene. They may be able to tell you only how many shots they heard or how loud the shots sounded, but you can't write great stories without those kinds of details.

Always go to the scene, **Part 2:** You hear a shooting broadcast over the police scanner. It's 1:30 a.m., an hour before you're scheduled to go home. You're exhausted. You call up the public information office (or more likely, the communications center, at that hour), and they tell you all they know is that a youth, apparently in his late teens or early 20s, was found shot to death in an alley in a bad neighborhood. You tap out a brief and go home to bed. You wake up the next morning and click on the radio to hear this: "A 14-year-old honor student was found shot to death outside a reputed crack house in southeast Washington early today. ..." You throw up your breakfast.

That's actually a true story (well, not the throwing up part). So always, always, go to the scene.

Never assume people don't want to talk: Sometimes, particularly after an especially horrifying crime, victims and their relatives—and a suspect's relatives and friends—*don't* want to

Continued

talk. But many, many times, they do talk to reporters. Sometimes, they even talk for hours. The point is: Don't try to
guess. Ask. You never know.

Spend time in neighborhoods: Particularly those known
for high crime. The temptation is to avoid these communities.
The truth is that they often offer rich stories—stories of people trying to save their children; stories of people trying to
drive out criminals; stories of people who've seen their
beloved communities crumble. Get to know the activists,
longtime residents, mothers (mothers talk because their top
priority is to save their children; so they're often willing to
risk the scorn of neighbors by talking to reporters). The best
police stories are almost always in the neighborhood.

Cops are human, too, Part 2: When the cops do something good, get it into the paper. Even if you think it's just going to be a scrawny six-inch story buried deep in the Metro
section, write it up. Police officers feel like they take a lot of
criticism but rarely receive praise when they do something
good. And they're right. So when they make a key arrest or
add some patrol officers somewhere, don't ignore it. Writing—
when it's appropriate—about when the cops do something
good is one easy way to build great sources and build lots of
good will (that, sooner or later, you'll have to draw on).

Know different sections: Develop sources around the department. The temptation is to spend most of your time
hanging out with the senior detectives, the ones who handle
the big cases. Spend time with the folks in the vice squad,
the burglary section, the robbery section, etc. They've got
good stories, too.

Look for patterns: Police departments often have daily
logs that they allow reporters to go through. Go through that
log. Check to see whether there's been an unusually high
amount of crime in a normally quiet neighborhood. Or maybe
you'll notice that a normally dangerous community turns
quiet for a few weeks. Or maybe you'll see that all the homi-
cides in a neighborhood seem to have the same m.o. (i.e.,
three cases over a few months in which young professional
women are strangled). Don't wait for the cops to put those
things together. Be your own detective.

Read police news in out-of-town papers: Often, crimes
move in trends. If you live in Harrisburg, Pa., and you hear
that heroin is making a big comeback in Pittsburgh, ask
detectives if they're seeing more heroin on the streets of

Harrisburg these days. Crime-fighting strategies also move in waves. If you read that the San Jose, Calif., Police Department has started to employ something called community-oriented policing, make a note of it. Chances are lots of other departments have either started to do the same or are considering taking that route.

Cultivate clerks: Get clerks and front-desk sergeants on your side. Chat them up when you've got nothing to do. Offer to take them to lunch. Treat them the way you would a homicide detective. You won't win over all, but you'll win over some. Sometimes they'll tip you off to something big happening (like a multiple shooting) or to a major arrest. Sometimes they'll get you a file you've been trying to track down for weeks. Sometimes they'll patch your call through to homicide rather than hang up and tell you that the detectives are busy. As with clerks and lower-level officials everywhere, they respond to people who've shown them respect and courtesy.

GLOSSARY: ESSENTIAL TERMS FOR POLICE REPORTERS

ARREST. Apprehension or detention of a person by a law enforcement officer.

ASSAULT. Attempting to kill or cause serious physical injury to another person. The threat of force is called assault as opposed to battery, which is the actual use of force.

BAIL. In criminal cases, a sum of money posted by or on behalf of a defendant to guarantee his or her appearance in court after being released from jail. May also be referred to as bail bond.

BAIL BONDSMAN. A person who posts bail in exchange for a fee, usually 10 percent of the total bail.

BATTERY. The use of force or violence to inflict an injury on another.

BURGLARY. Breaking into a building to commit a crime.

FELONY. A serious violation of criminal law punishable by death or a prison sentence of a year or more.

HOMICIDE. The killing of one person by another. Includes first- and second-degree murder and manslaughter.

JUVENILE. A young person who has not yet attained the age at which he or she should be treated as an adult for purposes of criminal law. Age varies by state.

LARCENY. The illegal taking of another's property.

MANSLAUGHTER. The unlawful killing of another without malice or premeditation. It may be either voluntary, upon a sudden impulse, or involuntary, in the commission of some unlawful act.

MIRANDA RULE. The Supreme Court ruling that confessions cannot be used to prosecute a defendant if the police do not advise the suspect in custody of certain rights before questioning. The rights include:

1. The right to remain silent and to refuse to answer any questions.
2. The right to know that anything the suspect says can and will be used against the suspect in a court of law.
3. The right to consult with an attorney and to have an attorney present during questioning.
4. The right to have counsel appointed at public expense, prior to any questioning, if the suspect cannot afford counsel.

MISDEMEANOR. A criminal offense, less serious than a felony, that carries a maximum penalty of less than one year in jail or prison.

MURDER. The unlawful taking of a human life with malice and premeditation.

RAPE. Sexual intercourse without consent.

ROBBERY. Stealing money or other property from another by force and intimidation.

Crime and punishment definitions in this chapter are drawn from The Associated Press Stylebook *and online glossaries posted by the Ninth Judicial Court of Florida, Utah State Courts and the* News Reporter's Handbook on Law and the Courts *by the Missouri Press-Bar Commission.*

COVERING COPS: FROM NEWS RELEASE TO BRIEF TO STORY

The criminal justice process begins when a crime is committed. Police respond to the scene and later file a report. The report is usually summarized in a news release, which is usually the starting point for a reporter.

Following you will find three items that trace the evolution of a typical crime story as it was reported in a newspaper.

1. The police news release on the next page. It provides basic information that often answers the five W's and "How?": type of incident, date and time, address, identification of victim, defendant and charge, circumstances, and the officer who prepared the release. Cops aren't professional writers or typists. The spellings may not always be correct, so double-check everything.

2. A brief that appeared in the local newspaper the morning after the incident. It doesn't contain all the details included in the news release, which may not have been available to the reporter before deadline. Some police departments make a tape recorded summary of the release that news organizations can listen to by telephone, or a police official will provide information in response to a reporter's questions.

A 16-year-old St. Petersburg boy was killed Sunday afternoon when he was shot by a friend playing with a shotgun, police said.

David R. Starkes, 524 16th Ave. S., was shot by Carlos J. Smith, 19, St. Petersburg police officials said.

The pair were at Smith's home, 658 1/2 16th Ave. S., when the gun fired, hitting Starkes in the head.

Smith was charged with manslaughter, police said, but he had not been booked into the Pinellas County Jail late Sunday.

St. Petersburg Times
July 13, 1998

3. A follow-up story on page 489, that appeared the next day. It is based on interviews with police and relatives of the dead teen-ager and the friend charged in connection with his death. It takes a storytelling approach, with a lead that compares the common ground of the boys' lives with the gunplay that ended in death for one and jail for the other.

ST. PETERSBURG POLICE DEPARTMENT
PUBLIC INFORMATION RELEASE

INCIDENT: Homicide   OFFENSE # 98-38781

DATE OCCURRED: 7/12/98   TIME OCCURRED: 4:05 p.m.

ADDRESS OCCURRED: 658 1/2 16th Ave. So.

VICTIM: David R. Starkes

RACE: black   SEX: male   D.O.B. 9/28/81

VICTIM'S ADDRESS: 524 16 Ave. So.

DEFENDANT #1: Carlos J. Smith

RACE: black   SEX: male   D.O.B. 2/12/79

DEFENDANT'S ADDRESS: 658 1/2 16th Ave. So.

CHARGE(S): Manslaughter

CIRCUMSTANCES SURROUNDING THE INCIDENT OR ARREST:

At 4:05 p.m., Sunday, July 12th, officers received a call of a person shot at 658 1/2 16th Avenue South. Upon arrival, officers found the victim had received a gunshot wound to the head. The victim was transported to Bayfront Medical Center, and died at approximately 7:10 p.m. The victim, suspect, and at least one other person were in the apartment at the time of the shooting. The suspect had acquired the gun (shotgun) recently and had been "playing" with it over the last few days. Today, it appears the gun discharged while the suspect was again "playing" with the gun. The spent round(s) struck the victim in the head.

RELEASE PREPARED BY: Sgt. Glen Moore
DATE: 7/12/98   TIME: 8:30 p.m.
cc: Chief of Police
    Public Information Officer
    Communications Supervisor

Many police stories begin with a tersely worded release issued by a law enforcement agency. The reporter will have to interview police, witnesses and relatives to flesh out the facts. (Courtesy of the St. Petersburg Police Department)

Friends' Gunplay Takes Fatal Twist

By Kris Mayes
St. Petersburg Times Staff Writer
July 14, 1998

David Starkes and Carlos Smith had much in common.

Both were living with their grandmothers in the same St. Petersburg neighborhood. And both had a fascination with the same sawed-off shotgun, blasting off rounds in a nearby alley for kicks.

But on Sunday, police said, the gunplay turned deadly when Smith trained the gun on Starkes and accidentally fired, killing the 16-year-old.

Smith, 19, on Sunday was charged with manslaughter in Starkes' death and was also charged with resisting arrest without violence. On Monday he was being held without bail in the Pinellas County Jail.

The tragedy between friends left family members stunned.

"I can't believe it was an accident, because why would he (Smith) point that gun at David when he first walked to the door?" said Virgil Beckford, Starkes' grandmother. "Why David?"

According to Beckford, Starkes had walked to Smith's home late Sunday afternoon to hang out with a group of friends.

The men often gathered together, according to Beckford, and had recently begun taking Smith's shotgun out for target practice.

At about 4 p.m., police said, Smith and Starkes were loading and unloading the gun inside Smith's apartment at 6581 1/2 16th Ave. S., when Smith accidentally fired one round into Starkes' head, according to St. Petersburg police department spokesman Bill Doniel.

Ironically, Starkes recently injured his hand when the gun recoiled during target practice, sending him to the hospital for treatment, according to Beckford.

"He had shot that gun, and it had messed his hand up," Beckford said. "But I told him, 'Don't touch that gun again.'"

She added, "I didn't want him to bother with guns at all, especially a gun as powerful as that."

Starkes was described by family members as a "character" who loved to joke and fish and planned to try for a spot on the Northeast High School football team during the upcoming school year.

Smith's grandmother and great-aunt said they were shocked by the incident and were unaware that he owned the gun. "I don't even know how to explain it," said Effie Lowe, Smith's grandmother. "He was a good boy."

Nora Campbell of St. Petersburg, who is Smith's great-aunt, said the family was deeply sorry for the accident.

"We don't know what to say," Campbell said. "Sometimes we do our best for our kids, and sometimes our best isn't good enough."

BEGINNER'S BEATS: COVERING COURTS

Covering the legal system can be, well, a trying experience. There are no require-ments of public notice, and participants are often not eager to talk to reporters. But lawyers and judges alike are more apt to open up if they feel the reporter understands what they are doing.

That sentiment, from the introduction to the section on the legal system in the *St. Petersburg Times* stylebook, is the best advice any reporter new to a beat could embrace. But it's particularly important for anyone reporting in the courts. The legal system is a process, with its own rules and lan-guage. You can also think of it as a landscape, a collection of territories, each with its own terminology and procedures. Broadly speaking, the le-gal system in America is divided in two parts. Think of it as the Law of Twos.

Two kinds of courts: federal and state

Two kinds of laws and legal actions: criminal and civil

Two kinds of crimes: felony and misdemeanor

Two sides in a legal case: plaintiff and defendant

FOR MORE IN-FORMATION ABOUT FEDERAL AND STATE COURTS ONLINE, VISIT THE CENTER FOR INFORMATION, LAW AND POLICY AT http://www.cilp.org/

Federal courts decide cases that involve the U.S. Constitution, such as taxes, bankruptcy, civil rights and federal statutes, or laws, passed by Congress. There are three levels of federal courts:

1. **U.S. DISTRICT COURT.** The first step. It holds trials and hears federal cases.

2. **U.S. COURT OF APPEALS.** Decisions made in District Court are appealed here.

3. **U.S. SUPREME COURT.** The highest court in the land. It hears ap-peals from federal and state appeals courts.

State courts decide cases that involve state constitutions and state laws passed by the legislature. Court systems vary by state, but often include these levels:

1. **MUNICIPAL COURT,** such as city, county or magistrate court. It handles misdemeanors, small claims, traffic offenses, preliminary felony hearings.

2. **STATE TRIAL COURT.** It handles felonies and misdemeanors, civil cases.

3. **APPEALS COURT.** It handles appeals from trial courts.

4. **SUPREME COURT.** Highest state court. It hears appeals from appeals courts.

There are two kinds of law in America: criminal and civil. Civil and crim-inal cases are heard in federal and state courts. In criminal court, the government, through the police or prosecutor, is the accuser. In civil court, actions are usually brought by individual citizens, corporations or organizations, although the government can also bring civil actions, for example, against polluters or civil rights violators.

CRIMINAL PROCEDURES: STEP BY STEP

As you learned in Chapter 11, libel actions often arise from what seem the most unlikely stories; not the hard-hitting investigative piece but rather the short crime story. Even if a libel suit doesn't go to trial, it can cost your news organization millions of dollars in legal fees and settlement costs. Mistakes often stem from misunderstandings about criminal or court procedures. Procedures vary from state to state, so you will have to master the process in your community.

1. **ARREST.** Arrest is the act of being taken into custody by the police. The police must have enough evidence to convince a judge that there was "probable cause" that a crime was committed and that the person arrested committed the crime. Police officers can arrest the accused at the scene of a crime, or later, based on a warrant issued by a judge who has been presented with a sworn complaint, or based on an indictment issued by a grand jury.

    Note: Be careful how you use the word "arrest." As Bill Walsh, a copy editor at *The Washington Post,* says in his Web site, The Slot: A Spot for Copy Editors, the common construction is inherently libelous. *John Smith was arrested for bank robbery* means Smith robbed a bank and was arrested for it. Rather, say he was *arrested on a charge of bank robbery* or *arrested in connection with a bank robbery* or something similar. Note that some jurisdictions may be picky about the word "charge"; if you're writing in a place where the charge doesn't occur until the indictment, you might want to use the *in connection with* wording or something along the lines of *arrested on suspicion of.*

2. **BOOKING.** After arrest, police book the suspect. Fingerprints and a photograph (known as a "mug shot") are taken, and possible charges and the suspect's name, age, address and other biographical information are recorded in the police "log." The suspect may also participate in a lineup where victims and/or witnesses are given a chance to make an identification.

    COPY EDITOR BILL WALSH OFFERS USEFUL HELP ON "THE SLOT" ONLINE AT http://www.theslot.com

3. **PRETRIAL RELEASE.** The police may release a suspect, depending on the severity of the crime, either on promising to appear in court to answer the charges or on posting bond—in cash or property. Otherwise the suspect will be held either at the police station or in a jail.

4. **FIRST APPEARANCE.** Also known as an advisory hearing. The suspect appears in open court before a judge who advises him or her of the charges, appoints a lawyer if the defendant can't afford one and

establishes whether probable cause existed to justify the arrest. The defendant may be released on bond or on a promise to appear or ordered held pending arraignment.

5. **INDICTMENT.** The formal document, issued by a grand jury, that contains the essential allegations of the crime. In some cases, a document known as an "information" may be signed by a prosecutor, accomplishing the same purpose.

6. **ARRAIGNMENT.** The main function of the arraignment is to call upon the defendant to plead to the charge(s) after the judge reads the charge(s) or hands the defendant a copy of the complaint, information or indictment. Some arraignments are held by closed-circuit television if the defendant is in jail.

7. **PLEA.** Required at arraignment, guilty or innocent are preferred pleas, but some jurisdictions allow *nolo contendere* (no contest) pleas. News organizations don't use the term "not guilty" because of the danger that "not" will be inadvertently left out in publication.

8. **DISCOVERY.** The state must turn over to the defendant the names and addresses of anyone with knowledge of the case, such as witnesses or victims, as well as statements they made to police or other items that will be used in evidence.

9. **TRIAL.** At the trial, the judge or a jury of citizens will decide whether the defendant is guilty or not. The burden of proof is on the state to prove the defendant's guilt beyond a reasonable doubt. This burden is designed to be difficult so that innocent people will not be found guilty. The state cannot carry the burden of proof without the effective cooperation of witnesses. The trial begins with opening statements by the lawyers. First, the state will present its evidence. Then the defense will present its evidence. Attorneys for each side will have a chance to ask questions of every witness. The lawyers then make closing arguments. The judge instructs the jury about the law, and the jury deliberates in secret before it delivers a verdict, or, if it is unable to do so, a mistrial is declared, and the state must decide whether to start the process all over.

10. **SENTENCING.** A defendant who pleads guilty or is found guilty at trial may be sentenced to prison, fine and/or community service. Victims are usually allowed to address the court about the impact of the crime on their lives.

LEARN MORE ABOUT THE CRIMINAL JUSTICE SYSTEM ONLINE FROM CRIMINOLOGIST CECIL GREEK AT http://www.criminology.fsu.edu/cj.html

CIVIL PROCEDURES: STEP BY STEP

Civil cases allow people to settle disputes between themselves rather than through criminal cases filed by a prosecutor. Here's how civil lawsuits work:

1. **PLEADINGS.** The first step occurs when a complaint is filed with the court clerk. The defendant must be formally served with notice of the legal action, known as a lawsuit, and generally has 30 days to respond.

2. **MOTIONS.** These are formal requests presented to a court. Lawyers use these to seek victory without a trial. Motions are entered into court at this time to ask the judge to immediately find for one side or the other based on a purely legal consideration of the case as developed from the discovery period.

   If the judge agrees that there are no genuine issues of material fact, he or she issues a "summary judgment" based solely on the legal issues, and that ends the case. If the judge feels there are still issues of fact to be decided he or she will allow the case to proceed to a jury.

3. **DISCOVERY.** Discovery is the time when each side gathers information it feels is necessary to win its case. The discovery process is governed by formal procedures monitored by the court. Each side collects evidence through formal questions, personal interviews and subpoenas, or through legal requests for documents.

4. **DEPOSITION.** The defendant has the right to seek information from the plaintiff through sessions, known as depositions, where lawyers have the right to question witnesses. The other principal method of discovery is interrogatories, which are written questions answered in writing by parties to the lawsuit.

5. **TRIAL.** A trial may be held before a judge or jury. In criminal cases, a defendant must be found guilty beyond a reasonable doubt. In civil cases, the standard of proof is lower: a "preponderance of the evidence"—or clear and convincing.

6. **DECISION.** The jury (or judge) decides in favor of either side, and damages may be awarded.

7. **WRIT.** A writ is a court order issued by a judge. An injunction is a writ compelling a private defendant to do or stop doing something and is issued after a hearing before a judge. A temporary restraining order may be issued by a judge without a hearing if the party requesting it can show that harm will occur without immediate action.

ONE OF THE MOST ACCESSIBLE EXPLANATIONS OF COURTROOM PROCEEDINGS IS THE VIRTUAL COURTHOUSE AT THE LOS ANGELES SUPERIOR COURT WEB SITE AT http://www.co.la.ca.us/courts/superior-auc/Lawday/Dept2000.htm

Find out how the court system in your community operates. Court administrators can provide you with background, and many jurisdictions now post this information on the Internet.

If you're a full-time court reporter, you will probably spend most of your time in the courthouse, observing trials and hearings, and studying the docket, which lists upcoming proceedings. You will need to build up a working relationship with the court clerk, whose office oversees the volumes of paperwork that the legal system produces: transcripts, motions, decisions, depositions.

"I figure my job is to write about what happened in court that day and if possible make the readers feel they were there when it

READ THE FULL TEXT OF CRAIG PITTMAN'S DESCRIPTION OF A COURTHOUSE REPORTER'S DUTIES ONLINE AT http://www.fsu. edu/~crimdo/ pittman.html

happened," says Craig Pittman, who wrote hundreds of court stories for the *St. Petersburg Times*.

"In covering courts, I get to write about a variety of human frailties. I get to point out how much we trust people in authority ... church deacons, for instance ... for everything from babysitting to investment advice and how some betray that trust. I get to write about how lives are ruined by greed and selfishness and jealousy. I have written about feats of heroism, acts of cowardice and the hard work of simply surviving day to day after a tragedy. These are stories that tell us about ourselves, as people and as a society."

Following you will find an example of Pittman's court coverage. Notice how he reports the news but also tells the story behind the case with economy and grace.

Pittman knows he's writing for the public, not a law review. He must understand the arcane jargon of the legal system, the difference between "a motion in limine and a motion to suppress ... I have to know those things to ask the right questions of the people I cover." Rarely do those details make their way into his stories, or if they do, Pittman does his best to describe them in language a nonlawyer understands.

As with any beat, the court reporter's job demands intensive study of the process, the terminology, the rules and history of the discipline. It's your responsibility to know the territory and all that comes with it.

Man Gets 9-Year Sentence in Friend's Death

By Craig Pittman
St. Petersburg Times Staff Writer
Feb. 4, 1998

LARGO—The plan Ronald Kenney and Joseph Mistretta came up with was a simple one: Steal a pair of jeans from one Kmart in Largo, then "return" the pants at another Kmart and use the refund to buy alcohol.

But the two drinking buddies got into an argument. Mistretta, 43, of St. Petersburg punched Kenney, knocking him to the ground. Kenney, 49, of St. Petersburg hit his head on the pavement and lapsed into a coma that lasted off and on for five months.

Mistretta was charged with aggravated battery and pleaded guilty last year. Before he could be sentenced, though, Kenney died. Prosecutors wanted to charge Mistretta with manslaughter, but his attorney contended that would be double jeopardy.

On Tuesday they worked it out. Prosecutors dropped the aggravated battery charge, and Mistretta pleaded guilty to manslaughter. Circuit Judge Frank Quesada then sentenced him to nine years and three months in prison.

Kenney and Mistretta might seem an unlikely pair. Kenney had been a nightclub guitarist in New Jersey, a casino dealer in Nevada and a draftsman in Miami. Mistretta was a high school dropout whose addictions to drinking and drugs left him with two failed marriages and three DUI convictions. He used marijuana at 15, moved on to heroin in his 20s and eventually tried crack.

By early 1997 Mistretta was hiring himself out as day labor, which is where he met Kenney. On Feb. 25, neither had a job to go to, and both had a powerful thirst. Although Mistretta's driver's license had been suspended, he swiped a friend's car so he and Kenney could drive around.

Lacking cash to buy alcohol, they concocted their plan and stole the jeans, Assistant State Attorney Thane Covert said. But in the parking lot of the second Kmart, they argued over whether Kenney should use his identification card in getting the refund, Covert said.

Mistretta "acted like he was going to walk away, then turned around and cold-cocked him," Covert said. Later he tried to justify the punch by saying Kenney had slapped him or flashed a knife, but witnesses saw nothing like that, the prosecutor said.

From time to time during the next few months the brain-damaged Kenney regained consciousness briefly, but complications ensued, and he died of pneumonia in July—before Mistretta could be sentenced to prison for aggravated battery.

Defense attorney Nathaniel Kidder contended prosecutors could not then change the charge to manslaughter, but Covert said prosecutors were unable to charge Mistretta with manslaughter until Kenney died.

Ironically, going to jail has proven to be good for the now-sober Mistretta. According to psychologists who examined him, his drug and alcohol abuse masked a serious mental illness, now being controlled by antipsychotic medication.

GLOSSARY: ESSENTIAL TERMS FOR THE COURT REPORTER

ADVERSARY SYSTEM. The system of trial practice in the United States and some other countries in which each of the opposing, or adversary, parties has the opportunity to present and establish opposing contentions before the court.

AFFIDAVIT. A written and sworn statement that may be admitted into evidence.

ARRAIGNMENT. In a misdemeanor case, the initial appearance before a judge at which the criminal defendant enters a plea; in a felony case, the proceeding after the indictment at which the defendant comes before a judge in District Court, is informed of the charges, enters a plea and has a date set for trial or disposition.

CALENDAR. A court's list of cases for arraignment, hearing, trial or arguments.

CAPITAL CRIME. An offense that may be punishable by death.

CIRCUMSTANTIAL EVIDENCE. All evidence of an indirect nature. Testimony not based on actual personal knowledge or observation of the facts in controversy.

CIVIL CASE. A lawsuit brought to enforce, redress or protect private rights or to gain payment for a wrong done to a person or party by another person or party. In general, all types of actions other than criminal proceedings.

CLASS ACTION. A lawsuit filed by a small group of plaintiffs on behalf of themselves and numerous other persons in a similar situation.

COMPLAINANT. Synonymous with "plaintiff," or, in criminal cases, the "complaining witness."

CONCURRENT SENTENCE. Sentence imposed for two or more convictions, under which two or more prison or jail terms are served simultaneously, and the prisoner is entitled to discharge when the longest term specified expires (i.e., sentences of 1 to 15 years and 0 to 5 years mean a maximum sentence of 15 years). Differs from a consecutive sentence, which is when the sentences are served back-to-back (1-to-15 and 0-to-5 consecutive sentences could mean up to 20 years).

CONTINUANCE. A court order postponing proceedings.

CONVICTION. In a criminal case, a finding that the defendant is guilty.

CRIME. A wrong that violates a statute and injures or endangers the public.

CRIMINAL CASE. A case brought by the government against a person accused of committing a crime.

CROSS-EXAMINATION. The questioning of a witness by the lawyer for the opposing side. This may be done by leading questions, questions that suggest the answer.

DEFENDANT. The accused in a criminal case; the person from whom money or other recovery is sought in a civil case.

DEPOSITION. The taking of testimony of a witness under oath outside of court, usually transcribed in writing by a court stenographer or, less frequently, recorded on videotape.

DISCOVERY. The process through which parties to an action are allowed to obtain relevant information known to other parties or nonparties before trial.

DOCKET. A brief entry or the book containing such entries of any proceeding in court.

DUE PROCESS. The guarantee of due process requires that no person be deprived of life, liberty or property without a fair and adequate process. In criminal proceedings this guarantee includes the fundamental aspects of a fair trial, including the right to adequate notice in advance of the trial, the right to counsel, the right to confront and cross-examine witnesses, the right to refuse self-incriminating testimony and the right to have all elements of the crime proven beyond a reasonable doubt.

EVIDENCE. Testimony, records, documents, material objects or other things presented at a trial to prove the existence or nonexistence of a fact.

GUILTY. The accused plead "guilty" when they confess to the crime with which they are charged, and the jury convicts when the accused are found guilty.

GRAND JURY. A group of citizens impaneled to hear evidence and decide whether a defendant should be charged with a crime.

HABEAS CORPUS. Latin phrase meaning "you have the body." A civil proceeding that is used to review the legality of a prisoner's confinement in criminal cases. Also, a writ ordering a law enforcement officer to bring a certain prisoner into court and show legal reasons to keep him or her in custody.

HUNG JURY. A jury that cannot agree on a final verdict. If a jury is hung, the court declares a mistrial and the case may be retried.

INDICTMENT. The document filed by a prosecuting attorney charging a person with a crime.

INJUNCTION. A writ, or court order, forbidding or requiring a certain action.

IMMUNITY. Legal protection from liability. There are many categories of immunity in civil and criminal law. For example, sovereign immunity protects government agencies from civil liability, and judicial immunity protects judges acting in their official capacities.

JURISDICTION. The legal authority of a court to hear a case or conduct other proceedings; power of the court over persons involved in a case and the subject matter of the case.

MOTION. A formal request presented to a court.

NOLO CONTENDERE. Legalese for a plea entered by a defendant in a criminal case. Latin for "I do not wish to contend," the plea means the defendant isn't admitting guilt but will offer no defense. Use "no contest" or "no-contest plea." The court can judge the person guilty and give the same punishment that someone would get if convicted or if pleaded guilty. However, the defendant can deny the same charge in another legal proceeding.

PERJURY. False swearing of a person under oath. A person inducing another to perjured testimony is equally guilty.

PLAINTIFF. A person who files a lawsuit.

PLEA. The defendant's formal response to a criminal charge (guilty, not guilty, *nolo contendere,* not guilty by reason of insanity, and guilty and mentally ill).

"The education beat can be the best there is. No other assignment sweeps across people's lives from infancy to old age. In most communities, education is a major industry. In most states, it consumes the largest share of tax dollars. A reporter or other journalist writing on education will cover everything from budgets to blustery encounters over values, from threatened local lawsuits to U.S. Supreme Court rulings, from clever products by students in woodworking to the role of education in competition for global markets, from back-to-school features to assessment of the worth of a college degree."

—COVERING THE
EDUCATION BEAT:
A CURRENT GUIDE
FOR EDITORS AND
WRITERS

PLEA BARGAINING. A process whereby the prosecutor and defense attorney settle a case without a trial. Under such settlement the accused may be permitted to plead guilty to a lesser offense or plead guilty to one or more charges but have others dismissed, or the prosecuting attorney may agree to recommend a particular sentence. The terms of a negotiated plea must be stated in the open court, and it will be effective only if approved by the trial judge. The way most criminal cases are decided.

PRESUMPTION OF INNOCENCE. A cornerstone principle of American criminal justice: Every defendant enters a trial presumed to be innocent. This presumption remains until and unless the state overcomes the presumption by competent evidence of guilt.

REASONABLE DOUBT. A person accused of a crime is entitled to acquittal if, in the minds of the jury or judge, his or her guilt has not been proved beyond a "reasonable doubt"; the jurors are not entirely convinced of the person's guilt.

RESTITUTION. Court-ordered payment to restore goods or money to the victim of a crime by the offender.

SEARCH WARRANT. An order issued by a judge or magistrate commanding a sheriff, constable or other officer to search a specified location for evidence suspected to be related to a crime.

SUBPOENA. An official order to appear in court (or at a deposition) at a specific time. Failure to obey a subpoena to appear in court is punishable as contempt of court.

TESTIMONY. Evidence given by a competent witness, under oath; as distinguished from evidence derived from writings and other sources.

VENUE. The particular county, city or geographical area in which a court with jurisdiction may hear and determine a case.

VERDICT. The formal and unanimous decision or finding made by a jury.

BEGINNER'S BEATS: COVERING EDUCATION

Greg Toppo was a grade school teacher for eight years before he decided to pursue a lifelong dream to become a reporter. After graduating from The Poynter Institute's summer training program in reporting and writing, he became the education reporter for *The Santa Fe New Mexican*. "When education reporters cover schools," he says, "we should focus on four questions, all foremost in the minds of responsible public and private school parents:

1. Does my child attend school in a decent building?
2. Is my child safe?
3. Is my child learning first-rate material?
4. Is my child challenged and excited?"

People care about school news. A survey commissioned by the Education Writers of America found that 40 percent of those surveyed are most interested in news about the public schools, outstripping the 36 percent interested in crime and another 22 percent who are most interested in local economic news.

The power of the education beat is evident in the following story by Holly Kurtz in the *Montgomery Advertiser,* for which she covered schools in the Alabama capital. It began, as so many of her school stories did, with a phone call from a disgruntled parent who complained about a racial quota in homecoming elections at the end of the football season—the homecoming court had to be half white and half black, and kids had to say which race they were. The problem for Bethany Godby, her father said, was that her mother is black and her dad is white, and she didn't want to choose between them. It ended, after Kurtz wrote a series of stories about the policies, with the Montgomery school board voting to end racial quotas for all school offices.

Mixed-Race Girl Not on Ballot for Queen

By Holly Kurtz
Montgomery Advertiser Staff Writer
Oct. 12, 1996

Bethany Godby considers herself white.

She also considers herself black.

When her ninth-grade class nominated her for homecoming queen a few weeks ago, the 13-year-old daughter of a white man and a black woman said a white teacher asked her to choose: Run for one of the black slots on the homecoming court. Or run for one of the white ones.

Bethany said she polled her homeroom classmates. She said they voted to nominate her for one of the white slots.

What happened next led her parents, Jeff and Kristine Godby, to seek help from Southern Poverty Law Center legal director Richard Cohen.

Bethany's name did not appear on the schoolwide ballot.

Cloverdale principal Jethro Wilson did not return calls Thursday and Friday.

Like several other Montgomery public junior high schools, Cloverdale elects a homecoming court that is half white and half black, or nonwhite. The queen is the ninth-grader who gets the most votes. Black and white runners-up from her grade serve as her two attendants.

The quotas started soon after desegregation, said Cathy Fowler, who oversees Capitol Heights Junior High School's homecoming elections as director of the city-run Capitol Heights Community Center.

Back then, few blacks attended formerly white schools such as Cloverdale and Capitol Heights.

The quotas gave minorities a fairer chance at election, Ms. Fowler said.

At Cloverdale, the quotas remain, but the demographics have changed.

In the 1995–96 school year, the school was 91 percent black and 9 percent nonblack, according to the board of education's *Annual Progress Report.*

Yet half the slots on the homecoming court are for whites.

"In the past, a lot of white students have won homecoming elections just because they were white," Bethany said.

Mr. Cohen said, "The racial desegregation in any kind of school matter or extracurricular matter is always something that's really fraught with problems." He said he met with school board attorneys on behalf of the Godby family. He declined to comment on what went on.

Mr. Godby said he rejected solutions suggested to him after the meeting.

One solution was having no homecoming queen. Mr. Godby said that would be unfair to the other students.

The other solution was to hold a new election. Mr. Godby said that would be too hard on his daughter.

"I used to laugh at the expression, 'pain and mental anguish,'" said the former Marine, who manages the sporting goods department at a local discount store.

"But my daughter is hurt by this. They've hurt her mentally."

Mr. Cohen has recommended the family see another Montgomery lawyer. Mr. Cohen said the Southern Poverty Law Center may continue to supply "technical and financial support" for the Godby case.

School board attorneys did not return calls Thursday and Friday.

School superintendent John A. "Pete" Eberhart said he had been unaware that some junior high school homecoming courts had racial quotas. He said he was unaware of the details of the attorneys' meeting. He said he knew nothing of the details of the case. The Godbys have not contacted his office, so the case remains between the family, the attorneys and the school, Dr. Eberhart said.

"I'm assuming they're either considering working to resolve it or that it has been resolved," Dr. Eberhart said.

Mr. Godby said the meeting did not resolve his concerns.

"I want a written apology," he said.

"I want whoever was in charge to be reprimanded. I want to try to allow the legal system to handle it. ... If I could pack up and move I would. But then it could happen somewhere else."

Bethany said the election upset her so much that she no longer wants to be queen when homecoming rolls around Oct. 19.

"If that's the way they do it, I don't want to run," she said.

A LIFE IN JOURNALISM

Holly Kurtz

It is hard for me to describe a typical day in my life as a reporter because every day is different. When it comes to

HOLLY KURTZ
WROTE THIS ACCOUNT
WHEN SHE WAS EDU-
CATION REPORTER
FOR THE *MONT-
GOMERY ADVERTISER* IN
ALABAMA. SHE IS
NOW AN EDUCATION
REPORTER FOR THE
ORLANDO SENTINEL.

stories, I try to keep three sets of goals. They are: something daily for tomorrow, something mid-range for next week and something long-range for next year. Like life itself, this doesn't always work out exactly as planned. Some days I am so busy with daily stories that I have time to do little else. Other days when it's slow, I concentrate on my long-range project following an honor student and a high school dropout.

Monday, Nov. 4, 1998, was a typical easy day. At 10:30, I met a high school teacher at a restaurant where one of her students was interviewing for his first job. I sat in on the interview, taking notes for a story on the new school-to-work program he was part of. After picking up lunch at Taco Bell and a cup of coffee at a nearby Barnes and Noble where I read *The New York Times*, I drove to a Catholic school where pupils were spending their first day in a newly built building. I spent about two hours there talking with students and chatting with the principal. At 2 p.m., I went into my office for the first time that day. I wrote the story about the Catholic school for the next day, made phone calls for other stories and left by 7 p.m. Once home, I ate some takeout food and read a library book.

A much more stressful day was Thursday, Nov. 21. That day, I arrived at a junior high school at 8 a.m. to watch Alabama Gov. Fob James teach a class on American history. At the school, I ran into a central office administrator who was angry at me over a story I had written about a school bus driver who dumped the noisy children on her bus into the middle of the road, then sped off. I confronted the administrator and asked him why he was mad. (He had had his public relations person call my editor the day before.) He told me he felt it was unfair to put that story on Page 1 when there were so many good bus drivers in the system. I offered to write a profile of a good driver. After a brief stop at my office to pick up messages and fresh notebooks, I went to the home of an Alabama State University alumna. I interviewed her for about an hour for a weekend story on the Turkey Day Classic, Alabama State's historic football rivalry with Tuskegee University. After another brief stop at the office to assign a photo of the alumna, I went to the Bell St. Mission Church. There, the high school dropout was getting an award at her GED program's annual Thanksgiving dinner. I ended up staying for more than two hours. The girls in the GED program had all loaded their plates with so much stuffing that some of the program's board of trustee members went without! An amusing etiquette lesson ensued.

Continued

> When I returned to the office at around 2:30 p.m., I found out that space in Friday's paper was so tight that the editors no longer wanted my story on the governor. They wanted only the photograph. I wrote the picture caption, then started to write the Turkey Day Classic story on the alumna while making phone calls for the second Turkey Day story on professors' interpretations of the event.
>
> At 5:45 p.m., I left for the school board meeting. These monthly meetings are quite stressful. Because the real action is often going on in the hallway outside the meeting room, I have to run in and out the entire time, handing out business cards to disgruntled parents while keeping one ear on what's going on inside. I stayed until the meeting ended at 9, then hurried back to the office to write the story, which I focused on a group of vocational students who showed up to protest conditions at their school. The story was done and edited at about 10 p.m. When I got home, I had something to eat for the first time that day, then went to bed.

"I always say to people, if you're a beat person, every day your goal should be to wake up and get a news story, a news story that's gonna get you on the front of your section. And most days you're going to fail, but at least that should be your aspiration."

—LEN PASQUARELLI, SPORTSWRITER, ATLANTA JOURNAL-CONSTITUTION

BEGINNER'S BEATS: COVERING SPORTS

In 1995, when the American Society of Newspaper Editors gave one of its Distinguished Writing Awards for the year's best sportswriting, judges described the beat as "not only a lot of fun, but illuminating of the human condition."

The advantages of writing about sports are obvious, Frank Deford, one of the nation's best sportswriters, once wrote. "The structure is heaven-sent. Every day, every game, every substitution, there is instant, well-formed drama: a beginning, plot development and climax."

For the sports fan, a seat in the press box might seem like a dream come true. But sportswriters know the reality: long workdays, impossible deadlines and the haunting realization that your audience may have seen the same game you're trying to write about. "Let's face it. You can log on your computer anytime, day or night, and get all the scores," says Mitch Albom of the *Detroit Free Press*. "And that's a lot easier to do than walk down your driveway in seven degree-below weather and get your newspaper, which had to be printed at 10:30 at night and doesn't even have the box score."

But as a teacher once told *Boston Globe* sportswriter Larry Whiteside: "A box score can say there was a line drive, but it doesn't say that a fan touched it or that it snaked around a wall. It doesn't say what anybody said or what anybody felt."

In the face of electronic competition, sportswriters have survived and thrived by relying on a combination that has always worked for reporters, whatever their beat: dogged reporting and stylish writing, fueled by hard work and passion.

"The main weapon is good reporting," says Lawrie Mifflin, who had to battle sexism in locker rooms as well as the demands of covering professional sports for *The New York Times*. "It's a matter of questioning and not taking people's words for things, being skeptical, pursuing it further, asking other people.

"Being a good reporter is as essential in sportswriting as in any kind of writing: getting both sides of an issue, verifying whether what somebody tells you is true, checking things with many sources."

Whatever the sport, there are three types of sports stories:

1. Game and event coverage
2. Human interest and feature stories
3. Columns

The game story is the most common sports assignment, especially for a beginner. Here is a list of tips for writing the game story, followed by an example of the form by an experienced sportswriter, Thomas Stinson of the *Atlanta Journal-Constitution*, who then discusses his methods in an interview.

- Sportswriters need to know the rules of the games they cover. "If you don't know the game you can't write a great sports story," said sportswriter Bob Ryan.
- Access to information. Use a scorekeeping system that you understand.
- Use a note-taking system.
- Start thinking about your leads as soon as the game begins.
- Write contingency leads before the game begins.
- Ideally, the lead is ready by the time the game is over, but it often comes from postgame interviews or even from an overheard remark.

STORY EXAMPLE

Braves Snag a 3-1 Victory

By Thomas Stinson
Atlanta Journal-Constitution
April 17, 1998

Maybe they weren't the cleanest innings; they were speckled with a triple here and a hit batsman there. But then, baseball doesn't have a white-glove test, and for the Braves, John Smoltz was doing a beautiful job.

Four months and four days after they pulled the surgical scope out of his right elbow, Smoltz beat the Pittsburgh Pirates 3-1 Thursday.

A club that takes aim at autumn has found joy in April.

"The old John Smoltz," said Javy Lopez, his catcher. "One-and-oh."

Intending to walk softly in his first start of the season, Smoltz found himself near the top of his form. He got stronger as the game progressed, striking out seven and giving up two hits in five shutout innings. That showed the Braves the way to a three-game sweep of the Pirates. It also showed that their No. 1 starter a year ago has put elbow surgery behind him. The effect was palpable.

"Right now, we haven't played that well the first two weeks," Chipper Jones said, "and just having John around helps keep the mood light."

"It thrills me just to see John in the clubhouse," manager Bobby Cox said. "If he never threw another pitch the rest of his life, it would still thrill me. He's that type of person."

The victory gave the Braves their fourth victory in five games, the most consistent run in the first two weeks. Atlanta is 9-6 and three games over .500 for the first time. The Pirates finally snapped their trance, scoring a run off reliever Dennis Martinez in the seventh, which halted Atlanta's run of 25 consecutive scoreless innings. That was all secondary, though, to refitting the Fab Four. Even Smoltz got a little carried away with that.

"My mind-set was to go after them," Smoltz said, "but then you get in a game, and you start realizing, hey, your curveball's pretty good and your slider's pretty good. I always pitch off that. So I put them away as early as possible."

Maybe it was contagious. Lopez, in an 0-for-14 slump, reached base on a Lou Collier error in the second, and Michael Tucker, who had not driven in a run thus far, brought Lopez in with his double. The next inning, Lopez and Ryan Klesko drove in one each, giving the Braves the early lead for the 13th time in 15 games.

That would be enough. Smoltz threw 47 strikes in 75 pitches and was replaced after five innings with a 3-0 lead. He might have gone more, but Cox said, "Enough was enough. I'd be stupid to have let him go longer. It was hot out there."

Martinez gave up a run in the seventh with just one ball hit out of the infield, but Mark Wohlers closed the case in the ninth for his fourth save.

Snow flurries were forecast for Denver as the club loaded the bus afterward for a weekend series in Colorado, but that didn't seem to matter.

"Everything has worked perfect," Smoltz said, "to now."

Stinson's story was part of a package named best beat reporting by his colleagues at the *Journal-Constitution*. As part of its writing improvement program, directed by training editor Michael Schwartz, the winning writer discusses how the story was reported and written. Excerpts from Stinson's interview with Carolyn Nizzi Warmbold follow:

HOW I WROTE THE STORY

An Interview with Thomas Stinson

Q. There's usually very little time between the end of a game and when your story is due, particularly if the Braves are playing out west. How do you go about collecting the news of the game, interviewing the relevant players and coaches and then writing a story on the edge of deadline?

A. I write two game stories—one a running play-by-play account for the four-star that I hope no one sees, the second a sub that should hold up for all other editions. Given most games run to three hours, that usually allows me to get to the clubhouse by 10:30. My sub is due at 11:30, which should give me plenty of time, barring extra innings or rain. I hate rain.

The farther west the team goes, the more complicated the process. With a 10 p.m. start, I will file a nongame news/feature story that will plug the hole on the front until the game ends. Usually, I'll send the first seven innings first, send a quick top with the last out and then write through as quickly as possible. Some nights, it all works. Some nights, it's angina.

Q. How do you keep your leads and your reporting approach fresh after covering games night after night and month after month? How do you plan your lead, particularly when the outcome of the game isn't known until the Braves' last bat?

A. Generally, a game will present a theme by the seventh inning. Of course, if something happens in the ninth, that theme is trashed. But last night (May 7), for instance, John Smoltz pitched poorly to start, drove in three runs to reclaim the lead and then pitched well after that. I love games like that.

It is helpful to work up some background each night—hitting streaks, pitching trends, personal vendettas—that might come into play. Tom Glavine hates pitching when Gary Darling is calling balls and strikes. Ryan Klesko still thinks he can hit left-handed pitching. A former Brave is in the other team's starting lineup. Any of these items could come into play any night. If you can recognize the situations as they come around, the reporting is easy. The preparation's a bitch.

Continued

Q. How do you manage a family life with the heavy demands of the beat?

A. You can't manage a family life. I have three kids (16, 15 and 10) who are very tolerant of what I'm doing. I try to be around for breakfast when they leave in the morning and try to drive carpool on my days off, just to show them I can still do it. But before I agreed to take on the beat, we had a family meeting about it, and they gave me their blessing. I wouldn't be doing this without that. I still made it to three of the girls' soccer games and have made three of George's 11 Little League games. I can even tell you what happened.

Q. Right after the May 4 game with Los Angeles, I wondered how Bobby Cox would feel after being ejected for arguing with an ump. You talked with Cox and reported in the next morning's story that he was sorry he hadn't just let it go. Do you consciously try to spin your stories ahead and go beyond mere play-by-play coverage?

A. With the average game story running 12–14 inches, if the morning lead doesn't get away from play-by-play, it's not worth reading. We feel that with a "How They Scored" segment on the inside Braves page as well as a detailed game report on isolated big plays, the lead should have elements beyond how the score got to be 4–4 in the third.

An ejection like Cox's or a hit batter like Michael Tucker last night, those had better be played up in the lead quickly. Most fans know the score by the time the paper comes. You better have something more to get them into the story.

Q. In what way(s) does the baseball beat differ from other beats, sports or otherwise? How important is it to develop contacts on the team/in the organization, gain the confidence of players/coaches, etc.?

A. Baseball is different because it's bigger—162 games, 30 teams, a six-month season and a voracious appetite by the public for information. I don't work harder than Len Pasquarelli (our NFL man) or Jeff Denberg (our NBA man), but I do a hell of a lot more games with the worst deadline problems in our industry. Getting inside with management helps, but gaining confidences is not as important as maintaining them. Baseball is a very closed society—the players don't trust the front office, the front office doesn't trust the agents, the agents don't trust the leagues. But the longer you're around, the more questions you ask, the easier it is to maneuver your way into stories. I'm not saying I understand it all. But I'm finding more of the people who really do.

WORKING A BEAT: THE COACHING WAY

- Try drawing a map of your beat. Nothing fancy, show the key places and people. Draw connecting lines to reveal the relationships that exist.
- Are you looking beyond the traditional sentinel posts of your beat to those places and people whose lives are most affected by the news?
- Identify a place or person on your beat you have never visited because the idea makes you uncomfortable. Ask yourself what bothers you. Then go and see for yourself what the reality is.
- Pledge to improve your writing every day. Every beat reporter can benefit from a test suggested by Lawrie Mifflin, a pioneering sportswriter for *The New York Times*: Read through the sports pages and see how many adjectives you can cross out, how few of them are serving any illuminating purpose. Usually you can convey more about the impressiveness of an achievement by simply describing it well.

EXERCISES

1. Keep a beat book where you record and describe your beat and what you discover there. Because you will also include class handouts, fliers and other materials you collect during your visits to your beat, use a loose-leaf notebook. Maintain three sections: Section 1 should contain dated entries of your observations, descriptions and notes of conversations you have with people on your beat. Section 2 should include lists of story ideas and your questions about people, events, buildings, businesses, agencies and other beat phenomena. Section 3 will be your journal proper, where you record your thoughts and feelings about your role as observer, reporter and writer. Date each entry. Your beat book is your own autobiographical record of your development as a journalist and a writer. (Note: Although these exercises were devised by Professor Christine Martin of West Virginia University for students covering a specific geographic area, they can also be applied in any other type of beat, such as police or politics.)

2. Arrange a tour of your beat for your classmates. First, you decide what your classmates need to see and experience to understand your beat community. Second (during class time), take your classmates (fellow reporters) on a guided tour of your beat community, highlighting those people and places that define and explain your beat. Select one person or group of people who, you believe, exemplify something significant about your beat (for example: the police chief, if the police station is on your beat; a nurse or doctor; or a concerned citizen with something to say). Schedule an in-class meeting between your beat representative and your class.

3. Based on the people and issues you discover on your beat, write a profile, a meeting story, a police or crime-oriented story, a speech story, a budget or financial story and a story that explores, questions, develops or celebrates the cultural diversity of your geographical beat.

4. Prepare yourself for the day when you must report on the legal system by taking advantage of every citizen's right to observe trials and other proceedings.

5. Describe the state court system in your state.

6. Study David Ho's council meeting story. Discuss how you might amplify the story with reporting outside the council meeting. Where would you go to do additional reporting? Who else might you interview?

READINGS

Armao, Rosemary. "Steps to Sterling School Coverage." *The IRE Journal,* July 1994, p. 4.

Askari, Emilia. "Readers Thirst for More About Their Environment." *The American Editor,* October 1995, pp. 14–20.

Brown, Karen F. "What Deadline Writers Can Learn From Sportswriting." *Best Newspaper Writing 1991*. St. Petersburg, Fla.: The Poynter Institute, 1991, pp. 253–257.

"Covering Crime: A Resource Guide." *Columbia Journalism Review,* January/February 1997, pp. 45–48.

"Covering the Courts." *Media Studies Journal,* Winter 1998.

"Covering the Environment." *Gannett Center Journal,* vol. 4, no. 3, Summer 1990.

"Covering the Violence: A Report on a Conference on Violence and the Young." *American Journalism Review,* September 1994.

Ford, Patricia. *Don't Stop There! Five Adventures in Civic Journalism.* Washington, D. C.: Pew Center for Civic Journalism, 1998.

Harrigan, Jane. *Read All About It!* Chester, Conn.: Globe Pequot Press, 1987.

Pulitzer, Lisa Beth, ed. *Crime on Deadline*. New York: Boulevard Press, 1996.

Sachar, Emily. "Teaching School for a Year Gave Reporter New Insights Into Reporting on Education." *ASNE Bulletin,* January/February 1990, pp. 22–23.

Selditch, Dianne, ed. *My First Year as a Journalist: Real-World Stories From American Newspaper and Magazine Journalists.* New York: Walker & Co., 1995.

Skolnick, Jerome H. *Justice Without Trial: Law Enforcement in Democratic Society.* New York: Wiley, 1975.

Stein, M. L. "Re-Establishing Relevance for Readers." *Editor & Publisher,* March 5, 1994, p. 16.

Stevens, Jane. *Reporting on Violence: A Handbook for Journalists.* Berkeley, Calif.: Berkeley Media Studies Group, 1997.

Sugg, Diana K. "Trying to Muzzle the Beat." *Nieman Reports,* Fall 1996, pp. 17–18.

Titone, Julie. "Ten Commandments for Environmental Reporters." *Editor & Publisher,* Sept. 22, 1990, pp. 35, 48.

"Tough on Crime: News Directors are Re-Examining the Role of Crime in Electronic Journalism." *Communicator,* October 1997, pp. 39–44.

Woodward, Steve. "Reporting Power Tools." *Second Takes,* vol. 8, no. 12, April 1997.

Zinnser, William. "The Sports Beat." *Speaking of Journalism: 12 Writers and Editors Talk About Their Work.* New York: Harper Collins, 1994.

HOTLIST

CRIME AND PUNISHMENT

http://www.freep.com/jobspage/academy/crime.htm

Courts spend years developing criminal procedure, but as *Detroit Free Press* development editor Joe Grimm notes, "newspapers sometimes have just minutes to describe them." And when they get it wrong the mistakes can be costly to their credibility and their bottom line. Two Michigan judges gave *Detroit Free Press* staffers a crash course in criminal procedure, including court jurisdiction, trials, pleas and sentencing. Obviously criminal procedure differs by state, but this is an excellent introduction to basic concepts.

http://www.udayton.edu/~grandjur/

Monica Lewinsky and Kenneth Starr made grand juries famous in 1998, but most people, reporters included, know little about this important institution. Two lawyers/teachers created this Web site to dispel myths. It includes information about the history and function of grand juries, frequently asked questions-and-answers about federal and state grand juries, as well as links to related state grand jury sites, news reports, essays, law review articles and the full text of relevant laws. Especially for those who have never seen a grand jury. Also interesting is a slide show of photographs and descriptions of an Ohio county grand jury at work.

http://www.fsu.edu/~crimdo/pittman.html

"Covering Courts." The full text of a presentation by Craig Pittman, former courts reporter for the *St. Petersburg Times*, for a crime and media course taught by Dr. Cecil Greek of Florida State University. A thoughtful view of the process by a careful reporter and graceful writer. Includes several stories.

See also:

http://www.criminology.fsu.edu/cj.html

Dr. Cecil Greek's list of criminal justice links. Greek is an Internet and media-savvy criminologist. His site is full of valuable information for police and court reporters.

See also:

http://www.fsu.edu/~crimdo/cj-flowchart.html

Navigate Dr. Greek's site with an interactive flowchart that provides a graphic view of the criminal justice system.

http://www.nvc.org/

The National Center for Victims of Crime. An important, and often ignored, perspective on crime and punishment. This site offers background information, news tips and other valuable links.

http://www.apbonline.com

"APB Online" is a Web site that hopes to become the ESPN of police and crime news. With 911 tapes a click away, it is an Internet version of the sensational police tabloids of the '30s. Still, its resources, such as statistics, FBI files and interviews with journalists and writers, make it a valuable spot.

http://reporter.org/

"Courts and law" and "crime and law enforcement" are two beats on the beat page at reporter.org., maintained by Investigative Reporters and Editors. Includes links to the FBI, U.S. Justice Department and other data sources, links to victims organizations, the American Bar Association and other law-related links.

GOVERNMENT

http://www.jou.ufl.edu/brechner/brochure.htm

The Brechner Center for Freedom of Information at the College of Journalism and Communications at the University of Florida provides a range of online resources about open government and related subjects for government reporters.

http://usacitylink.com/

The USA CityLink Project offers links to cities and towns around the country and the world. Although many links are little more than travel brochures, many cities offer information about local government that will be of interest to journalists.

http://www.pewcenter.org/index.php3

The Pew Center for Civic Journalism provides funding, training and other support for civic journalism experiments "to create and refine better ways of reporting the news to re-engage people in public life." Includes links to articles, projects and conferences.

http://www.brown.edu/Faculties/University_Library/subject/gov.html

U.S. Federal and State Information. Includes links to the White House, Congress, courts and the 50 states. A good starting point.

EDUCATION

http://www.ewa.org/

The Education Writers Association (EWA) is the national professional organization of education reporters. Its Web site is a must-browse for anyone covering schools: Links include current research reports, a rich archive of prize-winning education stories from news organizations around the country and story idea lists.

http://www.edweek.org/

American Education's Online Newspaper of Record offers a rich re-source for school reporters, including searchable archives, glossary of educational terms and "The Daily News," which provides links to edu-cation stories written that morning in newspapers across the country.

http://www.ed.gov/

Information about the U.S. Education Department and links to resources such as the National Center for Education Statistics.

http://www.ewa.org/eric2.html

ERIC Expertise for Education Writers. Looking for background for your education stories? A list sketches some of the particular areas of exper-tise you'll find among the leaders of the subject-area clearinghouses within the federally sponsored Educational Resources Information Cen-ter (ERIC) system. For referrals on other topics, phone (800) LET-ERIC (538-3742) or see the research syntheses available from the various ERIC clearinghouses at **http://www.accesseric.org/**.

http://govinfo.kerr.orst.edu/sddb-stateis.html

Government Information Sharing Project. The School District Data Book, from the National Center for Education Statistics, is an electronic library containing social, financial and administrative data for each of the 15,274 school districts in the United States for 1989–1990.

http://www.sportsjones.com/sportswriting.htm

Sportsjones, an online magazine, recommends examples of good sports-writing that appear in other publications.

http://www.reporter.org/beat/sports.html/

The sports beat page at reporter.org., maintained by Investigative Re-porters and Editors. Includes Web links by sports category.

http://www.sportspages.com/

Sportspages.com. The best way to learn how to write sports is to study how others do it. This page, maintained by Rich Jones, includes links to major newspaper sports sections in the United States and Canada, mag-azines and online sports publications.

http://www.sportseditor.com/

SportsEditor.com calls itself "the Web's home for online sports editors, producers and writers." It features information about jobs, seminars and an online forum.

CHAPTER

14

NUMBERS AND THE
BEGINNING JOURNALIST

CHAPTER FOCUS

For the 21st-century journalist, numeracy is as important as literacy.

CHAPTER LESSONS

- Why math matters
- Numbers in the news
- Basic math skills
- Advanced math skills
- Writing with numbers
- Reporting and writing about budgets
- Making sense of numbers: The Coaching Way

INTRODUCTION

You may have thought that you went into journalism because you're not good at math but you like writing. If you were good at math you would have gone into engineering, computers, medicine or science. But journalism is about words, a haven for the literate.

Wrong.

You need math skills. Whether you like math or not, numbers are going to come streaming across your desk every day—in polls and press releases, reports from government and advocacy groups, balance sheets and municipal **budgets.** No matter what your beat (sports, business, local government, public safety, courts, consumer, health and medicine, transportation), numbers are the lifeblood of a modern society.

This chapter introduces the concepts and skills that a beginning journalist needs to survive and points to resources where you can sharpen your skills. This means basic skills; it does not mean you'll be able to get a job with NASA, write computer code or do risk assessments for the EPA. It does mean you should understand the role numbers play in society, be able to assess their accuracy and significance and communicate their meaning clearly. It doesn't mean you have to be a mathematician.

WHY MATH MATTERS

Like many reporters, Roger Simon was never very good at math. "My SAT scores in math were so low that during my college interviews the interviewers said things like, 'Did you leave the room halfway through?' or 'Are you sure you understood the concept of multiple choice?'"

His poor math skills didn't keep him from getting into college. Nor did they keep him from landing a job as a reporter. Simon was an adult and, so he thought, he no longer needed math. But there was one problem.

"As a reporter," Simon recalled in a 1990 newspaper column, "I found I needed math all the time."

He needed math on police stories: "If the gunman entered the bank at 4:17 p.m., and the hostages were not released until 1:02 a.m., how long were they held captive?"

He needed math on tax stories: "If the average county tax bill was $3,334.47 last year, and this year it's $4,567.29, by what percentage did it increase?"

Simon found he needed math "on all kinds of stories. So slowly and painfully I had to learn in real life what I had not learned in school."

Simon went on to become an award-winning columnist for the *Chicago Sun-Times* and *The Baltimore Sun* and today is chief political writer for *U.S. News & World Report*. But as a beginning reporter, he suffered from a common journalistic ailment: **innumeracy,** defined by mathematician John Allen Paulos as "an inability to deal comfortably with fundamental notions of number and chance."

If Simon had been an illiterate—someone who lacks the ability to read and write—he never would have been allowed in a newsroom. But as an innumerate, it didn't matter that he wasn't good at math. If you don't know the difference between a noun and a verb, you could never get a job as a reporter or editor. But newsrooms are full of people who don't know how to calculate a percentage.

LEARN MORE ABOUT STATISTICS ONLINE FROM THE AMERICAN STATISTICAL ASSOCIATION AT http://www. amstat.org/

More than half—58 percent—of the job applicants interviewed by broadcast news directors lacked an adequate understanding of statistical materials, such as a municipal budget. That was the finding of *Tomorrow's Broadcast Journalists—A Report and Recommendations From the Jane Pauley Task Force on Mass Communication Education*, published in 1996 by the Society of Professional Journalists.

Widespread journalistic innumeracy is a serious problem.

"Deploying numbers skillfully is as important to communication as deploying verbs, but you won't find many media practicing that philosophy," says Max Frankel, a media columnist and former executive editor of *The New York Times*. Frankel complains that most schools of journalism give short shrift to **statistics,** "the science of learning from data," as defined by Jon Kettenring, president of the American Statistical Association. "Some let students graduate without any numbers training at all. In the professional world, it's a rare newsroom that provides any on-the-job training in the accurate use of numbers. How can such reporters write sensibly about trade and welfare and crime, or airfares, health care and nutrition? The media's sloppy use of numbers about the incidence of accidents or disease frightens people and leaves them vulnerable to journalistic hype, political demagoguery and commercial fraud," Frankel says.

"Aversion to all things numerical seems universal among journalists, and it causes nothing but trouble in today's newsrooms," says Deborah Potter, former CBS and CNN correspondent who is executive director of NewsLab, a Washington, D.C., group devoted to improving local TV news. "Simply put, journalists need math skills to make sense of numbers the way they need language skills to make sense of words."

The Poynter Institute includes numeracy as one of the skills today's journalists need to be competent. Competency with numbers requires:

- Basic working knowledge of arithmetic.
- Familiarity with statistics.
- Ability to calculate percentages, ratios, rates of change and other relationships between numbers.
- Ability to translate numbers into terms that readers and viewers can understand.
- Knowing the difference between median and mean averages.
- Understanding of margin of error in polling.
- Basic understanding of probability theory.
- Understanding of graphs and other pictorial representations of numbers.

Too often, says Potter, who developed Poynter's guidelines for numerical competency when she was on the Institute's faculty, "reporters and editors are suckers for numbers. To them, a number looks solid, factual, more trustworthy than a fallible human source. And being numerically incompetent, they can't find the flaws in statistics and calculations. They can't tell the difference between a meaningless number and a significant one. The result is stories that are misleading and confusing at best and, at worst, flat out wrong."

I sympathize with Roger Simon and all the reporters out there who get nervous when numbers come up in a story. Experts blame innumeracy on bad teachers, psychological blocks and what mathematician Paulos calls "romantic misconceptions about the nature of mathematics." That all sounds very familiar. In high school and college, I was a terrible math student. I flunked geometry, was totally bewildered by algebra. Trigonometry I ran from. I had trouble balancing a checkbook. As a reporter, I was painfully aware of my innumeracy every time a percentage appeared in my story. Budget stories made me cringe. Can you make it in journalism without math skills? As Brant Houston, executive director of Investigative Reporters and Editors and author of *Computer-Assisted Reporting: A Practical Guide*, points out, "journalists report on statistics every day with less-than-complete understanding," or we avoid them because we "don't do math."

Without math skills I was not as effective a journalist, and my readers weren't well served. It wasn't just the mistakes I made or the agonies I went through trying to figure things out. As a reporter I regurgitated statistics without understanding them because I didn't feel capable of interpreting them. I'm sure I missed stories and screwed up others because of my weak math skills.

You will use math as a reporter nearly every day. Whatever route you take in journalism—print, broadcast, online news—or whatever job you hold—reporter, copy editor, graphics artist, Web producer—you will have to count on math skills.

"Mathematics is not primarily a matter of plugging numbers into formulas and performing rote computation," says Paulos. "It is a way of thinking and questioning that may be unfamiliar to many of us, but is available to almost all of us." So Paulos recommends that reporters add a list of other questions to the five W's, such as "how many?" "how far?" "how likely?" "what percentage?" and "what rate?"

The biggest reason you need to know math as a journalist is so you won't be easily fooled. Your audience expects you to sort fact from fantasy. Your audience expects you to get it right. Just as a grammatical error, or an error of fact, undermines your credibility, so does a mathematical error. The 21st-century journalist will need basic understanding of mathematics and statistics.

"Simply reporting what someone said or did is no longer enough to ensure an information professional's career," says Robert Niles, executive producer of insidedenver.com, the Web site of the *Rocky Mountain News* and author of an online statistical primer. "Information professionals who wish to survive the Internet age must be able to synthesize and analyze words, deeds and data so that they can report to their readers and clients the reality of what is happening in their world today."

Lynne Enders Glaser, who writes a readers' column for the *Fresno Bee* in California, makes a passionate call for reform:

LEARN MORE
ABOUT STATISTICS
EVERY WRITER
SHOULD KNOW
ONLINE AT
http://nilesonline.
com/stats/

"For eons, it's been a standard line in newsrooms that journalists don't do math. It's been stated so often that many reporters and editors seem to accept it as a valid, logical reason for mistakes. And they seem to think that readers agree. But, readers don't. They repeatedly say it is not okay to give them numbers that don't compute ... something needs to change here, and it needs to start with attitude. The newsroom should take numbers as seriously as words."

NUMBERS IN THE NEWS: A RANDOM SAMPLE

Journalists use math skills to help their audiences make sense of the flood of numerical information that affects their lives: mortgage rates, school enrollments, crime statistics, municipal budgets, pollution standards, property taxes, unemployment figures, the stock market.

As an experiment, I looked through one day's edition of my local newspaper, the *St. Petersburg Times,* and counted how many of the 130 stories involved numbers. More than one-third did. They were in every section of the paper: news, sports, business, features, editorial page:

- Professional sports team purchase.
- Legislation to limit consumer lawsuits.
- Questions about local government revenues from new baseball stadium.
- Proposed antismoking cigarette tax.
- Presidential campaign donations.
- Social Security's future.
- Drug-money laundering.
- Health stories: prostrate and breast cancer screenings.
- Surveys of people in India about nuclear testing.
- State tax reports.
- Antitrust settlements.
- Mediterranean fruit fly spraying.
- Fees paid lawyers in tobacco lawsuits.
- Personal injury lawsuit verdict.
- Company mergers.
- Minority investments by bank.
- Company earnings.
- Sports statistics: salaries, scores, player performances.
- Feature on cystic fibrosis sufferer's financial woes.
- Statistics on male plastic surgery .

THE BASIC MATH SKILLS YOU'LL NEED

Whether you're adding up the number of burglaries that occurred over the weekend or calculating the percentage increase in a community's annual budget, you'll need math skills like these:

AVERAGES

An **average** is a way to summarize a set of numbers with a single number: teacher salaries, batting averages or perhaps the most familiar for students, grade point average.

If you talk with people who are familiar with math, they may not even use the word "average." Instead they'll talk about one of the three types of averages: the **mean,** the **median** or the **mode.** Confusing the types of average is one of the most common math mistakes that journalists (and many other types of people) make.

MEAN: The sum of all numbers divided by the number of numbers in the set.

MEDIAN: The one in the middle.

MODE: The most common answer.

Although any of the three can legitimately be called the average, most people are referring to the mean when they use the term "average." The mean measures the central tendency—and gives baseball fans an idea of what to expect when a batter comes to the plate.

MEAN.   The term: Mean (also known as the average)

The definition: The sum of a set of numbers divided by the numbers, or terms, in the set.

The formula: $\text{Mean} = \dfrac{\text{Sum of terms}}{\text{Number of terms}}$

The problem: In her first semester of college, Caitlin received one A, four B's, two C's. (An A equals four grade points, a B three grade points, a C two grade points.) What was her grade point average?

The solution: 1. **Add up** the grades (sum of the terms).

2. Then **divide** that total by the number of terms in the set.

$$\frac{4 + 3 + 3 + 3 + 3 + 2 + 2}{7} = \frac{20}{7} = 2.86 \text{ GPA}$$

Remember that numbers are tools for describing things, just as nouns and verbs are.

The problem with the mean is that it can mislead, especially when one of the numbers in the set is significantly larger or smaller. The example most often given to demonstrate this tendency is the salaries of a group of people in, say, a news organization.

MEDIAN.   The term: Median (also known as the middle number and the midpoint)

The definition: The value of the middle case when the cases are put in order of size.

Consider this example. At Hypernews, an online news site, the president makes $200,000 a year, the managing editor makes $55,000, the programmer makes $50,000, the ad sales representative makes $45,000, a reporter and a graphic artist make $35,000 each, and the office receptionist makes $20,000.

If you calculate the mean, 200,000 + 55,000 + 50,000 + 45,000 + 35,000 + 35,000 + 20,000, the mean = $63,000.

Try telling the programmer, ad rep, reporter or receptionist that the average salary at Hypernews is $63,000, and they'd choke on their latte. That's because the salaries at Hypernews aren't distributed equally—the president makes significantly more than the other employees—which makes the mean unrepresentative.

You discover the median by setting the terms in a line in order of size and picking the middle number.

20,000   35,000   35,000   45,000   50,000   55,000   200,000

Remember: When the set of numbers includes extreme cases, the median is more informative, more accurate and fairer. The median salary in this example is $45,000.

What happens when you have to find the median of an even number of numbers? In that case, it's the mean of the two middle numbers.

The problem: Burglaries in Pleasantville for each of the first six months of the year were 8, 10, 12, 35, 70, 45. What was the median number of burglaries committed?

Set out the numbers in a line, by order of size: 8, 10, 12, 35, 45, 70.

Notice that this is an even number of burglaries, so it's impossible to select a middle number. In that case, you add the two middle numbers and divide by two:

$$\frac{12 + 35}{2} = \frac{47}{2} = 23.5$$

The median number of burglaries during the first six months of the year is 23.5.

MODE.   The term: Mode

The definition: The number that appears most often.

The mode is the simplest to figure out, but it's the least useful, except in cases where the number that appears most often is relevant.

The problem: Seven friends were comparing ticket prices to music concerts and trying to decide which was the most common ticket price.

Sara paid $25 = 1.
Jay, Kevin and Que paid $30 = 1,2,3.
Kenetra and Willie paid $40 = 1,2.
Stella paid $45 = 1.

Which is the mode or number that appears most often?
The most common ticket price paid by seven friends was $30.

MEAN, MEDIAN, MODE: WHEN TO USE THEM.   In general, use the MEAN when you want to know the arithmetical average.

Use the MEDIAN when you are talking about a typical price or income. Use the median especially when the set contains a few extreme values.

Use the MODE when you are talking about the most common example, such as a favorite item.

RATES AND PERCENTS

A **rate** is a proportion that always expresses its numerator (the number above the line in a fraction) and its denominator (the number below the line in a fraction) or baseline as "so many per so many." Examples include miles per hour, deaths per passenger mile, false positive diagnoses per hundred cases, equipment failures per thousand uses.

Percents, the rate per 100, are a communication tool that enable you to convey how one value differs from another. Journalists wrestle with percent differences virtually every day. Real estate taxes went up from the previous year. By what percent? Crime is down or up from the year before. By what percent? A Saturn is cheaper than a Saab. By what percent?

"The inability to figure a percent increase is a chronic failing in most newsrooms, even though the formula is simple," says Philip Meyer, author of *The New Precision Journalism* and a pioneer in the use of social science methods in journalism. Meyer had a distinguished career with Knight Ridder Newspapers and is now a consultant to news organizations and professor of journalism at the University of North Carolina at Chapel Hill.

One way to remember what percent means is to know the root of the word. "Per" means "out of." "Cent" means "one hundred." So "percent" (or the symbol %) after a number means that many out of 100. Another way to think of percents is that they are the same as fractions with the same denominator—100, such as $\dfrac{25}{100} = 25$ percent.

The definition: Percent is one-hundredth. Percent increase is the amount of the increase expressed as a percent of the original amount. Percent decrease is the amount of the decrease expressed as a percent of the original amount.

The formula:

1. **Subtract** old value from new value to find out absolute number of increase or decrease.
2. **Divide** absolute number of increase or decrease by old value.
3. **Multiply** by 100.
4. **Add** percentage sign %.

The problem: Population in Fairweather County totaled 220,000 in 1988. In 1998, it totaled 355,000. By what percent did it increase?

The solution:

$$
\begin{array}{r}
355,000 \\
-220,000 \\
\hline
135,000
\end{array}
$$

$135,000/220,000 = .608108$

$.608108 \times 100 = 60.8$ or 61%

The population in Fairweather County increased by 61 percent between 1988 and 1998.

MATH WORKSHOP: PERCENTAGES

The assignment: The National Transportation Safety Board (NTSB), the federal agency that investigates major transportation accidents, including all aviation accidents, today released its annual figures on transportation fatalities in the United States. Your assignment is to write a story based on the figures. But first you have to determine what the figures mean.

Materials: Following you will find a table the agency released comparing the change in fatalities for a variety of transportation accidents that occurred between 1996 and 1997.

The problem: Using the formula for percentages, calculate the percentage change between 1996 and 1997 for *each* category (Highway, Marine, Pipeline, etc.) and each subcategory (Passenger Cars, Pedestrians, Airlines) as well as the percentage increase for the total number of fatalities.

The formula:

1. **Subtract** old value from new value to find out absolute number of increase or decrease.

2. **Divide** absolute number of increase or decrease by old value.

3. **Multiply** by 100.

4. **Add** percentage sign %.

After you are finished with your calculations and story, you can review your figures by checking them against the official press release issued by the NTSB. Compare your story with the one written by an Associated Press reporter. Both appear later in this chapter.

CHANGING DECIMALS TO PERCENTS AND VICE VERSA

To change a decimal to a percent:
  Move the decimal point *two* places to the right.
  Example: .50 = 50%
  To change a percent to a decimal:
  Move the decimal point *two* places to the left.
  Example: 50% = .50

PERCENT OF

Just as writers have language inadequacies, such as commonly misspelled words or grammatical mistakes, we can have mathematical inadequacies as well. For some reason, I've always had a mental block when it comes to figuring out percentages. For years, I kept the back of a calculator package because it listed formulas. Calculating percentages was the most common math problem I encountered as a reporter. What percentage of the school budget went to teacher salaries? What percentage of convicted arsonists

NATIONAL TRANSPORTATION SAFETY BOARD
1997 U.S. TRANSPORTATION FATALITIES

		1996	1997
Highway	Passenger cars	22,416	22,227
	Light trucks and vans	9,901	10,323
	Pedestrians	5,412	5,300
	Motorcycles	2,160	2,099
	Pedalcycles	761	800
	Medium and heavy trucks	621	711
	Buses	21	15
	All other	615	525
	Total	41,907	42,000
Rail	Trespassers and nontrespassers	570	584
	Employees and contractors	42	49
	Passengers on trains	12	6
	Light and commuter rail	128	107
	Total	752	746
Marine	Recreational boating	709	800
	Cargo transport	29	16
	Commercial fishing	76	54
	Total	814	870
Aviation	General aviation	631	646
	Airlines	380	8
	Air taxi	63	40
	Commuter	14	46
	Foreign/unregistered	5	236
	Total	1,093	976
Pipeline	Gas	48	11
	Liquids	5	0
	Total	53	11
Grand Total		44,619	44,603

THE PRESS RELEASE

Transportation Fatalities Hold Steady in 1997; Highway Deaths Hit 42,000, NTSB Reports

For Immediate Release: Aug. 10, 1998
SB 98-30

WASHINGTON, D.C.—The number of persons who died in transportation accidents in the United States and its territories remained virtually steady between 1996 and 1997, according to preliminary statistics released today by the National Transportation Safety Board. Total transportation fatalities, in all modes, were 44,619 in 1996, compared to 44,603 last year. Highway fatalities accounted for more than 94 percent of the transportation deaths (42,000) in 1997.

"It is encouraging that transportation fatalities did not rise in 1997, even though more and more people are traveling every year," NTSB Chairman Jim Hall said. "However, highway deaths, among the more preventable in transportation, continue to account for most transportation fatalities, emphasizing the importance of Safety Board initiatives in drunk driving, seat belt and graduated licensing legislation."

The largest increase in highway deaths occurred in the category of light trucks and vans, which experienced 422 more fatalities in 1997 than in 1996. This continues a five-year trend in which this category has accounted for a larger share of highway deaths each year, from 21 percent in 1993 to 25 percent last year. Passenger car fatalities have remained at about 54 percent each year.

The number of persons killed in aviation accidents dropped from 1,093 in 1996 to 976 in 1997, despite a large increase involving aircraft not registered in the United States. The 236 deaths in that category, compared with just 5 in 1996, are mostly attributable to the 228 persons who died aboard a Korean Air Boeing 747 that crashed in Guam in August. While general aviation fatalities increased from 631 to 646, airline deaths fell from 380 in 1996—the year of the ValuJet and TWA Flight 800 accidents—to 8 in 1997.

Fatalities involving rail transportation fell from 752 to 746 in 1997, with the vast majority (584) being persons walking along or crossing tracks. Deaths among train passengers dropped from 12 to 6.

Marine deaths increased from 814 to 870, due to an increase in recreational boating fatalities of almost 100. Fatalities in marine cargo transportation and commercial fishing declined.

Pipeline fatalities fell from 53 in 1996 (33 of them in one accident in Puerto Rico) to 11 in 1997.

Aviation statistics are compiled by the NTSB. Data on the other modes of transportation are reported to the board from the U.S. Department of Transportation. The attached table and chart provide a further breakdown of 1996 transportation fatality statistics. All 1997 data are preliminary.

-30-

NTSB Media Contact: Ted Lopatkiewicz (202) 314-6100
Source: National Transportation Safety Board

THE STORY

Transportation Fatalities Hold Steady in 1997

The Associated Press
Aug. 10, 1998

WASHINGTON—Travel in America claimed the lives of more than 44,000 people last year—roughly the population of Wilkes-Barre, Pa., Palatine, Ill., or Covina, Calif.

The 44,603 transportation-related deaths were nearly the same as the 1996 total of 44,619, the National Transportation Safety Board reported Monday.

As usual, more than 90 percent of the deaths occurred on the highways—42,000, up from 41,907 in 1996.

The aviation toll declined slightly from 1,093 in 1996 to 976 last year. Also following the usual pattern, the majority were flying in small, private planes.

The lone major airline crash on U.S. territory last year was that of a Korean Air Boeing 747 in Guam, killing 228 people. In 1996, the ValuJet and TWA 800 disasters claimed a total of 340 lives.

"It is encouraging that transportation fatalities did not rise in 1997, even though more people are traveling every year," said Jim Hall, chairman of the safety board.

He noted that highway deaths, the most preventable of accidents, continue to claim the most lives, with the largest increase involving popular light trucks and vans.

---

went to prison or got probation? "When you calculate percentage differences or percentage change, you are comparing two numbers and trying to determine the significance of the change from the first number to the second number," explains Lisa Miller in her book, *Power Journalism: Computer Assisted Reporting.*

Here's how to compute percentages:

The problem: 9 is what percent of 36?

The formula: 1. **Divide** the number you want to find the percentage of by the whole. 2. Then **multiply** the quotient times 100.

1. $9 \div 36 = .25$

2. $.25 \times 100 = 25$ percent

Therefore, 9 = 25 percent of 36

The problem: What is 20 percent of 84?

The formula: Percent × Whole = Part

The solution: .20 × 84 = 16.8 = 20 percent of 84

(For people who prefer words to symbols, it may help to think of "×" as "of." Thus 2 × 2 = 2 of 2 = 4.)

Example: Based on the preceding National Transportation Safety Board release, what percentage of highway fatalities in 1997 involved buses?

Bus fatalities = 525

Total fatalities = 42,000

525 is what percent of 42,000?

The solution: Percent = 525 ÷ 42,000 × 100 = 1.25 percent

Bus fatalities represented 1.25 percent of all highway fatalities in 1997.

RATES

Percentages, that is, rates per 100, are useful to communicate changes in values over time. But sometimes they aren't sufficient. In that case, choosing a different rate, such as per 100,000, is better. A good rule of thumb, according to Philip Meyer, is always use a rate that gives your significant numbers without decimals. Choose a rate that allows whole number comparisons.

In *A Mathematician Reads the Newspaper*, John Allen Paulos points out how descriptions of relationships between numbers vary according to the intentions of the person using them. Want to make something appear small? Stress its volume. Want the same object to appear huge? Describe its size in a linear measure. Take 4 million nickels. Sounds like a lot. But they would fit easily into a cubical box measuring six feet on each side. Doesn't sound too big, does it? But stack those same 4 million nickels on top of one another, and you'd have a tower that stretched from sea level to the top of Mount Everest.

Paulos offers another example, one with greater relevance to journalists: the number of people affected by an illness, accident or other misfortune. Want to make it seem like a huge problem? Use the number of people affected nationally. So if 1 out of 100,000 people suffers from some illness, that's 2,500 people around the country, a figure that could cause alarm, especially if the news reports include heart-breaking stories about individual victims. Want the problem to appear small? Report the incidence rate. Say that there would be just one victim in a crowd that could fill not one but two jam-packed sports stadiums, and the problem seems minuscule.

Rates—numbers that act as measures of value in relationship to other numbers—can give a picture of crimes in a certain area and let you compare them to other areas. They can help you compare the same values even though you are looking at groups of varying sizes, such as populations. A common rate used by journalists is the per-capita rate, or the number for each person in town. Percent is the most common.

PER-CAPITA RATE

The definition: Per capita is the rate per one unit of population.

The formula: **Divide** the value (crimes, heart attacks) by total population. To discover the rates per 100, **multiply** by 100.

Example: In a neighborhood of 1,000 persons, 20 speeding tickets were issued in one month. What is the per-capita rate?

The solution: 20 ÷ 1000 = .02 per capita rate

Rates per 100 = .02 × 100 = 2

A LIFE IN JOURNALISM

MAKING NEWS SENSE OF NUMBERS

Tiffany Murri
Reporter, KIVI Channel 6, Boise, Idaho

"Albertsons Compare and Save," my investigative report into deceptive pricing at Albertsons, started with a simple trip to the grocery store. As I did my personal shopping I noticed signs posted on Albertsons shelves asking shoppers to "Compare and Save." So I decided to compare and see what the savings actually were.

Albertsons pits national brands against their in-store brand to show you save money by buying the Albertsons label. For example, one "Compare and Save" sign claims you'll save $1 buying Albertsons laundry detergent instead of Tide Ultra.

But I noticed that the prices on the national brands seemed exceptionally high. I wondered if Albertsons was jacking them up to make their in-store brand look cheaper. So I wrote down the prices of 32 "Compare and Save" national products at Albertsons. Then I did the same at Boise's other two major grocery stores, Waremart and Fred Meyer. Of 32 national products, 30 cost more at Albertsons.

To find out just how much more, I entered all the prices on a spreadsheet. Using the percent difference function, I learned if you buy Tide Ultra at Albertsons you'll pay 15 percent more than at Waremart and 18 percent more than at Fred Meyer. The spreadsheet also quickly showed how much you'd save on your total grocery bill just by shopping at Waremart or Fred Meyer, instead of Albertsons.

At this point I'd like to say I consider myself a math and computer idiot. But a three-hour spreadsheet class conducted by Debbie Wolfe, technology training editor at the *St. Petersburg Times*, and a couple of pages in the Excel program manual were all it took. And was my news director impressed when I presented my data in the daily news meeting!

Still, we had to handle the story carefully. Albertsons corporate headquarters is in Boise, and it's a major advertiser on our station.

I interviewed the manager of the Albertsons store where I did my price comparisons. He said, "It's simply part of our competitive pricing." He denied artificially inflating national brand prices.

I also got the opinions of several Albertsons customers. Most said despite higher national brand prices they would continue to shop at Albertsons for the service, cleanliness and convenience.

The story ran during our "In-Depth" segment on our highest viewership night. I got a lot of positive feedback from viewers, saying the story offered the kind of news they can use.

Albertsons was furious. But they didn't call the news department. They called sales and threatened to cancel a $30,000-a-year advertising account. My news director stood by my story. We agreed to give Albertsons a copy of my spreadsheet. Once they saw the numbers they didn't have anything left to argue about, and they didn't pull their ads off our station.

As a first-year reporter I learned a lot from this story. First I learned that in your everyday life you find some of the best news stories that affect the most people. Second, I accepted the fact that math and computers are important tools for reporters and don't have to be intimidating. Finally, I gained the courage to go after big stories, no matter who the truth might offend.

REPORTING ON BUDGETS

One of the most important things journalists report on is how government spends public money. But news organizations often shortchange the public with reporting that is superficial and uninformed.

To offset that limitation, reporters and editors at *The Oregonian* are encouraged to consider the following topics in every story:

- Dollar amount of current year's budget.
- Dollar amount of proposed or new budget.
- Percentage change (increase or decrease) new budget represents.
- Impact of changes on individuals—taxpayers, teachers' salaries.
- Winners and losers in budget process—who wanted what, who got what?
- Sources who will balance what government officials say about their own budgets.

Reporters don't like writing about budgets. For many, says Dave Herzog, an investigative reporter at *The Providence Journal*, it's on a par with going to the dentist: It's something we know we have to do, we don't like doing it, and it's pretty painful while we are doing it.

This section draws on the account of a discussion Herzog led on budget stories at the Providence paper, which appears on its Power of Words Web site (**http://www.projo.com/**).

First, change your definition of a budget from a stack of computer printout littered with unintelligible numbers. It's an operating plan, Herzog says. It sets out the vision of the school or town. You learn what your political leaders value. What do they spend money on? A budget is a very political document.

Budgets may be filled with dry numbers, but there are powerful stories lurking behind those numbers. *Journal* reporters looked at the expense account vouchers of school committee members in one suburb. Their story reported that committee members put in for babysitting fees and donations made at funerals.

Budgets typically make news when they are presented, argued over and voted on. After that, reporters ignore them. Herzog advises reporters to go out and see what impact the budget is having. When a reporter toured a high school, he learned that students had to do their dissection on rotten frogs because the school did not have money for new ones. That image did a better job than a number would to convey the school's funding woes.

And remember: Not all math is complicated. Some important calculations can be figured out using the tools we all learned in elementary school. For example, you can use long division to determine how much your community spends for education for each child in town. If the school budget is $4 million, and there are 2,000 kids of school age, the per-capita spending rate is determined by dividing the budget by the number of children: $4,000,000/2,000 = $2,000 per child.

A Little Light Reading

There's more to a budget than rows of numbers. Herzog advises reporters to supplement their knowledge by studying other budget-related documents.

ANNUAL REPORT. This is the official feel-good document put out by the town, describing the good things that are happening.

AUDITED FINANCIAL STATEMENT. This will tell you what is really happening in the town in regards to its finances. It will say if there are any deficits, pending litigation, retirement account problems and will include the management letter. The latter describes problems the auditors have found, and often makes recommendations that are repeated year after year.

BOND OFFICIAL STATEMENT. Whenever a town needs to borrow money for a big capital project, it floats a bond, and it needs to prepare this document. It includes demographics and the financial condition of the town to help investors in deciding whether to invest in the bonds.

WATCHDOG GROUP REPORT. In Rhode Island, the Public Expenditure Council Reports analyze property tax rates in all municipalities in Rhode Island, equalizes them and then makes comparisons. Check to see if there is a counterpart in your state.

CREDIT REPORT. Moody's and Standard & Poor both prepare reports on the financial condition of a town. They can be extremely helpful. A good textbook on municipal finance might also be helpful.

LEARN MORE ABOUT BUDGETS FROM DAVE HERZOG OF *THE PROVIDENCE JOURNAL* ONLINE AT http://www.projo.com/words/tip415.htm

Budget Tips

Herzog offers reporters these tips for reporting and writing more effectively about budgets:

- Break out of the mind-set that a budget is a dry collection of numbers that you report on a couple of times during the financial season. Remember that it is a document that charts your town's plan for the coming year and reflects the political values of the people who put it together.

- Approach the budget and town financial reporting as a cycle that unfolds during the year. As you do the event-driven stories, keep an eye open for possible enterprise stories.

- Look at the bottom lines. If spending is greater than income, your town will run a deficit.

- Look for stories you can do before the budget is released. For example, you can analyze the budgets from the past five or ten years and discover trends that are important to readers.

- Always adjust for inflation when looking at budgets over time. This will save you from making the embarrassing mistake of

FIND OUT THE CONSUMER PRICE INDEX IN YOUR AREA ONLINE AT http://www.bls.gov

writing that spending has doubled in your town. The best way to adjust for inflation is by using the Consumer Price Index. The formula for adjusting 1988 spending to 1998 dollars would be: (1988 amount × 1998 CPI) ÷ 1988 CPI. In the example that follows, you can see that what looks like a 50 percent rise over the past decade really is a 5.7 percent rise. (The CPI for the New England region is available on the U.S. Bureau of Labor Statistics Web site: **http://www.bls.gov. ro1home.htm**.)

1988 spending: $1,000,000

1988 adjusted: $1,418,624

1998 spending: $1,500,000

CPI 1988: 119.2

CPI 1998: 169.1

Real difference: $81,376

Real change: 5.7%

- Put your budget-day stories into context by telling readers whether taxes will go up and by how much. Illustrate by showing what would happen to the tax bill of a "typical" property.

- Make budget-day stories meaningful for readers by telling them what services they're going to be getting or losing. Find out who the winners and losers are.

- Get wish lists from department heads and check to see whether their priorities got into the budget. If not, what are the implications?

- Pick one interesting or unusual part of the budget and write about it some time during the budget cycle. Tell readers something they didn't know before.

- Look at independent audits. These documents cast a cold eye on a town's spending and show what really happened in a fiscal year. Look for deficits in all the funds—not just the general fund.

- Check whether the budgeters are moving functions into enterprise funds. These funds are supposed to pay for themselves and cover government functions that you can measure. An example: providing water service.

- Read the management letters in the audits. There's where you will find criticism of the town's policies and practices.

- Read credit reports and bond official statements. The bond official statements will report, in gory detail, the financial condition of the town and possible risks to investors. The credit reports, available from ratings agencies (Moody's and Standard & Poor), do a nice job of outlining a town's finances in clear terms.

- Learn how to use a **spreadsheet** and use it to analyze your budgets.

- Get reports from the state's expenditure council or any other agency that monitors municipal finances and taxation.

- If your town has big year-end surpluses, ask why. Officials may say it's from conservative fiscal practices. It may actually be because they're intentionally asking for money in the budget and not spending it.

- Look to see if the town is setting aside money for legal fees and settlements. If that's happening the town may be planning to close a lawsuit by settling with a plaintiff.

- Find out whether municipal contracts are set to expire. If the town is negotiating contracts, what effect will these contracts have on the budget (and vice versa)?

- Remember that the budget is a living document that has application year-round. Keep it on your desk and refer to it often.

ADVANCED MATH SKILLS

STATISTICS: NUMBERS THAT TELL US WHERE WE STAND

Derived from the Latin word for "stand," "statistics" tell us where we as a society stand. Statistics transform large amounts of information into smaller quantities that are easier to grasp.

One economist calls them "the economy's flashlights," though he cautions "sometimes they illuminate poorly."

Statistics are used for a variety of purposes. But for reporters just two uses matter: statistics as a descriptive tool and as a method for testing inferences.

Descriptive statistics include the following:

1. Nominal measurement sorts things into categories, such as the number of men and women in a class, and counts them.

2. Ordinal measurement ranks things along some relevant dimension such as good, better, best.

3. Interval measurement determines by how much things differ from each other, such as height in inches.

Inferential statistics are important to journalists because they help "sort out the phenomena which seem to require explanation from those that have a good likelihood of being due to nothing more than chance," says Meyer.

Statistics also measure the extent to which two things vary together, such as sales of air conditioners and the number of 100-degree days in August. This measurement helps us find causation and/or make predictions.

VITAL STATISTICS: BIRTH, DEATH, HEALTH, DISEASE

The science of statistics was born in the mid-1700s. That was when an Englishman named John Graunt decided to study a weekly record of christenings, burials and causes of death that the government had been keeping since 1592 but had never interpreted. Back then the causes of death included "Affrighted, Dead in the Street and Starved, Executed and Prest to Death, French Pox, Grief, Teeth, Worms and Suddenly," as Victor Cohn reports in *News & Numbers,* a useful guide to reporting about statistics.

"**Vital statistics** are the statistics of life, health, disease and death, the statistics of much that we hold dear and much that we fear," says Cohn, a former medical writer and science editor for *The Washington Post.* "They tell us of the burden of illness and its costs. They measure our progress against disease and premature death, or should do so if properly applied. They are much misapplied, misused and misunderstood. We who report the news often misunderstand them or ignore them. They seem dull. We prefer to hear about ideas, subjects, people. Yet these statistics can yield fascinating stories if we learn something of their power and limits and the rather special vocabulary of human lives."

Stories with that power require their own vocabulary, such as "the rate."

In medicine, the two most common rates are incidence and prevalence. The **incidence rate** is the proportion of persons who contract a disease in a given population in a given unit of time. The **prevalence rate** is the proportion of persons who have the disease in a given population at a given point in time. The **mortality rate** is the incidence of deaths per unit of time in a given population. The **morbidity rate** is the incidence of a particular disease or all illness.

The incidence rate counts only new cases, whereas the prevalence rate is the total case rate, both new and old, in a given population at a given time. Remember Victor Cohn's analogy: "If incidence is like an entering class, prevalence is the whole school."

To judge statements in government, politics, economics or advertising, reporters can ask the same questions that researchers ask in medicine and science: How do you know? Have you done a study? What kind? What numbers lead you to your conclusions? How valid, how probable are they? Compared to what?

STANDARD DEVIATION

The **standard deviation**—which determines how much numbers vary around the average—is a useful tool that can help you find stories behind the numbers. Why, for example, are one school's test scores higher than another school's? At first glance, you might assume one group of children is smarter, but further reporting could discover that the school with higher scores has a bigger percentage of gifted students.

As journalist Robert Niles says, you'd probably never use the term "standard deviation" in a story because your readers might not understand it. Niles' Web site gives a reader-friendly explanation and an example—school test scores—relevant to journalists: **http://nilesonline.com/stats/**.

MARGIN OF ERROR

You see the phrase "margin of error" all the time in stories about surveys or polls, as in "the survey has a margin of error of plus or minus three points." But what does it mean?

Margin of error refers to a measurement of the accuracy of the results of a survey. For example: A margin of error of plus or minus 3.5 percent means that there is a known chance, usually 95 percent, that the responses of the target population as a whole would fall somewhere between 3.5 percent more and 3.5 percent less than the responses of the sample (a 7 percent spread). However, for any specific question, the margin of error could be greater or less than plus or minus 3.5 percent. It refers to sampling error. Other sources of error are not so easily specified.

ADJUSTING FOR INFLATION

Which movie was more expensive to make, *Waterworld*, the 1995 epic starring Kevin Costner, or *Cleopatra*, made in 1939?

Don't kick yourself if you picked *Waterworld*, Kevin Costner's watery box-office bomb. In 1995, before the movie premiered, with a budget of $175 million, the news media consistently described the flick as the most expensive movie ever made. Actually, at the time, that distinction belonged to *Cleopatra*, which cost $219 million to make—in 1995 dollars.

"How could responsible reporters get it so wrong?" asked David R. Henderson, a writer for the business magazine *Fortune*, who used the movies to highlight a common journalistic failing. The answer, he said, is simple. "In comparing costs and revenues over time, they typically leave out something that matters just as much as the raw revenues or costs of a movie. They leave out inflation. The plain fact is that a 1939 dollar bought a lot more than a 1963 dollar, which bought more than a 1982 dollar, which ... you get the point. In the 56 years after 1939, inflation has averaged 4.4 percent a year. Although that sounds small, even moderate inflation adds up over time. Actually, it doesn't add up. It multiplies up. Inflation, like interest, compounds. The net result: Since 1939, prices have increased by 998 percent." A reporter who fails to account for inflation when comparing dollar amounts in different years comes up, Henderson says, with one result: gibberish. Remember his rule: To compare accurately, you must convert all dollar amounts into same-year dollars.

Of adjusting for inflation, Neill A. Borowski, director of computer-assisted reporting for *The Philadelphia Inquirer*, says, "It's the thing that everyone *knows* is the right thing to do. But many media outlets often mislead because they do not adjust data to reflect the impact of inflation." The next time you hear someone say, "everything's going up," adjust for inflation.

For more information on inflation, visit the Bureau of Labor Statistics' Web site at **http://www.bls.gov/**.

POLLS AND SURVEYS: NUMBERS THAT TELL US WHAT WE THINK

Polls and surveys use numbers to provide information about attitudes, knowledge and behavior. Polls "attempt to tell us what we are thinking," says Victor Cohn.

Even though journalists and the public may complain that polls make politics into horse races, the fact is elections represent local, regional and national decisions about who will run the government. "Polling is knowledge, and knowledge, famously, is power, and polling knowledge, furthermore, is knowledge about power," says Jonathan Schell, a columnist for *Newsday*.

The problem is that polling, as one prominent pollster, Ken Dautrich of the Roper Center, says, is "an ABC science, Almost Being Certain."

Reporters take polls and conduct surveys. At *The Providence Journal*, we used to call them "walk and talk" stories. You'd go to a mall or prowl downtown streets buttonholing strangers to ask them who they favored for president or to get their reaction to a news event. But these are informal, decidedly unscientific and as a result not worth much except anecdotally. In the same way, the online polls that appear on many news sites are not scientific and in many ways worthless as measures of anything except what the people who answered the question believe.

To be statistically significant, a survey must have these characteristics, according to Philip Meyer:

1. The population being surveyed must be clearly defined in advance.
2. Every member of the population must have a known probability of being included in the sample.
3. Everyone must be asked the same questions, and answers must be recorded in the same way.

A major problem with many polls, especially national ones, is that they underrepresent the opinions of poor people and minorities. Make sure you know what the questions are, who was asked, by whom and how. And make sure if you write about a survey that you share that information with your audience.

WRITING WITH NUMBERS

As we've seen, numbers are not just a tool for analysis. Numbers also communicate. Once you've figured out the numbers for your story, the next step is to be able to use them clearly in your writing.

"No matter how rigorous your analysis, numbers aren't a story," says Jeff South, former database editor for the *Austin American-Statesman* who now teaches at Virginia Commonwealth University. "As politicians might say: It's the content, stupid. Words, not data, make a story. Your analysis will shape the story; it might be the foundation for the story. But you must tell the story in a way that connects with people who don't know a spreadsheet from a cookie sheet. And that means, ironically, telling the story almost as if it didn't involve computer analysis."

Mathematics is a precise science and requires semantic as well as numerical precision. Even experienced journalists get sloppy when writing about numbers. At *The New York Times*, reporters have been known to use the word "shortfall"—which means the quantity or extent by which something falls short—to mean shortage, decline, unpaid bill, difference, unmet budget, request, debt, remainder and deficit. Avoid jargon. Bureaucrats may use terms such as "revenue" and "expenditures"; keep it simple with "income" and "spending."

Here are some tips to help you use numbers effectively in your writing:

COMPARISON SHOP. "When you do use a figure in a story, put it in context by comparing it to something else. A number has little significance on its own; its true meaning comes from its *relative* value," says Paul Hemp, an editor for *The Boston Globe* and author of *Ten Practical Tips for Business and Economic Reporting in Developing Economies*. Whenever Hemp reaches up to the top row of keyboard keys for the numbers 0 through 9, he always stops and asks himself: Compared to what?

When you use a statistic, compare it to another time, such as an earlier year, or another place, to something people can relate to. That's what the writer for The Associated Press did in the story about transportation fatalities by comparing the previous year's transportation fatalities with the population of three communities familiar in three major regions of the country:

WASHINGTON (AP)—Travel in America claimed the lives of more than 44,000 people last year—roughly the population of Wilkes-Barre, Pa., Palatine, Ill., or Covina, Calif.

The Associated Press

ROUND OFF AND SUBSTITUTE. Economists and financial experts need exact numbers. Readers don't. So you can say "nearly doubled" or "about one-third" and remain accurate as well as understandable. You don't need to say that burglaries increased 105 percent when you could say they doubled. If 33 percent of the drivers in fatal crashes had alcohol in their blood, it will be clearer if you say, "one in three drivers had been drinking."

THINK VISUAL. To help readers understand numbers, it's often helpful to relate the numbers to something readers can picture. Make quantities visible in the mind's eye. In an article about the excavation of World War II planes that crashed in the marshes and swamps of the Netherlands, author Les Daly used this vivid picture to convey the enormity of the 7,000 crashes. "To put it another way, the crash of 7,000 aircraft would mean that every square mile of the state of New Jersey would have shaken to the impact of a downed plane."

TIPS FROM THE EXPERTS

Use statistical methods as safeguards, advises Brant Houston of Investigative Reporters and Editors. "They should not make journalists leap to conclusions, but they should prompt journalists to question the veracity of their perceptions and assumptions or those of the people the journalists are covering."

Get help. Copy editors are often the most numerate people in the newsroom. Ask a high school math teacher for help. Often knowledgeable sources will be glad to check the accuracy of your computations. After all, it's often in their interest that numbers in a story are correct. Kelly Ryan, who covers city hall for the *St. Petersburg Times,* says a top city budget official is willing to spend time to help clear up any confusion over budgetary matters, even late at night when Ryan is on deadline.

Questions to ask when dealing with data:

■ Where did the data come from?

■ Have the data been peer reviewed?

■ How were the data collected?

■ And a warning: Be skeptical when dealing with comparisons.

"If you're going to use a number, you'd better know where it comes from, how reliable it is and whether it means what it seems to mean. The garbage-in, garbage-out problem has been with us a long time," says *Newsweek*'s economics columnist Robert Samuelson.

If you're having trouble with numbers in your reporting or writing, mathematician Paulos suggests these techniques:

■ Use smaller numbers.

■ Collect information relevant to the problem.

- Work backward from the solution.
- Draw pictures and diagrams. "I can't think without a picture," says Greg Martin, a college teacher who specializes in training math teachers.
- Compare the problem or parts of the problem to problems you do understand.

REPORTER'S TOOLBOX: CALCULATORS

Are you a math-phobe, terrified of numbers? Philip Meyer recommends you get a grip by investing in a pocket calculator. First available in the early 1960s, by the 1970s calculators were small enough to fit in a pocket and became available to consumers. With 10 keys to enter numbers and additional operating keys, they allow the reporter to perform everything from basic arithmetic to complex mathematical functions.

Meyer prefers the kind that clicks when you press the keys. Whether the calculator is quiet or not, he advises buying the kind that, at least, does square roots. Better yet, he says, is a model that features parentheses, which will let you handle complicated calculations (this avoids having to keep track of intermediate steps on paper or memory that has to be fed manually). A good one costs $10 to $15 and should have a percent key and flip-flop key to transpose entries.

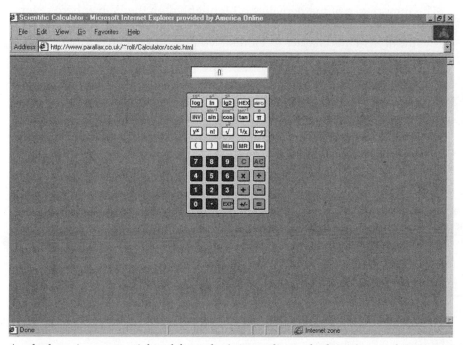

A calculator is an essential tool for today's journalists, whether it's a pocket type or this online version.

ONLINE CALCULATORS

Can't do math on your fingers? Forget your calculator at the coffeeshop? There's a calculator just a couple of clicks away on the Windows desktop of a personal computer. If you're connected to the Internet, you can also log on to the World Wide Web and find online calculators that will do all sorts of figuring: from mortgage rates to percentages, metric conversions, cost of living, even child support. Point your Web browser to the My Virtual Reference Desk site, which features a list of links to online calculators, at **http://www.refdesk.com/**.

GETTING SMARTER

Remember that these are the basics written by a nonmathematician. (I've had them double-checked by mathematically minded journalists and math teachers.) Consider this the beginning of your education and don't stop now.

You can go to the Web, buy books, take an adult education course.

On deadline you can go to Web sites that will calculate percentages.

Make cheat sheets. If, like me, you have trouble remembering the rules for math calculations, keep a cheat sheet handy with formulas for calculations that come up frequently.

The importance of mathematics is highlighted on the Web, where several sites for journalists offer primers and tools.

In addition, in this chapter's "Hotlist" you'll find Web links to several academic, educational and news organizations that offer help in mathematics.

MAKING SENSE OF NUMBERS: THE COACHING WAY

■ For a great "day after" story when the budget is approved, follow this lead from Dave Herzog: Before the vote, get a wish list from department heads. Compare it with the budget for a story that identifies the budget's "winners and losers."

■ Look for the reality behind the numbers. Find the people affected by budget cuts: the scholastic programs, the hospital patients, families of jobless workers. Try to put a face on every number.

■ Reduce clutter in your stories by taking some of your numbers out and putting them into graphics.

■ Brush up on your math skills. Take a course in statistics. Browse the Web sites listed in the "Hotlist." Make friends with a math-savvy colleague.

GLOSSARY OF IMPORTANT TERMS

Average. An average is a way to summarize a set of numbers with a single number: teacher salaries, batting averages or perhaps the most familiar to students: grade point average.

Budget. An annual financial plan issued by a government agency that sets forth estimated spending and income.

Incidence rate. In health statistics, the incidence rate is a proportion of persons who contract a disease in a given population in a given unit of time.

Innumeracy. Defined by mathematician John Allen Paulos as "an inability to deal comfortably with fundamental notions of number and chance." The opposite of numeracy.

Margin of error. A measurement of the accuracy of the results of a survey.

Mean. The average. The sum of all numbers divided by the number of numbers.

Median. The one in the middle. The value of the middle case when the cases are put in order of size.

Mode. The most common answer. The number that appears most often.

Morbidity rate. The incidence of a particular disease or all illness.

Mortality rate. The incidence of deaths per unit of time in a given population.

Percent. The rate per 100.

Prevalence rate. In health statistics, the proportion of persons who have a disease in a given population at a given point in time.

Rate. A proportion that always expresses its numerator and its denominator or baseline as "so many per so many." Examples include miles per hour, deaths per passenger mile, false positive diagnoses per hundred cases, equipment failures per thousand uses.

Spreadsheet. Computer software, such as Microsoft Excel, used to sort, organize and manipulate numerical data; mathematical functions range from basic arithmetic to complex calculations.

Standard deviation. Determines how much numbers vary around the average; a useful tool that can help you find stories behind the numbers.

Statistics. The science of learning from data.

Vital statistics. Statistics about health, disease and death. Useful markers of social conditions and the effects of poverty, drug abuse and other societal problems.

EXERCISES

1. Study a newspaper, broadcast or online news page and identify which stories involve numbers. What math skills did the journalists employ?

2. Numbers can numb. As a reporter for *The Wall Street Journal*, William Blundell, author of *The Art and Craft of Feature Writing*, says he always tries to avoid letting two paragraphs with numbers "bump into each other." Follow his guideline in your next story that includes numbers. Notice how carefully other news writers follow Blundell's guideline.

3. Using the National Transportation Safety Board report on transportation fatalities and the board's press release included in this chapter, write one or more stories about accident categories, such as airlines or marine fatalities.

READINGS

Cohn, Victor. *News & Numbers: A Guide to Reporting Statistical Claims and Controversies in Health and Other Fields.* Ames, Iowa: Iowa State University Press, 1989.

Heller, Barbara R., and Stanley Kogelman. *The Only Math Book You'll Ever Need.* New York: Facts on File Publications, 1986.

Hemp, Paul. *Ten Practical Tips for Business and Economic Reporting in Developing Economies.* Washington, D.C.: Center for Foreign Journalists, 1994.

Henderson, David R. "Fun and Games With Inflation." *Fortune*, March 18, 1996. **http://www.pathfinder.com/fortune/magazine/1996960318/expert.html**.

Houston, Brant. *Computer-Assisted Reporting: A Practical Guide.* New York: St. Martin's Press, 1996.

Kirtz, Bill. "Figures Can Lie." *Quill*, May 1998.

Meyer, Philip. *The New Precision Journalism.* Bloomington, Indiana: Indiana University Press, 1991.

Miller, Lisa C. *Power Journalism: Computer-Assisted Reporting.* Fort Worth: Harcourt Brace, 1998.

Paulos, John Allen. *Innumeracy: Mathematical Illiteracy and Its Consequences.* New York: Hill and Wang, 1988.

Paulos, John Allen. *A Mathematician Reads the Newspaper.* New York: Basic Books, 1995.

Simon, Roger. "Math Adds Up to Life's Biggest Problem." *Los Angeles Times.* July 29, 1990. Part E, p. 5.

Stanton, Robert, and the staff of Kaplan Educational Centers. *Math Power.* New York: Kaplan Books, Simon and Schuster, 1997.

HOTLIST

http://www.mathmistakes.com/

Here you'll find the most often-repeated mathematical mistakes made by journalists, along with advertisers, politicians and activists. There's also a link to quotes about mathematics. Check out the mathematical mistake of the month. It will improve your math IQ and maybe even trigger a story idea. In any case, you'll be able to at least hang out, in a virtual sense, with people who care passionately about numbers, and if you're a math-phobe like me, that's a useful experience.

http://saturn.vcu.edu/~jcsouth/

The J-Files at Virginia Commonwealth University: resources for computer-assisted reporting. Jeff South, former database editor at the *Austin American-Statesman,* has created a rich and math-phobe-friendly site devoted to computer-assisted reporting. It's a must-bookmark site for 21st-century journalists. Take the online math quiz and learn your strengths and weaknesses and how to overcome them.

http://www.math.temple.edu/~paulos

Check out John Allen Paulos' home page to experience the wit and wisdom of a mathematician who is also a terrific writer. The author of *Innumeracy: Mathematical Literacy and Its Consequences* and *A Mathematician Reads the Newspaper,* Paulos posts recent writings that will comfort math-phobic journalists.

http://www-groups.dcs.st-and.ac.uk/history/index.html

The History of Mathematics Page offers an informative background on the development of math from its earliest days in Babylonia in 2000 B.C. to what will replace the calculator.

http://www.newsengin.com

Here's a site, created by reporters, that knows the dirty little secret about journalistic innumeracy. The Newsengin site provides free computer tools for journalists and researchers. (It also develops software for newsrooms.) The cost-of-living calculator lets you convert dollar values between any two years to adjust for inflation. "Reporting historical dollar amounts without adjusting for inflation is boneheaded and sloppy. Good journalists don't do it once they know better," say the site's creators. The percent change calculator is a godsend for reporters, like me, who can never remember how to calculate a percent change, which is the math computation that keeps journalists busy the most.

http://cara.phillynews.com/

Neill Borowski, director of computer-assisted reporting at *The Philadelphia Inquirer,* is a journalist who knows numbers and how to teach reporters how to use them. His site covers such critical reportorial techniques as how to adjust for inflation and the importance of compounding.

http://nilesonline.com/stats/

"Statistics Every Writer Should Know." Robert Niles is a journalist who knows how to crunch numbers and, more important, how to take the mystery out of statistics. This site explains, in clear and plain English, the meanings and uses of averages (mean and median) and percentage changes.

CHAPTER

15

GETTING—AND KEEPING—A JOB

CHAPTER FOCUS

Getting and keeping a journalism job require the same hard work, accuracy and creativity as do reporting well and writing well.

CHAPTER LESSONS

- Job hunting step by step
- Crafting a résumé
- Online résumé
- Writing a cover letter
- Planning a job search
- Successful interviewing
- Job prospects, salaries and benefits
- The value of starting small
- Dealing successfully with editors
- Surviving your first year in journalism
- Getting—and keeping—a job: The Coaching Way

INTRODUCTION

You've learned—and begun to develop—the skills needed to succeed as a journalist. Now it's time to get a job. This chapter traces the steps necessary to find and land a job in the news business: preparing a résumé, planning and carrying out a job search, conducting yourself well in an interview, knowing what salary and benefits you can expect. But getting that first job is just the beginning. Once you've made it onto a news staff, how do you continue to ensure your success? You'll learn from veteran reporters and editors and newcomers like yourself a variety of strategies and techniques to survive your first year—and beyond—in the newsroom.

JOB HUNTING: STEP BY STEP

To get a job in journalism, in whatever medium, you must apply the same creativity, tenacity and accuracy that good reporting and writing demand. Here are some basic steps to increase your chances of success.

STEP 1: CRAFT A WINNING RÉSUMÉ

A **résumé** is usually a one-page typed summary of your achievements, education, experience and skills. It gives prospective employers a document they can scan in a couple of minutes, at most, to find out who you are and whether you are qualified for employment with their organization. Highlight your academic preparation, extracurricular activities, leadership skills and journalism-related activities, such as **internships,** or school news experience. Skill in a second language, particularly Spanish or Asian languages, is a plus. List your work experience even if some jobs have no journalism connection. Explain gaps; employers spot them and wonder whether you were sailing around the world or just goofing off. Use good-quality paper, in white or a neutral color. Keep the résumé on a disk so you can update it. Find someone to critique it. Check and recheck the spelling. Include telephone, fax numbers and e-mail addresses where you can be reached. Be easy to find. If your schedule, like those of many students, is hectic, let employers know the best time and place to reach you.

Try to keep your résumé to one page. If your academic achievements begin to crowd the page, cut them out. Don't pad your résumé with trivia. And double-check the accuracy of every fact. Don't inflate your experience, turning an internship into a staff job, for example. Lying on her résumé unraveled a web of deception that cost Janet Cooke, a talented young writer for *The Washington Post,* her job, her career and the Pulitzer Prize; the discovery that she lied about her educational background exposed the fact that she had made up the main character in "Jimmy's World," a story about urban drug addiction that won journalism's highest award.

Include two or three **references** on your résumé. (Don't write "References available on request." Busy editors want that information at their fingertips if your application interests them. They may also question whether you actually have any credible references.) Select people who know you well as opposed to someone with an impressive title who remembers you only from a cocktail party at your parents' home. Professional references, such as editors at publications where you interned, are best, followed by journalism teachers. I'd advise against using the editor of your college paper or a friend you worked with at Wal-Mart, as some students have done. Include each reference's name, title, place of employment, address, phone number and e-mail address.

Whomever you list, make sure the reference knows she or he is named on your résumé, and be sure to keep your references informed of your progress. State in your objective what you can *offer* rather than what you want, unlike this otherwise good example on page 545. Send them copies of stories you're

CHECK OUT RÉSUMÉS POSTED ONLINE BY JOB SEEKERS IN BROADCAST AT http://www.tvjobs.com/newres.htm

Dan Wiederer

Home: 177 Michael John
Park Ridge, IL 60068
(847) 696-4039

College: 803 S. Second
Champaign, IL 61820
(217) 328-4559

Objective

I am looking to become a writer, primarily in sports reporting at a newspaper or magazine.

Experience

Sports reporter, *Fighting Illini* newspaper
Champaign, IL
September 1996 to present

Profiled student athletes, football and men's and women's basketball in particular;
Covered 1997 and 1998 NCAA women's basketball;
1997–98 women's basketball beat reporter;
1997–98 men's basketball coverage, including the inaugural Big Ten tournament.

Sports reporter, *Daily Illini*
Champaign, IL
October 1996 to January 1998

Gained experience working in a daily newspaper environment;
1996–97 women's swimming beat reporter; also have covered men's tennis.

Education

University of Illinois
Urbana-Champaign
news-editorial journalism major
August 1995 to May 1998

Graduated in May '98 after only three years of college with a bachelor's degree in news-editorial journalism; course work included in-depth reporting, magazine article writing and news editing; made the Dean's List five out of six semesters. **Final GPA:** 3.705 out of 4.0

The Poynter Institute for Media Studies
St. Petersburg, FL
News reporting and writing fellowship
June 12 to July 24, 1998

Selected as one of 15 journalists to participate in a six-week news reporting and writing fellowship; attended classes given by professional journalists; beat reporter for Maximo and Broadwater neighborhoods of St. Petersburg.

Awards and Honors

Golden Key National Honor Society
October 1997

Recognized as one of the top 15 percent of college juniors and seniors nationally in terms of academic achievement.

National Dean's List
January 1997, April 1998

Awarded to $1/2$ of 1 percent of college students in the nation for academic excellence.

University High Honors
May 1998

Graduated from University of Illinois College of Communications with high honors.

References

Dick Barnes
editor—*Fighting Illini News*
(217) 333-3317

Ronald Yates
head of journalism department—
University of Illinois
(217) 333-0709

Kristen Leigh Porter
sports editor—*Daily Illini*
(217) 333-7025

A one-page résumé can give a prospective employer a snapshot of your education, experience and achievements. Always include references.

proud of or notes about your progress, including the lessons you've been learning about your craft. You might even want to send them a file folder with your name on it so they have it handy if an employer calls about you.

ANATOMY OF A RÉSUMÉ.

Your name

Your address

Phone number

E-mail address

- **OBJECTIVE:** The job you're looking for and what you have to offer a news organization. List what you can offer, not what you want.
- **EXPERIENCE:** Where you worked, dates of employment, job title and brief description of responsibilities.
- **EDUCATION:** Where you went to school, including the name, city and state of the college, graduate school and other courses, such as computer-assisted reporting training.
- **SKILLS:** Foreign languages, computer skills.
- **AWARDS AND HONORS:** Reporting and writing awards, scholarships or academic awards.
- **REFERENCES:** Include name, address and contact information.

CHECK OUT AN ONLINE RÉSUMÉ AT http://jon.dube.net/resume/

THE WORLD WIDE RÉSUMÉ. Post your résumé and **clips** on the Web. That's what Jonathan Dube did in 1996 when he began his job search as he neared graduation from the Columbia University Graduate School of Journalism. He created a home page that allowed interested editors to read his résumé and browse through his stories without leaving their terminals. Here's what Jonathan, who moved in 1999 from a job as a reporter with *The Charlotte Observer* to ABCNEWS.com as a senior associate producer, had to say about the pluses and minuses of an online résumé:

Obviously someone looking for a new media job would want to create an online Web site. But I think it could be useful for others as well. An online résumé also has the advantage of demonstrating to an employer that you have multimedia skills. I think it's also a particularly good way to go if you're looking for a computer-assisted reporting job.

By now there are dozens of online employment sites where you can list a link to your résumé, enabling employers to quickly scan your qualifications and clips. Although most newspapers probably don't look to these sites for journalists, the *American Journalism Review* does have a pretty good one on its Newslink site, **(http://ajr.newslink.org)** and I imagine posting your résumé there would get a decent response. In general, I'll guess that if you made a good online

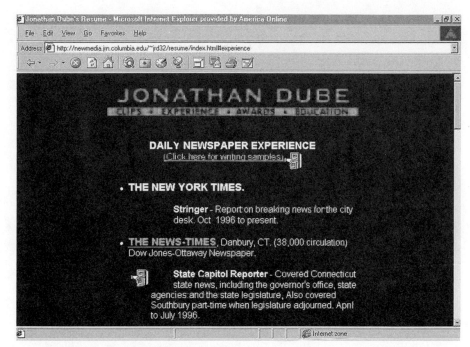

An online résumé can give prospective employers access to your work while cutting down on their paper pile. (Courtesy of Jonathan Dube)

résumé and did a thorough job of listing it around the Web, you'd get good response.

I think the best advantage of the online résumé is its permanence. Even after I got my job, I kept my résumé online and have kept updating it (when I'm not too busy with my job!). As a result, folks who want to follow my career can do so easily by looking at the Web site every so often and seeing what work I'm producing. Also, if I decide to look for a job, my résumé is already put together. And if I can't find old clips, I can just print them out off my Web site.

Another advantage of having an online résumé is that you can e-mail the address to editors and recruiters. Although there's no guarantee they'll click on the links and read your stuff, they may be more likely to notice it than if it's just one of hundreds of letters they get every day. And if they see you have an online résumé, that could also impress them and make it more likely they'll read your clips when you send them. The point being that I wouldn't recommend relying solely on the online résumé, but it certainly can't hurt to use one in addition to the old paper application process.

BUILDING AN ONLINE RÉSUMÉ.   Here are Jonathan Dube's tips to put your résumé online:

To create your own online résumé all you need is a basic word processor and knowledge of a few simple codes. Create a text file and use the following template:

<html><body>

<title>My Résumé </title>

Type your résumé here. At the end of each line, type <p>

That functions like a carriage return.<p>

</body></html>

- Every Internet provider is different, so once you've created the Web page you should contact your provider for instructions on uploading the Web page to the Internet.

- Once you've mastered the basics, you can easily teach yourself how to add graphics, improve the design or link to articles you've written. Bookstores carry dozens of books that teach basic HTML, the World Wide Web programming language. Any search engine will turn up many Web sites that also offer good instruction.

- But perhaps the best way to learn is from others. When viewing a Web page you'd like to imitate, click on the "view source" menu option on your Web browser, and you can see the coding for that page. Just as you can learn to improve your writing by reading great writers, you can learn how to improve your Web skills by studying great Web pages.

STEP 2: PLAN YOUR SEARCH

By now, you've had enough experience to know what appeals to you in journalism. Sure you want to be a foreign correspondent for the *Los Angeles Times*, but be realistic. Identify three to six news organizations that interest you. Include one long shot, but make most of your picks newspapers that are open to hiring newcomers. (We'll talk a bit later in this chapter about the advantages of starting in a small organization.) Don't blizzard every newsroom in the country with an application. You need to do some reporting on possible employers to avoid gathering an overly long list of potential jobs.

For newspaper reporters, your bible will be the *Editor & Publisher Yearbook*. Aspiring broadcast journalists should consult *Broadcasting & Cable Yearbook*. If you're interested in online journalism consult *E&P*'s new *Directory of Interactive Products and Services*, which lists newspapers with online services. Available in most public libraries, these yearbooks contain detailed listings for every daily and weekly paper and radio and television station in the United States and Canada and the growing online field. Here's where you learn the correct names of the newspapers and stations and where to send your application. Be sure to call the newsroom and check for the most up-to-date information, because turnover and promotions often make occupational directories outdated.

STEP 3: SELECT AND PACKAGE SAMPLES OF YOUR WORK

Your work will always be your best résumé. In the newspaper world, they're known as "clips," short for "clippings." Broadcast job seekers send a **résumé tape** that includes samples of their radio or television stories. Online job seekers can submit clips of their work, but employers also expect to see addresses for their home page or other Web sites they've created or contributed to.

How many clips should you send? Not an avalanche as too many people do. You don't want the newspaper to have to buy a filing cabinet just for your application. Send no more than six to eight stories with your application; an editor can always ask for more. Select clips that show your range.

In general, an effective portfolio should show an editor you can handle standard journalistic tasks: report and write on deadline, come up with your own story ideas as well as respond to assignments, produce a graceful feature or profile, cover a meeting with clarity. It will be a plus if you can also include a personal essay that can move a reader to genuine laughter or tears.

To be specific, try to include the following stories:

1. One or two stories that you reported and wrote on daily deadline: a meeting, speech or public safety story.
2. A story that you wrote on assignment from a teacher or editor as well as a story that you came up with yourself.
3. A feature story about a trend or a profile of a person.
4. A personal essay on a serious or light topic.

Sheryl James attracted the attention of editors at the *St. Petersburg Times* with a whimsical piece on pantyhose; hired in news features, she went on to win a Pulitzer Prize. Pick only your very best work. If you don't have published clips, provide samples of writing for class assignments or free-lance projects you have submitted for publication. By all means, make the package appealing, but don't overdo it. Keep it simple and make sure nothing in your package is bigger than 8 1/2 x 11 inches (the size of printer paper) so editors can easily photocopy the package for others in the newsroom to read. Instead of reducing the print so small an editor needs a magnifying glass, take the time to arrange the story on more than one page.

STEP 4: BEST FOOT FORWARD: WRITE YOUR COVER LETTER

After you've selected your clips, turn your attention to your **cover letter,** which will be the first item in your application. Like the résumé, it shouldn't be longer than a page, especially for an entry-level job. The tone should be sincere and to the point. You can be creative, but don't be cute or

---

LEARN EMPLOYERS' PET PEEVES ABOUT JOB APPLICATIONS FROM BROADCAST JOURNALISTS ONLINE AT http://www.tvjobs.com/peeves1.htm

---

"The secret to a good cover letter is to seize on the most interesting work you've done or experiences you've had and to tell about them in a brief, but compelling, way. Give your cover letter a strong lead. Remember to use nouns that people can see and verbs that they can feel."

—JOE GRIMM, RECRUITING AND DEVELOPMENT EDITOR, *DETROIT FREE PRESS*

overly clever. Looking for a job involves creativity as well as persistence. Select the aspect of your personality, your background or whatever feature best illustrates who you are and what you're capable of, and reflect that in your cover letter. Don't think you can wait for the interview to show what you're made of and why you're the best person for the job; you may not get the chance. So express enough passion in your cover letter to cause an editor to say, "I want to meet this person." You can also use the cover letter to comment on your clips, briefly, or you can attach a separate sheet or notes to individual stories that provide pertinent background, such as the fact that you had just two hours to report and write a breaking story. And if you were the only reporter to get the interview with the inmate on death row or if your essay was reprinted in *Harper's* magazine, don't be shy about it. If you're aware of a particular vacancy, you can mention it, but at this early stage in your career it's best to be open to anything. The last paragraph in your cover letter should be a promise to call the editor in a week to find out if you can arrange an interview.

ANATOMY OF A COVER LETTER.

Your name

Your address

Phone number

E-mail address

Date

Name

Title

News organization

Address

Greeting

Lead

Body

The body of the letter is the place where you can cover several key points:

Your qualifications

Experience

Special skills

Achievements: awards

Your knowledge of the news organization and what you think you can contribute

Concise description of your clips

Ending

Closing: Request an opportunity to meet to further discuss your skills and qualifications. Express appreciation to the person for considering your application. Include your phone number and the best hours to contact you. Also promise a follow-up call.

Signoff

Enclosures

Your cover letter has to do a lot in a small space: apply for a job and show why you merit consideration. First impressions count. The lead is critical. Here's a sample of good—and bad—openings collected by Joe Grimm, recruiting and development editor at the *Detroit Free Press*. You can find more examples and other job-hunting links at **http://www.freep.com/jobspage/ toolkit/cover.htm**.

Short, sweet, no nonsense:

In response to your ad on the JobsPage, please find my résumé and clips.
Please accept my application for a photo opening at the *Free Press*.

Leading with your experience:

I have 20 years' experience writing and editing sports.
My most valuable lesson in four years at the ...

Autobiographical:

I am a small-town girl with my eyes set on the world.
Every valuable lesson I ever learned about reporting I learned in a taxi—from the front seat.
They said it couldn't be done, but I ...

Sympathetic and helpful:

It's a pain in the neck, going through that stack of résumés.
You: Busy editor working late and staring at a growing mountain of job applications. Me: ...
I'm sure the ad for a [job] at the [paper] unleashed a torrent of applications ...

Confident:

I would be an asset to your newspaper staff because ...
I meet every one of the requirements in your job posting. [Bullet points follow.]

Brimming with confidence:

If you haven't filled the sportswriting position, look no further ...
Let me save you some trouble ...

Nonstarters:

Pursuant to our conversation ... [English, please.]
I read with enthusiasm your classified advertisement in *Editor & Publisher* that solicits applicants for community reporting positions. [Ditto.]

I am applying for an entry-level, general assignment reporter position. The reason I'm interested in working for your paper is I would like to move back to the area. [Better approach: Tell me how your knowledge of the area can benefit the newspaper. We hire people to make the newspaper better, not out of kindness.]

I am a recent graduate ... [Congratulations on your diploma, but lots of people get them every year. What distinguishes you?]

With four years of reporting experience under my belt, ... [Cliché alert!]

As a writer for a small daily who's more than ready to move on to an unqualified metropolitan daily, I'm responding to your ad for reporters. [I did not make this up!]

STEP 5: FOLLOW UP

After your interview, be sure to write a brief letter thanking the person who interviewed you. If you met the top editors or others you think may play a role in hiring, write them, too. It's common courtesy and also a way to keep you in the forefront of their minds. Repeat why you want to join the staff, and refer, if you can, to some aspect of the interview. Mention how you think you can contribute.

FREQUENTLY ASKED QUESTIONS ABOUT JOB INTERVIEWS

How do I get in the door?

If you're lucky, your résumé and cover letter will be so professional that your phone will be ringing off the hook with calls from editors who want to interview you. The reality, however, is that competition is stiff. Try to set up an interview at your hometown or community paper where you might be visiting on a break. Call ahead or write to ask, or even e-mail to ask for an interview. Walk-in interviews are a gamble sometimes worth taking. Job fairs, sponsored by journalism groups or minority journalist associations, allow you to meet lots of recruiters.

What do I wear?

Journalists are never mistaken for fashion models.

For men, a tie and jacket, shoes and socks. For women, a skirt and blouse, suit, pants suit or dress. Alternative papers may not mind your fondness for body piercing, but editors of many newspapers will worry whether you will be an effective representative in their community if your hair is purple and your tongue is pierced.

Who does the talking?

Answer questions directly but don't go on forever with anecdotes that only your roommates might be interested in hearing. Don't monopolize the conversation. An interviewer may have a number of things to find out about. Keep it short.

Make direct eye contact. Use good posture. Ask questions. Give honest, concise answers. Don't ramble. Take notes. Ask for a business card. Remember names of those you meet and use them in conversation. Smile.

What if they offer me a job I honestly don't want?

Be honest. If they ask if you'd be willing to cover the dog pound, handle all wedding announcements and death notices and tell you that there's no chance for promotion for five years, don't be afraid to say, "No, thanks." If there's something that you wouldn't do on a bet, don't mislead a potential employer that you're interested.

Should I try for an internship at a big city paper or take a full-time job in a small town?

Internships, usually summer stints in a newsroom, are ideal for students. An internship is a college course, usually a semester long, that takes place in a newsroom rather than a classroom. Interns earn academic credit while learning their craft by doing, make valuable contacts and, in some cases, lay the groundwork for a full-time job. Print internships usually pay, whereas broadcast internships typically are unpaid. "Virtually all editors agree that getting a summer internship on a newspaper while you are in college helps you land that first newspaper job," reports an American Society of Newspaper Editors advisory. (In the "Hotlist" at the end of the chapter you'll find several Web sites that will help you find a media internship in print, broadcast or online journalism.)

Once you've graduated, a job on a small newspaper is preferable to an internship or one of the growing number of temporary correspondent jobs offered by such large organizations as Knight Ridder Newspapers, the *Chicago Tribune* and the *Los Angeles Times*, for several reasons. At a big paper, your chances of being hired full time, no matter how good a job you're doing, are reduced by the fierce competition from experienced job seekers from other papers. Indeed, applicants for the *Los Angeles Times'* two-year temporary positions for reporters and photographers have up to four years of daily newspaper experience. Even if you become a news "temp," your chances of gaining permanent status are slim, a 1996 *Wall Street Journal* article reported. At the *Chicago Tribune*, the paper said, the hiring rate for one-year "residents" (who generally work in suburban bureaus) was 30 percent. At *The Philadelphia Inquirer*, about 50 reporters are employed in its two-year correspondent programs, but in the four years since the program was formalized, "the paper says it has hired only four" permanently.

At a small paper, you'll have the opportunity to tackle a variety of jobs. At *The Keene Sentinel* in New Hampshire, Erin Caddell began work as a business reporter, was promoted to the city hall beat and within a few months was covering the presidential primaries—interviewing U.S. Sen. Bob Dole in the back of a limousine. Consider the big news organization internship as a last resort.

Parting words

Before you leave, ask, "What are my chances here?" If they're not good, ask the interviewer for an assessment of your chances and for the interviewer's best advice: "What might you do in my place?" Follow up the interview with a thank-you letter: "I'm still interested."

Stay in touch. Send a few clips and call occasionally to let them know you're still interested.

JOB PROSPECTS, SALARIES AND BENEFITS: WHAT YOU CAN EXPECT

You may already know this, but if you don't let me be the first to tell you. I won't be the last. If you're looking to get rich, journalism is not the place for you.

The median salary for journalism and mass communications undergraduates in the class of 1997 was $23,000 a year for a full-time job, according to an annual survey by Professors Gerald M. Kosicki and Lee B. Becker. (Remember, from Chapter 14, the definition of "median": the middle number in a set of numbers, a figure that takes into account extremes at either end of the scale.) The pay is better if you have a master's degree: about $28,000 a year.

By contrast, the median starting salary for a lawyer in private practice who graduated in 1995 was $50,000 a year, the *National Law Journal* reported.

But before you throw your clips into the trash and apply to law school, consider this comment from Eric Crawford, an assistant sports editor at *The Evansville Press:*

"What we do as reporters isn't easy, and yet friends of mine from college in a variety of fields have bolted past me in earnings, benefits, etc. But an experience at a wedding I went to just yesterday helped put things back into perspective. I was seated at a table with people from a number of high-paying jobs, and while I was envious of what I imagined everybody's salary must be, every guy at that table would've traded a large portion of that salary to do what I do for a living. It is a special profession, and there are rewards beyond the money."

Following is a chart showing the median weekly pay earned by journalism and mass communication graduates.

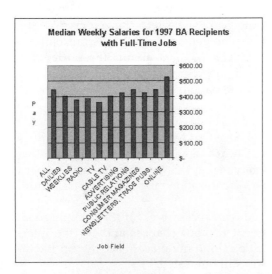

Professors Lee Becker and Gerald Kosicki track the state of salaries for journalism and mass communications graduations. For 1997 graduates, the median salary was $23,000. Reprinted with permission.

Source: Annual Survey of Journalism & Mass Communication Graduates

Crawford's experience is shared by many journalists who have willingly traded the higher salaries of other jobs for a career in news. Although salaries are low, the good news is they are getting better, according to the annual survey of job prospects and salaries conducted by Professors Becker and Kosicki. The median salary earned by 1997 graduates with bachelor's degrees is a gain of $1,500 from the year before. On top of that, graduates said they received benefits, such as basic and major medical coverage and disability insurance, that were better than those of graduates "at any time since at least 1992," the researchers found.

And the job market in the late 1990s continues to improve, with the level of full-time employment for bachelor's degree recipients higher than it has been since 1986. For graduates with master's degrees, full-time placement is higher than it has been since the survey began measuring that rate in 1989.

JIM NAUGHTON'S RULES FOR JOB HUNTING

Jim Naughton interviewed thousands of reporters and hired hundreds during his 18 years as an editor at *The Philadelphia Inquirer*. Today, as president of The Poynter Institute, he shares the lessons he learned with participants in its summer program who will be looking for their first full-time journalism job when it ends. Here are his rules for job hunting:

BE REALISTIC. It doesn't hurt to apply to the big paper, but as a beginner, you're not likely to get that dream job on the first try. Also at a small newspaper you have to do everything, and you make discoveries about your own work and yourself. You'll learn what you are good at but hate to do, and what you're not good at but love. If you make a mistake, it will probably have lesser consequences in a smaller newsroom. Smaller organizations may give the opportunity to take on many different tasks. You'll get to do everything there is to do. A smaller organization gives you an opportunity to test yourself in ways that are less threatening.

Jim Naughton
(Courtesy of
The Poynter
Institute)

BE ACCURATE. If you're not factual about your own background you may not be careful about your stories. Take the risk of understating rather than overstating your accomplishments.

BE A REPORTER. Find out everything you can about the news organization you're interested in. Make the materials you send appealing enough that its people will want to meet you. It's good form to direct your application to the top editor as well as sending one to the person who oversees the hiring process.

Call the main number, ask for the newsroom and ask who processes job applications. Ask also for the name of the top editor. Make sure you get the spelling of their names and their job titles. (Given the mobility of the news business, you can't assume the names in *Editor & Publisher* are correct.)

Call reporters at the paper: Most are happy to share, gossip and gripe. Ask about the personality of the person who will be getting your application or will conduct your interview. Know with whom you're dealing.

DON'T BE TOO PICKY. The best place to get hired may be somewhere you can be the best in a bad newsroom.

BE CREATIVE. Use your cover letter and résumé to display your writing ability.

NAUGHTON'S LAST RULE OF JOB HUNTING: THERE ARE NO RULES. What works works. If you can network your way to a job, that's great. If you don't want to use connections, that's fine, too. What may work for you at one newspaper may work against you at another. Listen to advice, but don't let somebody else decide what's right for you.

Rejection is an essential element of the writer's life. It's how you deal with rejection—the spurned interview, the rejected lead—that will determine your future.

DON'T GIVE UP.

START AT A SMALL PAPER

> Of 1,553 daily newspapers in the United States, more than 83 percent are considered "small" with circulation under 50,000. And that doesn't include weeklies and other nondailies.
>
> —AMERICAN SOCIETY OF NEWSPAPER EDITORS, SMALL NEWSPAPERS COMMITTEE

■

Like me, Karen Brown Dunlap, the dean at The Poynter Institute, started out at a small paper. As a college journalism teacher, she encountered many students who dreamed only of the big time, but as she argues next, there are many more lessons to be learned when you start out small.

Karen F. Brown Dunlap

My first journalism job after college was with a small newspaper. A very small newspaper.

I started as editor of the *Warner Robins Enterprise*, a Georgia weekly owned by a real estate tycoon. Not only was I editor, but also I was senior writer, intern reporter, feature writer, food writer, editorial writer and ghostwriter for the publisher's column.

In addition to writing, I was the photographer when the circulation guy wouldn't take pictures. At about 2 a.m. on production night, I became typesetter when the real typesetter's husband called her home.

What did I learn?

DR. KAREN F. BROWN DUNLAP IS DEAN OF THE FACULTY AT THE POYNTER INSTITUTE.

Karen Brown Dunlap (Courtesy of The Poynter Institute)

- I learned that I should have paid attention to my college classes in design and headline writing. In school my mind was only on writing, but now I searched my notes and memory for pointers on page makeup and copy editing.

- I learned to write quickly and on a range of topics. I covered business openings and city council meetings but also stories of individual success or family distress, as well as the ever-present "Kitchen of the Week."

- I learned to respect all jobs in the production process because, at various times, I had to do each job.

- I learned to respect all the people I worked with. We were a small group working in a compact office. If dissension broke out and someone stormed out, chances were I would have to finish that job. I was committed to peace and good will by respecting all.

- I learned that there is a thin line between editorial and advertising, but sinners can always find redemption with excuses about the bottom line.

- I learned to talk past differences. Warner Robins, with nearly an all-white establishment, awoke to find that the *Enterprise's* new editor was a 21-year-old black woman with an Angela Davis Afro. I needed their stories. They liked seeing their names in print. We talked.

- I learned I needed to know about the community to avoid making errors or just looking silly. The library and conversations with townspeople were my shortcut to learning the history and culture of the place.

- I learned that my labor in a small market provided an opening to a larger newspaper. For me, the next step was the *Macon News*.

Continued

■ Most of all I learned to appreciate the small newspaper that gave me a chance to learn and grow while practicing the craft I love.

Years later I taught journalism students who shunned small papers. They expected to start at a leading daily or at least a mid-sized newspaper. Some laughed when they learned of openings with smaller papers. I frowned and told them they would probably end up tossing burgers instead of reporting news. Then I would recall the production night of the *Warner Robins Enterprise*. My students didn't know the experience, the challenges, the fun that they were missing.

KEEPING A JOB

A LIFE IN JOURNALISM: LESSONS TO A NEW REPORTER (FROM AN ALMOST NEW ONE)
Erin Caddell

Okay, so you've finally landed the big job. The uncomfortable interviews are over. You don't have to stare at that pile of rejection letters anymore. You're ready to start your career as a professional journalist. Now what?

That's the position I found myself in. I graduated from Williams College in Massachusetts in June 1994 with a degree in English and some experience with the campus newspaper under my belt. Then I spent six weeks at Poynter in the news reporting and writing program for college graduates.

After that, I went looking for a job. Poynter helped me become a better reporter and gave me some helpful tips on getting a job. But I didn't have any other experience, so it was tough. I sent my résumé and clips to dozens of papers, hounding editors from Tennessee to Oregon. Most went nowhere. My first interview was a disaster.

But that first interview led to another and then another. West Virginia. Rhode Island. New Jersey. Wyoming. Even if the paper didn't have an opening at the time, interviewing made me feel I was getting somewhere.

After a month and a half, I was offered a reporting job at *The Keene Sentinel*, an afternoon daily in southwestern New Hampshire, with a circulation of about 15,000. I accepted the job and started less than two weeks after that.

In just a few months since then, I've covered the business and city hall beats. I've written dozens of stories and learned a lot about reporting, writing and life in and around Keene. And in that time I've learned several lessons that I think are particular to having a first reporting job.

1. **Build sources or die.** Building sources is a critical part of any reporter's job, but especially a new one. Get past the pat questions and answers to find out how long the city manager has been on the job, if he or she grew up in town or moved in from somewhere else. Talk to the city manager's secretary, find out the same information: He or she may know just as much as the boss and may be more willing to help you out when you need to track someone or something down.

Always call back. Even if it's past deadline, and the story you were working on for that day is done. Just call or stop by to thank that person for getting back to you. Ask a question that can help you with a future story.

News is about people and the relationships among them. In order to find and understand the news, you need to know the relationships. Read the histories of the town or towns you're covering. Know the biggest businesses, the most powerful families, whether the mayor is the latest in a long line of Republicans or the crusader who broke the stranglehold of the local Democratic party in the last election.

2. **Take advantage of the "honeymoon period."** Rather than pretending you're somebody you're not, use your ignorance to your advantage. Let *everybody* know that you're an outsider.

When I first started doing stories and people asked, "You haven't been here very long, have you?" I winced inside. I wanted to look and act older and ask questions that showed I knew what I was talking about. But when I tried to do that, I often found later when I sat down to write that I had no idea what I was talking about. I realized that if I admitted my ignorance to sources, more often than not they would give me the background I needed and more.

AFTER GRADUATING FROM THE POYNTER INSTITUTE COLLEGE FELLOWSHIP PROGRAM IN NEWS REPORTING AND WRITING IN 1994, CADDELL REPORTED ON BUSINESS AND POLITICS FOR *THE KEENE SENTINEL* IN NEW HAMPSHIRE, WAS AN EDITOR AT *INSTITUTIONAL INVESTOR* IN NEW YORK CITY AND IS NOW COMPLETING A MASTER'S DEGREE IN BUSINESS ADMINISTRATION AT COLUMBIA UNIVERSITY.

Continued

When you're starting out on a beat, you have a chance to ask the big questions: What are the biggest challenges facing the police department in the next year? How's morale among city employees? These questions won't be so easy to ask once you're writing difficult stories that may make sources upset and less reluctant to talk to you—or ecstatic, for that matter, and willing to tell you more of what they think you want to hear.

3. **Get the little things right.** Did that old church burn down in 1963 or 1936? Is that woman you talked to earlier today at the town hall the bookkeeper or the administrative assistant? Is Water Street north or south of Cedar Street? When you're starting out, you won't know every last little detail of the topics you write about. But you can bet that your readers and your sources do. The little things are easy to forget, but they can take the wind out of an otherwise great story.

As a reporter, particularly in a small community, all you have is your reputation. If people know that you will get it right, they will return your calls, drop hints for other stories and won't dismiss your questions. Conversely, if you gain a reputation as someone who misspells names, messes up quotes or makes minor factual errors, you can be branded faster than you think.

One other note: If a mistake should make it into the paper, and you catch it, try to notify the person or persons affected by the error before they see it, even if you should run a correction the next day. That way they know what's coming and know that you care enough to notify them. It's easier to avoid the personal apology and hope they don't call. But then, you're just another reporter who doesn't get it right.

4. **Surprise your readers, but not your editors.** Everybody wants to make a good impression. But remember that the newspaper didn't start publishing the day you arrived.

At a meeting I covered during my first month, a city official briefly mentioned that an old landfill in town had become contaminated and that it would cost up to $2 million in city money to clean it up.

With visions of wasted tax dollars and cover-ups dancing in my head, I began digging, looking up public records and going to talk to the official in his office. But a couple of days later, when I mentioned it to my editor, he said, "Oh, yeah, we've been reporting on that for months. What's going on with it now?" My front-page splash became a three-inch brief on the inside—albeit one that took hours to report.

Your editors can be a great resource to learn the paper's writing style and the way it covers stories. They also can provide context for the issues you're covering and what's already "out there."

At the same time, know when to say "no." You'll want to do all that is asked of you, particularly when you're new and trying to prove yourself. But know your limits. If you're running out of time, and you don't think you can get all your stories done in a particular week, say so. Your editors may be disappointed, but they'll understand. If they didn't believe in you, they wouldn't have hired you in the first place.

5. **Use the clips, but don't be wedded to them.** When I was assigned stories early on and didn't know much about them, I would look through the clip file and read them pretty thoroughly before I did my own reporting. I'd feel like I wanted to have a sense of the situation before I ventured into uncharted territory and talked to people who had never heard of me.

Everything you write about has a history. And chances are, if it's on your beat, your paper has written about it before. The reporter who wrote some of those stories, and the editors who assigned them, may even still be in your newsroom. The clips are in a room or on a computer a short, climate-controlled walk away.

But don't make that walk a habit, and make sure you don't let the clips or other people in your newsroom provide the answers to your questions. It's not called the "morgue" for nothing. The stories there are dead. Your readers and your editors have already heard them.

You will cover a story differently from anyone who has come before. Your personality, your background and your reporting ability will see to that. The less you use the clips, the more your own style will come through.

6. **Follow your instincts.** Your editors may be saying one thing. The reporters from the rival paper or the local TV station covering the same story may be doing something else. But a voice in your head is telling you to do a third thing that is altogether different. Listen to that voice. Do what you have to do to avoid giving your editor fits, and don't try to change things overnight. But don't ignore it. Think about what isn't said at the meeting. Your predecessor may have consistently quoted three of the seven planning board members. What do those other four members have to say? Zig while others zag. Look for what nobody is talking about yet. What bothers you?

Continued

What don't you understand? Following those impulses will make your stories distinctive.

7. **Be a salesperson.** Early on, you may get assignments from the bottom of an editor's list. But don't think that's where they have to stay. An editor likes nothing more than a brief that turns into a front-page story and will reward the reporter who makes it happen with better assignments next time around.

That doesn't happen easily. You've got to talk a good game as well as write one and explain to your editor why the story deserves more. Maybe it's a simple zoning dispute, but behind it you see a community grappling with the question of whether to bring in big business or leave the community untouched. Fight for the time to pursue that larger question. Then fight to get your story on the front page, above the fold, with the big headline and a photo. Get excited. An added bonus: As you argue your case, you're in part starting to write the story.

8. **Have fun.** But sometimes, it will seem like there is no end to the stories you need to write, the appointments you need to make, the facts you need to check. That piece you were so proud of got chopped in half at the last minute. The source in the mayor's office who helped you so much when you first started out hasn't spoken to you since you wrote that story about the mayor's campaign funds. Your apartment looks in worse shape than the two-car accident you covered on Tuesday.

Take a step back. Go for a walk in the park you've written about but haven't seen. Clip your best stories and send them to your mom or a former teacher. Reporting is a great business. It allows freedom to learn, explore, be creative and have an impact while getting paid. You can interview a rising political star, meet your favorite musician who happens to be in town and help a kid get a bone-marrow transplant—all in the same week, if you're lucky. Enjoy it.

DEALING WITH EDITORS: A BLUEPRINT FOR SUCCESS

Editors will play a crucial role in your career. A word of advice: When an editor makes a suggestion, consider it a command.

Jason DeParle, a graduate of Poynter's college fellowship program in News Reporting and Writing who is now a staff writer for *The New York*

Times Magazine, lavishes as much attention on his editor as he does on his sources.

Doing One for the Club: The Importance of Attitude

Attitude is everything.

David Maraniss is a Pulitzer Prize–winning reporter who often devotes months to investigations and series at *The Washington Post,* but when news breaks he's one of the first to pitch in. "Usually when there's some kind of major event happening, I either volunteer to help out, or they ask me. ... Even if I'm doing a series, I say, 'Look, if you guys need me, I'd be happy to do something.' I try to be in a position to say yes, and I try to volunteer so that I can have enormous freedom the rest of the time.

"I find that so many reporters keep banging away at their editors and having frustrating confrontations about what they have to do or don't have to do. I've always found it much more effective to do what I want to do by doing some things for them.

"I like newspapers, and I love to write on deadline. And so I volunteer. But one of the reasons I do that is so that there's a fair exchange, where they know that I'm always around when they need me, and then in return, I get a lot of freedom the rest of the time to do what I want to do."

TOP 10 WAYS TO SURVIVE YOUR FIRST YEAR IN JOURNALISM (AND EVERY YEAR AFTER)

Christine Martin

Your first year as a working journalist will probably be the most exciting, most educational, most memorable in your life.

On the other hand, you will face the realities of overburdened staffs, underprepared managers and directionless newsrooms. Some, perhaps many, of the editors you work for will be less talented, less motivated, less directed than you. Their lack of vision will thwart some of your best efforts.

Your best plans will face a steamroller of too little time, too many assignments, too much cynicism. In short, your first year can smash your best hopes and plans flatter than a june bug.

You just have to survive it—with the best of your dreams and wishes intact.

Continued

CHRISTINE MARTIN DIRECTS THE SCHOOL OF JOURNALISM WRITING PROGRAM AT WEST VIRGINIA UNIVERSITY, IS CO-DIRECTOR OF

Christine
Martin
(Courtesy of
West Virginia
University)

THE POYNTER INSTITUTE'S COLLEGE FELLOWSHIP PROGRAM IN NEWS REPORTING AND WRITING FOR COLLEGE GRADUATES, AND IS AN ACTIVE NEWSROOM COACH.

How?

Here are the top 10 ways young reporters say they survived their first year in journalism.

1. Adjust Your Attitude

First impressions are lasting. When you enter a new workplace contain your weirdness and pay a little attention to appearances—both superficial and substantive.

Wrap the whining. Don't be the bitcher, complainer, kvetcher. Journalists as a species tend toward whining. Some great journalists make a career of expertly, finely tuned whining. Dave Barry. Andy Rooney. Molly Ivins. But, they're talented columnists who've turned pitching a bitch into an art form. You, on the other hand, will just be known as the pain-in-the-ass whiner. Other reporters, editors and sources will come to shun and avoid you.

Can the cool. Wrapping yourself in a cocoon of cool insulates you, but it also labels you as unapproachable and uninterested. Good journalists are interested in everything—they are always open to awe. So to survive and to succeed you need enthusiasm. Lots of it. Be excited by everything. And if you don't come by enthusiasm naturally, generate it. Successful reporters (people) are excited by their work. And not just when the story is recognizably exciting. Newsrooms are filled with pessimists and nay-sayers. Be the optimist. Assume you can make any story a good one. It pays off—even if you come across like some Pollyannaish nerd. It's more important to be the dorky, excited guy than the cool, cynical one. Nobody ever won a Pulitzer or any other prize by deciding that his or her story was lame.

To borrow from Nora Desmond in *Sunset Boulevard:* "There are no small stories, just small reporters."

2. A Little Manners Goes a Long Way

Your mother was right. Good manners count and could help you to develop important and successful working relationships with other reporters and editors.

Don't be a space cadet. Respect other people's space, desks, cubes. At many smaller papers, you will probably share a desk—even a cube—with another reporter who works different hours. Don't leave coffee cups, candy wrappers, half-eaten hot dogs littered across a common desktop.

Try a little sensitivity. Remember that you'll probably be working with a group of people far more diverse than you realize and far more diverse than the group of young and mostly middle-class kids you went to college with. Age, economic background, race, gender, ethnicity and class will all factor into your workplace dynamics. Offending a co-worker early on could sour a potentially important partnership and brand you as a bigoted lunkhead.

Don't put your feet up on the editor's desk. This sounds obvious, but it's easy to get comfortable—and stupid. A reporter I know lost a promotion to a better position because at the end of his interview for the job, he relaxed and put his feet up on the editor's desk. The editor—a neat, quiet, perfectly manicured woman—was appalled. The reporter—a comfortable slob—lost the job.

3. Manage Your Time and Your Money and Write for Yourself

Don't cut off your best clips to spite your face. If you feel thwarted, overworked, overlooked—don't adopt the "I'm not doing anything for this crummy organization" attitude. That will only ruin your chances for good stories, good clips and a chance to leave that crummy organization. Instead, write for you. Report for you. It's all about learning and clips. Learn to think ahead. What can I do to build my résumé, clip file? Think of it as self-promotion, and it will be.

Give yourself at least one good clip a week, a month. You must. And that will probably mean working on your own time. I wanted to do a big investigative project that I knew would be an important story. My editor told me, "Terrific idea. We don't have the time to give you." So I did it all on my own time. Not for the paper but for me. It paid off. I won a national award and an enormous sense of achievement.

But manage your time. You have to avoid slave-labor burnout. It's all about balance. The first year, you will be tired a lot. Get used to it. But channel your best efforts and best energy to building your knowledge and your clip file.

Try to have a personal life. You won't have much, but try to set a pattern here from the start that allows you some sense of balance. Women, especially, need to think carefully about balancing career and family because few women will find men who are willing to become spouses solely devoted to raising a family and supporting and nurturing. So,

Continued

determine how much time you want to devote to your job and for how long. It may be healthy to obsess over your work for the first few years, but unless you start cultivating a personal life early on, you may never learn to balance ambition and success with family and happiness.

Manage your money. Map out a reasonable budget. You will have to because for the first few years, you will be poor. As students you became accustomed to poverty. So a regular paycheck can fool you into believing you are solvent and armed with discretionary income. *Don't be fooled.* Save some money. Allow yourself some economic leeway.

4. Find Mentors, Tutors, Writing Partners

This is imperative during the first year as you wean yourself from professors, advisers, parents and other people dedicated to helping you. In the real world, all that ceases. If you want help and advice, you have to seek it. So look for mentors and advisers. If you admire or respect someone, ask his or her advice. Seek out that person. Pick people's brains—interview reporters and editors you admire, even envy. Ask a lot of questions. People like to be expert. So when you make people feel important they will seek you out to offer help. They will want to mentor. Seek out positive, creative, energetic, driven people. Their enthusiasm is contagious and healthy.

And if you can't find any mentors, become your own. Learn to mentor yourself.

5. Avoid Sucking Black Holes of Negativity

There will be some people in every newsroom who create a whirling vortex of negativity. They spend their time and energy (and yours) complaining, criticizing, blaming and spitting bile. Avoid them at all costs. Their cynical aura may at first seem seductive. *But don't be fooled.* They will suck the life and energy out of you—like vampires. Stand back. Be warned. Run for your life. They *are* vampires. And once they suck you into their dark world, you become one, too. Twenty years from now, you'll still be sitting in the corner of the same newsroom, spitting bile and looking for your own new recruits.

6. Set Your Sights on the Job You Want and Do What It Takes to Get It—Even If It Isn't Currently Available

Have goals within the newsroom. You want courts? Volunteer. Want to cover cops? Look for crime stories on your beat.

Want to be a feature writer? Do features—find them, do them, offer them to editors. Fill in for people. Do enterprise. Let people know you're interested, able and dependable. You won't get the job if you don't do the job. The bottom line is usually extra work—but it pays off if you're working for what you really want.

7. Don't Develop a "They Won't Let Me" Mentality

Highly successful people—people who have high emotional IQ—never blame the system for holding them back. They take chances, take responsibility and learn from mistakes. So to survive your first year successfully, avoid blaming the company or the editor. Instead, understand your own power. When you take responsibility, you seize power. You make the calls; you do the job. And if it fails, you take the blame and figure out how to fix it. So take a few creative risks. And accept the consequences. Go out on a few limbs.

8. Make Some Friends Who Aren't Reporters

Journalists tend to band together in packs. I think it's because the job is so hard, the hours are so irregular, and the ethic is so weird ("Terrific—a double fatal!") that we have to befriend each other. No one else will have us. But when all your friends are journalists it gets kind of inbred and unhealthy. It's not conducive to learning the most you can learn. So widen your arena. Be a generalist in your social life as well as your professional one.

9. Always Work Over Your Head

This is the best single advice I ever got. It means simply that you should never let yourself become comfortable. You should always be struggling some. If it gets easy, you get lazy and, eventually, stupid. Always offer yourself a new challenge. Change beats, change styles, change jobs. If you don't escape the comfort zone, you get trapped there. And, eventually, it becomes mighty uncomfortable—confining and dead.

10. Start Out Being a Reporter—Learn the Newsroom's Political Landscape So You Don't Have to Spend Your Time and Energy on Politics

Find the power zones; find the trouble spots.
Know how people and groups relate to one another.

Continued

> Ask questions; learn who's hard to work with, hard to work for. Learn the long-standing battles, the blood feuds and the political stand-offs. But learn so you can avoid them—not join them. Office politics sucks up enormous time and energy. So take a little time learning the political landscape early on so you don't have to waste time in it, and with it, later on. The less time you spend embroiled in office politics, the more time you can spend on your work.

GETTING—AND KEEPING—A JOB: THE COACHING WAY

■ Write in one paragraph or one sentence the one thing that somebody you would want to hire you ought to know about you. Some examples written by my students: "I am still learning and anxious to keep the news business alive" and "I am the type of reporter who brings the same passion for reporting and writing to a flower show and a breaking news story."

■ At a job interview, pretend you're interviewing the interviewer for a story about the news organization. (Ask an editor what the paper's or station's needs are, for instance.) You'll impress the editor or news director with your curiosity. Remember that he or she is looking for journalists. Act like one.

■ Be honest. Don't call an editor and say you're So-and-So from *The Boston Globe* or CNN if you're just interning there. Don't inflate your qualifications or experience on your résumé. Employers want, and journalism needs, people with character.

■ Join the Society of Professional Journalists (you can visit its Web site at **http://spj.org/**) and/or one of the minority journalism groups listed in Chapter 7). With chapters in most states and many large cities, these groups are especially helpful if you're moving to a new area and are looking for connections or new friends in the business.

■ Once you get that job be the kind of person you'd like to work with.

Glossary of Important Terms

Clips. Published stories that accompany any application for a reporting job.

Cover letter. A letter, usually one page long, that serves as an introduction for a job seeker and accompanies résumé and clips or résumé tape.

Internship. A college course, usually a semester long, that takes place in a newsroom rather than a classroom. Interns earn academic credit—and sometimes get paid—while learning their craft by doing, make valuable contacts and, in some cases, lay the groundwork for a full-time job.

References. Individuals listed on your résumé who can vouch for your skills and character, including teachers, editors and former employers.

Résumé. A typed summary, usually one page long, of your achievements, education experience and skills.

Résumé tape. Also called "job tape." Videotape with samples of broadcast stories. Radio and TV version of newspaper clips.

Exercises

1. Write your résumé and cover letter using the guidelines in this chapter as a model.

2. "Apply to newspapers that you know something about," advises Lee Stinnet, former executive director of the American Society of Newspaper Editors. To develop that knowledge, prepare a research report on a news organization you'd like to work for. Prepare a one-page report that lists circulation and/or market, ownership, competition and political affiliation, as well as your analysis of one week's worth of its reporting and writing style and the major news stories covered during that week. Finally, answer the question "Would I want to work here?"

Readings

Becker, Lee B., Stone, Vernon A., and Graf, Joseph D. "Journalism Labor Force Supply and Demand: Is Oversupply an Explanation for Low Wages?" *Journalism & Mass Communication Quarterly*, vol. 73, no. 3, Autumn 1996, pp. 519–533.

Calamba, Shella P. "At Big Dailies, More News Jobs Are Temporary." *The Wall Street Journal*, Aug. 26, 1996, pp. B1–2.

"Expert Advice on Landing a Newsroom Job." *ASNE Bulletin*, September 1994, pp. 16–17.

Feola, Christopher J. "Making the Cut: Enhance Your Job Opportunities by Developing Your Computer Skills." *Quill*, March 1995, pp. 24–26.

Gabarro, John. J., and Kotter, John P. "Managing Your Boss." *Harvard Business Review,* January-February 1980, pp. 92–100.

Jacobson, Gianna. "For Journalism Graduates, Opportunities in New Media." *The New York Times,* May 20, 1996.

Pavlik, John V. "New Media Offer Growing Job Prospects." *Nieman Reports,* Summer 1996, pp. 26–28.

HOTLIST

Job hunting used to mean combing through *Editor & Publisher,* asking friends and teachers for tips. It still is a matter of networking, but now you can also do your job hunting online. A number of Web sites offer information about journalism jobs. The most comprehensive group of links can be found at the following:

http://www.newsbureau.com/journalist.html

Offers the Online Job Banks page maintained by the Internet News Bureau Press Release Services for Business and Journalists. As always, remember that the links may be outdated. Your best bet is to type in "journalism jobs" in a search engine for update links.

http://www.freep.com/jobspage/

"Jobs Page: Your Link to Newspaper Careers" is yet another great feature of Freep, the *Detroit Free Press* Web site created by Joe Grimm, the paper's recruitment and development editor. From this page, you can browse journalism job banks, learn about job fairs and internships and get tips on improving your résumé and clip portfolio.

http://www.medill.nwu.edu/people/placement/packets.html

"Crashing the Market: A Journalist's Guide to Cover Letters and Résumés." Written by Mike Reilley, a former sportswriter and founding sports editor of the *Chicago Tribune*'s Internet edition who is an adjunct lecturer at Northwestern University's Medill School of Journalism, this excellent guide covers the gamut of issues facing journalism job seekers: choosing a paper, marketing yourself, writing résumés and cover letters and choosing clips. There's also a section on assembling a broadcast résumé tape by Jim Disch, director of news and programming at Chicagoland Television (CLTV).

http://www.medill.nwu.edu/faculty/reilley/newmedia/onlinejobs.html

A page of links for jobs in online and broadcast news.

http://www.tvjobs.com/index_a.htm

TV JOBS. An online employment service dedicated to helping you find employment in the highly competitive broadcast marketplace. Includes practical tips from employers.

http://www.newsguild.org/

The home page of The Newspaper Guild, which represents more than 31,000 journalists and sales and media workers of all kinds in print, broadcast and online news organizations. It also offers a table of top minimum salaries for more than 100 daily papers where the guild represents workers. Top minimum is not, as it might seem, what entry-level reporters are paid. Rather, it is the minimum amount the most veteran reporters earn.

http://www.asne.org/kiosk/careers/carerdet.htm

The American Society of Newspaper Editors offers an online version of articles and other resources for beginners, among them a list of newspaper internships listed by state and application deadline date and a schedule of job fairs that offer newspaper editors and recruiters the chance to interview journalists of color.

http://www.missouri.edu/~jourvs/carecrww.html

Explore the possibilities of a career in radio or television news with Vernon Stone, professor emeritus at the Missouri School of Journalism, through invaluable online excerpts from *Careers in Radio and Television News*, a booklet available from the Radio-Television News Directors Association.

http://www5.infi.net/inland/research/nicsdata.htm

Find out how much journalists in the United States and Canada are paid by region, circulation size and as a whole from highlights of the Newspaper Industry Compensation Survey. (The complete survey, aimed at newspaper executives, requires a stiff fee, but the site provides general trend information.) The California Society of Newspaper Editors compares the national figures with salaries paid in its state at: http://www.csne.org/1997paysurvey.html.

http://www.rtnda.org/issues/salary98.htm

Radio-Television News Directors Association (RTNDA), the association of electronic journalists, shares the fruits of its 1997 salary survey and offers comparisons to the previous years.

http://www.grady.uga.edu/annualsurveys

What's the journalism job market like? What are reporters getting paid? For the most reliable information, check out this site. Professors Lee Becker of the University of Georgia and Gerald Kosicki of Ohio State University conduct an annual survey of journalism and mass communication graduates. The report covers the job market, salaries and benefits and measures job satisfaction.

http://studentpress.journ.umn.edu/internships/default.html

Internships. Associated College Press Guide to Internships at the Top Newspapers and Magazines.

http://www.snpa.org/internship/internship.html

The Southern Newspaper Journalism Internships site provides a state-by-state listing of newspaper internships in 14 southern states.

http://www.newsjobs.com/home.html

The National Diversity Newspaper Job Bank posts job openings at newspapers to make them more available to minorities and women. It allows job-seekers to post a résumé and offers job hunting tips.

http://www.daily.umn.edu/~mckinney/

The Mighty Internship Review provides state-by-state listings of internships for print and broadcast reporters. It includes reviews by former interns.

http://www.tvjobs.com/intern.htm

This site lists internships in television news.

http://www.siliconalleyjobs.com/

This site focuses on online internships in New York City.

APPENDIX

NEWS WATCH PROJECT STYLE GUIDE: DIVERSITY GLOSSARY

Judy Gerber, co-director of the News Watch Project at the Center for Integration and Improvement of Journalism at San Francisco State University, compiled and edited this style guide using the style guides of the Asian American Journalists Association, National Lesbian and Gay Journalists Association, The Associated Press and the *Los Angeles Times*. It is reprinted with the permission of the News Watch Project. It is also available online.

CONSULT THE NEWS WATCH PROJECT STYLE GUIDE ONLINE AT http:// newswatch. sfsu.edu/ StyleGuide.html

1.5 generation. Bilingual, bicultural Korean Americans who were born in Korea and then immigrated to the United States as children.

ACT UP. AIDS Coalition to Unleash Power, an activist organization with independent chapters in various cities. "ACT UP" is acceptable in first reference. The organization focuses on AIDS treatment issues and legal and social concerns connected with AIDS.

Africa. Avoid presenting Africa as a monolith. It's the second-largest continent in the world, containing over 40 nations with hundreds of distinct cultures and politics.

African American. Acceptable to use interchangeably with "black" to describe black people in the United States. When referring to specific people, use the term(s) that they prefer to call themselves.

AIDS. Acquired immune deficiency syndrome, a serious and often fatal medical condition that weakens the human immune system, leaving the body defenseless against life-threatening infections. Individuals may be HIV-positive but not have AIDS. Relatively new treatments mean some people are living longer with AIDS. Do not refer to AIDS as a death sentence, unless in a direct quote. Avoid equating gay men with AIDS. The number of AIDS cases is increasing fastest within the heterosexual population. More straight people have AIDS worldwide.

AIDS transmission. Relevant in a story only about how people can get it: unprotected sex, blood products or dirty IV needles. Otherwise irrelevant to a story.

alien. Avoid; derogatory term for an immigrant.

Alien Land Laws. Enacted by many western states in the early 1900s, these laws prevented Asians from owning land. Most of these laws were repealed in the late 1950s and 1960s.

all-American. Unless you're willing to apply the term to anyone who is a U.S. citizen, avoid using. A Eurocentric expression used to conjure up images of blond, blue-eyed people who represent traditional images of white Americans. In a U.S. population of every ethnicity, use of "all-American," until now, implies that anyone not of European descent is "other" and could not possibly be "all-American." Ideally, the term would be more inclusive of our national multicultural makeup. Unfortunately, that's not the case.

Amerasians. Children born of Asian and non-Asian parentage. The term often is used to refer to children born in Korea of non-Asian American fathers and Korean mothers, or Vietnamese mothers and non-Asian American fathers.

American Indian. Synonymous with "Native American." Some indigenous people in the United States prefer "American Indian" to "Native American." Best to ask individual preference. When possible, use national affiliation rather than generic "American Indian" or "Native American," e.g., Navajo, Hopi, Cherokee. To specify that someone was born in the United States but isn't a Native American, use "native-born."

Arab. Refers to nation or people from Arabic-speaking country. Not synonymous with "Muslim." When referring to events in a specific country, name the country rather than generalizing "Arab." Do not imply in headlines or text that "Arab" equals with Muslim, holy war or terrorist. Note: Iran is not an Arab country. The majority of Iranian people are Persian, and the language is Farsi.

ARC (obsolete). AIDS-related complex. Replaced by "HIV disease."

Asian Indian, Indian. Avoid. When distinguishing from Native Americans, use "people from India," or use "Indian Americans" when referring to people from India living in the United States.

Asiatic. Avoid. Implies enemy race. Instead use "Asian," "Asian Pacific American," "Asian Pacific Islander" or "Asian American."

bachelor society. Refers to the predominantly male social settings that dominated American Chinatowns before World War II, because few Chinese women were allowed to emigrate to the United States until after the war.

Balouch. Pakistani language spoken in the eastern Pakistani province of Istan.

Banana. Avoid (slang). Pejorative reference used by Asian Americans when referring to Asian Americans who identify more with whites than with other Asian Americans. Use only in direct quotes.

Banzai. A celebratory chant, like "Hip, Hip, Hooray," used by Japanese and Japanese Americans. To be distinguished from "bonsai," a miniature potted tree.

barrio. Avoid because the term conjures up stereotypes about Latino neighborhoods. Just use the name of the neighborhood (see **ghetto).**

Bharat. The official Sanskrit name of India.

Bharatiya Janata party. Political party in India often characterized as a "Hindu fundamentalist party." "Hindu nationalist" is more accurate. Its credo equates Hinduism with Indian culture.

bindi. The name for the decoration some women from India wear on their forehead. It is a decoration, like makeup, and comes in different shapes and colors to match a woman's wardrobe.

bisexual. An individual sexually attracted to both women and men. Does not presume nonmonogamy.

black Africa. Avoid (see **Africa).**

Black Muslim. A person belonging to the Nation of Islam in the United States prior to 1985. Dissolved to join the orthodox Islamic community. Members of the current Nation of Islam, led by Louis Farrakhan, are referred to as Muslims.

boat people. Refugees from Vietnam who fled in boats beginning in 1978. About half of the boat people were ethnic Chinese, who dominated small business and trade in Vietnam.

Bombay. India officially changed the name of this, its largest city, to Mumbai.

Bombay Stock Exchange. The oldest stock market in Asia. The benchmark indicator is the Sensex.

*Bowers vs. Hardwick/***the Hardwick Decision.** Landmark Supreme Court ruling that upheld Georgia's antisodomy laws.

brave. Avoid use of the word as a noun for Native Americans.

buck. Avoid this racial slur for a young black or Native American man.

buckteeth, bucktooth. Avoid. The stereotypical caricatures of Asians drawn with this feature are highly racist and offensive.

Buddhahead. Avoid (slang). Pejorative reference sometimes used by Japanese Americans to describe themselves or other Japanese Americans. Use only in direct quotes.

bui doi (boo-ee duhy). Vietnamese for "children of the dust," it originally referred only to homeless Vietnamese children who roamed the streets in that nation. But after 1972, it also referred to Amerasian children born between 1965 and 1972 (see **Amerasians).**

camel jockey, camel driver. Avoid (racial slur). Derogatory term for Arabs.

camp. When Japanese Americans refer to "camp," they mean the camps—also called relocation, detention, internment or concentration camps—into which they were forced to relocate during World War II.

Cantonese. Chinese dialect spoken in and around Canton, China, located near the South China Sea. It is spoken in one province in China.

Cao-Dai. Vietnamese religion.

caste system. Although discrimination based on it is banned, the social hierarchies of the caste system continue to be recognized in various parts of India, particularly in villages. These hierarchies were a corruption of a medieval system of classification that grouped people and families by their inherited trades—priests, merchants, soldiers and laborers.

Chaebol (jeh-bol). Korean multinational conglomerates, including such companies as Hyundai, Samsung and Daewoo.

Chicano/Chicana. Refers to people of Mexican American origin. Some say the term is outdated because of its link to the Chicano civil rights movement, though many younger Mexican Americans use the term today to describe themselves. For instance, MeCHa is a national student organization whose members routinely refer to themselves as Chicanos. For some, the term alludes to a spiritual and cultural link between Mexican Americans and Mexico's Aztec Indians—and the Indians' battles to resist Spanish colonialism. Some elderly Mexican Americans consider "Chicano" a derogatory term. Best to ask the person or group members what they prefer.

China doll. Avoid. Reinforces stereotypes of all Asian women as exotic and submissive sex objects. Use only in direct quotes.

Chinaman. Avoid (racial slur). A derogatory term for Chinese in America. Use only in direct quotes.

Chinaman's chance. Avoid. Signifies little or no chance to succeed. Believed by some to have derived from the fate of Chinese laborers building the transcontinental railroad. They were subjected to extreme physical danger and died at a high rate from placing explosives on steep cliffs and working in deep tunnels. Others believe it derives simply from the lynchings and other racist attacks by white mobs against outnumbered and often defenseless Chinese, beginning in the 1850s. Use only in direct quotes.

Chinatown. Any one of several Chinese American communities in the United States.

Chinese, Chinese American. Use "Chinese" when referring to anyone of Chinese ancestry, but use "Chinese American" when specifically referring to those of Chinese ancestry who are American citizens.

Chinese fire drill. Avoid. Racist phrase referring to chaotic situations. Refers to a game that often takes place at a stop light. Involves passengers in a vehicle getting out of one door, running around the vehicle and re-entering through another door in a haphazard way.

Chinese Zodiac. The Chinese Zodiac is based on a 12-year cycle. Each year is represented by an animal. These animals are attributed with certain characteristics that are applied to human behavior. The following is a listing of the 12 animals and their respective years for three cycles. Animals for other years can be determined by subtracting, or adding, 12 from, or to, the year.
Goat 1991, 2003, 2015; Monkey 1992, 2004, 2016; Rooster 1993, 2005, 2017; Dog 1982, 1994, 2006; Pig 1983, 1995, 2007; Rat 1984, 1996, 2008; Buffalo 1985, 1997, 2009; Tiger 1986, 1998, 2010; Rabbit 1987, 1999, 2011; Dragon 1988, 2000, 2012; Snake 1989, 2001, 2013; Horse 1990, 2002, 2014.

Chink. Avoid (racial slur). A derogatory term for Chinese and Chinese Americans. Use only in direct quotes.

Cho, Chow, Tsau. Chinese dialect that can be spelled in three ways.

closeted, in the closet. Refers to a person who hides his or her sexual orientation.

Coconut. Avoid (slang). A pejorative reference to Filipinos and Filipino Americans who identify more with whites than with Filipinos.

colored. Not synonymous with "people of color." Avoid when referring to people in the United States because it's considered derogatory. In parts of Africa, it sometimes means mixed race. If used, include an explanation.

combat language. Avoid the language of war when writing about people of color and the story is not about a specific war. Examples of terms to avoid: "Tokyo's fashion invasion," "on the warpath," "circling the wagons."

coming out. Short for "coming out of the closet": process of accepting one's own sexuality and then letting others know (see **closeted**).

Confucian work ethic. Avoid. Stereotypical term used to describe the tendency of some Asians to work hard and keep quiet. Many Asian Americans cringe when the generalization is made because it evokes images of Asians as mindless hordes unable to think or act creatively.

Confucius say. Avoid. Stereotypical saying that pokes fun at Asian Americans as always speaking in proverbs and not having original thoughts or actions.

coolie. Menial laborer. The term is believed to have derived from the word "koli," an aboriginal race in western India, or from the Chinese term "ku-li," meaning "bitter strength" or "bitter labor." The term came to refer to laborers who were transported from China to other parts of the world in the coolie trade in the 1800s.

cross-dressing. Wearing clothing most often associated with members of the opposite sex (see **transvestite**).

cruising. Visiting places where opportunities exist to meet people, specifically potential sexual partners. Not an exclusively gay phenomenon.

Dalit (capitalized). More respectful and current term for castes once called "untouchables." M. K. Gandhi coined the term "Harijan" ("children of God") to refer to these castes.

Dark Continent. Avoid. Derogatory term for Africa.

Democratic Republic of the Congo. Formerly Zaire.

Desi. A colloquial name for people who trace their descent to South Asia, especially India and Pakistan.

Diwali, Deepavali. One of the most festive holidays observed by Hindus, Diwali generally occurs during the autumn. Although it is celebrated in many parts of northern India as the start of the new year, Diwali should not be referred to as the Hindu New Year or the Indian New Year. No such thing exists. Nor is any one explanation of Diwali's significance applicable to all Hindus. Because of ethnic variations from state to state, the traditional new year is celebrated at different times in different parts of the country.

domestic partner. Unmarried partners who share living quarters. Typically used in connection with legal and insurance matters. See **gay/lesbian relationship** terms. "Domestic partner" sometimes refers to straight unmarried couples as well as gay/lesbian ones.

dotbusting. Avoid (slang). A pejorative term used on the East Coast by those perpetrating violence against people from India. It is derived from the practice of some women from India wearing a painted dot, or bindi, on their forehead.

drag. Clothing of the opposite gender.

drag queen. A man who dresses in female attire for show, often in order to perform. Not synonymous with "transvestite."

dragon lady. Avoid. Stereotypical image of Asian women as sinister and evil.

dyke. Pejorative term for a lesbian. Avoid, unless used in a direct quote or organization name. Example: dyke march.

East Indian. Vague geographic term referring to a loose grouping of countries in southeastern Asia. Not to be confused with people from India or with "Asian Indians" or with the Dutch East Indies, a former Dutch colony in the Atlantic. Because of the confusion, it's best to avoid the term and use the specific name.

Egg. Avoid (slang). A pejorative term used by Asian Americans to describe whites who are enamored with Asians or Asian culture (white on the outside, yellow on the inside).

emigrant. See **immigrant.**

Eskimos. When referring to Native Americans in Alaska, acceptable to use for Inupiat Eskimos or Yupik Eskimos. Do not use for Aleuts or Inuits.

Eurasian. Person of mixed white and Asian heritage. Also called "Amerasians." Not derogatory.

Eurocentric. Avoid geographic terms that place Europe at the center of the world. Examples: "Far East," "New World," "Old World," "Orient," "Occident."

Exclusion Acts. First, the Chinese Exclusion Act, enacted in 1882, barred immigration of Chinese laborers to the United States and prohibited Chinese from becoming naturalized citizens. At the time, about 105,000 Chinese—100,000 of them male—were living in the United States. The act was repealed in 1943, when Congress established a quota of 105 Chinese immigrants per year. The 1917 Immigration Act barred admission of natives of "islands not possessed by the United States adjacent to the Continent of Asia" and natives of most of Asia. The 1924 National Origins Act (sometimes called the Immigration Quota Act) barred immigration of all aliens "ineligible for citizenship," that is, Asian Pacifics. The 1934 Tydings-McDuffie Act imposed a quota of only 50 Filipino immigrants a year. Only in 1965 did the United States grant Asian countries equal status in immigration laws with countries in Europe.

Executive Order 9066. A presidential order issued by Franklin D. Roosevelt on Feb. 19, 1942, that led to the internment of 110,000 people of Japanese descent (see **internment**).

exotic. Avoid its use when describing Asian, African, Latino or Native American cultures, unless you also use the term for European and American cultures.

fag, faggot. Avoid. Pejorative term for a gay male. Comes from old English word for a bundle of twigs used to stoke a fire. During the witch hunts of the 1600s, male witches/druids were used as fuel (faggots) to burn witches at the stake.

Far East. Avoid. Denotes Asia, as viewed from London. Instead, use "Asia," "East Asia" or "Southeast Asia" (see **Eurocentric**).

Filipino/Filipina. Use "Filipino" in reference to males or mixed groups, "Filipina" in reference to females. Alternate spelling: Pilipino/Pilipina.

Flip. Avoid (racial slur). A derogatory term for Filipinos and Filipino Americans. Use only in direct quotes.

F.O.B. Avoid. Acronym for "fresh off the boat," a derogatory term for newly arrived Asian immigrants. Use only in direct quotes.

Foreign Miners Tax. First of many laws aimed at restricting the economic activities of Asians, this was enacted in 1856 against Chinese gold miners.

Four Tigers. A nickname for South Korea, Hong Kong, Singapore and Taiwan, whose economies have been growing rapidly.

Fu Manchu. A fictitious Chinese character, created by novelist Sax Rohmer, who came to reinforce stereotypes and fears by white Americans of the Chinese as an evil race.

fundamentalism/fundamentalist. A Christian concept implying a literal interpretation of the Bible. Sometimes used to describe people who base political actions on religious beliefs. Not synonymous with any religion, especially Islam.

gay. Acceptable and preferable in all references as a synonym for "homosexual," primarily male. "Lesbian" is preferred for women. When possible, use "gay and lesbian." Best to use "gay" as an adjective, not a noun, e.g., "gay man," "gay woman," "gay people." In headlines where space is an issue, "gay" is acceptable to describe both.

gay bashing. Violent hate crime motivated by anti-gay politics or homophobia.

gay killer. Avoid. Straight murderers are not called straight killers. Sexual orientation does not cause murder.

gay lifestyle. Avoid. There is no one gay lifestyle, just as there's no one heterosexual lifestyle.

gay relationships. Gay, lesbian and bisexual people use various terms to describe their commitments. If possible, ask the individual what term he or she prefers. If not possible, "partner" is generally acceptable.

gay slaying/homosexual killing. Avoid, unless in a hate crime, in which "anti-gay killing" could be used. Otherwise it's ambiguous whether reference is to killer or victim.

gay underworld/underground. Avoid. If it's not a closeted world, it's not a secret. Anyone can walk into a gay bar. Many bars are community institutions.

gay woman. Use instead of "lesbian" if preferred by the person interviewed.

ghee. *The New York Times* crossword clue refers to it as "Hindu clarified butter." But ghee is consumed by all communities in India (who can afford it and are not worried about cholesterol or weight gain).

ghetto. Avoid its use. Better to name the neighborhood (see **barrio).**

ghetto blaster, ghetto box. Refers to a portable radio. Avoid; implies stereotype about who owns the radio. Use "boombox" instead.

gold mountain. What California was called by Chinese who came to the state in the 1850s searching for gold. They intended to return to China with their new-found riches. Instead, many were driven off the mines into jobs in laundries, restaurants or on the railroads and never returned to their homelands.

Gook. Avoid (racial slur). A derogatory term for Asians, widely used by American GIs during the Korean War and again during the Vietnam War.

Gujarati. Indian language spoken in western India.

gung hay fat choy. Cantonese for "happy New Year."

hajj (not capitalized). A pilgrimage to Mecca, Saudi Arabia, the birth-place of Mohammed. Every Muslim able to afford the journey is expected to make the hajj at least once in his or her lifetime.

Hakujin (HAWK-u-jeen). Japanese for "white person." Not necessarily derogatory.

half-blood/half-breed. Avoid. Derogatory term for a Native American of mixed racial heritage.

Haol (hah-oh-leh). Hawaiian for "white person." It originally meant "foreigners." Not necessarily derogatory.

Hapa or **happa** (hah-pah). Hawaiian term for someone of mixed racial heritage, generally of Asian and white parents. Short for "hapa haole," or "half-white," it is increasingly used among mainland Asian Americans. Not necessarily derogatory.

Hawaiian. Refers to Polynesian descent in Hawaii. Also acceptable: "Native Hawaiian." Does not refer to everybody living in Hawaii. When referring to non-Native Hawaiians living in Hawaii, use "those in Hawaii" or "state residents" (see **Native Hawaiian).**

heterosexism. Presumption that heterosexuality is superior to homosexuality. Also: prejudice, bias or discrimination based on that presumption.

heterosexual community/straight community. Avoid. There is no one community in the United States encompassing all straight people.

Hindi. One of the two official languages of India and one of 19 distinct languages spoken around the country. Do not confuse "Hindi" with "Hindu," which is a religious designation.

Hindu, Hinduism. Designating the religion practiced by the majority of Indians and designating certain cultural features of South and Southeast Asia. Hinduism does not have a founder or defining text. Do not confuse with "Hindi," which is a language.

Hindustan. This term once referred to a particular empire in northern India but is now used to refer generally to the Indian Subcontinent or the Republic of India.

Hindustani. An unofficial language spoken in northern India, a mixture of Urdu and Hindi.

Hipsing. An old-fashioned Chinese family clan that developed the phrase "New Chinatown."

Hispanic. Umbrella term, may refer to people from anywhere in Latin America, as well as U.S. residents or citizens who identify themselves as having Latin American heritage. Some people prefer it to "Latino." Others use the two terms interchangeably or prefer a term indicating their national origin, i.e., "Colombian," "Cuban," "Mexican American," etc. On the West Coast, people tend to use "Latino"; in the Northeast and Southwest, more people use "Hispanic." Some people regard "Hispanic" as insulting because they consider it a term created by the U.S. government to lump together anyone of Latin American and Spanish origin. Best to ask the person or group members what they prefer.

HIV. Human immunodeficiency virus. Generally accepted as the cause of AIDS. "HIV-positive" means testing positive for the antibodies to HIV, which implies carrying HIV. Note: "HIV virus" is redundant.

Hmong (Mong or Mung). An ethnic group in southern China, Vietnam, Laos and Thailand. Approximately 50,000 Hmong came to America as refugees in the mid-1970s, uprooted from their homeland largely as a result of a civil war in Laos.

Hoa-Hoa. Vietnamese religion.

homo. Derogatory term for "homosexual."

homophobia. Fear, hatred or dislike of homosexuality and lesbians/gays.

homosexuals. Medical/clinical term for lesbians and gays. (adj.) Of or relating to sexual and affectional attraction to a member of the same sex. (n.) A person who is attracted to members of the same sex. "Gay" or "lesbian" is the preferred term in all contexts, except clinical.

Hui (WHO-ee). Revolving credit associations used by Chinese immigrants to pool money and help each other start small businesses.

hyphenated Americans. Many newspapers and others use a hyphen between the words "Asian" and "American" in "Asian American." Many Asian Americans, however, object to that usage, saying that it puts them into a subclass that's not fully American.

illegal immigrant. Avoid. Use "undocumented immigrant" instead when referring to someone who comes to the United States without legal documents. Do not use "illegal" as a noun. Avoid "illegal aliens" (see **alien).**

immigrant, emigrant. Both terms refer to one who leaves his or her country to settle in another country. Both terms refer to the same person. In reference to the United States, an "emigrant" is one who leaves the United States; an "immigrant" is one who enters the United States.

immigration. Use neutral terms—e.g., "arrival"—to describe immigration. Avoid words with negative connotations like "flood," "tidal wave," "horde," "deluge."

India. The largest and most populous nation on the Indian Subcontinent. Population: 975 million. Capital is New Delhi.

Indian languages. India has two official languages, English and Hindi, and 17 regional languages recognized by the central government. These languages are not dialects; they can be as distinct in their vocabulary and grammar as English and Chinese.

Indian names. Indian names follow different patterns, depending not only on the ethnicity of the person, but also on his or her caste, subcaste or other classification. Furthermore, some families modify their naming practices upon migrating to the West, to conform with local customs. The general rule is that there is no general rule. For second references on Indian names, the last name (whether it is the given name or the family name) is usually considered the surname, but it's best not to assume that is the case. Ask.

Indians. Use "Native Americans" to refer to indigenous peoples of the Western Hemisphere. Name an individual's identity by his or her nation (see **Native American**). Do not use "Asian Indian" to distinguish from Native Americans. Instead say "people from India" or "Indian Americans."

Indochinese. Refers usually to persons from Vietnam, Cambodia (Kampuchea) or Laos. The term is falling into less frequent use, however, because of its colonial context—the peninsula comprising these countries was once called French Indochina—and because it does not, strictly speaking, include persons from Thailand, Burma and other Southeast Asian nations. A more inclusive term is "Southeast Asians."

Injun. Avoid (racial slur). Do not use.

inner city. Avoid. Conjures stereotypical view of poor, supposedly crime-ridden urban neighborhoods where people of color are living. Would be acceptable only if it were also used to refer to wealthy neighborhoods in central cities.

Islamist. A Muslim who wants Islam to define a country's national and international politics. Not all Muslims are Islamists.

Issei (EE-say). First generation of emigrants from Japan, who generally came to the United States in the early 1900s. Sometimes spelled "issei."

J-Town. Short for "Japantown" (see **Nihonmachi**).

Jap. Avoid (racial slur). A derogatory term for Japanese or Japanese Americans, used widely by white Americans to whip up hatred against Japanese or Japanese Americans before and during World War II. Generally should not be used except in direct quotes. Abbreviations: The recognized abbreviation for Japan is "Jpn." Some Japanese American newspapers use "Jpnz." as an abbreviation for "Japanese."

Japanese American Citizens League. The nation's most prominent Japanese American civic and civil rights organization, based in San Francisco and founded in 1939.

Japanese, Japanese American. Use "Japanese" when referring to anyone of Japanese ancestry, but use "Japanese American" when specifically referring to those of Japanese ancestry who are American citizens.

Kampuchea. Khmer Rouge name for Cambodia.

Khalistan. Name used by Sikh militants for a proposed independent country in what is now the Indian state of Punjab.

Khmer. Alone, the Cambodian term refers to the language or the people. It is interchangeable with the term "Cambodian." "Khmer" should not be confused with "Khmer Rouge," which refers to Pol Pot's guerrilla forces.

Kibei (KEE-bay). Children born in the United States of Japanese immigrant parents who were sent to Japan for their education and who usually returned to the United States. During World War II, many Kibei were suspected of disloyalty to the United States, even though they were American citizens.

Korean American Coalition. The nation's most prominent Korean American bilingual civic and civil rights organization, based in Los Angeles.

Korean Federation. Sometimes also called Korean Association. Organization of Koreans outside Korea that provides services for newcomers. There is usually a Korean Federation in each major U.S. city or region where a significant number of Koreans reside.

Korean, Korean American. Use "Korean" when referring to anyone of Korean ancestry, but use "Korean American" when specifically referring to those of Korean ancestry who are American citizens or permanent residents.

Koreatown. Any one of several Korean American communities in the United States.

Kye (kyeh). Korean rotating credit unions used by Korean Americans to help members finance small businesses, housing, children's education and other family needs.

Kyopo (kee-yo-poe). Koreans living outside of Korea. Korean Americans are referred to as "che mi kyopo" (chay mee kee-yo-poe).

La Raza/Raza. Spanish word for "race." "La Raza" refers to Latino people. Some Latinos use "Raza" to refer to Latino culture and heritage.

Lao. A separate ethnic entity, apart from the Khmu and Hmong. It is also a language.

Laotians. Various ethnic groups including the Lao, Khmu and Hmong.

Latino/Latina. Umbrella term, may refer to people from anywhere in Latin America, as well as U.S. residents or citizens who identify themselves as having Latin American heritage. Some people prefer it to "Hispanic." Others use the two terms interchangeably or prefer a term indicating their national origin, i.e., "Colombian," "Cuban," "Mexican American," etc. On the West Coast, people tend to use "Latino"; in the Northeast and Southwest, more people use "Hispanic." Some people regard "Hispanic" as insulting because they consider it a term created by the U.S. government to lump together anyone of Latin American and Spanish origin. Best to ask the person or persons what they prefer.

lesbian. Preferred term for a female homosexual. The phrase "lesbian woman" is redundant because, by definition, lesbians are women.

Liberation Tigers of Tamil Eelam. A militant group in Sri Lanka that has been at war with the government since the early 1980s, seeking a homeland for the Tamil ethnic minority in the predominantly Buddhist and Sinhalese nation.

lifestyle. Avoid. An inaccurate term sometimes used to describe gays, lesbians and bisexuals. There is no one gay lifestyle, just as there is no one straight lifestyle.

Little Brown Brother. Avoid. A derogatory term used in reference to Filipinos.

Little Saigon. Any one of several Vietnamese communities in the United States.

Little Tokyo. A Japanese American community near downtown Los Angeles (see **Nihonmachi** and **J-Town).**

lover. A gay, lesbian, bisexual or heterosexual person's sexual partner (see **gay relationships** terminology).

mail order brides. Women, usually from the Philippines or Southeast Asia, who are selected as marriage partners by American males through catalogues.

Malayalam. Indian language spoken in southern India.

Mandarin. The official dialect of China that has a standard variety centering around Beijing.

Manilatown. Any one of several Filipino American communities in the United States. Unlike Chinatowns, however, Manilatowns are not very big and are in decline, as Filipino immigrants generally speak English and thus tend to disperse.

Manong (mah-nong). Title of respect for older Filipino males, used preceding their names, as in "manong Carlos." For older Filipina women, the term is "manang" (mah-nang).

Marathi. Indian language spoken in western India.

McCarran-Walter Act. Officially, the Immigration and Nationality Act. Passed in 1952, it allowed Japanese, Koreans and other Asian Pacifics to become naturalized citizens.

Meo or Miao. Avoid (racial slur). Derogatory term for Hmong (Mong or Mung).

Mestizo. A person of mixed European and Latino background. Avoid unless people identify themselves as mestizo.

Mexican American. U.S. citizens of Mexican heritage. Note: no hyphen.

Mi Guk Saram (mee gook SAH-ram). Korean for an American person, used most often to refer to white Americans; not necessarily derogatory.

mistizo/mistiza. Filipino term for someone of mixed Asian Pacific and white parentage. It also may refer to someone of mixed Filipino and Spanish parentage. Use "mistizo" for males, "mistiza" for females.

model minority. A stereotypical term applied to Asian Americans in the misleading belief that they have achieved success in the United States. Such references ignore the large groups of Asians and Asian Americans who have failed to achieve success or who suffer from poverty, unemployment, language barriers, drug abuse and other problems.

Mumbai. India's largest city and commercial capital, formerly known as Bombay.

Muslims. People of Islamic faith. Not all Arabs are Muslims; not all Muslims are Arabs. Not all Muslims in the United States are Arab or black.

Native American. Synonymous with "American Indian." Sometimes preferred term for indigenous peoples of the Western Hemisphere. When possible, use national affiliation rather than generic "Native American" or "American Indian," e.g., Navajo, Hopi, Cherokee. To specify someone who was born in the United States but isn't Native American, use "native-born."

Native Hawaiian. Refers to people of Polynesian descent living in Hawaii or descended from those living in Hawaii. Does not refer to everybody who happens to live in Hawaii. For non-Polynesians living in Hawaii, a more appropriate description is "resident of Hawaii" (see also **Hawaiian).**

New World. Avoid. It's a Eurocentric term that implies that no one was in the Western Hemisphere before Europeans arrived.

Nigger. Avoid (racial slur). Even though the word is used within the black community, avoid its use.

Nihonmachi (NEE-hon-MAH-chee). Japanese for "Japantown." After the World War II internment of Japanese Americans, the areas of American cities called "Little Tokyo" or "Japantown" shrank considerably. Today Japanese Americans are the most widely dispersed of all Asian Americans.

Nikkei (NEE-kay). A person of Japanese ancestry.

Nip, Nippers. Avoid (racial slur). Derogatory term for Japanese and Japanese Americans, derived from "Nippon," a Japanese word for "Japan."

Nisei (NEE-say). Second-generation Japanese Americans, the first generation born in the United States. Also "nisei."

Occident/Orient. Eliminate use of either term, unless in direct quote or name.

Ohana. Hawaiian term referring to family.

Old World. Avoid. Confusing term because it's Eurocentric, i.e., makes Europe the point of reference.

openly gay/lesbian. Preferred over "self-avowed," "self-admitted," "self-confessed" or "practicing" in instances where the sexual orientation of the individual is germane to the story. Example: The openly gay legislator voted against the measure denying civil rights to gays. "Acknowledged" is acceptable if context calls for it. Example: A person accused of being gay acknowledges it.

Oriental. Avoid. Use "Asian," except for objects such as Oriental rugs.

outing, to out. Publicly revealing the sexual orientation of an individual who has chosen to keep that orientation secret (from "out of the closet"). Some activists, political groups and media believe outing is justified or newsworthy when the person involved works against the interests of lesbians and gays. Others oppose it as an invasion of privacy. Also a verb: "The magazine outed the senator in a front-page story" (see **coming out** and **closeted).**

Pacific Rim. The regions and nations touching the Pacific Ocean. It often refers to East Asia, the Pacific Islands, Australia, New Zealand and the West Coast of the United States.

Pakhtoon (Pushto). Pakistani language spoken in the northwest frontier province of Pakistan.

Pakis. Avoid (slang). A derogatory term used in reference to Pakistani people.

Pan Asian. Refers to policies or other activities resulting from cooperation among Asian nations or among Asian American ethnic groups.

Pearl Harbor. U.S. military base in Hawaii bombed during World War II. Cries of "Remember Pearl Harbor" are still sometimes used to whip up anti-Japanese/Japanese American sentiment. Thus, references to Pearl Harbor should be used with extreme care because of the potential inflammatory effects upon an entire group.

Pilipino. See **Filipino.**

pink triangle. The symbol that gay men were required to wear in Nazi-occupied Europe and concentration camps. Lesbians were classified in various groups. Some were forced to wear black triangles. Starting in the late 1970s, the downward-pointing, equilateral, pink triangle was adopted as a symbol of gay pride. Lesbians sometimes also use a black triangle.

Pinoy (pee-noy). A Filipino American male. The term for women is "Pinay." Some Filipino Americans consider the term derogatory.

powwow. Avoid, unless referring to the title of a specific event. Evokes stereotypical image of Native Americans.

Pride. Short for "gay/lesbian pride," this term is commonly used to indicate the celebrations commemorating the Stonewall Inn riots. Example: One marcher said, "The day of the Pride march is the one day of the year we can all feel free."

Punjabi. Indian dialect spoken in northern India.

Pushto. See **Pakhtoon.**

PWA. Stands for "person with AIDS." Or AIDS patient, if the context is medical care. Avoid calling PWAs "innocent victims." It implies criminal guilt among some other PWAs.

queen. An effeminate gay man. Derogatory when used by people outside the gay community. Affectionate internally. Use only in a direct quote.

Queen Liliuokalani. The last reigning monarch of Hawaii, she was forced off her throne on Jan. 16, 1893, by U.S. businessmen backed by military might. The United States annexed the kingdom in 1898.

queer. Traditionally a pejorative term for gays. Now being reclaimed by some (particularly young) gays, lesbians, bisexuals and transgendered persons as a self-affirming umbrella term. Example: the group Queer Nation.

race. Leave a person's race out of the story unless it's necessary to tell the story. In racial conflicts, the identity of parties involved or quoted is important. Example: In police brutality cases, if the race of a victim is relevant, so is the race of the officer(s) involved. Contrast: The race of someone charged with robbery is usually not needed.

racially diverse. A group made up of people from different races.

racially mixed. A person whose ancestors came from different parts of the world.

racially mixed, racially diverse. The terms are not synonymous. "Racially mixed" means a person whose ancestors came from different parts of the world. "Racially diverse" means a group of people from different parts of the world.

Raghead. Avoid (racial slur). A derogatory term against Sikhs, for their wearing of turbans.

rainbow flag. A flag of six equal horizontal stripes (red, orange, yellow, green, blue and lavender or violet) adopted to signify the diversity of the lesbian and gay communities.

refugee. A person admitted to the United States from abroad due to that person's well-founded fear of persecution on account of race, religion, nationality, membership in a particular social group or political opinion. A refugee may apply for permanent status one year after admission to the United States (from the *John Marshall Law Manual for Community Developers and Social Workers*, Chicago 1991).

Refugee Act of 1980. Enacted in response to the arrival of refugees from Southeast Asia, this act gave resettlement agencies $560 for each refugee to help provide temporary housing, food and other services during the refugee's first 90 days of resettlement in the United States. Otherwise, refugees do not receive greater benefits than other welfare recipients, nor do they receive low-interest loans or grants to start businesses. The majority of Vietnamese, Cambodian (Kampuchean) and Laotian refugees to the United States have arrived since 1980.

religious zealots. Avoid this stereotype when referring to Arabs.

reservation. The Bureau of Indian Affairs (BIA) designation for lands in the western United States designated as belonging to Native American nations. Some Indians prefer "nation" to "reservation." Example: the Navajo Nation, instead of Navajo Reservation. Best to ask each nation which it prefers.

rupee. The monetary unit of India and Pakistan. In India, a rupee is 100 paise; one paisa equals 1/100th of a rupee. "Rupee" is abbreviated in the singular as "Re." (at a cost of Re. 1) and in the plural as "Rs." (Rs. 65 million).

safe sex, safer sex, protected sex. Sexual practices that minimize the transmission of infectious bodily fluids. Important for all sexually active humans, no matter their sexual identity, gender or age.

Samurai. A Japanese warrior. The samurai ethic is overemphasized when describing the Japanese mentality, particularly when describing Japanese business styles in competition with the United States.

Sandsucker. Avoid (racial slur). Derogatory term for Arabs.

Sansei (SAHN-say). Third-generation Japanese Americans who were children of the Nisei. They were born in the United States, mostly during the post–World War II baby boom.

Sanskrit. Language in which many ancient Indian texts are written.

sari (also **saree**). Described in the Western press as a dress worn by Hindu women, but Christians in India wear saris, too, as do many Bangladeshi women.

second parent adoption. Legal action giving same-sex second parent legal rights over children. Not permitted in all states.

seroconversion. Scientifically observable alteration of blood or other bodily fluids from HIV-negative to HIV-positive. The verb is "seroconvert."

seropositive. Synonymous with "HIV-positive."

sexual orientation. Innate sexual attraction and self-identity. Always use instead of "sexual preference" or other misleading terminology.

sexual preference. Avoid. Implies a choice to stray from the straight and narrow. Use "sexual orientation."

Sikh. Follower of Sikhism, a monotheistic religion that originated in northern India.

Sindi. Pakistani language spoken in the western Sind province of Pakistan.

slant, slant-eye. Avoid (racial slur). The stereotypical caricature of Asians with narrow, slanted, slit eyes, with no pupils showing, was first used by white cartoonists in the 1800s to whip up anti-Asian hysteria. The caricature also is used to demean Asians as mindless hordes. Cartoons drawn with this feature are highly racist and offensive and should be avoided.

Slope. Avoid (racial slur). Derogatory term for Asians and Asian Americans.

sodomy. Collective term for various sexual acts deemed illegal in some states. Not synonymous with "homosexuality" or "gay sex"; refers to noncoital sexual acts between males and females. Anti-sodomy laws are used to stigmatize and criminalize gay men and lesbians.

South Asia. The Indian Subcontinent as distinct from East and Southeast Asia. Includes Bangladesh, Bhutan, India, Maldives, Nepal, Pakistan and Sri Lanka.

Southeast Asia. Preferred over "Indochina" (see **Indochinese).**

sovereignty. Independence from external control. The question of status in relationship to the United States for current and former U.S. territorial possessions, such as Hawaii, Guam and Puerto Rico and also Native American nations, continues to be debated. Takes the form of plebiscites, political discussions and independence movements. In the case of Native American nations, many assert their sovereignty based on having entered into treaties (international agreements) with the United States that the Native American nations still recognize.

Spanish. Spaniards and many Latinos speak Spanish. Some Latinos speak Portuguese. People from Spain are Spanish, not Latino. People from Latin America are Latino, not Spanish.

Spanish names. Usually include both the father's and mother's family names in that order. On second reference, okay to use just the father's name, unless a person specifies otherwise.

squaw. Avoid. Derogatory term for a Native American woman.

Stonewall. The Stonewall Inn tavern in New York City's Greenwich Village was the site of several nights of raucous protests following a police raid on June 28, 1969. Although not the nation's first gay rights demonstration, Stonewall is now regarded as the birth of the modern gay rights movement.

straight. A heterosexual; a nongay person. Also used as an adjective.

Subcontinent, Indian (capitalized). Also known as "the Subcontinent" (see **South Asia).**

Tagalog (tah-GAH-log). The official language of the Philippines. Each province has its own language. There are eight major dialects and 84 other dialects.

Tamil. Indian language spoken in southern India.

Telugu. Indian language spoken in southern India.

Thai. Term used in reference to people from Thailand. This group should be distinguished from the Tai, who come from Taiwan.

Third World. Avoid. Eurocentric term. When referring to locations outside industrialized regions, preferred term is "developing world." When referring to people, "people of color" is the preferred term.

Toishanese. A Chinese dialect mainly spoken by the earliest immigrants. Toishanese is a subdialect of Cantonese. It is spoken in only six counties in China.

Tongs. Any of a variety of Chinese organizations. "Tongs" also could refer to a club, clan or a large residence. Used in combination with other words, it could also mean a church or a school. The term has come to be associated in America, however, with Chinese secret societies that engaged in illegal activities.

transgender. An imprecise term for individuals who cross gender lines. Sometimes synonymous with "transsexual."

transsexual. An individual who believes himself or herself to be a member of the opposite sex and who, by surgery or therapy, acquires the physical characteristics of the opposite sex. Individual can be gay or straight.

transvestite. An individual—not necessarily gay—who dresses in garb most often associated with the opposite sex. Not synonymous with "drag queen," "transgender" or "transsexual."

tree climber. Avoid (racial slur). Derogatory term for Filipinos, alluding to their climbing coconut trees.

tribal warfare. Avoid. Eurocentric term for ethnic conflict among people of color.

Example: The conflict between Hutus and Tutsis in Rwanda was called "tribal warfare," but the civil war in the former Yugoslavia between Serbs, Croats and Muslims was "ethnic" cleansing. They are both ethnic conflicts or civil wars.

tribe. Avoid. Use "nation" or "ethnic group" most of the time, except for specific entities like a "tribal council" on a reservation. Within the United States, Native Americans prefer "nation" because their people have signed treaties with the United States that recognize them as nations. Some Native Americans prefer their national affiliation instead of the generic term "Native American," e.g., Navajo, Hopi, Cherokee. In Africa, avoid referring to different ethnic groups as tribes. Hutu and Tutsi are ethnic groups, just like Serbs, Croats and Muslims in the former Yugoslavia.

Tsau. See **Cho.**

Twinkie. Avoid (racial slur). Derogatory term, like "Banana," used by Asian Americans to describe other Asian Americans who identify more with whites. "Banana" usually refers to Asians who grew up in a white environment. "Twinkie" implies that people knowingly reject their Asian identity.

Tydings-McDuffie Act. Enacted in 1934, this act imposed an annual quota of 50 Filipino immigrants and granted deferred independence to the Philippines.

undocumented immigrant. Acceptable and preferred over "illegal immigrant."

Urdu. One of the official languages of Pakistan, also spoken in many parts of India, especially in the state of Uttar Pradesh.

wampum. Avoid. Evokes stereotypical image of Native Americans.

warpath. Avoid. Evokes stereotypical image of Native Americans.

wetback. Avoid. Derogatory term for a Mexican or Mexican American.

Wong, Suzy. Cinematic Chinese prostitute whose image reinforced the stereotype of Asian women as exotic playthings for white males. References to "Suzy Wong" in describing Asian women should be avoided except in direct quotes and specific historical references.

Yellow Peril. Avoid. Derogatory term used to describe Asians as a great threat to Western civilization. The term gained appeal in the 1880s and was used by some newspapers and politicians to whip up racism against Asian immigrants, who were portrayed as taking jobs from whites or as being poised to invade the United States.

Yonsei (YAWN-say). Fourth-generation Japanese Americans.

Zebra. Avoid. Derogatory term for a person of mixed race.

CREDITS

CHAPTER 1

"Schwinn Bicycle Seeks Chapter 11 as Talks With Banks Break Off." *The Wall Street Journal.* Oct. 9, 1992. Courtesy *Wall Street Journal,* Dow Jones & Co. Inc. Reprinted with permission.

"Schwinn Files for Chapter 11." *USA Today.* Oct. 9, 1992. Copyright *USA Today.* Reprinted with permission.

"Schwinn Bicycle Files." *The New York Times.* Oct. 9, 1992. Copyright 1992 by *The New York Times.* Reprinted with permission.

"Schwinn: It Was The Wheel Thing." *The Washington Post.* Oct. 9, 1992. Copyright *The Washington Post.* Reprinted with permission.

CHAPTER 2

"An Accuracy Checklist," by Michele McLellan. *Second Takes: Monthly Reflections on The Oregonian,* edited by Jack Hart. Sept. 1998. Reprinted with permission.

CHAPTER 3

"In shock, loathing, denial: 'This doesn't happen here,'" by Rick Bragg. *The New York Times.* April 20, 1995. Copyright 1995 by *The New York Times.* Reprinted with permission.

"Some fathers won't pay, on principle." Knight Ridder Newspapers. June 24, 1993. Reprinted with permission.

"Jed Barton's Story: Mainstreaming a Blind Child." *The Providence Sunday Journal.* Nov. 7, 1982. Reprinted with permission.

CHAPTER 4

"Gunmen Make Getaway on City Bus." The Associated Press. May 10, 1997. Reprinted with permission.

"2 Guards Delivering Cash are Ambushed in Queens," by Barry Bearak. *The New York Times.* May 10, 1997. Copyright 1997 by *The New York Times.* Reprinted with permission.

"Ambush and a Miracle," by Dan Morrison and Margaret Ramirez. *Newsday.* May 10, 1997. Reprinted with permission. Copyright Newsday, Inc. 1997.

"The Lexicon of Leads," *Second Takes: Monthly Reflections on The Oregonian,"* edited by Jack Hart. March, 1997. Reprinted with permission.

"Israeli Prime Minister Yitzhak Rabin is killed," by Barton Gellman. *The Washington Post.* Nov. 5, 1995. Copyright *The Washington Post.* Reprinted with permission.

CHAPTER 5

CHAPTER 6

CHAPTER 7

"A story of the season," by Peter King. *The Los Angeles Times.* Feb. 26, 1995. Reprinted with permission.

"Coach skates past rumor mill," by Gwen Knapp. *San Francisco Examiner.* Feb. 15, 1998. Copyright *San Francisco Examiner.* Reprinted with permission.

"Wheelchair athletes do more than roll along," by Aly Colón. *The Seattle Times.* July 4, 1996. Reprinted with permission.

"Speechless in Seattle," by Aly Colón. *The Seattle Times.* Nov. 20, 1994. Reprinted with permission.

CHAPTER 8

"Boy, 13, charged in man's death." *St. Petersburg Times.* Dec. 30, 1998. Copyright *St. Petersburg Times.* Reprinted with permission.

Murder arrest report. News script. WFLA-TV. Dec. 29, 1998. Reprinted with permission.

"Meth Bust" package and brief, news script by Tiffany Murri. KIVI-TV, Channel 6, Boise, Idaho. Used with permission.

"This Morning On Your Business" news script. Holiday gift-giving segment. Fort Lauderdale *Sun-Sentinel.* Used with permission.

CHAPTER 9

"Dispatches from along the Coast," by Jonathan Dube. *The Charlotte Observer.* Aug. 26, 1998. Copyright *The Charlotte Observer.* Reprinted with permission.

CHAPTER 10

"Nitro man unhurt in crash." July 13, 1998. *Charleston* (W.Va.) *Daily Mail.* Reprinted with permission.

"Take-charge effort turns deadly on I-65," by Carol Robinson. *Birmingham News.* June 2, 1998. Reprinted with permission.

"Fire hits apartment; man injured," by Bob Banta. *Austin American-Statesman.* Jan. 29, 1998. Reprinted with permission from the *Austin American-Statesman,* copyright 1998.

"Record-Seeker Wants a Fair Shake." *Delaware State News.* July 14, 1976. Reprinted with permission.

"Putnam Commissioners get earful over abandoned house," by Heather Svokos. *Charleston* (W.Va.) *Gazette.* Sept. 10, 1996. Reprinted with permission.

"Putnam board gives definite maybe to proposals," by Heather Svokos. *Charleston* (W.Va.) *Gazette.* Aug. 30, 1996. Reprinted with permission.

"Poca water project gets off ground," by Heather Svokos. *Charleston* (W.Va.) *Gazette.* Nov. 1, 1996. Reprinted with permission.

"Creating a Quality of Life Checklist," by Jerry Davich. *The* (Munster, Ind.) *Times.* June 3, 1998. Reprinted with permission.

"Kissinger critical of Clinton," by Karin Fischer. *Charleston* (W.Va.) *Daily Mail.* Dec. 17, 1998, Reprinted with permission.

"Earl excoriates Press," by Jørgen Wouters. ABCNews.com. Sept. 6, 1997. Online at **http://more.abcnews.go.com/sections/world/DailyNews/oration906.html**. Reprinted with permission.

"How I Wrote the Story" account by Erin Hoover. *Second Takes: Monthly Reflections on The Oregonian*, edited by Jack Hart. June, 1994. Reprinted with permission.

CHAPTER 13

"Anything goes at Lutz celebration," by Bill Coats. *St. Petersburg Times.* July 3, 1998. Copyright *St. Petersburg Times*. Reprinted with permission.

"Police: Teen killed when friend plays with gun." *St. Petersburg Times.* July 13, 1998. Copyright *St. Petersburg Times*. Reprinted with permission.

"Friends' Gunplay Takes Fatal Twist," by Kris Mayes. *St. Petersburg Times.* July 14, 1998. Copyright *St. Petersburg Times.* Reprinted with permission.

"Man gets 9-year-sentence in friend's death," by Craig Pittman. *St. Petersburg Times.* Feb. 4, 1998. Copyright *St. Petersburg Times*. Reprinted with permission.

"Mixed-Race Girl Not On Ballot For Queen," by Holly Kurtz. *The Montgomery Advertiser.* Oct. 12, 1996. Reprinted with permission.

"Braves Snag a 3–1 victory," by Thomas Stinson. *Atlanta Constitution.* April 17, 1998. Reprinted with permission from *The Atlanta Journal* and the *Atlanta Constitution.*

"Writing Awards for Beat Reporting and Writing." Interview with Thomas Stinson. Reprinted with permission from *The Atlanta Journal* and the *Atlanta Constitution.*

CHAPTER 14

"Transportation Fatalities hold steady in 1997." The Associated Press Aug. 10, 1998. Reprinted with permission.

Excerpt from "Budget Basics." *Second Takes: Monthly Reflections on The Oregonian.* Edited by Jack Hart. March, 1998. Reprinted by permission.

"Writing better budget stories," by Dave Herzog. Online at "The Power of Words Web" site. *The Providence Journal.* **http:powerofwords.projo.com/ words/tip415.htm**. April 15, 1998. Reprinted with permission.

CHAPTER 15

"Killer Cover Letters," by Joe Grimm. Posted on "Jobs Page," on **www.freep.com**. Copyright Detroit Free Press. Reprinted with permission.

APPENDIX

News Watch Project Style Guide. Edited by Judy Gerber. Center for Integration and Improvement of Journalism. Reprinted with permission.

The Poynter Institute. Various photographs of Poynter faculty and alumni and excerpts from Poynter publications, including *Best Newspaper Writing* interviews, and *Points South* and other publications of the College Fellowship Program in News Reporting and Writing. Copyright The Poynter Institute. Reprinted with permission.

St. Petersburg Times. Various article excerpts. Reprinted with permission.

PHOTO AND ILLUSTRATION CREDITS

p. 42. Screen shot reprinted by permission: Lexis-Nexis.

p. 276. Courtesy of Kenny Irby.

p. 545. Dan Wiederer résumé. Used with permission.

All other literary, photo and illustration credits are listed in the text.

INDEX